The Elementary School Teacher

THE

ELEMENTARY SCHOOL TEACHER

VOLUME VI

JULY, 1905—JUNE, 1906

CHICAGO
The University of Chicago Press
1906

PRINTED AT
The University of Chicago Press
CHICAGO

INDEX TO VOLUME VI.

INDEX TO ARTICLES.

INDEX TO AUTHORS.

INDEX TO BOOK REVIEWS.

(Only signed reviews are noted.)

VOLUME VI NUMBER I

THE ELEMENTARY SCHOOL TEACHER

SEPTEMBER, 1905

CHILDREN'S SELF-ORGANIZED WORK AND THE EDUCATION OF LEADERSHIP IN THE SCHOOLS

COLIN A. SCOTT
Boston Normal School

To the earnest parent and teacher of the present day two conflicting ideals must always present themselves. On the one hand, to be properly educated a child must be prepared for the life which he is to lead when he becomes an adult. Society provides skilled teachers and material equipment in order to protect itself. The way in which people act and feel and think in adult society, as it exists at present, is thus to be taken as an example and imitated. Presumably typical human beings meet together in school boards and decide upon the manner in which the child shall be made in their image. The teacher is delegated to carry out their wishes. Since the ways by which the various members of the school board, or those whom they represent, themselves succeeded are quite various, one will insist upon one way of education, another upon a second and different way. Two tendencies arise: one, to compromise by introducing a little of all the different subjects anyone has found to be of value, and thus crowd the program and dissipate the attention of the child; another, to compromise by cutting off all differences and leaving a devitalized residue common to all. It is manifest that the ideal which confines itself to the imitation of individuals of the present or even past generation is confronted by serious practical difficulties, and it is in the main these difficulties from which the future is bound to suffer.

This situation I might illustrate by an Indian story. Once upon a time a council of all the animals was called to decide as to how they might ask Nanebosho to create the new generation of animals so that they would all be better able to cope with the difficulties which pressed upon their fathers and mothers. The bear spoke first and dwelt particularly upon size, a flat foot, and a sensitive nose. He thought a tail was quite unnecessary. The fox politely pointed out that, unless one slept through the winter in a hollow tree, a tail made an excellent wrap with which to cover the feet. The beaver thought the fox was moving in the right direction, although he hadn't gone quite far enough, and suggested that by a proper use of mud (the details of which he could find in Mr. Long's books) there was yet hope that he might have his children or even himself provided with flat club-like appendages, much more useful and more beautiful than anything he had dreamed of. After all the animals, and even the birds, had spoken, they began to quarrel, as they could see no common ground upon which they could appeal to Nanebosho. The sly fellow, however, had been listening to this dispute all the time, and now appeared with an entirely new animal which he had made out of a little mud from the river bottom. It was a comical but harmless creature. Every point which any animal had objected to was omitted in its make-up. It had no feet, no tail, no eyes, no hair, but did have a sharp voice and an enormous stomach. All the animals began to laugh, when suddenly a second creature which Nanebosho had made suddenly appeared upon the scene. This was as terrible as the other was comical. It had every kind of tail, claw, wing, and tooth that anyone had ever seen. The animals were so frightened that each began to run in a different direction, and the council was completely broken up. No one was left but Nanebosho, who laughed heartily as he took his two new creations and drowned them in the river.

Opposed to the ideals founded narrowly on the imitation of present or past members of society are those who use all individuals and present society itself merely as guide-posts to the much larger ideal of growth. It is not a fact that society is already grown, and that its present institutions and its present individuals are safe models for implicit imitation. Society is in process of growth, and it is particularly from the young that we may gather the direction of this growth. We must learn to read the new impulses which arise, and to estimate their viability in other terms than those of the present and the past. The child is a social embryo, and ought to be more than what he can imitate. He is protected, as is the physical embryo, from the destructive stimulation of a too complex environment, so that inner forces can operate more freely. He is being created, not molded. The home and the school are the amniotic membranes and the womb by which he is nourished and within which he lives. It is not the infringement of society upon the child, it is the push of the child upon society, which measures his growth. Fortunately, the physical embryo is concealed from our eyes, and there is nothing to do but wait. The spiritual and social embryo, on the contrary, is in direct relationship to all our mental and moral powers, and grows by means of them be these consciously or unconsciously applied. When we rise to conscious education, it would be well if we did not contradict what has already been done unconsciously, and press upon the child from without the products of our adult egoism. French experimenters find that when an egg is varnished in certain patterns, chicks of various kinds of monstrosity are hatched. To quit varnishing the egg, to prevent hindrances — these are the mottoes of the educator: to give such protection and provide such means that the child is able to react favorably upon his present environment; and then to wait.

To apply such maxims sanely it is necessary to take both sides of them. If the protection and the means are not provided, it is idle to expect a favorable reaction. It is also highly important that there be no mistake about what is a favorable reaction. Who shall judge about the reaction? Shall it be the child, or shall it be the teacher? To leave it exclusively to either would presuppose both a lack of love and a lack of reason. Love and reason both act, like all evolutionary processes, by a series of sketches or approximations. Tolerance of what is not quite understood is essential in such a process. "It doth not yet appear what we shall be." But when the hearts and hopes of both child and teacher are in the future looming large, but not yet realized, there we have the conditions which make such tolerance necessary. Unlike the mothers whom Solomon judged, neither will wish the offspring divided. To give the child a future near enough to be laid hold of, and to quit feeding him with the husks of the already determined part or of what he will be expected to do when a man as seen by the teacher, which is the part once again, these are essential conditions of his growth. If this is done, the problem of who shall judge the reaction is already solved.

To find futures for the child is the teacher's mission. Many of these are, however, already in the child himself. All of those capable of present real activity are to be found there, and of many of them he is already conscious. Why, then, should the teacher hunt for all possible kinds of future needs, and neglect the needs and aims which the child is actually feeling at the present? On the contrary, the proper satisfaction of those near at hand will lead most naturally to those that are farther off. And, without finding out how he can satisfy present ideal needs, how will the habit of exerting himself to satisfy these future needs ever arise? We must exercise such habits as will later on be used. If, then, submission to those over him, and dulness to the conduct and movement of the rest of society, even if this should be beneficial, are wanted, the teacher may safely be continuously authoritative. If, however, the power to create society is wanted, experience in doing this thing either as leader or as voluntary follower is necessary to the result.

Where can the opportunity for such an experience be found? It is, no doubt, already begun in the instinctive play of children, especially where the members of two or three families come together in a neighborhood. Here clubs, either called by such a name or merely virtual, are often formed which succeed in carrying out various schemes. The elders are often interested in these, and thus get an opportunity not so much "to divert" as to yield up to the young some of their stored experiences in the art of life. These activities, however, have upon them for the most part the ban of civilization. Like the innocent lives of primitive people, they must hide in obscurity. Pick up what time can be squeezed out between the serious demands of the school and the home, and finally suffer from the stigma in the mind of the elders, and in the higher consciousness of the child himself, of being merely play.

If such experiences are to be dealt with effectually so as to yield a reasonable revenue of educational value, the child's institution, the school, must take hold of them. The teacher must see in them an opportunity, and the highest opportunity, for her sacred office. She must learn to put out at interest, to willing borrowers, those sums of social heredity with which a rich and scholarly culture has put her into contact. She must learn also to refrain from pressing upon her customers wealth which they seem to consume, but do not use. To permit such waste is to produce a nation of educational paupers.

The attack upon such problems can doubtless be made in many ways, and the whole of the new education is a history of more or less indirect and flanking movements toward such an end. Nor will these indirect approaches ever be superseded. A portion of the work of any school must always be "directed," or even controlled and compelled, by the teacher. A good education ought to give intellectual insight and habitual response to both these sides of a well-rounded character. The individual ought to be able to submit willingly and intelligently to authority, even authority which he has not constituted. But he ought also to be able to use authority, even absolute authority, with true wisdom and success. In every walk in life an individual gets some opportunity for each of these attitudes; opportunity, however, in which his education has too frequently not fitted him to succeed.

Of these opposite poles, the power to organize, to use resources, to place purposefully and to execute, with no further compulsion than the natural failure of places if they should prove unsuccessful, has seemed to the present writer to be the most neglected in the schools. Some five years ago an attempt was made in the Chicago Normal School, and afterward carried out in Colorado, Wisconsin, and Boston, not so much to carry out preconceived ideas, as to give a chance for the development of some of the plans and ideas that children already possessed, and to adopt an attitude toward them on the part of the teacher of help and subordination, to study them and bring to their aid such material and spiritual resources as they themselves cared to use. From one standpoint this was an attempt to afford an opportunity in the schools for natural child-study, although going beyond the mere examination of individual details and their consequent scientific combination by the investigator. In order to carry out such a notion, the teachers needed to divest themselves of most of their presuppositions as teachers. On the other hand, it was quite fatal for them to fall into the attitude which is often supposed to be that of the scientific investigator, who, after having arranged the conditions, folds his arms and looks on. At every moment, on the contrary, the teacher must realize that she cannot divest herself of actual participation, but it must be, within the limits prescribed, that kind of participation in which she is authoritatively a follower and not a leader. Her position is that of one of the nourishing membranes of a social embryo.

Since, however, the school begins in authority, the first thing is to find a point of connection for the new departure. In the actual conditions this resolved itself into a division of time upon the school program. A clear demarkation on the program was thought to be the most practical for many reasons. It reduced the difficulties to a minimum. The smallest working time — half an hour two or three times a week — was offered to such children as preferred to have plans which they reasonably believed they could carry out either in the school, the school-yard, or the surroundings. This was a condition which depended upon natural social selections and challenged responsibility. At the beginning the teacher is in a position to move tentatively and accept only those plans which appear quite reasonable and likely to succeed. As their common experience widens her knowledge of the children's possibilities, and also strengthens their own power of overcoming difficulties, her indorsement may be given with an increasing degree of confidence. It may be that at first there is only one group, or perhaps even one child, who can be allowed to carry out self-organized plans. This, however, is not without its effect upon the other children who are meanwhile pursuing work wholly directed by the teacher, especially if the teacher has permitted such activities as have a stimulating social effect. Our experience for five years has been that very soon there is no dearth of plans, and the teacher will be rather crowded with the labor involved in the estimation of the plans which are presented to her. Here the children should be asked to participate in proposing ways by which the preliminary consultations with the teacher can be facilitated. They often propose or freely agree to reduce them to writing and making them more definite, so that long conversations become less necessary. Part of this work is furthered by previous discussions on the part of the children before they approach the teacher.

I have here been supposing cases where the idea of such a work has been clearly, practically, and sometimes enthusiastically grasped by the children. A high degree of such an attitude cannot be expected at first, no matter how many words are used. Actual experience is the only effective teacher, and such work, if real, will grow, like a snow-ball, from very small beginnings. As the work grows, the advantage of a measured time upon the program will begin to make itself felt. It will soon be seen, and the idea may be expressed at first either by teacher or by pupils, that it would be better if there was more time given to this work. Do not let the teacher be either too eager or too stiff in adopting this idea. This is really a plan involving all the other plans. Only when the class as a whole, or at least a working majority, can satisfy the teacher that such work can hold itself together, and perhaps really overcome the difficulties involved with greater success by such a change, is she justified in giving her consent. The children must feel that this is a judgment for which they must themselves produce a reasonable probability.

Such a method of advance in extending the time on the program gives an objective measure of the work, and thus attains a certain degree of scientific precision. To what extent the time might be successfully extended could in the beginning of their experiences not be known for any of the various grades, any more than could the inventor of the thermometer know to what extent the mercury would rise when placed in boiling water. After five years of such work in various grades, a measure has not yet been obtained for all, but a reasonable degree of probability has, I believe, been reached in the case of children about nine years old. In five different classrooms of about this average age the children continued to press upon the program up to about one period of three quarters of an hour a day. Beyond this they never cared to go. The psychic powers involved in such work seemed exercised and contented. The children's imaginations seemed satisfied, and their executive resources exhausted. Outside of that time they appeared to be more willing than previously to be carried by the teacher. Their attitude seemed a little like that of a child who is learning to walk; a short period of an upright position is all that he craves for or can use advantageously. Professor Dewey's criticism that, if a self-active spirit is good at one period of the day and for some of the work, it is good for all periods, and ought to be introduced in such a way that the whole work is equally permeated with it, does not seem, in view of the actual constitution of the school, or in view of the best possibilities of the growth of self-activity itself, to be either practical or ideal.

It is, however, not to be supposed that, although in the more directed portions of the program the children submit more readily to authority, they do this because they are not appreciative of the meaning of freedom. On the contrary, they understand it better. They have been behind the scenes and have found out by their very failures that authority is necessary to the carrying out of any free conception. They have a greater respect for it, and consequently sympathize, in the sense of acquiescing, more profoundly with the teacher's efforts. The teacher, too, comes to find in proportion as she meets with a willing response that her authority needs not to be so strenuous or backed up by compulsion either suggested or enforced. She can actually be somewhat more dictatorial and direct without weakening confidence. On the other hand, she can free herself from unduly persuasive or so-called suggestive methods — the very pitfall of weakness, and productive of mental and moral flabbiness and inertia — and still meet with an effective and reasonable co-operation on the part of the pupils.

While such command is rendered more possible, and is desirable and economical, for part of the time, a middle stage also easily differentiates itself in which the teacher, although she may propose the plans, gives the children the greatest freedom in suggesting modifications and in carrying them out in their own way. This is a custom which is gaining ground in all the best schools, but a true understanding of its possibilities is more quickly and more thoroughly attained by both teacher and pupils if work is differentiated so as to provide for authoritative planning on the children's part, as well as for work commanded without debate on the part of the teacher. Such a differentiation is logical and natural, and each part mutually supports the other.

A word further may be said about the introduction of self-organized work in a class. In calling for plans or schemes on the part of the children, the method of approach may readily vary with every class and with every teacher. The method of real approach to any child or group of children is indeed a whole science of itself. If the teacher should feel that the instructive plan of many of her children, if freely expressed, would be to get out of school at any cost, and as far away from the teacher as possible, or, failing that, to ignore her help or the help of each other in ambitious plans, and thus to relapse to mere idle play or what they could do just as well without the school as with it, it is plain that she is not in the best position to approach the children with any such proposition as I have described. How many of my pupils would remain with me if they were perfectly free to go, expresses an ideal which must find some root in the heart of anyone who would succeed in such an undertaking.

I have suggested some of the general ideas and some of the practices governing the more general aspects of this kind of work, and must now turn to more intimate details.

In all these experiences, although nothing was said about whether individuals or groups should offer plans, it was found that only rarely purely individual plans were submitted to the teacher. The resources as well as the responsibilities necessary not only to success, but to vivid planning, were better provided for in a group. The idea, however, which started the group, and which was to be worked out, was, I think, always the possession at first of a single individual. A germ of this had been obtained, no doubt, by previous contact with the home, school, or other portions of the environment. The value of an idea does not depend upon its isolation from every previous influence. Its value is rather to be measured by the degree with which it sticks and lives spontaneously in the mind. There is, for example, no author more saturated with the influences of his time than is Shakespeare, who, nevertheless, succeeded in giving a personal stamp to a large part of what he absorbed and organized. It is not so much so-called originality, viewed in a narrow way, but rather the extent to which the individual or the group is willing to stake himself on the issue which is characteristic of self-organized work. To do this is to have a real originality of spirit. There is a feeling that they are effective and actually causing something worth while in the outside world. In this respect such work differs from play which does not come up against the real resistances of the outside world, and causes changes which are ineffectual except within the body or the imagination. Of course, in view of such a distinction, what is work at one stage of development becomes play at another.

Even when plans were at first apparently individual, they usually either were concealed or took on later some conscious social reference. I may illustrate this by a single case. A fifth-grade boy, rather belated in his development, wished to go with a number of others who were modeling in clay. He was not, however, connected with them in any organized plan. His idea of what he wanted to do was proportionately indefinite and at first looked forward to but half an hour. He seemed to care very little about what he was going to model, but mentioned a definite object, perhaps more to get an opportunity of handling the clay than for any other reason. As he was working, I came up to him and asked him if I could assist him in any way. The fact that he had no particular problems in mind led to a rather indefinite answer. Now, it is plain that if a plan has not sufficient life in it to stand a struggle for existence with other plans that may come easily to mind, it is not sufficiently intense to be worth while. A resolution that cannot stand a certain amount of temptation is not very well adapted for a hardy life, nor is it very likely to be well carried out. It is better that such weaknesses be discovered at an early stage, if possible. I accordingly set myself to see if I could not, using a moderate stimulus, tempt the boy to desert his plan. I think a cup or vase was the object he was modeling. I said: "What's the good of making a cup? You have plenty of them at home, haven't you?" and so on. I said this, of course, somewhat tentatively, so as not to suggest in the slightest any feeling of authority on my part. The boy at this stage was, I felt, too weak to resist a too powerful stimulus. He went on modeling without giving much of an answer. I then said: "Why don't you make a rest for a pen or something like that? You could make it just long enough to hold pens so that the ink wouldn't fall on the desk when you laid it down. You could put in a little cup for ink, too, make it like a fern leaf and have the stem wind round the little cup. Or you might, perhaps, make a frog looking into the little pool of ink;" and so on, giving a number of different scattered suggestions. One of these appealed to his imagination, and he said: "Yes, that would be better;" and he started to sketch out on the clay the new idea. (I may say here that we had a kiln in the school, and that these utensils could actually be burned and afterward painted and used.) The next day he was working quite vigorously at his pen-holder. When the teacher of the room, hearing the story of his change of plan, said: "That boy is so shilly-shally that if I would go and ask him to change to something else, I believe he would do it." I said to the teacher: "It would be good to try. If he is to develop the power to resist temptation at all, he must get just such experiences." She provided herself with a little china pin-holder, and showed it to him, thus presenting him with a sense-perception as against his mere image. She pointed out the advantages of the pin-holder as well as she could, including the ease of its manufacture. The boy was again quite taken with the new idea, but remained somewhat disturbed. He finally said: "Well, I would make the pin-holder if I hadn't said I was going to make the pen-holder." "Oh, Mr. Scott won't care," said the teacher. "No, I suppose he won't;

but I kind of thought I would make it and give it to him, so that he could use it on his desk." And he went on with the work he had in hand.

It is evident here that what enabled the boy to resist the second temptation was the self-elected social motive, in which he had chosen me as a member of his group. Unfortunately for me, the pen-holder never got finished. A checkerboard (I think it was) which he had started in the sloyd-room weighed on his mind, and the next day he proposed that he use this time which had been given for modeling to finish the checkerboard. He said that the holidays were near by, and that if he did not get some extra time the checkerboard would never be finished. The teacher permitted him to make the change.

I saw him next day, and said rather humorously to him: "You're a nice kind of a fellow, changing around all the time. Is that the sort of man you're going to be when you grow up? I suppose now you would change again for very little. Suppose I give you ten cents, would you go on with the pen-holder?" "No," he said, "I wouldn't." "How much, then, would you take?" "I wouldn't do it for less than the price of a pair of boots." As the little fellow came of a poor family and was sadly in need of boots, I could readily appreciate this measure of his present resolution. Further temptation was not offered, and the checkerboard was finished in time.

A course in temptation may be a new thing for the public school, but it is a necessary part of the power of finding oneself. It is but the negative side of character-building. After all, in the most spiritual sense of the words, everyone has his price. The tragedy of it is, as George Eliot says, that many sell their souls and fail to get the price.

One of the first groups formed in the third and fourth grades in the Colorado Normal School consisted of two boys. One of these spoke to the teacher, and told her that he wanted to make a haystacker. He explained how he wished to make it, and said that he had another boy to help him. The teacher gave him a piece of paper so that he could draw out his plans, which he did. The two boys finished the work in about six weeks, having at the beginning of this period only one hour a week in which to work. There was during the work no hitch or uncertainty of procedure. The next important plan in the same grade was offered by a boy who wished to construct a two-room cottage. The plan of this was brought in at the beginning, and showed a full comprehension of what was needed. He had selected four or five boys to help him. The principle difficulty was one of cost. He estimated that the cottage would cost $23. There was some talk of raising this money among the pupils, but a very small amount only was forthcoming. The idea from the beginning had been that the cottage could be used by all the members of the grade, as a playhouse or even for the purposes of some recitations. The group were asked to go over their calculations carefully and see if they could reduce the proportions of the house so as to make it less expensive. They changed it to a small one-room house with a shingled roof, a door, a large window, and a small window at the back. The cost of all the material was obtained from dealers. About $10 was found to be the very lowest figure. At this point I obtained a grant of $8 from the school, to be given to the grade on the condition that there would be nothing further given that year. This changed the actual conditions somewhat, and, since the whole grade was concerned, I described this offer to them, giving them to understand that the money could be used in other ways than the building of a house. Representatives of the building group spoke on the advantages of having a house, but others wished to buy a cabinet, and others wished to have an aquarium with gold-fish. I even went so far as to suggest that they could buy candy. They calculated the amount of candy that would come to each at my suggestion, but the proposal, although taken seriously, was not accepted, and indeed never gained any adherents. The building group proposed that if the house were built, other groups could be formed to make various things that would be needed to furnish it. Chairs, beds, and tables were necessary. The girls, they thought, might make curtains and bed-clothing. The house, too, ought to be papered, and a garden laid out. The small window ought to be provided with a stained-glass design (done in paper). No decision, however, was reached that day. The day following further influence of the group had evidently been exercised, for all were unanimous in wishing to devote the money to the building of the house, and to supply what more money would be needed.

In the carrying out of this (see sketch) there were many difficulties to overcome, and many mistakes were made. The time estimated to complete the work was found to be altogether too short, so that work was stopped during part of the winter; but the house was finally finished, and stood resplendent in its thick coats of green and white paint. Meanwhile furniture and other furnishings had been made, the stained-glass window put in, and the garden laid out ready to be planted and irrigated. It was viewed with pride and affection. The faults in measurement of beams and laying of the shingles were pointed out by the pupils, but these defects, which were not at all apparent to an unskilled eye, did not prevent the satisfaction of everyone concerned.

Sometimes thoroughly self-organized work starts from work planned by the teacher. This is frequently so in the cases where groups are occupied in making and acting little dramas to be given before the class. In the fourth grade, e. g., the story of Damon and Pythias had been told by the teacher. A group was formed to write out the story in dramatic form, and to play it as well as write it. They decided to ask in other members of the fourth grade and teachers to witness the play. In the words of the teacher:

> As this was Friday, and they had decided to give the play on Monday, they must get their invitations out at once. When the teacher entered the room (a small room adjoining the classroom), all were rushed with work, some writing invitations, others programs, and a few the drama. Groups had been formed within the group; division of labor was felt to be the most effective plan.. . . . The committee requested the room for practice after school that evening. The parts were learned and very simple costumes were planned, each girl telling what she could bring or make. Only a few things were to be made; a crown for the king was one of these. On the following Monday the play was given at the regular hour for the literature lesson. The audience was requested to offer criticisms. These were kindly accepted, and the cast decided to improve upon the play and present it before the whole school at general exercises, if the permission of the principal of the school

BUILDING THE HOUSE

PLAY WITH THE DOLLS

could be obtained. One of the criticisms made was that when the wife of Pythias received the note containing the king's decree that her husband must be executed, she fainted; but the audience had no way of knowing the cause of her faint. The next time it was played she read the note aloud before fainting.

The same kind of work has recently been carried out in some of the Boston schools. Miss Shaw, of the Wells School, and Miss Clark, of the Charleston High School, have both succeeded well in this undertaking. The narrow limits of this article will prevent my giving more than a hint of this work. The conditions surrounding Miss Shaw's school are not the best for the development of initiative and resource. The school is situated in one of the most crowded quarters of the city, and the children (mostly foreigners) come from poor homes. The making and acting of plays has been one of the most favored activities, especially with the Russians, Jewish, and Polish children. This may be because material resources are limited, although a great deal is done in organizing even simple material for a play. A little ten-year-old author, who had written a play mainly about two dolls (see cut), said that one of these dolls was her own. There was a kind grandmother in this play. I asked her if she had a grandmother. She said "No," but that she would like to have one. This was one reason for putting her in the play. Some of the original tableaus made by the groups were excellent even from an adult standpoint. Many of the subjects were drawn from the history the children had been studying. Among these were "The Execution of Nathan Hale," "Waiting for the News of Washington's Army," "Soldiers' Farewell," etc. Others, such as "Tag," and "Blind Man's Buff," represented the imaginative quintessence of their usual games and other home and street activities.

On the basis of a freer and more participative conduct of the regular class in history, Miss Clark's high-school pupils organized three clubs. One of these is a camera club for the purpose of photographing scenes, statues in the Art Museum, etc., relating to the history. Another club produces drawings in the same way, while another calls itself "The Sidelights Club," because it hunts for and brings into the class information not discussed in the regular textbooks.

I have spoken of the differentiation of these classes of work in the schools. That part involving absolute command and implicit obedience is hardly necessary to touch upon, however valuable it is, especially as a training for times of strain. It is evident that war could not well be carried on without a training in such habits. The same may be said of other operations organized like those of war. This is not all, however. On the ground of economy of thought and time, absolute authority is advantageous as an element in most civilized affairs. There is a threshold of authority, marking off its favorable effects from its unfavorable. This is to be found in every case by experience. An illustration may be advanced in the case of the authoritative laws surrounding the medical profession. In certain states none but those having passed a certain standard are allowed to practice. The public is not left free to select anyone, but must choose within the limits laid down by law. The effect of this, however, is practically to increase the freedom of the public, by economizing time, especially at a period of strain. When life is at stake, one is not in a position to deliberate and choose the best physicians, nor would many take this precaution beforehand. The authoritative protection directly aids the individual in the line of his own deepest desires, and thus also gives him more energy and more time to pursue his liberty in other directions. The threshold here might be formalized by saying that, in as far as authority increases liberty, it is an undoubted good. The maxim, "Use authority only to prevent hindrances," if interpreted fairly and generously, would express the same idea from the imperative or motor side.

The midway stage, where the teacher, or society back of her, insists that certain definite things shall be done, but leaves the pupils free to carry these out in ways of their own invention, although used in the schools, is not yet extended to the limits of best effectiveness. When self-organized work is carried on, this midway stage is greatly benefited. The children are more ready to lay hold on details capable of cheerful effort and success. An example from a second-grade class will illustrate this feature. The subject undertaken by the teacher was nest-building; the

the time was in the spring. The teacher, a young man, had got up a plan based on the McMurray ideas, and arranged according to what he thought would be the law of apperception. He would ask questions about the children's experience. How many had seen birds nesting? Etc., etc. The application was to be a moral one, and would emphasize the evil of robbing birds' nests.

After some discussion, I got the teacher to join together a few of the Herbartian stages and proceed a little more naturally, while keeping in mind the children's great motor capacity; not attempting to plan the lesson exactly as it would come, but to have a number of possible ways in which it might run. The outcome of the lesson showed that the children proposed doing several unexpected things. The proposal to do something rather than to talk about something was the first step on the teacher's part. (As a matter of fact, actual doing is more thoroughly apperceptive than anything else, neglected as it has been by Herbartians and non-Herbartians alike.) The teacher said simply: "I've been watching some birds building their nests, and wondered whether any of you could make nests like theirs." As will be seen, this suggests a whole program. The children discussed it readily, but not lengthily. One said: "The birds have bills, which are better than hands; but if I had a needle and thread, I think I could do it." Many did not know, and asked the teacher if he would show them a nest so that they could tell how hard it would be to make. He did not have a nest of the kind he had been observing, but one in the class asked where this nest was, and, since it was near, proposed that they go out and see it. This was done immediately. (The class was only about twenty in number.) They got a stepladder and went up one by one, each to see how the nest was made and what it was made of. The teacher proposed that they do not tell what each had seen till all were through, but perhaps write it down. Many did this latter, while some started to look around to find where the birds had got their material. They found nearly all of it — dried grass, pieces of excelsior, etc. Each thought now that he could make a nest. The next day the teacher provided them with branching twigs, which he had stuck in their ink-wells, but the children proposed to go outside and stick them in the ground. They also proposed to work two by two, but none of them paired off as boy and girl. The pairing was done simply for the sake of rapidity and other effectiveness. During this hour they all made birds' nests many of which were very successful, although the children pointed out discrepancies. Pictures of birds were provided, and books with descriptions. It is evident that such work gains both the knowledge and the moral sympathy aimed at in the first plan; but by following the children's proposals frankly where they seemed sensible, even although unexpected, a deeper and more permanent element had been liberated by the teacher.

A word in closing ought to be said as to the effect of such work as we have been advocating in strictly graded classes. We may say frankly that the tendency is to break up this rather mechanical and thoroughly authoritative institution. In the self-organized group the selective attractions of children themselves, apart from their formal knowledge, as well as their motor efficiency, lead to the strong and weak, from a scholastic standpoint, being often drawn together. When the work that is done under these conditions is successful, there is no reason why such associations should not be continued beyond the usual period of promotion, especially as the world that the children go out into is not rigidly graded, except in manufactories, where we are already beginning to regret it. Out of this there ought to come, not a grade as we now understand it, superficial and artificial as it is, but a natural grouping of children resulting from their combined attractions, mutual helpfulness, and the teachers' correcting judgment, which, it would be expected, would roughly follow an age measure, and would not ignore intellectual differences, but would much more thoroughly than at present reflect the growing development of heart and hand as well as head.

Such a natural institution or series of them would form a real school, and give the children an opportunity to find themselves in presence of each other, rather than too exclusively in the presence of the ghosts of even Euclid, Newton, Mommsen, Longfellow, or Shakespeare, especially as reflected in the single facet of the teacher's personality. The children would thus be able to grow much more along their own lines, instead of always imitating the past, or the narrower present which reflects it. For them there would come to be a present, not gray with much mere learning, but joyful with futures about to be realized. In such a spirit the part itself is better understood; and, as one pine-tree imitates another, not by looking at it, but by obedience to the law of its own growth, so we may expect a future generation comparable in some degree to the heroes who have made our world and our country what it is.

ON THE STUDY OF ENGLISH COMPOSITION AS A MEANS OF ACQUIRING POWER[1]

GEORGIA ALEXANDER
Supervising Principal, Indianapolis Public Schools

In modern education the tendency is to train for power through self-expression, particularly for expression through the medium of art. The emphasis that is now placed upon the manual arts, including drawing and color, upon music, and especially upon English composition, or expression in language, is indicative of this tendency. Of all these avenues of expression that of language is the most fundamental. All thinking is done in words by a self-conscious mind, and the language that a man uses is the measure of his thought.

By virtue of its very intangibility, language is the most direct mode of communication from soul to soul, and attains a power over the mind of the listener beyond that of the more concrete expressions of thought. Beautiful as is Westminster Abbey, it has never swayed the hearts of men as has that hymn so often sung within its walls:

> So long Thy power has blest me, sure it still
> Will lead me on.

The first means of developing power is conceded to be association with nature. That man who has seen the majesty of the mountains, or the shimmer of the sea, who has known seed-time and harvest, has forever had his thoughts ennobled by the great Thought of which these are but the symbols. But nature alone does not suffice for the development of power. The first man, Adam, in a complete environment of nature, contributed only negatively to the world's advancement. The centuries through which man has toiled since then have testified that the curse of labor pronounced upon Adam was but a blessing in disguise.

[1] Paper read at the meeting of the N. E. A. at Asbury Park, N. J., July, 1905.

Man has learned that he earns not only his bread by the sweat of his brow, but his heaven also.

Looking farther along, we see Abraham a colossal figure towering over the great plains of Moab, surrounded by nature, yet not subdued by it. The care of flocks has given him food and shelter, has established the family and the altar. Truly, Abraham was a man of power. "The Hebrew patriarchs had small libraries, I think, if any," says the Autocrat, "yet they represent to our imaginations very complete ideas of manhood, and I think if we could ask in Abraham to dine with us men of letters next Saturday, we should feel honored by his company."

We have, however, the greatest embodiment of power in that man who had added to his personal experience with nature and in society, the experience of the great men of all time, found in literature and in art. In other words, the scholar is the man of power. Is not David a perfect example of one in whom these forces met? Did he not have contact with nature, the discipline that comes from labor and social intercourse, and in addition the culture of scholarship? We see him a shepherd lad wandering over the green hills of Judea, lying at night under the stars; a minstrel with music so sweet he comforts King Saul; a warrior so mighty his triumphs become a song; a king of wisdom so beautiful that he is forever the ideal of the Jews; but above all the divine Psalmist whose words express the most exalted thought of God ever conceived by man. Do we wonder that the man who was able through the alembic of his nature to distil such language from his experience in life was the progenitor of Him who said "Consider the lilies"?

With this idea that the power of any man is dependent upon the virility of his thought, and that his thought is the product of his living, we have come to a new notion of the relative importance of a number of things in the school. The old-time school with its barren drill upon the three R's has been incorporated into a fuller, richer school which attempts to develop the child by giving him life through nature, labor and scholarship and by training him in the use of language, the expression of that life in words.

This modern school is working under new conditions, the result of our rapidly increasing urban population. Its problem is how, on the one hand, to give to the city child that association with nature and that discipline of labor which his home environment does not supply, and how, on the other hand, to help him to realize upon the riches of literary culture with which he is surrounded. The child from the city tenement can have no such experience with nature as had the roving shepherd lad David, but he does have Tennyson and the

Flower in the crannied wall

and under happy conditions may just as truly know

What God and man is.

So much for the nurture of power in the child. Perhaps I have dwelt too long upon it, but the child in his lisping, and the statesman in his power delivers each in speech just what he has garnered from living. It is common enough to hear, "No impression without expression," but "No expression without impression" is a truth more fundamental, and one that is peculiarly true of expression in language.

This modern school is consciously organized as a social community in which each child as a member in full standing discusses his work freely and spontaneously with his fellows. This is in marked contrast to the old-time method in which the child recited his lesson from the book verbatim and solely to the teacher, and was not encouraged to reorganize its thought and make it fully his own. Now every lesson is consciously a language lesson, in which the teacher judges of the definiteness and accuracy of the child's concepts in arithmetic, in history or in geography, by the aptness of the words in which he clothes them. Moreover, the child himself is helped to clarify his thought in these subjects by expressing them in words of his own choosing.

In addition to this general work in language there is usually in the day's program a period devoted exclusively to the study of English composition. During this period there is practice in short themes as the most efficient means of developing facility and power. These themes fall into two main classes — the reproduction of classic models, and the composition of original exercises. Reproduction exercises are not, strictly speaking, exercises in composition, but they are invaluable in giving the child those necessary tools of composition, vocabulary and style. Such exercises, however, are irksome to the child, who has naturally a passionate desire for self-expression. Following the dictates of modern thought in education, that a child best learns form not as a thing apart in itself, but as a necessary and most convenient mode of expressing his thought, original exercises have become the chief part of the composition work. In these he embodies all he has learned from the study of literary models and from the more formal instruction in the making of sentences, rules of syntax and the mechanics of writing. Thus he reveals to his teacher just what he has mastered, both in thought and form, and better than he could possibly do in any other way.

The recognition that language serves a distinctly social purpose has transformed the requirements in composition. The child no longer bends over long essays on "Friendship" or excerpts from encyclopædias which neither he nor any one else ever wishes to hear. Rather his exercise is the recital of some little thing which he has found interesting in his daily life, and which he knows his schoolmates will wish to hear.

Further, the mode of delivery has also changed to meet this social requirement. It is now often oral, or when written it is directly addressed to some person or persons. This social training is most stimulating to the child and helps him to find his place in the world. He learns that he must not only present his thoughts in logical order and in agreeable phrase, but also in that modulated voice and with that poise of body that accompany the speech of the well bred.

The choice of subjects for this composition work is limited only by the experience of the child and his power of comprehension. He talks or writes of what has appealed to him, and his teacher skilfully correlates his language expression with his observation work in his nature-study and geography, with his manual work and his little home tasks, and with his culture work in history and literature. The child writes on the opening of the spring buds as he saw them on his way to school, tells how he made a sled, or dramatizes an episode from his history lesson. Of these exercises the last class gives him by far the greatest delight, because it affords his imagination free play.

Perhaps letter-writing is the most distinctly social form of written composition. A letter pre-supposes a person to whom it is addressed and between whom and the writer there is a common bond of interest. The following letter from Hans Christian Andersen to his little niece, Marie, was given at the mid-year test to our fourth-grade classes who had been preparing to celebrate the centenary of his birth, and they were asked to answer it:

DEAR LITTLE MARIE:

I am in the country now like you. . . . . It is so nice, and I have had some strawberries — large, red strawberries, with cream. Have you had any? One can taste them right down in one's stomach. Yesterday I went down to the sea. . . . . and sat on a rock by the shore. Presently a large white bird that they call a gull, came flying along. It flew right toward me, so that I fancied it would have slapped me with its wings; but, mercy on us, it said, "Mamaree!" "Why, what's the matter?" I asked. "Mama-ree!" it said again, and then, of course, I understood that "Ma-ma-ree" meant Marie. "Oh," said I, "then you bring me a greeting from Marie, that's what it is, eh?" "Ya-ya! Ma-ma-ree, Ma-ma-ree," it said. It couldn't say it any better than that, for it only knew the gull language, and that is not very much like ours. "Thanks for the greeting," said I, and off flew the gull. After that, as I was walking in the garden, a little sparrow came flying up. "I suppose you now have flown a long way?" said I. "Vit, vit" (far, far), it said. "Did you see Marie," I asked. "Tit, tit, tit" (often, often, often), it said. "Then give my greeting to Marie, for I suppose you are going back?" I said. "Lit, lit" (little, little), it replied. If it has not come yet, it will come later on, but first I'll send you this letter. You may feed the little bird, if you like, but you must not squeeze it. Now greet from me all good people, all sensible beasts and all the pretty flowers that wither before I see them. Isn't it nice to be in the country, to paddle in the water, to eat lots of nice things, and to get a letter from your sweetheart?

H. C. ANDERSEN.[2]

The personal appeal of the letter was so strong that though many of the children had never seen the sea or the sea bird of which Andersen wrote, though it was a cold January day with ice and sleet on the ground and more than all, though they knew that Hans Andersen is dead, their power of imagination under

[2] From Dye's *Letters and Letter Writing.*

the influence of the letter overcame all difficulties, and they responded astonishingly well. The following is typical of many others of equal quality:

INDIANAPOLIS, IND., January 11, 1905.

DEAR UNKIL:

Yes, I am in the country. I love to pick wild flowers. I found a bird nest full of young birds. But I dident touch them for fear I would make the bird angry. I was sitting under the tree when presently the mother sparrow came and fed her young ones. Then she flew towards me and chirped. I could not understand. But after I got your letter, I knew that she brought a message from you. I gave the message to the gull to give to you. As you were speaking about strawberries and milk, I like to pick them myself, put them in my own saucer, skim the cream of the fresh milk, and put it on the berries, and have a little dinner. Then I am a fine lady with a cabbage-leaf hat. I pretend my bare feet is two big white horses and I ride acrost the stream. Once a craw fish pinched my toe and I fell down. I thought I would take a ride in the little boat, so I took the boat down to the deep part and jumped in. I sailed smoothly for a while. But directly I hit a rock, tumbled out and got all wet. You may be sure that I never sailed in that boat again.

Goodby Uncle Hans.

From your niece, Marie.

A recent experiment in story-telling in which the same picture was used in every grade, from the first through the eighth, was an interesting one. The picture chosen was the frontispiece to Henry Van Dyke's *Fisherman's Luck.*

A study of the construction of the compositions showed a steady increase in power and complexity of thought and form from grade to grade. The children were allowed to write for as long a time as they chose. In the second grade, the average composition contained three sentences, in the fourth grade nine sentences, in the sixth, twelve sentences, and in the eighth, fifteen sentences. The number of simple sentences decreased from 88 per cent. of the whole in the second grade, to 35 per cent. in the eighth. In the sixth, seventh, and eighth grades the sentences were very long and involved, showing that the child was grappling with thoughts which he could not yet fully express. From the beginning the adverbial clause was used, but there were not many adjective clauses until about the fourth grade, and then there continued to be about three times as many adverbial clauses as adjective clauses. If this is universally true, as it probably is, it would indicate that the mind instinctively uses the relations of time, place and cause as more fundamental than embellishments through description.

A further study of the papers showed an increase in imagination and thought power from grade to grade, developing markedly about the fourth grade and gradually rising to the sixth, but showing a decided decrease in the seventh and eighth grades, where the child had grown self-conscious. In the earlier grades there was no past nor future to the stories. The social relations between the boys in the picture did not prompt explanation, and there was a painful recital of just how many fish each boy caught. In very few instances in any grade was the lunch omitted, and at night all had fried fish for supper.

Here is one of the stories written by an eight-year-old girl. You will notice what a direct and distinct style it has:

THE KIND BOYS

Once there were some boys who were very kind. One boy's name was Tom, and the other boy's name was John. They had a little brother. One day there mother called boys, the boys came.

Take your brother to the brook, she said.

They went back a little way from the brook. After a while they heard a cry.

That is brother, they said. They looked, yes it was. They ran and got him out. They would not let him sit so close to the brook any more.

There was a marked difference between the style of the boys' compositions and that of the girls'.

"How about a fishing trip, Tom," said Ned.

"I never caught anything when I went fishing," said Tom.

That was written by a boy. Quite in contrast to it is the following extract from a composition by a girl:

Harry is sitting in silence on the river bank with quiet leaf shadows running over his anxious face.

The idea of an ethical purpose necessarily underlying every story was evidently, though unconsciously, in the minds of many of the children. Carelessness and disobedience met sure and swift punishment. The boy who disobeyed his mother was stung by bees or caught on his own fishhook. The children were significantly silent as to rewards of merit, picturing the world as it is often presented to them that a child should be good anyway. Indeed, if one had the insight, one could by reading these spontaneous exercises, find all that the child has stored from his life experience. He will express it there in concrete form, just as in the Psalms we find all the life of David: shepherd boy, minstrel, warrior, king, philosopher, poet.

The teacher's responsibility in this work cannot be overestimated. "Who is the Master?" says someone. "The one who awakens." "Who is the Scholar?" "The one who answers." What responsibility then rests upon him who dares to call forth a child's thought in language! How must he ever conceive himself as creator and artist making for this child his spiritual body! He must have what Froebel has called the "Glied-ganzes," the view of the whole, and he must plan that this child, his creation, shall fill it beautifully, graciously, unctiously. Nay more, he should gradually awaken his pupil to a sense of his own destiny, that he may begin to mold himself in conformity to the great Ideal; so that day by day and year by year he may grow in foresight, in judgment, and in desire to serve the world. In other words, that he may become a man of power. And how shall you know a man? Says Confucius: "A man can never be hid."

AN APPLICATION OF NUMBERWORK IN NATURE-STUDY

SPENCER JARNAGIN McCALLIE
The University of Chicago

A paper twice as long as this could easily be written as a polemic against the too prevalent practice of teaching arithmetic *in se* and without proper reference to the other subjects of the curriculum. It is not my purpose, however, to enter into an extended argument against the formal methods of teaching numberwork, such methods have already received stronger condemnation than I am able to give them.[1] I shall assume, therefore, as evident that a purely formal subject like arithmetic should be closely integrated—incarnated as it were—with subjects of more intrinsic worth. It is in the development and the clarification of these subjects that numberwork finds its real value. Wherever there is a quantitative relationship to be determined, and whenever the pupil finds it necessary to his progress to make this determination, then the use of numberwork finds its justification.

Numberwork cannot be successfully *injected into* the material, but it must arise out of the conscious need of a solution of the problem. Indeed, this seems to be a truism in actual business affairs. The banker and the broker use percentage, discount, commission, etc., because these arithmetical relationships are felt necessities in the furtherance of their work. Their interest is primarily in a familiar content and only incidentally in the form which embodies this content. To them, then, the solution of the problem in percentage is interesting, because worth while.

[1] For an able and critical review of the formal presentation of numberwork in the elementary school, I would refer the reader to an article by W. S. Jackman, the editor of this magazine, appearing in *Educational Review,* 1903, Vol. V, p. 35.

Yet it is just here that the presentation of arithmetic in the ordinary school breaks down. Bank discount, brokerage, stock exchange, etc., *in se,* are not interesting to the young pupil, since their content is totally unfamiliar. The pupil, moreover, has no real purpose in the solution of the problem; consequently the interest — if there be any — is that belonging to mental gymnastics. The makers of arithmetics have copied the forms of business life, but have missed the spirit. At the risk of repetition, I urge that numberwork must be evolved out of a content in which the pupil is vitally interested. Ordinary problems, such as, "If a hound can take two leaps to the hare, then," etc., are species of mental folderol.

Aside from the lack of real interest and loss of time involved in the formal presentation of numberwork, another serious evil is to be noted: Arithmetic taught as a discrete subject tends to remain discrete. Unconnected and uncorrelated with the larger and richer subjects of the curriculum and of the daily life of the pupil, its use does not become habitual, since its accustomed content is not that of daily experience. Hence, the average person drops the use of mathematics just as soon as school days are over.

On the other hand, however, the incorporation of numberwork in an experienced content insures for it all the interest, and all the stability and permanence that belongs to the content itself. The interest, moreover, originally felt in the subject-matter is strengthened, since new relations are brought out and fresh determinations are made. The result is increased accuracy and clearness of conception — which is the essence of science.

I have stated the above principles very succinctly, yet I trust sufficiently clearly for the purpose of putting forth the ideas that have been the controlling motives in the presentation of numberwork as an organic part of a series of lessons given in the fifth grade of the Elementary School of the University of Chicago. The central topic of the series was "The Cereals of North America." It is not essential to state here the outline used in the development of the subject-matter; let it suffice to remark that maps, pictures, drawings, reading lessons, actual planting of seeds, etc., were freely used as the work progressed. The problems given below arose out of a visit to a flour mill. They are in no sense manufactured, but are rather questions arising out of the relationships existing in the material. Consequently they may lack the order and the logical symmetry belonging to a prearranged set of problems found in the arithmetic, yet they possessed for the pupils a real quickening interest as instruments in the successive unfolding of the main topic of study—an interest accompanying clear and purposive conception.

An entire morning was given over to an excursion by the class of about thirty pupils to the flour mill of Eckhart & Swan, 377 Carroll Avenue. Through the courtesy of the officials of the mill the pupils, under the able guidance of Head Miller Rachel, were enabled to see the entire process of transformation of the wheat into flour. Beginning with the unloading of the cars on the side track, the storing and weighing of the grain in the elevators, the observation was carried out through each move until the final product was reached. During this observation work the pupils and teachers asked certain questions that were the data for subsequent quantitative determinations. Every problem, therefore, is based on the actual conditions found in the business of Eckhart & Swan.

1. If a car holds 1,000 bushels of wheat, how many pounds will it hold?

2. How many carloads will it take to fill Eckhart & Swan's elevator, holding 800,000 bushels of wheat?

3. How long a train will these cars make, if each car is 36 feet long? Answer in feet, yards, and miles.

4. How long a time will it take to fill the elevator, working eight hours a day, if a car can be unloaded in 20 minutes? Answer in days, hours, minutes.

5. What is the value of the wheat in Eckhart & Swan's elevator, when wheat is worth — (market price) per bushel?

6. If the daily capacity of Eckhart & Swan's mill is 2,500 barrels of flour, what is its annual capacity, based on 300 working days?

7. If it takes 4⅔ bushels of wheat to make one barrel of flour, how many pounds does it take to make a barrel of flour?

8. A barrel of flour weighs 196 pounds; how much of the wheat goes into bran, middlings, and "waste"?

9. One twenty-first of the by-product (bran, middling, etc.) is "waste," how many pounds is this to each barrel?

10. How many pounds are wasted each day? How many bushels? How much is wasted for the year of 300 days? Answer in pounds and bushels.

11. How much bran and middlings in pounds are made each day? During the year?

12. Bran and middlings are worth 85 cents per hundred pounds; what is the value of the output of Eckhart & Swan's mill for one day? For one year?

13. Flour is worth $6.25 per barrel; what is the value of the daily output of Eckhart & Swan's mill? What is the value of the yearly output?

14. What is the value of the output of flour, bran, and middlings for the year?

15. If wheat is worth — (market price) per bushel, how much is it worth per pound? How much is flour worth a pound? How much is bread worth a pound? How much more is bread worth a pound than flour? Than wheat?

16. If one acre of ground will raise 18 bushels of wheat (based on Government Report on Indiana, where most of wheat used in Eckhart & Swan's mill came from), how many acres will it take to raise enough wheat to fill the elevator of Eckhart & Swan? How many acres will it take to raise the wheat for the yearly output of the mill?

It was not expected that each pupil should work every example in the above set; yet every pupil worked some of them and was interested in all. An information was gained by the use of these problems that could not be obtained in any other way.

Underlying, and in a sense supporting and increasing, the interest arising out of the development of knowledge concerning the flour mill, was another interest of even more significance and depth—an interest inherent in social service. That is, the pupils looked forward to, and were inspired by, the idea that they were to tell the rest of the school this information that they had worked out. For it is customary in the University Elementary School for reports to be made from time to time by the various classes on certain phases of their work at the period of the morning exercise before the entire school. For instance, one class may present a drama that they themselves have created, as was done by the members of a French class; at another time a report may be made of a visit to an art gallery. So a morning exercise was set aside for this class to present to the school their visit to the flour mill.

It is outside my purpose to note the features in detail that the pupils worked up and presented at this exercise. Briefly, each pupil of the class had a part in the exercise, and felt that he or she was an active participant in the social life of the school—nay more, was an indispensable agent in its social progress.

The mathematical relations, however, that were brought out in connection with this exercise were as follows:

It takes 800 carloads of wheat to fill the elevator once, and it requires thirty-three days, two hours, and forty minutes to do the work. The elevator requires 4⅜ fillings to run the mill for one year, or a total of 3,500,000 bushels of wheat. It would require a train of over 28,000 feet to fill the elevator once; a train of over twenty-three miles to supply the elevator for one year. The acreage used to supply this one mill alone for a year is 194,444 +, or over 300 square miles.

Again:

The yearly output of flour in barrels is 750,000, worth $4,687,500. The yearly output of bran and middlings is 60,000,000 pounds, worth $510,000; while the "waste" amounts to 3,000,000 pounds a year, or over 50 carloads. A comparison of value of a pound of bread was made with value of a pound of flour, and with value of a pound of wheat. [This will be taken up in detail after the pupils visit a bakery.]

The above quantitative relationships were concerned with one mill alone; the emphasis was upon that mill and its capacity and output. This left the pupils with a strong impression of its vastness, and of the reasources required to run it. Naturally this led to a comparison with the still greater capacity of the mills of Minneapolis and the matchless resources of the wheat belt ministering to them. It is not necessary to suggest that the study of this mill as a type-form opened the way for incursions into related fields of even richer content.

DRAMATICS IN THE TEACHING OF A FOREIGN LANGUAGE

EDWARD L. NORTON
The University of Wisconsin
and
LORLEY ADA ASHLEMAN
School of Education

The value of dramatics in the teaching of a foreign language is so apparent that one is surprised to find how seldom it has broken through the narrow conservatism of the traditional school and won for itself an honorable and enviable position. Experience has shown that as a method in foreign-language teaching it can supplant the toil and mechanical habit-forming of the old methods — not only with groups of limited numbers, but with large classes. A natural method, discarding translation, it is, with its vividness, concreteness, elimination of undue constraint, and adoption of various expressive channels, especially adapted to the young.

The social value of such work can hardly be overestimated. The social life of the school is too often confined to the playgrounds, where it may remain uncontrolled by any ideal suggestions, while within the class-room the atmosphere most cultivated is that of toil, perhaps in an anti-social rather than a co-operative spirit.

School dramatics develop imagination and sympathy; form standards of thought, feeling, and practical reaction, conduce to self-control and, by enriching the child's inner experience, furnish a more concrete basis for moral judgments.

In all these ways they are socializing. Note how the young student's sympathies must of necessity be enlarged. He must sympathize with the author (if a finished production is used), with the character that his acting is to portray, and with his fellow-actors. He must feel as they feel, if his own part is to be rightly articulated in the whole; but especially he must have the genuine feelings which in his particular rôle he purposes to express.

Thus in the course of the action the performer is both himself and another. He takes up into himself, as it were, the character and motives of another; in short, in playing the rôle of a Frenchman he becomes a Frenchman. He thus broadens his horizon and enriches his personality. Not only does he absorb new ideas, but emotional reactions which are those of another people are added to his stock.

A child's attention is largely sensuous and motor. This opportunity of free movement must be utilized, if later control is to be normal and efficient.

Evidently imitation must be the method on the linguistic side; it is mainly by this means that the pupil acquires the right vocabulary, pronunciation, grammar, and intonation. Direct, conscious imitation is of less certain utility in developing gestures and action. Yet the foreign atmosphere, which is so desirable an acquisition, includes some particular gestures and emotional manifestations. Particles like *n'est-ce pas?* and expressions like the shoulder-shrug must be classed together as symbols, and imitation seems the best way to catch them; they belong among the irrational idioms which are to be copied rather than explained. Indeed, this whole atmosphere must be absorbed from the native teacher; in the early stages at least it is a matter of suggestion rather than explicit instruction.

The dramatic method, of course, is not without its dangers. There is danger of an overdevelopment of imagination and emotions, and of severing these from their function in real life. Both stimulation and inhibition of these mental processes are involved in their culture, and this can be effected properly only in view of a developed ideal which the teacher, as guide, has in mind, and which is or becomes embodied in the play. The drama is the schoolmaster of the susceptibilities; it must therefore be an idealization of social life. It must be typical, so that, without conscious intention on the child's part, the imagination and feelings trained by it will function later in his actual experience.

Again, playing a part may become a habit, leading to affectation, "bluffing," insincerity, and deceit. This very complicated psychological and moral question cannot be dealt with here. In fact, one never is quite the same person in different surroundings; one always, consciously or unconsciously, assumes what seems to be the fitting rôle. Dramatics can avoid this difficulty only by aiming to instil always a feeling for what the entire situation demands: to take a given dramatic rôle on the stage, but to act out one's own noblest, broadest, deepest purpose or self in the affairs of real life. Another danger arises from the fact that the performer imitates the dramatic character which is his part, and this reacts into his own character, developing it for good or ill. The question is in part whether his own character, assimilates that of the dramatic rôle, or *vice versa*. In this connection the ideal structure of the play is most important. We must be somewhat puristic in dramatics for little folk. To assume even in play a mean or villainous rôle may be harmful. Young children are less able than their elders to resist, to react negatively upon motives into which they have first gained positive insight; they feel less the true proportions and larger relations of things; each actor is more apt to be sunk in his own part, while the spectator is better able to subordinate it. There is danger of presenting to the child a problem for which he is not prepared and which he does not feel. All problems, intellectual, moral, or æsthetic, should, so far as educative influences can bring it about, be approached from the standpoint of wholesome habits already formed.

The danger of display and egotism — prominent motives in the children — is avoided by using every means to induce a social atmosphere and show the value of team work or organic unity. The inspiration to do something well as a group is quickly caught. Each child can be led to play his part well as a member of an organic group or dramatic constellation, not as an independent star.

As to the content of the plays ,it should in the earlier grades deal with the children's daily interests at home; but gradually a distinctively foreign content can be used, introducing the pupil to French life, myths, history, customs, and ideas. Take, for example, the French festivals, *Noël, Les Vendanges;* or, in history, *Jeanne d'Arc, Les Croisades, La Fayette, En Amerique, La Salle, Joliet, Guillaume le Conquérant, Versailles, etc.* This leads to broader sympathies, and is still an expression of the child's growing self; he *is* (in ideal, at least) no longer a mere American, but a citizen of the world, a cosmopolitan with French traits. Thus with progress the plays will also receive a more completely foreign interpretation, and the children, whether in language, gesture, or conception, will be controlled by the foreign atmosphere.

Evidently in the earlier stages of the work a ready-made play must be provided, adapted to the needs of the pupils, and therefore best written by the teacher.[1] For ability to comprehend and imitate the foreign tongue precedes ability to speak or write. In a play for students already familiar with French the pupils are to do everything possible themselves, with such checks and guidance from the teacher as are necessary to eliminate the grosser errors. The teacher should be considered a member of the group rather than an external force, and thus may be expected to contribute something. In the elementary school, the basis of the play should be a story with which the children become very familiar, and which they as a group then dramatize. In the high school, the starting-point may be a brief outline which the pupils, grouped according to scenes in the proposed dialogue, fill out themselves. Such training would make it possible in college work to start from a mere theme or idea and demand individual dramatic production.

In the elementary work, after the children have heard, read, and studied the story, the class may make a brief abstract for guidance, and then work out either the first couple of scenes or the whole play together, individuals suggesting and criticising. Various pupils may be asked to work out particular scenes at home; when these are read in school, the class may select the best, criticising and correcting them.

[1] Any teacher who has worked with dramatics rarely finds the play, when a finished product of the children, the one her imagination had created.

A first-year high-school class of the Chicago Institute was struck with the dramatic possibilities of Daudet's *La dernière classe.* The class worked out the following three scenes together, and the successful presentation of this co-operative production was an inspiration to pupil and teacher alike:

LA DERNIÈRE CLASSE

La scène se passe en 1871 dans un village d'Alsace.

SCÈNE I

Personnage: Frantz, un petit écolier du village.

Scène première: Un matin de printemps. La lisière d'un bois au fond du théâtre. Un petit garçon entre, marchant très lentement avec des livres sous le bras. Il regarde autour de lui avec envie.

FRANTZ: Qu'il fait chaud! Le soleil brille bien fort, et les oiseaux comme ils chantent! En vérité, il fait trop beau pour aller à l'école. D'ailleurs, si j'y vais, je serai grondé, car je ne sais pas ma leçon au sujet des participes! Que ces choses sont stupides! *(Il s'arrête et semble écouter.)* Ah! voilà les Prussiens qui font l'exercice dans le pré Rippert. Je crois que j'irai les voir. Non! Il faut aller. . . . . Oh! il fait trop beau. Je n'irai pas à l'école. *(Il entend l'horloge du village qui sonne le quant.)* Déjà neuf heures et quart. Je suis trop en retard pour y aller maintenant. Mais . . . . que dira Monsieur Hamel demain, et que dirai-je moi-même? Ce sera bien désagréable. Après tout, il vaut mieux aller a l'école! *(Il se met à courir dans la direction de l'école.)*

SCÈNE II

Personnages: Une vieille femme; Deux jeunes filles; Un homme et sa femme; Un apprenti; Un forgeron; Un facteur; La fille du facteur.

Devant la mairie, la foule s'est arrêtée près du grillage aux affiches.

Devant la mairie, la foule de gens s'est arrêtée près du grillage aux affiches.

LA VIEILLE FEMME: Maintenant que font ces Prussiens! Ha, Ha! *(Elle lit l'affiche.)* Vous voulez donc que nos enfants n'apprennent pas leur belle langue. *(Tout le monde secoue la tête en désapprobation.)* Misérables que vous êtes! Mais, vous allez voir! Mes petites *(prenant un enfant dans ses bras et l'embrassant)* apprendront le français.

(Deux jeunes filles passent.)

LA PREMIÈRE FILLE. Voila les dernières nouvelles. Il nous faut parler allemand.

LA DEUXÈME FILLE: Quoi? vous dites, qu'il faut maintenant toujours parler Allemand. Je ne le veux pas. D'ailleurs, je ne le ferai pas, non non jamais jamais de ma vie!

(Un homme entre avec sa femme, qui tient un bébé dans ses bras.)

L'HOMME: Ma pauvre femme, ce sont là de mauvaises nouvelles! Notre pauvre enfant! Mais, non nous irons à Paris.

LA FEMME: Oui, nous irons à Paris; mais ce sera si écœurant de quitter notre vieille maison!!!

(Le forgeron Wachter et son apprenti entrent en scène; le forgeron se met à lire l'affiche.)

L'APPRENTI: Monsieur Wachter, que dit cette affiche, s'il vous plait?

LE FORGERON *(lisant)*: Il faut qu'après le 15 Mai, tout le monde parle Allemand en Alsace-Lorraine. Tous ceux qui n'observerront pas cet ordre dans les écoles seront punis. Signé, "Bismark."

L'APPRENTI: Qui est Bismark?

LE FORGERON: Le chancelier de fer.

(Frantz s'arrête en voyant l'affiche.)

FRANZ: Qu'est-ce qu'il y a donc encore? *(Il court vite vers l'école.)*

LE FORGERON *(criant après lui)*: Ne te dépêche pas tant, petit; tu y arriveras toujours assez tôt à ton école. Ha! Ha!

(Le petit garçon regarde derrière lui et court toujours vers l'école.)

(L'ancien facteur, accompagné de sa fille, lit l'affiche.)

LE FACTEUR: Depuis deux ans, ma fille, toutes les mauvaises sont venues de là.

LA FILLE DU FACTEUR: Eh bien, mon père, toi et moi, nous parlerons toujours français chez nous. Nous pouvons au moins garder notre langue.

The amount of grammatical work accomplished in these class corrections and criticisms is astonishing. It is important that the students get the feeling that the play is a gradual evolution, not finally perfected until its last presentation. Therefore the action and dialogue should be worked out *pari passu,* each serving to modify the other. This is the surest means of making the play at once a self-expression of the group and an organic whole, ideal and objective. Thus the pupils feel the difficulties in language and dramatic construction; they may feel the need of some *trouble* in a drama, some obstacle, some collision of characters with each other or with circumstances — the need of evil in some kind or degree — if the drama shall at all represent life. They get an insight into the nature of dramatic crisis and *dénouement;* they study the desirable proportion of action to dialogue. In these and other respects they are learning the principles of dramatic art, as well as the language in which they work. This all would be of little interest to them, were they not planning a performance; and such study must have great influence in forming both their language and their dramatic taste.

Manual training, scientific ingenuity, drawing, and painting may be put in requisition to supply the necessary stage fixtures and scenery. The study of pictures and sculpture will furnish ideas regarding costumes and poses. Literature in some form is either the inspiration or the finished material of the dialogue.

Such correlation is not an external juxtaposition of certain studies. The elements of the performance are welded into an organic unity by the interest of those who take part. For here is exemplified at its best the value of *play* as an instrument and method in education.

In availing itself of the aid of dramatics, foreign-language teaching is merely falling into line with the educational tendency of the day: it is discarding the textbook for the laboratory method.

The dramatic rendering of the life and ideals of another people, whose mode of expression is the key which the student must make his own, is in the truest sense laboratory work, and this actual living with another people which dramatic expression demands cannot but result in that emotional appreciation of such a people which is the forerunner of the gospel of Christ — charity toward all men and universal fellowship.

A DEPARTURE IN CONSTRUCTIVE PUBLIC HYGIENE[1]

E. B. DE GROOT
Director, Physical Training, South Park Commissioners, Chicago, Illinois

The influx of people who make their permanent homes in the large cities, the rapid material development of these great centers, and the specialization in all fields of labor, give rise to many questions concerning the preservation of life and health of these people.

To enlarge upon this thought is only to repeat what Doctors Sargent and Gulick have written from the physical training point of view, and what Jacob Riis, Jane Addams, and others, have told us from the sociological aspect of the subject.

The rapid strides we have made in sanitation have done much to make the city a safe place in which to live. Caring for our people *en masse,* with proper sanitation, to caring for them more individually by means of the hygienic agencies of physical exercise and bathing, is but a short and logical step, and one which we believe should be taken as fully and as rapidly as possible in every community. In this latter respect our public schools seem to lead, as we see school systems everywhere making more and more extensive provision for physical training. Public school physical training, however, no matter how excellent, is inadequate when it is confined, as is usually the case, to the classroom and the four walls of a small gymnasium.

There must be extensive facilities for unconscious physical training, and for bathing, if the physical and social advancement which we believe to be necessary, is to be obtained among our common people. Statistics show that the vast majority of children leave school at, or soon after, the grammar-school period. It is open to doubt that the amount and kind of physical training

[1] A paper read before the Department of Physical Education at the Annual Meeting of the N. E. A. at Asbury Park, July, 1905.

received in the grammar grades produces results of more than the merest temporary nature.

The persistent appeal everywhere, for more and better facilities for physical training in the high schools, indicates that we are not yet prepared to give even a small number of children of the school age an adequate physical training service. And in our schemes of physical training, what becomes of the vast number of children not in the schools? There is no more pitiable sight in our great cities than the boys and girls whose playtime has been cut short by the necessity for work in office, factory, or shop, there to become a cog in the machinery of modern specialization in labor. This is a class in as great need of physical training activities as the student class.

The South Park Commissioners of Chicago are endeavoring to meet the problem of an adequate physical training service for all the people in the South Park district, and are thereby incidentally demonstrating the possibility of park boards leading the way in matters of constructive public hygiene. I do not mean to say that park boards are likely to lead the way in research work in public hygiene, but the South Park system of Chicago, indicates the possibility of park boards leading the way in making use of the store of knowledge gained by experiences and experiments in schools and under health boards. Park boards have large grounds and money, and are well able to start the wheels of legislation in favor of public hygienic agencies.

To accomplish what has been done by the South Park Commissioners of Chicago needs only a non-political park board, composed of "big" men and a park superintendent who loves to achieve things for the public good, and not for a political gang.

In that portion of Chicago known as the South Park district, the South Park Commissioners are constructing fourteen new parks, ranging in size from ten to three hundred acres. Each park site has been selected with special reference to density of population, location of schools, and other factors of similar nature. In each of twelve of these parks a field house is erected, costing on an average $90,000, exclusive of equipment. Each field house contains separate gymnasiums for men and women, locker rooms, shower and plunge baths. Each field house also contains an assembly hall, office, reading room, rooms for neighborhood clubs, lavatories, and toilet rooms, a laundry, and a refectory where pure foods, modified and sterilized milk are sold at cost.

The men's gymnasiums contain basket-ball and hand-ball courts, traveling and flying rings, stall bars, bucks, jump standards, jump boards, mats, especially designed horizontal, vaulting and parallel bars, climbing ropes, miscellaneous equipment for games, and an instructor's movable platform and chest.

The women's gymnasiums contain stall bars, flying rings, a basket-ball court, bucks, mats, jump boards, jump standards, Swedish ladders, specially designed Swedish boom and bar saddles, miscellaneous equipment for games, and an instructor's movable platform and chest.

Competent men and women, graduates of normal schools, are employed to take charge of the men's and women's gymnasiums respectively.

Six thousand steel lockers are installed in the locker rooms, and the women's locker rooms are amply supplied with dressing booths as well as with steel lockers. All lockers are equipped with devices making it possible to use any one of three locks — a combination, rim, or padlock.

The outdoor space is divided and used as follows: The central portion of each park is laid out as a "flat," or large field for football and baseball. A twelve-foot cement walk surrounds most of these fields for roller skating. In winter the fields are flooded for ice skating.

In two of the sixty-acre parks lagoons are being made, and a fleet of row boats will be launched and ready for use this summer.

On the side of the park next to the men's locker room is a cinder running-track, with a "straight-away for the sprints and hurdles." The tracks range in size from one-eighth to one-fourth mile to the lap. They are completely equipped for all sorts of track and field work. At one end of the running track inclosure there is a large iron pipe frame containing gymnastic apparatus in sets of eight. In winter, toboggan slides are erected in the running track inclosures.

On the side of the park next to the women's locker room is a space set apart for out-door work for women. This space is amply equipped with gymnastic and play apparatus.

Beyond the women's gymnasium is a space set apart for the exclusive use of small children. This space is equipped with suitable gymnastic and play apparatus. A large wading pool, surrounded by sand courts, is also a part of the equipment for small children.

The running-tracks, women's gymnasium, and children's playgrounds are surrounded by iron fences, and each group has the exclusive use of a space for such activities as are of special interest to the group.

Each park has a large open-air swimming-pool, surrounded by sand-courts of large dimensions, thus bringing the bathing beach to the people in the city. The smallest pool is about 4,000 square feet; and the largest is about 35,000 square feet.

The matter of lighting the parks, the planting of trees and shrubbery, the laying out of walks, fences, lawns, etc., has been treated in most artistic and practical fashion, and all combine to make a beautiful and an attractive place for all physical activities.

Before an attempt had been made to lay out a detailed plan of work, the buildings had been planned and the dimensions and character of the structure of the gymnasiums had been determined, so the plan of work and the equipment selected has reference to these factors as well as to what is considered the physical training needs of the community.

A tentative plan of work has been laid out for both in-door and out-door activities.

During the in-door season, work in the gymnasium is conducted somewhat as follows: Early in the afternoon classes are organized for small children, and later in the afternoon for larger boys and girls. In the evening, school children are excluded, and classes are conducted for working boys and girls and adults in general.

The program for men and boys consists of marching evolutions (confined to the school of the company); free exercises, selected primarily for their hygienic effects, and free exercises selected primarily for their corrective influences. A scheme of progressive mat and very simple tumbling exercises is used for both boys and men.

In addition to the above mass class work, squad work upon the apparatus is conducted, and special efforts are made to put to fullest use all in-door games and the development of group games.

The plan of work for girls and women is much the same as that outlined for boys, except that dancing steps take the place of mat and tumbling exercises, and apparatus work is of a different character.

Dumb-bells, wands, Indian clubs, and chest weights have been omitted from the equipment, and their use from the plan of work.

Aside from the advantage gained in having all walls free of this apparatus, and consequent obstruction when playing games, the omission of the so-called calisthenic drill enables us to lay special emphasis upon a slightly different character of work from that pursued in the schools. In this way we hope to supplement and enrich the school program for school children, as well as to offer work calculated to meet the needs of the adult population.

In order to make the gymnasiums as nearly "fool proof" as possible, all pieces of apparatus are locked in place or up out of reach, so that improper use of apparatus and danger of injury in the absence of the instructors is reduced to the minimum.

To encourage systematic work, the entire change of clothing when exercising, and attention to bathing, lockers are, and gymnasium suits may be, furnished free of cost or deposit money to those who register and report for regular class work. As there is a laundry in each building, all gymnasium and bathing suits will be laundered at regular intervals, free of cost. Towels are furnished free of cost to all bathers, and no towels are allowed to hang in the lockers.

During the winter months the assembly halls will be used frequently for demonstrating gymnastic work, and for lectures on physical training, and related subjects.

The plan for out-door work contemplates instruction on the gymnastic apparatus, the organization of baseball, football, and track teams. In addition to holding numerous graded contests in each park, a league will be formed comprising all the parks, and inter-park contests will be held in all branches of sport in their seasons. The same amount and kind of supervision will be given to the activities of the girl's gymnasiums and to the small children's playgrounds.

No efforts are made, at the present time, to conduct aquatic sports, but the swimming pools are open daily for the freest possible use. Bathing suits and towels are furnished free of cost.

All lockers and locker rooms are disinfected periodically, and special efforts are made to keep the bathing suits, gymnasium clothes, swimming pools, and sand-courts in a perfectly sanitary condition.

Four parks are now open and are being extensively used by the public. Six more parks will be ready for use in August.

In the autumn of this year the South Park district of Chicago will be supplied with a system of public gymnasiums, baths, swimming pools, and playgrounds that will rival the ancient Greek institutions of similar character.

Chicago, more than any other American city, has grown so rapidly that there has been little or no time for correlation of the units of public service. We shall, it is hoped, some day reach a period when the unification of the efforts and expenditures for physical and social advancement of our people will take place. At such a time, the physical training departments of the public schools and parks might be brought together under one comprehensive system. Conscious physical training might be carried on in the schools without the use of many expensive gymnasiums—the school children obtaining their unconscious and informal physical training in the parks, after school hours, and under either (or both) school or park instructors.

Here is perhaps an economical as well as an ideal solution of a great and complex problem of the modern city.

The juvenile courts of our great cities are institutions of recent origin and of positive value to society. The great problem of the juvenile court is what to do with the boy or girl when convicted of an offense. Isolated institutions where such children are cared for under the direction of the court are so rapidly filled that a startling economical problem soon presents itself. Here again a unification of the agencies for physical and social betterment might work a solution of a great and complex problem, ever growing more complex. Under a unified system such children might be parolled to the school at stated hours, to the park gymnasium, natatorium, playgrounds, and pure food restaurant at other stated hours, and to one other public institution to sleep and eat. Such an environment would be likely to defy positively bad heredity.

To enlarge upon the thought of a unified public service for physical and social advancement, we have only to pass in review the city police force composed of fat and slovenly units, and how an hour each day spent in the park gymnasium, natatorium and athletic field would make the policeman a better appearing, and more efficient public servant. A unified system would require our firemen to exercise and bathe daily, and thus maintain a high standard of physical efficiency. Our militia organization would be better prepared to serve state or nation if weekly drills in military gymnastics and athletics were a part of the training of these organizations.

Thus we see the possibilities of the park gymnasia. The work now being done in these gymnasia is truly constructive in the fullest sense of the word.

Children are taken from the streets and alleys and given a better environment and safer place in which to play. Parents, truck drivers, policemen, and others involved in the care of children are relieved of anxiety and care. Working boys, girls and adults are encouraged to spend their idle hours in a wholesome environment and away from questionable amusements.

Both children and adults are encouraged to give attention to personal hygiene—exercise, and bathing especially.

Wholesome amusement is furnished to those who do not participate in the activities of the gymnasium and athletic field. Bent frames are "set up;" physical skill, courage, and a wholesome respect for the rights of, and respect for, others are acquired.

In fine, there is, perhaps, no other public institution better calculated to raise the standards of good citizenship, and this is by common consent the problem of the great city.

A DISCUSSION OF HIGH-SCHOOL FRATERNITIES AND SORORITIES

GENERAL STATEMENT

At a special meeting of the Parents' Association of the University Elementary and High Schools (School of Education), April 13, 1905, it was voted to ask for a referendum vote on the question of sororities and fraternities in the University High School, to be sent as advice and recommendation to the faculty of the High School. It was voted also to ask two committees to prepare briefs of arguments for, and against the societies, to be handed to all who vote. It was further decided to ask for the vote of all parents of students in the High School, and the four upper grades of the Elementary School. This was done that all persons concerned might be fully provided with materials for a deliberate judgment, and that those whose children are soon to come into the school might help to decide what kind of school it shall be. All parents are urged to vote, since our action will be widely quoted and influential in the country, and will be a help or a hindrance in establishing the ideal school of the future.

To vote in the affirmative, put a cross in the square opposite the word YES; to vote in the negative, put a cross in the square opposite the word No.

Votes not signed by name in full, or not in the hands of the secretary by May 15, will not be counted.

Each parent (both father and mother) has one vote. Women will kindly sign husbands' names, as well as their own, to avoid confusion. Kindly give address, as well.

CAROLINE W. MONTGOMERY,
Secretary Parents' Association.

Mrs. Frank Hugh Montgomery,
5548 Woodlawn Ave., Chicago, Ill.

May 7, 1905.

BRIEF IN FAVOR OF FRATERNITIES AND SORORITIES

STATEMENT

The question under consideration is whether or not fraternities and sororities shall be permitted among the students of the University High School upon the following conditions, to-wit:

No freshmen shall be admitted.

No student shall be admitted without the consent of his or her parents or guardian.

No fraternity houses shall be maintained.

Every fraternity shall have as a counseler a member of the faculty.

At a meeting of certain of the parents of the students and of members of the school faculty, it was deemed advisable to learn the views of the parents upon the proposition with the conditions as above set forth, as to whether or not they favored the continuation of said societies.

This argument is submitted with the firm belief, that a great majority of the parents will, without hesitancy, promptly return their votes in favor of the fraternities and sororities.

ARGUMENT

THE FACULTY SHOULD NOT INTERFERE

We respectfully call attention to the fact that from our viewpoint, the question is one for the parents of students who may be members of such societies, and not one for the faculty or the parents of scholars who are not members.

If we were dealing with a boarding school, it might, with some degree of wisdom, be contended that the faculty should decide the question, but here the faculty is not responsible for the conduct and associations of the students when without the school.

Any attempt by the faculty to dictate what shall be the social conduct of the student in his home-life, would certainly be an invasion of the rights of the parent to whom, and to whom only, is logically given the privilege of governing the student when not in school. It would be equally just were the faculty to dictate what church or Sunday school the scholars shall attend.

CHARACTER OF MEMBERS

Good standing in their studies is necessary for the scholars to become eligible to membership in the societies, and any outward appearance of snobbishness is not only not sanctioned, but in most instances is quickly eradicated, greatly to the betterment of the individual.

SOCIAL COMPANIONSHIP

Social quality, so essential to good morals and good citizenship, develops in youth. Consequently persons to each other congenial will drift together, and as soon as the faculties of order and self-control develop, such association is formulated in societies such as fraternities, sororities, clubs, lodges, and the like. Recreation so necessary to all is, by fraternities and sororities, afforded to the students by congenial companionship, directly under the advice of the faculty and directly under the influence of the home circle.

Therefore, all such friendly relationships and associations among the students should be encouraged in every possible manner, because it broadens the minds of the scholars, and teaches aspirations for leadership, which tends in after life to the elevation of womanhood and manhood.

SCHOOL SPIRIT

Whatever arouses school spirit is beneficial to the school—the association of the students in fraternities and sororities leads to an interest in the welfare of each other, particularly in school spirit and school enthusiasm. Such companionship can only be congenial and successful in its purpose when voluntary, as democracy and equality cannot be forced.

In this age almost the entire social life of a school is furnished by the sororities and fraternities, and if a school be robbed of its social spirit, then indeed will it fail of advancement.

THE SOCIETIES RIGHTFULLY EXIST

Fraternities and sororities undoubtedly, rightly exist, and there is no doubt that they will exist in fact, if not in name. Why should they not be permitted an open, rather than a secret, existence?

Is it possible for anyone to admit the rightful existence of any religious, political, or civic society, and then to honestly and truthfully deny the rightful existence of fraternities and sororities?

The argument that all students are not invited to membership in the societies is not pertinent—parents are not above their likes and dislikes, why then should students be criticised because they are similarly constituted?

It has been said that members of the societies receive most of the elective offices and honors in the school. This may be true, but it is equally true that there are many instances wherein non-members receive the honors in the literary field, debating organizations, and athletic positions, etc.

In the world at large the active and energetic individuals receive the rewards.

Congenial companionship, friendship, and loyal co-operation are of right matters of choice and never have been, and never can be, successfully forced upon a people or an individual. The free and untrammeled exercise of such right by the people in matters of this kind should not be invaded to the extent here sought to be exercised.

CONCLUSION

If a student stays too long or too late at fraternity meetings, it is not the fault of the society, but of the student personally, and likely is chargeable to his early training, or rather to the lack of same. So if a parent, by remaining at his club, neglects his family, would anyone say the fault was with the club rather than with the individual?

It must be recalled that a member of the faculty is to act as counselor to each fraternity; that no freshman shall be eligible to membership; that no pupil shall be admitted without the consent of his, or her parent, or guardian; and there shall be no fraternity houses, but that the meetings are to be held at the home of some member of the societies. Could the students be in attendance at a better place than the home of a fellow student? Surely the parents will not deny their sons and daughters social relationship under such good and favorable auspices.

In submitting this argument we request a vote on the proposition from every recipient hereof, because we believe our contention herein expressed will be upheld by an overwhelmingly large majority.

JOHN G. DRENNAN,
ROBERT L. HENRY,
CHARLES F. DAVIES,
Committee.

OBJECTIONS TO SECRET SOCIETIES IN THE UNIVERSITY HIGH SCHOOL

I. SOME FUNDAMENTAL PRINCIPLES INVOLVED

1. They are not needed. Students live at home, under direct care of parents and teachers. They are mere imitations of college societies without their justification.

2. They are selfish, unsocial and exclusive, working for their members' welfare as against that of the community.

3. All secrecy among young people except the protection of private rights is dangerous, inevitably harboring evil. A reasonable chaperonage is necessary in developed societies. The young must learn to have their pleasures in the open neighborhood of those who care for them.

4. Educators work for the prolongation of the spirit of childhood and youth. Fraternities tend toward early sophistication, imitation of elders, worldly social success, manipulation of community politics and experimentation in vice.

5. They are undemocratic, preventing the free formation of social groups. Students cannot leave them without accusations of dishonor, "disloyalty," even if a mistake has been made.

6. These societies cause a too early fixing of social choice.

7. High-school students should meet many people of varied character and experience and keep a broad social horizon. The secret societies are narrowing.

8. Secret societies likely to suggest, stimulate, and spread immorality. "Loyalty" and group protection against outsiders keep it secret. No self-cleansing principle in the system, and discipline uncommon except on outside pressure.

9. No such thing as adequate supervision; supervision is opposed to the very nature of the societies. It makes teachers spies, and injures their usefulness.

10. They create false notions of social life as consisting of (1) a few private friends, (2) "society" functions, (3) constant amusement, instead of co-operation in all school activities.

II. HARMFUL TO THE MEMBERS THEMSELVES

1. High-school students are immature, unable to profit by social mistakes without interpretative help of home and school. Secret societies avoid this help by deliberate isolation from social life to the whole, and resistance to, natural community criticism.

2. The effects of "rushing" are bad, causing anxiety, excitement, confusion of interests, and waste of time.

3. The mystery surrounding secret societies and the social eminence supposedly conferred, give false estimates of their value to immature students.

4. They are a common cause of strife between rival fraternities, and between fraternities and "barbarians."

5. High-school fraternity members develop a narrow spirit of partisanship; and also partisan manipulation of school activities. Out of this rises the school "boss," whose pernicious activity hides too often behind the fair name of "school spirit."

6. They choose largely persons of wealth, social position, and striking personal gifts. This develops exclusiveness, snobbery, and neglect of many schoolmates.

7. The fraternity and sorority life forces a premature "society" life between boys and girls, filled with personal and social dangers.

8. The wide testimony is that these societies among young people tend to lower the general moral tone of members, that idling, expense, trivial conversation, indulgence, love of display, and the spread of gossip all accumulate in these protected eddies of school life.

9. The special moral evils of boys' fraternities are always possible, constantly likely, and actual and notorious enough to frighten serious parents. These evils are keeping late hours,

ribald language, obscene songs, smoking, drunkenness, gambling, and social vice.

III. THE EVIL TO STUDENTS NOT MEMBERS

1. All students have equal rights to school advantages. The small secret, aggressive groups take an unfair share of these advantages, and make most of the students outsiders, "barbarians."

2. When secret societies are permitted there is a vast amount of social pain among non-members from feelings of accidental or organized neglect, and from natural timidity, and social inexperience.

3. This brings great pressure on students to join the societies, when many would prefer to remain out.

4. Special bitterness arises from the not uncommon experience of being "rushed" and then not elected.

IV. SECRET SOCIETIES A MENACE TO THE SCHOOL

1. They are almost uniformly opposed by teachers—a sufficiently convincing argument alone.

2. They are commonly centers of rebellion against school regulations. Witness the well-authenticated report that the fraternities of our high school during the past winter have persisted in initiating members against the clearly announced rule of the faculty forbidding it.

3. They are opposed to a genuine "school spirit."

4. Though self-appointed, they assume to take charge of student activities, they tend to monopolize them, to interfere with free initiative of other students, and with proposals from the faculty.

5. They tend to destroy student interest in literary, scientific and art societies.

V. IN RELATION TO PARENTS AND HOMES

1. Parents who have the best developed home life and show most interest in education almost uniformly oppose secret societies. These societies break up the perfect understanding and kindly co-operation between parents, children, and the school, which is the new ideal.

2. It forms the habit of leaving home to find society, amusement, and other than family standards of conduct.

VI. SOME MINOR CONSIDERATIONS

1. No private rights are involved in prohibition, since the societies are clearly school societies, originate there, prosper there, and have their evil influence there.

2. They are increasingly opposed by their own graduate members, and by college fraternities, and sorority members.

3. The ramifications of the societies through other schools is a confusion and danger to the ideals of the local school.

4. These arguments look toward the future, toward an ideal yet to be developed, and especially toward cautious parents whose children are yet to enter the school.

VII. OUR PROPOSALS FOR DEVELOPING THE SOCIAL LIFE OF THE SCHOOL

1. That the school provide a Student Club House for boys and one for girls. That these houses be placed under the care of intelligent, well-bred persons, and be open to all students on equal terms.

2. That the school develop, when they do not now exist, many clubs of objective interests—literary, debating, art, music, collections, outing, athletic, dramatic, scientific—and furnish them meeting places.

3. That the school furnish a systematic series of school parties, varied to suit the age and social experience of many students. That these be chaperoned and managed by a combination of students, faculty, and parents.

4. That the school and the Parents' Association devise a large series of home parties, co-ordinated so as to prevent intemperance and neglect.

5. That all school honors and leadership be kept open, and administered by the faculty.

W. D. MacClintock,
Arthur J. Mason,
Eva R. Greeley,
Committee.

MEETING OF THE PARENTS' ASSOCIATION

MRS. FRANK HUGH MONTGOMERY
Secretary Parents' Association

APRIL 19, 1905

After the minutes of the preceding meeting had been read and approved, the Executive Committee was enlarged by adding four parents, nominated from the floor in accordance with an amendment to Article IV of the constitution, proposed at the previous meeting.

The report of the Education Committee was read by Mrs. John O'Connor, chairman. She said that the value of the Parents' Association depended largely upon the interest it succeeded in arousing in the school on the part of the parents, in order to make them more familiar with the principles of the school, and thus secure their co-operation in bringing the school into closer and right relationships with the ideal of the school. The work of the Education Committee was to aid this result by the stimulation of its own special phases of the work. According to the by-laws the work of the Education Committee was "to direct the educational interests of the association, particularly in the study of the educational principles of the school, and the ways in which the association can aid in carrying them out." The committee, as appointed by the chairman, has consisted of mothers from each grade in the elementary school and the first year in the high school, who called and presided at the meeting of their special grade or class. The plan has been to discuss the particular educational question of the class. The attendance has varied from six or seven to eighteen or twenty. The class teacher has always been present, and sometimes the special teachers, which made the meetings of much more value.

The first and third grades discussed the question of reading. Despite varying opinions on the part of the mothers, all expressed confidence in the judgment of the teacher. The consensus of opinion was that, at the end of the third school year the child should have acquired the ability to read matter suitable to that age. The mothers of the second group took more ethical subjects, as selfishness, discourtesy, untidiness, carelessness, their causes and remedies. The school excursion was also discussed, and the suggestion made that the mothers join in the excursion in order to lessen the responsibility of the teacher. It was also advocated that a study of trees and birds be a feature of these excursions. The discussion of excursions extended throughout all the grades. It was felt by some mothers that the excursions overtaxed the strength of young children. It was clearly shown that the work of the school necessitated excursions, and that the knowledge gained could be secured by no other means, not only in knowledge of facts, but in training of the mind. It was felt that the number of teachers should be sufficiently large to secure the safety of all, and that the parents should receive notice in advance in order to have children better prepared. Another subject of discussion was the dramatic work. It was shown by the teacher that the work was valuable in developing the imagination, the power of expression, and the command of language. It was thought that more of the best poetry should be learned by the children, and more of the best literature be read to them. In the fifth group an additional topic was the question of more systematic work in arithmetic and spelling. A vote resulted in a tie on the question of arithmetic, and a majority in favor of spelling.

At the sixth-, seventh-, and eighth-grade meetings, much attention was given to the development of closer unity between the elementary and high schools. This was also expressed in the meetings of the mothers of the first year of the high school. The sense of the high-school meeting was that the work was too formal and abstract; that an arrangement by which children might choose some handwork, other than the complete course in manual training, should be made; that they should have some physical science adapted to their needs; that classes in art, drawing, modeling, and painting should be open to them, and music for the whole school. It was felt that both the elementary and high schools could help to bridge the gap between the eighth grade and first year of high school. It was also the sense of the meeting that the first-year high-school pupils needed more superintendence from the school, more oversight, and personal advice and supervision, that the children should have easier access to their instructors and be encouraged to consult them. Also that there should be some system of assigning home work.

Mrs. O'Connor made the following deductions from her report: (1) That the Home and Education committees should be merged in one. (2) Regular meetings at prearranged and stated intervals, say, one at the beginning of each quarter. (3) That some plan be devised by which the suggestions of the meetings be brought to the notice of the Faculty, perhaps by having a representative of the Parents' Association at the meetings of the Faculty.

The report of the Home committee was made by Mrs. W. S. Jackman, chairman. Mrs. Jackman gave as results of the year's work: (1) Closer knowledge of one another and recognition of the fact that the problems of one are the problems of all. (2) The necessity of following the child to school, and also the need for the teacher to know the child in his home environment. (3) Growth toward the conception of the Parents' Association meetings as platforms for the discussion of educational principles, involving environment, characteristics, and tendencies of young people, looking for definite action which shall better them, and not as an opportunity for fault-finding or discussion of the personality of the individual child. Most grades had held two meetings, some three under the Home Committee and one meeting each in the first and second years of the high school. Attendance had been one-half to one-third the parents in each grade. A great point for consideration was to gain the interest of the parents who sent children to school between fourteen and sixteen years of age, without inquiring as to what they were doing. Interest must be a matter of growth, and the character of the meetings must be improved by presenting subjects of vital interest, and by inviting speakers who should make the presentation of the subject possible. She suggested regular days for meeting or dates for meetings that should be known two or three weeks in advance. She recommended that the meetings of the coming year be planned together by the chairmen of the committees, keeping in mind always the presentation of the two sides of the home and the school. The special work of the Home Committee should be the physical and hygienic conditions surrounding their children, and also their social life. Two meetings of the chairmen and secretaries had been held, one in October and one in March. The subjects were "Responsibility" and "Excursions." It was voted that the teacher should be invited to be present and present the work for the ensuing month, suggesting supplementary reading or indicating in what way the parent might assist the children. This had met with general appreciation and gave the best opportunity possible for studying the actual work of the school in all its relations. About half the meetings had been held in the homes and half in the school. She suggested that the papers that were a distinct contribution to the subject, as a number of those on responsibility had been, should be preserved, and as others were added put into pamphlet form. The discussions showed a great diversity in the amount of responsibility put upon the child, varying from no work at all to a carefully planned co-operation in most of the home functions. Various methods of developing responsibility, as the care of pets, some regular, simple duties, going on errands, gardening, the expression of taste in the selection of home decoration and clothes, etc., were advocated. It was suggested that the difficulty of securing willing service when there were paid employees, might be offset by the return in vacation to very simple living, requiring the working together of all the family. It was urged that beside entering into the life and interests of the children, parents should permit and encourage the children to enter into their plans. It was asked that the children be given an opportunity to carry out the work done in the school in cooking, textiles, and woodwork in the home. It was further agreed that home work occupying twenty minutes might be given for the fourth to sixth grades, and from thirty to forty minutes in the seventh and eighth. In regard to the discussions on excursions which were still in process, it was thought that they contributed greatly to the social life of the children. The mothers of the seventh grade were anxious to secure simple dress at the parties of the children.

The Home Committee had had an especial interest in guarding the health of the children, and it was interesting to note that arrangements had been perfected to give more special attention to the spread of infectious disease. Parents were asked to co-operate.

The treasurer, Mr. A. V. Booth, made his report for the year. One hundred and forty-six members had paid two dollars each, making $292.00. The expenditures had amounted to $208.34, leaving a balance of $83.66.

The secretary made an informal report and suggested ways of securing and keeping more accurate lists.

It was voted that the Executive Committee be asked to prepare a plan for closer co-operation between the Parents' Association and the Faculty.

The Nominating Committee made the following report. The officers named were afterward duly elected:

President — Charles A. Heath.

Vice-Presidents — Arthur J. Mason, Mrs. Frank J. Miller, Dr. John M. Dodson.

Secretary — Mrs. A. W. Moore.

Treasurer — A. V. Booth.

Chairman of the Education Committee — Mrs. James H. Tufts.

Chairman of the Home Committee — Mrs. Frank Hugh Montgomery.

Chairman of the Finance Committee — Mrs. Frank R. Lillie.

Chairman of the Social (House) Committee — Mrs. E. Fletcher Ingals.

The Executive Committee was completed by the nomination from the floor of Mrs. Charles F. Harding, Mrs. William Kent, Mr. Samuel Foss, and Mr. William D. MacClintock, in accordance with the amendment passed earlier in the evening.

The meeting adjourned.

MAY 18, 1905

After the reading and approving of the minutes of the preceding meeting, the address of the evening was given by Mr. James Rowland Angell, Professor of Psychology in the University of Chicago.

Mr. Angell's subject was the problem of properly treating the moral and physical natures of the young people of high-school age, in other words, the general problem of adolescence. Speaking from the standpoint of a parent interested in the school and looking back on his own experience, he felt stimulated to a fresh sense of duty in the matter. This was a period of (1) great physical changes, which were very remarkable in their nature, as, for example, (*a*) the enlargement of the heart, (*b*) changes in circulation and digestion. In some cases the physical changes were very rapid, and therefore must affect the mental and moral sides of the young person. This was the reason why this age was especially a prey to disease. What should be looked out for: (*a*) The diet. What are we doing in this? How controlled? In this respect common-sense was quite as rare as common. (*b*) Sleep. Surely, here we had not a clear conscience. (*c*) Exercise. By this was specified out-of-door exercise, but not athletics. He was opposed to contests such as football, in boys of this age, although they might be harmless for some boys under some conditions. In this particular we were on the verge of transition and in process of paying bills to the cashier of competitive athletics.

In addition to the physical changes were (2) mental changes, which were tryingly obvious. They were evidenced by an upheaval in emotional life, for which there were physiological reasons. The girls were irritable and obstinate. The boys were self-willed, suspicious, and jealous. All the emotions were not bad. Some were very striking in their possibilities, as altruistic motives, development of sympathetic interest, larger interests in humanity. They must be recognized. We must not bear down too hard, but help the young people to form their own lives. (3) Emotional and intellectual changes, perhaps rather, religious and philosophical interest in life (shown often by scientific interest in nature). We must see to it that these interests are fed, not left to run wild or become perverted. It was a matter that could not be left in the hands of others. (4) Sexual life, which unfolds itself in most trying forms. It must be treated properly. If not, it will bring ills of all sorts. It cannot be slurred over. Only a small fraction of parents strive to meet the dangers. They have no panacea to offer. He urged the necessity of meeting the issue frankly with our own children.

The report of the Executive Committee, for closer co-operation between the Parents' Association and the Faculty, was read by the secretary, as follows:

In accordance with the instructions of the preceding meeting to prepare plans for closer co-operation between the Parents' Association and the teachers, the Executive Committee respectfully submit the following:

I. That the Parents' Association send representatives to all meetings of the Faculties of the University High and Elementary Schools in which subjects of interest to the Parents' Association are to be discussed. Further, that these representatives be the chairmen of the four standing committees.

II. That the Faculties of the three schools (Elementary, High and Teachers' College) send representatives (one from each school) as an Advisory Committee to the regular meetings of the Executive Committee of the Parents' Association.

Further, that the Parents' Association, while expressing its appreciation of the assistance which has been rendered it on the part of the teachers, bespeak their more general interest, not only by attending the meetings, but by taking part in the discussions, believing that the full value of the Parents' Association, as well as the work of the school, can be reached only by the earnest and sincere co-operation of teachers and parents. These recommendations were unanimously adopted.

The report in regard to the referendum vote on fraternities in the University High School was read by the secretary as follows:

A canvass of the votes for and against fraternities and sororities in the University High School resulted as follows: for, 172; against, 389; a majority against of 217.

[Signed] CAROLINE W. MONTGOMERY, *Secretary.*
W. D. MACCLINTOCK,
JOHN G. DRENNAN.

Mr. Owen called attention to the importance of the action in regard to fraternities and its consequences. The Parents' Association must see if it can devise a larger and better social system. Their action against fraternities must be followed by something positive, sensible, and definite. The young people did not like to lose the pleasant social life they had organized. Something must be done.

Mr. Jackman said that he felt that the matter was very important. He thought that there should be a joint committee of parents and students. He should dislike to see the students put in a position of waiting for the Parents' Association to do something. The meeting should not be adjourned before definite action was taken.

It was voted that the Home Committee of the Parents' Association, who had in charge the social life of the school, should be instructed to appoint a special committee to work with committees from the Faculty and students in regard to substitutes for fraternities.

The meeting adjourned.

EDITORIAL NOTES

Education Not a Science

Education is not yet a science. We cannot predict — we but guess at the result of the teaching process. The theory of education supposes the consistent development of high moral character; practice produces types radically different, representing every degree of virtue and iniquity. The outcome of a given course of instruction, of certain methods of teaching, in terms of human life, no one can foretell. When the alchemist sought to transmute the baser metals into fine gold, slag was the uniform result. The teacher can do little better; his products are at best but alloys of uncertain value.

The occupation of the craftsman is different. With given materials and proper tools, his results are definitely predictable. His processes, once fixed, may be represented by formulas which may be carried out ever after by a machine.

Marks of a Craft and a Science

The methods of science are exact. The chemist combines and dissociates the elements according to an established order. When the order is discovered, he is relieved of concern as to the nature of the result. The flame will always explode gunpowder, and water never will. The electric spark under fixed conditions will combine hydrogen and oxygen, forming water. Such transformations of matter belong to the domain of true science. The processes, because regular and exact, are scientific. The operations may be relied upon implicitly to give a definite result. In this they are wholly unlike the guesses of alchemy.

Complexity of the Teacher's Problem

The teacher's problem is peculiar. He is required to produce spiritual results of a definite type from material things. The agency by which this is accomplished is the transforming power of the child's mind. Given the subject-matter of science and history: by the intellectual digestive processes of the pupil, change this into virtue —

into character. To develop justice from geography, to evolve love from history, and to turn chemistry into honesty—these are the problems that confront the teacher, and for him there are no others.

When measured by the standards of science, teaching is a Black Art. Materials are selected at random, methods are a venture and the result a hope. Whether the spiritual output will be righteousness or the reverse, no one can predict. Education, therefore, is not yet a science.

Emphasis on the Wrong Thing

Teaching can never be reduced to mechanics, nor can its principles have the inflexibility of mathematical formulas. It is possible, however, to increase vastly the certainty of the product. This can be done by fixing the attention and by laying the emphasis upon the thing which society really needs—individual character. Most of the stress is now laid upon subject-matter—upon the *means* and not upon the *end*. Pupils are judged, finally, when it comes to promotion, by the knowledge they possess; whereas the chief concern should lie in what they have done with their knowledge. In school as well as outside, the individual should be required to stand, not upon what he is able to do, but upon what he has actually accomplished in contributing to the welfare of the whole. There is no reason why the teacher should longer deceive the pupils by holding up before them false standards. Society is not much interested in the actual amount of knowledge which the individual possesses, but it is mightily interested in what he does with it. When the teacher shows a like concern for this same thing, there will be less uncertainty as to the result of the educational process.

Education a Black Art

Chemistry grew from alchemy only as the chemist discovered all the facts involved in his processes and learned to give them due weight. Education will grow from Black Art into science only as the teacher learns to take into account all the factors that enter into growth, and as the processes of growth become understood. Teachers usually teach as though growth depended upon what the child can take in. So his chief concern is to select and present attractive material that the greedy senses may lay hold and suck their fill. But growth depends no less upon the spiritual result that comes out and again enters the original source of supply. As the leaves of the tree fall about its roots, and in turn stimulate and nourish new growth in its buds and branches, so it is what the pupils put back into their lives through virtuous action, no less than what they take in, that determines what the new growth shall be, and, indeed, whether there shall be new growth at all. Dammed-up knowledge turns stale and sour, and breeds moral disease. It clogs the wit that acquired it, and it benumbs the sympathies that would direct its use.

Growth Measured by Action

The first care of the teacher, therefore, is to see that the pupil's knowledge is kept moving out into virtuous action. Education will become a science when methods of instruction insure, in every case, this result. The teacher therefore must look continually to the *motive*. It is the motive that transmutes the material things of the environment into the spiritual products of righteousness. As the motive becomes strong and well-defined, the outcome of the teaching process becomes predictable. It is only as we acquire the power to determine the motive that education can become a science.

Motive the Reagent

The establishment of the motive is a part of growth itself. It depends upon the preservation of a delicate sensitiveness to genuine needs. Without this, there can be no motive, no certainty of action, no growth, and education remains a Black Art. The average school presents few actual needs to the pupils, and, consequently, they work without proper motive, and there is but little educative action. The life of the school is still stiffened by forms and traditions that originated in an era when the training of childhood was a matter of command, and when the teacher depended upon someone in authority rather than upon his own good judgment as to the needs of the pupils for the direction of his work.

Growth of Motive

The emphasis of the day must be laid upon the quality of

action which the pupil puts into the school, rather than upon the quantity of knowledge which he gains. No curriculum can fully prognosticate this, nor can any set examination adequately find the measure of its worth. Extraneous tests are needless and irrelevant. Inside the school, as elsewhere, life must justify itself through its quality at every step; its worth must be self-demonstrated every moment.

W. S. J.

FIG. 1.—The completed work. See article "Manual Training and Good Citizenship."

VOLUME VI NUMBER 2

THE ELEMENTARY SCHOOL TEACHER

OCTOBER, 1905

MANUAL TRAINING AND GOOD CITIZENSHIP

IRENE CLEAVES, CATHERINE CLEMENTS, IRA M. CARLEY

For the use of the eighth grade of the Francis W. Parker school, in the fall of 1904, the room formerly furnished as a library was turned into a grade room. The library shelves on the south wall were boarded up to afford space for blackboards; but since there was no cupboard in which to keep materials, those covering the whole east wall were left—an unsightly length of open shelves, eight feet high. In all other respects the room is a very attractive one, with the north wall broken by three dormer windows which give a pleasing view of the park and there is a satisfactory absence of cross-light.

At the beginning of the year the pupils of the grade saw at once the admirable features of the room and its disfiguring shelves as well, and recognized the necessity of amending the appearance of the east wall. This became the problem of the class for the winter quarter in their work in art and manual training.

A few of the designs which were made and rejected are shown, to make clear the advance in taste which the children undoubtedly achieved before they found a plan which pleased them. The canons of taste which they established for themselves show constantly in their attitude toward interior decorating and their interest in it. The visible result of their work in design and execution is to be seen in the photograph of the finished work shown at the head of this article. There were other results which were also of some interest.

The class has been engaged all the year in a study of Chicago. It is possible in an eighth-grade civics class to study the problems of a great city, and the way such a city as Chicago is trying to solve some of these problems. It is far from desirable to call the attention of such a class to the distressing aspects of municipal conditions. That is to say, it was worth while to make an excursion down the Drainage Canal, and another to the cribs; to study the history of our drainage and water-supply; to see why our problem was more difficult than that of seaboard cities; to make maps and diagrams for the use of next year's class; to see the expense attendant upon correcting our terrible mistake of draining sewage into the lake; and to find out how taxes are levied to pay this expense, and why the state government had to authorize the organization of our drainage board. But to see the opportunities for corruption which this form of organization afforded was no furtherance to the end of influencing the pupils to good citizenship.

To the lesson that good citizenship consists in actual constructive service to the community—for which lesson their year's work in civics was meant to give a background—their work in manual training in the winter quarter gave the desirable practical application. For three months they put all the skill they had into a piece of work which was not to be taken home, but to remain in the school, to be of use to all succeeding eighth grades, and a pleasure to all who should see it; and they had worked together, each doing the kind of work he best liked and could best do, and feeling responsible for the quality of his particular contribution, and all interested in the excellence of every part. And where manual training can give a class an opportunity to render a valuable service to the community, in a task which develops individual taste and ability, and engenders interest in the work of others and respect for the achievement of others, it seems to be the greatest single influence toward sympathetic, responsible, active good-citizenship.

The description which follows is intended to show how the details of the work were planned and carried out, together with something of the gain in the technique of design and woodworking which was acquired.

The pupils of the grade, after some discussion as to the best

FIG. 2.—Design not accepted

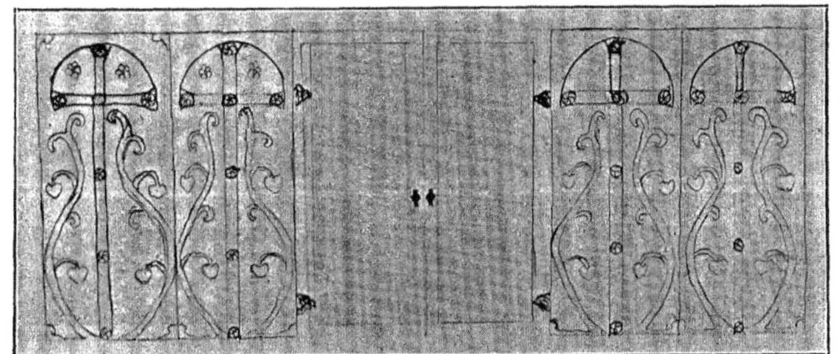

FIG. 3.—Design not accepted

FIG. 4.—Design not accepted

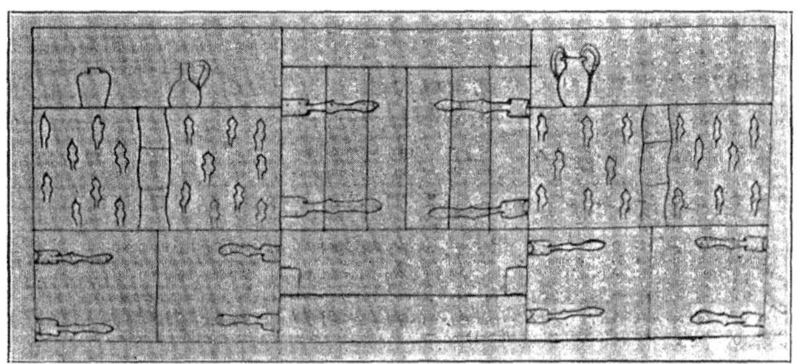

FIG. 5.—Design not accepted

general method of treating the shelves, with a view to securing both sightliness and utility, made several different plans, each child, in fact, contributing at least one. Other members of the school, both pupils and teachers, also were invited to offer suggestions, and this invitation was accepted to some extent, one grade in particular contributing a complete set of sketches.

At this point in the progress of the work, the discussions in the class were upon such questions as the best and most beautiful way to divide the space; the proportion and shape of the divisions —how much space to give to the inclosed cupboards, and how much to the curtained shelves; etc. Rough gray paper was tacked up over the shelves, and different plans were sketched out on it full size, to see how each would actually appear. Some of the suggested plans, which were most favorably considered, and the one which was finally adopted, are shown herewith.

When the arrangement of the closed cupboards and curtained shelves had been decided upon, together with the more important details of construction, such as, notably, the form of door to be used and the style of the bench, (a bench or settle for visitors, to be placed in front of the shelves, had been added to the plan as a hospitable after-thought), the children took different parts to design in detail, and assumed the responsibility for their making.

This selection was made, partly in accordance with the preference of the individual for work of a certain kind, and partly— perhaps to a greater degree—by the consensus of opinion of the grade as to the member of the class best fitted successfully to carry out a certain part of the work.

In working out the design and colors for the curtains, the children made a considerable incidental study of design. They visited Marshal Field's to look at beautifully designed curtains, and the Arts and Crafts shops to see how designs are made and put on.

In designing their own curtains, they tried borders, panel effects, and all-over patterns. After much experimental sketching of this nature, in pencil and color, full-size drawings of sketches most favorably considered were made on the blackboard.

Meanwhile much attention was devoted to the study of color

in general in the effort to select colors which would go well with those of the walls and woodwork. The north lighting, too, was necessarily taken account of in the color scheme.

The final decision was for an all-over pattern of green on tan-colored linen, using the Lombardy poplar for motif, the pattern to be put on with stencil.

In designing the hinge-plates, much the same methods were employed. Some of the children visited the Newberry Library to see designs of hinges, and many drawings were made, and full-size paper patterns cut out, before anything which at all satisfied the class was produced. When the form was finally agreed upon (see Fig. 9), a stiff pattern was carefully made, and the hinge-plates were marked by it upon sheet copper of medium weight. They were then cut out and raised in the center by hammering into a wooden mold made for the purpose.

A number of the members of the class were somewhat dissatisfied with the use of hinge-plates merely for decoration, but as true hinges of decorative type have had to be forged in iron, for which work none of the pupils was prepared, it was decided to use the plates, temporarily at least, as the general style of the doors demanded something of the sort.

For a time the class was anxious to have the space above the large doors of the center cupboard finished in leaded glass, but finally the suggestion was made that it should be finished with copper panels, set into an oak frame, the panels to be decorated in a way to carry out the scheme of decoration used on the curtains. This idea was adopted, and one boy was given charge of that work. The tree designs were carefully drawn on the face side of the copper and outlined with a chasing tool; then the design was raised up from the back, the copper sheet being supported on soft wood, which furnished a sufficiently yielding surface into which to beat the design.

In the woodwork the chief difficulties were encountered in making the long joints required in the doors and bench. As some of these were four feet or more in length, and the wood used was oak, a great deal of care and patience was demanded, and a good degree of skill in accurate planing was developed.

FIG. 6—Accepted design

FIG. 7.—Design for curtain not accepted

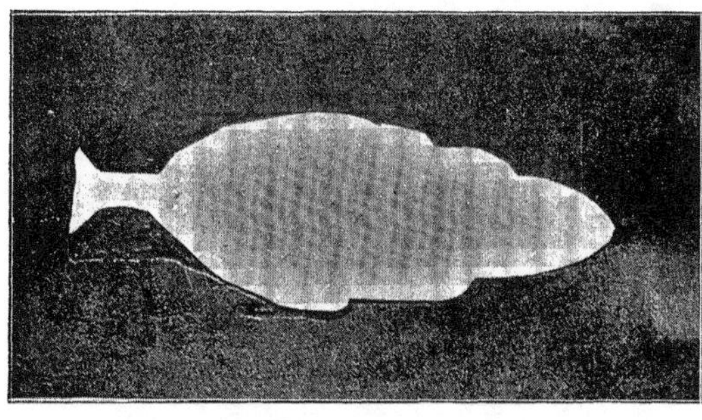

FIG. 8.—Stencil used in decorating curtain

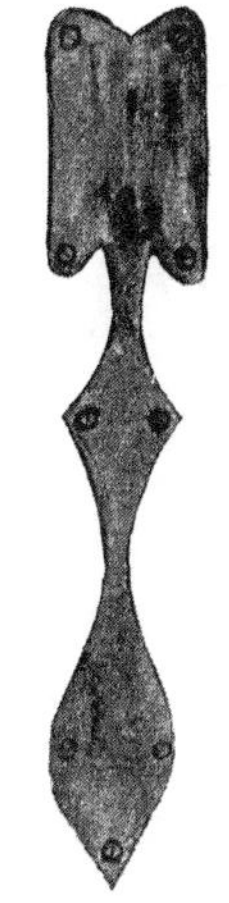

FIG. 9.—Design used for copper hinge

Each joint was amply doweled to insure permanence and rigidity, and cleats were screwed across the inside of the doors to keep them flat.

The children also had considerable trouble in fitting the hinges and hanging the doors so that they would swing properly. Although both the operations were tolerably familiar to them in previous pieces of work, the size and weight of the work added greatly to its difficulty.

In looking over the results of the work, it would seem that the greatest gain, from the technical point of view, in the wood working, was in the handling of larger pieces, the making of the long joints, the setting up and plumbing of the door frames, and the squaring and hanging of the comparatively large and heavy doors, all of which, though really repetitions of operations with which the pupils were familiar appeared, in this larger piece of work, in the nature of new undertakings.

In design, the greatest value of the work was in the incentive it furnished to the children to find out the laws and principles governing good design. The pupils saw that in making their own designs they arrived at pleasing results only after a great deal of experimenting, and that with no certain knowledge to guide them. Even when one of the class chanced upon something which he liked, it was often discovered, upon critical examination, to possess faults and weaknesses which easily might have been avoided, had he possessed some knowledge of the fundamental principles underlying all good design.

The organization of the work, as effected by the children, in a very informal and almost unconscious manner, was very interesting. The interest of the grade as a whole was so thoroughly enlisted in the undertaking that no child thought of not contributing. The natural leaders gradually assumed direction of the work, and carried the responsibility of it, while the less capable members of the group were aroused to their greatest effort.

In a word, the work was great enough, and inspiring enough, from the children's point of view, to incite each member of the class to the highest quality of thought and action.

CHEMISTRY IN THE ELEMENTARY SCHOOL

INGA A. ALLISON
Lake Erie College, Painesville, Ohio

[In the development of nature-study within the past decade, no branch of the subject has received so little attention as chemistry. There are several reasons, good and bad, for this neglect. Nature-study has always been more or less clouded with the story-book method, and this branch of the subject does not lend itself easily to such treatment. Fortunately, nobody yet has attempted to introduce the children to chemistry by reporting in story form a familiar conversation between "Mr." and "Mrs. Atom;" nor has anyone yet worked out the infinite literary possibilities that may lie in the detailed tribulations of the little "baby atoms." It is not to be expected, however, that we shall much longer escape a dramatic presentation of the lives of "Papa" and "Mamma Microbe," the effect of which will be to impress upon the vivid imagination of childhood the picture of something like a cross between a rhinoceros and a crocodile.

There is some difficulty in the fact that many of the phenomena belonging to the field of chemistry arise from changes that are obscure in their origin and difficult to observe. But the chief trouble is that most teachers seem to think that the only way to begin the subject is to start with certain experiments relating to chemical change which through endless repetition have come to be known as "classics." Whoever heard of beginning chemistry in any other way than by decomposing mercuric oxide and by combining iron filings and sulphur!

There are, though, many ways in which pupils come into contact with chemical phenomena. When proper attention is given to it, no other aspect of nature is more profoundly interesting to children. The following outline is intended to illustrate some of the points of contact which the child makes with the subject in his ordinary experiences, leaving it to the sense of the teacher to see how such work should be carried out in detail.— Note by the Editor.]

OCTOBER

THE COMPOSITE NATURE OF FRUITS; RELATIVE AMOUNTS OF CONSTITUENTS; PROPERTIES OF THESE CONSTITUENTS

First Grade	Second Grade	Third Grade	Fourth Grade	Fifth Grade	Sixth Grade	Seventh Grade	Eighth Grade
Compare different ripe fruits as to general proportion of water (juice) present. Dry the fruits; note loss of moisture.	See First Grade. Preservation of fruits and vegetables; first, as begun in the gathering, packing, and transportation of fruit. Conditions presenting decay and fermentation.	Constituents of fruit or plants: water, organic solid, ash. Note relation of ash in fruits with that part of the soil that will not burn. Determine the presence of water in the soil. Trace a fruit from growing place to consumer; note method of preservation. Plants: parts, functions. Evaporation as a means of preservation.	Fruits and vegetables: constituents. Sugar: presence in fruits and vegetables as a preservative. Relation of soil constituency to growth. Temperature relations to growth. Thermometer.	Plant growth: conditions of. Study of plant fiber: action of *acid* and alkali upon fibers (dyeing). Canning of fruit: conditions. Vinegar from apples: formation of acid. *Acid* and *alkali* tests.	Preservation of fruits and vegetables: salt, spice, heat, sugar. Preparations for change in season: by plants, in light of chemical change.	Seed formation: result of chemical change. Rise of industries. Common metallic elements. Cu, Ag, Au, Fe, Pb; occurrence, properties, compounds, metallurgy, uses. Continue in November.	Changes in vegetable life: result of chemical change. Weather observation: barometer.

NOVEMBER

CHEMICAL CHANGE SEEN IN DECAY (VEGETABLE AND ANIMAL); RELATION TO PHYSICAL CHANGE; CONDITIONS OF DECAY

First Grade	Second Grade	Third Grade	Fourth Grade	Fifth Grade	Sixth Grade	Seventh Grade	Eighth Grade
Conditions of decay: means of preservation by nature; by man.	Weather observation; effect of frost in decay. Temperature below surface of ground several feet; value of this fact in preventing decay in hibernation. Grains: kinds. Flours: kinds. Properties of different products of wheat grains.	See Second Grade for first half of outline. Constituents of soil. Metals: Cu, Fe, Pb; where found; mining; melting; casting. Continued in December.	Swamps: how formed. Constituents of soils in general: formation of. Clay beds: formation of; Use of clay in brick; the making of bricks.	Milling of flour. Chemical properties of milled products. Soap making; action of *acid* upon *alkali*. Properties of resulting salts. Term: *neutralization*.	Product of fermentation: CO_2; experiment. Yeast: effect of temperature upon; yeast under microscope. Vinegar making. CO_2 a product of direct chemical action, as in baking powders.	Make and identify O and CO_2. Respiration $\rightarrow CO_2$; decay $\rightarrow CO_2$; chemical compounds $\rightarrow CO_2$ (baking powder). Substitutes in cooking, for baking-powder, as molasses (if acid) and soda; sour milk and soda.	

DECEMBER

LIBERATION OF ENERGY; RESULTING FROM CHEMICAL CHANGE; OXYGEN

First Grade	Second Grade	Third Grade	Fourth Grade	Fifth Grade	Sixth Grade	Seventh Grade	Eighth Grade
Butter-making: constituents of milk; properties of fat; steps in butter-making. Making of flour: wheat ground in schoolroom. Compare the properties of fine, white, final product with coarser intermediate product as to thickening properties, etc.	Butter: see First Grade. Primitive methods of churning. Flour: continued from November.	Starch: vegetables used as source of supply. By experiment make starch; cooking temperature of starch; properties; test for presence of.	Combustion giving rise to heat and light; combustible materials. Resulting product of combustion, CO_2, compared with breath. Necessity of oxygen for combustion.	Making candles: primitive, modern. Fats used: wicks, snuffers. Structure of flame. Products of combustion in candle flame. See *necessity* of oxygen.	Heat the result of chemical change. Various methods for the production of heat. Heating of houses—methods. Lighting of houses. Light the result of chemical change. Compare primitive with modern methods; relative values.	Respiration: relation to body heat. Ventilation: necessity for—principles of—	

JANUARY

FOOD PRINCIPLES; PROPERTIES; TESTS

First Grade	Second Grade	Third Grade	Fourth Grade	Fifth Grade	Sixth Grade	Seventh Grade	Eighth Grade
Continue work outlined for December. In cooking the fruits dried in the fall, note the large quantity of water required for cooking; compare by cooking fresh fruit of the same class.	Soils: note the comparative amounts of organic matter present; note moisture in different soils.	Constituents of flour: test for starch; separate gluten. Starch under microscope. Effect of high heat upon starch; e. g., sweetened crust of bread.	Extract starch from vegetables; test vegetables for starch; properties of starch. Gluten in flour a proteid. Egg-albumen a proteid. Cooking temperature of proteids. Sugar: kinds, distribution, manufacture of, use.	Starchy foods: value. *Solubility* of starch; effect of heat upon starch; of moist heat, dry heat. *Solubility* of egg-albumen. Effect of heat. Gluten in flour; value in bread-making.	Conversion of starch into sugar. Albumenoid in milk, compared with egg-albumen; how coagulation is effected.	Starch: structure of grain. Compare carbohydrates and proteids as to food value. Dietary studies: rough food analyses.	

FEBRUARY

CARBON: SOURCE, FORMS; CARBON-DIOXIDE

First Grade	Second Grade	Third Grade	Fourth Grade	Fifth Grade	Sixth Grade	Seventh Grade	Eighth Grade
Fuel on farm; fuel used in city. *Thermometer:* the reading of; read the freezing-point.	Fuels in primitive life: turf, wood, etc.; compare with fuel of today.	Combustible materials. Incombustible materials. Preservation of meats and fish a winter industry as well; preservation by salt, smoke, drying.	Systems of heating: relative values. Heat transmission: methods. Metals: smelting.	Presence of *carbon* in all combustible substances. Review: candle dipping; comparison of flame. Alloys: making of; those suitable for dishes.	Forms of carbon: sources and uses of CO_2	Combustion defined in broad sense. Use of matches: sulphur match, lucifer match, phosphorous match. Phosphorous: (1) properties, (2) kinds. Principle of safety mach. Gaseous product of drawing match	Heating, lighting, ventilation of the modern house.

MARCH

COMBINATION (OXIDATION), CONDITIONS OF; KINDS OF; FLAME STRUCTURE

First Grade	Second Grade	Third Grade	Fourth Grade	Fifth Grade	Sixth Grade	Seventh Grade	Eighth Grade
Conditions of combustion — general. Recognize a few of the materials (substances that will not burn).	Review February outline. Combustible materials. Conditions of combustion.		Old methods of "starting" a fire: flint, steel, tinder. (Sacredness of hearth.) Relation of heating system to system of ventilation.	Structure of flame: necessity of oxygen. Conditions under which plants grow; hotbed. Decaying matter generates heat.		Sources and uses of CO_2.	

APRIL

WATER: SOURCES, PROPERTIES (CHEMICAL AND PHYSICAL), PURIFICATION

First Grade	Second Grade	Third Grade	Fourth Grade	Fifth Grade	Sixth Grade	Seventh Grade	Eighth Grade
Forms of water: rain, melted snow and ice. Experiments in germination of plants; needs of plants.	Compare "city" water and "well" water with that obtained as rain, melted ice, snow, etc. Needs of plants. Try the different soils in January study; how do they meet the needs of plants?	Sources of water; properties of "hard" and "soft" water. Something in the one requires the use of more soap.	Sources of water: (1) conveyance, (2) properties, (3) characteristics. Purification: by distillation, filtration. Drainage.	Forms of water: value of soap in using "hard" water. Soap-making reviewed. Distinguish "hard" and "soft" soaps.	Water: boiling point, freezing point. Fahrenheit and Centigrade. Needs of plants. *Nitrogen* supplied by some.	Action of certain metals upon water. Sodium — + water; sodium hydroxide; + hydrogen. Note alkalinity; NaOH formed. Collect and test *hydrogen*.	Form in which water occurs in substances: (1) water of crystallization (alum); (2) integral part of substance (sugar); (3) water inclosed between crystals, salt.
Maple sap: boil to obtain sugar. *Evaporation:* Power of chemical change in tree; building up sugar. *Dissolve* much sugar; note consequent hardening in solution.							Use of terms, hygroscopic effervescent, etc.

MAY

ATMOSPHERE: COMPOSITION; AFFECTED BY RESPIRATION, HENCE VENTILATION; PRESENCE OF MOISTURE; PRESSURE; TEMPERATURE

First Grade	Second Grade	Third Grade	Fourth Grade	Fifth Grade	Sixth Grade	Seventh Grade	Eighth Grade
Reading thermometer.	Composition of atmosphere very variable.	Relation of plants to soil, light, and air.	Relation of plants to soil.	Weight of air; constituents of air.	Air in room, in upper and lower part.	*Analysis of air:* Burn phosphorus in inclosed space.	
	Discover the presence of water, dust, gases in air.	Experiments indicating the result if either in insufficient quantity or quality.		Determine roughly the relative proportion of these constituents.	As result: what import in ventilation?	Remaining gas does not support combustion; is not O, not CO_2, but ***nitrogen.***	
					Devise system of ventilation:	Determine relative proportions of CO_2, *N*, and O, and moisture in the air.	
					Necessity of pure air for blood.		

JUNE

ELECTRICITY; RESULT OF CHEMICAL CHANGE; EXPERIMENTS IN GENERATING ELECTRICITY

First Grade	Second Grade	Third Grade	Fourth Grade	Fifth Grade	Sixth Grade	Seventh Grade	Eighth Grade
						Make an electric battery; principles of; magnets, magnetism.	

Proper understanding of chemical terms. All of outline illustrated and worked out experimentally.

CORRELATION OF MATHEMATICS AND SCIENCE[1]

CLARENCE E. COMSTOCK
Bradley Polytechnic Institute, Peoria, Ill.

A foreword in regard to the point of view of this paper may be of service. I take it that any interplay between the school courses in different subjects to be of lasting value must spring from underlying relations which serve as essential links binding those subjects into one. This interplay must result in mutual helpfulness, or else it fails of its purpose. Science is not to be lugged into mathematics as an outsider, nor is mathematics to be foisted upon science as an added burden. If it can be found that the one is indispensable to the other, then and only then can there be any reasonableness in the remarks offered in this paper. I trust that you will find the position of the speaker a thousand miles removed from that of the teacher in a grammar school of a decade or two ago, who, holding up a bird before her bright-eyed pupils, asked them to count its eyes, its legs, its toes, its wings, etc.; and then propounded these elucidating questions: "How many eyes and toes does the birdie have? If it had three more toes, how many would it have in all? If you multiply the number of its eyes by the number of its toes, what would the result be?"

From the point of view of the scientist, mathematics is a tool of science; from the point of view of the mathematician, science is a field for the application of mathematical truth; from the viewpoint of both, mathematics is a method of science. In fact, it may be called the ultimate method of science; the more perfectly a science is developed, the more mathematical does it become, until it reaches a stage when it is classified as mathematics. Away in the past was it when the sciences of arithmetic and geometry assumed their mathematical names. In comparatively recent years mechanics has reached this same development,

[1] Paper read before the Department of Science Instruction of the National Educational Association,, Asbury Park, N. J., July, 1905.

and is now classed as mathematics. The various branches of physical science, astronomy, meteorology, and chemistry are rapidly being subjugated by this method of exact investigation; while the biological, mental, and social sciences are still in a very unmathematical state of evolution. The method is of such power and value that it must itself be made the subject of investigation; its inner relations must be scrutinized, and the inevitability of its conclusions established on a firm basis. There has thus arisen the most wonderful and enthralling science of them all—that science which defies definition, for it transcends all limiting bounds; that science which rears unto itself in imagination a palace whose walls and turrets know not the limiting thraldom of time and space; the queen science of them all, abstract mathematics.

If this view of the relation of mathematics and science in general be true, then it would seem that there should be a corresponding intimacy between the courses offered in schools and colleges for instruction in these subjects. Of course, there is and always has been a certain degree of interplay between such courses; but the query obtrudes itself: Cannot a more vital and effective relation be maintained? It is easy to see that the study of mathematics is absolutely essential to anything but a very superficial knowledge of the sciences. Physical laws of action, the laws of chemical action, and the laws of the formation of crystals are derived from observed data and verified by the methods of the higher mathematics. It is the very language of science. To read Shakespeare, one needs to know the meaning and the use of words. To read Hilton's *Chrystallography,* Preston's *Theory of Light,* or the works of the masters in chemistry, a very considerable acquaintance with mathematics is a prerequisite, if they are not to be sealed books.

But it is not to the scientific man alone that mathematics is indispensable; the engineering profession, that vast army of workers in applied science, is equally in need of such knowledge.

The minute differentiation of the engineering profession which has in very recent times resulted in the separation of the countless pursuits which require technical education, has opened an ever-increasing field for the operation of human activities. The specialists who concern themselves with problems of sanitation, water supply, highway construction, marine architecture, bridge-building, the telephone, tannery, refinery, and manufactory, the machinist and the designer—all these, and a thousand more, call for expert technical knowledge. It is becoming more and more apparent that success in these technical professions is conditioned upon such knowledge and training. In a recent meeting of the National Association of Electrical Engineers it was the generally expressed conviction that one prerequisite for success in that profession is a thorough training in mathematics. It is clear that science is an indispensable part of modern civilization. Of course, science is not the only element in education, for culture is broader and must include much more. And yet it is certainly true that when so large a part of modern human activity is based upon scientific knowledge, it becomes necessary that the schools furnish ample opportunity for adequate instruction in science. I here use the word "science" to include both natural and mathematical science.

An examination into the teaching of science in the schools and colleges of America for the past two hundred years or so reveals some interesting things. Until very recently the study of science was considered of little importance. The amount of mathematics required in courses in astronomy and natural philosophy in early American times can be inferred from the amount of mathematics taught. At Harvard in 1643 the mathematical course began in the senior year, and consisted of arithmetic, geometry, and astronomy. The science of algebra was unknown on the continent. The importance ascribed to mathematics is shown by the time devoted to different studies: philosophy, 10 hours; Greek, 6; rhetoric, 6; oriental languages, 4; mathematics, 2.

In 1726 natural philosophy was given in the junior year, but was metaphysical rather than mathematical in form; nor could it be otherwise, as arithmetic and geometry were still taught in the senior year. By 1742 algebra was taught at Yale, and the mathematical studies were put earlier in the course. The freshmen had arithmetic and algebra; the sophomores, geometry; the juniors, mathematics (probably trigonometry), conic sections, and natural philosophy. By 1766 fluxions had been introduced as an optional study.

Since 1816 the whole of arithmetic has been required for entrance to Harvard. The catalogue of 1825 adds algebra through simple equations, with roots, powers, and the progressions. In 1843 a little introductory geometry was added. The mathematical course at Harvard in 1818 was as follows: freshmen — algebra and geometry; sophomores — algebra and trigonometry, with application to heights and distances and navigation; juniors — natural philosophy, astronomy, mensuration of surfaces and solids, surveying; seniors — conic sections, spherical geometry.

The physics taught in the colleges of the eighteenth century required very little knowledge of mathematics. To master Olmsted's *Natural Philosophy,* which was extensively used during the middle of the nineteenth century, a fair knowledge of algebra and geometry, with a very little trigonometry, was sufficient. Almost no mathematics was used in the treatment of heat and electricity, whereas now calculus is commonly used in college courses in physics. In former days, when the college course (classical) chiefly trained for the so-called learned professions, the student found very little or no field in which his mathematics was needed. There was no application for it in his serious work, and it was therefore studied purely for a cultural value, as a means of training the general logical and reasoning powers of the mind. But with the growth of scientific study, and the rise of scientific courses and technical schools, the study of mathematics has assumed a much more important rôle. It now becomes an essential prerequisite to the future work of a large number of students; it becomes highly functional rather than decorative or gymnastic. We begin to learn that the real worth of mathematical study is not the general training of the mind, but the training of the mind in mathematical thought, to the end that our ignorance of the phenomena about us may be lessened and our impotence in the face of the forces which surround us may be reduced.

One would naturally suppose that such an important change

in function ought to have considerable influence in determining the form in which mathematics is presented to the student. It is having some effect in the dethronement of the mathematical fetish; the increasing tendency to make mathematical study optional is traceable, I think, in some degree to this cause. And yet the courses themselves are too little affected. In most cases the vital connection between mathematics and science is not dwelt upon, and the student fails to find any place for his mathematics in his scheme of life. He learns to cipher, but sees in it nothing but an artificial pastime. Now, ciphering is of value when ciphering leads to some desired end. The ability to solve a quadratic equation in itself is worthless; it is only when the equation is solved for some other end that the ability to solve it has meaning.

It appears to be true that under present conditions the student is not properly prepared in mathematics for his work in science. A training which does not furnish the student with the best and most efficient mathematical equipment for such work is certainly misdirected. It would seem to me that the statement just made must be acceded to, no matter what view is taken as to the end of mathematical study in the school. This brings us to the main question of this paper: How can courses in mathematics be organized to better meet the needs of science?

A speaker in a recent convention of electrical engineers said: "What we need most is a common-sense mathematics." This voices what seems to me to be an imperative need. We need a mathematics stripped of its artificialities and direct in its purpose. It is often a far cry from the mathematics of the schools to the mathematics of actuality. Our texts are filled with cunningly devised exercises which are remarkable for nothing but their intricacy, tangles, and labyrinths, the like of which are found nowhere save in the brain of the drill-master. They are meaningless devices, "which," to use Beltrami's language, "make the student's mind sterile through the everlasting exercises which are of no use except to produce a new Arcadia where indolence is veiled under the form of useless activity."

Such artificial exercises, it is true, afford a certain training, but a training in nothing else than dexterity in the manipulation of impossible formulæ — "brain-spinning" as the Germans call it. Now, although a high degree of dexterity in the use of algebraic forms is essential to successful study of higher mathematics and science, yet that dexterity is not the main thing to be sought. That which is of the most importance in mathematics as well as in science is the interpretation of the mathematical forms used. In the higher mathematics there are countless forms that do appear and call for transformation or simplification. Let such forms be used as exercises in lower reaches of algebra, instead of the useless forms so prevalent in our texts. A few illustrations may make clearer this distinction between mathematics as it is taught and mathematics as it is used.

A recently published algebra tells us that "an unknown quantity is usually denoted by one of the last letters of the alphabet, as x, y, z." Now, this is far from being the fact, unless you restrict the field to elementary algebra. Open any book on astronomy, physics, chemistry, meteorology, or higher mathematics, and the exact contrary is found to be the case. Such equations as these meet the eye on every page:

$$\frac{a}{b} = \frac{\sin A}{\sin B} \cdot$$

$$A = \pi r^2 \;;$$

$$s = vt - \frac{1}{2} gt^2 \;;$$

$$c = \frac{E}{r + R} \;;$$

$$p = ae \;;$$

$$w = c \log \frac{v_2}{v_1} \;;$$

$$v = e^{ay + Bx} \;;$$

$$I = \int p^2 dM \,.$$

In fact, in the higher mathematics x and y have a meaning largely restricted to the Cartesian co-ordinates. The constant use of the x, y method is harmful in that it relieves the student of the necessity of scanning an equation, for the unknown for which the equation is to be solved is at once recognized, and the solution follows mechanically; whereas some attention must be given to such an equation as

$$D = \frac{w}{v} \quad \text{or} \quad s = vt - \frac{1}{2}gt^2 .$$

And right here lies a fundamental of great importance. From the standpoint of science, an equation is looked upon as stating a relation between certain numbers of co-ordinate importance. The significance of the equation rests in this, that if some of these numbers be known, the others can be found. Now, in order that algebraic training shall be of advantage to the student of science, this view should be firmly impressed upon him. Too often the equation is regarded as a formal puzzle to be solved, rather than an essential relation to be perceived. It is in the interpretation of the equation and the result of its solution that true algebraic thought resides. It were better to solve a limited number of equations understandingly than a large number mechanically. Nor will this thorough consideration of a few examples prevent the acquiring of dexterity in solution. For if all steps are understood to have a meaning, and are thoroughly mastered in their relations, the very clearness of perception thus produced will induce a better performance. Clear seeing is more than half in the doing.

Again, the scholastic method so prominent in all our texts produces the result pointed out by a recent scientific writer: "The regular textbooks of mathematics rather perplex than assist the chemical student who seeks a short road to a working knowledge of higher mathematics." The scientific student needs a thorough insight into mathematical methods, as well as a working knowledge of them; but to obtain this it is not necessary for him to go through all the artificial rubbish with which so many works are incumbered. A man can gain his exercise and develop his mathematical muscle among the green fields and wooded lanes of God's universe, rather than on the tread-wheel in a man-made gymnasium. I protest against a condition of affairs because of which it is possible to say that instruction in mathematics befogs the issue and cheats the scientific student out of the very results for which he began his study of mathematics.

As a second element in the improvement of mathematical training, I would suggest that the best mathematical methods be used as early as possible. As mathematical science advances, it produces better and better methods for solving given problems. It was a long step in advance when multiplication was substituted for a large class of additions; and one can hardly express the debt the world owes to Napier and Briggs for logarithms. Descartes, Newton, and Leibnitz have forged for us titanic instruments with which to work. The progress of civilization is conditioned to some extent upon the application of these discoveries to the needs of mankind. Without a murmur, the most of us replace our tallow dip with the incandescent fiber, the messenger post with the copper wire, the copper wire with the wireless telegraph. But there is a great outcry when any of us propose to use logarithms in arithmetic, trigonometry in geometry, or calculus in the secondary school. I even know of a college professor of mathematics who lives in a world long since outgrown, for, as he says: "Long ago I discarded from my teaching the doctrine of negative numbers." But the history of mathematics is but the story of the victorious march of new and better methods: new ideas and processes replace the old. New discoveries increase efficiency. A search in the algebras of a generation ago would not reveal the presence of the remainder theorem, the graph, or the determinant. Only within late years has the ratio definition of the trigonometric functions become current in our teaching. It is a waste of time and of perspicuity to teach simultaneous equations without graphs and determinants, or the geometry of the triangle without trigonometric functions. The calculus offers instant relief among the antiquities of college algebra and analytic geometry. Says Professor Jules Tannery, of the École Normale Supérieure, in speaking of the use of integral calculus in the secondary school: "After these lessons, say, nine or ten, one half-hour is sufficient to establish the expressions for all the volumes of elementary geometry." Why not use the best instruments the mathematician can turn out, at the first opportunity that offers? Says one, because the student cannot understand all the fundamental theory of the subject; especially is this urged in the case of calculus. But would you throw the equation out of algebra because it is impossible to prove to the child that every rational, integral equation has a root? Shall we give up multiplication because we cannot construct a definition that will include all cases of multiplication? Indeed, we never get to the bottom of anything. What is number? No one can tell us, not even Professor Peano. We are often led away by that will-o'-the-wisp, thoroughness, until we lose our pupils in the maze and perplexities of the more advanced reaches of a subject much too abstract to be within their powers of comprehension; whereas the beginnings of trigonometry, analytics, calculus, and differential equations open a field of clear and simple ideas, well within their power of understanding. It is folly to insist that a problem be worked by a certain method of elementary arithmetic, when it can be done in a better way by algebra or calculus. It is high time to strike off such shackles as those with which Euclid bound elementary geometry, the ruler, and the compass.

The sciences—astronomy, physics, chemistry, and mechanics—can make powerful use of these higher forms of tools. What waste of effort to treat the composition and resolution of forces without the help of the trigonometric functions! The ideas of differentiation and integration are wonderfully productive in the hands of science. We can best benefit the student of science by giving him an early mastery of these powerful agents. He must have that mastery if he is to have anything but a superficial glimpse of the fields of science, or if he is to be of material service in the application of that science to the subjugation of the world.

But there is a third way in which mathematical course may better fit for service—the consideration of real scientific problems. The stating of a problem in algebraic form, its solution, and the interpretation of the result is rightly regarded a valuable part of algebraic study. All our algebras contain long lists of such problems, and it is to the character of these problems that I wish to call attention. They are for the most part manufactured, unnatural. A few illustrations, taken from an algebra published in 1904, will serve to make this point clearer: "A lady purchased 20 yards of one kind of cloth, and 50 yards of another, for $30. She could have purchased 30 yards of the first kind and 20 yards of the second for $23. What was the price of each?" This is artificial, as no lady would ever meet such a problem. Or this: "A fishing-rod consists of two parts. The length of the upper part is 5-7 that of the lower part. The sum of 9 times the length of the upper part and 13 times the lower part exceeds 11 times the length of the whole rod by 36 inches. Find the length of the rod." This was evidently manufactured for consumption in simultaneous equations. It is thoroughly unnatural and impossible, and is a mere rehabiting of that old problem supposed to have been given by Euclid in 300 B. C.: "A horse and a donkey, laden with corn, were walking together. The horse said to the donkey: 'If you gave me one measure of corn, I should carry twice as much as you, but if I gave you one, we should carry equal burdens.' Tell me their burdens, O most learned master of geometry." As a contrast to these problems consider two. "A stone dropped from a balloon rising at the rate of 32 feet a second reaches the ground in 17 seconds. How high above the ground was the balloon when the stone was dropped?" "It is desired to find the height of a town or hill above a level plane. A 6-foot pole is set up, and the point determined where the line connecting the tops of the town and pole strikes the ground. The pole is used at this point, and a second point determined in the same way. The distance between these two points is measured. What is the height of the town?"

Objection is often made to this sort of a problem, that it brings in matter that is unfamiliar to the pupil, and it is said that in the first class, such as deal with ages, money, capital, partnership, legacies, "there is an especial advantage in that the attention is not distracted from the algebraic side of the problem while the acquaintance with algebra is as yet slight." After considerable experience in using both kinds, I find that students will solve the second class as readily as the first kind. They may require more thought, but this is to be commended; for the thought is productive thought. Respect for mathematics can hardly be maintained if its interpretation is given in terms of how old is Ann, and if it seems to have no more serious purpose than the solution of a mathematical rebus. It were much better to present the dignity of a mathematics evolved to solve real problems; and the world is full of such problems—problems of number, mensuration, statics, and dynamics, which need offer no distracting ideas. The two problems just mentioned, the balloon and the town problems, were solved with little difficulty by a class in first-year algebra, and several solutions were given. These natural, real, vital problems should be spread through the whole course of school and college mathematics. I cannot refrain from quoting a rather humorous problem found by my calculus class. The problem was no doubt an attempt to be practical: "A train starting from a station has after t hours a speed of $t^3 - 21t^2 + 80t$ miles per hour. Find its distance from the station; time when it repassed the station; the distance the train had traveled when it passed the station the last time. The train passed the station after starting the first time at the rate of 1,200 miles an hour."

Mathematics is an abstract science. Its glory is that it can proceed to the profoundest generalizations without appeal to the world of the senses; and yet its ideas at the start are abstractions from that world. From one point of view, geometry is a system of logic entirely independent of a physical world; yet our Euclidean geometry is but a classification of observed facts and the generalization arising therefrom. The difficulties of a geometrical proposition may often be dissipated by the study of a model. In our geometrical teaching we are making constant use of diagram and model. The transit has come to be of service for furnishing material for the class in trigonometry to work upon. But this is about the extent of any appeal to the world of the senses, made in our classes in mathematics. To me this seems unfortunate, especially in view of the steady pressure by which mathematical study is being crowded into the earlier years of a student's growth. It appears to be undeniable that capacity for abstract thought develops late. Now, it takes thirty-six or forty-eight weeks to cover the same ground that was covered in twelve or sixteen weeks when geometry was a college study. Although we have lengthened the time for the boy, we have made but little alteration in the method, forgetful of the fact that "boys are not men of a lesser growth." Boys are men in the process of making, and there the likeness ends. The impetus given to the study of physical, chemical, and biological phenomena by the recourse to actual observation and experiment has been most remarkable. It would seem to me that a similar vitalizing movement may be of service to mathematics. There are dangers connected with the use of experimental methods in instruction, and laboratory work has often been carried to absurd lengths; and yet the study of the world at first hand can never cease to be the fountain-head of all serious study. I firmly believe that the study of mathematical relations in concrete form by students of elementary mathematics is of great value. Last fall I asked a class beginning algebra to cut from a strip of cardboard 10 by 1½ inches a piece containing 12 square inches. Not more than two out of a class of thirty could do it. I found that very few of them had ever used a scale or a tape-line. All of them could answer the abstract question: "The area of a triangle is 15 square inches; one side is 3½ inches; what is the other side?" The divorce between the abstract and the concrete had been so complete in their case that the connection had been entirely lost. This is but an instance of a widespread condition—the failure to embody mathematics.

As a fourth means of meeting the needs of a scientific age, then, I would make the suggestion that more use of actual experiment and observation be made in our classes in mathematics. You will pardon a reference to some work with which I am intimately connected. I make it with the thought that a bit of testimony from actual experience may be of service in this connection. In Bradley Polytechnic Institute we have introduced such experimental work to a greater or less degree for five or six years. The results lead us to increase rather than diminish such work. There are certain experiments usually performed in the physics laboratory that are really mathematical in form. But little physical knowledge is needed for their performance. A number of these are now performed in our mathematical classes; credit is given for reports upon them by both the departments of mathematics and physics. It is not so much the purpose to teach physics as to teach mathematics in a setting of physics. In the beginning algebra class the balance and lever are used; observations on the movement of a street car are made. The law of falling bodies, $s = \frac{1}{2} gt^2$, is tested by a stone dropped from the tower. Heights and distances are calculated, and then actually measured. This gives confidence in mathematical processes and control in their application. In the second year, devoted especially to geometry, the work is a little more serious. Careful reports are required on about thirty experiments, chosen because of the geometrical ideas involved. Among these may be mentioned reflection of light and formation of images in plane mirrors, refraction of light by prism, composition and resolution of forces, and inclined plane involving use of trigonometric functions. The same care and accuracy that are demanded in the physics laboratory are insisted upon. From this kind of work the student gets a more real and intimate hold on the meaning of geometric and algebraic truth. It is often objected that there is a waste of time in such work; it is said that "the geometrical results can be arrived at more expeditiously in other ways." Is it not true, however, that the geometrical result is not the only thing to be sought. Fully as important is the setting, the value, and the utility of the fact. A boy may not see the use of filing a piece of metal to the exact diameter demanded by the teacher; but when he finds that the piece is too large or too small, by the thousandth of an inch, to fit into the engine or machine he is helping to build, and has to be made over or thrown away, he learns something of great value. Just so the student who finds that exceeding care must be taken if the lines determining the image in the mirror are actually to meet on his drawing, learns something from his own experience that the insistence of the teacher can seldom impart.

Our experience seems to point to two definite things. We are often told that, "no matter how geometry be taught, the student must be able to pass the entrance examinations set by the colleges and the universities." Now, while I demur to the view that the typical entrance examination is either a fair or a desirable test of mathematical ability, I am willing to admit that, since the examinations exist, they must be met. We determined to make a test in the examination just held two weeks ago. There were two classes in geometry to be examined: One, a class of boys, was given the entrance examination for one of the large eastern universities; the other, a class of girls, was given an entrance examination of one of our best-known woman's colleges. The instructor in charge of the classes did not see the papers until they were given him at the time of the examination. The class had reviewed but a very small portion of the work of the year. There were in the classes a few students whose general standing as students would debar them from being college timber. Of those who were at all eligible for going up for college entrance, but two out of forty were unable to pass, and those two were good students who always fell down on examination from emotional or nervous reasons. Some of the papers were of a very high order. At least this can be said. After a training involving a large number of physical experiments, they were no less able to handle the reasoning of the abstract originals than are those who are not so trained, while at the same time they have in addition a real and intimate knowledge of mathematics as revealed in natural phenomena.

The other point of interest comes as testimony from the classes in physics. Said a boy who entered the physics class from another school, to his instructor in physics: "You talk to us as though you expected us to know mathematics, and I seem to be the only one that has very much difficulty in using mathematics." Now, this is a crucial test.

This is the real service that instruction in mathematics may render to science. Not that science be taught as science in classes of mathematics, but that the language in which science speaks shall be taught, and as far as possible mastered, so that the science teacher may proceed with his teaching unhampered by the inability of the student to understand the language in which he can most clearly and accurately put the ideas and laws with which he is dealing.

By such means it would seem to me possible to make mathematics a more efficient instrument in the hand of the student of science or engineering. Nor would the student who is to become the pure-mathematician receive a less worthy training. It is from a rich mathematical soil that the great mathematicians of the future will arise. It is Fourier who said: "The deeper study of nature is the most fruitful source of mathematical study;" and we remember that it was the effort to solve some particular problem of science that gave birth to most of the great advances in mathematics. In our study of mathematics, the queen of science, let us not get too far from that world which, to quote Kelvin and Tait, "is replete with astonishing theorems of pure mathematics such as rarely fall to the lot of those mathematicians who confine themselves to pure analysis or geometry, instead of allowing themselves to be led into the rich and beautiful fields of mathematical truth which lie in the way of physical research."

A CONSIDERATION OF GEOGRAPHY TEXTS

WALTER J. KENYON
State Normal School, San Francisco, Cal.

No other elementary textbook costs the publishers so much to make ready for the market as does the school geography; and none comes in for a greater share of abuse, by teachers and schoolmen generally. If the teaching force of the country really know what they want in this particular, they have never succeeded in making it clear. The criticisms in the main have been iconoclastic rather than suggestive. The present paper, while frankly stating a personal view-point, will attempt, in the end to contribute something on the constructive side.

DO WE NEED A TEXT AT ALL?

The belief is held by many educationists that if our grade teachers were properly equipped in training and scholarship, there would be no place for the textbook. We have set up, in our pedagogical shrine, an ideal teacher, of high conceptions, high attainments, and high mettle, to whom we conceive the textbook merely as an impediment, prescribed by an undiscerning superintendent.

That this is a dangerous fallacy, however, it requires but a glance over the situation to show. Not all initiative is dependable, and not all the roads of individuality lead to Rome. Our profession is full of people with crochets and hobbies, and perhaps you and I are among the number. Too many of us poke hairpins into the course of study, to see the wheels go round, or possibly to make them turn the other way. Occasionally there arises one who can blaze a new trail, but there are not many. For the rank and file of us tradition is by far the safest working platform; and with it under our feet we in the long run render our best service. So far as geography-teaching, at least, in concerned, no scheme superseding the textbook has ever been offered which has proven, in the estimate of schoolmen at large, acceptably inclusive and exclusive.

The textbook appears needful also for a diametrically opposite reason. It not only answers as a corrective against crochets and distorted perspective, but, on the other hand, it sustains, in a fair degree of continuity, the work of the great army of teachers who are troubled neither with crochets nor perspective. In a word, it is the only safeguard we have against the chaos of genius, on the one hand, and the barren wastes of indifference, on the other. Those upon whom devolves the task of shaping the materia and methods of elementary teaching must ever be conscious that they are purveyors, not to a few geniuses and zealots, but to a great body of average toilers, tolerably alike, and numbering, in our own country, nearly four hundred thousand head. Viewed in this practical light, the textbook, be its failings what they may, appears as a veritable life-buoy in the deep.

THE CHARACTER OF EXISTING TEXTS

A painstaking examination of all the school geographies now offered for sale leads to the conclusion that, in a large way, all geography texts are the same texts. The authors have been too respectful of tradition to launch out into any marked deviations looking to a radical improvement in geography-teaching, Notwithstanding the broad claims of each new prospectus, all of the contemporary texts (with the two exceptions noted[1]), together with their predecessors for the past seventy-five years, are seen to be virtually repetitions, one of the next. There is a relieving variation in cover design and preface, but there the differences virtually stop short. Indeed, there are certainly six contemporary geographies (three by the same house) which are so nearly identical in plan and content as utterly to nonplus the superintendent who would choose a text. Only the publishers themselves could supply the reason for this duplication.

This pervading likeness greatly facilitates comparison. Taking them as they stand, there would seem to be five particulars upon which to base a choice among the current texts. These are

[1] The Tarr and McMurry series is a partial, and the Chisholm and Leete scheme a complete, exception to this statement, as later noted.

(1) make-up, (2) maps, (3) illustrations, (4) content, (5) method.

1. *Make-up.*—The claims made for the novel make-up of the Tarr and McMurry geographies are in part justified. The reduced size[2] proves a convenience, and a test of two years' wear and tear in the schoolroom shows these books to have a superior endurance. The one point in which the small page is at a disadvantage lies in the impaired value of the maps, despite the claims made to the contrary.

A more important matter, in which the Tarr and McMurry series scores an advantage is the psychology of the printed page. Certainly the most serious criticism to be made upon textbook make-up is the confused medley which the usual page presents to the reader's baffled eye. Opening a Redway at random (and it might as readily be a Frye, Butler, Morton, Roddy, or other), I find (p. 86) five fonts of letters disposed in a very mêlée of typography, and located in odd nooks amid the jumble of illustrations. This page is quite typical of those in any of the large-form geographies. The Tarr and McMurry books also yield to this fondness for kaleidoscopic type effects, but the small page and single column make the results less disastrous to the reader's concentration.

Finally, the table of contents is as available in the Tarr and McMurry as it has always been unavailable in other texts.

2. *Maps.*—With regard to political maps it is argued that the standard reference maps of the old-line textbooks are unduly crowded with names of unimportant towns, provinces, etc., which are not germane to the content of the geography lesson, and therefore serve only to complicate the map without rendering any return service; and that by a wholesale elimination of these cartographic minutiæ a result is attained which better serves the end in view. It is worthy of consideration, however, that in the typical schoolroom the text geography must serve also as an atlas, whenever an atlas becomes necessary. All the geographical references arising in the history lesson, the literature lesson, and

[2] A reversion to Jedidiah Morse, whose excellent geography flourished a century ago.

the daily news must have recourse to this book, in default of a more richly informational source. We have then to decide whether the extreme denudation of the political map is of sufficient import, psychologically, to offset its diminished value for purposes of general reference.

A comparison of leading texts suggests that in the Tarr and McMurry series this elimination has been too sweeping, and that the maps are thereby lessened in usefulness. It is true that the detail maps make up for the omissions in the continents. But it is a matter of much importance to locate a given feature upon the map in hand instead of searching further for it. Some of the other texts have been a trifle more conservative in this matter of eliminations, and the result is in their favor.

Whatever may be the decision upon this point, there is another which must not be confused with it. After having determined just how far the simplifying of the political map is advisable, we must not, in the same act, denude the physical map of what at first thought may be set down as worthless details. I refer to minor lakes and rivers, descriptive elevations, and deviations of coast-line. Unfortunately, a theory has gained some foothold that by robbing a map of its descriptive coast-lines, and by omitting the unnameworthy but richly descriptive small rivers, lakes, and minor relief, we have served some pedagogical principle. By the same logic we should have to expunge the stars from the firmament, that the pupil might with greater facility locate and identify the moon.

Of the texts examined, Morton's on the whole, has the most desirable maps. To begin with, each continent is introduced by a full-page physical map, followed by a political map with the physical features underlying. This initial separateness of the physical map is of some moment in a step-by-step, or cumulative, plan of teaching. Also in Morton the physical maps have a more realistic relief than those of any other text. These maps use the pictorial, or light-and-shade, device for mountains with a surpassing effect. It is used also by the Tarr and McMurry, but with less success. In the latter its quality varies from the moderately effective relief in Fig. 177, First Book, to a faint and undescriptive stain in Fig. 183. Compare either with Morton. The Howell reliefs, for which much is claimed in the Tarr and McMurry, are fraught with significance to the tutored eye of the physiographer, but they are utterly without grasp on the imagination of the child. The Howell marine relief, p. 2, Second Book, is an example of a (to the child) quite meaningless and uninviting illustration.

Maps for school children should afford some sort of transition from simon-pure pictures to the aggregations of symbols which carry a message to the eye of the physiographer or engineer. Redway's maps use the hachure symbol for mountains, and his relief, while valuable reference for the teacher, is unintelligible to any but mature students. The black-and-white reliefs of Frye vary from the mechanically effective United States on p. 68 to the unspeakable creations in the Supplement, pp. ii–iv. But even the best of these reproductions from photographs of wax or putty models are very barren of that genuine suggestion of a teeming area of land. Structural models have scant effect in stimulating the child's imagery, and photographs of the same must have even less. These black-and-white reliefs can be given a superlative value, however, if they are *drawn,* thus receiving the suggestive touch of the artist's hand.

Frye's political maps are superimposed over the old-fashioned hachure, or symbolic relief. His colored physical maps, are equal to Redway's, inferior to Morton's and smaller than either. The picture maps in Frye, however, are a very valuable revival of an old device, and will be considered later.

Compare[3] Morton, p. 48, with Frye, p. 65, or Redway, p. 44, or Tarr and McMurry, Second Book, p. 121. These Morton maps appear to be the most richly descriptive that have ever been produced. Compare Morton, p. 60, (New England), or p. 89 (California), with the corresponding maps in Redway, pp. 60, 88, or Frye, pp. 91, 117, or Tarr and McMurry, Second Book, pp. 124, 281. In the Tarr and McMurry the transition from the pictorially conceived earth through several intermediate stages to the detail maps of political areas is to be commended.

[3] In each case the advanced book.

3. *Illustrations.*— Since the legitimate use of pictures is to enhance the descriptive effect of the text, presumably the highest artistic skill will give the most richly descriptive illustration. But we have allowed ourselves to fall into the curious belief that the camera lens cannot lie; and that therefore the most direct product of photography is necessarily the most descriptive picture. On second thought, however, it is apparent that a photograph is, in the general rule, the least descriptive of all pictures; and that the half-toning process of reproduction is very apt to reduce its descriptive value still more. The photographic lens in average hands exercises no selective power; neither does it lay that intelligent stress upon the right spot which only the *bona fide* illustrator can secure. Pen-and-ink, woodcuts, and wash drawings cost more than reproduced photographs, but they are of incomparably greater descriptive value.

Redway's and Frye's geographies use woodcuts throughout. These pictures are satisfactorily descriptive. The Morton pictures are half-toned, but they are reproduced from drawings, not photographs, and the result is surprisingly brilliant and descriptive. On the whole, they are superior to Frye's and have something the advantage over Redway's.[4] But the animal and landscape picture-maps of Frye's are peculiar to that series and cannot be too highly indorsed, either as a teaching device or as to workmanship.[5]

The Tarr and McMurry illustrations are half-toned from photographs. Even with matchless workmanship, the outcome of this combination is always lacking in virility. But somewhere in the process the work has been ill-done, and the results are, in the main, muddy, dim, and undescriptive. These half-tone photos are without that piquancy of light-and-dark and atmosphere, which gives to woodcuts and pen-drawings their descriptive quality. Turning to p. 5, Tarr and McMurry, First Book, this distinction is clearly seen. Compare the pen-drawing, Fig. 4, with Fig. 3, on the page opposite. Or, compare the iceberg, on p. 193, with the icebergs in Redway, Advanced, p. 19, or the

[4] *Vide* "Gathering Cinchona," p. 114, Morton.

[5] See Frye, pp. 44 ff.

Elementary, p. 9; or Morton's Advanced, p. 24, or the Elementary, p. 69.

4. *Content.*— In the matters of arrangement and content, the Redway and Morton geographies are remarkably alike, and appear to have been built in a common mold. In the table below it will be seen that these two books give almost page for page the same attention to the various divisions of subject-matter. Frye elaborates considerably in the direction of physiography and United States. He is unduly scant on foreign *civilized* areas, notably other North America and Europe. Tarr and McMurry, on the contrary, while dealing more abundantly with all the divisions, are especially attentive to Europe; this is a point of considerable value in the latter book. It is the German policy to teach the young subjects of the Kaiser a great deal about the Fatherland and its dependencies, and as little as is convenient about the rest of the world. This inbreeding of the national ideal and ideas is observable in an even greater development in China. The true fruitage is slow in revealing itself, but it comes at last. It has come to China, and it will come to every nation that deliberately narrows the outlook of its school children. No geography course is justifiable which tends to emphasize rather than correct the provincialism which no community ever wholly escapes. We cannot afford to teach any geography that does not, in a generous sense, provide or imply a substitute for world-wide travel. Still, on the other hand, such instruction must not crowd a fairly intensive study of the home country. Considering the fact that the elementary school claims eight thousand hours of the pupil's life, there should be ample room for both.

During the latter part of the last century an avalanche of physiography descended upon the elementary school, from higher institutions, and invested its course of study. This has not influenced the textbooks, however, as much as might have been expected. The physiographic minutiæ of earth structure occupies ten pages of Frye's Advanced book and twenty of the Elementary; of Redway's, somewhat more in the Advanced, and considerably less in the Elementary. Morton's contains less than Frye's by half in the Advanced, and none at all in the Elementary.

Tarr and McMurry devote an equivalent of seven of the large pages to this material in their Second Book, and the first eighty pages in the First Book. But in the latter case the material is skilfully made local to the average child's experience, and each unit of thought is summarized in a pregnant sentence immediately following and printed in italics.

NUMBER OF PAGES DEVOTED TO EACH DIVISION

	General Geography and Principles	United States	Other North America	South America	Europe	Asia	Africa	Australia, etc.	Appendix
Redway	41	43	15	10	18	14	6	4	26
Morton	39	44	22	10	20	14	8	6	17
Frye	65	63	12	9	16	15	10	5	8
T. & McM. 2d and 3d books *	57	80	16	14	55	16	12	10	16
Roddy	19	42	14	10	20	14	9	7	4

* Figures corrected for difference in size of page.

5. *Method.*—There seems good reason to concur with Tarr and McMurry in their argument abandoning the uniform map scale—more particularly as no textbook has ever succeeded in maintaining such a scale. And, as someone has said, it should be a part of the pupil's training early to recognize and accept scale variation in maps, since in a multitude of his experiences he will encounter it.

The reaction from our late over-attention to physiography points toward an increased regard for descriptive geography, especially on the human side. The Tarr and McMurry books, by reason of their expansion, are the only series that can claim really to abandon the definition and desiccated statement and enter the task of description. The foregoing table discovers in the treatment of Europe a proportion of 55 to 16 in favor of Tarr and McMurry as against Frye. In spite of the more intensive treatment of the subject-matter, however, the Tarr and McMurry text is hardly less dry and didactic in its style than the others. It is descriptive in a purely informational way, but lacks the color and atmosphere which are a prime requisite in the best geographical reading. A little more attention to the art of word-painting and a little less to the didactic ideal of causal relations would have lessened the necessity for supplementary reading.

The expedient summarizing of each topic is an important consideration. Of all the information imparted by the geography course, our expectation is that the pupil will forget the greater part. But in connection with each topic there is a nucleus, or generalized notion, which we hope he will remember. For the purpose of selecting from the topic this precipitate of essential matter, a topical summary is needful.

The Frye and Redway texts have come nearest to supplying this organic thing. Morton is wholly lacking in this respect, depending upon a fly-leaf suggestion (p. 4, Advanced, and another on p. 61) to fill the need. Tarr and McMurry have a valuable series of summaries in the First Book, but thereafter this plan is abandoned and no substitute furnished. The "Questions and Suggestions" are of great value as searching exploitations of the text, but they have no movement toward focusing upon a nucleus of essentials. The "Summary and Conclusion" appearing at the end of the Second Book, and substantially repeated at the close of the Third, is excellent, but too long delayed, and too remote from its immediate text to equal the value of an oft-recurring topical summary.

An important point in method is the treatment of characteristic, instead of political, areas in descriptive geography. The old-time textbook taught that Minnesota raises wheat; and as an entirely distinct and unrelated item the pupil memorized from another page that Dakota also raises wheat. Thus the simple organic units of description were chopped up into meaningless fragments by the "square-inch" method. Redway and Morton make a free use of this treatment still, contenting themselves with an exceedingly brief unifying survey at the opening of each areal study. Tarr and McMurry, on the contrary, make the areal treatment the substance of their scheme,[6] following it with a short square-inch treatment under the political headings. The necessary result is that in the one case the pupil's descriptive fund is received

[6] *Vide* Second Book, pp. 200–33; cf. Morton, pp. 81 ff., or Redway, pp. 80 ff.

in unorganized, unstable fragments that are soon lost to him; while in the other there is every reason to believe that he will retain an essential knowledge, organized and related in a few large, simple units.

Frye uses the areal treatment, but less intimately and intensively than do Tarr and McMurry.

In the Tarr and McMurry books the relation between physiographic processes and man's affairs is constantly brought to the pupil's attention. So much as a book alone may do in this direction appears here to have been accomplished; always excepting the photographic illustrations, which should be replaced by woodcuts or pen-drawings.

Having thus looked into existing texts upon their own grounds, it remains to consider in what respects and how radically the textbook of the future may profitably differ.

Those now in use fall into the fundamental error of trying to furnish a description of the earth and its inhabitants within the limits of a single volume. They are thus compelled to serve up their contents in a highly concentrated form. Their desiccated statements are at once barren of imagery for the pupil, and unwieldly as a course of study. In a high endeavor to be both a syllabus for the teacher and a book of content for the pupil, they fall short of achieving both aims. They are, in any real sense, neither textbooks nor descriptions; and they are not easily adapted to any known scheme of teaching. Our present question is, therefore, not as to whether the task, within its limits, has been well done, but whether, such as it is, it has ever been worth the doing.

The Tarr and McMurry *Geography* is a departure in that a determined—we may say heroic—effort has been made to expand the text into actual content. The result, while certainly an improvement, in the end simply goes to clinch the conclusion which was already obvious: that a satisfactory treatment of geography can never be compassed in one volume, be it never so bulky, and be it in one or several parts. The Tarr and McMurry series is a strenuous and thorough exploitation of a blind alley—

a blind alley into which competing texts entered and remained much nearer the entrance.

A *bona fide* geography text will have two essential parts; one of these an atlas, made up of maps and such tables of statistics as are needful in ordinary reference; the other, a minutely specific course of study, for the teacher's guidance. Then, in addition to this textbook, there will be added, in a complementary relation, a copious fund of geographical readings, such as fifty volumes could scarce include. Fortunately, this complementary material is to a great extent already at hand, in the splendid supply of geographical readers lately appearing. The list is far too large to enumerate here, but the Carpenter Readers and the Youths' Companion books are typical of the best. We must not, however, confuse these highly available books with the flood of juvenile adventure, which has the consistency only of foam, and leaves no precipitate.

The proposed textbook itself is seen in prototype in the Longman's Atlas, taken together with the Chisholm and Leete handbook. Unfortunately, these books, as a unit, have not been promoted by their publishers with the zeal which they merit. Considered in combination with the complementary reading above mentioned, they certainly appear to point out a happy solution of the vexed problem of geography-teaching, so far as books are involved at all.

THE PUBLIC SCHOOL AS A SOCIAL CENTER

OLIVE E. WESTON

There is no American institution that wields so great a power for good as the public school. By the public school is meant the elementary and high schools, including the kindergarten. This great institution is really the most democratic of all our democratic institutions. It is the cradle of the deepest principles that underlie our government and our religion. In its conception it is no respecter of persons. The highest and the lowest may share alike its beneficence. Fame and glory in the public school, if that school be not in the clutches of politics and politicians, come to the one, who within himself, holds the elements of success and of greatness. The rich is as good as the poor in the public school, if he does his part and plays fair. A clean, bright, honest little fellow from the poorest hut, may sit or stand beside the millionaire's son whom riches and love have surrounded with luxury and beauty. If the poor boy be industrious he may even put the other one to shame in their mutual tasks. On the other hand they may be equally skilful and great chums in the public school. The rich man's son will throw himself into the water to save a drowning companion, though he be poor and unlettered, if he be a schoolmate. As the sun in heaven shines upon all alike, so the true spirit of our public schools would shed equal benefits on all its children.

Look at our night schools. Go visit them. You will see fine buildings warmed and brilliantly lighted from roof to basement, and every room open. Enter and you will think you are in classic halls. You feel like taking off your hat and moving with light step, for here you are in a great community where no one is idle or unhappy. All are doing what they love to do. Here is a white-haired man studying chemistry. He never had a chance when he was young, although he evidently had a taste for it.

Here is a boy who works down town all day in a factory. He comes here at night to study electricity, so that he may learn to understand the power that runs the great machine he tends all day. But look farther. Here are young men and old, middle-aged business men, girls and women, all too busy to see you. All these may for the taking, gather the riches of knowledge and study the law of the universe, without money or price. This is the public school, and instructors come here to give out the best they have, at this banquet of mind.

I wonder if we thoroughly appreciate and rightly understand what this great public school system is doing for the future citizens of our city and our country. It is high time that we make use of our opportunity and acquaint ourselves with it in all its phases; for instance: Let us inquire, How did this come to be a free school? Who is responsible for its excellence, and who may be charged with its failures? What is its purpose, and what does it accomplish? What is its curriculum and who makes it? Where do the teachers come from? Who are they and how are they prepared for this great work? Who selects them and on what basis are they chosen? What are the essentials of a good teacher? What is the relation of teacher and pupil, or teacher and parent? What are the responsibilities of the home and the school in the education of the young? What should the school do for our children socially? What is it doing now for this essential part of their training? What can we, fathers and mothers, club members, and thinking men and women everywhere, do to bring this greatest institution of our land to its highest function? How may we co-operate, and with whom shall we co-operate?

These are some of the questions that we should study with great care, and with deepest interest; and then proceed to answer them by doing something. Every father and all mothers are needed right now to seriously undertake the solution of these and like problems. The great trouble is that parents do not know their children. Then how can they be expected to know their needs, or how to meet them?

The home is the first and primary institution for the study and development of the child; but the school is next and very close to it. Out of the heart of nature comes the raw material for the making of God-like beings. The home is the womb, where the embryo statesman, philosopher, scientist, artist, or great teacher and leader are nurtured. When the seeds are sown and the budding begins, the child is transplanted to the school or kindergarten to be developed or dwarfed as the case may be. Who should know so well what that school should be, and what it is, as the parents? In the home the process of absorption has gone on; the child has gathered sense-impressions and experiences by the million, each leaving its effect upon the child somehow and somewhere. Here emotions of all kinds have been awakened for the first time, ideals have been forming, aspirations and ambitions have been aroused and ties have been fastened to the tender heart. Now he goes to the school to develop all these into usefulness or to have them changed or crushed and killed. In the home he has learned to co-operate, to be one of a social fellowship, to think of others while seeking his own happiness; and if the home be a true one, he will have learned that the good of all is the good of each. At home he had first an unconscious, then a subconscious, will. He goes to school to become conscious of his growing power, and in proportion to develop a conscious will, a new force, a directive force. At home he has been under the direction of others. In the new surroundings he feels a desire for self-direction and the direction of others. This is legitimate. It is a needed experience in forming the man who may be able to take a high place in the world where such power is needed. We are said to be made in the image of God. The truth is, we are making ourselves into the divine image, and if the child has half a chance he will do it. God created the universe and directs all its forces, seen and unseen. To be God-like, man must be a creative being and learn to direct the forces of nature. To do this he must understand the laws of the universe. Watch any child and you will see the expression of this divine nature. With the discovery of his powers comes the desire to use them. He wants to make something, to test and manipulate all the materials and forces within his environment. He feels that he is surrounded by many wonderful forces and he longs to discover them. He wants to touch, handle, and name everything he sees. This is perfectly legitimate. It is God-given instinct. Now what do we do? Why, we are inclined until we learn better, to combat and suppress all these instincts and tendencies. We are forever saying to the child, "Don't touch," "Don't try to do this or that," "Don't go here or there." Is not this true? The child feels a precious individuality within himself and longs to assert his inheritance. He attempts to be self-directive and we head him off and assume the directive power, and so dwarf his being. When we send him to school, he feels anew this impulse, and at once gets into trouble, because some one else who does not understand the impulse is unable to respond to his needs. You say, "He should learn obedience." Yes, if you can show this thinking being the justice of it he will gladly learn it.

In the public school, the little ones find ways of physical development in their free play, and the social instincts are easily satisfied; but about the sixth grade a great change comes over the whole nature. Not a sudden change, however, but at the threshold of adolescence the demands of the child are greater physically and socially, if not mentally. The creative power asserts itself in a new way; life opens up to the boy or girl with an intensity, which, if not understood is alarming. Now the child begins in earnest to study the law of cause and effect and to inquire into the relations of life. He asks for his own origin and would become acquainted with processes and causes. He or she as the case may be, chooses some confidential companion who is in the same state of mind, and together they try to solve the mysteries of being. Often they gather about them others of their own age and sex in segregation; clubs and fraternities are formed, and the legitimate business of their lives, which is to know and understand themselves, is often carried on in an illegitimate way. Parents, teachers, and friends begin to worry and try by hook or by crook to overcome and circumvent all this business, while all the time the youth are fortifying themselves against every attack. They even resort to the law and combat the powers that be with their own weapons.

Now, parents and teachers, this is your business; your duty

unveils itself at this point. What is the trouble? Is it with the home or the school, or with both? First of all, I think the responsibility is with the parents, to see to it that each child should be informed, should be enlightened upon these vital and natural questions. If possible this knowledge should come through the parents by a mutual study of the life of plants and animals. Watching the habits and methods of a few plants in their round of germination, development and perfection for one or two seasons, carefully noting the effect of heredity and environment, would awaken a deeper reverence in the heart of the child than any amount of preaching would do. Here is the basis of this plea for practical nature-study in all the grades of the public school. If directed in the right way it cannot be done too early.

Watching the process of development of the seeds, bulbs and flowers, the child will meet many vital questions which should be answered with great care, but truthfully and in correct and scientific terms. In all cases the universal laws of nutrition, self-preservation, and reproduction, should be pointed out, and when the interest seems to center in any one direction, the emphasis should be placed there. Inch by inch, as it were, the truth of the law of all life will work its way into the child's mind and heart. It is this law that the child is consciously or unconsciously searching for. When the interest passes over to animal life and human life, do not hush it up, but follow the lead of the question and when you come to the conclusion say "All life comes in this way, from a seed, which is life's cradle." Then when once you have opened the door, you must prepare to give your very best interpretation of life, and you may have to go to your *Encyclopædia Britannica*, your Darwin, Spencer, and many other heavy books, that you may give the sacred truth. But give it, and without delay. Children will not wait; they are immediate and exacting. They instinctively feel that time is precious. We know it is, and yet we waste it. Children observe and know much more than we realize, but they get false ideas, and it often takes years to correct them. Let us start them out with the banner of truth. "Know thyself" is a divine injunction.

When the time comes for definite questions, there should be

a carefully prepared course of study on the origin and the methods and relations of life. Every boy and girl ought to study such a course with an expert teacher. Small groups of girls who are friends, and groups of boys in the same manner, with an earnest, gifted instructor might thus be given the key to high thinking and lead them to right living.

If our schools should have nature-study as an essential part of the curriculum for every grade from the kindergarten up, with planting, tending, observing, and studying, with first-hand experiment, and all under the guidance of a lover and student of nature, the problems that so vex parents and teachers now would nearly all be solved. We talk down to children too often. Let us turn our faces upward toward them and borrow a little of their enthusiasm. All other studies might better be neglected than this. How they like the words "biology, chemistry, zoölogy, science," and all the rest. I asked a ten-year-old what he was having in school that was fine. "Chemistry of foods," was the prompt reply and he proceeded to enlighten me on the sugar and starch found in certain vegetables. I was not surprised at this because I know that children are interested in things related to life in a practical way. So would they be deeply interested in civics as a practical study. Witness how they love to plant and tend and harvest the gardens; especially the vegetables that can be taken home and used. Children are eminently practical, and there is no doubt that they would order their lives to live in harmony with the laws of life if they had the knowledge needful. The fires of the passions that are often uncontrollable in the boy, or girl, or the youth, being once understood might be turned to great account.

Instead of being a misfortune the possession of this power may become a great blessing. It is a fact that all great art, all great achievement in any direction is simply the output of this creative element in human nature. It is this deep surging sexual passion turned to good account that moves the world. Think what harm the steam engine might do if it were not well understood and controlled. Electricity would send the world to destruction if it were not directed under the laws of the universe by man's intelligence. Now this wonderful force which makes so much trouble and breaks so many hearts is nothing more or less than a great electric dynamo. Shall we, then, keep the child in ignorance, or shall we give him his birthright and enable him to use it for making his way Godward? But how may we know when to lead him to this fountain of knowledge? Watch your child. He will teach you. When you see the self-consciousness, self-assertion and awkwardness that comes to every child; when your boy throws out suspicions and pugilistic tendencies; when he forgets to give you the good-night kiss, then be sure he is well on the way. He feels the change within him, a welling of something he does not understand. He is petulant, seems less loving, and less thoughtful for others; less obedient to individual authority. He wants to be alone or to go out with the boys; or if a girl, she wants to go to stay all night with her best girl friend. If a boy, he scorns girls, while perhaps in the secret recesses of his heart he feels, somehow, a deeper interest in them; studies them more closely, judges them more severely; scorns and loves them at the same time. He fixes his ideal of a woman far above any one he knows; seems to care for girls older than himself. In a thousand ways he is unconsciously telling you what is happening, if only you are able to read this wonderful book of nature.

In the moods and new manifestations of the young girl, she also is revealing the dawn of her womanhood and the wise mother will read the demands of this enlarging soul. The paramount needs for both boy and girl at this time are social needs. More than one-third of their waking hours are spent away from home and usually in school. Now what is the school as a social center doing for the child? First, and above all things, the school should administer to the social needs of the children, for only as he is related to the world as a social being can the child hold any place as an adult. Society is a unity and can be no better than the units of which it is composed. Each must find his true relation and contribute his character and work to bring the whole to a perfect unity. The school belongs to the fathers and mothers, and it is their responsibility to make the schools just what they should be. They are supported by the people. They were made for the children and are the legal ward of the state, but the parents are the natural guardians of the institution.

The public school was not established for a source of revenue, but for a commodity far higher, viz.: for the making of men and women, noble and useful citizens. The Board of Education, the superintendents, principals and teachers are all agents or employees of the people. And from this point of view it is clearly seen that it is the duty of the people to look after this work of education; to see that all investment of money, time, and thought is made wisely and to the greatest good of the greatest number. The returns must ultimately be measured in character and ability.

Let me urge that this question of the public schools, especially the high schools, is the burning question today. It is the most important and immediate duty of every man and woman in the United States, especially in Chicago, to guard and manage well this inheritance of the children now with us and the children yet to come.

The true function of the American public school is to educate the people. It is the poor man's college, a preparatory school for the university work, and a place for social culture for all. It belongs to the children and youth in the morning hours, it should be the center of club and community life of the mothers in the afternoons, and a school for the workingmen, and boys, and women, five evenings in the week, and a true neighborhood center for the balance of the time. Like the institutional church its doors should never be closed. Library centers, art centers, and amusement halls of the highest character ought to be housed in our school buildings. In this way would be secured the greatest prevention of crime. The time has come when no man or woman can occupy a high place in the world's work, or in places of trust, who is not equipped with a fair education and a true sense of the relationships of the race. There is no way to find these relations except by living a life of interdependence. One must be in the spirit of giving and taking kindness and responsibilities, especially giving.

While the school makes excellent provision for the physical

development by manual training, domestic science, gymnasium and athletics, it should also contribute to that other side of human nature, the emotional side, which demands music and an all-round art training, rhythm, grace, in movement as well as thought. Grace, vigor and strength help to make the perfect man or woman. Again, all the race loves a story and loves to live over the experiences of the race. So dramatic art is a most essential element in a curriculum for the social life. The school building, I repeat, should be always at the service of the people. Parents should organize associations, and co-operate to cultivate a living spirit of unity, thus giving the children's growing powers the legitimate outlet.

Oh, fathers and mothers, open your eyes and see what great privilege is yours by fulfilling your duty to your public schools. The public school, I repeat, is your own business, and the public school buildings are your places of business. Do not neglect them.

Now that the time is approaching when thousands of little children, and older boys and girls will be turned into the street with nothing to do but learn vice and wrong, let us make a heroic effort to keep the school buildings open for business, and so enter into competition with the saloons and street corners. In this way we shall save our city from a generation of criminals. These little minds are eager to know, the hands are aching to do something, and the dear helpless mothers are begging us to save their children. Our recent terrible strike troubles that have cost so much life, happiness, and money, would never have been, if every one of these men had been thoroughly educated in the principles that underlie our public-school system. Every child saved from the street this summer will save ten times what it costs to keep him in the vacation school, for the street is the school of crime. Let us bond our city or do something to meet the expense of placing a vacation school in every public-school building.

EDUCATION FROM THE GENETIC POINT OF VIEW[1]

WILLIAM H. BURNHAM, PH.D.
Assistant Professor of Pedagogy, Clark University, Worcester, Mass.

The genetic conception of education is not new. The fundamental principle of genetic pedagogy — that of adaptation of education to the sequence of the stages of individual development — is at least as old as Comenius; but a point of view means nothing unless it enables one to see facts as well as to dream dreams. The result of modern child-study has been to give the insight that the only way to make this principle of adaptation vital is to find out by careful inductive study just what is the actual condition of children at different stages of growth and development. My purpose this morning is to recount some of the facts that have made the genetic point of view vital.

Fortunately, you are all familiar with the modern doctrines that education is a process; that the child is a different creature from the adult; that the child differs from the adolescent; that the child differs from the child at different stages of its development; that stages low and imperfect may be significant because preparatory to higher stages; that the child should be a child before he becomes a man; that the best guarantee of normal maturity is normal immaturity; that, as Froebel put it, the full and complete development of each stage is necessary for the development of succeeding stages; and again, on the social side, that the child is not so much fitting himself for society, but that he now is a member of society; that the school may represent society in embryo; that the teacher is primarily a member of this social group; that, as Professor Dewey puts it, the school life and the home life should be one and the same; that the purpose of the school is to introduce to the fundamental, constructive, productive

[1] Paper read before the Department of Child Study of the National Educational Association, Asbury Park, N. J., July 7, 1905.

social activities; and that here, too, everything must be adapted to the child's own social experience.

Such familiar doctrines are based upon the genetic interpretation of facts. There are some other truths with which you are not perhaps so familiar. First of all, certain physiological facts.

Besides the obvious facts of growth and development which are of vital importance to education, there are certain more specific characteristics of the child's organism which are of practical importance. The child, for example, has a different circulatory system from the adult. The child's heart is relatively small, his arteries relatively large. During the period of development the heart grows very rapidly, and after adolescence it is relatively large, while the arteries are relatively small and narrow; or, more concretely, measurements have shown that during the period of growth the volume of the heart increases twelvefold, but the width of the aorta only threefold; or for 100 cm. of height in case of the child the heart volume is 50 c.cm.; in case of the adult it is 150–190 c.cm. Thus during the school period there is a complete change of the circulatory type. This is a fact of great practical importance to be considered in all manual work and physical training, as well as in the ordinary work and play of the child. Cardiac disturbance is quickly compensated for in the child's organism in a way impossible with the adult; hence short and rather violent activity is quite harmless for the child, although prolonged activity and feats of endurance are dangerous.

Again, in case of the child the constituents of the blood are different from those of the adult; especially is the protection against contagion less in case of the child. In the child the blood is less alkaline, and thus offers less resistance to micro-organisms, the germ-destroying or bacteriacidal power of the serum, according to Weill, is not so great, and the white corpuscles of the blood with bacteriacidal power are less. In case of the adult they are estimated at 70 in 100, but are only 28 at birth, 40 at the end of the first year, 54 in the third, 64 from the eighth to the tenth. That is, the protective power of the blood is twice as great in case of the adult as in case of the young child. This difference, together with the child's inferior protection in other ways, makes contagious diseases especially dangerous in the kindergarten and early primary grades. This is not a mere matter of theoretical speculation, but statistics show that 90 per cent. of all deaths from the common contagious diseases — such as measles, whooping-cough, and the like — occur before the age of ten; and an extensive study of measles in Munich shows that while between the years two and five the fatal cases were 5 per cent. of all, between the ages of six and ten, they were only 0.4 per cent. In other words, if an epidemic of measles occurs in the kindergarten, the chances are that four children in one hundred cases will die; if the epidemic can be postponed until the primary school, the chances are that only four in one thousand will die.

Another specially important difference between the child and the adult is in the activity of the lymph. This gives a child added protection from certain contagious diseases; but, on the other hand, carries its own dangers with it. Experiments upon animals are instructive here. An artificial opening made into the thoracic duct of a young dog furnished lymph to the amount of between one-sixth and one-tenth of the body weight within one day, while from an adult dog lymph amounting to only one-tenth to one-sixteenth of the body weight was obtained. In the same way the lymph apparatus in the young child and adolescent is more active than in the adult.

Says Dr. Jacobi:

> This is why the condition of the lymph glands in the young is of such importance. Whenever there is any infection of the mucous membrane, the infecting poison is carried off to the next gland, where there is a stopping-place. That gland will become the seat of irritation or swelling. That is why . . . . whenever there is only a slight diarrhea, no matter from what cause, ... lymph bodies in the neighborhood will swell. Unless such a diarrhea is soon stopped, the irritation will continue, congestion, inflammation, swelling of the glands will ensue, and the structure of these neighboring glands will be changed.

Other facts of practical significance are the different growth-rates of different organs at different periods, the immaturity of special organs demanding special care, the undeveloped eyes of young children, the danger to the naso-pharynx, ear, and mouth from hypertrophied tonsils, and the like, the undeveloped voice of the child, and the strain especially upon boys at the period of mutation.

On the physical side, then, the aim of education from the genetic point of view is to give a child the opportunity for growth and development, and to foster the acquisition of habits of healthful activity. Many other things are desirable, but a child's first business is to grow. He may have another opportunity for the acquisition of knowledge, but the demands of development cannot wait.

On the mental side the contribution of genetic psychology and physiology is perhaps equally great, although it cannot be stated so concretely and definitely. As popularly believed, the child has less power of attention than the adult; contrary to popular opinion, he has also less memory power; but the chief differences may be summed up in one word—lack of experience.

The studies of children are in some important respects revolutionizing pedagogy. Attention is shifting from methods of teaching to methods of learning. The work has already passed from the stage of mere observation and crude speculation to the stage of analysis and experimentation. Concrete problems of school work and of economic and efficient methods of study are being investigated by careful methods in the laboratory.[2] Meyer has studied the difference between the methods and results of school work done in a group of children,and similar work done by the children alone, finding that usually the group work is superior. Schmidt has studied the home work of children as compared with the school work and found, on the one hand, that in the more mechanical work pupils do better in the school because of the stimulation from other pupils, while in original essays in the mother-tongue and the like they do better in the isolation of the home. Meumann has studied the most economical and efficient methods of learning by heart. A single concrete example must suffice. Suppose the school task be to learn a stanza of a poem; children, as well as most adults, usually adopt the method of learning by parts—first a few words or a line, with many repetitions, and then another phrase or line. Is this a good method? Which is better—to learn the stanza as a whole, or to learn it

[2] See *Archiv für die gesammte Psychologie*, passim.

by parts? By which method will it be learned in less time, with fewer repetitions, be remembered more permanently and accurately? Investigations upon many children, extending through several years, show clearly that, as a rule, with them as with adults, the method of learning as a whole is decidedly better. Somewhat less time is required by this method, a very much smaller number of repetitions suffices, and most important of all, confusion of association and possibility of error are lessened, while correct and healthful habits of association and of study are developed.

Such are some of the facts as I understand them; we have in the child a psycho-physical organism, unstable, immature, growing and developing irregularly at different periods and at different rates in different parts and organs. These are facts of the utmost practical importance in the everyday work of the school. But, while we are primarily concerned with such concrete facts, we may stop for a moment to glance at the wider relations of these facts. Modern biological study has enormously enlarged the genetic conception of education. It is hardly fanciful to draw an analogy between the adjustment of the individual that we call education and the adaptation and mutation of species in plants found by De Vries and others. And if this investigator is right in concluding that when a species is in the period of mutation, as he found the evening primrose, new species are easily formed, and, after this period is passed, new species cannot be formed, then something similar seems to be true of the individual. Without pushing the analogy too far, in general it seems to be true that during the nascent period new acquisitions and adaptations can easily be made. After the nascent period is passed, new acquisitions are made only with great difficulty or not at all. The great lesson is one that teachers and parents are slow to learn — that nature works by times and seasons. We cannot forestall her without danger. We cannot let the moment of opportunity pass without irrevocable loss. Perhaps each organ has its nascent period when the conditions are most favorable for the acquisition of function, and the skill of the educator is put to its greatest test in determining when the favorable opportunity for training occurs.

When one says that hygiene and sound pedagogy fear premature and unrelated developments, and that the best guarantee of normal maturity is normal immaturity, it means very little; but when one studies the developing nervous system of young animals, all this becomes very concrete and emphatic. I know of no more interesting illustration of this than the studies of the guinea pig, made by Miss Allen. The guinea pig develops rapidly, and it is mentally precocious at a very early age. The white rat, on the other hand, develops relatively slowly. At birth the guinea pig has all its senses, pretty well-developed muscles, and is psychically mature at the age of three or four days. The white rat at birth, on the other hand, is undeveloped, blind, deaf, naked, his nervous system unmedullated, his muscular system without control. He does not gain the power of vision for sixteen or seventeen days, of hearing for perhaps thirteen days, nor become psychically mature for from twenty-four to twenty-seven days. The result of the precocious development of the guinea pig as compared with the slower development of the white rat appears in the education of the two animals.

As Miss Allen puts it:

When the guinea pig has forced his way through a labyrinth, he has reached the end of his psychical powers. He cannot pull a latch nor push a bolt; he will not depress an inclined plane, chew a string, nor stamp his foot. . . . . The experience of the white rat extends to strange combinations of wires and springs, and all the delightful surprises revealed by secret doors; but when the guinea pig has turned the proper number of corners, his dinner must be waiting for him or he does not get it. The white rat at three days is just learning to crawl, has never seen an object, and remembers nothing. The guinea pig at that age has triumphantly recalled a complex path, at the end of which he sits eating his well-deserved carrot. At twenty-three days the rat is lifting latches neatly and forming what Hobhouse calls "practical judgments" as to the value of an inclined plane, in a situation at the center of which is his food—a desired thing, an end. The guinea pig is still wearing out the floor of the same labyrinth.

And, again, to quote Miss Allen:

The contrasting features in the two animals are their nervous systems. In the one a mature nervous system is accompanied by psychical maturity; in the other, neural immaturity permits great psychical development.

If more were needed to show the importance of the genetic point of view, the errors that result from the lack of it would be enough. I have time for but a single illustration. In medicine and hygiene there is always danger, if one lacks the genetic point of view, of treating the diseases incidental to growth and development, especially the nervous diseases — neuroses of development as they are technically called — in the same way that one would traet similar diseases in adults. In a word, there is danger of mistaking incidents of development for neuroses of degeneration. A concrete case in point has recently come to my attention.

An hysterical boy of fifteen was committed to a hospital. It was found that he had certain cardiac symptoms, precordial pain, and the like; and the physician to whom the boy's case was allotted, apparently having had more experience with old men than with children, treated him by giving one-hundredth of a grain of nitroglycerin three times a day. The probability is that the boy's heart will be injured for life; whereas with care, and a judicious use of iron and other tonics, the boy would have outgrown the cardiac trouble along with his hysteria. Such treatment of an adolescent is so atrocious that it is hardly credible that any reputable physician could be guilty of such an error. Apparently it was a case of mistaking a neurosis of development for a disease of adult life, on account of lack of the genetic point of view.

Teachers, as a result of their special work, are very likely to fall into similar errors. The defects and even the wickedness of children and youth, usually mere psychoses of development, are often taken too seriously by both teachers and parents, and the error of mistaking a psychosis of development for a sign of degeneracy is perhaps no less serious than that of a physician who gives nitroglycerin to the adolescent. If child-study had done no more than to give teachers the genetic point of view, all the labor expended would be well repaid; for here they are prone to err. If they do not adopt the nitroglycerin method of discipline, they are apt to desire a guinea-pig form of prematurity.

Everywhere today teachers and students are studying children; some in the laboratory with carefully controlled conditions; some by the questionnaire method — *la méthode démocratique,* as the French call it; others by mere observation and reminiscence, often by methods crude and unreliable. What is the result of all this? What does it all amount to? Some of this work has yielded practical results. Some of it has illustrated the genetic point of view. All, I believe, has been valuable. For a single illustration, in the city where I live, the students of the normal school observe children as they have opportunity, and record isolated facts, sometimes the significant, more often the trivial and banal. There are tens of thousands of such reports in the archives of the school. Each year adds something to this store. Is that all? By no means. The students in this work acquire the genetic point of view, the right attitude toward children; and Principal Russell says that reports from graduates are to the effect that the bad boys and the defective become objects of special interest and study.

It is difficult to describe a point of view, but the point of view is everything. It determines what we see and what we are unable to see. In every profession, especially perhaps in the teacher's calling, the development of the professional point of view soon inevitably makes it impossible for one to see things as they really are. The attainment of the genetic point of view would save teachers from much of this scholastic blindness. It would save them from worry over defects and imperfections, and give the insight that education is a process, and that normal development implies imperfection and the gradual approximation to higher stages and higher ideals. It would revolutionize the teacher's calling, and the teacher's task would become a part of the great world-process of evolution in human life and human society. Again, it would save the school from what Professor James calls "the modern textbook of Moloch, in whose belly the souls of living children are turned to ashes," and from the mechanism of artificiality and traditional examination, classification, and grading. It would emancipate them from the idolatry of methods. It would save them from overstimulation and overpressure, and from that overstraining which means arrest of development. In a word, it would make the aim of the modern school development, health, individualization, and the opportunity for spontaneous intercourse with nature and society.

ANNOUNCEMENT

Among the most significant educational events of the year is the annual meeting of the Western Drawing and Manual Training Teachers' Association. This organization, which for ten years was limited to the drawing teachers, found it advisable, two years ago, to expand by a union with the manual-training teachers. This fact in itself indicates the trend of modern education.

The keynote of the meetings held in Chicago this spring, is denoted by the address by Miss Jane Addams on the "Social Value of Handicraft." The problems of modern industrialism are forcing themselves upon the educational profession.

That art is regarded by these people as a factor in daily life, was apparent in all the discussions of these most interesting meetings.

The members of this association are usually compelled to do pioneer work in the movements toward better educational conditions. Their exhibitions and discussions are therefore of value as denoting what has been actually accomplished under the average school conditions. The School of Education therefore looks forward to an interesting and profitable conference when it entertains the Association next year.

The twelfth annual meeting of the Western Drawing and Manual Training Association was held in Chicago April 25–28, inclusive. The session was a most successful one both as to program and attendance. It was voted to accept the invitation of President Harper to meet at the University of Chicago next year.

The following officers were elected:

President — Florence E. Ellis, Grand Rapids.

Vice-President — Charles A. Bennett, Peoria.

Secretary — Mary E. Chamberlain, Saginaw.

Treasurer — Louis A. Bacon, Indianapolis.

Auditor — J. E. Painter, Minneapolis.

Executive Committee — Lillian S. Cushman, Chicago; Frank A. Selden, Chicago; Charles S. Hammock, Cedar Falls; Welhelmina Seegmiller, Indianapolis.

Chairman Press Committee — Emma March, Chicago.

EDITORIAL NOTES

The usual school curriculum is a misfit. Much of the material proposed cannot be presented properly, and much that is presented the youthful mind is in no condition to apperceive. In organization and arrangement it does not correspond to the natural processes of thinking, and it fails to stimulate and nourish mind-growth. There is, on this account, indefinite waste in the work of teaching.

Waste in Teaching

The operations of nature often follow the path of a circle with a recurrence in cycles. The stalk of corn takes up from the soil small quantities of materials which, after serving their purpose, are returned to the earth again, and the process is repeated in endless generations and cycles of vegetation.

The educative process, too, when complete, follows the path of a circle, and in some respects the growth of the human being is like that of the plant. But there is a difference — an important difference. In the plant the materials are organized into complex compounds, which in time become separated and reduced to the simple and original forms. At every stage of the process the transformations deal with materials, and nothing but materials. But in human growth, in the transformations of the materials which minister to it there is a by-product in the shape of a spiritual output that at once lifts the development of a human being above the growth of a vegetable.

Educative Process a Circle

Spiritual By-Product

It is this spiritual by-product of material transformations that is the chief concern of the teacher; and the trouble is that nobody is able to understand it. The lime, the carbon, and the water, having performed their function in the corn, passively return to earth and air, leaving no trace behind. But in the human being there is accompanying these changes a spiritual output that may be good or may be bad — it will never be neutral and passive. It is here that the teacher finds his problem. It is his special business to see that the uncertainties that are ordinarily involved in the spiritual result become certainties in the direction of righteousness.

Toward this end comparatively little has been accomplished. Some of our philosophers have turned pessimists and given it up.

Outcome of Education Uncertain

The most diabolic and fiendishly artistic crimes are frequently perpetrated by those who were long treated in childhood and youth with the educational process as it is commonly practiced. It seems that not only a little learning, but also a great deal, is often a most dangerous thing. Somewhere in the educational process there is a break, a lapse; something is overlooked; something is left out.

Looking at the educational process under the similitude of a circle, there are several things needed to make it complete. The

Parts of the Educational Process

omission of any one of these will make the spirit of man a wanderer upon the face of the earth, and open up to it all the possibilities of villainies that detract and defile.

Upon one part of the circle that describes the educative process lies the environment of the learner. This includes every-

Evironment

thing that is capable of producing any kind of an impression through any or all of the senses. This part the schools in the past have much neglected. The face of the scholar was turned from the face of nature. All the machinery of the school was devoted to strengthening this attitude. But the situation is improving. Through object-lessons, and nature-study, and in countless other ways, the pupil is placed in direct touch with the influences of his surroundings.

At another point on the circle is the individual himself. It is his function to transform the impressions received through the

The Individual

senses into a spiritual product. It is the sole office of the teacher, it is the chief business of method, to see that the impressions are so marshaled that the spiritual outcome shall be certain. Without this there is no education. Upon this point, too, the schools have been ignorant and indifferent. So long as the children were compelled to deal with symbols and empty formulas that possessed little significance for them, the impressions were faint and the spiritual result was weak. But the pupils are now in close touch with practically all matters—physical and intellectual—that can influence a human being, and the spiritual product is robust. This is due to two things: to the substitution of interesting material for empty forms and symbols, and to improved and more skilful methods of presentation.

The Proper Emphasis in Education

Up to this time almost the whole emphasis in school-teaching, from infancy to maturity, has been placed and still is placed upon these two phases of instruction. Science with its field-work and laboratories, and history in its work of excavation and research, are but emphasizing the importance of concrete and interesting material as a basis for instruction. Departments of education in normal schools, colleges, and universities express the importance that now attaches to philosophic and skilful methods. Yet, in the face of all this, the world is still half afraid of the educated product. Nobody knows just what it will do; we appear to be no more sure that it will be upright than we were when educational schemes were less elaborate. College and university men may be found who contribute to the general welfare—they may be found also tangled up in all sorts of nefarious schemes. Hence the public is hesitating, doubtful, and half-afraid of education.

Education Made Safe

It is evident that the educative process is not complete; the circle is not entirely closed. The only thing that can ever make education safe is to have the spiritual output, the by-product of those physical transformations of the living body, immediately enter as an influence for good into the environment which was the source of the original impressions. At present the school does not do this. It assumes that the spiritual result will some time later beneficently affect the environment; and in many cases it does; but it is largely a matter of chance, and our education is therefore not scientific. Character is not assured until the spiritual product has made itself felt in the uplift of the surroundings which gave it birth.

Weak Spot in the Schools

Here is the vitally, fatally weak spot in the schools. While they are furnishing an increasing number of opportunities through material and method for the pupils to derive ideas from their surroundings, they by no means furnish adequate or corresponding opportunities for them to work their impulses back into their surroundings again.

A man looks out over a plague-smitten city; from what he sees he forms an idea — a spiritual product — as to what should be done. He plans a system of drainage and other measures which finally dispel the pestilence, and his surroundings are left upon a higher plane than that on which be found them. The new generation begins where his work ended and repeats the process; thus through generation after generation in endless cycles the elevation of the race proceeds.

Educative Process Illustrated

In this illustration there is the perfect type of the educative process. The man not only blesses his city; he at the same time educates himself — constructs character. Nobody doubts him, nobody fears him; everyone knows just what he will do. He is the only type of a citizen that is absolutely safe, and but few of such appear in each generation. "By their *fruits* ye shall KNOW them." The schools are almost wholly lacking in opportunities and means by which the pupil can make this beneficent connection with his environment. He has no means by which he can close the circle, and his spiritual product, his impulses, waste themselves away in the ether. No human being was ever educated by such a process.

Meaning of Hand-work

Slowly are the schools waking up to this fact. By almost imperceptible degrees the pupils are allowed to exercise the means by which they may work their ideas out in their surroundings. This is the real meaning of all the forms of art, and of hand-work, that are gradually finding place in the curriculum. They are not there merely to make the fingers nimble, any more than the object is introduced simply to render the senses alert. It is their immediate purpose to afford the pupil a direct means of putting himself, his spiritual output, as a living impulse, into his environment that he may uplift it. When pupils are *all* trained in this part of the educative process, there is every reason to believe that *all* of them will become educated; that *all* of them will become safe and reliable citizens. It is the final step, the closing of the circle through the individual's reaction upon his environment, that actually assures character. The various forms of handwork are admirably adapted to this end. Domestic sci-

Educating all the Children

ence lies at the foundation of the health and happiness of the race. Its glaring need is evident everywhere. In this subject the pupils have the fullest opportunity of putting into immediate operation, for the benefit of all concerned, every lesson that is learned.

Through the artistic and industrial aspects of clay-modeling, woodwork, metal-work, textiles, sewing, bookbinding, printing, drawing, painting and design, no home and no school need be without work that is both useful and beautiful. Early ideas of taste in matters pertaining to dress and decoration exert constantly a powerful influence in the development of character. All of these activities meet the growing demand for finer adaptations and more delicate adjustments, that materials may be used with greater economy, more artistic effect, and for a more exalted purpose.

Function of the Occupations

These occupations in the school are intended to close the gap that ordinarily exists in the circle—in the educative process—between the individual and his environment. It is they that finally root in the human being the elements of character. There is no doubt what a man or woman so trained will do. He can be trusted to make things better, and through the making to become a stronger and finer character himself.

Creative Work

It is this part of the educative process that calls for original and creative work of the highest type. Imitation will not answer; for the environment is to be changed, made better, and new ways and means must be devised. It turns education from a copying process into one of original research. It insures a re-examination of the motive at every step, that the highest ends may be sought and attained. Through the continual search into the needs of his surroundings, the moral sense of the individual is immeasurably quickened, and the motive itself in time becomes firmly established. It is then, and not until then, that the right type of citizenship is assured.

W. S. J.

VOLUME VI NUMBER 3

THE ELEMENTARY SCHOOL TEACHER

NOVEMBER, 1905

AN EDUCATIONAL DEVELOPMENT IN GEORGIA

C. S. PARRISH
Georgia State Normal School

The city systems of schools in Georgia have been developing for many years in harmony with progressive educational thought. Some of them have had a marked degree of excellence, but the rural schools have not improved correspondingly. For the last ten years the attention of educational leaders and of the leaders in the women's clubs has been turned to the problem of making these schools more efficient, and noteworthy success has been achieved in several directions. The model schools established, and in part supported, by the women's clubs have done some good work, and the undertaking of Mr. Ira Williams, first at Sand Hill and then at Temple, Ga., in the consolidation of schools, transportation of children, and the introduction of better methods, has been and is worthy of very high praise.

The practice school of the State Normal School of Georgia, located at Athens, is beginning now to do a work which, from the nature of the case, could not be done by any other of the agencies mentioned. In the winter of 1902, President E. C. Branson requested the writer, who was then entering the school as teacher of psychology and pedagogy, to study the needs of rural schools in Georgia, and to reorganize the work of teacher-training at the State Normal School with especial reference to furnishing better teachers for those schools. Captain S. D. Bradwell, the founder of the school, had appealed to the state legislature for funds for its support, with the promise that this should be the primary object of the institution, and he had done one of the noblest pieces of pioneer work any state ever saw. Mr. E. C. Branson, upon his accession to the presidency, had pressed toward still greater efficiency, and it was his desire that the department of pedagogy which he was resigning should be expanded, kept in harmony with the best educational thought, and, at the same time, adapted to the needs of the country schools of Georgia.

On undertaking the solution of the problem, the writer believed that one of the most necessary factors was a practice school in connection with the pedagogical work of the State Normal School, this practice school to be itself an example of the working of the forces which were needed in the country schools. She did not believe that it would be wise to make it a model for country schools. It needed to be better than any country school in Georgia could be for years to come. The teachers who were best fitted for work in these schools were, it was believed, young men and women who could mold opinion and lead the people of Georgia toward a much higher type of school than any which they could establish or conduct under existing conditions, or in the present state of commonly received opinion. It was believed that the teachers in training at the State Normal School should work out in a practice school such a practical application of the theories which they accepted in their study of education as could afterward be modified, adapted to local conditions, and used in any school in Georgia. In April, 1902, in conference with Miss Lucy L. Davis, who had been called from the practice school of William and Mary College to be the principal of the new school, the writer made a plan for its conduct, which was submitted to President Branson and to Chancellor Hill, of the University of Georgia, and which, after its approval by them, was sent to Mr. George Foster Peabody, the constant benefactor of Georgia schools, with an appeal for a sum of money sufficient to provide a building and equipment with which the work could be begun. In May of the same year Mr. Branson submitted the plan to the board of trustees of the State Normal School, who promised to support the school when established. In June Mr. Peabody gave ten thousand dollars for a building, and three thousand five hundred for its equipment, the promoters of the scheme believing that this sum would suffice for a modest beginning.

Various untoward circumstances interfered with the accomplishment of the project, but in the autumn of 1903 the building was opened and the work begun. From the first, the policy of the school, and of the teacher-training which was to go along with it, was clearly defined. It was believed that all elementary education should grow out of and be centered around the life and experience of the child; hence the work was to have its basis in the industries which are essential to the home and the community. It was seen that all education in country schools should help to foster a sort of life which would be so attractive to the best young men and young women in the country communities as to furnish a strong check to the growing tendency to leave the country and rush into city life, without any real fitness for that life. Hence, the element of beauty was to pervade the school and to transform, as far as possible, what might otherwise be considered sordid. It was hoped that, through the teachers trained in it, the practice school might do something to make daily work a joy instead of a burden; that it might hasten the time when men and women would find their pleasure *in* their work instead of in its pauses, and fill it with so much honesty, truth, and beauty that it would be a contribution of worth to the world. Art, music, literature, and history were to be integral parts of the work; were to be infused into the habitual expressions of daily life, and to become, as far as possible, necessary parts of the life of each child. The history-teaching was to be planned so as to bring the children to a consciousness of institutional development, the growth of civilization, the evolution of the industries which underlie human progress and their relation to social conditions. As a matter of course, it was understood that all this could not be formulated for children, but the work was to be so shaped that they would grow into an attitude which would embody the truth sought. It was understood that no such attitude could be reached under conditions of forced action or violent restraint, and the principle of interest was to be dominant in both teaching and government. The self-control which is the result of developing character was to be sought, rather than enforced good behavior. The health, strength, and happiness of the children were to be well cared for, and, as aids to these, indoor and outdoor gymnasiums, playgrounds, and means for games were to be provided and the children encouraged to play. The organic unity of all stages of education was to be impressed upon the teachers in training, and it was desired that they should see all grades, from the kindergarten to the high school, so related that no sharp lines of separation could be drawn. The kindergarten of the practice school was to be only a grade of the school; the students were to observe and practice there just as they did in other grades, and without any other training than that given for the general work of elementary teaching. It was hoped that in the development of the work the same sort of continuity between the highest grammar and lowest high-school grades could be shown. The promoters of the scheme wished to enlist both children and practice-teachers in the service of civic beauty, and especially to stimulate the improvement of the buildings and grounds of country schools. As an example of what might be done with little or no expense, it was planned to have one section of the practice-school grounds made beautiful with the resources of the Georgia fields and forests. The absolute necessity of a library for every school was to be emphasized, and there was a distinct intention to plan all the work of the school so as to make it impossible of accomplishment without a library. At the same time, the teaching was to be such as could be done, with modifications, by an intelligent teacher in any country or city school. The work was not shaped with reference to a school of one teacher. The leading educators of Georgia were then, and are now, pressing the consolidation of schools and the transportation of children. The school of one teacher was disappearing with sufficient rapidity to justify confidence in its speedy extinction, and it was thought bad economy to train the students of the State Normal School for a decaying phase of education. There were minor points of emphasis, but those enumerated were made essential.

As a matter of course, all which was projected has not yet been accomplished. Some lines of work have not yet even been entered upon. The scheme was sufficiently new to seem an innovation, and no teachers trained for this particular kind of education and with experience in it were available with the means at hand. The enterprise could not fail to suffer from the skepticism which always clogs far-reaching aims, and from the opposition which any departure from the time-honored must brave. That so much has been done in spite of difficulties seemingly insurmountable is due largely to the tireless energy, patience, and skill of Miss L. L. Davis, the principal, to the self-sacrificing devotion of some of her assistants, to the helpful sympathy of some of the parents of pupils, and to the intelligent faith and unwavering loyalty of the senior classes of the State Normal School.

The building which has been erected contains four large schoolrooms, four small classrooms, a kitchen, pantry, store closet, dining-room, library, weaving-room, gymnasium, shop, a small anthropometrical laboratory, and a principal's office. There are now five regular teachers, including the principal, and this year the practice-teachers are eighty in number. There are eight grades of children, including two kindergarten groups, and another will be added next year.

The work is based upon fundamental industries. The occupations used at present are cooking, sewing, spinning, weaving, gardening, drawing, clay-modeling, basketry, and woodwork. There are no "courses" in these. They are simply parts of the children's daily lives. The arithmetic consists almost entirely of the problems arising from the various occupations, though the teachers utilize opportunities so diligently that more number work has been done than the time-honored methods could make possible. There are no separate writing lessons, but the children have so many records to keep, receipts to make, excursions to describe, summaries of information to preserve, and letters to write, that they do far more writing than is done in the routine school, and are writing well. Formal reading lessons are very little emphasized, that little being in deference to custom; but the children are reading almost constantly in connection with their various pursuits. The language work has been largely incidental, and yet carefully attended to. The spelling has been confined to words the children have needed to use, and has been taught when it was needed, not in set lessons. A record has been kept of words spelled, and every child is compiling his own dictionary. A great deal of elementary science has arisen from the cooking, gardening, and building, the teachers having lost few opportunities of bringing to consciousness the processes which underlie the daily work of the home and the community. The work in geography, in addition to its nature-study connections, has concerned industrial areas and centers, areas and centers of human development in this and other countries, and has dwelt with particular emphasis on Georgia as furnishing these areas or being able to furnish them. The history work has dealt with the developing life of the race, and has embodied a comparison of present conditions with the conditions of primitive life and with later stages of development. Primitive hunting, pastoral and agricultural life, as well as the later phases of city, commercial, and manufacturing life, are studied, not necessarily in succession, but as they seem to appeal to and arouse interest, and as they serve the purpose of cultivating in the children a consciousness of the steps by which the human race reached its present condition. The evolution of means of transportation, of roads and streets, of lighting and heating, of forms of food, clothing, and shelter, of gins, cards, spinning-wheels, looms, mills, sewing-machines, and other industrial implements and instruments, of books, paper, textile fabrics, and other accompaniments of human life, are being studied.

Excursions have been considered an important part of the regular work of the school. The children, with the help of the practice-teachers, have found and brought in from the woods near Athens, ferns, hepaticas, blood-roots, wood violets, asters, azaleas, sumacs, dogwoods, hawthorns, and hollies, and planted them in the piece of ground reserved for Georgia resources. They have brought yellow jessamine, honeysuckle, woodbine, Virginia creeper, and bamboo, and planted them against the walls of the building, or where other support could be furnished. These excursions have been utilized either in studying the life-history of the plants sought or in observing some other phase of nature. The expanding life of spring, the maturing life of autumn, and the sheltered and hidden life of winter have been brought to consciousness and closely watched. Life-histories rather than mechanisms have been studied. Insects and birds have been considered mainly with reference to their homes, modes of life, and functions in the economy of nature. Excursions have also been made to the various industrial plants in and around Athens. The fire department, the water-works, the cloth-mills, the electric power-house, the cotton-gin, the "batting"-mill, and other places of interest have been made the basis of arithmetical calculations, of studies of simple physical truths, of elementary studies in economics, and of valuable language and composition work.

The children are brought into contact with a great wealth of literature. They read freely in connection with all their occupations, and with their geography, history, and nature-study. In addition to this, each grade makes a special study of some masterpiece of the world's literature. Indian, Greek, and Norse myths, the Arthurian and Homeric legends, the *Nibelungenlied,* and stories from the Old Testament have alternated with modern masterpieces. The Arthurian work of a year ago was especially fruitful in its results. The fourth grade had, in the illness and absence of the principal, shown a degree of restiveness which was at once despair for the practice-teachers and interesting study for the teacher of psychology. It was felt that much must be endeavored before giving up the cherished plan of building character, and helping the children to self-control was allowed to yield to a system of force. Influence after influence was tried with very little result. At last it was determined to ask a new teacher, who was in full sympathy with the theory of moral development held by the teacher of psychology and the principal of the practice school, to tell the children the Arthurian stories, and to let them live the Arthurian life as far as possible. The teacher of literature in the normal school entered into helpful co-operation, and the result was watched with intense interest by all who were in the secret. Very soon it was found that all the Arthurian literature in the libraries of both normal school and practice school was not sufficient to meet the demands of the children and the practice-teachers. The Atlanta library, the recent gift of Mr. Carnegie, was called upon, and generously lent its resources. A jousting-place appeared on the playground, and was rarely without contending knights in the hours given to play. Helmets, shields, spears, swords, lances, and Arthurian costumes for both sexes were soon in process of manufacture, not only in the shop and the schoolroom, but in the homes of the children. Each boy in the grade assumed the name of one of Arthur's knights, and agreed to try to imitate his life and to gain his character. Each girl became a lady of Arthur's court, and was shortly acting well her part. No observer could doubt the value of the result. A noisy and restless school became orderly and obedient. Courtesy took the place of self-assertion on the playground, and evidence was obtained that many of the children were carrying the new spirit into their home conduct. "That is unknightly" became a strong deterrent; and, with the exception of the lapse, when the boys organized to attack a gypsy encampment, and then asserted, in justification of their behavior, that the gypsies were conspiring to steal their Queen Guinevere, the transformation was lasting. A little drama for public presentation was aranged by the children with the help of the teacher, and given at the end of the year. In the preparation of this, the children studied mediæval life and customs, built a small Arthurian castle, made miniature suits of armor, copied for dolls the dress of ladies, esquires, and pages, and became so familiar with the legends that the drama was merely an expression of the knowledge gained in their regular work.

Dramatization has been a very effective instrument in the study of literature. Last year the fifth grade dramatized and acted *Rip Van Winkle.* This year a beautiful entertainment given to the grade studying *Rip Van Winkle* by one of the school mothers showed in a gratifying way the extent of her sympathy. She and her children had given a large part of the leisure of a month in making artistic decorations for the refreshment table, every detail of decoration and, as far as possible, of the refreshments themselves being illustrative of the story. The story of *Siegfried* is now in process of dramatization by the sixth grade. The first and second grades have dramatized the *Sleeping Beauty,* and the third grade the story of *Pocahontas,* for public presentation; but all the literary work, from the *Three Bears* of the first grade to the Greek stories of the sixth, has a large dramatic element, the dramatization of home life by the kindergarten children being a fit preparation for this. Story-telling has been a valuable instrument. The teacher of literature in the normal school has always co-operated, and has done such fine training work with the practice-teachers that most of them have been able to tell stories effectively. The children are encouraged to tell them, and like to use the privilege.

Play and other means of physical culture are receiving careful attention. Mr. Peabody's generosity made both indoor and outdoor gymnasium work possible, and provided space for indoor play in the occasional weather when outdoor life is not possible. The outdoor gymnasium was in place before the building was ready for occupancy, and has been used so constantly that it is already the worse for wear. An equipment for anthropometrical work has been provided, and the testing of the children for physical defects, with a view to remedial exercise in the gymnasium as well as of advice to parents, was begun last year. That it is not now in full operation because of the pressure of other work upon the director of the gymnasium is a source of deep regret to the managers of the school. Tests of sight, hearing, nervousness, and fatigue are, however, in progress under the direction of the teacher of psychology, who is projecting further tests in types of imagery and tone discrimination. Play has been encouraged and participated in by the practice-teachers. Last year the members of the junior class of the normal school played a number of time-honored games with the children, and invited suggestions from them for modifications. Afterward they worked over the plays with the purpose of giving them greater educational value, and then played again with the children, suggesting the changes and observing the results. The boys have made a baseball and football ground which is in constant use during the season. Basket-ball and tennis are available, but it is found that they do not appeal to children of the ages now in the practice school. The members of the senior class of the normal school are this year beginning an extension of the play-work, from which much good is hoped. On a visit to some children in the suburbs of Athens they began to play with them, and very soon the children in the neighborhood congregated to look on. The newcomers were invited to join the game, and enjoyed it so much that it was determined to give notice of succeeding visits and play with as many children as possible. This has been done in several localities, with gratifying results. It is intended to encourage and extend this work, and to add story-telling and singing. Last year a Story-Tellers' Club, composed of Athens boys and girls, met regularly at the residence of the teacher of pedagogy and, after listening to and telling stories for an hour, played in the grounds the remainder of the afternoon. The co-operation of the teacher of literature and one of the teachers of the practice school made the work interesting and profitable. An investigation of the play-preferences of children, and the reasons for these preferences, is now in progress in connection with the child-study work of the senior class of the normal school.

Æsthetic culture is not forgotten. There has been an earnest attempt to make both the interior and exterior of the building beautiful. The conditions have been too complex and the work too new to admit of best results; yet something has been done. Mr. Peabody's generosity made it possible to provide for each schoolroom a few good reproductions of fine pictures and masterpieces of sculpture. The central hall has pictures of the Egyptian pyramids, the ruins of the Roman Forum, the Roman Colosseum, the Alhambra, and one view of St. Peter's Church. A large amphora and a set of Greek vases are there, and a "Winged Victory" is to be added as soon as possible. Growing plants are to be found in every room of the building, and the children are encouraged to care for them. Clematis, wistaria, climbing roses, honeysuckle, Virginia creeper, bamboo, yellow jessamine, and Boston ivy have been planted against the walls, and are beginning to cover them. Flowers, shrubs, and ornamental trees, which have been planted with a view to artistic effect, are growing. The children are encouraged to make all their constructions as beautiful as possible, and attention is constantly called to the beautiful in nature. The care of the rooms, the decoration of the lunch-table, the care of their own persons, the work of the garden, the building and furnishing of playhouses, the decoration of pottery, the weaving of rugs, the dressing of dolls, and, indeed, all the occupations of the school, are utilized for lessons in beauty. Drawing and painting have been used as a means of expression in connection with nearly all the work the children do; but there has also been much art work with direct reference to the more purely artistic value. The children have painted landscapes, and made designs for the covers of their cookery and garden books, for Christmas cards, Easter cards, and valentines.

Tree-planting has been carried on very assiduously, the children and practice-teachers doing the work under the stimulation of the principal. There are now in the grounds water oaks, willow oaks, white and red oaks, elms, magnolias, cedars, hickories, walnuts, pecans, apples, peaches, pears, figs, and olives. A number of mulberry trees have been planted with a view to silk-culture in the future. Grape vines are growing on the walls of the building and on a frame made by the children. The planting of trees brought in from the neighboring woods, which has already been alluded to, goes on every spring and autumn.

The kitchen garden has been successful. The children have used vegetables of their own growing for their lunches, and have made presents of them to friends of the school. The growth of one or two varieties as a productive industry is being considered. This garden has been the center of many sorts of work. The children have thought out and drawn plans for it, as it has been changed from season to season and from year to year; have measured and laid it out, dug and prepared it for planting, studied its soil and fertilized it, calculated the quantities of seeds needed and their cost, macadamized its walks, watched the growth of its plants, painted its flowers, read with reference to the best methods of its culture, kept records of sowing, germinating, blossoms, and maturity, studied the insects that frequented it, and watched the effect of heat, cold, light, moisture, and winds upon it. They have studied the life-history of the plants which have been cultivated, and learned about their food-values, their functions in enriching or exhausting the soil, and the modifications produced in them by cultivation.

The woodwork has been very practical. The members of one grade built a log cabin large enough to admit one or two of their number in connection with the study of pioneer life in America. Another grade has made a pigeon-house and a wren-house which have been placed in position to entice the birds. Another still has made a scuppernong arbor and planted the vines. A Powhatan wigwam was built in connection with early colonial history. A syrup-mill, a primitive gin, and a wheelbarrow have been made by different grades. The children of the first grade always make and furnish a playhouse. Supports for vines, shelves, and boxes for flowers, tool-boxes, pencil-boxes, quilting-frames, and various other articles needed in the school life, have been made and used. In connection with their studies of primitive life, the children have constructed tepees, Eskimo huts, weapons, household utensils, canoes, dug-outs, boats, looms, and mills.

There have been no "courses" of sewing, "samplers," or "sewing-books," but the children have hemmed napkins and doilies for the dining-room, made cooking-aprons for themselves, hemstitched a set of napkins, and dressed dolls of various nationalities. A group of dolls in Arthurian costumes made by the children has been preserved. The first-grade children have made and stuffed small mattresses, hemmed sheets and coverlets, and made curtains for their playhouse. Baskets have been made of raffia, of the Georgia wire grass, of white-oak splits and shucks. Woolen rugs and straw mats for playhouses have been woven, pottery of various sorts has been modeled, and a number of other articles made.

As was said at the outset, all this construction has arisen from, or been closely related to, the needs of daily life, sometimes that of the children themselves, sometimes that of a people or period being studied. For weeks before last Christmas, for instance, the children were busy making gifts. In the kitchen they made enough candy for each child in the school to give away some. In the shop, baskets were made to hold the candy, and some of the lower grades cut tissue paper and wrapped it. Christmas in other lands was being studied, and dolls were being dressed in the costumes of those lands. Wooden articles of various sorts were being made for presents to parents or teachers. The result was a tree loaded with gifts made by the children for their teachers and parents, as well as for each other. At one time the first-grade children were interested in Indian life, and wished to bake corn cakes just as the Indians did. They were allowed to do this, and led to compare their methods with those of the present. Later, one of the upper grades gathered up the ashes, built a "hopper," and "dripped" some lye. Later still, a dye was needed for the raffia used in making baskets which the children had designed. One of the grades had an excursion in order to collect certain barks which had been suggested to them, and experimented with these until they obtained the color they wanted. The dye needed to be "set" with an alkali, and they used for this purpose the lye which had previously been made. In studying means of transportation, among other pieces of construction was a small Chinese wheelbarrow. Later, the grade united in making one large wheelbarrow of the present American type. This wheelbarrow is now in constant use in connection with the garden.

The correlation of other subjects with the industrial work has been constantly alluded to. The difficulty has not been in finding opportunities for correlation, but in utilizing the wealth of material suggested. A few weeks ago the fourth grade made some chocolate in their cooking hour. The teacher placed before them the powdered chocolate, the cracked bean, the whole bean, and a model of the fruit, and readily developed the process of preparing the powdered chocolate. She then led them to test it qualitatively for food substances, and showed a card giving the relative quantities of these. Some very simple calculations in percentages grew out of this, and other arithmetical processes were needed in calculating the quantity of milk and sugar needed for the beverage and the food substances which they would add. The action of heat upon the mixture, and the effect of the food substances contained in it on the body, were discussed while the chocolate was cooking; and when it was finished, the table was spread and a lunch served. A guest had been invited, and the children told stories for her entertainment. When they returned to the regular teacher, she showed them some pictures of the cocoa tree and of the fruit in various stages of preparation. These were discussed, and made the basis of several language lessons, without destroying the interest of the children in the knowledge they were gaining. As the work went on from day to day, the areas in which the cocoa tree is cultivated were discussed and their geography reviewed. In connection with Mexico, the children were told a story of Montezuma drinking chocolate from a golden cup, and they read about the Aztecs, their life and their subjugation by Cortez. A written account of the culture of the cocoa tree and of the manufacture of chocolate was prepared by each child before the close of the work.

Mr. Peabody's gift for the library was five hundred dollars, but a sum originally meant for another purpose was, with his approbation, diverted to the library, and, by using small sums obtained from other sources, books to the value of about one thousand dollars have been accumulated. The pupils and the practice-teachers have made good use of the reference books, and the children have constantly taken books from it for outside reading. It has become so indispensable a part of the work that each teacher in training will go away feeling that she cannot teach without a library; but it is still much too small to meet the need adequately.

The managers of the school have tried to keep the parents of the children in sympathetic contact with the life and aims of the school, and in the majority of cases they have met with a very gratifying response. Last year a mothers' meeting was held once a month. This year the mothers have been frequently invited to the school, and have come in good numbers. The classrooms are always open to them as visitors, and some use this privilege. Next year they will be invited to unite with the teachers in studying some of the problems of child-training.

As has been said, the work has had opposition and misunderstanding to face. There are many good people who, accustomed to older forms, have not had time to keep in touch with current educational theory, and are afraid of innovations. The work is yet too new for its best results to be manifest, and some parents prefer methods which have stood the test of many years. Nevertheless, there have always been more applicants for admission than could be accommodated, and a number of parents have been steadfast in their intelligent confidence.

The senior class of the normal school numbered eighty last year. The majority of these young men and young women were from the country, and have returned to it. They have formed themselves into groups of two or three for the purpose of establishing schools in needy rural communities. They intend to try to become parts of the community life and to make the school a social center. They want to improve schoolhouses and grounds, consolidate schools, transport children, establish libraries and shops, plant gardens, secure the co-operation of parents, and conduct their schools so as to develop the community life in the best possible way.

A SCHOOL GARDEN

NINA LEUBRIE
Francis W. Parker School, Chicago

FOURTH GRADE — FRANCIS W. PARKER SCHOOL

In October, when our school opened, we found many flowers still blooming in "Grandmother's Garden" at Lincoln Park. The children were anxious to have hollyhocks, hardy chrysanthemums, and some bright autumn flowers in front of our building. We consulted the seed catalogues, gardening books, and the park gardener, to find when such things should be planted. Some of us had had experience with bulb-planting, and it was decided that, since it was too late for fall flowers, our front yard should have flowers in the spring. Bulb catalogues were sent for. Pictures and flower descriptions were studied. The children were surprised to find that so many of the plants familiar to them came from bulbs.

In order to plant properly, directions by experienced gardeners had to be read, understood, and followed. These directions had to be referred to again and again, intelligent and accurate reading being absolutely necessary. Color schemes and size of the flower had to be considered. This was one of many suggestions: A bright group was to be planted in the farther plot near the wall; when the children of the school, attracted by this color patch, went over there, they would find the fragrant lily-of-the-valley, too.

Taking gardening books, catalogues, trowels, and rulers with them to the yard, the children planted the bulbs. Sometimes two or three children wanted to work together. They took turns, one reading the directions while the other dug, the third going for the sand or gravel needed.

In the yard we planted roots of Tritoma Pfitzerii and Dicentra, two vines, Clematis paniculata and matrimony, a clump of lily-of-the-valley, and bulbs of tulips, crocuses, scillas, daffodils, jonquils, poet's narcissus, iris, snowdrops, snowflakes, grape hyacinths, and Chionodoxa Lucillae (glory of the snow). Bulbs of hyacinths, freezias, stars of Bethlehem, Easter lilies, and Chinese sacred lilies were planted in the house. The cost of the bulbs and roots was about eight dollars.

For spring planting and fall blooming it is believed these will prove satisfactory: Seeds: canarybird vine, nasturtium, coreopsis, digitalis (fox-glove), mignonette, alyssum, ten-weeks stocks (sow late), cosmos, marigold, single annual wall flower (sow early), corn flower, phlox, zinnia, poppy, nicotiana affinis, Chinese and other larkspur, and seeds for next year's hollyhocks. Plants: gaillardia, baby rambler, Alleghany hollyhock, hardy chrysanthemum, and hydrangea. The Betchel double crab and three-year-old plants of oriental poppies, if planted early, will blossom the same spring.

The following papers were written by the children:

GARDEN BULBS

NOVEMBER 9, 1904.

"Different bulbs should be planted different depths and distances apart. They need good drainage; generally stones or sand are used. When bulbs are planted, they should not be stepped on.

"Some bulbs need rich soil, and others do not need such good soil. Most bulbs should not be left in water, for if they are, they will rot.

"This is a list of the bulbs we planted outside: Grape hyacinth, crocus, scilla, iris, daffodil, jonquil, poet's narcissus, snowdrop, snowflake, single tulip, parrot tulip, and glory of the snow. In the house we planted: freezia, Easter lily, hyacinth, star of Bethlehem, and Chinese sacred lily.

"CARLTON PRINDIVILLE."

BULBS

"We planted bulbs out in the garden in front of the school. Different bulbs have to be planted at different depths, and they all have to have good drainage, or they will not grow well.

"So we looked in some bulb catalogues and found out the depth that the bulbs should be planted. We put sand under the bulbs, that would let the water come through the ground more easily, and the water would not stay by the bulbs and rot them. The different bulbs have to be planted at different distances apart as well as different depths; we found that in the bulb catalogues, too. We planted some bulbs in the house.

"Outdoors we planted hyacinth, crocus, scilla, iris, snowdrop, snowflake, glory of the snow, tulip, jonquil, and narcissus.

"Indoors we planted freezia, Easter lily, star of Bethlehem, Chinese lily, and hyacinth. The Chinese lily and the hyacinth we planted in water, but the rest of the indoor plants we planted in pots.

"LUCY SMITH."

Paintings were made of the bulbs, and in the spring of the flowers that came from each kind of bulb.

In February Josephine wrote:

"November eighth we planted Chinese lilies in our room. They grew quite fast. The book said that they would bloom in six weeks, but the reason ours did not blossom was because we put the plants on the window-sill over the radiator and the florist said that we roasted them.

"At Christmas time there were a great many buds on each of them, but none of them came out."

In May, Doris' record says:

"Our Easter lily came up about the first of April. It did not come up for Easter, but is blossoming today.

"Our tulips are red and yellow ones. They are along the side of the house. Our lilies-of-the-valley are in bud and will be open soon. We planted them in March. The scilla is a little blue flower. It has come up and died down again.

"We planted three hyacinths in the house. They all came up, but they had very short stems. We tried an experiment on one. We took an opaque piece of paper and put it around the plant. But it died. We thought it would try to grow up to the light and so have a longer stem."

We were fortunate in having, as we planned, a succession of blooms, from the early scilla to our late parrot tulips, when it was time to put out spring plants. Many of our bulbs, however, did not mature.

In the fall each child made two plans of the front yard to a scale, showing grass plots and flower beds.

The first plan was used for individual suggestions as to where the bulbs should be placed. The class often went to the garden to better judge distances and proximities of color combinations. The plan of placing was changed again and again. The final plan was made to a larger scale, showing where the different bulbs were planted.

Our wild-flower corner was supplied with particular care. As the woods and ravines along the north shore have suffered from ruthless root-pulling and flower-gathering, we depended upon having excursions enough to become familiar with the wild flowers in their haunts.

The children planned ways of keeping records of these flowers showing the kinds found, dates and places. The blue-print herbal which was suggested to them became the chief means of record. The name of the flower, date of finding, and place found growing were often written on the back of the print.

COATING PAPER FOR BLUE PRINTS

Materials needed: balance scales, graduate, one ounce of red prussiate of potash (ferricyanide), one and one-half ounces of citrate iron of ammonia, five ounces of warm water, five ounces of cold water, glass rod, brown or yellow bottle (twenty-ounce bottle is good size), small shallow dish, small soft sponge or absorbent cotton, four or more sheets of unlined white paper, three thumb-tacks, four or more clamp-hooks, stout string and stove, lamp, gas burner or any heating apparatus that can be taken into the dark room.

Do the following in a dark room. Incandescent light will not harm. In a brown bottle dissolve one ounce of red prussiate of potash in five ounces of warm water. Stir with glass rod. Add to this solution one and one-half ounces of citrate iron of ammonia, and then add five ounces of cold water. Stir until crystals are dissolved. Pour a small amount of the solution into the

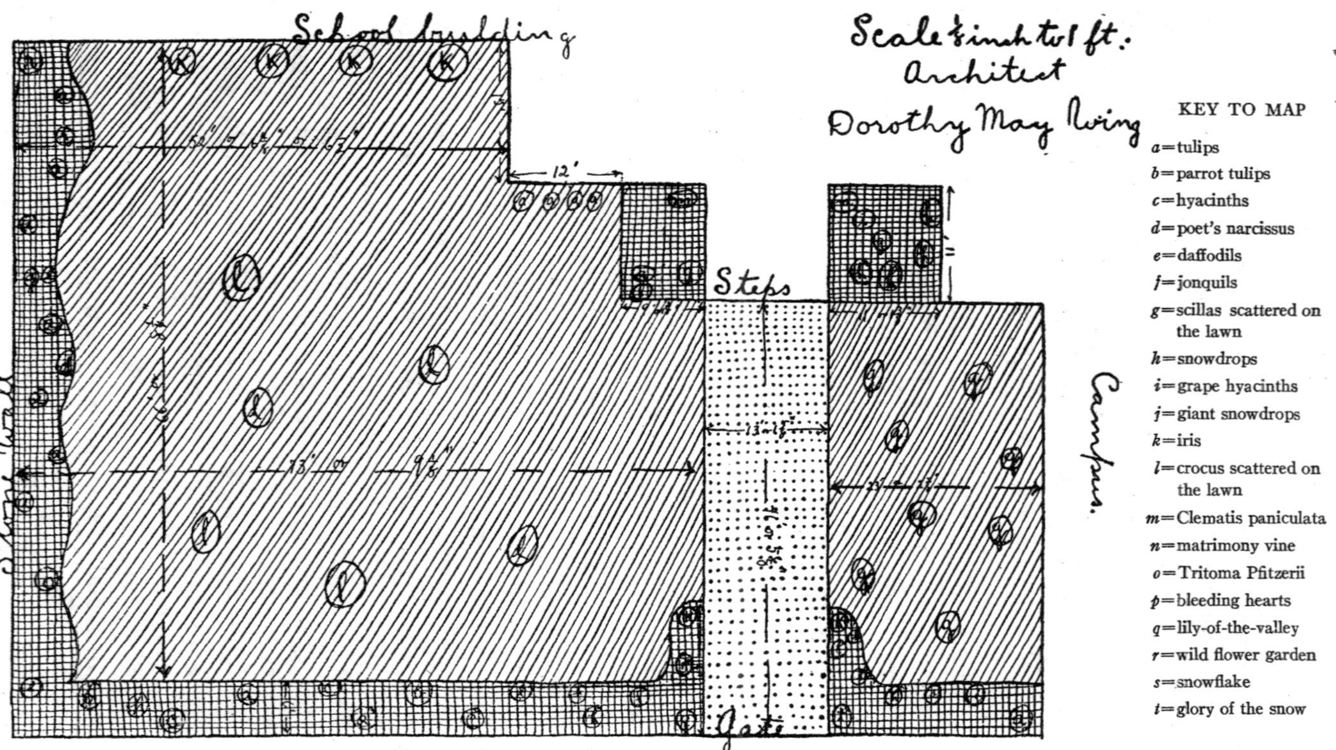

A CHILD'S PLAN OF THE GARDEN SHOWING WHERE BULBS WERE PLACED

shallow dish. Wet the sponge in this (do not have the sponge dripping), and coat the white paper evenly on one side. (The paper will stay better in place if thumb-tacks are used. The paper can be held by the tacks without being pierced.) Hang the coated paper by clamp-hooks over good heat. In about five minutes, or when *thoroughly* dry, the paper may be cut into the desired size and used for printing.

Keep this solution in a cool, dark room. It will not keep more than three or four days. If the solution is too thick, an ounce or two of water may be added. Use the paper the day it is coated, if possible. Keep it in a dry, cool, dark place. The paper is good as long as it is yellow.

As the solution stains the fingers, it should be washed off immediately after coating the paper.

BLUE PRINTING

Materials needed: printing-frame, clean plate of glass to fit the frame, blue-print paper, fresh water.

Place the flower on the glass in the frame. On this put the yellow side of the paper, close the frame, and expose to the sun (the time for exposure depends on the intensity of light). Wash and rinse well until no yellow shows in the parts that ought to be white. Place on a newspaper to dry.

An effort was frequently made at placing the flower artistically in the frame. The children were told of principles usually held by artists in arrangement, and they examined their own results, criticising them with these principles in mind.

The prints, I hope, will not only serve for a record throughout the year in different localities, but will suggest to the children designs for their clay tiles and pottery, and their work in textiles and illustrating.

In connection with the work the children read or committed to memory the following poems:

"The Snowdrop," "Flower in the Crannied Wall," Tennyson; "A Morning Song," "Where the Bee Sucks There Suck I," "Under the Greenwood Tree," Shakespeare; "Home Thoughts from Abroad," song from "Pippa Passes," Browning; "Let Me Go Where'er I Will," Emerson; "An Apple Orchard in the Spring," Martin; "Summer is i-cumen in," Old English.

REFERENCE READING ON BULBS: *The Practical Garden Book,* Hunn and Bailey; *Practical Floriculture,* Henderson; *Gardening for Pleasure,* Henderson; *Flower Bulbs,* Rexford; *A Woman's Hardy Garden,* Ely; fall catalogues of The Fair, Vaughn's Seed Store, and Petersen's Nursery, Chicago; The Elm City Nursery Co., New Haven, Conn.; J. Wilkinson Elliott, Pittsburg, Pa.; J. L. Childs, Floral Park, N. Y.; and catalogues of other nurseries and seed-stores. Send to the Mayflower Publishing Co., Floral Park, N. Y., for *Mayflower* magazines, August and September, 1903.

SCHOOL ARCHITECTURE[1]

SEYMOUR DAVIS
Philadelphia, Pa.

The old ideas of school construction, with the poor ventilation, inadequately lighted rooms, and their many other inconveniences, are rapidly being discarded. In many of the new buildings scientific principles of modern school architecture are incorporated. Of recent years this development has extended to every part of the civilized world, not only in the vital points just referred to, but in all points of construction. We have but to glance over the prize essay of Dr. Alcott, written in 1831, to find that his ideal for a schoolroom was one lighted on opposite sides. George B. Emerson, in 1842, advised less than 118 cubic feet of air per pupil in schoolrooms. Burrowes published in 1855 a treatise in which the heating and ventilating of schools were gone into in great detail, and for a room to accommodate fifty pupils he allowed vent ducts only ten by eighteen inches.

These gentlemen were the authorities of their day, and their suggestions in the construction of school buildings were widely circulated and followed; but the revolution in all matters pertaining to school construction and administration has changed the requirements for the modern school. A great factor in the advance of school work is due to the public demand for better things. Our school commissioners require that buildings shall be planned on correct architectural and sanitary lines, and so long as this educational movement advances, we can expect still greater progress.

Our new buildings are being properly equipped, and are hygienically and architecturally in keeping with the advance in education; heating, ventilation, and sanitation have been reduced

[1] Paper read before the Department of Business Education at the National Educational Association meeting, Asbury Park, N. J., July, 1905.

to such an exact science that there can be no excuse for an inadequately ventilated, poorly heated, or unsanitary school building. The sanitary conditions of the schoolroom having such an influence for good or bad upon the health and morals of the children, and bearing such weight in the success of the teacher, it is to the interest of everybody to be satisfied only with the best that science can produce.

The details of the modern school plan should be as carefully considered as the details of a hospital. It is encouraging to note that the school boards of the present day make themselves familiar with what is best in school planning, the result being that each year we see buildings that are better planned, better constructed, and properly designed, at an initial cost not greatly in excess of that under the old requirements.

Certain countries, states, and cities are fortunate in possessing laws governing the planning and construction of their school buildings. To assure these laws being carried into effect, it is required that plans be submitted to competent heads of departments for approval before any contracts are entered into. These laws are doing much good toward the development of school architecture, and their influence extends far beyond their own jurisdiction, neighboring states and cities benefiting by their influence. For an example: An architect who has designed a building under the foregoing restrictions, or a superintendent who under them has planned its details, will, when called upon to assist in the erection of a new building, in communities not possessing such laws, naturally use his influence to secure the best.

The laws controlling school construction succeed in establishing good conditions for the safety and health of pupils and teachers. This includes the fire-proofing of stairs and other parts of the building; the placing, construction, and number of exits; fire towers and outside escapes; the square feet of floor area and cubic feet of space that shall be allotted to each occupant in schoolrooms; the minimum height of ceilings; the amount of outside glass area; the proper lighting of the schoolrooms; the swinging of doors; construction of ceilings; heating, ventilation, sanitation, and other points of equal importance.

The underlying principles of modern school architecture may be divided into several different heads, such as the orientation, planning, construction, designing, and equipment.

The building site must be well considered, especially in respect to proper sanitary surroundings. Every precaution should be taken to avoid the possibility of dampness. The future possibility of obstructing the sunlight and the hazard of having surrounding buildings in close proximity should not be overlooked. The best-arranged plan will be a failure if these questions are not properly considered and solved. If the conditions are such that surrounding buildings preclude the proper lighting of schoolrooms, then reflecting prisms may be used to advantage. I do not recommend them, however, except as temporary assistance for old buildings. In a new building, if such conditions exist, I would prefer to design the rooms narrower, and place in the rooms lighted from one side a smaller number of desks. This brings up the old question of the exact number of pupils that should be accommodated in the schoolrooms used for the graded pupils. The tendency is to make forty pupils the maximum for any one room, especially in primary grades, and there are many good arguments in its favor.

In arranging a plan much depends upon the size of the ground allotted to the building, the number of pupils to be accommodated and their grade. An elementary rule is to avoid light walls, and use light courts as sparingly as possible, and never where the sunlight cannot at some hour of the day find its way into each room. The successful plan is the simplest in its disposition of corridors and rooms. Where possible, the entrances for the boys and girls should be near the ground level, avoiding the long flights of outside steps.

Keep the basement well out of ground. This space, if properly lighted, is valuable for playrooms, manual-training and other like rooms; which space is lost for successful use unless this condition is complied with. When the building is two stories in height, a high basement can be made to add materially to its dignity and architectural appearance. Ground-floor entrances should open into a commodious rotunda, and the rotunda should communicate with the principal rooms on this floor, including locker-rooms, toilet-rooms (if placed in the building), and also the stairs leading to the floors above. In addition to these ground-floor entrances, one or more entrances should be provided from grade direct to the first floor. All stairways should be so planned that the bottom flights end in close proximity to the outside entrances. They should be of ample width, easy of ascent, with intermediate landings wide enough to avoid jamming or crowding; they should be fire-proof, and always well lighted.

Corridors must be generous in width, bright, and with as few turns or breaks in the walls as possible. Hat- and coat-rooms for the lower grades are properly placed when adjoining to and communicating with the schoolroom; but for the higher grades it is frequently more convenient to centralize them. Cloak-rooms must be ventilated and receive direct light. Their surrounding walls should extend to the ceiling, and the rooms provided with a separate compartment for each pupil.

A schoolroom having its length a little less than one and one-half times its width is well proportioned and admits of a good arrangement of desks on the long axis. Thirty-two feet in length allows eight desks to a row and ample space for the teacher, who can, without effort, speak to a pupil at this distance. Twenty-three feet is a satisfactory width, which allows of five rows of seats and generous aisles. A room twenty-three feet by thirty-two feet approximates eighteen square feet of floor area to each of the forty pupils, and with a story height of twelve feet gives 200 cubic feet of air space for each pupil.

The English, French, and Dutch school laws, published for the guidance of architects in planning school buildings call for a smaller width of room, some fixing the height equal to two-thirds of its width plus the thickness of the walls in which the windows are placed. To obtain the best of results, the schoolroom should be thirteen feet in height. Some advocate a greater height, but I believe it inadvisable, as it unnecessarily adds to the expense of construction and increases the distance in traveling from floor to floor.

Seldom does it happen that too much light is secured. The

greatest amount should unquestionably come from the left of the pupil. In corner rooms, where it is desirable to place windows at the rear, they should be placed near the angle, in order that teachers will face wall surfaces as much as possible. The upper portions of windows furnish the most desirable light; therefore the windows should extend close to the ceiling. The glass surface should not be less than one-fifth of the floor area. The inside vertical jambs should be flared, and the windows should be spaced in the walls at regular intervals. Transoms and circular head windows are to be avoided, as they obstruct the light. A few wide windows are preferable to a number of smaller ones. Wood wainscoting should be eliminated from the schoolroom. By keeping the window-sills, chalk-tray, and chair-rail at the same height, together with the picture-mold, a division of the walls is secured that is both effective and economical. A large unobstructed area of slate blackboard is essential to the schoolroom. The space immediately back of the teacher's desk is especially valuable for this purpose, and should be kept free from obstruction.

Double sash and weather stripping are to be recommended in cold climates; while they add somewhat to the initial cost of construction, they save in fuel and add to the comfort of those occupying the room.

No schoolroom is complete without a teacher's book-closet, provided with shelves and hooks. Every school building should be planned for a teacher's room, properly equipped, where in cases of emergency it can be used as a temporary hospital.

The plumbing should have the most careful consideration, as the health of the children may be affected if this work is not properly installed. Tests of the plumbing should be made at stated intervals. The sanitaries, if placed in the building, should be automatic in their flushing, and ventilated independently of other parts of the building.

Pupils in class- and study-rooms should be supplied with not less than thirty cubic feet of fresh air per minute, and an equal amount of vitiated air should be exhausted to the atmosphere at a point most extreme from where the fresh air is taken into the building. To do this successfully, and at the same time obtain properly warmed air, a mechanical system of indirect heating and ventilation must be installed in buildings containing more than four classrooms with both supply and exhaust fans, and where steam is used for the motive power the exhaust can be utilized as supplementary heat to temper the air before passing over the heating surface. Where furnaces are used to warm the fresh air, the exhaust from the motive power can be used to advantage by direct radiation, to heat the rooms used for administration work which allows of their comfortable use without starting the fans. In designing the heating and ventilating apparatus economical results can be secured by revolving the air in the building until occupied, and also by controlling the tempered and warm air delivered to the rooms.

In buildings devoted, wholly or in part, to the higher branches of education, the plan naturally becomes more complex, but the general principles of school-planning remain the same. Such buildings are larger and more pretentious, the details of which should have the most careful thought and study. It is necessary to plan for the assembling of all pupils at certain intervals, to provide for the diversified class work, together with accommodations for the society and athletic work, all of which are important. It is in this class of building that you will frequently find accommodated the administrative branch of the schools, rooms for the board of education, the secretary, and the superintendent. This department should be of easy access to the public, and provided with toilets, fire-proof vaults, and rooms for the unpacking, sorting, marking, and storage of supplies. The assembly-room, owing to its large floor area, naturally dominates the plan. This room should be placed on the first floor, where it is easy of access, and where any danger in dismissing large assemblages is reduced to the minimum. There is also the advantage of simplicity of construction and economy of space.

The plan of the assembly-room depends largely upon the purposes for which it is to be used. It can be of the amphitheater pattern with galleries, where commencement and institute meetings may be held; or it may be much simpler in form, when used solely for the daily opening and closing exercises. By placing the scientific branches and other departments of special work on the top floor, the lower floors are left for a good arrangement of class-, study-, and recitation-rooms.

It may be of interest to describe here a high-school building, now under construction at Reading, Pa., in which the plan has been most carefully studied. It is one of a very large number of similar buildings that are now contemplated or under the course of construction.

The Reading building is to accommodate 800 boys, three stories and basement in height, thoroughly fire-proof. The auditorium is placed on the first floor with dividing partitions, giving a total seating capacity of 1,500. Two of these divisions may be used for large classrooms, and the two center divisions for lecture- and assembly-rooms. On the first floor are also provided rooms for the library, visitors, principal, and faculty; also classrooms and cloak-rooms. The second floor is entirely devoted to class- and recitation-rooms, and the gallery of the assembly-room. The third floor is divided into laboratories with their class- and lecture-rooms, commercial, banking, and typewriting-rooms, and professor's private rooms, drawing- and modeling-rooms, and room for photography.

The basement accommodates, besides the rooms for manual training, lunch- and drill-rooms, and rooms for athletics, the necessary space for the heating and ventilating plant, consisting of a double-fan combination steam and warm air heating and ventilating apparatus, with a complete system for regulating the temperature in all parts of the building.

The construction throughout is the best. The exterior is of granite, brick, and terra-cotta. The interior is of iron and concrete construction, with metal and hollow tile partitions. The floors and walls of corridors, cloak-rooms, and toilets are of white tile. The stairs are built of iron and slate; soapstone is used for the finish of walls in classrooms, and the floors are of narrow maple boards. The little woodwork used is of quartered oak. Each corridor is equipped with sanitary drinking-fountains, fire lines, janitor's closets, and supply rooms.

The construction of the modern school building, where possible, should be fire-proof. Where sufficient funds are not available, every precaution should be taken to make the building slow-burning. This can be accomplished, to a large extent, by using metal lath in place of wood stripping and wood partitions, and supporting the ends of all beams on masonry walls. With this construction, together with the use of fire-proof stairs built between brick walls, the building is made safe, but the many annoyances due to the shrinking of wood would not be overcome, but can be greatly reduced by subjecting the building to a good trial of the heating plant for a few weeks before the building is plastered.

I have stated before that the school building should be as carefully planned as a hospital. It also should be as carefully constructed and finished; everything that is difficult to keep clean should be avoided. Finish the floors above the basement in schoolrooms with narrow hard lumber, and the walls with a smooth tinted surface. The walls of cloak-rooms, toilets, halls, and basement rooms should be wainscoted with enamel brick.

The finish building materials should be non-absorbent; and combustible materials should be used only where absolutely necessary. Avoid as much as possible all unnecessary projections which catch the dust.

As to the exterior, it should be simple and refined in design, materials only being used that are substantial and lasting, and each building should have that dignity and beauty obtained by simple and straightforward means, without sacrificing economy or the requirements of utility. The beauty of the building should reside in its proportions, and in the lines and grouping of the doors and windows, without superfluous ornamentation.

It is not necessary or desirable to go into an elaborate expenditure of money in the construction or equipment of school buildings. They should be built well and equipped substantially. The desire to surround the children with the beautiful during their receptive age can be materially assisted by supplying each building with a well-selected collection of beautiful pictures and casts.

In closing, I will make a plea for the enactment of more

BLUE PRINTS MADE BY THE CHILDREN ON PAPER WHICH THEY HAD COATED

effective legislation pertaining to the erecting of our school buildings, and in this legislation I would suggest that a fire limit of forty feet or over, including streets and alleys, be left between the building and the adjoining properties. Such a law would not only protect the building from outside fire, but would always assure the proper lighting and air space, and would be the means of adding to the architectural effectiveness of the structure.

A STUDY OF THE SAND-DUNES ON THE SHORE OF LAKE MICHIGAN

IRA B. MEYERS
School of Education

[Perhaps the most popular and most interesting field trip of the year for the School of Education is to the dunes in northern Indiana on the shore of Lake Michigan. Beginning with a narrow strip of low sand ridges near South Shore within the limits of Chicago, they increase in height in a gradually widening belt which circles the lower end of the lake. In the widest part, the farther edge of the dunes is about two miles from the shore.

Opportunity is frequently offered for pupils to study the work of water in its action upon the earth's surface, but striking examples of wind-action are far more rare. In the dune area, however, the work of each season is easily measured by observing the growth of the annuals at the base of the advancing sand flood. Many of the taller kinds, such as bulrushes in the marshes, will be found buried to their tips and to a depth of three or four feet. Since these began to grow this season, the amount of sand moved, and its rate of movement may be easily observed. If not too moist, the movement may be detected before one's very eyes. By turning a pail or box on its side facing the wind, it will soon catch a quantity of sand that is being shifted by the breeze. By placing the face close to the surface on a dry day, one can notice that the air six inches to a foot above the surface has a fog-like appearance owing to the sand that is being carried along.

As may be imagined, the plants that grow here show many interesting adaptations to these uncertain and extreme conditions. The same may be said of the animals. Roots in treetops are not uncommon, while branches now protruding from the sand give a clue as to the cause of this strange and apparently unnatural growth.

The industrial aspect of the dunes is of no less importance. Thousands of carloads of sand, removing hundreds of acres of dunes in some places a hundred feet deep, have been brought to the city for the purpose of railroad track elevation. Without this enormous supply of filling close at hand, it is difficult to see just how the railroad companies would have met the track-elevation problem.

The scenic side of the trip is not the least of its attractions. The dark verdure of the pines, and the yellow sand against a background of deep blue in the lake and sky, form a picture never to be forgotten. While one might be inclined to associate the dunes with burning sands of the desert, the fact is that one is rarely uncomfortable from heat, as the lake breeze almost invariably holds the temperature within reasonable limits.

To assist the older pupils in a study of the dunes they are provided with the following outline of suggestions.— NOTE BY THE EDITOR.]

AN OUTLINE FOR FIELD-STUDY IN THE MILLER'S-DUNE PARK AREA

I. MATERIALS.— Provide yourself with a basket or strong pasteboard box, a strong knife, a garden trowel, a wide-mouthed bottle or pint Mason jar, a compass; if possible, a clinometer; a notebook with writing and drawing paper.

II. PREPARATORY.— Find the geographic location of the region with reference to Chicago and Lake Michigan; the distance from Chicago, and the course of the Lake Shore Railway in reaching it. See topographic map, "Tolleston Quadrangle" (*Twenty-second Report of the Indiana Geological Survey,* Lake & Porter Co.).

III. OBSERVATIONS EN ROUTE.— Topography of the country between Chicago and Dune Park: (1) area dominated by level, low prairie; (2) area of alternating flats or depressions and ridges; (3) area of irregular hills and depressions; (4) area of raw sand-dunes. Relation of depressions or lagoons, as to direction, to each other and to the lake. The character of the plant life dominating the various type areas (prairie, ridge, marsh, wet flats, dunes). Get a view of the Calumet River valley.

NOTE.— Always designate the place of observation as, Indiana Harbor to Pine, low dunes, long river-like lagoons, scrub pine, etc.; or indicate the station at which the observation is recorded, as, *Pine:*

IV. AT DUNE PARK.— (1) Get a good impression of the topography of the whole country around Dune Park. (Upon reaching the crest of a hill, locate the directions by using your compass, and make a note of the character of the country, as far as you can see, to the north, south, east, and west.) (2) Try to determine how large an area has been stripped of sand by the Sand Company. Note the plants found growing on this portion from which sand has been taken.

Hills.—(1) Note the general character of the wooded hills. (2) Find where a cut reveals a section of the hill, and examine the mineral material, the height of hill, the character of slopes; inference as to how these hills were formed; proof. (3) Examine the fringe of plant roots at the surface part of the cut; length, depth, abundance of roots. (4) Look for old soil lines along the sides of the cut. (5) Make a list of the dominant plants found on the wooded ridges. (6) Is there any difference in the vegetation on the south and north slopes of these hills? (7) Notice and account for the cone-shaped depressions among these hills. (8) Watch for signs of animal life in this region.

Marshes and flats.—(1) From the crest or side of the hill get a view of the whole marsh. (2) Notice the various groups or zones of vegetation. (3) Approaching the marsh, make a list of the plants dominating each zone. (4) Note where the plants of the hills cease and the plants of the marsh begin; is this change gradual or abrupt; examine the soil, collect samples to a depth of eight or ten inches. (5) Examine the swamp for animal life—birds, reptiles, frogs, insects, etc. (6) Examine the soil thrown up while cutting the ditch through this marsh; from the nature of this material and the position of the marsh try to determine its origin.

Bare dunes at base.—(1) Estimate the height of the dune. (2) Measure the steepness (angle) of the slope. (3) Notice any movement of the sand on the slope, how and why it moves. (Note: Find a place where sand has not been disturbed by the Sand Company.) (4) Examine the border line between the bare dunes and the vegetated area. (5) Compare the plants found on the old or vegetated area with those growing within the barren dune; what inferences? (6) Examine the roots of trees, where bared, along the crest of the bare dunes; estimate the volume of earth penetrated by the roots.

On the bare dune.—Where does all this sand come from? (1) Notice the surface appearance of the bare dunes; steep slopes, gradual slopes, cuts, crests. Do the ridge crests extend in one direction or in various directions? Do the steep slopes face in the same direction or in various directions? Do the depressions,

THE ADVANCING DUNES COVERING A FOREST

"blow-outs," extend in the same directions or in various directions? Work out how this surface was made, and show how these regularities or irregularities of surface came to be. (2) Observe along the surface of the sand evidences of sand being moved by the wind; how moved? (3) Where is sand being blown by the wind? where deposited? how is this determined? (4) Try to determine how this sand first begins to pile up or drift (look for evidence around clumps of plants, old logs, and stumps). (5) On which side does the sand drift with reference to the direction of the wind (6) Show how one of these small drifts may grow into a large dune. Give the story of the growth of this dune region.

V. (1) Account for the presence of growing trees on these barren dunes. (2) What is the meaning of the groups of dead, decaying tree trunks? (3) Make a list of the plants (*a*) that can grow on these barren dunes; (*b*) that can live while being buried or unburied by the sand; (*c*) that are killed when sand begins to bury them. (4) Examine the base of growing and dead plants, to see whether they have been affected by the wind-blown sand.

VI. "The Crater."—(1) Get a good view of the country from the top of "The Crater;" of the shore-line. Try to locate South Chicago and Michigan City, the Calumet River, the Valparaiso Moraine. Are there any dunes south of the Calumet River? (2) Try to account for this crater-hill so near to the lake. (3) The character of the hill and the condition of vegetation on the east and northeast sides of the hill, on the south and southwest sides, on the inside of the crater; account for these differences. (4) The meaning of the depression at the west base of the crater; your evidence. (5) The meaning of the high barren dune just west of this depression. (6) The kind of plants growing on this high dune; how do they influence the dune?

VII. The Beach.—(1) Can you find any evidence that the water delivers this dune sand? (*a*) Can you see the waves actually depositing any sand on the beach? (*b*) Do you find any materials in or along the edge of the lake from which sand might be made? (*c*) Can you detect any wave-action which would manufacture sand out of this material? (2) When waves approach the shore, do they bring any materials with them? When the water of the wave returns, does it take any material back with it? (3) How wide is the beach? Do the waves ever wash over the whole beach? Evidence. Make list. (4) What plants are able to live on this beach? (5) What animals find a living along the beach? What food do they find along the shore?

VIII. Collect and bring to the classroom the characteristic plants of (1) the beach; (2) the barren dune; (3) the vegetated dune; (4) the pine flat; (5) the marsh; (6) any animal life found in these areas; (7) the principal varieties of stones found on the beach; (8) kinds of soil.

MEETING OF THE PARENTS' ASSOCIATION

ELLA ADAMS MOORE
Secretary

The October meeting of the Parents' Association was devoted to the discussion of medical supervision in the School of Education. Dr. J. E. Raycroft, the principal speaker, talked of the necessity for medical supervision, and outlined the plans for carrying it on in the school. He quoted President Eliot and President Butler on the subject of the failure of schools and colleges to conserve and build up the physical life of their students. Dr. Raycroft attributed this failure to three causes: (1) The pressure due to introducing new subjects into the curriculum. The course of study is constantly broadening to meet the ever-growing demands of modern life. (2) The crowded condition of schoolrooms, due to the fact that school facilities have not kept pace with the rapid increase in school population. In the last fifty years the number of school children has increased from 11 per cent. of the entire population to about 30 per cent. at the present time. (3) Changes in the physical conditions of the children themselves brought about by decreased physical activity. They have fewer "chores" to perform, and in general fewer opportunities for physical activity, than the children of an earlier generation.

The principal factors to be considered in attempting to modify these conditions were enumerated as follows: (1) school environment; (2) the curriculum; (3) school activities outside of formal school work, such as athletics, play, etc.

Under the modification of school environment, the speaker included supervision of sanitary conditions in general, inspection of schoolrooms and premises, methods of cleaning rooms, blackboards, etc., heating and ventilation, attention to water-supply, etc. In the School of Education the matter of fitting the seats to the particular children occupying them is given special attention. Measurements are made and seats adjusted twice during the year. It is one of the distinct aims of the medical staff of this school to make a specific study of the school environment of the child, and to make that environment in so far as possible meet the needs and requirements of the student.

On the second point it may be said that the only way in which the medical direction is able to touch the curriculum at present is in the case of individual students who for one reason or another are not in such condition as to be able to carry on the regular work of the school.

With this thought in mind, a physical examination is given each child at the beginning of the year, a second near the close, and others at such other times as may seem desirable in given cases, a close watch being kept upon children whose physical condition is below normal. This examination may be divided into three parts: (1) The *history* of the child in so far as it bears upon his present condition. Parents are asked to fill out a blank giving information in regard to the child's previous illnesses, his habits of eating, sleeping, and exercising, his functional habits, and other points which may aid the examining physician. (2) A small number of measurements are made in order to determine the physical development of the child in comparison with the average child of his age. (3) A medical examination is made, including careful observation of eyes, nose, throat, ears, heart, and lungs. Children are examined for spinal curvatures and other abnormal developments. Special attention is given to the vital examination of students who are candidates for places on teams in competitive athletics.

Whenever the examination reveals weaknesses or deficiencies, parents are duly notified and such recommendations made as to future treatment, changes of habits, etc., as may seem wise. Provision is also made in the school itself for such corrective work in the gymnasium as may seem desirable, and needed changes in the child's curriculum are recommended to parents and the dean of the school.

A careful medical supervision is exercised in order to limit and prevent the spread of contagious diseases. Children who look suspicious, as well as those who have been absent from school for any cause, are required to report to the school physician before going on with their work.

During the consultation hour of the school physician, parents are invited to come and give information and ask questions about the physical condition of their children.

Dr. Raycroft concluded by saying that the purpose in general of this medical supervision is: (1) to study, and in so far as possible modify, the school environment so as to reduce the bad physical effects of school life to a minimum; (2) by studying the individual child himself, to gain an accurate and detailed knowledge of his physical life, and to place him in that environment which will produce the best results during his school life.

Dr. Pitkin spoke of deformities in children. She said that 25 per cent. of the girls had more or less pronounced spinal curvatures. Some of these come from improperly adjusted seats, some from the carrying of books, and the majority from bad habits of posture. She spoke of deformities of feet, weak ankles, flat feet, etc., and of the special work of the gymnasium in correcting and preventing such deformities.

Dr. Freu spoke of the medical examination of boys who wished to enter competitive games. Each candidate is asked how long he has played the game. He is watched carefully by the physician as he dresses, as he plays, as he takes his bath; the way in which he reacts is noted, etc. He is then examined as to his heart and lungs. The way in which he breathes is noted, and a constant watch is kept upon him throughout the year.

Professor Kroh emphasized particularly the need for training teachers, first, to realize the necessity for attending to the physical requirements of their children, and, second, to a knowledge of what those requirements are and how to meet them. He believed that schools for the training of teachers should not offer credentials to those who cannot properly look after the physical life of the children.

Dean Jackman said the opening meeting was being devoted to perhaps the most fundamental matter in dealing with the child.

He spoke particularly of the work of the medical staff in preventing and limiting the spread of contagious diseases. Last year they had taken all cases early and had warded off many possible dangers. He spoke of the consultation hour of the school physician as being most valuable to the school.

Dean Jackman also raised the question of the ethical influence of physical training, the commanding and obeying-orders feature, and whether this could or should be readjusted in any way.

Dr. Belfield spoke of the physical conditions in the French schools which he visited. He noted many unsanitary conditions, straining of eyes, etc.

Dr. Belfield also emphasized the fact that children before coming to school in the morning should be inspected by the parents. They are often sent to school when not able to come.

Dean Owen stated that medical supervision as practiced up to date has been of great benefit to high-school students. He spoke of Miss Hinman's work in the school in gymnastic dancing. One day each week is given to this. Such physical training he believes saves the time of the child, and organizes the social life of the school around gymnastic and physical training.

Dean Owen stated that the high school has increased in numbers this year, and that the school spirit is much improved.

Dean Butler spoke of the relation of the College of Education to the Elementary and High Schools. The three schools are trying to solve one problem. He emphasized Mr. Jackman's thought of the importance of the ethical side of physical training. It helps to solve the problem of school discipline, and makes better boys and girls; the military command is an essential point of benefit.

EDITORIAL NOTES

Textbooks in Arithmetic and Drawing

Arithmetic-makers are in trouble. They are in the same predicament in which the makers of drawing-books found themselves a few years ago. Drawing began in the schools with a textbook. In this there were sundry forms and figures which were to be copied by the pupil upon blank pages. With the introduction of objects, a new and different demand for drawing arose, and the flat copy drawing-book dropped out. The textbook-makers and their publishers struggled on for a time to make themselves useful; but with the development of nature-study, and other subjects which offered directly a rich fund for art work, even their best efforts, embodying beautiful productions in color and form, availed nothing.

Machine-Made Arithmetics

The machine-made arithmetic is just on the outer confines of the same limbo. The necessity for quantitative work in the study of material things is slowly—very, very slowly—becoming apparent. To the teacher who has the insight to see this necessity, and the skill to meet it in teaching the children, the machine-made textbook in arithmetic, except as a work of reference, is useless.

Use of Type-Forms

When drawing shifted from the flat copy method to the use of objects, at first, only those so-called type-forms were employed which were supposed to develop the technics of the subject. The theory was that this, because it emphasized exactness, contributed most to "mental discipline." Figures, forms, and models were chosen with this end in mind, and but little consideration was given to a study of form in its relation to function. Most objects chosen had no apparent immediate function, and therefore the subject was but one degree removed from its first state. But now drawing is used as a means of getting at the meaning of things. It is a direct mode of studying the relation of form and function, and it therefore happens that the meaningless, unrelated objects, and the so-called type-forms, are gradually disappearing from the drawing lesson.

The past decade presents an instructive parallel in the changes taking place in the teaching of mathematics, especially arithmetic. There has been a vast amount of ingenuity displayed in the use of objects as a basis for work in number. It is the first step removed from the old gymnastics with arithmetical formulas. This particular brand of textbook seeks by means of blocks of wood, geometric figures, and other objects having definite ratios to each other, to ring in all the changes that are possible in the study of quantitative relations. Since the children do the work by handling objects and figures which have a foreordained reciprocal relationship, they soon acquire a prodigious facility in solving all sorts of problems of the usual stereotyped kind. Some of the later books, too, have taken a step in the right direction by presenting a consistent series of problems growing out of the study of some industrial or commercial topic. Most of the authors being good teachers, their books have much to commend them in their suggestiveness as to method, and as texts for reference they are valuable also.

Type-Forms in Number Work

But these arithmetic-makers have gone just as far as anyone can in the direction of textbook-making in this subject. Neither these gentlemen nor any others can ever make, on the commonly accepted plan, a textbook in arithmetic suitable for general class use that will be abreast of the best pedagogic thought. They are the last of their race; they will have no successors, for the same reason that the drawing-book makers of a generation ago have no descendants living in our time. Textbooks for class use in arithmetic belong to the day when the school curriculum was represented by an aggregation of unrelated topics. They have no place, except as a kind of dictionary or reference work, in a school where the course of study is used as a means of organizing the life of the pupils. This does not mean that mathematics will become of less moment in the schools than it has been heretofore. We shall have more of it and a better kind — it is to be hoped, real mathematics.

End of Textbook Making

Mathematics is simply unthinkable apart from the quantitative aspect of the things studied. It can not be separated from the study of an object any more than the object can be divested of its color. That is, the quantitative relations of an object are inherent, and they can be studied only through the application of some form of mathematics. Now, so long as the objects studied in school were merely an assemblage of convenient forms with no organic connection with each other, we could afford to play with that semblance of mathematics found in the machine-made textbook. But we have never had much real mathematics; we have had an endless deal of textbook arithmetic. The proof of this is that while there are plenty of people who know the "Tables" and the definitions, and to a lesser extent the rules, all of which the textbooks *did* teach, there is not one in a hundred who has not had his mathematical sense blunted, if not destroyed, by the omission of just that particular thing which the textbooks cannot teach—namely, mathematics.

Place of Mathematics

Mathematical Sense Destroyed

Most of the later textbooks justly emphasize the necessity of imaging in number work through the use of objects. But the trouble is that the objects generally selected have no earthly interest, in themselves, for the pupils. This at once reduces the exercises given to the basis of "number for number's sake." They are doing precisely what the drawing teachers did in using the "type-forms" in developing "drawing for drawing's sake." It differs not a whit from teaching "language for language's sake," "reading for reading's sake," and, in general, everything else that is taught for the sake of the process. Of course, the process is important; it is the process that determines the ease and the economy by which a thing is done. But the process always has a fixed and unalterable place in our thinking, and it is this fact that the machine-made arithmetic ignores. Underlying the process is the logic of thinking, and the process is but the tangible form through which that logic is expressed. The arithmetic-makers invert the matter; practically, every problem introduced is given for the sake of the process involved; they give the least possible attention to the all-around development of a subject which

Uninteresting Objects Used

Nature of a Process

is necessary to show what its mathematical relations are, and without which showing all mathematical processes are meaningless; whereas it is just such a development of the subject that should be emphasized above everything else. This is the way PROCESS always originates. Somebody in his thinking finds that there are certain quantitative relations that must be determined. Through the necessity of his thinking, *a* process, finally *the* process, is evolved, and the image that lacked clearness in the beginning, so far as its quantitative relations are considered, is now cleared up. Now, the machine-made arithmetics are almost wholly composed of a transcript of these processes, thoroughly devitalized through their separation from the natural conditions that gave them birth, and classified into certain groups, accordingly as they involve division, subtraction, decimals, percentage, and so forth. It is true that the later textbook-makers have endeavored to clothe these skeletons of dead thought with some rags and tags of subject-matter; but, like the figure once so familiar in our grandfathers' cornfield, the dry stuffing sticks out at every joint, and the machine-made textbook in arithmetic stands today as the scarecrow of every schoolroom.

Study of Processes Dominates

One false step always leads to another. To teach the processes in arithmetic (or any other subject), when they are not the outgrowth of a natural and immediate demand, is at best a stupid business and well-nigh impossible. Hence, in an attempt to meet this difficulty which they have artificially created, the textbook-makers have had to take a second unpedagogic step by introducing almost endless problems of a like kind to secure repetition. They hope by much iteration and drill to fix the processes in mind, ignoring the fact that the repetition of a meaningless thing, being in itself senseless, is disastrous to actual thinking.

Bad Pedagogy

Repetition in itself is as hateful to children as bad medicine. This has led to the invention of more tricks to beguile the pupils into thinking they are really doing something else; it has given occasion to more sugar-coating of pills, that the real thing may not nauseate them, than can be found in the teaching of any other subject. Children who

Bane of Repetition

would gag at the thing itself are now charmed with the tricks. Teachers are enabled to endure from year to year because of the novelties that are annually introduced which vary the monotony, In fact, one of their chief concerns at the county institute and summer school is to find out, for example, the latest fashions in long division and the spring styles in multiplication of fractions.

A Misguided Effort

The most awful dose of machine-made arithmetic gotten up apparently for "drill for drill's sake," that has been let loose lately upon hapless children is now being prepared by "Forty Teachers" for the schools of one of our large cities. So far as one can discover from the advance sheets of these exercises, the work is illumined by scarcely a ray of pedagogic insight. There was great outcry a while ago because some teachers favored the reintroduction of corporal punishment into the schools. This was bad enough, but I would almost as soon have every youngster soundly bastinadoed every week, and then turned out into the parks for the rest of the day to recuperate, as to have him sit through the toilsome days under the arithmetical régime that is now being prepared for him. There are some things that are worse for the intellect and morals than a body-beating. If the work of these "Forty" collaborators were intended to be a cyclopedic dictionary of criminal antiquities in psychology and pedagogy, to be kept in a glass case under lock and key along with thumb-screws, it might have some value; but as a modern textbook it is nothing less than a municipal calamity.

Arithmetic the Center of Dread

The machine-made textbook-makers deserve credit for one thing: through the lapse of years, and by dint of incessant effort, they have succeeded in shoving the subject into such prominence as to keep it uppermost in everybody's mind. The thoughts of teacher, child, and parent all revolve around this center, not with a common affection, but in a common dread. Those who can easily master the tricks are regarded prodigies; others are doubtful or dull. The part it has played in the promotion of pupils has caused incalculable wrong simply because it is not a true measure of what we want in a human being.

Sometimes it is urged that we have too much of arithmetic;

but the ability of most people in the use of the subject scarcely indicates that they have been over-taught! How many years, perhaps centuries, of school life are wasted every year in this country by the multiplied discussions upon this and similar points, not even mathematics itself can tell.

Too Much Arithmetic

Shall we have arithmetic in the first grade or not? Like every other process, it depends upon the *thinking* which we have. Look to the *thinking*, then, for the answer. Children of that age when not in school do excellently a good many things that involve estimating, measuring, and counting. They naturally acquire and control these means to some extent in carrying forward some aspects of their thinking. If the first-grade pupils have work in school, therefore, which actually involves thinking, we then cannot put arithmetic out of the grade by "act of Parliament." We might as well try to legislate away a lobe from their brains. Mathematics is implied and understood to be necessary in what we are talking about, namely, *thinking*. This remark is not intended to make an opening through which the machine textbook-maker may run in a lot of his artificial forms and models to be used as subjects of thought; for the purposes of thinking, none of his tricks are half so interesting as dominoes or dice.

How Much Arithmetic?

We have here, then, the reason why the machine-made textbook in arithmetic cannot do the work in the schools needed in mathematics. No author can foretell just what the thinking will be, nor how much there will be. Nobody can tell this except *the teacher and child as they work together*. This is the way the mathematicians determine how much and what kind of mathematics they will use in a given day or year—they are not trying to get through a machine-made book—and this is the way the child and the teacher must determine it. Whether he shall know the numbers from one to ten in the first grade is an irrelevant question. Why are we so scary about large numbers for small children? A child of the first grade who travels from Chicago to New York on the railroad has a better notion of a thousand miles than he has of ten sheep or eight bushels that

Machine Textbook and Thinking

Large Numbers and Small Children

he has never seen. It is all a matter of actual *thinking*. We formerly made the same mistake about the use of words which were classified into short, medium, and long according to the length of the child. But nowadays the child learns the long German, Russian, and Polish names of his seatmates with much greater facility than he does the short monosyllables with which we try to educate him. It is all a matter of *thinking*, as to whether the form side of any subject shall give trouble or not.

Knowing Ten

When we set out to teach all there is in a number, as ten, for example, there are two things that should be remembered: first, it is never needed, and, second, it cannot be done. We shall only need it so far as we meet things which we wish to consider in such groups; and these groups will have to be made one by one as the necessity arises. You may be able to group everything you have seen in tens or in its subdivision; but if you will look out of my study window, I will show you a group of objects, and you will not be able to tell me whether it contains seven or nine or thirteen until, like a child, you begin all over again and count them up. This is a question quite apart from that of committing to memory all the formulas which express the combinations of numbers within ten; that is entirely a question of language, and it should be measured by its merit as a language lesson and according to the principles that here are being discussed.

The Psychological Need

Much of the confusion concerning number work can be charged up to those who have written upon its psychology. They have generally devoted themselves to a consideration of how the mind moves through the processes, ignoring or forgetting the fact that in practical school work the *movement* is the thing that is missing, and that it is absent because there is a lack of thought-stuff to start it. The psychological necessity for honest and abundant thought-material is the fact above all others that needs to be driven home to the consciousness of teachers. With plenty of this material at hand, with freedom to work, and with a motive to be realized, there need be neither difficulty nor mystery as to the place and part that mathematics shall take in education.

W. S. J.

BOOKS RECEIVED

Everyday Life in the Colonies. By STONE and FICKETT. Boston: D. C. Heath & Co. Cloth, 12mo. Pp. 119. $0.40.

A Little Garden Calendar. By ALBERT BIGELOW PAINE. Illustrated. Philadelphia: Henry Altemus Co. Cloth, 12mo. Pp. 329.

First Lessons in Food and Diet. By ELLEN H. RICHARDS. Boston: Whitcomb & Barrows. Cloth, 12mo. Pp. 52.

Builders of Our Nation. By ALMA HOLMAN BURTON. Chicago and New York: Eaton & Co. Cloth, 12mo. Pp. 260. $0.60.

The Blodgett Primer. By FRANCES E. BLODGETT and ANDREW B. BLODGETT. Illustrated. Boston: Ginn & Co. Cloth, 12mo. Pp. 115. $0.30.

The Blodgett First Reader. By same authors. Illustrated. Ginn & Co. Cloth, 12mo. Pp. 131. $0.30.

The Blodgett Second Reader. By same authors. Illustrated. Ginn & Co. Cloth, 12mo. Pp. 173.

Spelling Lessons for Intermediate Grades. By AARON GOVE. Boston: Ginn & Co. Cloth, 12mo. Pp. 104. $0.25.

Graded City Spellers: For Seventh Grade. Edited by WILLIAM ESTABROOK CHANCELLOR. New York: The Macmillan Co. Paper. Pp. 80. $0.12.

Black Beauty. By ANNA SEWELL. Edited by CHARLES FRENCH. Illustrated by CHARLES COPELAND. Chicago: Rand, McNally & Co. Cloth, 12mo. Pp. 319.

The Approved Selections for Supplementary Reading and Memorizing. First Year. By MELVIN HIX. New York: Hinds, Noble & Eldredge. Cloth, 12mo. Pp. 59. $0.25.

Word Studies. Primary Book. By EDWIN S. SHEPPE. Richmond: B. F. Johnson Publishing Co. Cloth, 12mo. Pp. 96 + 10.

Our Language. First Book. By LIDA B. MCMURRAY and F. T. NORVELL. Richmond: B. F. Johnson Publishing Co. Cloth, 12mo. Pp. 204.

La Mare au Diable. Par GEORGES SAND. With Introduction, Notes, and Vocabulary by ADELE RANDALL LAWTON. New York: American Book Co. Cloth, 12mo. Pp. 137. $0.35.

Das Amulett. Von MEYER. With Introduction, Notes, and Vocabulary by C. C. GLASCOCK. New York: American Book Co. Cloth, 12mo. Pp. 165. $0.35.

Problems in Woodworking. By M W. MURRAY. Illustrated. Peoria, Ill.: Manual Arts Press. Paper. Pp. 49.

Seat Work and Industrial Occupations. Primary Grades. By MARY L. GILMAN and ELIZABETH B. WILLIAMS. Illustrated. New York: The Macmillan Co. Cloth, 12mo. Pp. 141. $0.50.

A History of the Pacific Northwest. By JOSEPH SCHAFER. Maps and Illustrations. New York: The Macmillan Co. Cloth, 12mo. Pp. 321.

Heath's Beginner's Arithmetic. Boston: D. C. Heath & Co. Cloth, 12mo. Pp. 182.

The Principles of Rhetoric. By ELIZABETH H. SPALDING. Boston: D. C. Heath & Co. Cloth, 12mo. Pp. 275.

VOLUME VI NUMBER 4

THE ELEMENTARY SCHOOL TEACHER

DECEMBER, 1905

THE TEACHING OF APPLIED DESIGN[1]

JAMES PARTON HANEY
Director of Drawing and Manual Training, Public Schools, Boroughs of Manhattan and the Bronx, New York City

In any attempt to describe the practice of an art the briefest demonstration is of more value than the most elaborate statement. The demonstration can be made concrete and specific, the statement must often be general. Without objective illustration there is a great temptation to elaborate explanation, hence it is that writers who bravely start to treat of performance not infrequently stray from the straight road of practice and lose themselves and their readers in the mazes of theory.

Effort will be made to confine the following discussion to the limitations of the title—the teaching of design. There will be few definitions of elementary principles and it will be assumed that the reader is familiar with the subject's terminology.

ESSENTIALS TO SUCCESSFUL PRACTICE

Design is a technical subject, and some of the difficulties in its teaching rise from its technique. More, however, are born of poor teaching—of a failure on the teacher's part to recognize the factors which in any specific problem determine the steps necessary to its comprehension and solution by the pupil.

A design which is to be applied, must consider both the purpose of its application and the nature of the form it is to decorate.

[1] Paper read before the meeting of the National Educational Association, July, 1905.

The first question must always be: Is the problem a proper one? Should this form be decorated; and if it should, what shall be the nature of the decoration?

An adequate form of decoration decided upon, one must make the problem plain to the pupil, and set for him the limits within which he is to display his invention and individuality. The greater part of the difficulty experienced by the average teacher arises from her failure to define and definitely to limit the problem which the pupil is to undertake. Success lies in such precise definition.

Ability to design depends in no small measure upon a store of impressions of decorations seen or made. The young designer has but a scanty fund of such pictures in his mental exchequer, and of the few he has, the greater part are reflections of bad examples which everywhere surround him. If he is to do good work, he must be offered many and good illustrations that these may serve to illuminate the problems he is to undertake. Further, it may be said that she is a wise teacher who carefully divides the steps of procedure, and insists that each be developed in turn. Proceeding in such fashion, she has it in her hands to control progress and to enforce critical consideration of each step by each pupil.

The above principles stand as essentials to success in teaching design in elementary schools; summarized they state that:

1. The problem to be developed must be a proper one, i. e., one in which applied design is appropriate.

2. The limitations of the problem must be clearly seen by the teacher and must be precisely and definitely stated to the pupil.

3. Abundant illustrative material must be presented to the child.

4. Every problem must be developed in progressive steps and the pupil must be called upon critically to consider his work at each stage.

THE PROPRIETY OF THE PROBLEM

When designs are applied to constructed forms, the question of the propriety of the problem will be determined by the purpose for which the form is to be used. Simple forms require simple designs; many constructed objects are better without decoration. The question of the material used in the form to be decorated conditions the problem. The elaborate ornament which might serve a satisfactory stamp on a printed page is ill adapted as a problem for leather work, and totally unsuited as a decoration for a wooden model; the refined pattern pleasing when produced on some smooth surface, is often inadequate when duplicated on a coarse canvas or a heavy burlap. The decision as to whether design is to be applied or not must rest with the teacher and not with the child. The former must also determine the nature of the pattern.

THE DEFINITION OF THE PROBLEM

The problem decided upon, the teacher must define it for the child. As a problem it should be stated with the precision of a problem in geometry. Much depends on this. The child is not to be simply told to make a design, but must be informed exactly as to its nature and purpose. He must be prepared to understand both its necessity and fitness. As presented to him, the problem should be the development and refinement of certain space relations. He should be definitely limited in his work, and only within the limits stated, should he be expected or permitted to make personal variation. Unless so advised and restrained he will not be prepared to undertake comprehendingly any individual modification. The greater the opportunity afforded him for specific criticism, the greater the likelihood of his success. Beauty in line is a subtle thing; the beginner will have work enough to secure it in two or three main lines of his pattern. If he attempt this and no more, the teacher can aid him. Should he assay anything savoring of elaboration he is foredoomed to failure.

THE ILLUSTRATION OF THE PROBLEM

Adequate illustrative matter was noted as an essential to success. This is not to be offered to be copied, but to assist in clarifying the problem, in making plain just what is to be attempted. Not only should designs illustrating general principles be offered in the form of good prints or patterns, but others should be presented directly illustrative of the problem which the pupil is to solve.

It is not sufficient that the pupil merely observe these illustrations. He should be led to make an analysis of them that he may understand just what principles are shown and what steps have been taken by the maker of the illustration. Design is largely a matter of recombination. An original pattern is only one in which old forms have been re-used in new and personal ways. The most successful designer is one whose brain is stored with many elements and who is ingenious in their adaptation in novel form. For the child good examples are necessary that he may see how varied a design may be made within given limitations, but the examples offered should not be hung where they will serve as mere copies. It is better that they be analyzed and studied, then removed, that from the immediate background of experience the pupil may draw inspiration for personal practice. Thus good examples are necessary; but more essential still, is the orderly development of the steps or phases through which every design must pass in its proper evolution. That these steps must be understood, it will be well briefly to consider the nature of design and what makes for its successful application.

DESIGN — "PURE" AND "APPLIED"

Design defines the relations which maintain between associated masses. The moment any space is divided by a line, or has introduced into it a spot, masses are formed within it, that moment it becomes a design. The relations of the lines and masses used are expressed in terms of balance and rhythm, variety and unity. Pure design, so called, concerns itself with these terms and their illustration. As principles they should be taught to elementary pupils through practice. They should be presented not as abstractions — as illustrations of theory — but as the grammatical parts of speech of design to be practically learned through the necessity for their employment.

DEFINITION OF APPLIED DESIGN

Applied design concerns itself with a given space which has been divided into masses. The term defines the relations which are developed between the masses so formed. The more harmonious the relation the better the design. Pure design deals with the abstract; applied design involves reality. It offers abstract principles in concrete form: it is objective, and teaches beauty in use. It may, indeed, should, be used in beautifying things of service in the daily life of the pupil. So used it relates itself naturally to the teaching of other subjects of the school curriculum — construction, color and mechanical drawing — giving to their instruction point and interest.

STRUCTURE

The most important element in applied design is structure. Upon structure — the shape and boundaries of the space in which the pattern is to be developed — the nature of the design depends. In every applied design we look to see the structural elements of the space supported by the decorative. No matter how ingenious the use of conventional forms, no matter how striking the lines and smooth the rhythm, no applied design which is structurally weak can be satisfactory.

LINE IN DESIGN

The structure of a design is primarily dependent upon the number and movement of the lines which determine the masses. These lines control the observer's eye. One cannot help looking along them and being directed by them in one way or another. All lines condition movement, and where they parallel one another they strengthen and hasten it. Each additional line assists the eye to look in the direction indicated. This enables the designer to make movements both fast and slow. No line may, therefore, be ignored, nor is one to be added without careful consideration of its part in developing rhythmic relations between itself and other lines or spots.

The designer thus has it in his power to make the observer look where he will. He can lead the eye from one line to another, give strength and simplicity by emphasizing elements that bind together and support the form, and interest by felicitous rhythms and smooth transitions. Conversely, he can cause discomfort by forcing the eye to make abrupt changes, and positive dissatisfaction by leaving it to wander aimlessly in a mass of unrelated forms.

NATURE OF APPLIED DESIGN

Applied design concerns itself with the development of masses on a given surface. No mass can be introduced into a space without creating other masses more or less related, yet distinct. (See Plate VII, 1, 2, 3, 4, Fig. 1.) The simplest of applied designs consists of a single mass introduced within a space. In practice this mass may take the form of a bit of printing upon a card or page or in an ornamental unit placed within a border. In familiar language such unit is spoken of as "the design," but in itself it has no claim to the title. The design is the relation maintained by all the masses of the pattern.

Each separate mass exerts more or less attraction depending upon its size and nature, and upon the number and variety of the subordinate masses which it creates. Every design, therefore, has one or more centers of interest to which the eye is led by the rhythms among the masses. Unity requires that there be but one principal center, though subcenters may be developed. In practice multiple centers are to be avoided as they tend to distract attention, to weaken structure, and to destroy repose.

In the primary division of a space the masses to be developed will depend upon the nature or use for which the design is planned. If a single spot is introduced in a space and the eye grasps easily all the masses formed by the unit, then one center of interest is necessary. If, however, one of the related masses appears disproportionately large, the eye finds it empty and displeasing. That it may be adequately filled and the interests of the pattern balanced it then becomes necessary that a second spot be introduced. (See Plate VII, Fig. 2.)

STEPS IN DEVELOPMENT OF PROBLEM

The first step, in the practical development of any problem, is the creation of the main masses of the pattern. The pupil should be led to see the necessity for this, through the examination of examples based on simple space relationships. Simple book covers and programs will serve excellently for the purpose, while more elaborate patterns should be analyzed to make plain the fact that at base they are mass arrangements.

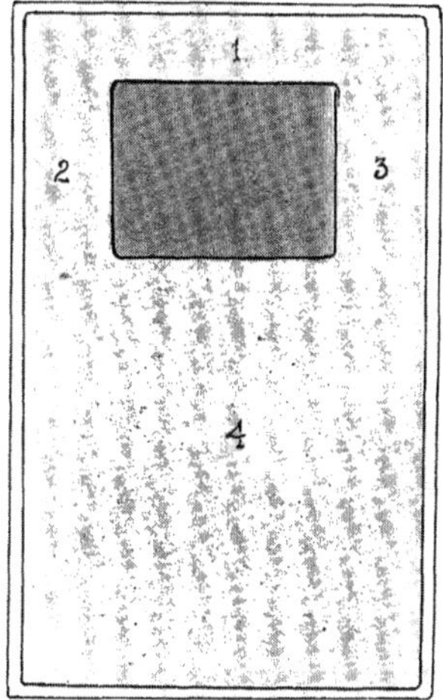

FIG. 1

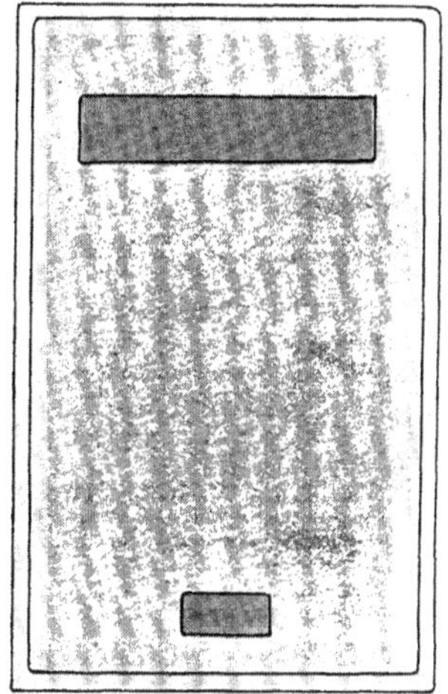

FIG. 2

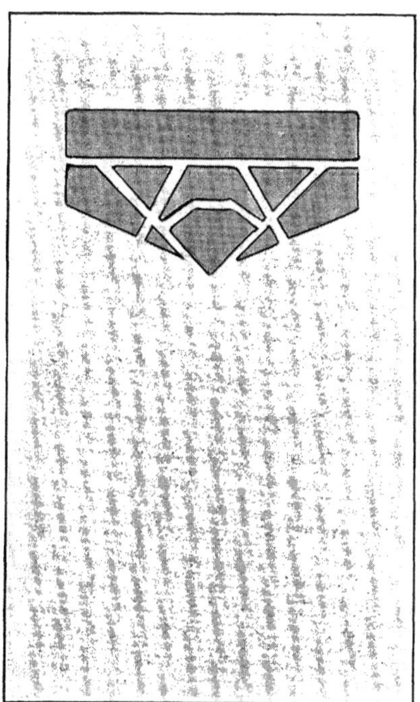

FIG. 3

In some very simple designs no elaboration of the primary mass arrangement is necessary, but in most cases the masses which are introduced to decorate a given space will require further division into spaces which may be filled by conventionalized natural elements. The second and third steps, therefore, in the making of a design must be the division of the decorating mass or masses and the refinement of the elements so formed, while the fourth step should be the introduction of conventionalized forms, if such are to be used, on the basis of the division already planned.

These four steps are to be developed in the order named. The pupil being required: First, to plan the masses of his design; second, to divide into related elements those which are to serve decoratively; third, to refine all the relations through the creating of subtle rhythms; and fourth, to adapt and introduce the subject-material elements it may be desired to present. So taught, he will learn to think as he should think — in masses, learn to work as the practiced designer works — constructively. His eye will become critical of form. He will develop what may be termed the decorative vision, the power to see all forms about him as elements of design. When this sense dawns, both nature and art will appear to him in a new light. He will see design where he has never seen it before; the world will be revealed in pattern.

STEPS IN CLASSROOM PRACTICE

The development of masses.— The first step in any design — the planning of masses — should be prefaced by a word of explanation to the pupils. They should be made to understand that, as a step, this is essential and that in itself, by cutting up the original spaces into forms of various shapes and sizes, it adds interest and results in space relationships. Emphasis is to be laid upon the fact that no matter what the resulting design, it must be characterized by structural qualities which will aid in maintaining the strength of the inclosing form.

Sequence of problems.— The first type of problem should be the simple division of any oblong which fills a given space, as the cover of a small card case or the front of a match box (Plate VIII,

Fig. 1, *a*); and the next, the introduction of a rectangular mass or stamp into a larger oblong, as a book cover (*c*), in which it forms a center of sufficient interest to make necessary no other element to attract the eye.

The third problem may properly be one which requires a balance of interests, to be secured by the introduction of two or more masses of different sizes and shapes (*d*). This may be followed by one in which the decorating unit is no longer a simple mass, but takes the form of a straplike element which extends about the edges of the inclosing form, and creates one or more panels within (*b*).

After the pupil has had practice in making designs of the foregoing nature he will be prepared to solve problems involving varied masses and panels. Each of the problems presented to a class should be illustrated by two or three typical solutions, and if more than one arrangement is satisfactory, those to which the choice is to be restricted should be indicated, and the pupils further apprised as to the limitations beyond which they should not proceed in making individual variations. All the emphasis will thus fall upon such variation. This is intentional. It is proper that the beginner in design should have the problem presented to him in a very simple and concrete way, and that he be brought to realize that his critical attention must be focused upon one or two important questions in it.

Structural questions.—In designs in which there are two or more masses care should be taken to secure the rhythmic relations of these masses. To insure comprehension of this idea, it will be found helpful to have the pupils illustrate their understanding of rhythm by arranging on the blackboard or at their seats small rectangular blanks of paper within outlines of different size. It is to be noted in this connection, that the constructed forms to which it is at times desired to apply designs may include elements —as binding and corner pieces—which enter into the design and must be included in any scheme of decoration.

In general it may be said that simplicity and strength will be secured by planning but few masses, by emphasizing rhythmic elements, by avoiding weak and uncertain curves, by limiting the

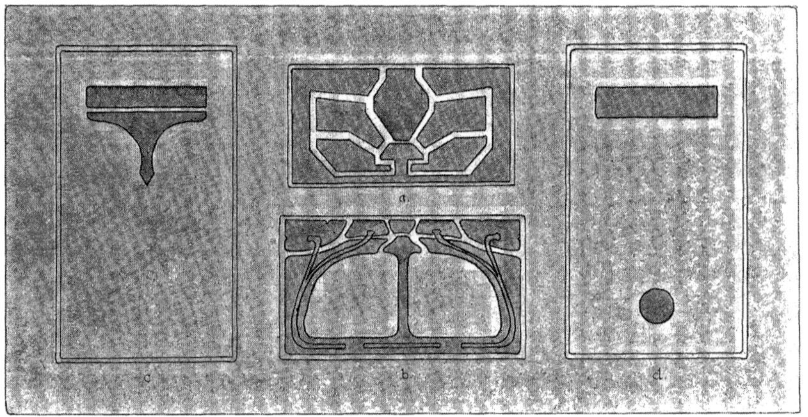

FIG. 1

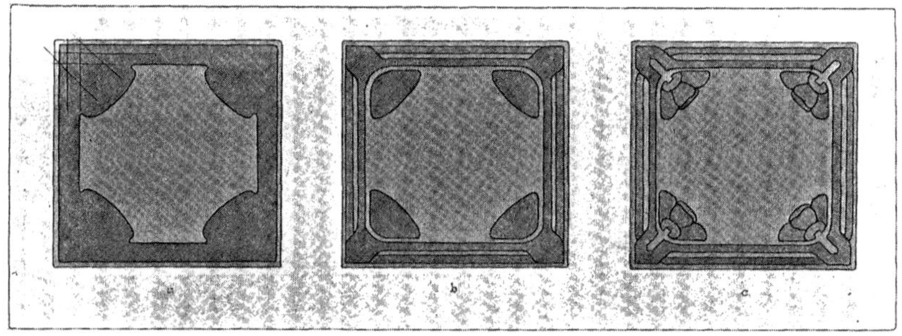

FIG. 2

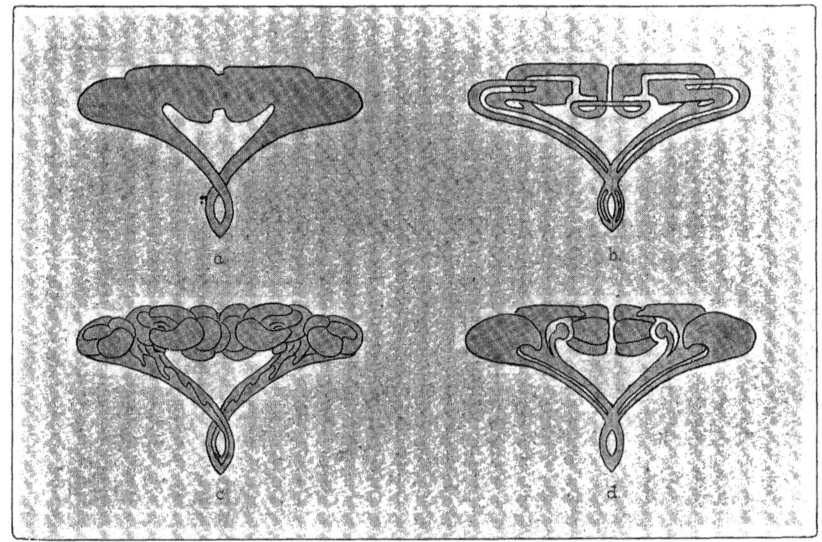

FIG. 3

size of the decorating units in all large spaces, and contrasting such units with large and simple masses. Throughout, the pupil should constantly be made to understand that it is the relation of the masses which constitutes the design. He must learn to think in masses and must learn to work with an eye intent on securing structural beauty as the first element in his pattern.

In the case of advanced pupils practice should be given in determining the masses which appear in completed patterns made by professional designers. These patterns should be presented, and the pupils led to see the mass relationships by closing the eyes until the smaller details are obscured and the basic elements of the design appear.

Throughout the first step in the problem emphasis should be laid on the principles of balance, rhythm, variety, and unity. The chief errors made by the pupils will be in arrangements which violate these principles, and show the design crowded or empty, monotonous or scattered. All possible errors cannot of course be named, but by referring the pupil to good examples and by causing him to analyze his own design in the light of their suggestions, he may be led to detect its shortcomings.

Division of the mass into decorating elements.— Once the size and placing of the decorating mass has been decided upon (as in the scheme for a box top or cushion cover Plate VIII, Fig. 2, *a*), there arises the question of its division into elements. The purpose of this is to give additional interest to the mass, and to attract the eye by pleasing lines and varied spaces.

A rhythmic relation of the elements created within the decorating mass is only next in importance to the relation of the mass itself to the other masses of the design. It must be understood that any movement within the mass should serve to relate the elements so created to one another and to the space which the mass fills; all such movements, in other words, must make for the rhythm and structural character of the design as a whole.

In the practical development of minor elements it will be necessary to illustrate to the pupil the desirability of working on constructive and connecting lines, the first supporting the edges of the outline, and the second carrying the eye between opposite elements. Lines of this nature the pupil should plan as tentative divisions. They should appear as mere threads upon the mass. In the more elaborate patterns of the higher grades they may cross one another in various directions, and so form what may be called "the net." (See upper left-hand corner of Plate II, *a.*) This is analogous to the square underlay offered by some teachers as a device to suggest possible divisions of the mass.

It will be necessary in this connection to illustrate the principles of growth, or the rising of one mass out of another. This in the form of radiation may first be shown in single units or spots and later in more complicated elements. Growth within a pattern assists in securing both rhythm and unity.

After the mass has been tentatively divided it should be searched carefully to determine which of the elements that now present themselves are to be retained. These decided upon, the lines which bound them should be strengthened, and the unused lines of the net erased.

If carefully developed, the foregoing steps will leave the pupil with decorative elements rhythmically related and exactly occupying the space of the original mass. To lend variety to the problem it will, as a rule, be better to separate the elements one from another. This may be done by doubling the lines which divide them. Care should be taken in so doing that the spaces or divisions formed are very narrow, that no element which is a part of a mass is left isolated. (See Plate VIII, Fig. 2, *b.*)

In the division noted above, opportunity will offer for refining the lines which bound the elements. Such refinement is to be secured by emphasizing the relations which exist between the separate masses, and by here and there altering boundary lines so that more subtle rhythms may be secured. Throughout this procedure the necessity of securing both harmony and variety of movement must be kept in mind. One of the most frequent errors is a sacrifice of unity by the pupil, that he may gain variety; instead of one characteristic line or movement appearing both in major and minor forms, it is not unusual to find in the latter movements quite unrelated to the general nature of the design. This is to be corrected by causing both large and small elements of the design to reflect the spirit common to the whole pattern;

there is no mixture of styles in the good design. Plate VII, Fig. 3, shows the scattered and disjointed effect which results from overelaboration of the decorative mass, and failure to develop proper structural and connective elements in it. Errors of this nature may frequently be corrected, if the general division lines are good, by uniting the minor elements into two or three well-related forms.

Introduction of subject-matter.— The introduction of conventional forms, or "subject-matter," into the elements planned is the final step to be taken in the development of the more advanced problem. It is a matter of adaptation, however, rather than of conventionalization. Few natural forms can be given to pupils to conventionalize, and it is quite sufficient to the purpose that the latter become skilful in the adaptation of those which are presented in charts, already much simplified. Seed vessels, bud, stem, leaf, and flower elements are all useful for this purpose; insect and animal forms may also be employed. (Plate VIII, Fig. 2, *c*.)

The adaptation of any of these requires that the specific form to be used, be introduced into the spaces which offer in the design without alteration of the general relations of such spaces to the pattern; that is, the mass arrangement may have the conventional elements introduced into it, but such introduction must not interfere to any considerable degree with such arrangement. It is to be noted in this connection that it is possible to introduce subject-matter into a mass arangement which has not had the elements separate one from the other. (Plate VIII, Fig. 3, *c*.) When this is done the design will appear as a solid base, made up of subject-matter, or with such matter superimposed upon the general mass below. Plate VIII, Fig. 3, shows a "stamp," or ornamental unit, consisting of a solid mass *a*. In *b* this mass is shown elaborated into straplike elements; in *c* subject-matter has been arranged completely to fill it, while in *d* it has been developed on the lines of a simple net, and the abstract spots thus formed have been translated into highly conventionalized plant forms.

COLOR

General considerations of color cannot be here undertaken. It may be stated, however, that success in the use of color in design will depend as much upon a nice sense of color values as upon the laws of color harmony. Applied designs, for the most part must partake of a mural character, that is, they must appear to be part of the surface on which they are found. This they can do only when the colors of the different parts of the pattern approximate one another in value. If all are identical in value, the most intense will attract attention, but even intensity will scarcely serve to distinguish the design unless a strong outline is used to separate the decorative mass from the background.

As a rule the colors of the decorating unit must be of approximately the same value, though as a whole they are higher or lower than the background. If such relation is not maintained, the design will not appear flat, but those parts highest in value will stand out in contrast to neighboring elements. In practice a design which lacks harmony, through differences in value, may be bettered by glazing down the highest elements. A skilful designer will sometimes intentionally lay in all parts of his design in intense colors and subsequently glaze them down with repeated washes. This gives a tonal quality to the design not to be obtained otherwise.

The development of critical power.—Taste, it was noted, is the development of a critical judgment through repeated discrimination. As one of the principal ends to be secured in the teaching of design is the development of this power, it should be the practice throughout the solution of every problem to require criticism at the completion of each step. This criticism is to be secured from the class by hanging up before it the best and poorest results secured. These should be reviewed in the light of the principles which have been presented, and the pupils should be required to criticize them in terms of such principles. Specific effort should be made to develop power to judge according to definite standards. It is not sufficient for a pupil to say that a design is bad or that he does not like it; he should be called upon to state why it is good or bad, and if unsatisfactory, how it is to be remedied by alteration in structural nature, in "balance," "rhythm," "variety," or "unity." These terms the pupils should learn to use comprehensively.

SUMMARY

Summarizing, one may say that the foregoing suggestions form a plea for the teaching of definite principles and for their definite application. It is not recommended that many problems be solved during the school term. In many cases all that is possible is the making of one, or perhaps two, designs. These should be for application to some article of use, as there can be no more significant factor in a lesson in design than a knowledge that such lesson is making for the beauty of a thing which is to play a useful part in our every-day surroundings. The problem once decided upon, the four steps named should be taken in order, the masses introduced, developed, refined, and filled with subject-matter. The making of the designs will thus take several lessons, and the development and application of a color scheme as many more. Far better, however, that one such good design be made than many desultory patterns leading to no specific power of execution or of criticism.

SCIENCE TEACHING IN ELEMENTARY SCHOOLS[1]

HUGO NEWMAN
Principal of Public School No. 33, The Bronx, New York City

What can the elementary school do in the teaching of physical science? What should be the aim, scope, and method of science work in the elementary school? What results may reasonably be expected? It is my purpose in this paper to set forth what is being done in the city of New York toward answering these questions.

About two years ago a new course in "nature-study" was planned for the elementary schools. It is stated in the syllabus:

> The aim of nature-study, particularly in the lower grades, is to cultivate a sympathetic acquaintance with nature and to develop the power of observation. To this end, the children should be brought into actual contact with the object of study whenever possible, either in or out of the classroom. The power gained by learning facts through actual observation or experiment will enable the pupils afterward to picture to themselves facts which it will be feasible to make known to them only by description. . . . The phenomena of life in the world about the pupil should be made prominent. The presentation of the topics in elementary science in the seventh and eighth years should, as far as possible, be accompanied with illustrative experiments. Classroom work should be supplemented by visits to the parks and museums, and by the use of pictures and lantern slides.

The course of study outlined in the syllabus divides itself into three cycles. In the first three years it is purely observational, consisting of lessons on familiar animals and plants, and observations of familiar natural phenomena, such as the weather, winds, clouds, storms, the sun, changes of season, etc. In the fourth and fifth years a more intensive study of animals and plants is required, together with some elementary classification. In the seventh and eighth years (the last two years of the elementary-school course) nature-study becomes "elementary science"—

[1] Paper read before the Department of Elementary Education of the National Educational Association, Asbury Park, N. J., July, 1905.

practically a complete course in elementary physics. It is this last phase of our nature-study work that I purpose to speak of somewhat in detail.

The aim of the course in "elementary science" is not only to acquaint the pupil with the fundamental laws and principles of physics, but to train him into habits of careful doing, close observation, accurate thinking, and correct expression; in short, physics is taught for its disciplinary as well as its practical value.

The scope of the course is somewhat comprehensive, as may be seen from the following outline: seventh year, first half, gravity, mechanical powers; second half, the mechanics of liquids and gases; eighth year, first half, the phenomena of sound and heat; second half, the phenomena of light, electricity, and magnetism. For the interpretation and practical operation of this course, a special syllabus has been prepared which contains a suggestive list of experiments that may be performed by the teacher and the pupils. Throughout the course emphasis is laid on the experimental presentation and development of the subject. Constant correlations with the other subjects of the grades and with the experiences in the daily lives of the children are required. It is sought not merely to make the course a collection of isolated facts, but to organize the experiences of the pupils into a connected, logical, unified whole. The practical applications and illustrations in the industries are an essential feature of the course; in fact, the keynote is found in the injunction to "make the work practical and interesting."

The time schedule calls for two periods of forty minutes each per week, but the permissible addition of a "study period" makes the available time to be given to physics three periods per week.

Many discouraging conditions were met with in the introduction of this experimental course in science into the public schools. There was no equipment whatever for the work; no apparatus was available; the classes were too large for laboratory work, and, most discouraging of all, the majority of upper-class teachers had no preparation whatever to teach properly an experimental course.

It is gratifying to note that these unfavorable conditions are being overcome as rapidly as it is possible in so vast a system of education as that of New York. There is a growing realization of the importance of natural science as a legitimate branch of the common-school curriculum. Treated at first with contempt, as another of the "fads and frills," it is now generally admitted that the study of science has a high claim for recognition as a factor in the common-school education of every boy and girl, not only as an object in itself, but as a means of general culture and discipline.

Our board of education has recognized the importance of laboratory work in science-teaching by providing for a "science room" in the plans of all new elementary-school buildings, and by placing on the supply list apparatus and material for fully equipping such a room for demonstration and individual laboratory work. In a number of the older schools regular classrooms have been equipped with demonstration tables for the teachers, and a sufficient supply of apparatus to carry on successfully a practical laboratory course.

The introduction, two years ago, of the "departmental system" of teaching into the seventh and eighth years has been a powerful aid in developing and perfecting the course in science. Under this system, each teacher becomes, to a certain extent, a specialist devoting his time exclusively to one subject, or at most to a small group of related subjects. It is thus possible, in many cases, for the principal of a school to assign the subject of physics to a teacher who has some special qualifications for the work. This system also conduces to economy of equipment and a unification of the entire course in a school. It makes possible the division of a large class into small laboratory sections, or the assignment of an additional teacher to aid in supervision and instruction.

Finally, the teachers, as a whole, are realizing the educational and disciplinary value of science instruction, and are striving, by all means in their power, to equip themselves for the work. Perhaps in no other subject of the course of study do the results to be attained depend so much upon the teacher as in the subject of elementary science. Not only must he be enthusiastic and thoroughly conversant with pedagogical method in general, but in addition, he must possess a comprehensive knowledge of the subject-matter and its technique. It is useless for a teacher to attempt to teach physics unless he can *do* as well as tell. This practical knowledge he can obtain only at first hand, as the result of his own experimental work. University and summer-school courses in practical physics are being attended by a goodly number of those teachers who feel the lack of training in laboratory methods. As a further proof of the desire on the part of the school authorities to obtain the best results in this branch of instruction, it may be stated that all applicants for license to teach in the elementary schools of the city must now pass an examination in physics.

It will be seen from this rapid survey of the field that much has already been accomplished toward the establishment of a rational course in physics in the elementary schools, and that the outlook for future development is very bright.

Regarding the method of teaching physics to be followed in the elementary school, it is my opinion that the work should be conducted along three lines: (1) presentation or demonstration by the teacher, assisted, whenever practicable, by some pupil or pupils; (2) individual laboratory work by the pupils; (3) recitations upon the topics of the demonstration or laboratory work. Let us consider briefly these three phases.

1. It is assumed that the school has an ample equipment of apparatus and material to enable the teacher to present experimentally the fundamental principles of the science. Every experiment to be performed by the teacher before the class should be rehearsed carefully in private, no matter how simple it may appear or how often it has been done before. The teacher, when he stands before his class, should have absolute confidence in the successful outcome of the experiment he performs. Nothing can be more subversive of the aims of science-teaching than the exhibition of an experiment performed in a bungling manner. An occasional failure may occur, even when the teacher has the highest technical skill. In such a case, no particular harm is done; in fact, the failure may prove even more instructive than a successful outcome, provided the teacher retains his composure and quickly turns the attention of his class to a careful examina-

tion and consideration of the new and unexpected phenomena observed.

During an experiment (which should always be performed with deliberation, never in a hurry) the teacher should, by skilful questioning, guide and direct the attention of his pupils, and stimulate their observing and reasoning powers. Toward the end of the period the teacher should write on the blackboard an outline giving in concise form the object, method, results, and applications of the experiment. This may be copied by the pupils in their notebooks, together with a sketch or diagram of the apparatus. I would not let the pupils of the seventh year take notes during the progress of a demonstration. It is my experience that pupils at this age (about thirteen years) are too young and unprepared to take notes intelligently in this way. Their attention is divided between the experiment and the notebook, and the lesson of the experiment becomes obscured or lost entirely. Besides, a habit of scribbling is easily formed, and may seriously cripple their work in other departments. With the eighth-year pupils I would omit the outline on the blackboard, but would pause in the demonstration, at frequent intervals, to enable the pupils to record observations and inferences, and to arrange their notes logically and neatly. All this may seem like doing too much for the pupil, but experience has shown me that the average pupil of thirteen to fourteen years needs much more help than the teacher is apt to realize.

As to the kind of experiments that should be performed by the teacher, I would say that, in general, he should perform: (*a*) experiments that may be considered basic or typical; (*b*) experiments that are wholly, or almost wholly, qualitative in character, and which it would be a waste of time to have each pupil perform; (*c*) experiments requiring apparatus not easily or conveniently duplicated for individual work; (*d*) experiments requiring a degree of manipulative skill not to be expected of the pupil; (*e*) experiments or exercises illustrating methods of manipulation or computation.

The question as to whether the teacher's demonstrations should precede or follow the laboratory work will depend for its answer upon the nature of the topic treated, the method of treatment, the equipment of the school, the capacity and previous training of the pupils, etc. In general, I would say that a fundamental principle or law should be developed by the teacher before the class, to be followed by verification and application in the laboratory by the pupils. If a series of minute observations has to be made in order to establish a law, these observations may well be made in the laboratory by the pupils individually, and then discussed with the teacher in the recitation or "study period."

The experiments selected by the teacher for demonstration should be the simplest that can be devised for the purpose in view. It is a mistake to use complicated apparatus with beginners, to call attention to all the details of manipulation and the multiplicity of minor phenomena that have no direct bearing on the object of the experiment. It is a good plan to call upon the more apt pupils to assist the teacher whenever possible. This gives an added interest to the demonstration, and is a stimulus to the other pupils to do their best in order to secure the coveted privilege of assisting the teacher. In this way the teacher may be able to train some pupils to be of valuable aid to him in the preparation of apparatus, and its distribution and storage.

No opportunity should be lost to impress upon the pupils the practical applications and illustrations of the principles they are studying. The basement of the modern school building usually furnishes a storehouse of useful and interesting information regarding furnaces, boilers, heating and ventilating machinery, pumps, elevators, dynamos, motors, etc. An inspection and explanation of this valuable school equipment should form a part of the demonstration work. Whenever and wherever possible, the class should visit neighboring manufacturing establishments, power-houses, etc. In fact, the field-work of "nature-study" in the lower grades may here find its counterpart and extension in the more advanced work of the upper grades. By this means an intense interest is aroused and maintained in the pupils.

2. Regarding the pupils' laboratory work, I think there can be no question of its necessity in science-teaching, even in the

elementary school. Satisfactory results in this, as in most other branches of study, can be obtained only by having the pupil *do* something, by providing that most potent means in the acquisition of knowledge—physical contact with, and manipulation of, the thing to be studied. During the first five years of the course in "nature-study" the attitude of the pupil was largely, if not wholly, that of a passive observer of given phenomena or conditions. Now in the seventh and eighth years he *creates* the conditions, adds experiment to observation, and learns to use for the first time this most powerful and fruitful of all aids in the aquisition of knowledge. He learns how to put "a question to nature, as it were, which she must herself answer—a kind of observation under definite and deliberate conditions." This being a new and untried process for the pupil, it is no wonder that he often finds it difficult to "get his bearings," unless the skilful and experienced teacher sets him right at the start. I have no sympathy with that use of the inductive method which places before the untrained pupil a physical problem to be solved experimentally, without giving him the slightest cue as to purpose, method, and results to be looked for. An unconscionable amount of time may be wasted in this way. Life is too short for this sort of thing.

Let the experiment to be performed by the pupils be most carefully considered by the teacher before assigning it. Let it be the most simple that can be devised, and absolutely within the comprehension and capacity of the pupil. Let it have some practical bearing, if possible, on his everyday life. State in clear terms the object or aim of the exercise, give explicit and minute directions (particularly at the beginning of the course), and, if necessary, call attention by means of suggestive questions to those phenomena which have a bearing on the conclusions to be drawn. After the pupil has been in the laboratory for a term, there will be less need for minuteness of directions, for he will have acquired then some skill in technique, and he will be able to observe more closely and accurately without guidance at every point. But at the beginning definiteness and clearness in statement of aim and method are essential to his later success. "Nature can only give a correct and unambiguous answer to the question you put it, when it is clearly and definitely proposed. This is very often not the case, and the experimenter loses himself in meaningless efforts, with the foolish hope that 'something may come of it.'" Aimless, desultory work in the laboratory, a mere pottering and playing with test-tubes, bottles, magnets, etc., is the worst possible introduction a student can have into the realm of physical science. On the other hand, a carefully selected series of experiments, adapted to his capacity, and performed with intelligence and earnestness, will develop in him a power of doing and thinking which no other single study can give him so well. There is no better means for training in observation, reflection, judgment, and expression than judiciously selected and carefully executed work in the laboratory. An eminent German philosopher says: "The accurate and discriminating observation of facts, supported by careful experiment, is certainly a great advantage that modern science has over all earlier efforts to attain the truth."

The kind of experiments to be performed by the pupils may be classified as follows: (*a*) experiments that verify laws demonstrated by the teacher; (*b*) experiments wholly, or largely, quantitative in character; (*c*) experiments or exercises that will impart a certain degree of mechanical skill. These may properly be repetitions of the teacher's model demonstrations.

The so-called "even front" system of laboratory work is, in my opinion, the best for elementary-school pupils. Under this plan, all pupils work at the same exercise at the same time. It requires, of course, a complete outfit of apparatus for each pupil, and hence is somewhat more expensive than the plan of assigning a different exercise to each pupil. However, the "even front" plan enables the teacher to utilize to the best advantage the all too short time at his command; it permits of general directions and explanations to the whole class, facilitates supervision, and simplifies the management of the laboratory. Indeed, since the classes in the city schools are apt to be large, this seems to me to be the only feasible plan to adopt.

One of the essential requisites in laboratory work is the keeping of a written record of the details of an experiment. This record should be made in a notebook of convenient size, and should contain the following data: number and date of experiment; object or aim; a description or diagram of the apparatus used; a statement of manipulations performed; the observations made (tabulated or graphically illustrated when possible); and the conclusions or inferences drawn from the experiment. It is best to use two pages for each exercise, reserving the even-numbered pages for a description of the experiment, and the odd-numbered pages for diagrams, tabulations, and computations. A device for facilitating the examination and criticism of notebooks, which I have seen used with some success, consists of a rubber stamp by means of which the instructor stamps the following items on the lower part of the odd-numbered pages: description; diagram; observation; inference; grammatical structure; neatness. A word or two opposite an item will serve to call the attention of the pupil to those particulars in which his record is deficient. The teacher should only indicate the errors; the pupil himself should make the corrections. Much attention should be given to the language employed by the pupil in making his records. There is a good opportunity here for emphasizing the work of the English department.

A good plan for presenting the laboratory experiments to the class is to typewrite and mimeograph the directions on a set of cards, about five by six inches, and to distribute these among the pupils during a "study period" for careful perusal, and for preparation of the form to be used in the notebooks in the following laboratory period. No portion of the time allotted to laboratory work should be given to reading up the experiment. This should always be done in a previous "study period," thus giving the full time of the laboratory period to the actual performance of the experiment.

The supervision of laboratory work is no easy matter, especially if the class be large. One teacher cannot handle effectively more than fifteen to twenty pupils, even when they are all working at the same exercise. Under the "departmental system" it is possible, by a judicious arrangement of the program, to divide a large class into two or more sections; or it may be possible to assign an assisting teacher to aid in supervision and instruction of a large class. The latter method has been tried in the school under my supervision, with excellent results. Both teachers are in close touch with the pupils and their work in the laboratory, and can give counsel and direction with facility and dispatch. These two teachers also divide between them the labor of examining and criticising the written work.

3. In the recitation periods the topics of the laboratory periods and demonstrations should be carefully reviewed and discussed, errors indicated and corrected, correlations made with the other subjects of the grades, and very simple problems given illustrating the principles or laws derived by experiment. This period should usually take the form of a "quiz," both teacher and class asking and answering questions. In this way a greater interest can be maintained in the class than by a formal recitation, and it is possible for the teacher to gauge more accurately the mental status of his class. If a textbook be used, it should be a real textbook, not a manual of "inductive questions." The textbook should supplement and extend the knowledge gained by the pupil in class and individual work. In New York a textbook is not used, but the pupil is encouraged to use books provided "for reference." In my opinion, much time could be saved if a textbook were used. I consider a good, simple textbook, if rightly used, an important aid in the teaching of physics. Without it, the pupil is likely to become possessed of a mass of isolated facts which he has not the power to correlate or classify. The textbook will provide the connecting links which he needs to unify his knowledge. The absence of a textbook increases very materially the work of the teacher, and restricts somewhat the scope of the course.

Written tests should be given about once a month. These will serve to indicate to the teacher the general grasp which the pupil has of the subject as a whole.

I cannot, within the limits of this paper, do more than merely indicate a few of the correlations of science with the other branches of study that can be made, if the teachers of the "departmental" classes work together as a unit. Mathematics, physical geography, physiology, composition, drawing, shopwork—all these departments may draw upon the science work, and the latter may in turn draw upon all the others. It is essential to the success of the whole system that such correlations be properly made. The practicability of this is one of the tests of a well-made curriculum.

It is too early as yet to say what will be the effect of this new course in science on the later science work of those pupils who enter the high school. It is safe to assume, however, that they will be better prepared to do the advanced work, even if some of the earlier work has to be repeated. There can be no doubt as to the value of this work in science to that vast majority of pupils who never enter the high school. It is for them, more particularly, that the whole course is planned. That the work is already producing practical results is evidenced by the fact that several recent inventions of considerable merit were made by elementary-school pupils. Among these is a plan to relieve the congestion at Brooklyn Bridge, and a new receiving apparatus for a wireless telegraph system. These inventors claim to have obtained their initiative and inspiration from the physics lessons in the schools.

Thus we are not only acquainting our pupils with the great truths of science, but we are creating and fostering that most desirable and productive quality, the "scientific habit of mind."

THE NEED OF ELEMENTARY MATHEMATICS

WILLIAM SCHOCH
Crane Manual Training High School, Chicago

The ordinary course of study in elementary mathematics is commonly stated not so much with reference to what we are to do as with reference to what we are to accomplish. It sets forth an aim and leaves to the teacher, or to the writer of the textbook, the choice of the means. Now, with a subject-matter selected and organized in the interest of the child we have the conditions of growth, the factors which cause him to exert himself to the best of his ability; but, on the other hand, if there is no such relation between him and the subject-matter, then he can have no internal, or intrinsic, motive in his work, and all genuine effort on his part will become stifled. So we see how much depends on a proper choice of material. We hear so much of the distaste children acquire during their school life for the study of mathematics. Can it be that the material of instruction is not properly adjusted to their needs and life-interests?

The scope of this inquiry is rather large, embracing, as it does, a course of study extending over eight years. Hence, it is hardly feasible to give a general answer. Besides, whatever may need to be said about one part of the course does not necessarily apply with equal force to another. So, for convenience, we will divide the subject of discussion into the following subdivisions:

1. Kindergarten and Grade 1: the teaching of the number-concept.

2. Grades 2, 3, 4, and 5: the teaching of the operations with numbers, both integral and fractional.

3. Grades 6, 7, and 8: *(a)* the applications of number in trade and business; *(b)* laying the foundation for algebra and geometry.

1. *The teaching of the number-concept.*—The first lessons in arithmetic, which involve counting and measuring, have for

their immediate purpose the development of the number-concept. We wish the children to form an idea of number as a discriminant of relation. However, exercises in mere counting and measuring are not of themselves sufficient for this purpose. A boy may be asked to count the spools on a table, and he will gladly enough respond to the task. But ask him to count the apples in a basket which his mother has just brought home, and he will do that more eagerly, probably also more accurately, because in this he has a personal interest, while in the former he had none. He perceives the number of apples in relation to something else—his appetite, for instance—and is thus led from one problem to another, the division of the number of apples into parts.

We may judge from this illustration that our general purpose, the development of the number-concept, will be served best, if we can arrange the work so as to fit in with some thought which the children are carrying on of their own initiative, or with some problem arising out of their plays and occupations.

Briefly stated:

a) Every exercise should be a real problem for the child so as to fully engage his attention.

b) It should give him something to do which will incidentally necessitate measuring and counting.

c) It should lead him on to a new problem.

Naturally, the task of choosing suitable exercises is no light one. In fact, it demands the most careful thought and study on the part of the teacher. There are no textbooks to help him. He must explore for himself the particular sphere of interest of the children under his care, join in their plays and occupations, and derive from these a series of problems related to their life-interests and needs. These problems should involve exercises in constructive activity, and present the conditions which will make it necessary for the child to count and measure, repeated processes of this kind leading him to a correct appreciation of the relations, "more or less," "greater or smaller," etc., and involving the fundamental ideas of addition, subtraction, multiplication, and division.

2. *The teaching of the operations with number.*—While

counting and measuring so as to learn that number is not a property of objects, the child unconsciously acquires some knowledge of the fundamental operations, though only within a small number limit. When he passes into the second grade, this limit is gradually enlarged, the complete mastery of the fundamental operations, both with integral and fractional numbers, by the time he finishes the fifth, becoming the objective point of instruction. It is here that drill is especially in place; but it is here also that mere figuring is likely to be overdone, and becomes tedious and destructive of interest, tending to make of the pupil a mere calculating machine.

Glancing over the history of mathematical teaching, we find that the remedy for this has been sought and found in the use of concrete problems, both in the beginning and in the end. These are made to serve (1) as a basis for the unfolding and learning of the processes, and (2) as a means for the application of the principles taught.

The first phase of the use of concrete problems has been worked out very well and to general satisfaction. No teacher nowadays attempts to teach, e. g., 6 divided by ½ without offering it first in some such form as "How many half-dollars will pay a debt of six dollars?" The pupil is given an opportunity to visualize the process. Conditions are provided which stimulate his self-activity and lead him to arrive at a solution *quasi* through his own effort. Another problem or two from the pupil's little world of trivial relations, offering like opportunities for visualization, and the pupil is ready to generalize that all 6's divided by ½ give the same result. When a process is thus developed, work with pure numbers, with these concrete problems as a dim background, will then have a distinct value as drill in fixing it permanently.

We have not been so fortunate with regard to the second phase of the use of concrete problems. For that has been only partially developed. We have come to see that the educative element in mathematics does not lie so much in gaining accuracy and rapidity with figures as in acquiring the power to discern which operation to use in a given case, and we have accordingly given up the grouping of problems under "cases" so characteristic of the old textbooks. However, our modern texts are yet by no means satisfactory. Instead of the old-time formal connection between the problems, objectionable though it was, we now have no connection at all, either in form or context. The books remind one more of a speller than a reader. You may select almost any two consecutive problems, and you will hardly find any connection between them in thought or in points of interest to a child. It is true, the pupil has to decide for himself what processes to use in the solution. He is certainly not robbed of the opportunity to think. But as to his motive for doing this work, is the desire "to figure" sufficient to sustain his interest?

It seems to me that these "applications" should be arranged in some order, in groups, so that each group follows up some central idea growing out of the environment of the child, leading out from some of his experiences, and teaching him something new and worth knowing. There are a good many interesting relations in the child's immediate environment about which he wants to know, and which the use of numbers may help to explain.

Problems selected along these lines would surely engage and hold the interest of the pupils, besides awakening in them a sense of the usefulness of arithmetic as a tool in dealing with the ordinary affairs of life. The purposelessness of figuring would disappear along with the distaste for it. There would also be ample opportunity for the exercise of the power of analysis before mentioned; and since the pupil's interest is bound up in his work, he will come to appreciate this power of his own accord.

3*a*. *The applications of number in trade and business.*—When the child passes into the sixth grade, it is presumed that he knows the fundamental processes, and hereafter his work is directed toward broadening and deepening this knowledge. In the selection of material, the time-honored custom of giving business subjects a prominent place still prevails; and there is no doubt that this choice is also in accord with a popular demand. Indeed, everyone who would be a useful member of society wants to form an intelligent acquaintance with them.

The difficulty usually encountered in teaching these subjects hinges on the point of departure. Textbooks start each topic with a lot of definitions of terms and relations unfamiliar to the child, and often also to the teacher. Then follow the problems without sequence of thought, that is, such a sequence as would unfold the subject. They lack the connection with the actual experiences of the children which would make them real problems for them and engage their interest. The much-lamented failure of our boys and girls to make any headway with commission, exchange, or taxes is largely due to this lack of interest on their part. It is because they see no relation to any problem of their own.

The average child knows very little about these subjects. Is it probable that a few definitions, no matter how well they may be put, however simple the language, can supply this deficiency? Is there no better way? Take, for example, the subject of taxes. Can we not find in the child's previous experience a problem that presents ideas akin to those of taxation, from which we may gradually—by linking problem to problem— develop the whole subject in all its aspects?

SUGGESTION OF A PLAN TO TEACH TAXES

I. Connection with the experience of the child. Problems involving the ideas of assessment, levy, and tax.

a) The pupils of a school consisting of 4 rooms, numbering 27, 48, 30, and 55, respectively, wish to buy a picture valued at $8. What is the best and fairest way of raising the money? (Chance to define "assessment.")

b) Four newsboys in the business district clubbed together to "run a newstand," agreeing to take turns in attending to the business and to share the expenses according to their respective earnings. They earned $30, $10, $20, and $40, respectively; the expenses were $20. How much should each pay?

II. Discussion of some civic function familiar to children, such as street-lighting, street-cleaning, police and fire protection, maintenance of schools, etc.

Questions: (1) Why does not every citizen light the streets

surrounding his property, maintain a school for his children, etc.? (Show that it is cheaper and better for him to divide the expense with others and obligate himself to pay his share, called "tax.") (2) Who pays the policeman and the fireman? (3) How is the money obtained?

III. Development of idea of "tax-rate." Problems: Supposing the 5,000 inhabitants of a certain town want to raise $50,000 to equip a fire department. How should this money be raised? (Emphasize the equity of determining the tax in accordance with property values.) If the estimated (assessed) value of property in this town is $2,000,000, how much should be paid on property valued at $10,000, $575, $7,987, $15,750, respectively? What is the best way of figuring on this? (Show that it is best to find the rate per $1 valuation. This is called the "tax-rate." In this case it is 2½ cents on the $1 valuation, or 25 mills, as it is usually expressed.)

IV*a*). The necessity of employing assessors and tax-collectors as public officials. (Different kinds of taxes: city, county, and state; tediousness of the work; use of "tax-table" to lighten the work of computing amounts.)

b) The tax-bill. Practical problems involving the use of the forms.

c) Why should tax-bills be paid promptly and cheerfully? (Penalty.) Problems.

V. Support of the federal government. Questions: (1) Who pays the postman, the weatherman, the army, etc.? (2) What is meant by internal revenue, tariff, duty? How are these regulated? How collected? (3) What is meant by "smuggling"? (Give a table of customs duties; free-list.) Problems.

3*b*) *Laying the foundation for algebra and geometry.*—Practice and drill in the principles of arithmetic is only part of the work in the upper grammar grades, for the course of study embraces also the rudiments of algebra and geometry. Added to the curriculum within the last twenty years in response to the demand for its enrichment, these subjects have not yet become thoroughly established, nor is there a sufficiently definite understanding as to the proper mode of presenting them. This is especially true of geometry. Its specialized treatment in the high school, questionable even there, though probably the only treatment known to many of the grade teachers, has been discarded as beyond the capacity of the pupils. However, in trying to refrain from giving and requiring formal proofs, we have drifted into the other extreme, the method of telling or "dictation." Think of giving, in the eighth grade, minute instructions for the drawing of a circle with the compasses even to the placing of the points, when a few well-directed questions would elicit the necessary information from the pupil! Yet courses of study and textbooks prescribe "dictation" as the method of teaching all the fundamental problems of constructive geometry. Is not the act of acquiring knowledge worth more to the child than the knowledge itself? There is nothing for him to do when the material is given him in ready-made form, except to absorb, and memorize, it in its logical wrappings. As in all education, so here

> the process of self-development should be encouraged to the uttermost. . . . . Children should be told as little as possible. . . . . Any piece of knowledge which the pupil has himself acquired, any problem which he has himself solved, becomes by virtue of the conquest much more thoroughly his than it could else be.[1]

Both algebra and geometry have side-lights in the life-interests of the children which furnish excellent supports to the study of these subjects, points to start from, as well as factors in sustaining an active and progressive interest. So there is no reason why the proper conditions may not be presented which will enable pupils to work out every one of those problems, seeking and finding the reasons for the steps in terms of their previously acquired experiences.

Education is the interaction of the old experience with a new experience felt as valuable. It presumes that the principle of self-activity is basic, inasmuch as the best results in teaching are gained when the child becomes active through a desire to solve a problem growing out of his needs and interests. We have pointed out in the foregoing that this thought has been given too

[1] Spencer, *Education*.

little attention in the construction of our courses of study and the textbooks in use. May we not conclude, for that reason, that both are in urgent need of revision? We have also recognized the desirability and possibility of grouping problems around some central thought emanating from the child's environment, and teaching him something besides mere figuring. There are many subjects scattered over the program which are available for this purpose. May we not relieve the crowded condition of the curriculum by taking these up during the time given to mathematics? We are breaking away from conventional lines in other subjects. Why not in mathematics?

CHICAGO VACATION SCHOOLS

MRS. GERTRUDE BLACKWELDER
Chicago

The idea is gradually gaining ground in our city that society has a responsibility toward the children of the crowded districts which does not end at the close of the regular school year in June. Teachers have long been aware of the need of some kind of wholesome training and restraint for the young ones who are literally turned into the street at this time, but the public is slow to realize the conditions under which thousands of them exist during the summer vacation. Driven from their crowded homes by the heat and general discomfort, the children, from the baby carried in the arms of some "little mother," to the adolescent boy or girl, find their social life in the streets. This life is as different from the natural, playful existence of children in the country or small town as can be imagined. Nothing which can be called "play" is to be seen; there is no possible chance for games of any sort. A municipal horse trough, or the dirty puddles after a rain, satisfy that mysterious longing for water which seems to be inherent in all children. The popularity of the swimming and wading pools in our new small parks proves that this youthful desire for contact with water, which may be reminiscent of ancient life-forms, is found in the tenement district as well as the country. Not all of the joy in childish pleasures has been rooted out by unwholesome and unnatural surroundings. The fact that vacation schools recognize and develop this desire for play, the birthright of all children, goes far to account for their popularity.

But the child craves something besides play; he likes to work, if suitable stimulus is given. This desire was recognized by the framers of the vacation-school curriculum and ample provision made for handwork. It was their intention to develop manual training along educational, rather than industrial, lines — to treat it as a form of expression, and for the first few years this branch of the work varied little from other schools. But the increasing demand for handwork has resulted in giving each year more variety in material, thus opening up greater possibilities for developing individual tastes. Last summer the metal and leather work was especially popular, and wherever it was possible to teach pottery there were plenty of workers eager to learn. At the Dante School (in the Italian district), the teacher of modeling gave to a group of boys some clay and asked them to shape with their hands some kind of a vessel—"Anything they thought pretty." The majority made beer mugs, with cuspidors and dice holding second place, and a solitary wine-glass completing the significant collection. The result was rather startling, but spoke plainly of the things most familiar to those boys.

The past two summers have seen a broadening of the work in domestic science. Not every available building has an installed plant for cooking, but for obvious reasons it is perhaps fortunate that our teachers have to exercise the greatest ingenuity in doing housework with the smallest possible equipment. At the Dante School we found all sorts of processes going on—girls on their knees scrubbing floors, others washing windows; a group preparing a simple meal, under the direction of the teacher, which was later served to a dozen girls decorously seated around the dining-table. The desire on the part of the girls to learn how to keep house is most encouraging, for it shows that the lack of good home training, the allurements of shop and factory have not entirely extinguished the taste for domestic life. One of the most pressing needs in certain parts of our city is for some strong influence which shall restrain the larger girls of school age from forming habits and interests which will unfit them to become good wives and mothers. The allurements of the streets and of the cheap shows are very potent at that age, and something should be done to check their influence.

In the sewing departments the teachers were often gratified to learn of the progress made by the girls who had been in the classes the previous year. In several cases they reported that they were making all their own clothes, and the neatness which marked their dress spoke plainly of the usefulness of this training in needlework. In most cases the girls are given something to make at once, a method which tends to hold their interest.

Music was as popular as ever, the bright, happy faces and vociferous tones speaking loudly of the possible influence of this art if given in a practical way. The children are taught songs; rousing martial songs, sweet and tender songs, music that arouses the emotions, that stirs the soul. The visitor can never forget the expression on the faces of some of the worst boys of the neighborhood when they are under the spell of the music—an uplifting but perfectly natural form of expression.

The methods of nature-study were as varied as the number of schools. Some of the teachers rose early in the morning, took the trolley far into the country where there was plenty of plant-life to gather from, and kept their rooms filled with interesting material for talks and investigations; others drew on the vacant lots overrun with weeds and insects. Here the children could be taught at least one of the fundamental ideas of nature-study—the adaptation of life to environment. In one school certain principles of physics and mechanics were given without the aid of material except a little simple apparatus for demonstration. One principal, a specialist in handwork, interested the children of one of the worst districts in the city in the successive processes of making textiles, beginning with the flax or cotton fresh from the fields and ending with the completed fabric—all the work of the children. Nature-work in connection with the excursions was far less serious than in former years. It is believed that better results are obtained by leaving the children free to roam about, to pick wild flowers, to find for themselves the interesting insects, or plants or stones, or to wade in lake or river.

The drawing and color work can be best appreciated by examining the hundreds of specimens which are now on the walls of the Municipal Museum in the Public Library. A large collection of articles made by the children of vacation schools last summer has been arranged there, with a view of showing to the public the variety of the work, and of developing an appreciation of the value of handwork in education.

As an instance of the possibilities in manual training, the

following incident is significant: Judge Mack, of the Juvenile Court, sent this summer four boys, who had been arrested and were in charge of Probation Officers, to one of the vacation schools. They at once became interested in the work, so absorbed in the delight of "making things" that their behavior was all that could be desired, and probably the wholesome influence of that joy and satisfaction has done for them what no amount of punishment could ever have accomplished.

The eagerness of parents and children for the privileges of vacation schools becomes greater each year. Last summer with nine schools there was a total enrollment of 6,583, and an average attendance of 4,360.

If it is true, as Mr. Cooley has said, in a late speech, that fifty vacation schools are needed in Chicago, it is safe to assume that there are $50,000 children who ought to have this help in the summer vacation. The expenses were again borne by a committee from the women's clubs, assisted by a small grant from the school fund. It seems to the women who have carried this burden for eight years, that the business men of Chicago, who cannot be wholly ignorant of the dangers, present and future, of juvenile crime, should give liberally in support of a movement which is proving its claims as a moral and educational force in Chicago.

It is safe to say that the members of the School Board are generally in favor of this work, and would vote the necessary funds if it were possible to do so without crippling other departments already established. It is to be hoped that other agencies may soon relieve the clubs of the responsibility of maintaining these schools, but until that time comes the women's clubs will not fail in their interest and generous support.

EDITORIAL NOTES

Is education business, or is business education? Can either one be the other, or is there any calling, trade, or profession that can be both? There is a deal of confusion just now in the public mind upon this point. There are those interested in the educative side of business, and those interested in the business side of education, who do say that business and education are one and the same thing.

Education vs. Business

Last year I received a neat circular from a business house of world-wide fame, in which the "Idea" of the firm was tersely set forth in a paragraph as follows: "To do the right thing at the right time, in the right way; to do some things better than they were ever done before; to eliminate errors; to know both sides of a question; to be courteous; to be an example; to work for the love of work; to anticipate requirements; to develop resources; to recognize no impediments; to master circumstances; to act from reason rather than from rule; to be satisfied with nothing short of perfection."

A Business House's Idea

I read this paragraph one day to the entire school, carefully explaining the big words, so that the younger pupils could understand them; and then I asked them to make a guess as to what kind of institution it was. They said it must be a very fine school. I then read further: "It is the purpose of the house to develop its organization of employees to be thinking men and women, capable of taking more and more responsibility, and each year becoming a greater credit to themselves and the house. To this end the rules . . . . are made with a view to utilizing as far as possible the individual judgment . . . . on a given piece of business rather than casting all his actions in one mold by making regulations which arbitrarily undertake to govern the minute details of his work. This business is noted for the enthusiasm, harmony, and effectiveness of its

The Children Are Deceived

organization." The children then said that it must be even a better school than they had thought it was in the first place.

A Model Factory

In another part of the country there is a great manufacturing concern, of equally wide renown, that has closely incorporated in its organization many things that are usually supposed to belong to the educational field in the departments of æsthetics, ethics, sociology, and political economy. These have been worked up into such a perfect blend with commercialism that it requires an expert to find out where education leaves off and business begins. Most people cannot discover any dividing line whatever. The firm itself talks as much about education as it does about business, and it claims it is the best of business policy to do so. The claim is made, also, that every educational feature that is developed adds materially to the percentage of profits. The theory underlying all this is very simple, and its soundness cannot be questioned: The better conditioned—body and soul—the employee is, the better the financial returns for the employer must be. The theory has led in practice to an excellence of physical, moral, and social conditions of workmen that is probably unequaled in industrial history. The buildings are sanitary and beautiful; the grounds rival in landscape effects the finest city parks, and the factories from almost every window command vistas of country scenery. The homes of the employees, elsewhere usually dreary and forbidding, are embowered in vines and flowers; schools, playgrounds, gymnasia, and gardens furnish recreation and lucrative employment for young and old when not otherwise engaged. Few schools approach the artistic taste displayed by this firm in its circular issued solely for the purpose of setting forth the educative side of the industry—yet this is all for the sake of business, because it actually pays.

The splendid organization on the business side that is maintained by these two firms may well be an example for educational institutions. There is hardly a school in existence that would not be immensely improved by just such sanity in business control. It is the lack here, as much as anything else, that tends to draw pupils at too early an age from school and to start them into business life.

Within the past decade the school apparently has been steadily assuming the character of the business house and the factory.

Business Practice and Educational Theory

Hitherto the relation of School to Business has been considered as that of Theory to Practice. But now, by the introduction of the arts and crafts, the School appears to be intimately incorporating within itself all the essentials of business Practice, while Business, likewise, is equally earnest in trying to adapt itself to educational Theory. These resemblances of each to the other are daily growing, and there is a cheerful optimism that predicts a not distant day when Business and Education shall be as one.

With no intent to dash these hopes—indeed, with full faith as to their final realization—it is important to observe that before

Selection of Employees

this union can be effected, it will be necessary for the business Leopard to change two or three of his spots. In a third paragraph of the circular already referred to occurs this statement: "Every applicant [for a position] receives careful consideration." A member of the firm in the factory described says that in the selection of employees there is no sentiment whatever; that it is simply a cold business proposition; if an employee proves himself incompetent in any way—mechanically, physically, morally, or socially—he is at once dropped.

People will generally agree, it is presumed, that this sounds like "good business," and for that reason I wish to contrast these

Admission of Pupils

statements with one that is made in letters big enough to be read half a mile away, and which is swung out across the street in front of the great school founded by the late Dr. Barnardo in Stepney Causeway, East London: ANY DESTITUTE PERSON, WITHOUT REGARD TO RACE, COLOR, CREED, OR CONDITION, IS ADMITTED AT ANY HOUR, DAY OR NIGHT. Here is an educational institution that seems by its "admission requirements" to be fundamentally different from a well-regulated business concern, and yet it is thoroughly industrial in its character. I noted the following occupations among the pupils: shoe-making, bristle-brush-making, mat-making, black-smithing, tin-working, printing, tailoring, baking, and carpentering. The business management of this institution, caring wisely for its thousands of inmates, would probably rival that found in either of the commercial enterprises already described, yet Business as we know it can claim no blood-relationship with such a school.

The Ninety-nine in Business

There is no *business* on earth today that dares to adopt Dr. Barnardo's "Admission Requirements"! And there is no *school* on earth today *that dares to adopt any other!!* There is the difference in a nutshell. It is the old question of the ninety-nine sheep that graze and gambol on the open hillside, and the hundredth lambkin sick and enfeebled which strays away perishing with cold and hunger. Business is mightily interested in the ninety-nine; it cares nothing for the hundredth—that does not pay! Graham Taylor tells this story: Seated in his room one day at work, he was annoyed by some boys who were playing on a vacant lot near by. Calling to them, he asked them to go away, whereupon one replied: "Say, Mister, if you make us leave here, we ain't got no ground to stand up on." Business can pick and choose; it can exclude the ineligible, the unfaithful, the unfortunate, and the incompetent. But these are they of all others that the schools dare not drop—else where will they find ground to "stand up on"?

The Difference in Ideals

The reason why Education at this time cannot make common cause with Business is that the IDEALS of the two are fundamentally different. The former is founded upon consideration for others, with fairness, justice, and equality for all; the latter is rooted in selfishness, upon which it feeds voraciously, and which it never ceases to engender even while wearing its most alluring and deceptive disguise of philanthrophy. Business is inherently selfish because its success is measured by the amount it "pays" in terms of the dollar. The dollar is the god that controls. When business therefore undertakes to care for its employees, it is only because, in its modern shrewdness, it is taking advantage of far-sighted methods and of more refined means of adding additional dollars to its till. While it is, on the one hand, pampering and "educating" its employees, on the other, it is practicing without compunction all the cut-throat schemes that human wit can devise to the end that competition may be destroyed—simply because a competitor interposes an obstacle between itself and the dollar it must have.

School not Fitting for Business

It follows, therefore, that in school we are not training the children for business—not in the University Elementary School, at least. They are being taught to take into thoughtful account the rights and privileges of others; how they may forego some of the advantages to personal self that others may have enlarged opportunity. They are taught how to work with their hands, to be industrious and useful, and how to live in harmony together. Business training would require that we add to these a study of the arts by which each can destroy the other. It is necessarily true, then, that when these young people step out into active life all the ideals that we have tried to engender will collapse at once into a moral scrap-heap, or else a new type of business will be inaugurated. It will be a type of business that must and will pay, but whose payment will not always be exacted in terms of the dollar alone.

New Business Era

There is good reason to hope for the dawn of a business era with higher ideals, because the business man of today is not altogether happy. His selfish methods of greed and plunder now come in for a measure of criticism and condemnation that is entirely new. Hence, he comes once more with the inquiry: "What shall I do to be saved?" And the answer to this through all the centuries has remained the same: *Sell all thou hast*—that is, the almighty dollar as an ideal must be given up! When the business man can see his way clear to do this; when he has studied out ways by which it can be made to pay to take the weak and inefficient into account; when he can see how it pays to keep in his employ the man who has but one talent as well as the one who has ten; when he can treat his brother in business with the same kindly toleration and consideration that we seek to have our pupils show to each other in school, then, and not till then, will it be worth while for him to consider the possibility of uniting education with business.

Money-changers in the Temple

It is not the first time in history that the money-changers have tried to become respectable by transferring their operations to the temple. So it is today; by encouraging in the schools all the mechanics of trade; by adopting in its phraseology the sounding terms of educational philosophy, Business is making a strenuous effort to become most exemplary and respectable. The schools, too, are equally assiduous in their efforts to become business-like. They are taking on the garb of industry and seeking to don the working apparel of the Practical. And, by these false appearances, as ever before, many people are being beguiled. It remains for the teacher today, as it was for a Teacher nineteen hundred years ago, to keep the ideals of the race clearly defined, and to see that the vision of the people remains clarified.

W. S. J.

A Unique Memorial

We are familiar with the memorial which takes the form of some beautiful object—the stained-glass window, the statue, or the picture; and we are also gladdened by the less æsthetic but more practical reminders seen in the endowment of hospital beds and rooms. But surely no more beautiful, more fitting, or more living memorial has ever been planned than the one designed to keep green the memory of a man who did much to put children in touch with the meaning of nature in its various forms. The Alpheus Hyatt Memorial Fund was created to aid in carrying out a cherished idea of the eminent naturalist. Mr. Hyatt was well known as curator of the Museum of Natural History in Boston, and as founder of the Teachers' School of Science. He labored untiringly for the advancement of science and of scientific methods in the public schools, and at the same time made a reputation by his original contributions to the body of knowledge.

Field-Work for City Children

The purpose of the fund is to make it possible for the children of the public schools of Boston to study nature first hand and out of doors. It meets partially that obstacle to out-of-door work, the expense of travel. The distribution of the money is in charge of Superintendent Seaver, and goes, of course, to those schools in which car fare is a large item to the pupils. As to the necessity for such trips, one needs only to consult a teacher who has taken them to be assured of the demand for them. Nature-study as it is seen in dislocated scraps drawn from articles taken out of their setting is a meager substitute for the nature-study to be gained in connection with these same things after they have once been seen in their setting. One good field trip will furnish nutriment for many days of study concerning things seen and processes noted. Here is a suggestive quotation from the letter of a fourth-grade philosopher:

> Some of our most interesting geography lessons were out of doors. I like them because they teach us to look at things and to learn about the world. Some of the things I saw were the ducks and the birds and the soil. It is better to study things outside than inside, because *inside you can only talk about it* and *outside you can see the things.* Next year I hope we will study more outdoors. We also saw the trees and bowlders and the plants.

Here is an extract from a letter written by one of the teachers that gives a picture of one class of children enjoying their outing and getting their fill of new experiences:

> Winthrop School, Tremont Street,
> November 25, 1903.
>
> Dear Sir: On one of the Jewish holidays in June I took those present, who numbered about thirty-five, to Revere Beach. I selected this day because less than half my class were present, and I could do much better work with a few. Moreover, there were so many unable to pay their car fares that I wanted to leave some of the fund for the other teachers. Some declared their mothers went to work, an hence no lunch could be obtained. This was especially true in the cases of the Syrian girls, whose mothers go out peddling. In these instances I supplied both. The car fares I took from the fund, but I paid for the lunches myself. I asked all those who could bring their own money to do so, and about three-fifths responded, though I knew that many of these could little afford to. My children come from the poorer classes, and are mostly all foreigners. A car ride was to them a novelty. When they saw the beach and the waves rolling in, they were beside themselves with joy and amazement.

We walked along the beach and noted the sand and farther up the rocks. They saw the tide when it was out, and then, to their great astonishment, saw it come in. They did not seem to realize that it would come back after receding so far. All my talking and explanation was done in very simple language, and those who understood interpreted for the others. They gathered pretty shells and stones, and took them home to their less fortunate sisters and brothers.

It was a gala day for all, and they could not tell me enough about it next day. I resolved, after seeing how much good I could do by taking them off on these trips, to do so again as soon as possible.

Our next field trip was to Franklin Park. I managed about the car fares and lunches as heretofore. The girls enjoyed this outing even more than that to the beach, if such be possible. The sight of the green grass on which they could roll and tumble at will filled them with ecstacy. When we reached the playground and I told them they might run on the grass, their joy knew no bounds.

We told them the names of a few trees. They picked acorns, and were delighted when we told them what would happen if we planted one. Many of the Italian girls brought home their handkerchiefs and aprons full of acorns to eat. We went to the duck pond to see the fowl, and here another treat was accorded them. On the way to the pond we climbed a hill, and the girls were questioned about it; some of them knew the name of the hill before.

We could not miss seeing the sheep, and, tired though the girls were, they insisted on going to Franklin Field.

What a tired party we were when we boarded the car at three forty-five — tired but unutterably happy! This little outing meant far more to them than any week's teaching could have done. It has gone down in their school annals as one of the happiest days ever spent. I only trust and hope that next year more money will be available so that we can take more trips, and more girls too.

Fund an Object Lesson

What has been begun by the organizers of this fund furnishes an admirable suggestion for active workers in any urban community. A generation of city teachers will rise up and call that one blessed who will hold up their hands in an endeavor to bring the children into contact with nutritious material for imagination and reason to feed upon. Wherever there are farms, with the fundamental economic problems therein suggested, there is an objective point for an excursion. Wherever there is running water, there will be problems in physiography and in physics. There is not a lake beach that does not present some opportunity for seeing the changes consequent upon wave-action. There is, indeed, no city which has not an adjacent countryside fertile in material for school children's study. A quotation from another letter illustrates the use made of physiographic material. This class went to Winthrop Beach:

> From here may be seen land forms, such as Deer Island, Point Shirley, the narrow isthmus connecting it with Winthrop, the Blue Hills in the distance, etc.; water forms, such as the Atlantic Ocean, Boston Harbor, Shirley Gut, an example of a strait. . . . . The horizon line is clearly seen, and, perchance, there may be vessels to show us one proof of the earth's rotundity.
>
> Then we clambered down the steep slope of the cliff to the beach. . . . . Under the cliff is a fairly good place to study wave-action. At low tide the finer material may be seen washed far out, while the coarsest remains at the foot of the hill.
>
> Sometimes there are very nice examples of deltas and river systems to be seen in the sand. . . . . On these excursions I believe that pupils should observe the trees, flowers, and birds all in the same lesson, in connection with the geography work, as these trips are necessarily few.

The fund cannot begin to cover the cases in which trips are needed and money scanty, and the trustees are devising ways of increasing its effectiveness.

B. P.

Spading and Hoeing Contests

The boys and girls who have had gardens during the past year at the School of Horticulture, Hartford, Conn., held a miniature agricultural fair on the afternoon of September 4. During the afternoon they had a spading and hoeing contest, and prizes were awarded to those who handled the tools and accomplished the required amount of work in the best manner and shortest time.

These gardens are among the most systematically conducted school gardens in the United States, and the gardeners receive instruction all through the summer. They are taught that the weeds are the enemies of the crop, and they learn to identify them from the crop. Because of this fact, one boy, whom Director Hemenway recommended to take charge of a garden in the city, proved himself so much more valuable than the ordinary workman whom the woman had been hiring, that he had an opportunity to work all his spare time, and placed in the savings bank to his credit over fifty dollars at the end of the season.

The work that the boys have done is giving the school a good name, and more persons have applied for boys than the school is able to supply. Two or three permanent positions are open to boys who have had garden work, and several teachers have received positions during the last year, upon being recommended from the school, to teach school gardening in other parts of the country.

The exhibit was probably of interest not only to every educator and teacher, but also to the farmers of the community, for there were many new forage crops growing, and eight plots showed the effect of the nitrogen-forming bacteria upon leguminous plants.

B. P.

NUTTING SONG [1]

CLINTON SCOLLARD — ELEANOR SMITH

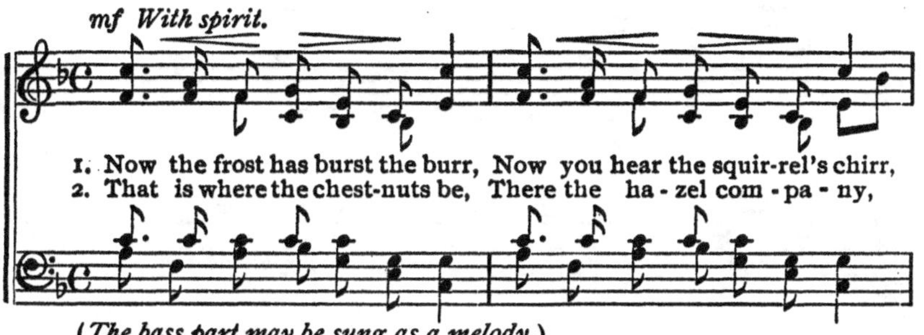

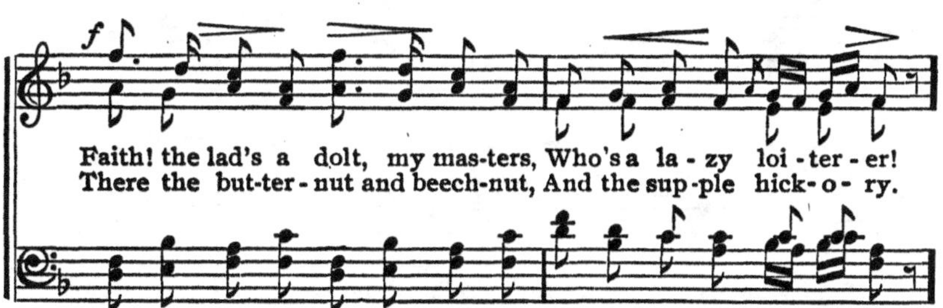

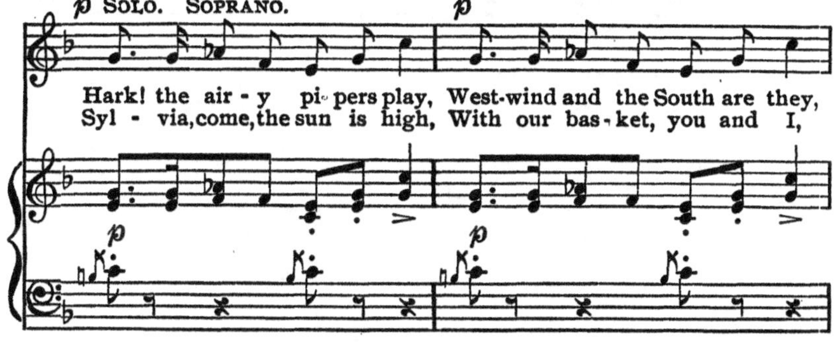

[1] From *The High School of Vocal Music* (Silver, Burdette & Co.).

Hear the tru-ant twain a-pip-ing "O'er the hills and far a-way!"
Shall we not the quest ad-ven-ture? Shall we not our for-tune try?
CHORUS.
Now the frost has burst the burr, Now you hear the squir-rel's whirr,
f
Poco rit.
Faith! the lad's a dolt, my mas-ters, Who's a la-zy loi-ter-er!

VOLUME VI NUMBER 5

THE ELEMENTARY SCHOOL TEACHER

JANUARY, 1906

L'ECOLE DES ROCHES

EDMOND DEMOLINS
Director

I. HISTORICAL

L'Ecole des Roches (literally, The School of the Rocks, from its nearness to a rocky cliff,) has been organized to answer the expressed wishes of a great number of heads of families little satisfied with the actual methods of education and instruction in French secondary schools. The program of the new school was set forth in November, 1898, in a volume styled *The New Education; The School of The Rocks*. The success of this volume prepared the way for the rapid success of the school. In fact, in January, 1899, the first pupils registered went to take a course of study in England or Germany, while awaiting the opening of the school. After Easter a second group of twenty pupils went to join the first. At the beginning of October of the same year L'Ecole des Roches, with fifty pupils, was opened in the House of Vallon, a building rapidly constructed. The school is situated in the domain of Roches, near Verneuil, Normandy; it is on the main road which leads from Paris to Granville, two hours from Paris. This domain, the extent of which is actually fifty acres, included at that time the Chateau of Roches, large commons, woods, prairies, and cultivated grounds.

The demands for admission being greatly increased, it was necessary to construct immediately a new house, that of the Pines. The opening of the House of the Pines took place at the beginning of October, 1900, one year after that of Vallon. At that time the school accommodated one hundred pupils, divided between two houses, having a distinct administration. In the course of the same year, in response to still greater demands, it was necessary to open a new house, La Giuchardière; then, in the following year, two others, Le Coteau and Les Tablans.

These five houses are grouped around a special building destined for the use of classes, and where there are also the chapel and the large assembly hall of the school. There are two isolated houses designed for infirmaries, and others for the machinery, electricity, carpentry, drawing, polishing shop, chemistry, laboratory, etc.

In bringing to this institution not only their moral but financial help, the founders of L'Ecole des Roches have given a great example, in that they have shown the power of private initiative. The development of the school was made by the construction of distinct houses around the central school building, and not by the enlargement of the houses. From now on, whatever may be the number of pupils in the future, we shall always avoid the danger of congestion. Every dwelling-house possesses a large measure of autonomy, being presided over by a principal, assisted by a lady and by several other professors. There the children take their meals, sleep, and have their study classes. It is truly a home, from which the children are sent to a day school situated in the vicinity.

This type of school avoids at the same time the inconveniences of the boarding-school and those of the day school. It avoids the confinement and the strict regulations of the boarding-school, because the children live in small numbers in the home of a professor. It avoids the carelessness, the loss of time, the crossing of the tracks, and the unhealthy sojourn in the city which the day school necessitates. This kind of school will find favor in France, and will be successful by its educational virtues. Its influence was first manifested by the volume *The New Education*. After the great parliamentary inquiry upon scholastic reform, the Educational Commission directed by M. Ribot, the eminent statesman, asked for some of the modifications which are now realized in Roches. Our school has had only four years of existence, and, thanks to the irresistible force of example, it has compelled the university to try certain improvements modeled after our program and our methods.

To remain at the head of the movement which we have so happily inaugurated, we must continually strive to improve our course of study, because this plan is our only reason for existence. One of the first improvements was found to be the study of science, not upon a theoretical presentation, as is the case everywhere in France, but upon practical work in the laboratory, begun in the lower classes and continuing throughout the school. It is only by this means that one can impart at the same time a taste for, and a serious knowledge of, science. The usefulness of this method of instruction will be understood if one considers that science has an increasing importance, not only in examinations, but in the daily life. A young man whose scientific knowledge is not only theoretical, but practical, will be the more needed and better remunerated since all our French schools produce exclusively theoretical men.

We have, besides, perfected our methods in physical culture and general hygiene, being inspired by the progress made in certain countries of Europe, especially in the schools of Sweden. This struggle must be undertaken methodically, and with all the resources of a better science of living.

II. THE GENERAL LIFE OF THE SCHOOL

Before speaking of the general life of L'Ecole des Roches, it seems desirable to give to our American readers a view of the type of the high-school teacher against whom our school protests. He lives with his family away from school; he comes only to attend the class; he takes his chair and lectures from there; and when the bell has rung that announces the end of the class, he leaves his chair and hurries to his home in the city. If the professor is a churchman, he hastens to his room. During the class-hour the professor has in front of him, at a considerable distance, an assembly of children. He has not, he cannot have, personal communication with them. The actual system creates no communication between the teacher and the pupils.

The monitors have more communication with the pupils, but generally of a disagreeable nature. These monitors are lodged at the school, it is true, but their permanent presence has for its excuse the need of continual watching. In fact, when so large a number of children are left to themselves by the absence of the teacher, it is necessary to inspire them with fear and to use punishments in order to secure obedience. The monitor is charged with this necessary but unenviable rôle. He has no serious authority over the children; he does not teach them; he has only the power to punish them.

Thus abandoned by his two educators, the pupil takes refuge in himself, and has no other resource than to turn toward his classmates. He finds an education in the invention of a thousand tricks by means of which he can outwit the vigilant monitor and rid himself of oppression. Naturally the prestige among the pupils goes to those who are more stubborn in resistance to authority; to those who are more skilful than others in running away from the guards, and in the invention of tricks. In the end authority rules and the pupils suffer. To re-establish the equilibrium of the situation, they take refuge in dissimulation and lying. This outcome is precisely the result of the scholastic régime all over France, and this is one of the reasons why the French school does not make men, because a man must never lie. Lying is not only a low vice, it is a proof that one is feeble and timid. A pedagogical system which inculcates the habit of dissimilution is condemned without any possible appeal.

In L'Ecole des Roches one meets neither such a professor nor such a monitor. Their functions exist, but in a type which is very different. Our teachers make their homes at the school, and take their meals together with the pupils in the common dining-room, where every table has ten pupils presided over by a teacher. In fact, if the professor is married, his wife has a function in the school, be it as a teacher or as domestic administrator. These teachers live from morning to evening with the pupils, not to watch them, but to educate them. They take a part in all their exercises—not only class exercises, but also games.

This long-continued contact between teachers and pupils has for its first effect the establishment between them of relations which much resemble those of a father toward his children — a father, who would take part equally in their studies, in their plays, in their everyday life. In this way is obviated the isolation of the child who has no other resource than the society of his comrades. The school, consequently, gives the impression of a real and complete life.

The character of the school is partly shaped by the presence of women teachers. It is believed that to attempt to educate a child without the presence and care of a woman is absurd. The presence of a woman is conducive to better manners. She introduces social habits into the school, and keeps the pupils away from mischief; and the young boy so educated is prepared to meet properly the feminine element in society after leaving school.

I must mention, in this connection, the moral influence of physical exercise and outdoor life. In our French scholastic system we try to lessen moral evils by moral and religious advice, whose effect is unfortunately lowered by the rigorous life to which the children are subjected, and by the supposition that they always do wrong. The best moral adviser is an active life, which creates an energetic disposition by wholesome physical fatigue during the day, and by a more profound sleep during the night. The manual training and the games, which exercise all parts of the body, the daily cold showers, and the frequent baths have a fine moral effect. By these means, and still more by appointing captains from among the oldest pupils, the teacher's task is made easier.

The school is, in fact, given to the care of the pupils; it is their task; they are responsible for its order and its cleanliness. The confidence and respect shown them develop self-respect and self-confidence. I do not think that there exist any more efficient means to build up men.

It is to reach this result that the teachers are in such continual contact with the children. For this reason also the older pupils are given some control over the younger ones, that they may influence them for good. The authority thus delegated creates a state of mind which stimulates everyone to advance himself rapidly. Even the smallest details are so arranged as to give to even the youngest of the children the sentiment that they are men. Thus the children never have that falsely humble attitude toward their teachers which exists so commonly in our country. To tell the truth, this latter is a necessity of our ordinary system of education, because we cannot maintain an unnatural régime among hundreds of children by simply displaying the flag of authority and suppressing every desire for independence. "Your son is humble and obedient"—this is the best praise which a French teacher can give to a pupil. Our ambition is to make strong boys, independent in character, and masters of themselves—boys capable of standing the hardships of life, and even of outgrowing them.

III. THE PROGRAM OF STUDY

The fullest details of our program of study are set forth in the volume, *The New Education.* We limit ourselves to giving here some general indications: In the classical instruction, Latin and Greek occupy most of the time of the children, while they neglect other and more important studies. In spite of that, the pupils know neither Latin nor Greek. Jules Lemaitre has said: "A master of arts is a brave young man, who knows neither Latin nor Greek, and who, in turn, does not know any better the living languages, nor geography, nor the natural sciences. He is a monster, a marvel of nothing." We have adopted for the study of ancient languages the most practical and rapid methods used for the study of living languages. The pupil prepares the text by the aid of a translation, and he explains it afterward in the schoolroom without the help of a dictionary. He can, therefore, prepare by this means several pages from the text, instead of some lines only. He thus memorizes many more words and phrases, which is the most essential point. When a pupil has read and understood—which, of course, is easy with a translation book—ten or twelve volumes of Latin, he will know Latin. The rules of syntax are disclosed here and there, as they need to be applied in the explanation of texts, thus facilitating the study of grammar.

This method is more rational, more practical, and at the same time more rapid. We begin the study of Latin in the fourth year — that is to say, when the child is able to progress rapidly in a study which needs reflection. This program has an advantage which will be appreciated by all parents. The child who enters the sixth grade knows absolutely nothing about the profession he will take up, and his parents do not know his tastes and his abilities. Nevertheless, when the child is only eight or nine years old, it must be decided whether he is to take the classic or the modern course. The future of the child is at stake, as in this way certain careers are closed to him forever. This is a matter of grave responsibility for the heads of families, and to it much thought is given. For the children it is a terrible limitation. On the contrary, if these decisions are postponed until the child is in the fourth grade, the parents can decide more intelligently, because they know the tastes and the abilities of the children which have then begun to manifest themselves clearly.

The time gained from Latin leaves about twenty study hours every week up to the fifth grade; in other words, about half of the time of the pupil. This time is used for French, for modern languages, for mathematics, geology, botany, zoölogy, physics, and chemistry, which are more or less neglected in the present system of instruction, in spite of their great and incontestable importance. For the living languages we have adopted the most efficacious method: All our pupils go to spend three months, six months, or a year in England or in Germany, in our corresponding schools. These sojourns are made between the fourth and the eighth grades, thanks to the time saved from Latin during this period. In four years we have sent to England and Germany about one hundred and seventy pupils, who stayed from three months to a year. When they come back, they understand and speak English and German. The study of the languages is facilitated by use. During the meals the pupils are distributed at tables, where either English or German is spoken. It is in this way that both these languages are used at the school.

A bachelor of arts often knows absolutely nothing about geology, botany, and zoölogy; his knowledge of the most common plants is so meager as to be absurd. Of physics and chemistry he knows little. He has only the first notions, acquired in haste usually a day before the examination, during the year devoted to philosophy. He ignores nature in its different and splendid manifestations. The world is for him as if it were not. This lack is so much the more unfortunate because the children, even the youngest, take an extraordinary interest in these studies, when they are taught practically and with intelligence.

The study of natural science in L'Ecole des Roches has for its starting-point direct observation. This is easy of achievement, as the school is situated in the country and the children can gather a great number of species from the mineral, animal, and vegetable kingdoms. Besides, the life, habits, and external parts of an animal are studied before the internal organs and the skeleton; the forms and construction of the plants, before their classification; the names and appearance of the stars and planets, before the laws of their movements. The afternoon excursions furnish opportunity for observation, and for gathering plants or insects, which are afterward carefully disposed and classified by the pupils themselves. Science becomes more natural, more comprehensible, more attractive, is better retained in memory, and is better assimilated. This study does not leave the distaste that often results from our exclusive methods. It gives the desire to extend one's knowledge, even after leaving college, thanks to the very lively interest awakened by actual contact and experiment.

These studies are valuable to the children from other points of view. The out-of-door exercise, under the stimulus of an adequate motive, and the gathering together in groups, are equally important features of the science lessons. To raise children between four walls, and under a rigorous régime that would be unhealthy even for old men, is a ridiculous and absurd proceeding, against which public indignation must be roused. Therefore the program of the school accords to natural science, physics, and chemistry about five hours per week in the lower classes, without counting the hours given to the same studies in the laboratory or during the excursions. Thanks to the time taken from that usually given to the ancient languages, we could go ahead with

French, the sciences, and the spoken languages from the fourth to the seventh grade. The children who begin their studies at Roches arrive at the fourth grade in less than a year, and in these studies are ahead of the pupils of other schools. We have been aided, in our desire to strengthen the classical studies, by the sympathetic help which we have received from the most eminent representatives of the university. They have allowed us to recruit from the faculty of the university professors who are willing to co-operate with us in our attempts at pedagogic reform.

IV. PRACTICAL WORK AND SPORTS

The several studies which we have just enumerated take up the whole morning and a part of the afternoon. The second part of the afternoon, from two to four o'clock, is devoted to practical work which is the direct outcome of the theoretical work, the plays, and the physical exercise. The pupil must not learn merely from books; he has much more to study than books. The instruction must not be only theoretical, it must be at the same time practical. Moreover, the child cannot be locked up the larger part of the day; he must have fresh air and exercise for his development. The children derive, indeed, much pleasure from this work, and acquire a great variety of knowledge; their intelligence is awakened, developed, and trained; it becomes more comprehensive.

The practical work contains several divisions.

1. *Gardening.*— Every well-informed man must know at least the elementary facts concerning the life-histories of plants and domestic animals. This is necessary for him not only in the event of his being occupied later with some such rural enterprise as the supervision of work on an agricultural estate, but these accomplishments are useful even to those who take up the liberal professions. Our bachelors of arts are indeed too ignorant about the most elementary things of rural life, as we often have occasion to observe when they are compelled to write or to speak on this subject. The politician and the clergyman must also have some acquaintance with the great agricultural interests which they compromise so often on account of an inexcusable ignorance.

L'Ecole des Roches, installed in the middle of a domain of about fifty acres, contains different grounds and various plantations, and is admirably located for the purpose of teaching the children the work of gardening and cultivation.

2. *The wood- and iron-work.*—This work, of course, does not aim to make carpenters or blacksmiths, but to develop in the child ability, and a skilful hand, so that he can in every contingency, no matter on what occasion or for what purpose, make use of this marvelous instrument, the hand. It goes without saying that this is an essentially healthful exercise, which strengthens the child, because it demands a certain expenditure of physical power. Much more, the resistance that these substances oppose develops in the child the habit of patience and perseverance in the work undertaken. Finally, the wood and iron, which are the most common materials employed by the people for general uses, can be modeled to different forms, thus devloping taste and the artistic powers.

A large shed is devoted to the woodwork. The pupils have at their disposal sixteen benches. They work under the direction of a professor who is a specialist, and of a carpenter of the school. The iron-work is taught in a foundry situated in the neighborhood of the school, under the direction of an engineer of arts and manufactures, who teaches also mechanics, physics, and chemistry. Thus this instruction is at the same time theoretical and practical.

3. *Visiting of farms and factories; collection of minerals, plants, and animals; land-surveying; treating of plans; etc.*—This kind of instruction has great importance, for it puts the child in direct contact with the different industries of real life. The regions about L'Ecole des Roches is well suited for this purpose, because it is at the same time agricultural and industrial. In regard to industrial visits our region is particularly favored.

Factories are established on the majority of the streams; several in line on the open field, using hydraulic and steam-power. One can therefore make varied observations from the mechanical point of view. The observations are not less varied from the point of view of manufacturers, or output. On a single river, the Stan, one arm of which encircles the neighboring village of Verneuil, we find the following: four sawmills, two forges, three tanyards, a brass and copper foundry, metal-plating works, two wire-drawing mills, a nail-forge, four hardware factories, two pin factories, one for the making of fine tools, a buckle factory, a sauce-pan factory, four construction workshops, several iron-polishers, five cleaning-places, two spinning-mills, a felt factory, eight fulers, a dye factory, a paper factory, a mustard factory, three elevators, and an electrical workshop. It is seen that this region contains a great variety of factories, which are so many object-lessons for the pupils.

By visiting methodically some of these workshops, the children can follow the successive transformations which the mineral, vegetable, and animal products undergo. Is there a study more necessary, more instructive, and more capable of interesting even the younger children? What they learn in this way they will never forget, and this experience reveals tastes and powers in the children which, without it, would remain poor or would be stifled. The children profit by these excursions across the fields, by collecting minerals, plants, or animals. These collections, arranged in order by each pupil, supplement in the most practical way the lessons in geology, botany, and natural science. Surveying and the execution of plans supplement similarly the lessons in arithmetic, geometry, and drawing. The principles thus carried out become a part of their lives, and help them to understand better what usefulness means.

We have organized two workshops, the polishing and modelling, in which the children take great interest. With the practical work is alternated physical exercises, especially football and the different winter sports. In summer the children play cricket and tennis, ride their bicycles, and row. The river Stan, which runs in the vicinity of the school, can be crossed without danger by small boats. The exercise of rowing, which develops the arms and the chest, supplements the exercises which develop the limbs. The small fleet of the school is just as necessary a part of the plan as it is a pleasant addition. Thus the various studies have for effect the giving of wings to all the faculties of the mind; and the great variety of physical exercises have for their aim to develop all parts of the body. A well-thought-out plan of education must neglect neither the mind nor the body. We must sacrifice neither the body to the mind nor the mind to the body, but must establish between the two a just and fair equilibrium. The school must develop breadth of intelligence and breadth of chest at the same time.

A part of the evenings is devoted to musical and literary meetings, and to social recreation. We wish to make social men—men efficient in the world. We want to differentiate them from the sad and awkward collegian. The young men must be neither awkward nor timid, but able to adapt themselves to the society of older people without shyness and with real enjoyment. They gather often in the parlor, where they meet the ladies of the school, and strangers who come to visit us. These evenings are devoted to the reading of selected pieces, to recitations or dramatic representations, to wood-carving or modeling, to dancing, or to lectures with stereopticon views. On Sundays the pupils attend religious services, or a moral lecture. We do not present religion to the children as if it were apart from life, but like an organic and harmonious whole, which must penetrate the individual entirely and direct all his actions. The school tries to help effectively, and to continue the teachings of, the minister, to whom the children are confided for their religious instruction. There are in the school both a Catholic priest and a Protestant pastor.

V. PROGRAM

6:00 Rising, bath, dressing, prayer.
6:25 Study.
7:25 First breakfast, very substantial.
7:40 Free time; the pupils make their beds.
8:00 First class.
9:05 Second class.
10:05 Free time.
10:20 Third class.
11:20 Fourth class.
11:30 Lunch.
1:00 Free time.

2:00 Plays, football, or cricket, according to the season; laboratory; excursions in natural science; modeling, carpentry, gardening, or music, according to the classes and the days.
3:00 In the cloakroom.
4:00 Tea.
4:30 Study or class.
7:00 Dinner.
7:30 Free time.
8:00 Study.
8:45 Prayer, and bed-time.

VI. THE STAY IN FOREIGN COUNTRIES

The visits of our pupils to England and Germany are one of the greatest successes of the school. The results are indeed better than we had expected. The children make these stays from the beginning of their school-life. Thanks to these methods, they begin to speak a foreign language after three or six months. Most of the children who are now at the school have already made a stay in a foreign country. This enables them to succeed in speaking English and German. When we inaugurated these stays at the beginning of the school, we were afraid to meet resistance on the part of the parents, especially of the mothers. Today we have won the case. Sometimes it is necessary to moderate the ardor of the parents, who are disposed to prolong the stays of the children beyond the necessary time. The most of the children leave between the ages of eight and ten years. This is the most favorable age. At this age the child learns the languages best and most rapidly, and obtains this important result without any serious neglect of his other studies. We could appreciate the results obtained, if we were to read in the *New Education* the extracts which were addressed to us by parents or children.

VII. PRACTICAL INFORMATION

1. *Situation of the school.*—The school is situated in a region of level land, having an altitude of fifty meters, which gives it particularly favorable conditions from the hygienic point of view. The buildings of the school are erected in the middle of a property of fifty acres, composed of a park, prairies, cultivated grounds, and fir woods. The school has the best improvements and the best

hygienic conditions. A system of steam circulation, with a low pressure, has been adopted for heating the buildings. Electric lighting is used. The electric force is produced in an annex building, and kept in accumulators; it moves also the water-pumps and the various accessories of the washhouse. The school is in itself a real workshop of scientific demonstrations—all the more because all these installations are made by a teacher of the school, the engineer of arts and manufactures, detailed to teach mechanics, physics, and chemistry. The school is in direct communication with the different parts of France by telephone and telegraph. The station at Verneuil is a junction reached by four lines of railroad.

2. *Object of the school.*—The school has for its object to educate men as rapidly as possible, from the moral, intellectual, and physical points of view. It endeavors to develop the love for work, which is made more successful and more attractive; the sentiment of responsibility, of respect, self-control, and the habit of energy. We wish to create good-will, and sound bodies and souls. This school is a classical and modern institution, but having a new course of study adapted to the child's nature and to the necessities of instruction. This course of study permits the pupils to prepare for the bachelor's degree, for entrance into different schools, or to take up directly agriculture, colonization, industry, or commerce.

3. *The division of the school year.*—The school year is divided into three terms, each of three months. Pupils are admitted at the beginning of each term. The year has three vacations: Christmas and Easter, about three weeks each; and in August and September, two months. Weekly and monthly vacations are not allowed. This division in three periods, with the suppression of the weekly and monthly vacations, gives real advantages. On the one hand, they do not interrupt school-life very frequently; on the other, these longer stays at home separate less completely the child from his family. He remains there long enough every time to receive an influence. Thus the family-life and the school-life remain associated, the more so as this type of school is really organized on the family plan.

THE DISCIPLINE-MASTER

JOHN ADAMS
London, England

Under the word "Discipline," in Dr. Murray's *New English Dictionary on Historical Principles,* we find the ninth heading running as follows: "*attrib.* as in discipline-master, a master in a school employed not to teach, but to keep order among the pupils." The first thing that strikes one on reading this paragraph is the definite limitation of the meaning of "discipline" to what may be called its objective aspect, the power of maintaining order in a class. Every teacher is aware that the word has another meaning, the subjective, in which it has to do with the training given to the mind by the various studies of the school curriculum. We talk of certain subjects as being of greater disciplinary value than others. Under this phrase lies a theory of very doubtful cogency. But apart from all theories there remains the broad difference between the two views of the meaning of "discipline."

The objective view is by far the more popular. When we talk of a teacher as being "a good disciplinarian," we attach a very definite meaning to the phrase, and distinguish sharply between the man's powers as a teacher and his powers of keeping order and controlling a class. The distinction, though clearly recognized so soon as attention is called to it, is very apt to be overlooked in ordinary life. In fact, in one very important connection it is almost invariably neglected. Wherever the problem of the training of teachers is discussed, the remark is sure to be made sooner or later: "The teacher is born, not made." If now the meaning of the saying is worked out, it will be found that the argument proceeds on the assumption that it is impossible for any training to supply the power of control. Some possess this power, it is maintained, and some lack it, and no amount of training can supply the want. Almost all the failures that come out of training colleges—and almost every class of students has one or two specimens—will be found to fail because of this defect. But it is worth noting that this applies only to the failures who are found out. For the experienced trainer of teachers knows full well that some of his students, who prove successful when judged by the rough and ready methods of the outside critic, are in reality very poor teachers. It is quite possible to be an excellent teacher, so far as the science and art of teaching are concerned, without being able to maintain order. For example, a student may give an admirable lesson to a class when the presence of the master of method and the other students in training, to say nothing of the official teacher of the class, renders it unnecessary to "maintain order." When such a teacher goes into the world and fails to control his class, he is said to be unable to teach; but clearly this is inaccurate. The question of his teaching has never been under discussion; he has never had the chance in school of showing whether he could teach or not; he never got the length of the teaching point. Critics of training are prepared at this stage to stop all further argument by the final statement that, since discipline is essential to the beginning of teaching, the lack of disciplinary power indicates incapacity for teaching. This argument is perfectly valid; as a practical criticism it is conclusive—unless there be found a place for the discipline-master.

Before examining the claims of the discipline-master, we must now turn to another fallacy that is so important as to justify the emphasis here laid on the distinction between teaching and maintaining discipline. Even if it be granted that without discipline there can be no teaching, it does not follow that because there is discipline there is teaching. There is a very common impression to the contrary. If a teacher is able to maintain excellent order in class, and secure instant obedience to all his orders, and is at the same time a fluent talker, it is generally believed that he is a good teacher. As a matter of fact, he has only mastered the conditions for the beginning of teaching. The power of maintaining discipline is only an essential preliminary to teaching; it is no part of teaching itself. It makes teaching possible; it prepares the way; but it is not teaching.

Is it, then, so distinct from teaching that it can be kept entirely separate from it? Can one person teach on the discipline maintained by another? The very existence of the discipline-master supplies an answer. The thing is possible; the thing has been done. But it does not follow either that the thing has been well done, or that it is ever worth doing. The natural action and reaction between the master-mind and the pupil-mind cannot be so free and direct when a third mind is always intervening. The energies of the pupils are dissipated because they are divided. The discipline-master produces a moral reaction at the same time that the subject-teacher is producing an intellectual reaction; and as a consequence there arises in the pupil a mild form of disorder known among pathological psychologists as double personality.

The problem of the place of the discipline-master in school is complicated by a confusion that is rather widely spread even among professional teachers — the confusion between teaching and education. It is too often assumed that because a man is a teacher he is therefore necessarily an educator. But it is only to a very limited extent that education is a necessary concomitant of teaching. It is true that no one can teach anything without at the same time to some degree educating; but the same is true about any of the processes in which human beings are brought into relation with each other. The writer of penny-dreadfuls, the manipulator of *Punch* and *Judy*, the woman in the truck-shop, are all educators more or less. It is only because the teacher usually sets himself out deliberately to influence the character of his pupils that he has come to be regarded as necessarily an educator.

If he is to be a real educator, the teacher must carry on the whole work of a lesson for himself. The real teacher, however, merely as teacher, must supply his own discipline, apart altogether from the higher educational aspects of the question. While teaching can never become a by-product of discipline, discipline may well become, and in many cases does become, a by-product of teaching. The teacher who knows the nature of his pupils, who knows the content of their minds, who presents his facts in the proper psychological order, who correlates the new facts to the facts already within the knowledge of his pupils, will certainly predispose those pupils to assume the attitude of mind that conduces to school discipline. There is a distinct gain through the unifying of all the forces at the disposal of the pupils, and the resulting teaching, merely as teaching even, is better than it would have been had it been superimposed on the discipline imposed by another will than that of the teacher.

But not only is the result better in the way of knowledge acquired by the pupil, but the effect in what is called "training" is much superior to that obtained under the joint influence of the teacher and the discipline-master. The mere imparting of facts is certainly instruction, but it is not in the best sense of the term educative instruction. Before mere teaching can arise to the level of education in the best sense of that term, there must arise that intellectual glow that accompanies the intimate interaction of mind upon mind. When this glow is present, discipline cannot be absent; it is a direct result of successful teaching. Real teaching includes discipline as the greater includes the less.

By admitting that the discipline that comes from successful teaching depends on the glow resulting from actual contact of mind with mind, it has been conceded that there is a personal quality without which discipline is impossible. A teacher may be able to express on paper in the most admirable way the course a lesson ought to follow, and yet in presence of a class may be quite unable to act according to his own directions. Accordingly, it has become fashionable to maintain that the power to maintain discipline is a natural gift that cannot be imparted to another, or indeed that cannot be greatly improved in the case of those who already possess it in some degree. Unless the teacher is born with this power, it is maintained that nothing will ever make him acquire it. So far as this statement is general, and means that none of our natural gifts can be improved as natural gifts, no objection need be raised. It may be cheerfully admitted that our inherited powers, capacities, possibilities—call them what you will—cannot be in themselves increased. It does not follow that they may not be applied with greater or less skill, and therefore with varying effect. The physiological basis of memory may be incapable of improvement, and yet the memory may be so used in relation to the material upon which it is exercised as to produce either good or bad results. An intrinsically bad memory may be so trained as to do better practical work than an intrinsically better memory that has had either a bad training or no training at all. So with the innate power of control. It may be impossible to impart such a power, or even to increase the intrinsic value of the power already possessed, and yet it may be possible so to regulate the use of the power possessed as to produce the best results possible under the given conditions.

Everything depends upon whether the original endowment is sufficiently good to warrant the expenditure of time and effort in training it. As with the other elements of original endowment, it is extremely rare to find a case where the power of control is quite lacking. It is the business of those who have to do with the probationary stages of young teachers to discover cases of abnormal lack of the power of control, and to weed out mercilessly all such cases. But it is quite possible by practice and training to increase the efficiency with which a moderate power of control can be applied in the work of an ordinary school. Increased familiarity with the subjects to be taught, and with the circumstances under which the teaching is to be carried on, greater knowledge of the nature of the pupils and their attainments, intelligent assimilation of the practical hints of experienced teachers, the observation of schoolroom devices of various kinds, the imitation of good examples set by skilful teachers — all these are quite powerless to affect the original endowment in the power of control, but are of the utmost value in enabling the young teacher to make the very most of that power. Perhaps the best test as to whether a young teacher has a sufficient amount of the power of control to warrant spending time on its cultivation, is to discover whether he can do without a discipline-master. A teacher who requires to be buttressed up in this way is by that very fact shown to be a professional failure. There is no longer any room for the discipline-master as a permanent member of the profession. Whatever may have been the case under the monitorial and other cheap systems, he has had his day, and must now cease to be.

GARDEN WORK

ELSA MILLER
Francis W. Parker School

The garden of the Francis W. Parker School occupies a plot of ground one hundred and twenty-seven by fifty feet, some fifty feet east of the building. The area is well adapted for the purpose, being open on all sides and shaded only at the southeast corner by some tall cottonwood trees.

Fortunately for the drainage of the plot, the subsoil consists of coarse sand and gravel, which was placed there when the excavation for the school building was made. Upon this foundation a heavy layer of properly fertilized loam was placed. Each succeeding year the garden has been plowed and fertilized. This has been the cause of one difficulty. The plowing excluded from our available plants all perennials. Each year the garden was planned anew without "an old year's brand to light the new." That deprived the gardeners of many experiences which are absolutely necessary in the growth of those who are to "love the green things growing."

According to the plan followed for the first three years, every grade planted a bed of some grain or vegetable for the common use of the school. A second bed was assigned to each grade, to be divided into individual plots. It is evident that under this plan the garden presented a motly appearance, since every child planted in his bed whatever he chose, irrespective of what was in his neighbor's bed. Sometimes several kinds of vegetables and flowers were planted in a bed two by three feet. Tall plants shaded and interfered with the growth of low ones; vines overran and crowded out other crops. The effect of the whole was not beautiful. The crop was limited in quantity and poor in quality. The care of the garden grew into a burden rather than a pleasant task. What is more important, the great opportunities which garden work offers toward unifying the school and enriching the social life were not realized.

After three years of such experience the children were ready to combine and organize their efforts, and last year, with the help of the teachers, a new plan was made, the teachers keeping in mind that the garden should be beautiful; that each child should be allowed to choose what he would plant; that he should have a feeling of ownership about his garden bed and the crop he would harvest; that all plants should be placed in the environment best suited to them; and that every part of every bed should be easily accessible to the smallest child.

First, every member of the school wrote a paper indicating in order of preference his choice of vegetables and flowers to be planted in the garden. The accompanying lists include all plants mentioned:

VEGETABLES

Lettuce	Spinach	Beets
Radishes	Parsley	Peanuts
Onions	Corn	Cotton
Potatoes	Popcorn	Watermelon
Tomatoes	Beans	Pumpkin
Cabbage	Peas	Cucumbers
Turnips	Watercress	Muskmelons
Carrots	Celery	

FLOWERS

Pansies	Bleeding Heart	Daisies
Sweet Peas	Forget-me-nots	Lilies of the Valley
Cosmos	Moss Roses	Morning-glory
Asters	Roses	Nasturtiums
Bachelor Buttons	Geraniums	Lady Slipper
Sweet Alyssum	Sweet Williams	Candytuft
Violets	Heliotrope	Coreopsis
Mignonette	Hollyhocks	Easter Lilies

To this list were added names which the teachers suggested of plants which would be of service in the science, industrial and art work of the school and which would add new acquaintances to the children's flower friends:

VEGETABLES

Wheat	Sage	Pepper
Sugarbeets	Bohnenkraut	Plum Tomatoes
Flax	Lavender	Asparagus
Kohlrabi	Kale	Gourds
Dill		

FLOWERS

Nicotine	Salvia	Sunflowers
Caladium	Ornamental Pepper	Celosias
Four o'clocks	Marigolds	Canterbury Bells
Ageratum	Amaranthus	Cypress Vine
Stock	Scarlet Runner	Zinias
Wallflower		

Committees were formed, composed in each case of children who had chosen the same plants. The first two choices of every child were adopted. If, as in several cases, these committees were too small, the third, fourth, or sometimes fifth choice of a child was considered and sometimes volunteers were called for.

After these groups had been formed, a detailed outline of the work necessary to make the garden a success was as follows:

a) Making of the general plan.

b) Drawing of a plan for each teacher, indicating the parts of the garden for which her pupils were responsible.

c) Writing lists of names of children to act on various committees, these lists to be posted in the hallway.

d) Making individual seed envelopes.

e) Labeling same with name of seed, name of child, and grade.

f) Apportioning seed.

g) Writing and attaching to each envelope clear and concise directions for sowing the seed.

h) Surveying the garden.

i) Digging out of the paths (marking beds with string has not been satisfactory).

j) Making garden stakes and labeling same to correspond with envelopes.

k) Making large stakes with small sign boards attached, to aid in readily finding the beds.

l) Placing of stakes in garden.

m) Making of a hotbed.

This list was presented to the school and the various kinds of work were either chosen by or assigned to the grades where they were best adapted. For instance, the plans were drawn by the seventh grade, envelopes made by the third grade, and directions for planting formulated by the fifth grade.

The making of the plan was the most responsible piece of work. It required consideration of many phases, most important among which were beauty, proper shapes of beds for convenience in planting, relative sizes of beds and their positions as to best conditions of light and moisture, and numbers of children acting on the various committees. For example, the favorite vegetable was lettuce. The amount of lettuce seed likely to be used was calculated, and this, with the size of the committee, was considered in determining the dimensions of the lettuce bed. In some cases an entire bed was assigned to one class, for the special study of some crop necessary to the work in that particular grade. For instance, the sixth grade took charge of sugar beets, the fourth grade of flax, the fifth grade of wheat, and the first grade of popcorn.

The work mentioned under *b* was important. The illustration given below shows how from these plans every teacher knew what was to be planted in every nook, and by the colored spots knew at a glance where she might expect to see some of her pupils working. The names of the children did not appear on the plans, because the teacher in charge had a plan which included the names, and directed the placing, of the individual stakes. The beds were marked off by means of a board, the edge of which was pressed into the ground. The depression made was filled with sand, which stayed in place long enough to serve the purpose.

The flower garden was more difficult to plant, because the rows overlapped, and the general arrangement was more complicated. Here the beginning and end of every row was indicated by a stake, the two stakes being labeled alike and facing one another.

With this plan every child had all the information necessary to make him independent in locating his bed and doing his work. All stakes were marked with paint or ink to make them proof against the rain. A red chalk mark was the means by which the children indicated that a bed had been planted.

Formulating directions for planting was an interesting piece of work. The motive of making all the directions so simple and clear that they might be read and understood by a child in the first grade made a demand for good concise English which the fifth-grade child could thoroughly appreciate. Directions poorly stated might mean failure, disappointment, and a mar to beauty.

The interest shown in making the hotbed is worthy of mention. The science work on decomposition, generation of heat, plant food, and germination was done with zest. The hotbed was so generous in its productiveness that there was a good supply of plants to give to all children who wished to start home gardens. Many children made small gardens along the edges outside of the big garden. All summer good reports came of tomato and cabbage crops, fine specimens of flowers, etc.

After the planting was accomplished a careful record was kept in writing and painting of the date of planting and the date of germination and appearance of plants in the first stages of growth, and the changes from week to week. This record was made in order to enable us another year to distinguish the young plants from the young weeds. Many mistakes in weeding were made this year. In some cases the children were temporarily discouraged because they expected the plants to appear too soon. One little girl who planted ageratum waited five weeks to see signs of growth. Just as school closed she found a few minute leaves. Four weeks later the plants were one foot high. This fall she supplied every classroom with blossoms for several weeks. Another year the data recorded will prevent this discouragement.

The school garden was a great benefit to the work in the art department, as it furnished abundant material and afforded the opportunity for continual use of flowers and vegetables in the study of elementary composition. The following are a few illustrations selected from the work of the sixth and seventh grades, as their work was done in black and white, and therefore is more easily reproduced than the color work of the other grades. The problem thus illustrated was to consider spaces in the background, masses of flowers and leaves, angles of stems, and their relations to each other.

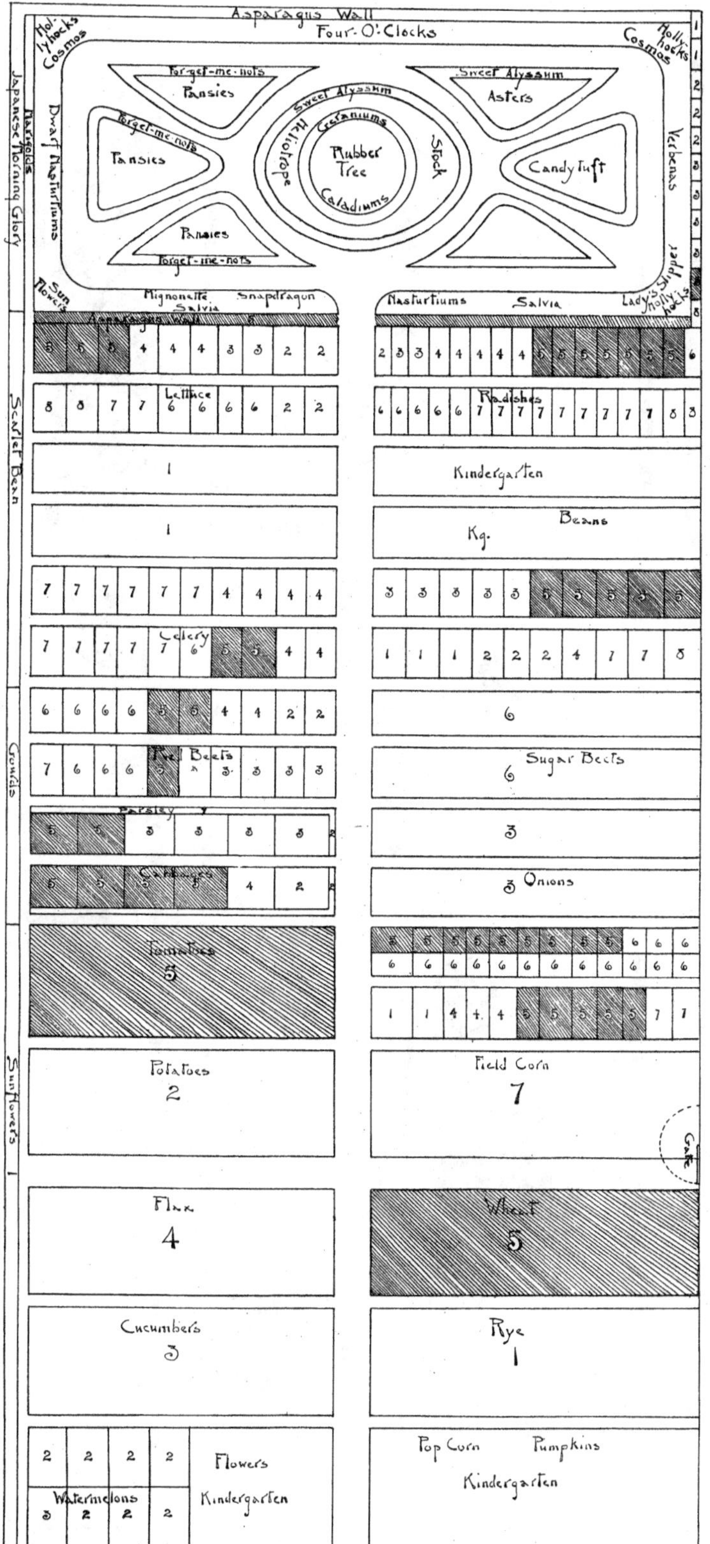

PLAN OF THE GARDEN

GARDEN FLOWERS USED IN ART WORK, SIXTH AND SEVENTH GRADES

BIRD'S-EYE VIEW OF GARDEN

FIRST GRADE HARVESTING THE POPCORN

THE SCHOOL GARDEN IN OCTOBER

Some of the sources of special pleasure to the children were: the asparagus hedge planted to separate the vegetable garden from the flower garden, this hedge having been planted in May and started from three-year-old roots; the bright red and yellow celosias, some of which grew four feet tall and waved plume-like on either edge of the long center path of the vegetable garden; the muskmelons, which grew so thick and luscious that from a bed of twenty-four by nine feet were harvested over forty melons; the watermelons, pumpkins, gourds, and green peppers; the celery bed, which supplied the school for seven weeks; the caladiums, which grew from bulbs two inches in diameter to plants five feet tall, with leaves two and one-half feet long. Last, but not least, the garden gate, and the benches which the small boys made from an old tree trunk which they chopped down, should surely be mentioned, for they would appear in any child's list of the special attractions of the garden.

One grade took complete charge of the grounds in front of the building. There they planted all favorite flowers, making every effort to have a variety great enough to insure blossoming plants throughout the seasons. Some children made frequent visits to the garden during the summer. They weeded and watered at those times, but coming irregularly could not give the garden proper care. The watering and weeding during the vacation time was kindly done by the man left in charge of the building, and by other interested people. Some children expressed a commercial instinct by selling vegetables to their parents and to other children. They agreed to put the income into a common bank, the money to be used in buying some of the seeds for next year's garden. The treasury was also increased by funds coming from a neighboring grocer, who bought at regular market prices what produce was not given away.

In August Canterbury bells, Sweet William, and hollyhocks were planted. The young plants have a good start, and there are enough hollyhocks to plant along the entire front of the building.

This fall the flower garden was cleaned and spaded. A large number of bulbs were planted and by this means the children may enjoy the garden for many weeks before June, while other years they have had few blossoms before the close of school. At present many children are nursing geranium cuttings and old stocks planted in window boxes. The pepper plants are adorning several classrooms. All are waiting for the spring when we shall make a much larger hotbed and supply the home gardens and perhaps some children in other schools.

Aside from the definite knowledge gained and its all-around educative value, if the work in our school garden adds a few names to the list of those who will always love and make gardens, it would seem that it has been well worth the time and labor expended upon it.

RAPIDITY IN ARITHMETIC

G. W. MYERS
The University of Chicago, The School ef Education

In the *Elementary School Teacher* for January 1905 the nature and office of accuracy in arithmetic were discussed. An attempt was there made to draw a line of distinction between arithmetical "cutting to pattern," or "target practice," and accuracy. It was there shown that the current reason assigned by grade teachers and principals that the boys and girls are more interested in arithmetic than in many other subjects in the seventh and eighth grades is that arithmetic problems are capable of more definite comprehension and answer, while the difficulties of other subjects are more vague with answers not so much of the pure "yes," or "no-variety," is in most cases an argument directly opposed to the high educational value of arithmetic, since it reduces arithmetic work to the "target practice" and "score-card" variety. It makes accuracy synonymous with mere *mechanical accuracy*.

In this paper the function of rapidity and the limitations under which it should be striven for in teaching arithmetic will be considered.

The practical man of affairs who supports, judges, and criticizes school work has an eye single to results alone, giving little or no heed to methods by which the results are reached. The teacher has his eye on results, but his chief concern is for methods that are economically and educationally sound. The maxims "Secure results without too great waste of the time and spirit of the learner," and "So teach that the act of acquiring is of more value than the thing acquired" to the teacher assume the dignity of great practical truths that cannot be disregarded with impunity. To the layman they are mere half-truths at least not to be taken too seriously, in case those mechanical results upon which the commercial and industrial world have put a high rating are not sufficiently numerous and manifest. The true teacher finds it wholesome now and then to disentangle himself from the glamour of the mart, and to seek the benefits of solitude to reassure himself of his educational moorings. Teachers need to practice this prudence often with regard to the meaning of the current arithmetical catch-phrase "speed and accuracy." It is the first part of the phrase that concerns us here.

It may conduce to clearness to state at the outset that a fundamental axiom of this discussion is that the purpose of every teaching act shall find sufficient justification in *the present needs of the taught.* "Hope deferred maketh the heart sick" is a more dangerous measure in the arithmetic class than in adult life. Not that no teaching act can be tolerated that does not justify itself fully *to the learner* at the time he is learning; for the place and meaning of much teaching have not yet been fully thought out. The science of teaching is still young. It has been and still is necessary to spend much time and energy justifying its claims to a place in professional curricula. The pre-emptors of the educational ground are so easily skeptical of everything new, that much time has gone to waste from the repetition and multiplication of argument for the sake of ancient and intrenched opinion that could be reached only with *a priori* reasons. The lethargy of our long pedagogical night is not yet entirely thrown off. But few of the *practical* problems of teaching are solved. The purport of our axiom is that no teaching act is more than tentatively justified until it can be freely admitted through the door of the learner's present needs.

Nor can the automatic promptness with which experienced teachers recite that one of the chief aims of arithmetic teaching is speed be taken as proof positive that the question of the educational office of speed has been solved even in individual cases. We must confess to the presence of much canting action as well as canting speech among teachers. The phrase "accuracy and rapidity" has been so long "canted" about that its possibility of estopping thought and disarming argument is the strongest reason for reviewing its legitimate bearing in arithmetic. Divesting ourselves of all notions of the sanctity of the phrase let us endeavor to find what of real educational merit there is in it.

Let one enter a grade room in the midst of the arithmetic period in almost any good elementary school and here is what he will at once see. A few pupils — perhaps one-third of the class — alert and attentive, another third will be loafing—" doing time "— and another third will be loafing because it is held in check by the half-hearted workers and slow, but hard, workers. The teacher is never-failing in insisting that everybody "hurry up." The textbook in a scarecrow note says: "A boy could not hold his job in a bank 24 hours who cannot foot that column correctly in 2 minutes." The teacher believing he is doing God's service, uses this as a spur on his class. The little ones, not comprehending the meaning or nature of the goad, though each imagining he is some day to try to hold a job in a bank, comprehend enough to understand that the teacher intends it as a whip, so they look a trifle worried, frown a little, and fidget a little, then as the reasons for the processes involved are hopelessly beyond them, each settles rapidly into his former place in the uneven ranks. Return a month later and behold the first and last thirds have shrunken to a scant fourth of the class, the one now hopelessly and helplessly behind, and the other far ahead of the average, and the second-mentioned third has swollen to a liberal half of the class.

This is not an overdrawn picture of what one may see in almost any good elementary school in the arithmetic classes. The teacher, after piling on enough formal work to nauseate an adult and keeping up the piling-process for from half to three-quarters of an hour, will tell you at the close of the period that he regards speed and accuracy as the primal considerations in arithmetic teaching. You would say, if you dared, that the tactics being pursued could not by any possibility secure either. You can only think that nervousness and feverishness on the one hand, and lounging and loafing on the other, all of which are the legitimate progeny of the aforesaid tactics, are the born foes of mental concentration, which is the *sine qua non* of speed and accuracy. The *modus operandi* you have witnessed can only dissipate any native incipient tendencies toward concentration. It inhibits and prohibits consecutive thought by dispeling all the relevant materials of thought, and substituting for them a mass of irrelevant ideas. One easily concludes that to be accurate about nothing in particular is as impossible as it is to be speedily correct in matters one cannot comprehend. Still some of those who are most insistent upon accuracy and rapidity urge that children cannot do thought-work in arithmetic. They would have us believe, in spite of the evidences of our plain senses, that real problems that have to be thought out serve only to confuse and muddle children. The most fortunate thing about this view is that it is altogether untrue to the facts in the case. If it were true it would be a clear case of the conditions of arithmetical education defeating education itself.

A little attention to the spontaneous activities of children, if parents and teachers were only wise enough and courageous enough to allow this spontaneity to remain unspoiled by the injection of self, long enough for a little study of it, will readily convince any one that each pupil, just as each adult, has a certain *norm* of speed at which he can dispatch work most economically and, at the same time, maintain a uniformly high grade of excellence of output. Each child has a normal mental, as well as a normal physical, gait, and at this gait he can secure most steady and certain concentration of thought. To undertake by extrinsic stimuli to force a pupil to work above his norm of speed is to make his mental acts flighty, uncertain, and jerky. To allow him to work below this norm is to permit his thinking to become "wobbly," ambling, and wandering and to encourage him to loaf, to accustom him to going at his tasks in a half-hearted way. This mulling over his work is again both the cause and the effect of permitting the pupil to work below his norm of speed and the end of it all is a loss of the power to concentrate.

It is the manifest duty of the teacher to seek by an individual study of his pupils to ascertain the *norm* of speed for each pupil and to hold him up to it religiously, but by no means to drag him beyond it. The pupil must and will raise his norm only *by working within it and close up to it, but not beyond it.* It is impossible to keep up work of this sort for long. If tasks of this nature are too long sustained they will defeat their own purpose.

Evidently, then, drill-work for speed and accuracy must be brief, brisk, and, what is very important but often ignored by the teacher, it must be thoroughly comprehensible to the pupil. It is evident, also, that the amount, kind, and continuance of it must vary with the individual pupil. To the teacher drill-work, if sane and thoughtful, furnishes a means of studying the individual habits and aptitudes of pupils. To the pupil drill-work, if properly administered, is a training in concentration of thought. The loose, flabby, and purposeless "quick-work," quite commonly seen in the public schools, is not drill-work, for the reason that there is not in it enough concentration of thought to constitute it work at all.

A HISTORY OF THE TEACHING OF NATURE IN THE ELEMENTARY AND SECONDARY SCHOOLS OF THE UNITED STATES. I

I. B MYERS
The University of Chicago, The School of Education

The following historical sketch on nature-teaching in the elementary and secondary schools of the United States includes the subjects variously known as natural history, nature-study, and biology (botany and zoölogy). The object of the study is to try to determine in a general way the aim and method of nature-teaching, and note the influence of the study upon educational purpose and practice.

The choice of subject and method of teaching, of any study, is largely determined by our conception as to the general aim or purpose of the study. In order to understand the full aim or purpose of a study, at the time of its introduction into the school curriculum, and to follow its development and influence from the period of its introduction to the present time, it is necessary to keep in mind the growth of those general ideas which shape the educational purpose as a whole. The complete educational purpose is most clearly revealed, because of its simplicity and directness, among primitive peoples. It consists of learning to perform acts necessary to living: to hunt, fish, prepare and use weapons and snares, prepare skins for clothing, construct shelter; and to do these things in such a way as to avoid offending the spirits which presided over the various objects of man's attentions.[1] The history of primitive races is largely the story of this twofold relation of man to the universe about him. The advance of man is marked by a gradual discovery and understanding of nature's secrets, and each discovery carries with it a gain in the feeling of mastery, and a loss of intensity in that quality of the emotions

Monroe, *Textbook of History of Education.*

which go hand in hand with mystery. Out of these conditions of living arise three, interlocked, groups of relations, varying in the dominance of their influence over man, but common in some degree to all men of all times: (1) that group of relations which has to do with supplying man's physical needs and comforts — the immediate securing of food, clothing, shelter, or their equivalent in wages; this represents education from a utility standpoint; (2) that group of relations which has to do with intellectual conceptions, æsthetics, and religions; (3) that group of relations which has to do with man's relation to man — social rights and needs.

Each of these groups has been recognized as having some place in the general educational scheme; the tendency being for one or the other to lead or dominate, according to the conception of the ultimate educational purpose. The general habits and environments of the people have had much to do in molding this conception as to the function of school work and the type of subjects to be studied. In a consideration of the study of nature it may be of importance to note this general change in nature environment: At the beginning of the century 4 per cent. of the people of the United States lived in cities, while 96 per cent. lived in rural districts, and were occupied, to a large extent, in some form of work dominated by the nature environment, and in which their living problems were directly related to this same environment. At the end of the century 48 per cent. live in cities, engaged in occupations dominated by social conditions and influences. During this early period children were in daily contact with their natural environment, and their acquaintance with the earth surface, climate, soil, animals, and plants, and the relation of these things to man, was gained at first hand. The people of the period were, on the whole, too fully occupied in supplying their immediate needs and simple comforts, and in subduing the earth to afford to experiment or theorize. They looked upon life from a "practical standpoint." It was only at a later period, when living became less strenuous, that the general-culture idea gained headway.

The study of nature was introduced into the schools of the United States near the beginning of the nineteenth century, but gained little headway during the first quarter of the century. The people of this period were quick to detect the instinctive interests of children in nature; they were aware of their insatiable curiosity, and the ease and pleasure with which they gained an acquaintance with natural objects and phenomena. But the conditions of living gave children a full acquaintance with these things, as to their uses and relations to man, and this knowledge could be better gained at home than in school. In their theoretic conception of nature the dominant idea was that of special creation, and these products of nature were for man's use and comfort. In this conception they found their motive for teaching nature to children. They argued that, by taking advantage of the early interests and pleasures which the child took in nature, he would be led to a fuller appreciation of the wonders of creation, and could thus more fully and reverently "love and admire a Being who could and did create such wonderful things for the children of men." All sciences were taught with this end in view, but none, unless it be astronomy, were calculated to accomplish this purpose so effectively as natural history (biology). Many of the natural-history lessons were in the form of reading stories, and were frequently queer mixtures of science, moral training, and religion. The following, from Lovell's *Young People's Second Book* (1836), is a type:

THE HEN

Of all the feathered animals, there is none more useful than the common hen. Her eggs supply us with food during her life, and her flesh affords us delicate meat after her death. What a motherly care does she take of her young! How closely and tenderly does she watch over them, and cover them with her wings; and how bravely does she defend them from every enemy, from which she herself would fly away in terror, if she had not them to protect. While this sight reminds you of the wisdom and goodness of her Creator, let it also remind you of the care which your own mother took of you, during your helpless years, and of the gratitude and duty which you owe to her for all her kindness.

Nature thus stood as a source from which could be drawn great moral and religious truths; and recognizing, as the people of this period did, the period of childhood as the time to impress the race with these truths, it was a logical sequence that the introduction of biology in "female seminaries" should find early favor. These students as mothers would hold the early influences upon children in their power, and with a knowledge of nature and the great lessons to be drawn from her, they would be the better prepared to guide children in the early years of their childhood. They argued that

The study of nature is a source of instruction and enjoyment from which no mind should be excluded, and least of all the minds which usually may give direction to the propensities of early childhood, and which ought to be supplied with means for attaining a pleasing ascendency over the dawn of character.

Popular sentiment seemed to consider the study of nature good, because of its pleasing and stimulating influence, for children not fully immersed in school work, but did not look upon it as a part of serious school study.

The study is regarded as an accomplishment, like the study of the fine arts, too inapplicable to the plainer and sterner duties of ordinary study. The system of utility and selfish views of immediate practical good come into action.

In the introduction of biology in the girl schools or academies, the work was confined wholly to the study of botany, by reason of its being

by far the most attractive, elegant, and precise, so well adapted to the refinement of female education; and the subject of its study so universally admired.

The general attitude of the educational public toward this study, as to its purpose, is best summarized by the various discussions of the period:

Botany is one of the most delightful and healthy amusements; but the entertainment afforded by this study does not arise from merely knowing the scientific name of plants, but in finding them out for ourselves.

Botany is peculiarly fitted for introduction in a girls' school; it is admirably adapted to the tastes, feelings, and capacities of females, as is demonstrated by the fact that the majority of botanists are females. Boys are less easily interested in it, more apt to be careless and harsh in their treatment of specimens, and too much attached to rude and boisterous sports.

Botany should be considered as a science of amusement; but with this strong recommendation, that it be acquired without stealing a single hour from more important studies.

The study of natural history is particularly desirable for children and young people, because it not only supplies them with an inexhaustible source of innocent amusement, but it is also extremely improving (if scientifically taught) by accustoming them to generalize their ideas and showing them how every subject may be simplified by regular and judicial classification. Children are generally delighted with everything that possesses life; they should therefore begin with *animal life* as being more interesting. Children may amuse themselves by classifying shells which, though of no use, will at least lead them to observe and admire the productions of nature.

These statements represent fairly well the general attitude toward natural history during the first half of the century.

Turning from theory to the actual teaching of natural history, we find that public and common schools excluded it entirely from their curricula. This was not so much on account of its inutility as from a lack of proper facilities for carrying it on. Teachers were thoroughly dependent upon textbooks in their teaching, and there were no textbooks to assist them in the most rudimentary work of natural history. The few books that existed, especially on animal life, were defective in that they were untruthful, fanciful, and were translations of foreign books treating of objects foreign to the pupil's environment, and did not serve to give him any introduction to nature around him. To add to the difficulty, teachers looked upon the text of these books as something to be memorized by the student. In botany the whole study centered around the Linnæan system of plant analysis and classification. This rendered the subject too difficult for study except in academies.

From too great a want of elementary textbooks and a greater want of proper instructors, the entrance to the delightful domain of natural history is rendered disagreeable. The student is disgusted with its technicalities before his zeal is awakened to its curious facts. He attempts to study its theory, and its theory is considered the end and aim of pursuit. . . . . Take, for instance, the single branch of botany . . . . as pursued in our schools it is generally a task. The students commit to memory page after page of some textbook so as to be able to tell the correct term of each organ of a plant without a single idea as to its economy. A specimen is put into their hands, and after being able to count the number of stamens, to determine without much hesitancy the size and form of the leaves, and by much trouble to discover through the manual the name — the mighty work is done. Pupils are now wise as the instructor; their labors and investigations must cease (1837).

There seems to have been little or no change, in either attitude or practice, in the work during the first half of the century. Apostles were abroad pleading for better things, but owing to the general lack of books and facilities for leading the way, and those available leading in a contrary direction, changes came slowly. Commenting on the study of botany, Gould (1834) says:

> The whole science of botany becomes little else than the counting of stamens and pistils; and if a student can tell whether a plant belongs to Pentandra or Didynamia, names to which he attaches no meaning, it is the height of his aspiration. . . . . It is of no consequence whether it is good for the food of man or beast, whether it is sanatory or poisonous, whether it may be cultivated on dry or wet soil. The kind of knowledge gained is neither practicable nor comprehensible.

The description of animals and plants as given in geography texts was, on the whole, considered ample for elementary schools. The idea of investigation did not exist in the schools; the only idea that existed was that of learning, and learning consisted of memorizing the text of a book. The attitude of the student counted but little; the rod and prizes were there to stimulate him into activity. The study, in the academies, was for discipline, and discipline consisted in working out some intricate system laid down in a textbook. The period was characterized by the natural-history phase of nature-study, and by a study of botany according to the Linnæan system of classification, both according to the textbook method. The aim in elementary work was to lead children "through nature up to nature's god," and to afford them innocent and pleasurable amusement, thus drawing them away from "frivolous and dissipating amusements."

In the academies the aim passed variously from a type of information essential in the care of children, to pleasure and refinement, until it got sufficiently severe and exact for discipline. In contrast to the work in the schools, we find a general unrest and protest against the character of the work going on in the schools; both Gray and Agassiz, the recognized leaders in their subject at that time, raised their voices in protest. Gray, in 1841, says:

> I do not suppose that the mere treasuring up of facts will effect the object of education . . . . I venture the assertion that, if the truth were known, the

child acquires a greater number of useful ideas, more real development and strength of mind, during his play hours with his rabbits, his kites, or from his story-books, than he does from the lessons assigned him during his hours of study; he is really educated more out of school than in school.

There is a general plea for a return to a freer study of out-of-door nature for the sake of a broader, healthier, and more pleasurable experience. The new theoretic attitude is well summed up in the following words:

The student should first examine, in all directions, the neighborhood of his residence, and should make himself so thoroughly acquainted with it that he can call up before his mind whatever he chooses. Such an acquaintance is the result of the unconscious and fresh pleasures which youth, joyful and free from scientific anxiety, will find for itself in such an examination, obtaining in this artless way a simple general impression not forced by a teacher. He is not teased while he is rejoicing in the blue heavens and the rapid motion of the clouds, in the oak wood and flowery meadows, where the butterflies play, by a professor with a kyanometer to measure the blue sky, nor by recommendations not to stare in the woods, but rather to ascertain whether the oaks are *Quercus rubus* or *pedunculata;* or, not to look at the flowers all at once, as if they were a yellow carpet, but to take his Linnæus and determine the species of this *Ranunculus;* no entomologist is setting him to chase butterflies and impale them. . . . . In this paradisaic pleasure is planted the seed of the perception of an intellectual world whose secrets will not be fully ascertained even after the longest and most active life of scientific effort. But most teachers, by the dispersion of these simple impressions of nature, destroy these earliest pleasures of children, the brightness of the imaginary which they see, or by our failure to bring them in contact with nature they fail the experience entirely.

The general tone prophesies a change for better things.

[*To be continued*]

EDITORIAL NOTES

'Tis time,
New hopes should animate the world, new light
Should dawn from new revealings.

—*Browning.*

New Principle in School Management

For the first time, *ab urbe condita,* the citizens of Chicago have had an idea set before them by one of the members of their Board of Education which embodies a new principle in school management and administration. The unique feature of this idea is found in the proposal to change from the primitive autocratic village educational system which now prevails the country over, in hamlet and metropolis alike, to a modern form more consistent with democratic ideals. The distinctive features of the plan proposed are given in the following statements, quoted, in substance, from the daily press:

1. Redivision of the city into districts each containing from ten to twenty schools.

2. Organization of all the principals and teachers in each district.

3. These organized bodies to act in a supervising capacity in the direction of the educational affairs of the district.

4. Nomination of principals by the district organization of principals and teachers; the superintendent to have the power to veto, and the Board of Education the power to elect.

5. Abolition of the Board of District Superintendents.

6. Substitution, for the present board of six district superintendents, of twelve teachers holding principals' certificates, to be selected by the organized principals and teachers of each district; these teachers to serve as critics.

7. Abolition of the promotional examination feature of the Normal School extension work, and the substitution of a differently organized merit system.

As a study of human nature, it is interesting to observe how these proposals were received by many members of the Board of Education and, editorially, by the public press. There was a great howl; nothing more intelligent, nothing more indicative of calm inquiry or of a disposition toward careful consideration — just a nine days' howl, for which, of course, the board as a whole must not be held responsible since the propositions were not placed officially before it.

Human Nature on Exhibition

The people generally express themselves as being anxious to have a "hard-headed business" administration of their schools. In this case, however, it is worth noting that the reaction of those who succeeded in getting themselves into print stands in strong contrast with the best modern business methods. There is a firm in this city, for example, the largest of its kind in the world, that has achieved its success after a different fashion. This firm pays a cash bonus for any suggestion which an employee can make that can be adopted with advantage to the business. There is a manufacturing concern in southern Ohio that in twenty years has made itself a world-monopoly. Throughout its factories many recording devices are distributed which the employees are invited to use as a means of bringing suggestions to the notice of the firm. Last year out of some fifteen thousand suggestions a majority were carried into effect by the board of administration. The plans adopted by these two firms reflect a far-sighted business policy that does more than anything else to insure in the employees a growing interest and a steadfast loyalty. That is to say, the best type of business man today has learned to quit howling at criticism, and, also, that it pays to leave no stone unturned to secure the intelligent moral support of all his workers.

Hard-Headed Business Methods

But with your "hard-headed business" board of education it is different. No other organization on earth is so skittish toward suggestions from the outside. Here is a peculiar phenomenon that is entirely beyond comprehension. Many a man in private life is most unobtrusive and unassuming; willing to get light from any source; modest and diffident in speaking on educational questions. But elect this selfsame man to a board of education and, in most

An Inexplicable Phenomenon

cases, within a month an angel from heaven would be unable to teach him anything — would be afraid even to try! Or, in private, he may be a sonorous defender of personal freedom; but once on the board, if he does not immediately begin to round up the teachers and to treat them like a herd, he is the shining exception. It has come to pass in most communities, therefore, that if a teacher were to make a suggestion to a school board, he would attract to himself unfavorable notice, if not suspicion; if he were to persist in such policy, he would be snubbed and probably "transferred" as a warning of even more serious things in store.

Degeneration of Teachers

Therefore, the thousands of intelligent men and women teachers throughout the country who are in the best position to know what the schools need have their lips hermetically sealed. And, still worse, their minds gradually close up and cease to work upon educational problems in their broad aspects, and they develop, or rather degenerate, into sycophants, cowards, and "stupids." The attitude of the ordinary school board toward its teachers, touching questions relating to the welfare of the schools, will, in time, turn all except the most stalwart into intellectual and moral runts. Such a policy is "hard-headed" enough; but, as a type of business method, it belongs among the trilobites in the fossil-bearing strata of the Lower Silurian.

In Chicago matters have gone farther. A member of the board was recently criticised in one of the meetings for making use of a communication which he had received from one of the principals. It was held to be in some way a violation of official courtesy due his colleagues. And it now turns out that if one of its own members, even, dares to work out a plan which he thinks might improve the school system, he does so at his own risk — that is, at the certain risk of being met with a howl!

A Well-Qualified Board Member

In the present instance Dr. DeBey, the author of the plan outlined above, is peculiarly well qualified to work with intelligence upon school problems. She is a trained teacher, and one of the very few members the board has ever had (I now recall but one other) who have filled and who still could fill acceptably positions in the elementary, high, and normal schools. Her actual schoolroom experience, coupled with her lifelong studies in education, if paralleled in some business enterprise, would entitle her ideas to close attention and respect. But the ordinary "hard-headed" business man, when he gets on the school board, has another and a time-honored way of dealing with anything resembling a new idea. He proceeds to show by vituperative methods how utterly impossible it is. It never occurs to those of his type that, if they were to devote as much energy to finding out the good points of a new idea as they do to proving that it is absurd; that, if they really were as anxious to understand a new plan when it is presented as they are to stamp it out; that, if they were as earnest in their effort to devise ways for carrying it into effect as they are to show that it is not practical; that, if they were to assume a position of friendliness and tolerance toward new ideas instead of an attitude of chronic hostility; that, if their influence, which now stands as a bulwark of eternal negation, were to be transformed into a positive force—it never occurs to them that then we should advance educationally as much in five years as we now do in fifty. No enterprise on earth ever grew up under the policy of the habitual objector; to adopt his methods in business is to become an easy mark for the sheriff. Let the objector, therefore, be cast into outer darkness.

New Ideas Tabooed

When one considers the characteristic attitude of the public mind toward new ideas in education, it need not be thought remarkable that not one of Dr. DeBey's critics, either on the board or on the editorial staff of the city press, gave much evidence of really comprehending the meaning of the plan which she proposed. How could they have given it that consideration necessary to understand it! Within an hour or two after it was presented to the public, these mighty folk, vociferous with objections, had shown to their own satisfaction the emptiness of the whole scheme. If anyone said, "Let me think it over for a day, or even for fifteen minutes, before I am called upon to express an opinion," no record of such plea for delay has appeared in print.

Plan Not Understood

The propositions laid down by Dr. DeBey, of course, only foreshadow a plan in its barest outline: she evidently intended nothing more. Before they can be wrought out into a definite working program, there are many details, involving matters of great difficulty, that will have to be studied with much patience and consideration. It is not so much the intention here, therefore, to discuss the numerous details which must enter into the completed scheme, as it is to treat of the spirit and purpose which the plan embodies.

The Principle Involved

The principle upon which the proposed plan rests is simple, but fundamental, and in its application to educational organization it is almost new. The meaning is this: Under its operation everyone participating in the educational work of the city, from the superintendent and the members of the Board of Education to the humblest teacher, will have a position of influence and worth measured and limited only by his ability to put brains into his work. The chief difficulty in the way of such a plan is that most people have no conception of public life except that under the administration of a boss. The press and public, generally, regard our common-school system as now administered in this country as being of necessity under the control of a boss, though whether this function resides in the superintendent or board of education is, in most places, still an unsettled question. The idea of the boss being uppermost, people jumped to the conclusion, therefore, that Dr. DeBey's plan means that the teachers shall be the boss, and that the collar now worn by themselves shall be placed about the necks of the superintendent and board. It has not dawned upon the average mind that there yet may be a plan evolved which will eliminate the boss, and under which all will have the opportunity and the privilege of co-operating and contributing to the common good up to the limits of their power to help! *That is the spirit of Dr. DeBey's plan, and that is all there is to it.*

Point of Objection

To be sure, nobody can object to this on theoretical grounds; it is the *practical* point that really rouses all opposition — it seals the doom of bossism in education. It demolishes bossism by the board and superintendent, and it destroys the hope of bossism by the teachers — probably many teachers themselves do not see this, *but that is what it means.* It substitutes for the system of bossism and fear the idea of co-operation and mutual consideration. An educational program based upon this principle is perfectly feasible, and it should be the business of all thoughtful people, on the board and off, to help work it out.

The Boss and the Employee

In a small village system the evils of bossism are minimized because the intimate relationship of the superintendent and board to the schoolroom work, which under the circumstances is possible, necessarily encourages and admits of more or less co-operation. But in large cities the evils are increased in proportion as the superintendent and board are removed from an acquaintanceship with the common teacher and the children, until the separation has rendered the situation intolerable for the teachers. For with the idea of the boss goes also the idea of the bossed, and the teacher becomes, in the eyes of the superintendent and board, an "employee" in a derogative sense of the word; whereas the teachers are not their "employees" in the sense that business makes use of this term, nor are they their servants or slaves; they are their colaborers, their colleagues, and their equals. In a lone sentence, a Chicago paper did express the truth when it said: "The trouble which Dr. DeBey finds with the school management is that it reaches from the top downward. She would have it come from the bottom upward." In holding to this view, Dr. DeBey falls in with history. No educational reform, nor any other for that matter, ever began at the top, because those at the top are generally satisfied. Friedrich Froebel struck the keynote of progress in education when he said: "Come, let us live with the children." Had he said, "Come, let us get into the board of education," we might have been without the kindergarten even today. Pestalozzi lived with the children as in a home; had he gotten himself elected superintendent, the regeneration of Germany might never have been realized. It is a profoundly significant fact that all educational progress is made through teachers who are actually at work with pupils. The reason for this is evident, and it brings to the surface once more the essential difference between a teacher and a mere business employee. The employee is in charge of a section, and may know more than the head of the firm about the details of gloves or shoes; his function, however, never requires him to have that breadth of view which to the head of the house is so essential. But the teacher, always in the presence of the children, *is immediately and eternally confronted with the whole educational problem.* In the store the glove department may be abolished without detriment to the department for shoes; but in the school system nothing can be done that does not profoundly affect for good or ill the teacher's work with her children, because it is for them, finally, that the whole organization exists. It is for this reason, therefore, that, in the future, the superintendents and boards of education will learn to exalt themselves by sitting at the feet of the teacher, that they may know what the children actually need. This will bring to them the true dignity that belongs to high service.

Teacher vs. Employee

Dr. DeBey's plans, as laid before the public, should receive the closest study and consideration by all friends of popular education for precisely this reason, that she brings to the board a wide and varied experience as a practical teacher. She forms a distinctly new element in the composition of the board, and is able to give her colleagues a point of view that heretofore they have been rarely able to gain.

The plan under consideration not only provides for everyone adequate opportunities for the development of new ideas, but it also secures to each the right to have his ideas duly considered, and, still further, to have a voice in determining whether they shall be carried into effect. Without the latter provision, of course, all else is vanity of vanities. It is too much to expect intelligent men and women to use their time and energy in thinking out reforms, if they are to be denied forever the privilege and opportunity of realizing them. This is the one point, perhaps, which above

Teachers Need Authority

all others arouses the bitterest opposition. The unspeakable hypocrisy of the public, that all through the years has been loading the teachers with a mawkish sentiment about the divinity of their work and mission, is baldly exposed by their instant opposition when the teachers seek some effective means of putting their divine ideas into practice. What the politicians and bosses are especially anxious for is that the dear teachers shall retain their divinity and —keep quiet!

Bald Hypocricy

It is not intended here to bear down with unnecessary severity upon superintendents and boards of education, nor is the purpose to belittle their great functions in the administration of a school system. Neither does Dr. DeBey's plan contemplate (as the public press assumed it did) reducing superintendents and boards of education to ciphers. On the contrary, it forecasts a higher field of usefulness than either can possibly attain under the present plan. It is frankly proposed that there shall be a general survey of all the functions that belong to a school system, with a view to placing the responsibilities for these functions upon the heads of those who, from the nature of their positions and work in the system, are able to meet them most intelligently. A hue and cry is raised at once because it is assumed that such a plan must diminish the chance for initiative on the part of the superintendent and board. Parenthetically, of course, as against this, the fact that thousands of teachers in the schools of the country are deprived of *all* initiative by the present plan counts for nothing. The truth is, however, that, if under the new plan proposed anyone should fail to find room for initiative, it would be because the individual himself is not blessed with the article. The stimulus toward personal initiative, as a matter of fact, would be immeasurably greater than it is under the present system: greater because, all working together upon common problems, the ideas of each, in order to impress themselves, would have to weigh more than they do now. The consequent uplift to the character of school work would be enormous and general. There would not be a place left in the entire system that a small man could fill.

Board and Superintendent Not Ciphers

The Initiative

A plan of school administration which "begins at the bottom instead of at the top" would develop that stability and steadiness in public-school work which are absolutely necessary to a healthy life and growth. The schools would be no longer so closely subject to the mutations of the board and the superintendent. Board members and superintendents must come and go, no matter whether they are elective or appointive. The teaching force is more stable, and its stability would tend to increase because of improved and more settled conditions. It is common at present to seek to secure this desired stability through a long term for the superintendent, or through his repeated re-election. Experience shows, however, that this plan alone brings a curse to the schools oftener than it carries a blessing. It is all because the man—any man—is too small and the school system is too large. A school system that is not so organized as to be bigger than any man in it is no system at all for the democracy of even a village. With the responsibilities for the schools properly distributed among all those who do the work, it would be possible no longer, for the meteoric superintendent, or the transient teacher, or the noisy fellow that by a political accident gets into the board of education, to shake the system of a great city, as he now may do, to its very foundation. The school system must be so organized that, no matter who is elected to any one position, or who is defeated; no matter who lives or who dies, the interests of the children shall remain free from the perils of those who seek public place in order to attain personal ends.

Greater Stability Insured

A School System vs. an Individual

The composition of a school board should be the strongest possible from a business point of view. In a city like Chicago, for instance, with its annual budget of many millions of dollars, the board should include, as it often does, the finest business talent it is possible for the public to secure. In a board of business men, however, one will not often find those who in the development of their commercial careers have been able to keep pace with the growth of pedagogic knowledge. It is for this reason that the teachers should not only have the privilege, they should be required to contribute from their studies and experience to the professional development of the school system.

The brief term on the board which is ordinarily granted to its members, renders it impossible for any business man, no matter how well disposed he may be, to acquaint himself thoroughly with the pedagogic aspect of the school system. No purely business enterprise could grow, or long endure, if it were made subject to the management of so changeable a directorate as that now having entire control of the public schools. It is as though some great business house on State Street were to select groups of teachers from the schoolrooms and place them for brief successive periods in entire charge of its commercial interests. In a word, those who perform certain functions in the school system must be permitted, nay required, to assume corresponding responsibilities; and, conversely, no one must be allowed to assume responsibilities for functions which he does not and cannot perform. Such an organization, through the gradual harmonizing of its teaching, its supervising, and its legislative functions, would develop a unity, a dignity, and an impregnable moral strength that our public-school system hitherto has never known.

Dr. DeBey's plan as yet is not understood, but, in the end, the principle underlying it will win. The time when it can go into operation depends very much upon the teachers themselves. The scheme does not propose benefits for the teachers alone, nor is it the purpose simply to make trouble for the board and superintendent. Neither teachers, nor school boards, nor superintendents have a monopoly of wisdom. They are all subject to the same racial, social, political, and religious prejudices that already have done so much to impair the usefulness of the public schools. Inflamed as many teachers are by present conditions it is not easy for them to see equally well all sides of the questions involved. If their movements are not controlled by a steady sense of justice, by deliberation, fairness, and consideration for all, and, finally, if they do not ever have an eye single to the welfare of the children, their efforts at reform will deservedly fail.

W. S. J.

AT LAKE GENEVA, WISCONSIN, SUMMER 1904.

Sincerely Yours

Feb 20th 1905 William R Harper

VOLUME VI NUMBER 6

THE ELEMENTARY SCHOOL TEACHER

FEBRUARY, 1906

WILLIAM RAINEY HARPER

WILBUR S. JACKMAN
The School of Education

[BIOGRAPHICAL NOTE.—Dr. Harper was born at New Concord, Muskingum County, Ohio, July 26, 1856, son of Samuel and Elizabeth Rainey Harper. Entered Muskingum College at eight years of age, and graduated in 1870, receiving the degree of A.B. at fourteen. Entered Yale College in 1873 for graduate study of Semitic and kindred tongues. In 1875, at nineteen, he received the degree of Ph.D., being the eighth in the history of Yale to attain that honor. In August, 1875, he was married to Miss Ellen Paul. In the same year he became principal of the Masonic College, Macon, Tenn., and the following year became a tutor in the preparatory department of Denison University, Granville, Ohio; later he became its principal. In 1880 he was called to the chair of Hebrew and Old Testament exegesis in the Baptist Theological Seminary at Morgan Park, Ill. In 1882 he became principal of the Chautauqua College of Liberal Arts—a position he held for six years. In 1886 he accepted the professorship of Semitic languages in Yale University, and three years afterwards he was also appointed Woolsey professor of biblical literature and instructor in the Divinity School. At the first meeting of the trustees of the University of Chicago Dr. Harper was elected president of the new institution, and on July 1, 1891, after a trip abroad, he entered on the duties of his office. His death occurred January 10, 1906.]

The School of Education is an enduring witness and it is a great monument to the breadth of interest which President Harper felt in the cause of education. With the kindergarten on its hitherside, and with its farther portals opening into the arena of life, the University of Chicago now spans completely the field of scholastic training.

Most men must content themselves with the upbuilding of a single department of a great school; but the mind and heart of Dr. Harper were large enough to include them all. He had the rare insight to see that an educational institution which did not provide for the training of children and youth, as well as for those of later years, must inevitably fail to fill the measure of its greatest usefulness.

The success of such a man, represented as it is by the splendid buildings that adorn the campus, by the sums of money that make up the endowments, and above all by his scholarly attainments that have indelibly impressed themselves upon the spiritual life of the University—such striking success so appeals to the imagination as to lift him who achieved it to a plane above ordinary mortals and to hold him aloof from them. Dr. Harper, however, won his place among men by the practice of those simple virtues which the life of our school itself should always represent. In revering his memory we think, first of all, of that careful consideration which he ever held in mind for others; of that self-effacement continually practiced, that principles might be fairly considered, and that the rights and privileges of all his associates might not be obscured or abridged.

In working out the organization of the School of Education, his interest was intense, his energy unbounded, and his counsel most stimulating and wise. He sought, and actually acquired, a great familiarity with the details of the school's affairs, that all interests might be properly considered. He showed a marked sympathy with the work of even the youngest children, and he often lamented the fact that time did not permit him to have a closer association with them. But a few days before the end he was particularly pleased with some of the pupils' handiwork, a number of pieces of which had been sent to his room. His message to the children was full of cheer and encouragement.

Dr. Harper's power of accomplishment came mainly from two things: a breadth of vision which enabled him to get the whole of a subject clearly in mind, and a remarkable ability to concentrate upon the matter immediately in hand. Having once decided upon a particlar problem, his pursuit of it was relentless until its solution was attained. He was most genial and accessible to men of all minds; and when emergencies in the line of duty arose with any of his associates, no hour of the twenty-four seemed inopportune for an appointment.

He was a lover of fair play; he never permitted himself to be pressed to a decision until the evidence was all in. And with the testimony in hand it was his habit to sleep over it and weigh it again before finally casting the die. Nor was this final—with him nothing was ever final; everything represented but a stage in an endless progression. His open-mindedness always welcomed an opportunity which demanded a reopening and a reconsideration of questions that would have appeared to smaller minds as being forever closed.

The most powerful and effective teaching is through the force of example. It is as the embodiment of these and a hundred kindred traits that President Harper will ever remain in the lives of those who knew him as a great teacher.

THE JEWISH TRAINING SCHOOL OF CHICAGO

O. J. MILLIKEN
Principal

Fifteen years ago the Russian Jews were coming to Chicago in large numbers, and to acquaint them in the shortest possible time with the English language, our American methods and American institutions, and to help them adjust themselves to the new order of things, the Jewish Training School of Chicago was established.

Centuries of persecution and restrictions in occupations had unfitted the newcomers to grapple with the strange conditions under which they were to live, and the school's curriculum was based entirely upon the necessary corrective tendencies, handwork becoming the central factor around which the other activities were grouped. For economic and religious reasons the new people naturally huddled together into what has become known as the "Ghetto," until they have built up a city within a city where, at the present time, if all buildings were removed, each person would have less than a square yard of earth upon which to stand.

During the last five years efforts in New York have resulted in scattering the emigrants over the whole United States; consequently there are not as many settling in any particular place. This has led the founders of this school to question whether its mission has not been fulfilled, and whether or not the public schools ought to care for the children who are receiving their education at private expense.

With these conditions before us, we have been gradually drifting into an industrial institution, selecting only those boys and girls who find it difficult to adjust themselves to public-school conditions and who do not take kindly to intellectual training alone. Every institution can point with

LATHE-WORK: MAKING A SHAFT FOR THE SHOP

THE PRINTING-PRESS

pride to its graduates, but the universal test must be sought in the masses who never reach the final goal—those whose economic circumstances compel them to become wage-earners before they arrive at any appreciable distance; and it sometimes appears as though we were doing but little for the large number of boys and girls, whose only diploma is a labor certificate.

We are placing before these children as many elementary trade activities as possible, in order to find out their bent, and then encourage and direct them along lines along which their natural abilities seem to trend. Carlyle says: "It is the first of all problems for a person to find out what kind of work he is able to do in this universe."

The school in its new mission is only in its infancy, but we see great possibilities, and, with a lengthened course covering two years of apprenticeship in trades, we hope to redeem many a drifting individual, and turn him into an active channel, where he can determine a direct purpose in life.

The academic work is to be made as practical as possible and brought in touch with the handwork. In fact, President Eliot, of Harvard, gave our creed in these words: "One-half of the education of a child should be manual education. Young people learn by doing. The soul-centers of many a young man can be reached only by having him work with his hands. I constantly see the fallacy of abstract theory in education."

A growing boy likes to do what a man does, in a man's way and with a man's aim. He soon tires working with toy tools or making useless things. He is utilitarian from the start, and usually is able to tell just what he wants. When he constructs an article, he has in mind one of three uses: for his play, for his home or school, or for profit; and it is a poor teacher who cannot direct a boy's interest so as to conform to the ability of the boy at the limitations of the shop. How often we squeeze all of the juice out of a boy's mechanical conception by following the pedagogue's law, as laid down by many manual-training teachers, that nothing shall be attempted until a working-drawing is made!

It is often better to allow him to make an article and then draw it. There are but few untrained adults who can read a drawing, and to compel a child to go through a formal imitation of meaningless lines at the time of an aroused interest is cruel and harmful. It will not be long, however, before a boy can be led to discover for himself that, in order to economize in time and material, he must first make a working drawing. The incentive is produced, and mechanical drawing ceases to be a meaningless drudgery.

There is a species of boy that we never turn from our doors, if we can possibly find room for him, and that is the one Ernest Thompson-Seton had in mind when, upon being asked what wild animal he liked best, he replied: "A wild boy." When he first enters the school, we enroll him in the shop, not allowing him to do any book-work until he asks for it; but we direct our efforts toward putting him in touch with something that will display his weaknesses in academic work, and it is not long before he asks permission to take the particular work in which he is found deficient, and this usually starts with arithmetic. We now have over sixty pupils of that kind, and, with two exceptions, at their own request, all are taking our full course in academic work. We feel that we have accomplished a considerable amount when we have supplied the incentive.

A course of work has not been so completely mapped out for our girls, but we are seeking to connect them with the domestic and commercial worlds. Much more attention has been given to boys than to girls, and the field is much newer, and not fraught with so many opportunities; but there is no question but what the needs are as great, and possibly greater. Within a year we hope to be able to give practical results from our work with the girls.

MORNING EXERCISES IN THE FRANCIS W. PARKER SCHOOL

JENNIE HALL

I. A REPORT OF MORNING EXERCISES

To the teachers of the Francis W. Parker School the morning exercises seem the most valuable work of the day. That period is sacred to the largest and best aims of the school, to the furthering of good fellowship among its members—good fellowship, that is, in all its phases from mere comradeship to an intellectual and moral co-operation in doing some piece of social work.

All the school, from the kindergarten through the twelfth grade, meets in the assembly hall at eleven o'clock. That time was chosen because some break in the regular work was necessary then, and because it was an hour convenient for the visits of friends and parents.

The exercises always begin with a song by the entire school. Usually there follows a short reading of verse or prose by a teacher. Then some class or group of pupils tells the school of some piece of work recently done. As an example we will describe an exercise about Eskimos given by the first grade. One child showed a clay model of an igloo, and explained the purpose of the long passage, gave the dimensions of the house, and told the process of building. Another child showed models of the furniture and utensils and explained their uses. Someone else had made a picture of a man catching a seal, and told the story of the capture and the later uses of the animal. Other children played Eskimo games for the audience to see. So twenty minutes were filled with interesting models, pictures, oral recitation, and dramatic representation.

This conception of the morning exercises grew up at the Chicago and Cook County Normal School with Colonel Parker.

There five hundred children and three hundred grown people met in a large room. With so large and so varied an audience, where, despite all efforts, there could not be a class acquaintance throughout the school, the meeting naturally took on a certain formality. There were not enough mornings in the year for everyone to have an opportunity to contribute; therefore the children could not form the habit of free public speaking. Moreover, the large hall was difficult to fill with the voice; and consequently, in order to make it possible for everyone to hear, it was necessary for these unaccustomed children to be drilled before the exercises in loud, clear speaking of what they had to say. Twenty minutes was all too short a time for a group of forty children to express itself; so the period was crowded full of this prepared work, and there was no opportunity for the audience to do anything but listen. The making ready of such exercises required much time and work; and, in consequence, the custom grew up of assigning mornings a month in advance to different teachers.

Such was the morning exercise in the Chicago and Cook County Normal School—a thing characteristic and inspiring. Colonel Parker's own words best describe it, and express, besides, the esteem in which the institution was held by his teachers and pupils: "In the morning exercises the entire school meets together for twenty minutes each day, and all the good things of class and grade are poured into the larger life of the whole school. Every subject presented to the assembled society should grow out—be, in fact, the efflorescence of the life in class and grade. Nothing should be in any way extraneous to the intrinsic movement of the school. There must be no attempt at show or mere exhibition. I have said that the morning exercises should spring from the work of the school, representing every class and grade from the kindergarten to the twelfth grade inclusive. All preparation should be made with care and deliberation; nothing should be done hurriedly. All preparation should be in the best literary and art forms. The morning exercises may be made the best period, educationally, of the day."

When the Francis W. Parker School was founded, its teachers

brought from the old Normal School not only a veneration for the morning exercises, but so strong a habit of having them that they were as essential to the idea of a school as was a curriculum. And they found their new pupils willing co-operators. In this little school, of perhaps a hundred and fifty people in its early days of unhabitual action, the morning exercises was at first a crude thing, but a pleasant one—a family meeting. But slowly, unaccountably, the attitude changed. After three years we awoke to find that many children were unwilling to appear before the school; that frequently a large part of the audience was inattentive; that occasionally there seemed to be a critical, almost unfriendly, attitude among the listeners; that sometimes an exercise did not ring true with genuine social action on the side of the participants. And yet such bald statements exaggerate the situation. Rather, these were fears on the part of the teachers instead of being established facts. Our morning exercises still seemed the most precious part of our program. But feeling that they were on a dangerous road, we began earnestly to consider the question. Every teacher who had a morning in charge made a special effort to choose an interesting and valuable piece of work, to plan carefully, and to give sufficient time for working out the exercises. Different seating arrangements were tried. The general idea and purpose of the morning exercises were discussed with the older children. Faculty meetings were given over to the consideration of the problem. But none of these actions had the desired result. Dissatisfaction grew. At last a committee was appointed from the teachers to work for the improving of the morning exercises. After many meetings and much discussion, this committee made a report to the faculty, outlining what seemed to the members the fundamental principles upon which the morning exercise idea and practice are based. This report was made merely for the purpose of directing discussion, and is of no value here. What is important is the later result of the thinking of the whole school. This paper is a new report from the committee upon that result.

The reason for the conditions was the first thing to seek.

Probably the difficulty at the base of the situation was that the type of morning exercises which had naturally evolved at the Normal School had been transplanted whole into quite different conditions. What the big school had needed was a meeting where people might learn what was going on in the school at large. What this small school needed was an opportunity to meet as a family and talk over common interests. The formal exercises, where one grade did all the talking, and that talking about its own work, seemed out of place, stiff, and unfriendly; so there had grown a cutting-off of listener from speaker, a habit of expecting to be entertained, a demand for finished, elaborate productions. Along with this growing disrespect for simplicity had come the lack of confidence about presenting oneself before the audience, which we have already mentioned. When the teachers once felt that they had the explanation of the situation, it was possible to act. We needed, both teachers and children, to get back to an understanding of first principles. Those principles were discussed in faculty meetings, and then the committee submitted them to the pupils for discussion at a town-meeting. From that meeting the teachers learned that the morning exercises, despite mistakes, were almost unanimously considered the pleasantest and most valuable part of the program, a precious thing, worth almost any sacrifice. The discussion was kept to constructive suggestion rather than criticism. And under all these suggestions showed a desire for less formality, for a return from the difficult thing that we had all together helped to produce, to the simple thing natural to the conditions. At the end of this meeting the children elected from among themselves a committee to act with a like committee from the faculty in following out suggestions already made in this meeting, and to plan further changes. As the result of the work of these committees, the following changes have been made:

Mornings are no longer assigned to teachers. Any person in the school, teacher or pupil, who wishes to give a morning exercise applies for time to the committee. Thus there is avoided the strain resulting from a division being forced to give a morning exercise whether the work has rounded itself to completion or not. Moreover, the feeling that it is rather a privilege than a duty to help in a morning exercise is emphasized. Plans for disposing of the unclaimed mornings have been suggested, but nothing has been adopted, because there is no present need, since all the exercises for two and a half months were eagerly taken.

The committee strongly advises that the prepared part of every exercise close five minutes before the end of the period, in order that the audience may ask questions or add contributions. When possible, the exercises should be planned with the purpose of encouraging such action on the part of the audience. It is of no effect to say: "Has anyone anything to add?" "Are there any questions?" The exercise itself must start new mental action, and then must give reason for expression. The people giving the exercises have sometimes asked help from the audience on questions too difficult for themselves to handle. One phase of the subject upon which the class is not fully prepared may be thrown open to the audience for discussion. As often as possible a theme of broad general interest is chosen for presentation, rather than one of limited appeal. To encourage general talking, the committee posts every morning the topic of the succeeding morning, that everyone may be considering it meantime.

The committee has made some definite efforts to bring the morning exercises into touch with the children's natural interest outside of the school. The members canvassed different grades, asking whether there were subjects about which the pupils would like to have exercises given. Airships, submarine boats, vacation experiences, Indians, and electricity were among the requests. Immediately six high-school boys, of their own initiative, took hold of the subject of airships, planned an exercise, executed drawings, and made an interesting presentation. It seemed to the committee, also, that the children's interest in collections might profitably express itself in exercises. On a chosen morning every child who may wish to exhibit his collection of stamps, coins, stones, pictures, or curios will bring it to school and set it up in some place. There will be different rooms for the different kinds of collections. People who wish to see exhibits of coins will go to the coin-room, those who wish to see stamps will go to another room. This plan has the added advantage of breaking grade lines and bringing together children of different ages into small sociable groups. At such times, in order to maintain the emphasis on the unity of our big family, we shall all meet in the assembly hall for a song and reading before separating into the different groups.

The newly interested audiences, the eager participants, the free discussion, the comfortable feeling, the general co-operation toward making the morning exercise period a valuable and pleasant one, make us all feel that at last our exercises have taken the right trend, toward informal family expression, and that our great task is to guard them from becoming formalized.

II. TWO TYPICAL MORNING EXERCISES

The following is a typical morning exercise by the second grade:[1]

MORNING EXERCISE

MONDAY, NOVEMBER 27, 1905

Singing of an opening hymn.

Reading of "Alice's Supper," by Miss Hall.

PAUL (second-grade child): Last year the first grade planted oats. The first time we planted them we didn't cover them up with earth at all. The second time we planted them we left them the same way, and then the third time we planted them and covered them up with earth, and then they came up. The two times before they didn't grow at all. They grew the last time, and Mr. Hendry picked them. Then we made a flail, and we flailed them this way. That is to get the oats out of the shells. Then we put them in a great big piece of cloth, and four children took hold of the cloth and threw the oats up into the air, and the husks flew away. This is to get all the chaff out of the oats.

FOWLER (second-grade child): Reading of "Threshing in Italy," as follows:

[1] Reported verbatim by the school stenographer.

THRESHING IN ITALY

The threshing-floor is out of doors.
It is a flat place paved with stones.
The floor is covered with yellow corn.
The men are going to shell it today.
Four of them come with their flails.
The flail is made of two sticks of wood.
They are tied loosely together at one end.
Two men stand on each side of the threshing-floor.
They swing their flails over their shoulders.
Down they come on the corn—first this two and then that two.
Whack! Whack! sound the flails.
The yellow corn flies.
The white cobs peep out.
After a long time the men stop.
They take wooden forks.
They lift the corn and cobs.
The corn falls through the forks.
The cobs stay on.
The men throw them away into a pile.
But some cobs still have corn on them.
The men take up their flails again.
So they work until all the corn is off.
It lies in a clean, yellow pile.
On another day the men will thresh wheat in the same way.

HELEN (second-grade child): I read a story of how the Indians got rice, and this is the way they got it: They took their canoes and rowed down until they got to a place that was filled full of rice, and then they bent the stems of the rice over into the canoe. And they had baskets in the canoe, and they pulled all the kernels of rice off, and they fell into the basket, and when they got the baskets full they took them home.

RUSSELL (second-grade child): The second grade read a story of how they threshed wheat in Greece. They would have a floor, and they would have horses hitched in a ring going around, and they would squash the wheat out. And then they would rake it up and throw it up with pitch-forks, and the chaff blows away and the wheat falls down. And then after that they take it and throw it onto a great big blanket, and women pick all the dirt out of it, and then they put it in bags.

MATILDA (second-grade child): The second grade made a lot of corn meal, and this is the meal (pointing to some jars on the table). We ground it with this coffee-mill. We are going to make corn-meal cakes.

MISS HALL: There are very few children in our grade who have seen modern threshing. We should be very grateful if someone would tell us how it is done; or, if you have seen some old-fashioned threshing, we should like to hear about that.

The following are spontaneous answers to Miss Hall's suggestion:

ELLIOTT (high-school boy): Two years ago, when I was out on a farm, they had two machines and a steam engine attached to the machines with belts. They put the wheat into the machines, and it made a great big pile of straw. The straw is used in winter for the cows.

WALKER (fifth-grade boy): When I saw them thresh, they had a lot of horses, and they made the machine go, and the grain came out of little funnels into bags. It wasn't a steam engine.

MYRON (sixth-grade boy): When I was in the country, we were going along, and we saw them threshing some wheat in a farm-yard, and we went in to watch them. A hay wagon would drive up beside the machine, and there were two men on each wagon and another that they kept there to load the wheat into the machine, and they shoveled it in as fast as they could with pitch-forks, and the kernels of wheat came out and fell into bags. The straw went up a kind of walking staircase and went into the barn. After a while they put buckets on, and the wheat fell into the buckets instead of into the bags, and the buckets carried it to a bin in the barn.

ELIZABETH (high-school girl): Last summer, when I was out in Lake Forest, I saw a silo. This is a big stone building, and they put in the green corn, stalks and all. After they put the corn in they put on a layer of dirt about three or four feet deep, and then they put on a heavy cover made of stone that squashes it all down. It is perfectly air-tight. We didn't find out how they got the corn out.

OTTO (seventh-grade boy): I saw them threshing, and there was a rod about four feet long that had knives on it, and the rod revolved. It was driven by a cog and chain. The bundles were thrown in, and they had a chute that was worked by another cog that had points on it so as to catch them, and that took the bundles up past the knives, and the knives cut the strings on the bundles.

The following is a typical morning exercise by high-school boys, assisted by high-school girls:

A MUSICAL PROGRAM

DECEMBER 11, 1905

NOTE OF EXPLANATION BY MISS GOODRICH

The steady, strong interest which the boys showed in preparing this program was due largely to the influence of the twelfth grade and the three teachers who joined the class, and to the variety, novelty, and virility of the songs. These songs, with the exception of the Latin hymns, were studied in class time during the fall quarter. The Latin hymns were sung last year in a program of historical songs. Translations of the texts of the hymns, and of the principal rule for their performance, were made by the boys with the help of the Latin teacher. Two very beautiful mediæval manuscripts were shown to the class, as well as pictures of cathedrals and an old engraving of monks at service in the chancel. The boys went to the Newberry Library to examine mediæval books and facsimiles, and some of them have made large manuscripts for the music-room under Miss Clement's direction. All of this work was voluntary. The training involved in learning to sing these songs with accuracy as to pitch, attack, and pronunciation was less valuable than the result to the boys in genuine musical feeling and in respect for the work. The dignified manner in which they presented the program reacted appreciably upon the whole school.

PROGRAM [2]

1 "Media Vita," tenth century; "Veni Creator," ninth century.

2. "The Volga," Russian boat-song.

3. "The Piper," Bohemian folk-song.

4. "The Lone Prairie," American folk-song.

5. "Henry of Navarre," French folk-song.

MISS GOODRICH: The first two of these songs are Latin hymns; the rest are folk-songs.

CLARENCE: "Media Vita" was written by a monk in the tenth century. The monk was walking along a road one day and saw some men building a bridge in a very perilous position, and their danger brought to his mind these words. The translation is:

> In the midst of life we are in death.
> What aid do we seek, O Lord, except thine,
> Who art justly angry at our transgressions?

MISS GOODRICH: At the time this was written they might have had a little crude organ, but they sang mostly without any accompaniment, and although it is a rather difficult thing to do, we are going to try to sing it in that way.

(Hymn sung by the boys.)

CLARENCE: The translation of the second song is this:

> Come, Holy Spirit, visit our souls.
> Fill with the highest gratitude
> The breasts of those whom thou hast created.
> Thou, who art spoken of as Paraclitus,
> Most High God, living fountain,
> Fire of youth, and Holy Spirit. Amen!

MISS GOODRICH: The rest are folk-songs, which have come from the people in a more or less spontaneous way and without scientific understanding of music. The first is a Russian boat-song:

[2] Reported by the school stenographer. The program was printed upon a blackboard.

On our Mother Volga's breast,
So proudly swelling,
  The Volga, the Volga.
Dark waves are upward welling,
Winds no more rest,
On our Mother Volga's breast.

Rowers all pull lustily.
The boat flies faster
  Adown the dark Volga.
There in the stern
The master calls cheerily:
"Rowers, all pull lustily!"

Then up spake our master brave,
Good Stjenke Rasin,
  On the wide Volga:
"Pull, lads, as rowers should,
And sing merrily,
On the river Volga."

MISS GOODRICH: The next is a Bohemian song, in three parts, and will be sung by the boys and girls:

When the jolly piper plays his tune,
Be it morning, eve, or sunny noon,
All the folks from far and near
Gather round, his pipes to hear.
When the jolly piper plays his tune,
Be it morning, eve, or sunny noon.

When the piper pipes so merrily,
I would wander forth as glad and free.
Over rivers deep and wide,
Through the blooming country side.
When the piper pipes so merrily,
I would wander forth as glad and free.

Wondrous tales the piper knoweth well,
Tales his droning bagpipe loves to tell,

Tales of castles rich and old,
Kings and queens with thrones of gold.
Wondrous tales the piper knoweth well,
Tales his droning bagpipe loves to tell.

Piper, might I go with you along,
To your pipes I'd sing a pretty song;
Then together would we stray,
Oe'r the hills and far away,
While your pipe, and e'en my little song,
Made too short the way that else were long.

KENNETH: The next song is supposed to have been made up by the cowboys on the western plains, and is one of the few folk-songs that American people have:

O, bury me out on the lone prairee,
Where the wild coyote will howl o'er me,
In a narrow grave, just six by three.
O, bury me out on the lone prairee.

And they buried him there on the lone prairee,
Where the coyote howls and the wind goes free,
In his narrow grave, just six by three,
And they buried him there on the lone prairee.

CHESTER: The next song is of Henry of Navarre, who was Henry IV of France. He was adored by the people of France, and they wrote this song entirely for his benefit, to do him praise:

Long live Henry, our glorious Henry Fourth!
Lord of high valor and monarch of true worth,
Conqueror invincible, hero of Navarre.
Let us praise him, Henry, king in peace and war.

Long live King Henry, our glorious Henry Fourth!
Lord of high valor, of laughter and of mirth,
Lover of revels, and blithe in peace and war.
Let us praise him, Henry, our hero of Navarre.

III. A HALLOWE'EN MORNING EXERCISE

OCTOBER 31, 1905

ELSA MILLER, TEACHER FIFTH GRADE

A story appropriate for dramatization for a Hallowe'en morning exercise was selected from the collection *Legendary Fiction of the Irish Celts,* by Patrick Henry. The legend is one named "Palace in the Rath." It appears in the Irish and Breton versions. The Irish version was used. It was simplified and much modified in presentation to the children. The story was first told to a fifth-grade class, which did considerable work in constructing a simple play and writing the necessary melodies. Each member of the class wrote a play.

To convey an idea of the story as it was presented, and at the same time to give an example of the work done by the children, the following is quoted:

THE HUNCHBACK

On the night of Hallowe'en a hunchback weaver is coming home from his work. He is very tired and sits down to rest awhile. He sings:

He hears strange music that comes from the little people. He stops his own singing and listens to theirs. He looks around to find them and sees a great hole in the ground. There they are.

LITTLE PEOPLE:

WEAVER:

The little people come out of the ground.

LITTLE PEOPLE: So it is you! We are so glad you finished our song for us. We have been singing it this way so long, and we could not find anyone who would finish it for us. You have finished it. Now, we are so grateful to you that we will give you a wish that will be sure to come true.

HUNCHBACK: I am so glad I could finish your song for you. I know what I wish already.

LITTLE PEOPLE: What is your wish?

HUNCHBACK: I wish that I were just as straight and tall as other men.

LITTLE PEOPLE (*take hold of hands and dance around and around him until he is just as straight and tall as other men*): Your wish has come true.

Further to intensify the feeling for the Irish fairy and give the children an idea of the Irish customs on May Day and Hallowe'en, selections from "Land of Heart's Desire" were read. The children recalled and recited poems and stories with which they were familiar, such as "Fairy Folk," by Allingham, and "The Brownie," by Graber-Hoffmann. "The Kildare Pooka" was also told, which may be found in the book of legends once before mentioned. More careful and intelligent work was done from day to day, until the point was reached where the class had contributed its best. A few children, however, wished to try to write the play in verse. This they found too difficult, and here they asked the teacher to contribute. Following is a copy of the play in its finished form:

A HALLOWE'EN PLAY

Characters: Hunchback Weaver, Fairy Queen, and Fairies. Scene: On a rath in Ireland.

HUNCHBACK (*gathering primroses in a basket*):

A black cat crossed my path tonight.
Misfortune follows me.
A weaver works and sings all day,
Why should he unhappy be?

I ran across the fields and raths,
I must not linger long,
For the good folks come when the moon is high
To find the paths where the primroses lie
That lead to each man's door.

If the fairies ask for aught in vain,
Some trick unkind they'll play.
A big, strong man need fear them not,
But trifle with me they may.

(*The hooting of an owl is heard.*)

The good folks ask for milk and fire,
And he who gives to them
Is in their power for one long year;
His heart is filled with dread.

(*The hooting of the owl is heard again.*)

What strange sounds!
It may be the Pooka hidden hereabouts.

(*The hooting is heard again.*)

I must go. I must go.

(*The hooting is heard again.*)

No wind sings tonight.

(*The hooting is heard again.*)

The hooting owl calls through the darkness.
Strange that the night has come so soon!
The bats are flying,
And the sun is hardly set.

(*Singing is heard. Chorus of fairies behind scenes sing the "Barley-Brownie," by Reinecke. Hunchback's fear increases. Fairies enter dancing.*)

FAIRIES:

HUNCHBACK:

FAIRIES: Oh! Oh! (*Dancing with joy and laughter around the hunchback.*)

FAIRY QUEEN:

> So you have finished the song
> That we have been singing so long.
> A good man! A good man!
> What shall we give you
> For a song with an end?

FAIRIES: (*Suppressed laughter and pantomime, imitating the hunchback's attitude. They stoop and straighten, stoop and straighten.*)

A FAIRY: We know what your wish is! We know what your wish is!

HUNCHBACK: I see you know what I would be—as straight and strong as my fellows.

(*Fairies dance around. Fairy Queen approaches with magic step, sways scepter, and touches hunchback.*)

HUNCHBACK (*slowly straightens up and solemnly says*): As straight and strong as my fellows.

FAIRY QUEEN:

> We must away to the paths
> Where the primroses lie,
> Milk and fire to find.

The actors were chosen from the various grades. The hunchback was a high-school boy; the fairies, about twelve in number, were chosen from the third, fourth and fifth grades. A dark-blue curtain formed the background, and brown screens to conceal the fairies and the hooting owl were the other articles of scenery. To add color, a large decorative lantern of Irish design, made by the children, was hung on either side of the stage.

The hunchback was dressed as a weaver, in a dark-blue frock and leather apron. To appear as a hunchback he bent his shoulders round and low. This seemed a more simple and natural way than using a clumsy make-up which would later be in the way. The fairies wore green jackets, red, white, or yellow tights or long stockings, and red caps with a white feather. The jackets were children's cotton shirts, dyed apple-green. These fitted closely and lent a sprightly look. The caps were ordinary red stocking caps stuffed with paper. At the top of each was fastened a soft white turkey feather. The fairy queen wore a small golden crown and carried a scepter.

THE OPPORTUNITIES AND RESPONSIBILITIES OF THE MANUAL TRAINING TEACHER

LOUIS C. BUTLER
St. Louis, Mo.

The manual training writer of today, being no longer taken up with apologies for his subject or explanations of it, may well consider the pioneer stage of his profession as past and turn his attention to details of beauty and finish heretofore sadly neglected. The ax of the woodman is followed by the plow of the farmer; the rude trail of the trapper, by the road of the merchant; and the successful introduction of a new line of thought or activity, by its refinement and polish in the smallest details. Volumes have been written and spoken in defense of the "why" and "what is" of manual training; and later the energy has turned to the question of what we shall teach—or the case is opened of models vs. models. Here the end is not yet in sight, nor does it seem as though one were possible; for, on the one side, the champions of the tools clamor of joints, tool sequence, and accuracy; while those who see the boy only murmur of water wheels, boats, and intellectual tinkering. This very divergence of opinion would be a most favorable sign were it not for the fact that they represent, in both cases, small extremes while the general run of schools seem to constitute a very large, solid, and immovable mean.

A few progressive men have ideas and give them out, and we feel that strides are being made; but, in the long run, the work—and I confine myself to elementary bench-work—of the schools of the country is typified, if not actually represented, by the ubiquitous plant-stick, coat-hanger, towel-rack, hammer-handle, etc. And my authority for this statement is a somewhat careful study of the various state and city exhibits at the great exposition held in St. Louis so recently. There, at least, the manual training teacher could feel at home, for on every side he was greeted by old friends with measurements and even decoration like unto his very own.

Now the reasons for this lethargic and static condition are doubtless many and subtle, and I feel that several of them are outside of the field of the average teacher; so I pass on to a point in our profession upon which little has been said, and maybe it will throw some light upon this first problem.

Our pioneers met and mastered the question whether we ought to teach manual training in our schools; their followers are still busy with the next logical question to be met: What manual training shall we teach in our schools? It is my purpose to propound the third critical question: How shall our teachers teach manual training in our schools?

As it refers to public school work, our subject may be divided into the hand-work stage, up to the seventh grade; the elementary bench-work stage, and the high-school stage; and it is the purpose of this paper to speak of the second entirely. I select this not only because of my experience there, but because I feel that here, as differentiated from the play element on one side and the occupational element on the other, my subject has its broadest and deepest pedagogical and artistic outlook, and that here lies the proper field for the asking of the question as to the opportunities and responsibilities of the manual training teacher.

At its inception, this, our branch of educational effort, was looked upon and approached from the standpoint of technique or technical training, and Old World systems were drawn upon for materials, regardless of their fitness for so wholesale a transplanting, and sometimes for workers as well.

No matter how brilliantly the faculty psychologists argued in its favor as a cure-all for the ever-prevalent diseases of carelessness, disorder, inaccuracy, and the like, the heart of the movement rested upon the conjunction of boy, tools, and skill; and in "sloyd," that truthful old name, the practical educationalists found their great opportunity.

With this emphasis upon skill and tools, what wonder is it that it came at once to be looked at as a subject apart from the usual curriculum, that its teachers were considered specialists in the extreme, and that those teachers were recruited from the ranks of the mechanical trades? Given benches, tools, and wood on one side, with active boys on the other, who was more fitted to combine the two into a broad and flowing stream of models than the carpenter, pattern-maker, or general shop practice man?

He knows a whole bagful of good tricks that the layman never saw; he can keep tools and shop in excellent order; he can make a model with his trained hands before the boys in true commercial manner; next to the janitor, he will be the handiest man about the place, and—he is cheap. (This latter, of course, entirely by way of parenthesis.) And if one mildly suggests that the man in his relation to the boys be considered, the reply will probably contain three absolute fallacies: first, that the children will respect the manual skill, and therefore the worker; second, that the subject is technical and requires a minimum of personal intercourse between pupil and teacher; and, third, that the subject is so popular a one among the boys that it carries itself along even with the most ordinary assistance. Why I consider these statements incorrect I shall take up later, but right now I wish to disclaim any reflection upon the many excellent teachers in our ranks who have come from the profession. Many of them have been well trained and are skilled teachers, but my point so far has been to show the early filling up of the ranks by many whose sole qualification for the teaching profession has been technical skill in some particular line. This idea still holds in some quarters; and it is to dispute it, and to show some of the real duties or opportunities of the manual training teacher, as opposed to the shop instructor, that this article is written.

At the seventh or eighth-grade age the boy is passing through that stage in his development when childish things are beginning to fall behind and the faint call of manhood begins to make itself heard. He sees a vista of rooms and grades in his district school through which he has passed, and close ahead the four magical high-school years. At the high school the boys wear bands on their hats, yell at football games, escort girls, make fun of the faculty via their own publication, and are altogether quite men. So it behooves the thirteen-year-old boy even to look about him for what the school has to offer as a suggestion toward the ideal of a gentleman and a scholar. The principal is a man who wears a white vest, writes unpleasant notes to one's parents, talks ethics, scolds little boys, is police court in perpetual session, and is altogether awful and depressing. He is doubtless a human being, but rarely within miles of one of his boys. Teacher is fine, and we thoroughly respect and, better yet, love her; but as a manly type we feel that something is lacking. This leaves only the janitor, who smokes a pipe in the basement when the principal goes out; and somehow his appearance is against him.

No, not all hope is gone, for once or twice a week we are separated from the depressingly good influence of the girls and, all by ourselves, turned over to a man and to do a man's work. In dress he is ahead of the janitor, though a little lower than the principal, and his authority and direction are personal like teacher's; but he is a real, live, human man, and he is here for the big boys only, and will treat us as such—not as masculine girls.

I hear you, my critics, label this as fanciful, but have you gotten near enough to your boys' hearts to find out their attitude toward their manual? If not, try it. How are our teachers dealing with this eagerness, none the less true for its frequent expression?

Some time ago I was present at a school where a beginning boy brought his thumb gauge to the teacher and asked for instructions as to its use. His introduction to the tool began, as nearly as I can quote from memory: "Do you see that, kid?" pointing to the scale on the beam. "Well, the man who put that there was a nickel-plated jackass, and if you ever meet him, you tell him so." The teacher was an excellent mechanic, but hours of work could not make up for the respect he lost in one minute. It explained why discipline was enforced at times in his shop by the application of a style of handwork not listed in the course of study. Again I visited a beautiful shop full of bright, cultured boys to hear the instructor finish a demonstration by saying: "Now you seen how I done it, try it yourselves." All this to illustrate my first point, that if young and highly impressionable boys are to be given by our schools into the authority of men, care should be taken that those men are of such refinement and education that the harm of association may not overbalance the good of the subject. The adherents of the tools will decry all this and claim a teacher's manual ability sufficient; but I claim that no man is fit to stand before small boys, with their keen eyes and sharp judgments, who is not able to do so as a gentleman of refinement and culture at best not inferior to their own.

Given, then, a man whose external personality meets my requirements, I would wish him to add to it a genuine love of his boys and interest in all their concerns. Now, it will be objected that these two considerations (in effect practically one) require a closer contact than the shop affords; but I deny it. I do admit that where every period starts with a twenty to thirty minute demonstration, and the rest of the time is spent by the boys in a mad attempt to catch up with the instruction, little is left for the teacher but his own bench and general police duty. But where the demonstrations are short, thoughtful, and entered into by the boys, there is plenty of opportunity for the teacher to visit, criticise, help, or encourage each individual boy, and so come much closer even than the grade teacher in her fixed location. Maybe you see that the child spoiled a corner, and you make a sympathetic, brief comment and go on; but he saw that you cared, and some day he will wait after school with a plan of a wind-mill he is going to make, and wants you to offer suggestions upon. That is a victory for you, do you but know it; and pretty soon he waits to help you clear up, walks home with you, and suggests a skating trip when it gets cold. Then you notice his never-failing pleasant look every time he meets your eye, his disposition to tell you of home and the family secrets, and finally his telling you his own boyish troubles—and he is yours. The chances are even, then, that you have done more good to that boy, and the community of which he is a member, than either you or your board will ever know, and at absolutely no expense of said board's time.

It may be objected here that we are paid to teach manual training, and this is out of our line; but to this I object. I am teaching boys, not manual training, and I do not propose to mix up the means and the end. As well say, when the boy cuts himself, that you are a teacher, not a surgeon, and so let him bleed, as to refuse a moral hand to a boy on the score that you are a teacher, not a man. From the strictly practical and technical side, however, we can arrive at the same conclusion, should our senses be dulled to more subtle influences, because this attitude toward the boys pays in models as well as manliness. To illustrate let me tell of a boy in one of my finishing classes who was just completing the towel-rack. It was very poorly done, and I could not seem to lift, or get at him at all. One day I noticed him limp and, after some delay, discovered he had hurt himself on the way to school. I took him from the room, bound up his leg in two places, and fixed him up in considerable comfort—though it cost me some twenty minutes from my class to do it. He was grateful and I saw my chance, and there began a fight to win him. He was the last boy in the grade on his towel-rack, and I spoke my mind. For the first time it was heeded, and he went for a tough old stick of maple, resolved to carve out of it a hammer-handle and his own salvation. When he started he said to me: "I'll try for you this time;" and he was a man and as good as his word. His model was the best in his class, among the best ever made in the school, and a beautiful piece of work; and as a result of the pride and interest of his parents he now has a fine bench and tools at home. This was not a spurt, for up to this day his work is steadily and thoroughly good, and I feel glad that by the exercise of some methods not suggested in the outline I made a true friend and a good worker.

In addition to this, the teacher should be a man of infinite resource, or the work will sadly suffer in interest. Popular though it may be, manual training will no more carry itself by the simple repetition of definite sets of models than the same sets of questions would serve the grade teachers for years; but it has to be watched, the local needs studied, trifling changes made, and the dry bones covered by real living—i.e., growing—tissues. From experience in a shop of over five hundred boys a week I find the average of interest in work fluctuates as follows: In the start the pressure is way up, and steam is always blowing off. and more often various forms of safety-valves come in handy; at the middle of the first year the engine is going smoothly and time is being made; with the start of the second year (eighth grade) the pressure begins to drop now and then; and at the middle of that year the wise man will keep the stoker busy and read up on the patent fuel. The reason is, I believe, that at the beginning the work is so new and pleasant that the model excites no discrimination or criticism; while at the close of the course skill and thought give a basis for judgment, and we are dealing with boys of considerable taste and critical ability. If the course, at this point, consists of small, fussy, detail work, let the teacher introduce a large, well-designed, and thoroughly practical and desirable model, and see the result. The writer has just made such an experiment with results far beyond his wildest expectations, and has seen his young men working with the keen interest of the most enthusiastic beginner.

Finally, my ideal manual training teacher must be in it

as his life-work, study it and the entire school work of which it is simply a part, and follow it alone. I thoroughly believe that one great stumbling-block of our profession is the men in its midst who are teaching for the time being only, using the school as a stepping-stone to other things. They may be men of ambition who, as one man told me, leave the front door at 3 P. M. when the boys leave the back, and so find time for law, insurance, real estate, cabinet work, music, and the like; but they are not teachers, and never can be. To such men this article, of course, has no message or interest, for their work is but routine drudgery to themselves and their hapless charges. But it is well to note them for their influence in lowering the salaries and the general intellectual and pedagogical standing of our hard and conscientious workers.

My omission of technical skill as a requirement is simply the admission of it as an obvious fact, and requiring no championship of mine.

In conclusion, my appeal is to the earnest members of my profession to demand higher intellectual and cultural standing of its members; to encourage the student-worker to enter the field; and so to constitute the rank and file of our profession that the manual training teacher many demand and hold the educational position to which the importance, scope, and possibilities of this subject entitle him.

A POINT OF VIEW IN THE TEACHING OF ELECTRICITY IN THE UNIVERSITY ELEMENTARY SCHOOL

HARRY ORRIN GILLETTE
Teacher in Tenth School Year (Eighth Grade), The School of Education

One of the much-discussed questions in the teachers' world today is "waste in education." All agree that there is a waste, but there is no unanimity of opinion as to just what constitutes the waste, and therefore suggestions of reform are legion. I do not intend to advocate a certain group of studies, the omitting of some or the adding of others, although it seems that our curricula need some revisions; but I wish simply to repeat the old suggestion that it is not the subject-matter which educates, but the mental effort consciously directed to the utilization, and hence organization, of that subject-matter. We do not educate the child; we help the child to educate himself. In our problem of teaching him to think, we wish him to use those means which will insure the best results in the shortest time. We all recognize *interest* as one of the great impelling factors in developing one's self; for genuine interest implies purpose and urges the application of all the faculties to the problem. Interest begets motive, and the motive guides the child. Both interest and motive profit from their being so closely related. Transient, shallow curiosity must not be confounded with genuine, lasting, deep interest. The point of view is that the impelling force must come from the child, not the teacher.

It may be only a result of tradition, and the modern school not at fault, that upon entering the school building many children feel that they must abandon all they really like to do. Where manual-training shops are introduced, and the boy feels that at last there is one study in which he may put something of himself, his hopes are often crushed by his being set at work making models "to learn technique." His own motive has been taken away; his guiding principle is gone. But if the piece of work which he wishes to do is so difficult that he cannot do it until he has learned the necessary technique for that piece of work, he attacks the preliminary work eagerly. The manual-training shop is a place where obviously the interests of the child may give a great interest and direction to the work; but I believe that the other studies also can be so organized about the interests of the class that there will be a distinct gain in the educational efficiency.

It is strange that it is in the teaching of science in the elementary school that the child's natural interests are most ignored. Children begin the study of nature and science with interest. But when they are led into formal abstractions about nature before they have any material upon which to generalize, the interest wanes. Where there is such a wealth of material which the children are eager to use, if guided and encouraged, it is too bad that the results are so poor. Perhaps it is the very wealth of material which confuses teachers. Without the organizing and unifying motive in the child by which the newly discovered facts may be related, it is difficult to get order out of the mass.

One of the lively interests of boys of twelve and thirteen is in electricity. If they receive the slightest encouragement at home, they attempt to repair the electric bell or recharge the cells, and will go to infinite trouble to learn how. They attempt to make bits of electrical apparatus, usually with failure, but this only increases their interest. When the course in electricity was introduced into the curriculum of the seventh grade, two years ago, an effort was made to let it consist of experiments along the lines of the interests of the class—experiments mostly suggested and devised by the children themselves toward the solution of their own problems. Naturally only the simplest apparatus was used, because the children knew of no other. They made most of the apparatus themselves.

The first two- or three-lesson periods were given to a report of what they had attempted at home, what difficulties they had encountered, and what they wished to know about electricity. Many had a real interest in electrical apparatus and machinery, and were willing to work hard to learn more. In the preliminary discussions they found that nearly all the electrical machines with which they were familiar embodied the principles of magnets. Our first work was therefore with magnets. I did not have to put the questions; for the class in the discussions asked many. These questions were organized in class as a basis for the laboratory exercises. The children used their own magnets largely in the laboratory experiments, and this was encouraged. Of course, many could answer most of the questions without having to experiment; they advanced to other work. No attempt was made to keep the class together in the experiments, but a strong class unity was noticeable in the frequent "report" lessons. Each child contributed something to the whole.

The work with electro-magnets was preceded by several hours' work with the electric current. As before, the apparatus was of the crudest—ordinary thick-walled drinking-glasses, small strips of zinc and copper from the tinsmith's, copper wire, and dilute sulphuric acid. In these experiments the problems expanded as the work continued: the proofs of a current, the bubbles being given off, the origin of the electric current, the expense at which it was being generated, the circuit, amalgamating the zincs, adding something to the acid to remove the annoying hydrogen bubbles, and ways of increasing the current by joining cells. These cells were, of course, very inefficient, and even when modified did not offer a convenient source of electricity for later experiments; but they had served their purpose. For later work we used the current of storage cells, or of ordinary wet cells belonging to the school equipment. The discovery of the effect of an electric current upon a magnetic needle suggested a convenient "current detector." Each child made one for use in future work.

It is not necessary to describe all the work in as much detail as is given above. It is sufficient to say that by following the same plan of letting the class organize the questions through discussion, and expecting individuals or groups to organize ways and means of answering these questions experimentally, we not only covered considerable subject-matter in the twelve weeks, but encouraged considerable mental activity toward definite ends. The class really thought to a purpose.

The experiments with the simple electric cells were followed by experiments with electro-magnets (nails, iron and steel rods wound temporarily with insulated wire), and with two of the common electro-magnetic machines—the electric bell and the telegraph sounder. We considered motors and telephones too complex for the class as a whole. Each person made a miniature electric heater, and did enough of copper-plating to understand the principle.

Last year the class set up an electric gong in the school, laying the wires and making the connections themselves, expended the circuits of the signal buzzers to other rooms; and several learned to operate and adjust the electric stereopticon. The interest extended back into the home, and there a majority of the boys set up telegraph instruments from house to house or from room to room, and learned the code, or put up elctric bells and buzzers, or wound motors; and one boy constructed a telephone.

CO-OPERATION BETWEEN LIBRARIES AND SCHOOLS—THE NEED IN CHICAGO.

HARRIET E. PEET
Chicago Public Schools

The public library as an institution has had a growth in its function within the last few years, and is fast becoming a great civic and educational force. It not only responds as of old to the needs of cultured people by handing books over a counter, but it is aggressive in its policy, and is going out to all classes by co-operating with clubs and societies, by sending books to places of recreation and public amusement, by including music and pictures in its circulating departments, by holding art exhibits, by giving study and reading courses, and by doing away with time limits and fines in books. It is not only relieving the overburdened school with its graded reading lists, its school bulletins and traveling libraries, but it is working directly with the children through its children's rooms with their specially trained attendants, with its story hours, and in the slums, with its library missionaries.

One of the causes of ill-feeling, sin, and crime in this world is the poverty of interests. There is too much absorption in the petty and trivial, and things are not seen in their proper perspective. Human ideals and the beauty of the past disintegrates, unless the institutions which conserve them are alive and aggressive.. Books unlock the treasures of the past, and give to us the wisdom of the ages and the ennobling thoughts of great personalities. What culture comes from a thorough knowledge of the works of even one great poet, what inspiration from reading biography and history, and what practical knowledge and the entrance into the innermost meaning of things from an acquaintance with science and philosophy!

A pretty sight can be seen at any time in Chicago's Blackstone Library. The low shelves which line the children's room are filled with a thousand or more attractive books. The two low tables are usually surrounded by children. The other day I saw an interesting group about the tables; one boy was studiously, though rather shame-facedly, taking notes from a book on electricity; another was buried in Robinson Crusoe; a third was lost to his surroundings in an account of a seafight; one little girl was attempting the impossible in her eager enjoyment, by trying to see at the same time all the pictures in her own book and in her neighbor's; and two girls in the corner were having quiet spasms of amusement over a book of fun.

In Northampton, Mass., the Forbes Library sends out envelopes of fine photographs. The people, rich and poor, are expected to take them home and use them to decorate their houses. The other day a little boy of nine went to an attendant and asked for some pictures on Greek art. The attendant asked him if he was studying it at school. He said: "Well yes, but I want to have them at home." If more of our boys were inspired to similar desires, the state would have to provide fewer reformatories and other expensive institutions. No community, either from a moral or from an economical standpoint, can afford to do without a good library.

A typical institution of the advanced kind is that in Newark, N. J. This library reaches out and co-operates with clubs and societies, sending ahead for club programs that the right books may be on hand. It has an attractive children's room. It does special work with the firemen. It publishes bulletins, and encourages the public in every way to avail themselves of their library privileges. It sends classroom libraries to the schools, so that every teacher in the city has at her command a library of from twenty to fifty books for the use of the children in her own classroom. It also sends to the schools collections of pictures on nature-study, historical events, foreign countries, architecture and sculpture. (Think of the labor saved by having these collected once by a public institution instead of hundreds of times by many different teachers, and how much better the result would be!) It also sends out single poems printed on slips in sets of fifty. It reserves books on special topics for the use of the children at the libraries, when notified by the teacher. Many of the schools have special messengers, who leave at night a list of the subjects which the children are studying. The librarians look up suitable material, and have books in readiness for the messengers when they call in the morning. The eighth grade classes are trained in the use of the library. The classes go to the library in sections between nine and ten o'clock in the morning, and as a part of their school work are taught by the librarians how to use the library. The lessons are arranged in this order: (1) how to find books on the shelves from the book numbers; (2) use of the card catalogue; (3) subjects with the card catalogue; (4) Poole's Index.

The spirit of the new library is well represented by the Boston Public Library. The teachers are invited to hold their classes in the branch libraries. When a request is sent in, space and books are reserved for the purpose. The teachers and children are cordially invited and even urged to come; and that they may come, the library does away with all possible red tape. The surroundings are beautiful, the service perfect. No need, from the most trivial one of the youngest child to the most serious, is passed by without due attention. There is inspiration and culture in the very atmosphere and spirit of the place, and the path to learning is made easy and attractive.

The Newark type of work is done on a varying scale in Buffalo, N. Y.; Springfield, Mass.; Cambridge, Mass.; Hartford, Conn.; Pittsburg, Pa.; Cleveland, Ohio; Minneapolis, Minn.; Indianapolis, Ind.; Milwaukee, Wis.; St. Louis, Mo.; Evanston, Ill.; and in many other cities.

The common method of co-operating with the schools in this system is to employ trained attendants to study the needs of the schools, to furnish from time to time graded lists of books, to publish frequent school bulletins, to inspire the children to right reading by sending to the schools gifted story-tellers, but best of all by sending to each classroom from twenty to fifty books. These are left in the school rooms varying lengths of time—in Milwaukee eight weeks in many places five months, in some a year. The libraries in almost all of these cases provide for the transportation of the books, furnishing cases which fold and lock like trunks, but open into bookshelves.

You observe that the St. Louis Library is among the ranks of the advanced libraries. It not only furnishes classroom libraries, for which we in Chicago would be grateful, but it takes charge of the supplementary reading for the city, sending out books in sets for periods of thirty days. The old story of the two frogs in a milk can would have had to be told the other way around if the frogs had been library frogs. It was the St. Louis frog that made for himself a pat of butter upon which to float. The Chicago frog was drowned!

The chief advantages of the Buffalo-Newark system are (1) There is economy in it. No books are put away on top shelves because ill-adapted to the class that happens to have them, and the books are kept in repair. (2) The books are better selected than they can be by the individual teacher. Buffalo has two expert assistants, who devote themselves to the school work, spending their time visiting the schools and looking into the problem.

Conditions in smaller communities seem more favorable for the development of good libraries. Small cities all about us have finer facilities than we have in Chicago. New York, however, must have problems similar to our own. The public library there is active for the benefit of the schools, but the board of education furnishes the schoolrooms with libraries. It maintains a bureau of libraries, which has this feature in charge. Three-fourths of the classrooms in the 484 public schools in New York have been furnished with permanent libraries of from thirty to fifty books, or 450,250 volumes in all. The circulation last fall term averaged about eight times per book. This is the sixth largest library in the country. It is operated with no expense but the cost of the books. The bureau of libraries also furnishes the schools with topical and reference lists.

The public library in New York in the meantime furnishes traveling libraries to schools as well as to recreation parks, playgrounds, etc., on any reliable person's guarantee. The expense of transportation is sometimes borne by the library, and sometimes by guarantors. It has fifty-five deposit stations in the public schools. It has a special attendant in each one of its thirty-four branch libraries, whose business it is to keep in touch with the teachers and the children. Chicago has not one. This attendant follows the course of study and monthly plans for teachers, and sends bulletins to the schools for the use of the children. These are posted on bulletin boards provided for the purpose by the board of education, and the result is that thousands of children flock to the sub-stations and avail themselves of the reference books there. The public library furnishes an unlimited number of books to the teacher for her own use. These may be kept six months on monthly renewals. Furthermore, when a teacher indorses a child's card, she is not held financially responsible for losses or fines.

The system in use in Indianapolis most resembles the one which Chicago has unsuccessfully tried. The library furnishes the schoolrooms with fifty books each. These are delivered by the school wagons. Such care has been taken that the total loss for the last ten years has been twelve books. Two of these are about to be recovered! Teachers have special cards upon which they can draw six books. The Chicago Public Library allows thirty books to a school to be delivered by the board of education supply wagons. That is the plan, but the libary has not felt that it could carry it out, partly because the books have not always been well cared for by the schools, but more because the means of transportation has not been a convenient one. Indianapolis has been successful with the plan. Moreover, Indianapolis has several deposit stations in the outlying schools, and fifty per cent of its work is for the teachers and the children. Story hours are held by a gifted attendant, who goes out three of four times a week to the fifth, sixth, and seventh grades in the schools.

Librarians everywhere say that the work with the children is made valuable when the schools co-operate with the libraries and direct the reading. The problem in Chicago is how to bring about a co-operation between schools and libraries, and put our system on a par with work done elsewhere. What can be done to bring library privileges to over two hundred and fifty schools?

The necessity of adequate library facilities in a community composed of a heterogeneous foreign population is three-fold. In the first place, there is the moral need of bringing the children not only to a consciousness of the seven cardinal virtues through contact with good literature, but to a clear understanding of the American ideal of liberty and service in contrast with that of license and graft. The latter is obtained in reading history and such biographies as that of Abraham Lincoln. In the second place, there is the necessity of forming the reading habit at the reading age of fourth and fifth grade to give those of foreign parentage in particular command of English. Many of our pupils do not pursue a higher education from their inability either to obtain or to give the thought from the printed page. In the third place, there is the necessity for more books to aid the scholarship of the schools. It is making bricks without straw to ask teachers, in these days of laboratory and library methods, to educate their pupils in history, literature, science and mathematics, and not put at their command a variety of books. Many, if not all, teachers here are greatly hampered in this way.

Several of the Chicago schools have, by dint of a great deal of hard labor and self-sacrifice, got together large libraries, which do them great credit. But we all know that there is a great poverty of books in many schools, and those possessed are not properly used. In fact, the school library problem has scarcely been touched in our city. A year or two ago Massachusetts had but two small hamlets that were not supplied with libraries. There is a town among the Berkshires which consists of two houses, a church, and a cemetery, and yet the circulation of its library reached a thousand volumes the first year. South Chicago has over 60,000 people within its limits. Its library privileges consist of one small substation in the rear of a flower store.

What Chicago should have is many branch reading-rooms, such as the Blackstone Library, and some way of furnishing the class-rooms with libraries of suitable books. The substations should be furnished with children's rooms, with trained attendants to help the children look up references, and inspire them to read good literature. The surroundings should be refined and attractive, story hours should be held, and there should be low, open shelves filled with books, puzzles, and games. The substations, if they could not be connected with every school, should be so situated that they could be used by a number of schools. The classroom libraries should contain fifty carefully selected books in attractive binding, picture-books for the youngest children, stories of adventure, history and literature, and good reference books for the older ones. The atmosphere of our libraries should be such that the self-conscious, shy students are not discouraged in their endeavors to use the libraries, but such helpfulness should prevail that the children all feel that the libraries are theirs for a wise and considerate use.

There are some movements on foot to bring about better conditions here in Chicago. Mr. Hosic, of the Normal School, has a new library list for the schools in preparation. The Public Library was to have opened three new branch libraries in the recreation parks the first of November. It is bending its energies toward perfecting its substations and is preparing new reading lists. The library has seventy substations, and is of course an expensive institution to run. We all hope, however, that the need of enlarging its work with the public schools will some time be so apparent to the public and to the library that means will be forthcoming and the schools supplied with books. Many libraries use a great deal of their energy and means in providing mediocre literature demanded by the public. It is possible that if the need of the schools was made apparent, some less deserving work of the library could be somewhat abridged and this work substituted for it. One of the first steps toward a proper co-operation between the schools and library would be a new rule governing the transportation of books to the schools. Although the library has not sufficient books to meet the demand which would come from the schools, the distribution of even twenty or thirty books to a school would be a movement from which great things might grow.

EDITORIAL NOTES

The Lures of the Impossible

With what serenity of soul most people at one time or another have undertaken the impossible! Certain of these lures to the imagination are classic. No boy ever lived, perhaps, who in his first top boots did not try to lift himself by the straps. The problem of perpetual motion has unbalanced many minds, while that of squaring the circle has held in thraldom many more that were capable of better things. The field of mechanics seems particularly enticing. I once knew a rather bright young man who thought he had solved the problem of railroad transportation: he proposed to place the load in a slanting position on the axle of the trucks, on the theory that the wheels would then be pushed forward! He said: "The heavier the load, the harder it will push." As usual, argument availed nothing. He had to waste much time and strength, and some money, in working it out. I once saw an "inventor," an old man, who had constructed a locomotive that would lay its own track ahead of the wheels, and then, as it went along, lift it from behind and pass it overhead again to the front! And it worked, too—on a smooth board walk. There was only one thing wrong with the invention: when it struck a place where a track was really needed, it stuck in the mud just like any old wagon that had no track.

There was, years ago, a country boy of my acquaintance who proposed to make water run uphill to a point above its source by attaching an air-chamber to the lower end of the pipe. This also worked; but it took more strength to pump the air into the chamber than it did to carry the water itself by other means—that one thing was all that prevented the machine from coming into general use and making a fortune for the boy. That is what makes this quest after the impossible so fascinating: generally all the difficulties can be eliminated down to just one—the last one—which for some reason refuses to budge.

Business is not without its illustrations of the same kind. In a neighboring town a man recently advertised that for fifty cents he would send a watch guaranteed to last for at least ten years. This man actually sent the watch and his guarantee was good—only one thing wrong: the watch had no works! A matter of detail, of course, but sufficiently important to put the enterprising advertiser out of business, when Uncle Sam heard about it. There are thousands of people who say they are in business who are not; they are merely trying to get something for nothing, and they bear the same relation to business that the perpetual-motion man does to mechanics.

Is This Business?

In education we are not clear of similar types. We still gaily attempt impossibilities with children which have been given up long ago with plants and other animals. Indeed, we are trying to grow children under conditions never thought of in connection with the cultivation of vegetables and the nursing of beasts. For example, there is not a "hayseed" from Eastport to Guatemala so ignorant that he would think of trying to raise a crop of oats or corn, or wheat, or peaches, or apples, or parsnips, or onions, or any other green thing, in the heart of our down-town districts. There is not a shepherd from Tampa to Puget Sound that would select the site of the Jones School in Chicago, for instance, as a suitable location for his sheepfold. Nor is there a living stockman who would choose the Adams School yard as affording the proper conditions for raising calves; nor would a swineherd select any one of a half-dozen such sites in the city that might be mentioned as a possible place for the rearing of pigs. These people—these big-fisted sons of toil are too wise, too scientific, to waste any of their valuable time on such obvious impossibilities. But the educa-

Wisdom in Horticulture

tors, both the practical and the philosophic, and the philanthropists with unwearying persistence have sought through the centuries to grow children under these impossible conditions. Verily, they are all own brothers to the perpetual-motion man.

A Personal Inquiry

Before anyone even begins to work out a solution for the problem of education in the congested districts, the ghettos of our cities, he should sit down and quietly try actually to sense the conditions that invest these children, from which the warp and woof of their lives are woven. This present generation of the streets has a life entirely barren of those early experiences which play so important a part in the development of truly educated people. Suppose you were to take from your own childhood-picture all the green grass upon which you romped and played as a child. Then take away all the trees, whose swaying branches gave the voice of song to the wind. Take out all the birds; imagine day dawn without a welcoming note and the fall of evening without the swallow's twitter or the song of thrush or whip-poor-will. Banish from memory those stretches of landscape, wooded and open, that sprawled and tumbled between you and the rising and setting sun. Take the blue from the sky; take the odors of fresh earth from your nostrils which Walt Whitman says "tastes so good," and then say what you have left of early memories that is worth while.

Consider This Picture

Now replace the green carpet of your early years with the hard and unyielding paving-stones. Instead of trees, let there be the stolid and naked chimneys. Bound your horizon with walls of brick and stone not fifty yards away, and beyond which you never see. Besmirch the sky with soot. Instead of song of birds, let there be the rattle and rumble and all the infernal delirium of the street. Instead of the perfume of fresh earth, fill your nostrils with odors unspeakable that have never yet been catalogued in any list of smells. Torment your throat and lungs with the fumes of sulphur—

imagine that you were born under such conditions, that you are growing up under them, and that you know no other—and then explain how a schoolmaster is to build out of such an experience that character which we want in human life! Dogs, sheep, horses, oxen, subjected to such conditions for a term of years, would no longer acknowledge themselves to be dogs, sheep, horses and oxen —they would beg for other names more befitting to their degeneracy. Neither can children under such pestilential influences grow into beings worthy of the titles belonging to man; an extravagant percentage must always answer to the names of dependent, delinquent, tramp, thug, thief, and murderer.

Shamed-Faced Cattle

This is not the first time the observation has been recorded that we are more reasonable in the case of our live-stock than we are with our children. It dates back at least as far as Roger Ascham, who in the time of Queen Bess expressed himself thus: "And it is pitie that commonlie more care is had, yea and that emonges verie wise men, to finde out rather a cunnynge man for their horse, than a cunnynge man for their children. They say nay in word, but they do so in deede. For to the one, they will gladlie give a stipend of 200 crownes by yeare, and loth to offer to the other 200 shillinges. God, that sitteth in heaven, laugheth their choice to skorne, and rewardeth their liberalitie as it should: for he suffereth them to have tame and well ordered horse, but wild and unfortunate children: and therefore in the ende they find more pleasure in their horse than comfort in their children."

The Jockey Better Paid Than the Schoolmaster

Well-Broken Horses, Ill-Taught Children

Roger Ascham had in mind the inferior ability of the teacher; the present observation bears upon the unfavorable conditions which surround the children, but the results in both cases are the same. Our school system is probably second to none in the world; it has school boards, superintendents, principals, teachers, houses, books, and all else, lacking just one thing: it fails to provide for the pupils of the congested districts that natural nourishment that is necessary if children are to grow to the stature of men. Only one thing lacking to make the impossibility possible; but as ever before, it is the vital thing which, at present, is missing.

The case, however, is not without its remedy. Instead of huddling the children into down-town buildings with scarcely more space than that upon which the structure stands, these schools should be established upon the outer rim of the city, in the forest reserve in Chicago, if it shall be acquired; if not, then in suburban parks. Each school should have at least five acres of ground (about the size of a city block in Hyde Park), which would not only insure good light, fresh air and a reasonable freedom from noise, but would also provide a fair space for different industries, for various phases of horticulture, and for field study. Such surroundings, sanitary and beautiful, would at once change the attitude of the children into one of friendliness toward all kinds of learning, and it would be possible to open up for them many ways of earning an honest livelihood that now are undreamed of. With an abundance of ground it would not be necessary to erect buildings with so many stories as is done now, where land is expensive. The shops, workrooms, and laboratories could be in separate buidings, well lighted and ventilated, and apart from the quieter literary work of the school.

Outer-Rim Schools

The rapid and marked improvements in urban transportation facilities that have been made within the past decade have removed the most serious difficulties that hitherto would have stood in the way of such a plan for suburban schools. Even as they are now, the down-town trolley lines radiate out and reach many points in the country in the city's circumference that would be entirely suitable for school houses. And when a little later, the people shall get full possession of the city's

Transportation

street car system, new lines can be laid, having the transportation of the school children directly in mind. The time is not far distant when people will establish their car service not only with reference to the localities where the parents work, but also with a just regard for the places where the children are being taught. At the worst, this proposed carrying of school children in the cities cannot possibly be fraught with greater difficulties than those which have been met and overcome in the country districts in several of our states—where the schools have been centralized. On the face of it, nothing could seem more nearly impossible to many people than the proposition to gather up in wagons and to carry to one point, in all weathers, the scattered school population of a country township; yet it is being done, with practically everything in its favor which relates to the education of children.

Cost of Outer-Rim Schools

The cost of establishing and maintaining these suburban schools need not exceed the expense of those already existing down-town. The grounds could be purchased for a much smaller sum than the sites are worth where the schools are now located, and the buildings, of course, need cost no more. The pupils should be carried free of charge, as far as they are personally concerned, in accordance with the same principle under which they are now furuished with free textbooks.

In order to provide for this part of the traffic, it is not likely that the means of transportation would have to be materially increased beyond what it should be at present in order to accommodate fairly well the general public. For, in the morning, when the children would be outward bound, the principal movement of the street car patronage is towards the central business districts, while in the afternoon, when the children would have to return, the people generally would be traveling in the other direction. Suburban schools or not, every city should see to it that school children in charge of teachers should have free car-fare on railroads as well as trolleys, on all field trips and excursions. In due time we shall have railroad officials who will see that it pays better to carry trainloads of children to school free of charge than it does to haul packed trains of adults to the race-track at full fare.

It is well to observe, too, that this scheme would insure certain important economies. The truant officer could be dismissed instantly, and in a decade the very name of this function would be stricken from the dictionary. The uninterrupted streams of miserable and unfortunate childhood that now flow out from the juvenile court to the different penal and reformatory institutions would be gradually dried up at their fountain-head, and the expense of maintaining this part of our educational (?) system would be greatly reduced. Nor should it be overlooked that the suburban schools operating under normal conditions would be able to turn back into the community productive citizenship, whereas, at present, these same pupils become a menace to society, and its constant care and burden.

Economies of Outer-Rim Schools

The main contention here, however, is not that the schools will be cheaper, but better. Should it be shown that they cost even more than at present, they need not fail for lack of funds, if what is now collected from the people is properly applied. A few days ago the governor of this state discovered that in about thirty years our state treasurers have filched public funds amounting to over three hundred thousand dollars. A little later it was discovered in Chicago that in a certain piece of public work six hundred thousand dollars had been stolen. At the present time an official's books are being overhauled, and a shortage of one hundred thousand dollars is reported. These three steals alone, which the people have been able to pay, would go a long way toward meeting any extra expense that might be involved in car-fare and other matters pertaining to the maintenance of suburban schools. When we become smart enough to inspect

How to Get the Money

our officials before they steal, instead of afterwards, we shall then have money enough.

Bearing on the Slums

It is unnecessary to detail how much "outer-rim" schools would mean for the immediate welfare of both teachers and pupils. The most important thing to consider is that it would lay the ax at the root of the slum question. So long as we try to educate children by using slum conditions, we shall have slums—it is practically impossible to create any other ideals. The outlook for such pupils must always be narrow and discouraging; but, train one generation in schools of the character described and none will wish to return to these haunts of wretchedness, and but comparatively few will do so.

Amelioration vs. Cure

No word of this must be construed as a criticism upon the work that is now being done for the welfare of the unfortunate people who are herded together like animals in parts of our cities. Nothing can adequately express the debt which the community owes to these teachers and workers. But their labors under present conditions must always be ameliorative and not finally curative. It is time, therefore, that the public came to their rescue. These people are struggling against tremendous and overwhelming odds, simply because they are trying to grow men and women where nature has decreed that nothing but vermin can grow—vermin, none the less, even though it should have the human shape.

Where Hope Lies

The majority of people who read what is here proposed for suburban schools will instantly dismiss the project as a dream; this signifies nothing except that the majority of people are asleep. What has been written here is intended for the minority who are awake. Most of those who shall consider the plan will begin at once to show why it never can be worked out; but a few, at the same time, will contrive ways and means for doing it. Nine men out of ten will immediately cast the plan aside—but the nine count for nothing; hope, efficiency, and resourcefulness, all reside in the tenth alone, and this appeal is made to him. It is through the waking minority, the active few, and the sagacious tenth man that finally the plan will be realized.

W. S. J.

VOLUME VI NUMBER 7

THE ELEMENTARY SCHOOL TEACHER

MARCH, 1906

THE CHILD'S WORLD OF IMAGINATION

STEPHEN S. COLVIN
University of Illinois

The term "imagination" in its popular sense often conveys a different significance from that which it has when employed in psychology. In everyday language it is not uncommonly used to describe an impractical state of mind, given over to illusion and the contemplation of uncertainty. From this point of view the imaginary world is a realm of shadows and ghosts, divorced from contact with vital living and fruitful thinking. Such a conception as this is unfortunate, because it is not true, and has caused no little confusion in the discussion of the desirability of imagination in the mind of the child, and the use of imagination as a means of education. What psychology means by imagination is quite simple. To illustrate:

Before me as I write is this manuscript. My knowledge of its presence is due in part to rays of light existing in the physical world as vibrations in the ether, and conveyed to my eye, where they are focused on the retina, and then carried to the cortex of the brain through an excitation of the optic nerve. This nervous discharge is correlated with a state of consciousness that may be described as seeing the paper which I have before me. Through other senses there also come other reports of the presence of the manuscript. I touch it; I hear the rustle of the pages; I recognize that it has weight when I lift it; and so on. The knowledge that comes in this way through the direct presentation of an object to the senses is called perception. Now, if I lay the manuscript on the table and shut my eyes, it is no longer present to the senses as an object, but may exist for me as a memory. My mental state of perception is then changed to one of imagination. In this change there is no question of reality or unreality, or delusion or falsity, but of immediate sensory presence, or the lack of such sensory presence.

Commonly thought also credits imagination as being a peculiar state of mind; one which is not always present, but which comes and goes; yet psychology assures us that there is no form of consciousness which is entirely without it. Let me illustrate further by returning to the consideration of the paper before me. I perceive that it has form, that it is covered with characters, that it has weight, and that its pages give forth sound when grasped by the hand; and yet that is not the end of my knowledge of the manuscript. Blended with what I directly sense there is much in regard to it that belongs to past experience, but which in reality makes no small part of my knowledge in regard to the manuscript. Take away all these elements of past experience now present only as images, and the very object before me loses much of its reality and significance. This is true of all objects presented to the senses. And thus it is that imagination in such cases as these, instead of being something removed from and distinct from reality, is a very essential part of reality. If the image were out and out unreal, then the universe of concrete things would likewise be unreal, since all objects that compose this universe are in part made up of elements of the imagination.

If imagination, then, be so fundamental a constituent of reality, how happens it that the widespread notion of its illusionary character should have arisen? The answer is not far to seek. Simple imaginary elements, in themselves symbols of concrete realities, are capable of combination which yield products that do not correspond to any actual or possible experience. This complex of imaginative elements owes its existence to the productive imagination, while to the recalling of single sensory experiences not immediately present to the senses is the function of reproductive imagination. For example, consciousness may combine elements of past sensory experience into products utterly fantastic and absurd. Such are often the dream images of our sleeping states, and the weird visionings of the paranoiac, or of others mentally deranged. Our images of a horse and a man are results of a reproductive imagination that are essentially real; but when they combine into the picture of a centaur, they constitute a productive image to which our experience denies reality. It, however, does not follow, because some of these constituents of the productive or creative imagination are unreal, that all such images are. Indeed, since there can be no image that is merely a copy of past experience, and to which intelligence has not added something, never mind how little, it follows that, if all productive images are unreal, then every bit of mental imagery has a taint of unreality about it, and that, further, each object perceived (since in it, as already said, there must be some elements not directly perceived, but merely imagined) is likewise to that extent unreal. No, we cannot say that, simply because an object is imaginary in part or as a whole, it therefore is unreal.

The test of the reality of an object, whether perceived or imagined, is its agreement with our individual and social experience. Why do I say, for example, that the centaur is unreal? Because I have never experienced such an animal, and because I believe no other being ever has or ever will. Surely the centaur is inherently no more fantastic than certain other products of the imagination in whose reality I have the most firm belief. Let us take some of the almost contradicting animal forms of prehistoric times which the scientific imagination has constructed. Do we believe they really exist? We do, because they fit in with the extended experience of those scholars who from a few scattered remains here and there, by a rare feat of productive imagination, have reconstructed in imagination the animal.

We may now turn from this general discussion of imagination to the question for our scientific consideration, the imaginary world of the child. Here we are concerned primarily with the child's productive imagination, of his combination of past experience into original mental products, although there are not a few facts of interest which relate to his simple reproductive imagination. It is obvious that from the very beginnings of his life the simple images of past experience play an important part in his mental growth, and certainly at no very late stage of his development he begins to combine freely the simple images into higher compounds and starts to build a world of fancy, which differs from that of his ordinary experience sometimes in an astonishing degree. The study of the imaginary companions of children has revealed the fact that they come early in the child's life. The imaginary companions are sometimes the most vivid realities. They are distinctly visualized, have definite peculiarities such as manners of dress and speech, have well-known moods and mental characteristics, and converse with and aid those who have created them.

The imaginary world of the child in his early years Dr. Hall describes as follows:

> In childhood credulity amounts almost to hypnotic suggestibility, not only is everything believed, but the faintest hint starts the exuberant imagination to vividness often halucinatory. This power to believe the false and even the absurd, in infancy, is not a defect, but excess of psychic vitality. The narrow horizon of reality within juvenile ken is not enough, and the world of fancy and myth is needed to supplant it. Never is receptivity so near to creative energy, and this is why genius is defined as the preservation into mature years of the fecund mental spontaneity of childhood.

Much of the mental imagery of the child resembles the fancies of our myth-making forbears. The clouds and the stars, the sun and the moon, the snowflakes, and other of the great elemental phenomena are often explained by children in a way that suggests the poetic conceptions of nature common to primitive peoples. Here, as in other directions, the child repeats the history of the race. He peoples forest and stream, field and fountain, with conscious beings. Elves, pixies, goblins, fairies, and gnomes are as real to him as parents, brothers, and playmates. They are an essential part of his wider world.

Since the knowledge of truth and falsehood, of reality and illusion, depends on experience in which the present is formed to agree with or to contradict the past, it clearly follows that in his early years the child has no definite criterion by which he can test his world of images, and distinguish those which refer to the actual or possible from those which represent the fanciful and contradictory. The child no more doubts the existence of the beings that people his myth world than he does the forms that belong to the world that we adults call fact. Further than this. his images are often so distinct, vivid, and persistent that he readily confuses them with objects actually present to the senses. The extreme suggestibility of little folks makes them subject to manifold delusions, such as come to grown-ups only in dreams, hypnosis, or pathological conditions. Who of us has not tried the experiment of making a bitter dose taste sweet or a pain vanish by suggesting to the child that the medicine was pleasant or the ache was gone; and we have often succeeded in our mild deception.

The fact, then, seems to be that children possess more than adults the creative imaginative faculty; that it shows itself at an early age; and that only by degrees does the child learn to distinguish between his image-world and the world of actuality. There naturally arises the question as to the value of this imaginary world, and the proper attitude of education toward it. Should imagination be cultivated in children, and, if so, in what direction; or should it be eliminated as rapidly as possible from the lives of the little ones, in order that they may be better prepared for the serious life that some day must come to them, if they survive the years of childhood and arrive at the development of adults?

There are not a few who would incline toward the second alternative. Fact is fact, and there can be no compromise with it and falsity. So the teacher of history hastens to banish all such delusions as the existence of William Tell, and the instructor in science urges the unreality of the nature-myth and fairy-tale as explanations of events in a world of orderly phenomena. Likewise, too, the professor of ethics may insist that truth is to be secured at all hazards, and that there can be no compromise with falsehood. Hence Cinderella, and Jack and the Beanstalk, and even Santa Claus must go; for the child must be made a moral being at all costs.

Doubtless people of this turn of mind are not in the majority, and their numbers are yearly growing less; however, they still are heard protesting against the mass of myth and fairy-tale which of late years have been especially prepared for the education of the child, and their point of view deserves consideration and an intelligent answer. If we believe in the cultivation of childish fancy, we should be able to give a reason for the faith that is in us, to satisfy our own legitimate questionings, if for no other purpose. It may be that in our emphasis of its value we have gone too far, if we have not erred in principle.

Seriously, what reply can we frame to the objection that myth is intellectually and morally wrong because it is not true? Our answer to this statement will be aided, if we consider again the point of view taken in the introduction to this paper; namely, that reality and truth depend upon the agreement of our present state of consciousness with our total experience and the experience of others. This is a position that today is being affirmed with ever-increasing vigor by such eminent students of the human mind as Professor James of Harvard and Dewey of Columbia. That which, on the whole, fits best into experience, which most uniformly satisfies the intelligence, is the truth; and since experience must ever change, there is no truth that is absolute and will stand the test of ages. For later antiquity and the Middle Ages the system of the universe evolved by the Greek-Egyptian astronomer Claudius Ptolemy was true because it fitted the then known fact; but the wider experience of the fifteenth and sixteenth centuries made its views unsatisfactory, and the Ptolemaic system gave place to the Copernican; but who will be so rash as to affirm that this is a final point of view? The individualism of the eighteenth century proved a sufficient philosophy for Rousseau and the doctrinaires of the French Revolution; is satisfied the framers of our own Declaration of Independence; but today it is giving way to a theory of social dependence that cannot find truth and satisfaction in what was once accepted as an ultimate statement in regard to the nature of man. So, too, the mechanical atomism of the science of yesterday is no longer able to hold its place in the newer conceptions of the physics of today. But why multiply examples? On all sides we see a significance in the statement now so often heard that a thing is true as long as it proves satisfactory and no longer, and that quest for ultimate truth is an unending quest, a goal that always removes, the rim of the horizon to whose mystic borders we can never attain.

So myth which satisfied the intellectual and moral needs of the savage was true for him, but false for us, just as our science will be false for some future generation; so the fairy-tale of the child, which for him offers the most reasonable explanation of the world about him, is far more true for him than our adult conceptions could possibly be. Some day he will be an adult and will have put away childish things; but as long as he remains a child he must think as a child, if he thinks at all. As his experience extends, he will slowly cast aside the fancies of an earlier day, now grown inadequate, but not so suddenly that there will be a jar, or a break in the continuity of his reality. Think as I may, I canot tell when Santa Claus became for me a reality of another order than that which my earlier imaginings had made the venerable saint; when I first learned that he had no place in this dull prosaic world, I cannot remember; I am sure, however, that the change was not in the twinkling of an eye. New truths come like the dawn: first the pale auroral tints that brighten and broaden, and before which the stars and the moon gradually grow dim and finally pass from view. But the stars and moon lit the night, and made the path clear. The myth-making period of childish imagination is necessary, because it best satisfies the childish conception of the world, and therefore is the true conception. It is good for the child as a child; and we must remember always the momentous thought of Rousseau, that the child is to live for itself. What has it to do with that great world of practical life that it may never attain? Its present enjoyment must not be unthinkingly sacrificed to a future that it may never know.

Further, even if the present of the child were of no value in itself, and the future were assured, it would not be wise to banish from his life those images of his creative fancy which the future will pronounce unreal. Child-study teaches us one fact at least with sufficient certainty, and that is that each stage of development is necessary for that which follows. Just as the gill-slits in the human embryo—those worse than useless appendages for the child in its post-natal existence—serve a very necessary purpose in contributing to the organs yet to be formed, so the mythopoeic fancy of childhood at its proper time in development enters into the adult experience in many subtle ways, and enriches the life of the man. The fairy-story of childhood still counts in the healthful fancy of the grown-up. Can we enter into sympathy with the great imaginative writers of the ages, if our early training has found no place for Grimm and Andersen, and others of that noble company of myth-makers? The language that Homer and Virgil and Spenser and Shakespeare and Dante and scores of others of the past have spoken is jargon to him who has had no understanding of the simpler, obscure, and forgotten masters who in the folklore of the people of all times have left a world of rarest story for the children of ages yet unborn. In this humdrum world of ours how the heart yearns for these oases of fancy in the desert of the real, but to drink from the sparkling waters is a privilege given only to those who have discovered the hidden fountains in the days of childish simplicity.

My boy of nine who has outgrown his implicit faith in fairy-tale, but who still finds them a satisfaction to his emotional life, often says: "I wish they were true; I wish that when you opened your mouth gold would fall from it. Wouldn't it be fine if just by thinking you could make castles rise in the air? How nice it would be if there were real giants that brave boys could kill and beautiful princesses who could be rescued from wicked witches and watchful dragons! I must confess that I sympathize with the youngster, and I am not ashamed that I still have a love for fairy-tale and the supernatural. But this sympathy and love could not exist if at one time these tales had not been for me a satisfactory *Weltanschauung*; if they had not constituted for me a realm of reality, more satisfactory and as suffcient as my present view of the universe. And when some child, on hearing a story of wonder, asks, half believing and half doubting, "Is it true?" I cannot with a clear conscience reply "No;" for it is true in a sense that the little questioner does not comprehend; perhaps not for the head, but for the heart. Indeed, as a mere intellectual proposition I am not at all convinced but what the myth-world of the child and the primitive man does not more exactly correspond to ultimate reality than the mechanical universe of the materialist, filled with whirling atoms, but without purpose or design.

Although the myth-making fancy of the child is very vigorous in the early years of its existence, it gradually loses its dominance, and the imagination tends to develop in other directions. Allen[1] found that school children showed a gradual loss of interest in myth and fairy-tale in the following ratio: third grade, 82 per cent.; fourth grade, 38 per cent.; fifth grade, 42 per cent.; sixth grade, 36 per cent.; seventh grade, 11 per cent.; eighth grade, 15 per cent. Other observations and studies seem to indicate that there is a gradual lessening of this type of imagination, and a development in the direction of interest in heroes and great deeds of courage and daring; while still later there is an accentuation of imagination along more practical and less fanciful lines.

In order to discover more exactly the course of this development, I collected several years ago compositions written by pupils in various schools of Illinois, and later three thousand of these were read and tabulated by Mr. I. F. Meyer, graduate student in psychology in the University of Illinois. The compositions studied were obtained from the four upper grades of the grammar school and from the entire four years of the high school, were prepared as a part of the regular school work, and were not revised or in any way corrected by the pupils after they had been submitted to the teacher. The aim was to make the work entirely spontaneous and as original as possible, with no suggestion as to content or treatment, and particularly with no hint that the compositions were intended as anything beyond a regular school exercise.

These compositions were carefully examined, and a record was kept of the visual, auditory, tactile, pain, olfactory, gustatory, organic, and muscular images among the more simple forms of imagination; while the more complex types, representing the

[1] *Pedagogical Seminary,* Vol. VIII, p. 259.

productive imagination, were studied under the heads of scientific, fairy-story, nature-myth, heroic, dramatic, religious, and melancholic.

The first eight types may be passed over with little explanation. All images reproduced from the sensations coming through the eye were termed visual; through the ear, auditory; through the skin, tactile and pain images; through the nose, olfactory; through the taste cells of the mouth, gustatory; from the contraction of the muscles and the working of the joints and tendons, muscular; and from the internal organs of the body, such as the heart, the lungs, and the alimentary canal, organic.

The remainder require further comment. Under scientific imagination were considered those images which related to invention, discovery, the construction of machines and devices, and the use of electricity and other natural forces. The fairy-story dealt with that class of imagery which had to do with elves, pixies, gnomes, goblins, etc., and the nature-myth with those mythopolic fancies common to primitive races and to children. Under the heroic were treated those images that had to do with overtowering personalities, such as Alexander, Napoleon, George Washington, and with ideas of magnanimity, self-forgetfulness, and courage; under the dramatic, striking situations, stirring events, and climaxes, such as the slaughter of the suitors in the *Odyssey* of Homer; under the religious, the supernatural and devotional, ideas of God, angels, and the devil; under the melancholic, feelings of sadness and depression.

The most striking feature of the curves representing the first four types of imagination was their marked decline at about the outset of puberty, with the single exception of the visional type, which shows a steady rise for both boys and girls through the entire eight years studied. The tendency to fall at this crucial period in childlife is likewise to be noted in the four lower types of reproductive imagination, with the exception of the olfactory, which, however, runs so low for all the years that it may practically be ignored. In the case of the visual, auditory, tactile, and motor types there is a partial recovery during the years of the high school; but in the case of the pain, organic, and gustatory, types the tendency is to grow less and less in the years following. The same general tendency of the curve to fall at the beginning of the adolescence is further to be noted in the fairy-story, nature-myth, heroic, dramatic, and religious types of imagination; while the scientific type, particularly with the boys, and the melancholic, which latter hardly exists before the adolescent years, alone shows a rise. Thus it is seen that out of the fifteen varieties of imagination dealt with in the study, all but four show the fall at about the beginning of adolescence, and of the four that show an opposite or neutral tendency, one is so slight for all grades as to be of little importance.

The cause of the fall I believe to be significant for psychology and pedagogy alike. It is probably to be explained by the general upheaval that accompanies the onset of puberty. The years roughly from eight to twelve are years of a low-grade stability a period of habituation and building up. The marked changes that come at the end of this period destroy this stability. Old brain-centers cease to function, or function in different directions. Thus images of earlier experiences tend to fade out and to be replaced as the adolescent years progress and renewed stability comes to others. The visual escapes this tendency, it seems reasonable to assume, in part at least, because it is not so deeply centered in the affective life of the child, and it is in the affective sphere that the greatest upheaval takes place. It is an interesting fact that the curves for formal correctness, which was also tabulated in the study, run practically parallel for the boys, and nearly so for the girls, during the entire eight years under consideration. This probably means that visual imagery is more objective and symbolic than the other types studied.

Another cause that may be operative in the fall of the curves is the increased reticence of expression which comes in early adolescence, especially in connection with the inhibiting influence of school environment in regard to spontaneity.

The explanation for the rise of the curve of scientific imagery is to be found in the immense interest that the American boy, in particular, takes in all forms of invention and discovery. This interest is so strong that it overcomes the tendency potent for the most part toward the disintegration of the image at the outset of puberty.

We may turn to a more specific discussion of those types of images which are included under the head of the productive or creative imagination. Highest in this class stood the heroic. For both sexes it seems to be a more constant form of imagination than many of the others studied, and it stands the shock at the onset of puberty better. There is little difference in the average for the four years of high school and in the grades. This shows that the interest in the heroic is continued throughout the school years—a significant fact for education to consider. The girls show a slight superiority over the boys in this form of imagery. For the dramatic imagination the results are similar, the girls, however, showing a more marked superiority over the boys than in the heroic. This is doubtless to be accounted for by the greater intensity in girls of those feelings which center around these two types. In this connection may be mentioned a study by my colleague, Professor E. G. Dexter, who has shown that on the stage recognition is much earlier for women than for men.

As has already been said, the interest in scientific imagination shows an increase at puberty. The average for the boys is much greater than for the girls. The highest point reached by both sexes is in the last year of the high-school course, and indicates the increasing tendency toward the practical and away from the mythopoeic and fanciful. Indeed, there seems to be an inverse relation between the curves representing these two types; doubtless the increase of one means the falling off of the other. The fairy-story and nature-myth find their highest expression in compositions written in the grades, and the figures show that this type of imagination tends to disappear as the age of the pupil advances. The question might then be raised as to the result of emphasizing the mythopoeic type. Does it not tend to check the development of the scientific? As far as this latter type is concerned, would it not be better to banish from the home and the school all mention of fairies and like supernatural beings, so that, when the time for the growth of the scientific imagination comes, the latter shall not be hindered in its development? I am not at all sure that such is the case, and I am still so far an adherent of the so-called dogma of formal discipline (a very serious psychological and pedagogical heresy in the minds of many) that I can conceive the possibility of the imaginative habit developed in fairy-stories being in part transferred to the construction of steam engines and flying-machines. The very rankness of the growth of the mythopoeic fancy may enrich the soil from which the scientific sprout is to develop.

Religious imagination is at its highest in the fifth grade for both boys and girls. In the case of the boys it falls off rapidly the last two years of the grades, and sinks to a still lower point in the high school. With the girls the curve shows a general tendency to fall, though it is not so pronounced. In the face of the well-known facts in regard to the religious emotions at adolescence, as set forth by Hall, Starbuck, James and others, this decline means, not that the high-school pupil is lacking in religious emotions, but that the school environment is hostile to the expression of such feelings. In the grades the expression is formal and conventional to a great degree, but in the high school there is a genuineness of emotion in relation to religion which precludes its expression in an environment which does not encourage it. The pedagogical influence here is so obvious that it need not be commented on.

Feelings of melancholy do not belong to the pre-adolescent years. In the grades such images are practically absent. In the high school they begin to appear, and are more than double in the case of the girls. Doubtless the compositions studied revealed but to a slight extent the actual intensity of the melancholic, which sometimes reaches the pathological in young people of a nervous temperament.

In connection with the development of the imagination a record was made of the sense of humor as revealed by the compositions. Here the boys show superiority over the girls, and the curve reaches its maximum in the seventh grade. A resemblance in the curve is to be noted for the boys between the pain images and humor. A connection here may be found in the fact that the type of humor possessed by the boys is largely of the teasing and bullying variety, which takes pleasure in the torture of animals and persons. The curve for the organic images shows also a resemblance to the curve for humor, as does farther the curve for motor images. This all goes to emphasize the low type of humor possessed by school children, and is in entire accord with a previous study on the "Sense of Humor in Children" made three years ago by me and reported to this section of the Association.

The study shows that, on the whole, the imagination of school children tends to decline during the years considered, and from this it may be legitimately concluded that our present system of education does little to foster the imagination. Indeed it is not improbable that the school course tends to crush out certain elements of imagination. In the premium placed on the visual type of imagination by the school education emphasized the more external and formal to the exclusion of the spontaneous and vital, since the visual image, as it appears on the printed page, easily substitutes itself for the concrete image behind it.

The tendency manifested at the outset of puberty for neuromes to become disassociated and for the old images to drop out, necessitates special effort on the part of the teacher to cause the new images formed to be of deep and vital character, and to stimulate the mind of the pupil along lines of higher creative endeavor. Hence all formality in education is to be particularly deplored at this age. It is not the time to appeal to desultory memory, and the period for formal logical drill has not arrived. Literature should be taught largely in its vital relation to the pupil's experience, and not as a grammatical, historical or philological cram. Descriptive prose and poetry to be enjoyed must call up vivid images in the mind of the reader or hearer. If a description appealing to the eye suggests no picture, if the words standing for sounds are mere dead symbols, if vivid narration arouses, among other things, no motor images, the whole subject is stale and profitless, if genuine interest is the goal aimed at in such teaching. Pain images, too, have their value, since without them genuine sympathy is dead, and a training in morals is then only formal. Even tactile, gustatory, and olfactory images have certain value in our higher life, and their loss to any great extent would be a misfortune.

The fact that the heroic and dramatic imagination is still strong at this period throws a light on the teaching of history. As I have maintained elsewhere[2], the attempt to make historical study in the early years of the high school an investigation in politics, or a training in methods of historical research, is dangerous. History should still be a narrative, a good story, an appeal to the love of the heroic and dramatic, and to the fundamental elements of morality based on human sympathy.

The school offers no training in the emotion of humor, the cruder types being the only ones that find expression to any considerable extent. Education thus ignores one of the most vital phases of human experience. The individual teacher should see to it that this emotion finds opportunity for legitimate expression in the school work, and that an appeal is made from the lower elements to the higher.

Education again ignores another fundamental element in the lives of all normal individuals by passing over the deep religious needs when they are most in evidence. It is a serious commentary on the character of our school work that just at the time when the spiritual universe comes closest to young natures there is practically no evidence of it in the schoolroom, which itself should be a very important part of the life of the boy and girl, and not something one-sided and particular. Of course, there can be no sectarian or dogmatic instruction in religion, but to those basal experiences of the human heart that constitute the essence of all true religion there should be a constant appeal. Hero-worship, sympathy, idealism, altruism, veneration, obedience, self-forgetfulness—all these are elements of religion. There should be a larger place for their cultivation in the schools than exists today.

The final conclusions of this paper may be stated as follows:

The imagination of children, both productive and reproductive, shows throughout the entire period of development, growth and change.

[2] "Teaching of History in the First Two Years of the High School Course," *Journal of Pedagogy*, December, 1901.

All of its forms are valuable and should be utilized at their proper time. The question of truth or falsity should not be raised as long as a certain form of imagination constitutes for the child the most satisfactory means of harmonizing his intellectual and emotional experiences.

Since there are no sharp breaks, under normal conditions, between one state of imagination and another, there will be no violent contradictions or struggles. Each stage of imagination is essential to the next, and no one stage can be left out, and no stage can be shortened or continue too long, without injuring the child.

Throughout the entire school course the attempt should be made to make the imagination as vivid and vital as possible. Images should not degenerate completely into mere visual or verbal-motor symbols of a reality behind them.

Above all, in the adolescent years a more effective appeal should be made to the religious elements in the young person's life, now manifesting themselves with an intensity that before was unknown, and that will never again be equaled.

THE SCHOOL CAMERA.[1]

LEWIS W. HINE
Ethical Culture School, New York City

It is difficult to realize what conveniences and necessities we owe to the photographic art. In the home photo reproductions adorn the walls and bring in the distant world of history, geography, and art. The modern newspaper and magazine would be seriously hampered without the aid of the camera, with its wealth of material and realistic illustrations brought within our reach by the inexpensive and rapid methods of reproduction. In the commercial world also it is indispensable, reducing the cost of manufacturing in so many ways; and still more necessary is it in the scientific world, from the astronomer discovering invisible stars with the photographic plate, to the microscopist recording bacterial life upon the slide. We may well stop to ask now whether we are taking advantage of the many opportunities which this pictorial art offers to increase our efficiency by appealing to the visual sense and recording for mutual benefit, the school work.

For several years this school has tried to build up a collection of school photographs to show some of the phases of school life, and at the same time to have the pupils' interest in photography fostered and directed. It is the aim of this paper to give some results of our experience.

As a record of school life we have found the camera to reach into every nook and corner of real activity. Indoors the opportunities are innumerable to catch bits of life in the classroom, at the bench or forge, in the laboratory, kitchen, and studio. Social events—class parties, festivals, and assemblies—have not been neglected; for in this way they may be shared with many who cannot otherwise participate in them, and the prints do

[1] Photographs by the author;

serve as mementoes of these happy events which are highly prized by the pupils.

Out of doors the necessity becomes even more imperative that we preserve some record of this side of school life. We succeed in keeping in this permanent form some part of the joyous contact with Mother Nature. The record of the progress of the garden products through the several stages is of great value to other classes, as are also the methods of carrying on the work through the passing seasons. The life and environment of many products of the soil may thus be clearly followed.

The value of bringing back from an excursion views of points visited and regions explored for nature-study, geography, and history is not realized fully until actually tried. This is of great assistance to both teacher and pupils in selecting the salient features of the trip; the central thought is emphasized and the relative values are brought out, thus teaching the selection of fundamentals which is so difficult and so vital to the work. Natural-history material which cannot be brought back to the schoolroom may be in the form of the photograph, and a continuous study of a tree, a rock, etc., through the seasons is made possible. In this way we have found many ways of illustrating the environment of different plants, and the results of wind, shade, crowding, etc. Evidences of physiographic activities are brought in showing the structure of the Palisades, the character of rocks disturbed by this intrusion, the crumpled layers of ancient rocks on Manhattan Island, etc. Changes now going on may also be recorded, showing the forward movement of a sand-dune from year to year, the encroachment of swamp on water area in a pond, and changes in a brook valley after a storm.

On industrial trips to the dairy-farm, the potter, the miller, etc., the camera has helped us to follow the steps of the different processes after the observation, which often has been hurried, has gone by.

Perhaps the greatest value of the school photograph as a record has been in giving to parents, visitors, teachers, and others interested in the school a brief but comprehensive view of the school activities which otherwise would not be preserved.

NATURE STUDY ON THE PALISADES

BOTTLING MILK AT THE DAIRY

It is a great problem to a visitor who has only a few hours to spend with us, to know how to begin and where to turn. A brief examination of a well-selected and representative collection of photographs will give a bird's-eye view, and then the visitor may select the lines with which he wishes to become familiar. At the annual school exhibit the photographs taken during the year have become quite indispensable as reinforcing and varying the written explanation, just as they have become so necessary in magazines and books. Here also the visitor's time is limited, and we strive to give him in condensed and attractive form what has been going on through all the year.

As a record of the past history of the school, the school collection is also valuable, showing past conditions, changes, and growth. From the standpoint of pupils' participation, the camera is a great help. In the kindergarten and lower grades the pupils make its beginning use of the photographic process in the blue-prints which are made of leaves, ferns, grains, pressed flowers, etc.,—an inexpensive and inexhaustible source of enjoyment and value. They make frames for these, and for the photographs of their school pets, to use for Christmas and birthday gifts. After a while they realize that impressions of their excursions are often fleeting, and thus learn the value of the photograph to refresh the memory during the review that follows the trip—that it is a record for future use, and, best of all, that it enables them to share with other pupils and other grades, that have not participated, the enjoyments and benefits of these experiences. When this sharing is more fully realized, it is possible for a grade to get many of these excursions by proxy, which of course greatly increases the value of the camera to the grade that finds the necessity to reorganize the essential points gained in such a way as to be clearly understood by others. Here the individual cameras come into the fullest play, with a proper motive and stimulus to make the most of what too often is considered a mere toy.

It is reserved for the camera club to transform many mere "button-pressers" into real amateur photographers. Our club, though small, has several vital interests. The fundamental one is in the comparison of work done, and the exchange of suggestions and criticisms. Another is the helping one another to develop and print, and the school dark-room becomes an educational and social center of wide influence. The exchange of ideas and experience as to different kinds of plates, paper, etc., which are best for certain kinds of work, plays an important part in the club work. Then there is discussion of the physical and chemical laws underlying work with the camera; anything that will directly or indirectly help in exposing, developing, and printing is interesting and valuable. The camera outing should be the basis of much work, especially in the application of the principles of exposure, composition, etc., discussed in the meetings. When the child realizes, even to a very limited extent, that success in this line cannot be attained by the snap-at-everything method, but by careful, patient, orderly work, he has taken the first important step toward real success in all lines of work, and he receives a genuine feeling and respect for laws that might not be gained in any other way. The pupils find that this work helps in other school lines. In the art work it is of great assistance in the appreciation of beauty, and is especially valuable in gaining a realization of composition. The recognition of what is good composition in art never becomes so vital as when one is able to select from the infinite variety of objects about him some bit that is pleasing to the eye, and then transfers to the photograph the lines and groups in the form of his idea of composition. This reacts again by helping in the next photograph to improve on former efforts. This sharpening of the vision to a better appreciation of the beauties about one I consider the best fruit of the whole work. In chemistry and physics it helps to appreciate many chemical changes and physical laws as few lines of work can.

The social value of the work of the club may be an important factor in class spirit. The idea of helpfulness is fostered; appreciation of the right kinds of competition, and the taking and giving of suggestions and criticisms, are developed; while each gains the social idea of working for the benefit of the group.

All this work is still in its infancy. We feel it can reach

PILGRIM FESTIVAL; THE FIRST SINGING SCHOOL

A WOODPECKER'S HOME IN CENTRAL PARK

into many more lines of school activities. It may be of great help to the History work by representing historic places visited by some members of the grade and not available to the rest. It may serve also as a record of the history trips taken during the year. The photographs taken on various excursions may be made into stereopticon slides, which open up another field of usefulness. With the assistance of the projection apparatus it is often possible to use the print itself without the trouble of making a slide. In the laboratory micro-photographs of specimens may be made, enlarged, and also used as slides in the stereopticon. When the pupils are making books showing some line of English history, or geography work, the photograph makes an excellent mode of illustration.

It is often of great assistance to school people to study the equipment of various schools which they cannot visit, and the school camera lends itself admirably to this field of work. An increasing problem in school management is to provide interesting and profitable work for the pupil during the long summer vacation. The camera may be made a most efficient assistant, giving at the same time an attractive form of outdoor work, and a means of recording and sharing the summer's experiences with the others after school begins again. The opportunities here are innumerable—travel, recreation, participation in industrial life, etc.

While these experiences and suggestions are based upon conditions in this particular school, many of them may be applied to any school. There is no one but will find, if he attacks this problem with enthusiasm and patience, that the result of his work is improved, and the enjoyment and value to teachers and pupils greatly increased.

WOZU EINFACHE ERZÄHLUNGEN FÜHREN KÖNNEN

EIN OSTERSPIEL

ANNA T. SCHERZ

PERSONEN

Heidi, Olga, Lieselotte, Heinz, Werner, Ulrich, Ludwig, Moritz. Hilde, Felix, Karl, Otto, Stephan, Kuno.

I. AKT

1. SCENE

(Ein Platz im Walde. Ringsherum steht Gebüsch.)

ULRICH: Hier muss die Quelle doch sein, aber ich seh' sie nicht.

MORITZ: Sie liegt auch ganz versteckt im Gebüsch. Ich will sie suchen.

HEINZ: Brr, wie kühl es ist. Aber hört ihr nicht die Quelle rauschen? Auf dieser Seite muss sie sein.

MORITZ: Ja, ich höre das Tröpfeln des Wassers.

ULRICH: Hier ist sie, hier, ganz tief im Gebüsch.

MORITZ: Das Wasser ist eisig kalt.

HEINZ: Und nun versteckt euch hier im Gebüsch, denn hierher müssen die Mädchen kommen.

ULRICH: Wie nass das Gras ist.

MORITZ: Das macht der Tau. Die Sonne ist ja noch nicht aufgegangen.

HEINZ: Nein, aber die Mädchen müssen ja auch hier sein vor Sonnenaufgang. Wie geht doch die Sage, an welche die dummen Dinger glauben?

MORITZ: Geh' zu einem Waldbrunnen früh am Ostermorgen vor Sonnenaufgang. Warte bis der erste Sonnenstrahl das Wasser trifft. Wasche dich dann mit dem frischen Quellwasser, so wirst du immer schöner und niemals krank werden.

HEINZ: Ach, ja, richtig. Wie kann man nur so etwas glauben? Aber still, da kommen sie.

(*Drei Mädchen treten auf. Alle sind in dunkle Tücher gehüllt, um sich gegen die Kühle des Morgens zu schützen. Sie tragen Krüge in den Händen. Sie sprechen kein Wort, setzen sich bei der Quelle nieder und warten bis die Sonne aufgeht.*)

OLGA: Ich höre ein Kichern. Da steckt der Heinz, der unnütze Bube.

HEIDI: Aber, Olga, da fiel grade der erste Sonnenstrahl und jetzt ist der Zauber gebrochen. Du hättest doch nicht sprechen sollen.

LIESELOTTE: Daran sind wieder die unnützen Jungen schuld. Da ist natürlich auch der Moritz.

OLGA: Natürlich die beiden Taugenichtse zusammen. Nun ist alles umsonst.

HEIDI: Dann ist auch der dritte nicht weit. Richtig, da ist Ulrich.

HEINZ: So lass mich doch endlich los. Du zerreisst mir ja den ganzen Rock, Olga.

MORITZ: Und du meinen, Lieselotte.

LIESELOTTE: Wir sind extra so früh aufgestanden und in diesen kühlen Morgen hinausgelaufen.

HEIDI: Und nun musstet ihr alles verderben.

HEINZ: Ja, wie konnten wir aber auch wissen, dass man bei dem Wasserschöpfen nicht sprechen darf.

MORITZ: Wir wollten euch ja nur necken, aber nicht alles verderben.

ULRICH: Ich glaube aber, das Wasser wirkt auch so. Ich würde mich an eurer Stelle damit waschen, und wir füllen euch die Krüge inzwischen.

HEIDI: Na ja, vielleicht wirkt das Wasser auch so.

(*Die Mädchen waschen sich.*)

LIESELOTTE: Brr, das Wasser ist eisig kalt.

OLGA: Es ist überhaupt kalt heute Morgen.

HEIDI: Meine Füsse sind ganz nass von dem nassen Gras.

ULRICH: Was knackt denn da in den Büschen?

HEINZ: Vielleicht sind es Werner und Ludwig.

LIESELOTTE: Die wollten euch wohl gar helfen?

MORITZ: Ja, die wollten auch mitkommen, haben sich aber verschlafen. He, Werner und Ludwig, ihr kommt zu spät.

WERNER: Ah, guten Morgen. Es tut mir leid, dass wir zu spät kommen. Ihr habt wohl ordentlich Spass gehabt.

LUDWIG: Wie schade.

HEIDI: Netten Spass. Sie haben Olga zum Sprechen gebracht und dadurch alles verdorben.

WERNER: Ach was, ich glaube überhaupt nicht an die Zauberkraft des Wassers.

LUDWIG, HEINZ UND MORITZ: Wir auch nicht.

ULRICH: Es ist ja alles Unsinn.

HEIDI: Na ja, ihr könnt ja glauben, was ihr wollt, das ist uns ganz einerlei.

OLGA: Uud abscheulich war es doch, uns alles zu verderben.

LIESELOTTE: Ja es war abscheulich von euch.

HEIDI: Jetzt lasst uns aber endlich nach Hause gehen. Ich bin schon ganz durchgefroren.

OLGA UND LIESELOTTE: Halt, Heidi. Vergiss nicht deinen Krug.

HEIDI: Ach, ja den hätt' ich beinahe vergessen.

LUDWIG: Habt ihr den dreien etwas von unserm Plan von heute Nachmittag gesagt?

HEINZ: Nein.

WERNER: Vielleicht tun sie mit. Ihr habt ihnen nun diesen Spass heute Morgen einmal verdorben, so ladet sie doch zu unserm neuen Streich ein.

MORITZ: Da hast du eigentlich recht. He, Lieselotte, Heidi und Olga.

MÄDCHEN: Na, was wollt ihr?

HEINZ: Hört zu, wir wollen euch was sagen.

LUDWIG: Ja, seht! Felix, Hilde, Karl und das Kleeblatt ihr wisst ja.

LIESELOTTE: Ach, du meinst Otto, Stephan und Kuno.

LUDWIG: Na ja. Also die haben irgendeinen Plan, von dem sie uns nichts sagen wollen. Der Plan hängt auch mit Ostern zusammen.

WERNER: Ich glaube, sie wollen etwas suchen. Wir haben das namlich zufällig überhört.

HEIDI: Na, und——

HEINZ: Und wir wollen nun sehen, was sie machen wollen, und ihnen dann einen Streich spielen. Tut ihr mit?

LIESELOTTE: Ja, ja, wenn es nichts Böses ist.

OLGA: Aber wie soll das denn gemacht werden?

MORITZ: Na, passt auf. Wir wissen, dass sie hierher gehen werden, denn sie haben von der Quelle gesprochen. Nun kommen wir heute Nachmittag zum Eierspielen hierher. Dann warten wir hier, bis sie kommen, und sehen was sie machen. Tut ihr mit?

WERNER: Wir werden viel Spass haben.

OLGA: Ich tu' mit.

HEIDI UND LIESELOTTE: Ich auch. Wann sollen wir hier sein?

WERNER: O, so gegen drei Uhr.

HEIDI: Nun gut, und nun adieu.

OLGA UND LIESELOTTE: Also bis heute Nachmittag.

KNABEN: Halt, wartet, wir gehen mit.

2. SCENE

(Dieselbe Scene. Heidi, Olga, Lieselotte, Heinz, Werner, Ulrich, Ludwig und Moritz kommen singend auf die Bühne.)

Osterhäschen, kommst du bald,
Oder schläfst du noch im Wald?
Hockst du unter Tannenbäumen,
Tief versteckt in süssen Träumen?
Schau, der Frühling naht mit Macht.
Osterhäschen, aufgewacht!

Osterhäschen, spring empor,
Spitze nur dein lange Ohr.
Osterklang durchweht die Lande,
Nimm die Kiepe mit dem Bande.
Manche Eier tu' hinein,
Viele Kinder warten dein.

HEIDI: Nun kommt, lasst uns spielen.

OLGA: Aber was zuerst?

HEINZ: Eier rollen.

ULRICH: Ja, hier ist die Grube, und nun rollt los.

LUDWIG: Ach, Werner, dein Ei war nicht hart genug; es ist zerbrochen.

WERNER: Dass schadet nicht, dann ess ich es auf.

ULRICH: Hast du noch mehr?

WERNER: O ja, noch zehn. Wieviele hast du noch?

ULRICH: Hier, zähl mal. 1, 2, 3, 4, 5, 6, 7, 8, 9, 10, 11, 12.

LUDWIG: Ich habe nur noch sechs. Fünf habe ich schon gegessen.

LIESELOTTE: Ha, mein Ei ist drin. Versuch doch Moritz, ob du es nicht kannst.

MORITZ: Da, meins ist auch drin. Nun versuch du es, Ludwig.

LUDWIG: Ich habe keine Lust dazu. Lasst uns lieber Eier tupfen.

ULRICH: Ob die andern noch nicht kommen? Was meinst du, wann werden sie hier sein?

MORITZ: Ich hörte sie sagen, dass sie um drei Uhr fortgehen wollten. Aber sieh lieber nach, Ulrich.

ULRICH: Ja, ich will schnell nachsehen. Fangt unterdessen mit dem Eiertupfen an. (*Ab.*)

LUDWIG: Ich habe ein steinhart Ei, das kann gar nicht zerbrechen.

OLGA: Dieses Ei ist auch furchtbar hart. Versuche es.

LUDWIG: Da, das war aber nicht hart. Es ist ja schon zerbrochen.

LIESELOTTE: Hier, probiere meins.

HEINZ: Warte, Lieselotte, ich will mein Ei versuchen. Da, meins ist doch härter als deins.

ULRICH: Sie kommen, sie kommen, versteckt euch.

WERNER: Steckt eure Eier in die Taschen, damit niemand sie sieht.

HEINZ: Halt, Werner, das blaue Ei gehört mir.

OLGA: Macht schnell und zankt euch nicht.

ULRICH: Ja, macht schnell.

LIESELOTTE: Sieht man uns noch hier?

ULRICH: Nein, euch sieht man nicht. Aber deine rote Mütze guckt da heraus, Werner. Still, da sind sie.

3. SCENE

(Dieselbe Scene. Hilde, Felix, Karl und Otto kommen auf die Bühne.)

HILDE: Ich glaube, wir brauchen nicht weiter zu gehen. Es nützt doch alles nichts.

FELIX: Du hast recht, wir finden doch nichts.

KARL: Aber seid doch nicht so verdriesslich. Wenn Ihr die Augen zumacht, findet Ihr sicher nichts.

HILDE: Aber wir haben schon so lange gesucht.

OTTO: Ja, aber wenn wir heute die Stelle nicht finden, müssen wir wieder ein ganzes Jahr warten, denn man kann den Schatz doch nur am ersten Ostertag finden.

HILDE: Warum eigentlich nur am ersten Ostertag? Ich weiss, die Grossmutter hat davon gesprochen, aber ich habe es vergessen.

KARL: Der Ritter starb doch am ersten Ostertag, und er hat geschworen, dass es einem Menschen nur möglich sein sollte, den Schatz am ersten Ostertage zu finden.

FELIX: Aber vielleicht hat die Grossmutter sich in der Stelle geirrt.

(*Karl und Otto haben fortwährend umhergeschaut.*)

OTTO: Du Karl, sieh doch hierher. Da ist das Schloss, und dort führt der Weg entlang. Hier steht ein gewaltiger Eichbaum mitten zwischen den Tannen. Von hier aus überschaut man des ganze Tal. Scheint es Dir nicht——

KARL: Als ob dies die Stelle sein müsste? Ja, das glaube ich auch fast.

OTTO: Hilde und Felix, kommt doch schnell hierher. Ich glaube, ihr sitzt auf dem Goldschatz.

HILDE: Was, wir sitzen auf dem Goldschatz?

FELIX: Redet doch nicht solchen Unsinn.

KARL: Na, nun schaut her. Wie hat die Grossmutter euch die Stelle beschrieben?

HILDE UND FELIX: Der Goldschatz liegt am Abhang eines Berges, dessen Gipfel eine Ruine krönt.

OTTO: Seht ihr wohl die Ruinen da oben?

HILDE UND FELIX: Ja, da sind Ruinen, aber——

KARL: Und ist dies nicht der Abhang eines Berges?

HILDE UND FELIX: Ja, ja, aber——

OTTO: Na, nun erzählt weiter.

HILDE UND FELIX: Der Goldschatz liegt unter einem Eichbaum, welcher inmitten dunkler Tannen steht, und von wo aus man das ganze Tal übersehen kann.

FELIX: Aber wo ist denn nun der Eichbaum?

KARL: Aber Kinder seid ihr denn blind? Seht euch doch um.

HILDE: Wahrhaftig, Felix, wir stehen grade unter dem Eichbaum.

FELIX: Wirklich, das ist ein Eichbaum.

HILDE: Der einzige unter all' den Tannen ringsumher.

OTTO: Und nun seht euch die Aussicht von hier an.

HILDE: Man überschaut das ganze Tal. Und dort ist der Weg. Kinder, das muss die Stelle sein.

FELIX: Ja, hier muss der Goldschatz liegen.

OTTO: Nicht wahr? Das glauben Karl und ich auch.

KARL: Und nun lasst uns anfangen zu graben.

OTTO: Halt, Karl, Stephan und Kuno sind noch nicht hier.

HILDE: Ach, wozu sollen wir auf die warten? Die lachen uns ja doch aus.

FELIX: Sollen wir denen überhaupt etwas sagen?

KARL: Das müssen wir wohl. Sie würden uns ja doch bei der Arbeit überraschen.

HILDE: Ja, die Beiden wissen immer alles; ich glaube, sie hören das Gras wachsen. Aha, da sind sie.

FELIX: Schnell, Stephan und Kuno, hierher.

HILDE: Wir haben ihn gefunden.

STEPHAN: Warum schreist du denn so? Was habt ihr gefunden?

KUNO: Habt ihr vielleicht die blaue Wunderblume gefunden?

KARL: Nein, sondern viel was Besseres.

ALLE: Ja, viel was Besseres.

OTTO: Ja, nämlich den——

ALLE: Goldschatz.

STEPHAN (*lachend*): Den Goldschatz!

KUNO: Den Goldschatz, welchen ihr suchen wolltet?

HILDE: Ja, und von welchem die Grossmutter uns erzählt hat.

KUNO: Ach so, wie lautet doch noch die Geschichte?

STEPHAN: Ja, gehört habe ich die Geschichte auch. Ich weiss, sie hängt mit Ostern zusammen, aber sonst habe ich sie ganz vergessen.

FELIX: Na, dann hört zu. Ihr seht da die Ruinen eines alten Schlosses, nicht wahr? Nun, vor langen, langen Jahren—ich glaube, es war zur Zeit der Kreuzzüge—wohnte da ein sehr reicher Ritter. Er besass einen grossen, grossen Goldschatz. Der Ritter musste plötzlich in den Krieg ziehen. Ehe er ging, vergrub er den Schatz unter einem Eichbaum, welcher ganz einsam inmitten dunkler Tannen steht. Der Ritter wurde im Kriege getötet. Er starb grade am Ostertage und schwor, dass es einem Menschen nur am Ostertage möglich sein sollte, den Schatz zu finden. Und nun glauben wir——

STEPHAN (*lachend*): Dass ihr den Schatz gefunden habt!

KUNO: Was für ein Unsinn.

KARL: Warum denn Unsinn? Die Grossmutter hat uns genau beschrieben, wo der Schatz liegt.

OTTO: Und alles stimmt. Der einzelne Eichbaum zwischen den Tannen am Ahbang des Berges. Da oben die Ruinen, dort der Weg und die weite Aussicht.

KUNO: Aber habt ihr denn schon nachgegraben?

KARL: Ich wollte grade anfangen, als ihr kamt.

STEPHAN: Aber Kinder, bei Tageslicht könnt ihr doch keinen Schatz finden.

HILDE: Warum denn nicht?

STEPHAN: Nein, das muss man bei Mondlicht machen.

FELIX: O ja, das ist schön spukhaft.

KUNO: Und man muss schwarze Kappen umtun und den Geist des verstorbenen Ritters bannen.

HILDE: Hu, wie gruselig. Dann lasst uns doch heute Abend zurück kommen.

OTTO: Und ich lerne einen Zauberspruch gegen den Spuk,

HILDE: Aber Stephan und Kuno, ihr sollt niemand etwas davon erzählen, hört ihr?

FELIX: Das müsst ihr uns versprechen.

STEPHEN UND KUNO: Wir schwören es.

OTTO: Um wie viel Uhr geht der Mond auf?

STEPHAN: So gegen acht.

KUNO: Dann sind wir um acht hier. Und nun kommt mit nach Hause.

(*Alle ab.*)

4. SCENE

(Die Ersten. Es ist Nachmittag.)

ALLE: Ha, ha, ha! !

HEIDI: Habt ihr das gehört?

HEINZ: Das ist ja zum Totlachen.

ALLE: Ha, ha, ha! !

MORITZ: Zum Totlachen. Die närrischen Dinger glauben wirklich, was die Grossmutter ihnen erzählt.

WERNER: Da soll ein Schatz liegen.

OLGA: Den ein alter Ritter vergraben hat.

LIESELOTTE: Lächerlich.

LUDWIG: Kinder, ich habe einen Plan.

ALLE: Heraus damit. Was für einen?

LUDWIG: Hört zu. Wir nehmen einen grossen Kasten, vielleicht *so* gross. Legen etwas recht Schweres hinein, denn Gold ist doch schwer, nicht wahr? Dann vergraben wir den Kasten unter dem Baum. Dann verstecken wir uns heute Abend hier in den Büschen und sehen zu, was geschieht. Das wird ein Hauptspass. Was meint ihr dazu?

ALLE: Hurra, juchhe. Das wird ein Hauptspass.

ULRICH: Kinder, ich erscheine als Geist.

HEIDI: Ja, als Geist des verstorbenen Ritters.

ALLE: Hurra, was für ein Spass!

MORITZ: Und ich werde sonderbare Töne machen wie ein Uhu. Das macht es noch besser.

HEINZ: Dann lasst uns jetzt aber schnell gehen, damit wir alles vorbereiten können.

KINDER: Ja, nun schnell nach Hause.

(*Ab.*)

II. AKT

(Dieselbe Stelle im Walde. Es ist Abend.)

1. SCENE

MORITZ: Kinder, ich kann nicht mehr. Der Kasten ist aber auch gar zu schwer.

HEINZ: Halt, Moritz, lass ihn nicht fallen, sonst zerbricht er. Komm, Werner, fass mit an.

WERNER: Nein, lass Ulrich lieber helfen. Ich habe genug zu schleppen an diesem Sack voll Sand. (*Er wirft den Sack auf die Erde.*)

LUDWIG: Wo soll ich das Loch graben?

LIESELOTTE: Hier grade unter dem Baum.

HEIDI: Warte, ich will erst den Rasen abstecken, damit wir ihn wieder darauf legen können.

OLGA: Und ich leuchte dir mit dieser Laterne.

HEIDI: Und ich höre zu, ob auch niemand kommt. Aber macht schnell und seid ganz still.

LIESELOTTE: So, nun grab das Loch.

LUDWIG: Die Erde ist schrecklich hart.

HEIDI: Ja, wirklich furchtbar hart, grade wie Stein.

HEINZ: Jetzt will ich doch probieren, ob ich ein Geist sein kann.

MORITZ: Nein, das mache ich. Klingt das wie ein Geist?

HEINZ: Nein, gar nicht, mach' es so.

MORITZ: So?

HEINZ: Das ist schon besser.

MORITZ: Hu, hu, hu!

OLGA: Moritz, wie schrecklich, du wirst sie furchtbar erschrecken.

ULRICH: So, das Loch ist fertig. Nun her mit dem Kasten.

HEIDI: Er geht nicht hinein.

ULRICH: Warte, ich grabe noch etwas nach.

MORITZ: Bums, da steht er. Nun schnell die Erde darauf.

HEINZ: Nun noch den Rasen. Nun sieht es gar nicht unnatürlich aus.

HEIDI: Leuchte, bitte, Olga.

OLGA: Das habt ihr gut gemacht.

MORITZ: Macht, dass ihr fortkommt. Ich höre jemand kommen.

2. SCENE

HILDE: Hier ist der Platz. Hu, wie spukhaft.

FELIX: Wenn es jetzt Mitternacht wäre, würde ich sicher nicht hierher kommen.

KARL: Still, jetzt müssen wir den Geist beschwören.

OTTO:

Wall' auf und ab,
Schwebe hin und her,
Zeige dich, Geist.

(*Horcht.*) Es bleibt alles still

MORITZ (*hinter den Büschen*): Hu, hu!

KINDER: Der Geist, der Geist!

KUNO: Ach, was, das ist ja Unsinn.

OTTO: Es ist hier wirklich etwas unheimlich.

STEPHAN: So fangt doch endlich an zu graben.

FELIX: Ich fürchte mich vor dem ersten Spatenstich.

STEPHAN: Ach, du furchtsamer Hase. So, nun grab.

HILDE: Hu, da ist wieder der Geist.

(*Otto, Karl und Hilde graben. Stephan und Kuno besehen prüfend den Boden und das Gebüsch.*)

STEPHAN: Du, schau her, Kuno, hier liegt ein Spaten.

KUNO: Und sieh, wie zertreten das Gras ist.

STEPHAN: Ja, besonders da unter dem Baum.

KUNO: Und was liegt denn da? Ein Taschentuch. Das ist doch merkwürdig.

STEPHAN: Und mir klingt die Geisterstimme etwas sehr menschlich.

KUNO: Das geht nicht mit rechten Dingen zu. Aber wir wollen ihnen doch den Spass nicht verderben.

KARL: Ich stosse auf etwas Hartes.

FELIX: Ich auch. Der Schatz, der Schatz.

(*Alle drei versuchen den Kasten herauszuheben.*)

HILDE: Das ist ein Kasten voll Gold.

KARL: Ja, voll Gold. Leuchte doch, Hilde.

FELIX: Der Kasten ist voll Gold. Ich glaube nicht, dass wir ihn heben können.

KARL: Nein, das Gold ist zu schwer. So helft uns doch, Kuno und Stephan.

KUNO: Ja, schwer genug ist der Kasten. Ich hoffe nur, dass wirklich Gold darin ist.

HILDE: Natürlich ist Gold darin. Was denn sonst?

FELIX: So mach' ihn doch auf, Karl.

(*Otto, Felix und Hilde versuchen den Kasten aufzumachen.*)

STEPHAN: Du, Kuno, glaubst du, dass der Kasten fünf hundert Jahre alt ist.

KUNO: Fünf hundert Jahre alt. Unsinn, der Kasten ist keine zehn Jahre alt.

STEPHAN: Du, da ist ja ein Zeichen dran von unserm Bäcker. (*Lacht.*)

KUNO: Na, die werden viel Gold finden.

FELIX: Der Deckel sitzt zu fest. Hilf' doch, bitte, Stephan.

STEPHAN: Auf!

FELIX: Hilde, da ist richtig der Sack mit Gold.

HILDE: Richtig, da ist er. Nehmt ihn schnell heraus.

OTTO: Das Gold ist furchtbar schwer.

HILDE: Stecke die Hand zuerst hinein, Karl, ich fürchte mich.

KARL: Nun gut, dann gehört mir auch die erste Handvoll.

OTTO: Komm mit der Laterne, Hilde.

KARL: Ich fühle Gold.

KUNO: Das ist ja Sand.

KINDER: Sand!!

KINDER: Sand!

FELIX: Wirklich, nur Sand. Aber vielleicht ist das Gold ganz unten.

HILDE: Nein, nur Sand, nichts als Sand.

ALLE: Nur Sand.

OTTO: Warum lacht ihr, Stephan und Kuno?

KARL: Schämt euch, ihr habt uns einen Streich gespielt.

STEPHAN UND KUNO: Nein, wir nicht.

HILDE: Aber jemand sicher.

OTTO: Wer mag es getan haben. Da ist der Geist wieder.

KUNO: Und ich sehe ihn. Heraus mit dir, du Bösewicht!

KARL: Und da ist noch jemand.

STEPHAN: Nette Geister!

HILDE: Unnütze Buben!

FELIX: Da steckt Lieselotte.

(*Alle kommen jetzt lachend hervor.*)

HILDE: Pfui, ihr seid abscheulich.

ALLE: Ha, ha, ha.

OLGA: Kinder, ihr wart aber auch zu dumm, an die alte Geschichte zu glauben.

MORITZ: Na, wieviel Gold habt ihr gefunden?

KARL: Wartet, das sollt ihr büssen.

(*Die zweite Partei jagt hinter der ersten her und jagt sie schliesslich von der Bühne.*)

MEETING OF THE PARENTS' ASSOCIATION

MRS. ELLA ADAMS MOORE
Secretary

The regular meeting of the Parents' Association was held on Thursday evening, November 16, at eight o'clock. The following topics were discussed: (1) "Would a More Elastic Curriculum Better Serve the Interests of the School and the Children?" (2) "How Far Should the Policy of Special Teachers for Specific Subjects be Carried, Especially in the Lower Grades;" (3) "How Far is it Desirable and How Far Possible to Maintain the 'Small Group' System in the Elementary School?" (4) "Home Work."

The discussion was opened by Mrs. James H. Tufts, who had prepared the program. Mrs. Tufts said that in regard to the first question the problem was how to ease up the school work when necessary or desirable; that always somewhere in the child's life there came a time when he could not do the full amount of school work without too much physical strain, or a parent may wish a child to devote more time to music, and so would lighten the school program; or a mother may wish her daughter to carry out more fully in the home the domestic-science training. There were many reasons why it was desirable that there should be some arrangement whereby the school work could be lightened without the child's feeling the onus of dropping behind his class.

As touching the second question, Mrs. Tufts said that as a parent followed a child from one thing to another, the question arose whether, in the desire to get the best possible instruction, we were not sacrificing unification and concentration. Looking for the origin of the condition which reflects itself both in the home and the school—namely a willingness to undertake a task, but an unwillingness to pursue it to an end—would it not be better to give more into the hands of the grade teachers, even if some expert knowledge were sacrificed? A mother undertook to help out all along the line; why not less rather than more specialization in the school in the teaching force.

Both the first and second questions overlapped the third. The best-teaching work was done on an individual basis. In a laboratory ten or twelve were as many as could be well managed. In languages, small groups were necessary. Was it not possible that, with the increasing number of pupils and the school's increasing popularity, we were losing sight of the theories on which the school was based, and which had contributed so much to its success?

As regards the home work, it was a ghost which ever rose and would never down. Mrs. Tufts hoped that in the discussion it would be possible to get at the logic of the questions and find out why or why not.

The meeting was thrown open to discussion. A very full discussion followed, in which the following points were made:

Mrs. Allinson said that the individual child should be the unit of the group. There was the need of recognizing different temperaments. In the seventh and eighth grades the pupil should go as rapidly or as slowly as advisable. How could this be adjusted? The number of children to the teachers should be limited. There should also be a difference in tuition for the amount of work. We must break up and loosen the lines. It was not a question of finishing the work in a given time, but of adapting the work to the individual child. Parents are apt to feel more than the school that the generous repast offered to the children is sometimes more than can be assimilated.

Mr. Owen said that there had always been a number of the Elementary School children doing work in the High School in some special subjects, in which they were particularly advanced, from the fifth grade up.

Mrs. Harding said that what had impressed her was the desirability for some change on account of the great sensitiveness of those children who could not keep up. Such children should do partial work and perhaps take the eighth grade in two years, but so explained and arranged that there would be no feeling of disgrace. Perhaps this came from the strong feeling in the public schools.

Dr. Montgomery said that, from a physician's standpoint, he had found that a child's health often suffered from a mental state induced by a return to school behind his grade or class. If a child is taken out of school for a time, there is the same feeling of discontent and unhappiness, all of which influence the health. If for the seventh and eighth grades and the first two years in the high school a course could be laid out by which a student could take as many years as he wished to complete the course, it would be a wise plan.

Mr. Owen said that in the University High School what had been spoken of was a regular custom; that there were people all the time who finished in anywhere from three to six years.

Mrs. Allinson asked if there were not a great discrepancy between the elementary and high schools in this respect.

Miss Stillwell said that the criticism of the school had usually been that it did not have a curriculum, rather than that it had too much; that the curriculum was perfectly flexible; and that any child in the eighth grade could take full or part work. The curriculum was based on the powers of the average child, and those who could do the work were given the opportunity.

Mr. Gillett stated that, as regards the sensitiveness on the part of any child as to keeping up with the work, not more than one-tenth of the class knew of any difference in the handling of a child who was not carrying out the full schedule. The teacher did not think of it. Promotions came any time.

Mr. Jackman said that he was continually beset by parents who wanted their children to have more work. He had been standing against the tendency of parents to rush their children. The course should be a matter of natural growth. He considered the grading system artificial and bad. There were practical difficulties, however, in the way of a child who was in the fifth grade reciting in some one subject in the third or the eighth. In order to get out of the grade ruts, he was forming various clubs, such as the camera, microscope, etc., whose membership should include students from all grades.

Mrs. Harding reported an experiment in the old Laboratory School, where the work of a number of children in about the seventh or eighth grades was very greatly lightened and much out-of-door occupation given. The work was increased a little year by year, and that group of children entered college with no loss of time, with the average abilities and preparation, and much better health.

The second question then came up for discussion.

Mr. MacClintock said that we were all drifting in the direction of the teacher who knew what he was teaching. He thought the trouble was in carrying too many subjects at one time.

Miss Port suggested that with very young children, if a teacher knew how to handle the children, it was not so much matter what she taught. She was afraid that her first-grade children might grow dizzy with eight new people to take them in charge. The critic-teacher must see that the eight people are working together. If the work stands as a whole, and not in parts, in the minds of the children, then the teacher has made the necessary union.

Miss Wygant said that all who had been watching children had seen signs of too much rush. The question was: Are you willing that your child should have no experience in clay, color, music; or are you willing that they should not have the help they need? How make the work simple enough and quiet enough? Is it possible that the special teacher should spend some of the time she spends in training the children in training the critic-teacher so she could do the work.

Mrs. Thomsen thought that it lay in the grade teacher's work so to unify the work that the children would not be dazed. She did feel that often, on account of the number of special teachers and stops, the room teacher had come to cut her work off short.

Several parents testified as to the keen interest of their children in the school, and that the work was not overtaxing, but healthful and stimulating.

The meeting adjourned.

EDUCATION VERSUS BUSINESS

A DISCUSSION

FRANK A. MANNY
Ethical Culture School, New York City

The editorial in the December issue of the *Elementary School Teacher* is needed. The problem is with us, and it is time that we become conscious of it to a greater extent than we have been. It is not my experience that the line can be drawn between these two types of social interest as is stated by the editor. I will not attempt to show that there are business enterprises which have the broader outlook—although that can be done, I am sure; but there are many schools which do dare to adopt "admsision requirements" other than those of Dr. Barnardo. Only today I spent some time in a great school which has room only for those who are wealthy. Thirty per cent. of its income is profit, yet some of its salaries are scarcely living wages. Another school, which provides a large number of places at free tuition, is carefully examined by observers to find what mercenary motive is hidden behind this plan. The commercial spirit is strong in our private schools; college-entrance requirements are a definite bar to certain students who would profit by higher education of the right kind, and they even dominate the secondary schools, establishing the same exclusion there.

In some cases exclusion is too little practiced. I remember one social reformer whose household constantly suffered because she would take in to her own service those strays whom she could not locate elsewhere. I have known public schools in which teachers and pupils alike were unable to do reasonable work because of the presence of defectives who had been disturbing elements for years without receiving any benefit. Of one school it was asked: "Is this a school or a hospital" In such cases I have not hesitated to remove the cause of trouble, even when I had no better place for the child in question. I believe, however, that this is a temporary condition, and that we shall have schools in charge of a group of men and women whose work it will be to meet every type of educational need, whether of child, or of adult, normal defective, or delinquent. But I do not now know the community where this is done. A number of social institutions are working, sometimes in complementary relations, sometimes at cross-purposes, but as yet in most cases separately and at haphazard. School systems can as yet only look at the better state as an ideal. No one of them has yet shown us that it can be done.

A teacher recently said of a schoolman: "I am surprised to learn that he was once a railroad man. I cannot think of him as dealing with those selfish interests. His work belongs in the broader field where human beings are concerned. The listener then contrasted to her the work of two brothers, one in railroad service, the other in a school. He pictured the duties and opportunities of the former, the men he had helped to grow, the positions for which he must employ men, a certain percentage of whom were sure each year to be killed in serving the public. He ended by saying: "There are two classes of men—those who work selfishly and those who have a broader vision, and both are found in business, and both are found in the school."

Hazing in schools, church decisions, insurance and political graft among many pressing issues show a defect common to our social institutions and not confined to business alone; we have a responsibility not only for a meeting of conditions as we find them, but for doing our best to make advances—to change conditions for the better.

AN EXPERIMENTAL SUMMER

CAROLINE M. HILL

A year ago a theory of vacation for upper elementary and high-school pupils was published in this magazine, followed by a plan to be tried in the summer of 1905 at Wheeling, Ill. This plan was in operation from June 20 to September 30, with twenty boys and girls who remained for periods varying from one week to fourteen weeks each. Judged by the satisfaction of the boys and girls while they were there, their unwillingness to leave, and their desire to return next summer, the experiment must be called successful. The judgment of the grown people who carried it on affords material for this article.

The theory, in general, was in harmony with the theory of the University Elementary School as to the place of industry in elementary education, and called for the revival of pioneer conditions as a means of development in the child of individual efficiency for community ends. The conditions which confronted the two families of settlers on Prairie View Farm in April were as primitive as could well be found near so modern a city as Chicago. Wheeling is only twenty-one miles distant as the crow flies, but in habits and ideas the country surrounding it is nearer to some parts of Germany. This, however, had little influence on the new settlers, except that it forced them to depend more upon themselves. There was no forest to fell, but there was a wilderness to be cleared, land to be brought into tillable condition, and a home to be created. The ground was full of thistles, there were no fences, and for a short time the children were sent out to herd the domestic animals.

Much arduous labor was done in the spring quarter by all the persons concerned in the scheme, and the children showed an excellent understanding of the plan and the greatest willingness to co-operate in whatever was to be done.

June 20 found at the farm a number of boys and girls from good families, with the most conscientious home-training, who had had the best educational advantages. Half of the total number present during the summer had had the advantages of foreign travel. The children were first put to work at painting an old house on the farm, which, it was hoped, would develop into a country club-house, and in fixing up the yard about this house. Both of these employments were quite popular, but there was no expert in either line to direct their efforts, and the results were not all that could be desired. The need of a landscape gardener was especially felt. Hoeing corn and plowing corn were excellent occupations for small and large boys respectively. Cherries were soon to be gathered, and the haying season came on, while chickens, cattle, and pigs were always to be cared for. Occupations involving the use of farm machinery, the driving of horses, and the care of all the animals were the "jobs" most sought after. Cutting thistles was another necessary occupation—not a popular one. Hot weather brought harvesting and threshing, in which the large boys arose to the occasion, the smaller ones ran errands, and the medium-sized ones tended more to reading or to play. Two hours of manual labor per day was insisted upon as a minimum, but the natural tendency to relax during July and August was taken to indicate a physical and mental need of rest at that time.

A sincere effort was made to carry out a literary program in the afternoons, and instruction in biology, geology, and botany was provided at the end of each week; but the scientific excursions which had been considered delightful during the school year were irksome in the summer, and avoided whenever possible. Instruction in agriculture was welcomed at table or in the field, but avoided if it came in any form that suggested a class.

An abundance of reading matter was provided, and those who were readers availed themselves of their opportunities, while those who were not literary in their tastes did more work. The reading aloud of *Innocents Abroad* was tolerated, the reading of Scott met with no success at all, and the only thing called for was Sherlock Holmes's latest exploits. Great interest was taken in dramatic efforts, and this fact, together with the class of reading preferred, is very suggestive as to the lines along which progress may be made another summer.

From the grown-up point of view, the greatest lack was in organization and expert assistance; from the point of view of the children, this seems to have been the greatest attraction. Regular hours for rising and retiring, and for meals, were insisted upon and quite successfully maintained—they breakfasted at 6:30 A. M., dined at 12 M., had supper at 6 P. M. and retired at 8:30 P. M.—but the proper care of person and rooms (they were expected to care for their own rooms), and proper behavior at the table, were only approximated, and that with the greatest wear and tear on the nerves of all the grown people in charge. The children delighted in the possibility of wearing overalls all day, of renewing primitive man's friendship with the animals, of living out of doors nearly all the time, and of being abundantly fed by a motherly darkey whom they christened "Ma."

The most successful feature of the organization was undoubtedly the fact that the children were paid by the hour for their work, if it were satisfactorily done. To add to the incentive to work, some parents doubled or even trebled the amounts which their children earned. The absence of temptations to spend money kept the earnings almost clear, and the children learned its value in terms of labor.

The farm life proved just as attractive to girls as to boys, although their smaller physical strength and greater nervousness made it difficult to find suitable things for them to do out of doors. The addition to the force of a competent gardener, a music teacher, and possibly a teacher of domestic science will make it possible to have more girls next summer.

The farm is not endowed, and few educational institutions expect to be self-supporting. Certainly no great amount of expansion is possible without an endowment. If it were possible to command the services of just the right persons trained in agricultural colleges, an ideal vacation place might be made out of Prairie View Farm. Most of the features so attractive to children may be retained, and others of genuine value may be added, if another summer is more successful financially.

The outcome of the experiment, then, has been that a score of boys and girls—sixteen boys and four girls—have found a healthful and pleasant place to spend their vacation. Whether any more than this is ever made of it depends upon how much Chicago parents wish their children to have of this kind of education—how much they feel the vacation problem and wish to see it worked out. Parents must make a great sacrifice of comfort if they wish to lead the simple life in the country with their children, and most of them would like to delegate it to someone else. The experiment will be tried another summer under as favorable circumstances and with as much assistance as can be commanded. The directors of the school will spend most of the spring quarter in visiting other places where the industrial features have been worked out. The Hillside School in Wisconsin combines country life with preparation for college the year around, while the Tuskegee Institution and the best agricultural colleges will give much to one who observes them with a definite purpose in mind. If it is possible to make distinct progress educationally as well as to get reasonable financial compensation for the time and labor expended, it may develop further in future summers. In the beginning the directors hoped that the plan would develop into a permanent institution open all the year. They believed, and still believe, that there is room in the educational world for another kind of school in the country and that the crowded conditions of Chicago schools demand some such outlet. They would be glad to hear from any parents and teachers who are interested in making a plan by which the education of boys and girls can be conducted partly in the city and partly in the country. Applications for the coming summer should be in as soon as possible.

EDITORIAL NOTES

Everyone now believes in education through some form of activity. The amount of activity, however, is no measure of what we want in an educated man or woman. The MOTIVE is the measure! Human progress toward better living hinges entirely upon the development of high, enlightened moral purpose. No one can be civilized above the height of his motive, though his activity may enable him to live in a boulevard mansion. Nor does any one remain imbruted below the level of his highest purpose, though sloth may domicile him under a thatch in the jungle.

Function of Motive

Upon these propositions there is no dispute. They are truismatic and trite. Why not, then, brush away all irrelevancies, all matters of minor importance that vex the day and get at once face to face with the great question—the fundamental one in education—*How shall the proper motive be developed?*

Face the Question

Sensibility toward right action is universal. There is no tribe so uncivilized as to ignore totally all the considerations of righteousness. Efforts at government are but the measure of the recognition which people give to the necessity of right doing. The methods, however, which now prevail in the world from Illinois to Afghanistan are arbitrary in their character. They depend more or less upon an appeal to force, and they invoke the stimuli to be found in the ideas of external and tangible rewards and punishments.

False Stimuli

These methods require that the individual shall be educated chiefly through negation. His behavior is determined by the prohibitions that hedge him round about. When Moses codified Jewish law into ten brief negations, he did the best, no doubt, for a primitive people. To my own mind, when a child, Moses appeared as a noble benefactor in that he had made life so simple for a boy. Just ten things not to be done! The remainder of life in all of its richness was open. In scanning the decalogue in search of all the fine legal discriminations that might be made in favor of a larger liberty, with one exception, the problems of living, to me,

Life Made Easy

seemed easy. To refrain from the pursuit of false gods, from the manufacture of graven images, from stealing and so forth, seemed self-commendatory. But the command not to covet, to a youngster who had but little, and who therefore possessed a bulging want for everything—that indeed seemed a hardship. Only when it was carefully explained that one should not *want* a thing up to the point of stealing it, did the rigor of the law seem mollified so as to make it even tolerable.

Teaching, founded upon a code of prohibitions, may have some bearing upon action, but it has little or nothing to do with the formation of motive. Neither is motive engendered by exhortations of a positive character; nor is it yet a matter of inoculation. Moral purpose is not generated by transferring a slice of the teacher's own good intentions to the mind of the pupil. It cannot be grafted into or upon the life of anyone. The motive that really civilizes, that actually lifts the race, comes from within as a matter of growth.

Motive Not by Vaccination

Most teachers beg the whole question at the outset. That is, in order to make a beginning they assume the presence of motive—the very thing it is the function of their teaching to establish. Or, if this assumption is not made, they proceed by the hortatory methods of a lecture in the attempt to create a motive through a process that inverts the principles of good pedagogy.

Begging the Question

In the beginning there is no motive present. In nature study, for instance, there is simply the child and nature. On the one side there is the sensitive organism, and on the other are the materials and forces that make an impression upon it. If there is no obstacle between these two—a defective sense or a witless teacher, for example—these at once originate, and indefinitely continue with cumulative intensity, action and reaction that are usually described in terms expressing growth. It must not be overlooked that this growth includes the motive itself. *It must grow too.* A motive can be derived, therefore, only though *the immediate and perpetual presence of the thing toward which one's actions are to be directed.*

Foundation of Motive

Here then, in nature-study, is the final argument for field-work. People generally suppose that school excursions are for the purpose of sharpening the senses, or for improving the circulation of the blood, or for developing the muscular system. Even so; field-work is for all of these things, *plus*. It is for everything enumerated, and also for the one thing still more essential, if even these physical results are to be attained—it is, finally, for the development of motive. This is a plan that always works, and no other one ever does. With Hottentot, Chinese, Sioux, and white man the result is ever the same. The presence of nature always begets its own motive for study through an aroused feeling of need, conscious or unconscious, and nothing else will do it. No method, as an artificial invention of pedagogy, can compensate for the lack of the masterful and impressive presence of nature. A little boy, once brought for a day from the Chicago slums to a shady grove in Normal Park, longed for his alley; he said he wanted to see the patrol wagon run through the streets. He was almost beyond the reach of teaching from the view-point of nature.

Function of Field-Work

The development of motive depends upon the presence of something that speaks of a need. It is the application of this principle that controls the arrangement of a program which provides, not only for trips to the country, but also for visits to the varied industries of the city. The great stores, the markets, the groceries, the mills, and the factories all tell of the needs in human life. Beginning with the initial challenge which they make to the curiosity of childhood, the continued presence of these interests will steadily grow a motive to participate properly in the world's affairs that, as the years mature, will become an intelligent and an imperative demand.

Adaptation of Program

Upon one trait in his pupils the teacher may forever reckon: they will always respond to a need which they can really feel and understand. It is this that makes the present plan of education possible. Children who would fail thus to respond would have to be educated according to some other principle.

A Fixed Trait

Illustrations

A study of our city parks showed how impossible it was for certain useful and beautiful birds to find suitable nesting-places in the trees and shrubs. Forthwith practically every pupil in the school volunteered to make a box for the nests. Whether the smaller children could make the boxes or not mattered but little; the strength of their *want* through a real sense of the need added cubits to their moral stature. Word came in the fall of a home school for waifs where clothes and playthings were needed; in a day or two the corridor was piled high with boxes which they had lovingly filled.

Caution Needed

At this point there is need of caution; there is danger that the tender sensibilities of childhood may be overwrought. Lacking in breadth of view, perspective, and philosophy—in a certain hardness of heart, it may be—too constant a presentation of the great needs of the world's unfortunates may produce a morbid and pathological condition of soul. This never arises through the touch with nature. Nature never makes one heartsick or sad, but it acts as a gentle tonic bringing hope and good cheer. The constant presence of nature, therefore, is needed as the ballast and the counterpoise of the educational system.

Hatefulness of Work

There is a serious practical difficulty in the way of teaching children to realize their motives in some useful end. To many people it looks too much like common work; there are parents, therefore, who strenuously object. They say their children can get that at home, and that the school should stand for something else—for culture! This is a curious fact, in view of the glorification that Labor is now receiving at the hands of the people. However, the large storekeepers do say that this great revival of enthusiasm for labor

Blessed be Labor!

has not as yet appreciably increased the demand for overalls and jumpers. No one has reported, so far, that the cuts of these elegant and useful trappings of toil are appearing in the latest fashion plates of our high-class tailors. From this it may be inferred that with most people the labor question has not yet gone beyond the stage of academic discussion. Hence the difficulty of getting the pupils actually to work either in school or at home. A few weeks since the children wished to have blooming plants in their school-room windows. They thought to improve matters by substituting for the unsightly pots the more beautiful creations of their own hands which they could easily make in the clay-room. Immediately a parent wrote that if our pupils could find nothing better to do than to make jardinières to beautify the University of Chicago he would take his son from the school—and he did! The kind of school which this type of parent really wants is one where his boy can insensibly acquire curvature of the spine, a sallow complexion, spectacles, and—culture!

Indignant Parents

The final test as to the value of any piece of educational work in the development of children of whatever intellectual capacity is determined by their appreciation of its worth in meeting a natural demand. Unless their energies are constantly directed toward filling a recognized want, the pupils put forth their efforts in vain, and the routine of the school becomes merely the rattle and grind of empty machinery. The social life of the school and home brings the pupils face to face with questions of moral values; the curriculum must be so ordered that the studies therein prescribed may help them to realize the importance of establishing these values in their minds as the fundamental basis for action.

Conclusion

W. S. J.

THE FRANCIS W. PARKER MEMORIAL

At the call of the chairman, Mr. O. T. Bright, The Francis W. Parker Memorial Committee met at the Normal School Thursday, February 15, 1906.

A report read by the secretary on funds collected showed substantial progress. In laying plans for future actions, Mrs. Hefferan was appointed to present the matter to the Englewood Parents' Association. Various plans were discussed looking toward a wider spread of interest in the movement. It is the hope of the committee that the thousands of teachers throughout the country who are glad to declare their debt to the great influence of Colonel Parker will do something to assist in establishing a suitable memorial at the Normal School. The memorial will not be for the man alone; it will stand also as a mark of approval upon the general movement to emancipate the child and to uplift the teacher, in which work Colonel Parker took so conspicuous a part. The fund, therefore, should represent wide-spread contributions from pupils and teachers in small amounts, rather than larger sums from a few, and the committee feels that teachers everywhere should interest themselves and their pupils in the work.

Contributions may be sent to Miss Sadie Griswold, Chicago Normal School, Chicago, Ill.

VOLUME VI NUMBER 8

THE ELEMENTARY SCHOOL TEACHER

APRIL, 1906

DEMOCRACY IN EDUCATION[1]

DAVID KINLEY
The University of Illinois

Nearly every foreign observer of American social and political affairs has commented on the prevalence of ring rule and bossism in our political life. It is commonly acknowledged that in our large cities the conduct of political matters is generally in the hands of one or a few people who manipulate the financial and other departments of the city government principally for their own benefit. Indeed, the corruption of city government in the United States has become notorious. The people seem to have abrogated their municipal rights and to have become afraid to assert themselves against the dominion of the machine, the dictates of the ring, and the commands of the bosses.

Whatever the causes of this state of affairs—and different ones are assigned by different people—we all agree that the condition is a disgrace to the public, a reflection on the manhood and integrity of the people, and a source of corruption and immorality in our public life.

But it is not only in political life that the existence of the power of the bosses has come to be recognized as a determined factor. The presence of one-man power, with its influences for evil and for good, has forced itself upon the attention of the country in the demoralization of business enterprises also. We are standing aghast at the revelations of low moral standards

[1]Address delivered before the Northern Illinois Teachers' Association, October, 1905

and utter lack of sense of responsibility for other people's rights and property shown in the attitude of the great insurance companies that are now under investigation; in the illegal and morally illegitimate conduct of many corporations, like the Standard Oil Company; in the indifference to public welfare shown by our railroad managers in their occasional defiance of law when it suits their purpose. The tendency among business corporations to concentrate power in the hands of one man is in many ways legitimate and necessary, but it has been in many ways illegitimately facilitated and extended in cases similar to those which have given birth to the power of corrupt political bosses. Stockholders, like voters, are aroused to declare themselves concerning the policy of a corporation only when their immediate interests are endangered, or when some strong and unusual issue presents itself to them. The resort to one-man power in politics was caused on the surface at least by a desire for clean government. We neglected to perform our duty at the polls, and our duty as common citizens in watching the men we elected to public offices and seeing that they discharged their duty well; and when we found ourselves in the midst of inevitable corruption, we took it for granted that the cause of the corruption was lack of proper power in the hands of our mayors and other high officers. We insisted that division of power in city government made it impossible to hold the mayor responsible, and that, since he did not have practically supreme power, we could not secure good government. In other words, we elected bad men to office, and then expected one good man to counterbalance all their influences and acts, and give us the kind of government which could only come from the concerted action of a large number of good officers. We had flung aside our own sense of responsibility, and we sought to escape the consequences of our act by putting the responsibility more heavily on one of our representatives. The experiment failed, as it was bound to fail in the long run; for when a group of democratic people shirk the responsibility which properly belongs to them by putting it upon some other people, their own sense of duty and obligation, their own interest and activity, become enervated, and the men on whom they thrust this power are subjected to temptation to use it for their own ends. When in a business corporation, a bank, an insurance company, or what not, the president, or highest officer, is left without supervision of the directors or the stockholders, and allowed to conduct the business in his own way, on the plea that concentration of power brings greater efficiency and larger results, need we be surprised if the results are of a character shown by the insurance investigations now going on in New York? If we sacrifice individuality, initiative, and responsibility for the sake of efficiency, we may get the efficiency with its larger results for a time, but it will be at the expense of higher morality; it will be at the expense of the impairment of the public sense of right and wrong, and at the expense of the lowering of general ethical standards of conduct. You cannot cure corruption in public life or in business life by concentrating power in the hands of a ring or of one—certainly not in a democracy, for the people are responsible on the one hand to the shareholders and the directors, and on the other they must take an active part in determining the policy and the operation of the machinery of politics and the machinery of business.

Now, this same tendency to leave the direction of things to a few or to one has been showing itself more largely of late in educational matters. We seem to have evolved in late years in this country a passion for organization for organization's sake. We have been busy in educational circles in constructing systems of administration and machinery of organization, and there has been a growing tendency for the power which formulates educational policy and administers educational organization to come into the control of a smaller number. One of the most astounding things in educational life is that it is in the most democratic country in the world, and in the most democratic parts of that country, that the most autocratic systems and methods of school administration have grown up and are growing up. If you go to Massachusetts, you will find the schools close to the people and managed by officers elected by the citizens in their own communities, advised and helped by superintendents and by a state board of education which has no immediate authority over them. If you go to some other states, as New York, you will find at the head of the system a state officer with a hierarchy of officers under him, having so wide an authority that the local authorities have little to say or do about the management of their schools, and the teachers have least of all to say. In some cases the organization seems to be theoretically so perfect, on paper, that no individual teacher or officer in the system can go wrong without being immediately checked up by the center or head of the system, and that no individual teacher or officer in the system can do anything without the direct authorization and approval of the head of the system. He determines the policy and method of the work; everybody in the system must conform to his standards and methods.

But it is not only in the few cases of "system" that I have in mind that the teacher and his personality seem to have been reduced to a minimum; the same thing is true, in a greater or less degree, throughout the country. It seems, for example, to have become the high privilege of the teachers in different states throughout the United States to attend teachers' associations to carry out the will of a ring or small group who make the slate of officers, determine the policy of the association, make its programs, and leave the rest of us the privilege of paying the bills. It is commonly said, for example, that our own National Educational Association is controlled by a small group of leading educators; controlled, that is, in the sense that the great body of members have little or nothing to say about the general policy of the association or its officers. Certain occurrences at the last meeting seem to an unbiased public to furnish evidence of the truth of this statement. What opportunity is there in that organization, as it is, for the vast body of teachers throughout the country to exert their will and make themselves felt, except by taking the disagreeable attitude of critics or rebels against the system?

Similar things may be said about many of the state and smaller organizations of teachers. The teachers are expected to assemble, to pay bills, hand up their membership fees, listen to the speakers whether they are good or bad, be bored by the writers of papers, and then to gather at an appointed time and place to cast their votes for the election of officers previously made out by a group who did not consult them and who have had their own ends in view in making up the slate, whether these ends were such as the body of their constituents would approve, or not. The small coterie that does this business adds to its power from year to year to control the affairs of the teachers' organizations, unless and until the spirit of rebellion becomes too great and the prepared slates are smashed. That they are seldom smashed is not surprising, because he or she would be a rash teacher who would rise against an authority, whether self-constituted or otherwise, when his superintendent or some friend of his superintendent was in the ring.

In consequence of this state of affairs, it is not infrequent that one man or a few men come to think and feel and act as if they owned the school systems of their communities or their states, and a subservient publc acquiesces in their assumption of power, so long, forsooth, as they seem to fulfil that fetish requirement of the American public—efficiency.

The evil reaches, however, not only through the teachers' association, but into school boards, into individual schools, and into colleges and universities. Here is a city superintendent, or a principal, or a president, who is an autocrat. He has the sole control of appointment and dismissal, and he exercises it in a way which makes it necessary for a teacher to suppress his individuality, if he would save his place; to forego initiative and spontaneity, and to follow slavishly the dictates of his superior officer, if he is to furnish sufficient proof of the "personal loyalty" which that kind of a man always demands. He speaks of the teachers as if they were his personal servants, and I have heard superintendents and college presidents talk about "my force," "my teachers," "my schools," "my institution," as the Czar of Russia or the emperor of Germany talks about "my people," "my army," "my ships," and "my soldiers." I have known some who insist on the power of summary dismissal at their own wish, yet who would resent hotly the assertion of any right on the part of the teacher to terminate his contract at will; who resented any efforts on the part of other schools or colleges to get members of their teaching corps, and laid it up against a member of their corps if he was known to be making an effort to better his condition in salary or rank by seeking a new position. Too much and too strong administration almost inevitably has such results and degrades the teacher. Either he rebels against the system and takes the consequences of a struggle with someone officially stronger than himself, and usually to his detriment; or else he submits at the sacrifice of his self-respect and dignity. If he does the former, he is accused of being a nuisance and of causing dissension in the school, and is marked as one whom it is not safe for superintendents and presidents to employ. If he submits, the degradation which he suffers from his loss of self-respect makes the teacher less of a man or a woman, and impairs the influence that he otherwise could have exerted in developing the character of the boys and girls under his charge.

We hear of men agreeing to accept a superintendency, a presidency, or a principalship on conditon that they may have a "free hand," as it is called, in "reorganizing" the faculty. To grant the propriety of such a request is to forget that an educational institution is an organic growth; that the continuance of its life and policy and present character depends upon its past career. They ask the right to hack and sever and cut deep into the life of the institution in order, forsooth, that they may impose upon it from without a preconceived policy, formed in their own minds and without reference to the continuity of the life and the historical past of the college or school; without reference to the moral obligations that have sprung up; forgetful of the fact that they are dealing with human beings and not with machines, and that any act which lowers the standard of self-respect of the teachers of the school—which makes them feel for an instant that they are not regarded as responsible and trustworthy individuals—is likely, by lowering the standard of work to lower also the standard of conduct and impair the quality of teaching.

In short, there is a tendency in certain quarters to insist that the teachers of the country shall have nothing to say or do about the organization of our educational system. The advocates of this policy insist that "it is the business of the teacher to teach;" such a statement is mere play upon words and ignores the fact that teaching cannot be isolated from administration, and the tendency is to deify the machinery of organization and to forget the human element, to organize and run a complex system beautiful in its completeness, smooth in its workings, but smooth because it is impelled by a force from outside that crushes and overthrows internal, spontaneous influences which, although they may not work so smoothly, would give a more human, beautiful, and lifelike movement to the system. Put in plain English, the tendency of this view is to relegate the teacher to a position of subordinate importance in the educational system; and it raises the question: Which is the important thing in education —administration or teaching? Are the teachers of a country or a community, taken as a whole, incapable of giving good advice regarding educational policy? Should they be cut off altogether in the matter of giving advice from access to boards of directors, boards of trustees and superintendents, and the whole determination of the educational policy in a community be left to a single officer, like a superintendent or a president or a small board? Are the teachers of the country worthy of confidence?

At one of the meetings held in Urbana a week ago, in connection with the conference of college and university trustees, I am told that it was stated by a distinguished speaker that the faculties of colleges and universities could not be trusted to give sound advice in the shaping up of educational policy; that mere teachers are impractical, visionary, and unable to meet men of affairs and take their part in the world's activity outside the schoolroom. Such a statement is an insult to the teachers of the country, and should arouse them to a sense of the danger that they are in, if the system advocated by the speaker should prevail. If the time ever comes when the public shall lay more emphasis upon the importance of a complete and smooth administrative machinery in our schools than it lays upon the efficiency of the teaching; if public opinion ever comes to the point where it believes that the teachers as a body are incapable of giving sound advice on educational matters, it will mean the degradation of the teaching profession. It will mean that self-respecting men and women, the equals of any officers in any administrative position, will seek other fields for their life-activities, and will refuse to subject themselves to the whims and dictates of men who might have been good slave-drivers in the days of slavery, but are hardly fit members of the educational system of an intelligent community, where men and women believe that individual initiative, spontaneity, sense of responsibility, knowledge, intelligence and sympathy, individuality—are more important factors in education than smooth administration or strong executive action. The question before us, then, is whether the tone and character of our educational systems in this country are to be determined by the great body of the teachers of the country; or are to be imposed upon the teachers by a relatively small number of men of autocratic temperament, who sneer at the teacher and insist that his proper place is a subordinate one of obedience to higher authority.

The demand for so-called strong administration is based largely on the alleged necessity for uniformity of method and smoothness in the work of the administrative machinery. The desire for uniformity is a curse in every department of educational matters. The ideal school would be one which had no uniformity of method or administration, because each individual pupil would be treated according to his specific characteristics. The only place where method and system would be needed would be in the keeping of accounts, in order that thereby the progress of the pupil might be noted. To crowd every teacher into the same mold is to destroy personality; to cast every complex character and undeveloped life into the same frame is to destroy individuality. A flower that has been pressed for herbarium purposes is, after all, only a mummy; however well it may serve as a specimen in a collection, it cannot be compared for beauty, or for the discharge of the service of flowers to mankind, with a flower in its natural condition. Its fragrance is gone, color is lost, the lights and shadows of its surface have disappeared; it is dead. So with teachers who are crowded too closely in the press of administrative machinery.

The time for dogmatism and for coercive uniformity is past. Administrative school systems, like all institutions, are good only so far as they give opportunity to all the influences within them to contribute to the growth of the people whom they affect.

The substitution of a higher form of control for a lower, of voluntary obedience and intelligent acquiescence for external control, marks a step in social progress. It always involves higher moral training, and therefore a more developed individuality and a better character, to offer more alternatives and trust a man to make the right selection, than to deprive him of all choice and compel him to walk in a prescribed way. What we need in educational administration is the replacement of coercive control and authority with free action, combined with a responsibility for the consequences of that action.

When a superintendent distrusts his teachers, or a college president distrusts his faculty; when either says that the teachers are incapable of advising with reference to school policy; when he says that they are without sound judgment, and that they need to have their ways of action pointed out to them, and kept well within the limits of a system laid down for them by their superior officers; the only conclusion that can be drawn is that that superintendent or that president has not yet learned the superiority of the organic over the mechanical. He has not learned that the flower expanding to the sun, blooming and shedding its fragrance and beauty in response to internal forces, is more typical of moral character and of the ideal individual life than the steam engine, however smoothly it runs, which is driven by a force outside of itself and is absolutely under the control of the manager of that force. He has failed to grasp that great truth of evolution that responsiveness to influence is a higher form of action than action in response to coercion. He has failed to see that spontaneous action is better than compulsory movement. He has failed to see that leadership is a higher form of authority, and is productive of far better results for the world, than is driving. He has failed to distinguish between a leader of men and a driver of slaves. He has failed to grasp the great moral and economic truth that the product of free labor is greater in quantity and far better in character than that of slave labor. He has failed to learn that in many cases influence is more powerful than authority.

A favorite illustration of some school officers, when speaking of their faculties and teachers is that of the stage-driver. They look upon and liken the corps of teachers to a group of unruly horses which need a driver to control them and make them pull together. The figure is a vicious one. If we are to go to the animal kingdom for an example, rather should we go to the dogs pulling the sledge of the arctic traveler. The movement of the team is controlled by the leader, who is at the front of the line. He it is who, setting the example, pointing the way, blazing the path, rouses his followers to enthusiasm and brings about that unison of action that results in the highest speed. The former figure is gratifying to the men who, by accident of office, have been led to feel themselves superior to their fellow-workers, but who, by the very use of the figure in question, show that they have not grasped the first principle of sound administration.

Mere differentiation and co-ordination of function, mere complexity of organization, mere exercise of authority to compel uniformity of action, does not prove that the system under which it is done is a good system or that it is making for progress. There is an order and peace that may be attained in the streets of a city under martial law; but it is not to be compared for a moment in its effects on human character, or in its results for the progress of civilization, with the peace that comes from the acquiescence of the citizens of the town in the laws of the land. The peace and order and system that make for progress are those that command voluntary obedience and the willing co-operation of those who are subject to them. The best system of administration in school work, as in all other work, is that which does indeed work smoothly, but which attains its results from and through the acts of intelligent voluntary co-operation of all the individuals working in it, because all these individuals see its beneficent character, and because it supplies them with multifarious opportunities whereby all their differing individualities can work out a congenial development.

As I have pointed out before, too much emphasis on the authority of administrative officers tends to degrade the teacher. There are evidences of this on all hands, although conclusive proof of it is likely to be late in coming. It will come only with the next generation of teachers, when we find that the personnel of the teaching profession is lower than it was, because self-respecting individuals, with ideas of their own, have refused to enter a profession in which they are denied freedom of action and initiative. There are institutions where the moral tone of the teaching corps is deplorably bad because they have submitted too long to coercive authority that suppresses their individuality.

If, instead of submitting and degenerating, the teachers rebel, we are likely to see a wider movement for affiliation of the teachers of the country with organizations of labor. They will organize and seek the strength that comes from affiliation with other labor organizations in order to protect themselves against the autocratic authority of administrative officers. It would be deplorable to have such a movement general, for the conditions of the teachers' work and life are in too many ways different from those of the members of ordinary labor unions; and the causes which justify the organization in the one case in many respects do not apply in the case of teachers. But I do not know what other explanation to give for the tendency which seems to be growing for teachers to seek connection with organized labor. The movement cannot be stopped by force, since there are men and women of independent minds in the teaching profession, and who choose to remain in it and fight against autocratic administration; and they will call to their aid all resources available, even if it brings them into affiliation with class organizations.

Sometimes when a superintendent or a president goes to a new place, as I have remarked, he asks for a free hand in the reorganization of the faculty and in determining policy. A demand of this kind either implies that the man who makes it lacks confidence in himself as a leader; that he does not feel that it is in him to gather together the existing forces in the institution and bend them to his will by the power of his influence and character; or else it implies that he mistakes the relative value of influence and authority. A leader of men is greater than a driver of slaves. The man who is truly strong is not the man who, on coming into a position of authority where he can dictate, cuts into the lives of such of those under him as happen not to please him or to come up to his personal standard, however satisfactory they may be from the common standard of the community. But rather that man is strong who, taking the influences and forces of the situation as they are, can combine those that are powerful for good by the influence of his character and superior education, and secure the willing co-operation of all toward the end he wishes to accomplish. Autocratic authority implies that there will be lack of continuity in the policy of the school system or institution. The policy will change with every newcomer. It implies for the teachers, uncertainty in their tenure of office; it sometimes subjects them to the caprice, prejudice, and ignorance of men to whom the work of experts does not appeal, because they do not know either its character or its value. It tends to the upbuilding of a personal clientele, and the development of envy, subservience, and toadyism. Which, then, is the more important in educational work—strong administrators or good teachers?

In truth, no one who considers the matter intelligently can hesitate a moment in answering the question. The purpose of the schools is not to give power to superintendents, principals, deans, and presidents; it is not to afford glory to teachers. It is simply and wholly to promote the welfare of the public. But even that is not a complete answer. Rather should we say that it is to promote the welfare of the pupils; and sometimes it is desirable to do things for them in which the existing state of the public opinion might not altogether acquiesce. Any system of school administration, and any system of teaching, which does not conduce to the welfare of the pupils has in some way failed; but certainly teaching is the more important of the two divisions of a school system.

As the trustees of Leland Stanford University recently said in comparing the internal organization of their university with the organization of the trustees and the president's office: "All that we have dealt with hitherto is merely the framework that surrounds and supports it [the real university], while upon this internal organization depends the vital institution itself: this is the true body as distinguished from its mere clothing and housing."

Anything that hampers the influence and personality of the teacher; anything that degrades that personality; anything that suppresses his spontaneity or checks his initiative in the interests of his work, or makes the teacher less of a man or a woman in his own estimation or in the estimation of the people of his community or of his school, is a vicious element in the school system, and one that should be crushed out.

We have often heard a college defined as Mark Hopkins on one end of a log and a boy on the other. The point of this is that a great personality, a teacher of high character and mighty influence, is a far more powerful agent in training the young without any system of administration than a person of mediocrity in a most finished, perfect, and complex system of organization. It is the teacher that is the center, the core, the heart of our school system.

The administration necessary for any school system or for any educational institution is the minimum necessary for the most effective teaching. The simplest administration is the best. An unnecessary wheel in a machine means less power and a diminution in the product. There is, indeed, danger in too little organization, but that danger is far less than the danger of too much. Too much administration leads to too much red-tape; too much of the teachers' time is spent in making reports and in writing instructions and in attending meetings that might well be omitted. The attention of the public has recently been called to the efforts of the president of the United States to cut some of the red-tape out of the administration of the national government. So complex had the administration become in some of the departments that many men employed in them seemed to think that their chief province was to read and indorse papers and tie them up in bundles with red tape. In formulating the business upon paper, they forget that the matters with which they deal are issues of life; and the content, in their minds, is lost in the framework.

There is danger that it may be so in our schools. Too much administration brings about a waste of time and knowledge that should be used by the teacher in studying and devising better methods of teaching, and to personal attention to individual students. These are the things which help to form life and character, although they may leave less perfectly written records. There is too much emphasis in some places on clean record sheets, on record books that show complete lists of tardiness and absence, with the causes.

There are three divisions, or parts, necessary to a school system or college. In order of their importance, they are the general educational policy, the teaching, and the administrative organization. Who shall determine these? The first deals with external, public, policy, and the system of instruction, in their relation to other school systems or colleges in the same community or state. It is a question of general educational policy, and the town or city or state must determine its details by the demand of the public. What things does the public wish the pupils to study? The answer would be different in Turkey from what it is in Illinois. No authority in one man, or in a group of men, in a democratic country like our own, can determine, or should be permitted to determine, the general policy of our school systems or any part of them. The schools should be close to the people and they should have local color; they should reflect in a measure the traditions, history, and character of the community. It is true that differences in the educational standards of communities in the same state and country are fast disappearing, but this disappearance should be brought about by the exchange of ideas and a closer connection between the people themselves, and not by the imposition of uniform standards by some external authority, whether a state superintendent, a commissioner, or a national superintendent.

It may be objected to this theory that there are communities with low standards; poor communities that cannot afford to have as good schools as they should have or want to have. This is true, just as there are individuals who are less well off than other individuals. If the interests of the rest of the state require that a particular community shall have higher standards, which it wishes but cannot afford, then it is the business of the rest of the state to help it by a state tax. If a community has low standards and poor schools, although the people can afford better so far as money is concerned, the question arises whether it is the business of the public to coerce that community into better methods, or to educate it to a higher life. I take it that some good results can be attained by leading the people of a community to see that they are losing in the race and falling behind because of their low educational standards.

If these statements are correct; if the theory of freedom and public control that I have briefly laid down is sound, then the schools should be kept close to the people by the election of school boards. Appointed school boards are an anomaly in our country and can be justified, if justifiable at all, only by the peculiar exigencies of some local situation.

The denial of this theory of democracy in our school system, the attempt to put autocratic power in the hands of one or a few men, whether superintendent, commissioner, presidents, or directors, is a phase of the distrust of democracy which has become too pronounced in this country of late. Cannot the people be trusted to determine for themselves what is for their highest welfare, educationally? If it be proved, as some say, that it is necessary for the authority to determine for them what is good in education, then our democracy is a farce. If the standards are low, will these be raised and the people strengthened by depriving them of the exercise of judgment and responsibility?

How, then, shall we draw the lines that are to distinguish the functions of the various parts of the administration and organization of our school systems and our colleges? What shall we assign to our boards of education, our trustees, our superintendents, presidents, and other officers? Clearly enough, the boards of education must determine, as representatives of the public, the general educational policy of the schools. They are the authority that must say whether the high school shall have a classical course or a commercial course, or both. They should seek advice of the superintendent; they should call in to their help the state superintendent, and any other state educational officer whom they can reach. They should also call to their assitance the advice of their corps of teachers. These are the experts. They are likely to have the best judgment as to the adaptability of a practical course of study to the constituency for which they are working.

Similarly, when a superintendent, having been instructed by his board of education, or when a president having been instructed by the board of trustees, as to the general character of the educational policy of the schools or the college, sets out to devise an administrative system or organization which will carry out these plans, he will get the best results if he consults those who are to do the work. To devise a scheme on paper, "out of his head," and without reference to local conditions and the experience, education, and personality of the teachers, is to invite failure.

To say that faculties and corps of teachers are incapable of giving advice on school matters or college policy is to say what is not true. This remark could be made only by one who is blinded by his own conceit or ignorance of educational history. The internal organization of a system which is to carry out the policy of board of education or boards of trustees should be made by superintendents and presidents only after they have consulted, so far as possible, the teaching corps, and have incorporated the ideas of the latter with their own. No school system can otherwise be sound or well administered.

The teaching itself, of course, can be done only by the teachers, but teaching involves more than merely "imparting instruction." Teaching cannot be intelligently done unless the teacher participates in the way that I have already described, in shaping the policy of the school system of which he is a part. We are dealing with boys and girls, men and women, human nature. It is not necessary for one cog in a machine to know anything about the character of another cog; both are dead matter, and the machine as a whole will do its work notwithstanding. Not so with teaching. The teacher must know something of the general policy of the school and of the community in which he is to teach, if he is to do his work in a way that will conform to the system and promote this policy. The teacher, however, must not make the mistake of supposing that he can do it all. He must rely on his superintendent. He must have access through his superintendent to the school board, or through his president to the board of trustees. The teaching corps represents that part of the public that are experts in these matters. To deny the teachers the right of being consulted, and of consulting with all their superior officers in the proper manner, is to stifle the sense of responsibility. "Public spirit dies where the people are debarred from public action."

The third part of the school system is its internal organization and administration. Here are the offices of the superintendents, the principals, the presidents, the deans, the registrars, and what not, in our various educational institutions. Their business is to devise the machinery which will give opportunity to the living body, the educational system, to grow to perfection. They are to furnish the sustenance, the sunlight, the framework, the earth, and all the collateral material equipment. They are to guide— and sometimes it is necessary for them to prune; but the pruning should always be an incident of their office and not the purpose. This phase of their work must not be magnified. The proper phase of their work is to construct and develop, not to destroy and repress. It is false to say, as a certain well-known educator has often remarked, that it is the real function of the college president or the superintendent to repress action. Their general function is to encourage action in the right directions. It shows a lack of knowledge of the vast amount of waste involved to take the other ground.

We come now to the consideration of democracy in the educational process; democracy in the school and in actual training; democracy in the immediate sphere of the teacher.

The whole character of our education should be democratic. The general aim, or rather the emphasis of the educational aim, changes from time to time, and this fact makes us lose sight of the importance of keeping its democratic character. The aim of education changes with the current of public opinion. The phase of life upon which the public, at a particular time, is laying emphasis is the phase that finds prominence in our educational systems. In the past, general culture and intelligent training of the individual—the production of polished members of the upper classes in society—was the aim and function of our school sytem and our educational training. In the last century the key-note of philosophical thought was the emphasis of political equality and democracy in government, and our education, in its organization and subject-matter, assumed a political character. Civic training, training of citizenship, training for membership in a democratic political community, was emphasized. Today the successful pursuit of business is regarded by the community and the country and the world as the test of a fully equipped man. Accordingly, our educational systems have been turning more and more to what is called practical training. Training for business, for engineering, trade, the law, and other practical pursuits, is the determining note of our educational course. The present demand that our schools shall train for economic success is particularly dangerous to the maintenance of our democratic ideals. The very test of excellence, economic success, tends to promote the formation of classes to the destruction of our democratic equality.

We need, therefore, to guard more carefully than ever the democratic spirit of our educational aim. We need to remember constantly that, after all, we are equal citizens of a free country, and that it should be our constant purpose to open the way for equal opportunity to all in all walks of life; that our schools, therefore, should afford training for all classes and all individuals to pursue any career for which they are particularly fitted. The establishment of trade schools for the children of people in particular trades is undemocratic, because it tends to stratify society; it tends to make and perpetuate trade classes. I have no sympathy, therefore, with the demand sometimes made that the children of a mechanic should be put to industrial studies, while the children of a lawyer need not be. Mechanical, industrial, training should be open to all, whatever the social class from which they come; but it should be open as a special means of yielding that all-round education which every boy and girl should receive, and not for the purpose of enabling or encouraging the mechanic's boy to be a mechanic, the grocer's boy to be a grocer, or the lawyer's boy to be a lawyer.

Over and above all, the general and most important aim of any school controlling and dominating the immediate purposes of curriculums and particular studies, whether commercial or classical or industrial, should be kept constantly in view; and this general aim is social service. Every pupil in the school should have the idea instilled into him that, while he is taking a course of study that will make him an economic success, he is to strive for that economic success, and the school is maintained to let him achieve that economic success, for the main purpose of serving society and promoting human progress. He will do this if he achieves his own success in the highest sense.

In the next place, the curriculum should be democratic in character. A course of study should be close to the demand of the community, and no community should have forced upon it, by boards of education or superintendents or trustees, courses of study that are foreign to its tastes, ill fitted to its life, or alien to its moral and philosophical beliefs. So far as possible, the school curriculum should be suited to all classes in the community; and if a community can afford it, several courses should be offered to meet the demands of the various groups, or classes.

Moreover, within the school itself the student, under the guidance and advice of parents and teachers, may well be allowed some liberty. Opportunity for selection of studies develops the judgment and the sense of responsibility. Personally, I do not believe in large liberty of choice so low down in the school system as the high school; but it is not the amount of choice, but the principle of choice, for which I am contending.

In the next place, the disciplinary arrangement of a school should be democratic. The school should be so organized that the pupils shall feel responsible for its orderly conduct, and it should not be so organized that order is preserved simply as a result of the coercion of the teacher. I do not mean by this that the government of the school should be left to the boys and girls;

nor am I blind to the fact that there are many cases where the sense of responsibility must fail and coercion must be used. What I am insisting on is that they should be used only when persuasive measures cannot be relied upon, and that they should be abandoned as fast and as far as accountability is developed.

Finally, over and above all the points that I have mentioned, in its far-reaching importance, is the necessity of a democratic spirit on the part of the teacher. I have said that a college has been described as a great teacher on one end of a log and a boy on the other. The personality of the teacher will determine the school, and will largely control the point of view and the mode of thought of the pupils and will give trend to their course of study and actions. If the teacher is not broad, generous, and democratic in spirit, the school will not be, and the pupils will not be. There is no higher duty upon teachers, not only in the public schools, but in all the schools of the country, than to emphasize and perpetuate and spread the spirit of democratic equality—the equality of social and economic opportunity in all lines of life. I know that this doctrine has gone a little out of fashion; but if we permit it to go too far out of fashion, we shall have to reckon with dangers to our democratic institutions—dangers which it will be hard to control, because we have allowed the spirit of democracy to decay.

Fellow-teachers, there is no profession on which rests a greater responsibility than upon our own for the preservation of the spirit of democracy. The discharge of that duty calls for self-sacrifice; it calls for obedience to duly constituted authority; it calls at times for the abrogation of our personal interests, the suppression of our personal desires, the giving up of our personal ambitions. The influences that go out from the schoolrooms of the country are more far-reaching, more lasting, and make a deeper impression upon the character and life of our people, than the influences of any other institution excepting the home. Just as the fathers and mothers of the land give their lives in a very real sense for the upbuilding of the lives and careers of their boys and girls, and for the maintenance of that country whose establishment and preservation have cost so many lives and entailed so many sacrifices; so the teachers of the land find their best success and do their richest work and attain their highest glory in the self-effacement that comes from pouring their lives and their spirit into the current of life of the pupils that are committed to their care, though their names may never be known beyond their own communities, nor their memories cherished except in the grateful hearts of a few who feel that without their teaching they would be worse men and women than they are.

Most of you have given up many things to be teachers; some of you have left careers that would have brought you fame and a larger measure of success, as success goes, than you have attained or ever will attain in the work you are doing now. But there is a success that cannot be seen; there is a reward of the spirit; that success and that reward come to the humblest of us when he sees that the boy or girl he has been trying to train has turned out a true man or a true woman, and that, however humble the career he may fill in his community, his life will ring true, his ideas will be sound, and the community life will be better, because he has caught something of your spirit and is a product of your sacrifice.

THE VERNAL EQUINOX

WILBUR S. JACKMAN
School of Education

Suppose it were given to man just once in one hundred years to see the opening of spring. Suppose it were true that every third generation, that only those who lived in a centennial year, should see this new birth in nature. Suppose that we were now living in that eventful year; that for fifty long years the trees had shivered in the cold, wintry blasts. When last they spread out their canopy of leaves, when last the summer birds sang in their branches, our grandfathers were mere boys. And suppose they were to tell us how their grandfathers told them, when they were boys, the way they saw nature rouse herself from her deathlike stupor and put forth a new life. How they tried to describe the way the leaden clouds grew gradually thinner, and how the sky became softer. How the fierce blasts became more subdued and mild, and more friendly to living things. How the birds, taking courage, came back, singly and in droves, to visit the haunts of their ancestors long ago dead. How the furry denizens of the burrows in the ground and the hollow trees rubbed their sleepy eyes and, stretching their stiffened limbs full of the rheumatism of the long winter, came forth to frisk and bask in the welcome sunlight. How the insects seemed to come from everywhere and from nowhere, until the air was teeming with a glittering host and the ear was filled with their droning bass. How the brooks and rivers, for fifty long years held by frosty bonds, now threw off their icy fetters, and how the water leaped and sparkled and sang with delight in its regained freedom.

Suppose that we should be able to get merely scraps of this wonderful story from our grandfathers, who received it in scraps from their grandfathers; with what bated breath and attentive ears would we listen while they told it! Suppose here and there in old books we could find a few pages of the story, as we now get fragments of the history of John Smith, the Salem Witchcraft, King Phillip, and the Boston Tea Party, with what sleepless interest would we read it!

But beyond and above all, how boundless would be our delight to know and feel that even we are to see this great change for ourselves; with what pity would we remember our grandfathers; King Phillip, and the Boston Tea Party; with what sleepless in-would bless the day that gave us birth!

With what interest would we scan the horizon in the morning to see just when and where the sun began his work, and follow his course at midday and evening that we might know the means he employs! Every tree, bush, shrub, even the meanest plants, would become the center of a living interest. Every bud would be numbered and watched; and when the green leaves came forth, the nation would give itself over to a week of celebration and festivity. How softly would we steal through the woods and thickets, that we might actually see for ourselves just how the birds weave their cunning nests! How we would admire and wonder at the dexerity of these delicate builders! And then the first flowers: with what diligence would we search field and wood for them! As now the astronomer makes himself ready by weeks and months of careful preparation to witness the transit of Venus, or for the observation of an eclipse, so would we in like manner prepare ourselves to witness the bursting of the bud into the full-blown flower.

But every year we and our children may behold the natal day of spring—this New Year's Day of Nature. What invader ever crossed the hemisphere on such a mighty revolution bent as the great sun who every spring enters ours? And as the gods of old used to send to mortals by winged messengers their promises of aid and succor, so this great king sends to us each spring by the birds and flowers the promises of a season which, though ten thousand times repeated, yet is ever new.

READING MATTER FOR SECOND GRADE

ELSIE A. WYGANT
The University Elementary School

Experience as the basis and dynamic center of all the work of the children determines the subject-matter of their reading. But not all the most intense experiences or enthusiastic interests of children lie within any outline covered by history, science, and geography. Any hard and fast conformity to these subjects brings about that pernicious form of correlation which makes one hesitate ever to use the term, that is, the correlation of subject-matter, rather than the correlation of children's interests.

Love of stories as stories which have no bearing upon either food supply, seed distribution, or the cardinal points of the compass are essential interests of childhood. Therefore stories, rhymes, and riddles are used in and out of season. The following have given much pleasure to one group of children. These are taken from *Sing Song* a volume of children's verse by Christina Rossetti. The book is out of print save in the author's complete works. Yet it is one of those rare, good things which should go on the shelf with the *Child's Garden of Verse* and *Mother Goose.*

Mother Goose herself never took more charming flights than does Christina Rossetti in some of her *Sing Song* verses; but like the *Rhymes of Mother Goose* a culling process is necessary, because, among these wholesome childlike jingles, are some so morbid, so full of hopeless misery, that one would hesitate ever to put the volume, as a whole, before children.

Because of this need of selection and the difficulty in procuring the volume a few are here printed. These will serve during the fall and winter as a part of the reading-matter for the second grade.

I

Mix a pancake,
Stir a pancake,
    Pop it in the pan;

Fry a pancake,
Toss a pancake,
Catch it if you can.

IV

Fly away, fly away over the sea,
Sun-loving swallow for summer is done.
Come again, come again, come back to me,
Bringing the summer and bringing the sun.

V

A peach for brothers, one for each,
A peach for you and a peach for me.
But the biggest, rosiest, downiest peach
For grandmamma with her tea.

VI

O wind, why do you never rest
Wandering, whistling to and fro,
Bringing rain out of the west,
From the dim north bringing snow.

VII

If a pig wore a wig
What could we say?
Treat him as a gentleman
And say "Good day."
If his tail chanced to fail
What could we do?
Send him to the tailoress
To get one new.

VIII

If all were rain and never sun,
No bow could span the hill;
If all were sun and never rain
There'd be no rainbow still.

XIX

What does the donkey bray about?
What does the pig grunt through his snout?

What does the goose mean by a hiss?
Oh, Nurse, if you can tell me this,
I'll give you a kiss.

XX

A pin has a head but has no hair;
A clock has a face but no mouth there;
Needles have eyes but they cannot see;
A fly has a trunk without lock or key.
A hill has no leg but has a foot;
A wineglass a stem but not a root;
Rivers run though they have no feet;
A saw has teeth but it does not eat;
Ash trees have keys yet never a lock,
And baby crows without being a cock.

XXI

There is one that has a head without an eye,
And there's one that has an eye without a head;
You may find the answer if you try.
And when all is said,
Half the answer hangs upon a thread!

XXII

Three plum buns
To eat here at the stile
In the clover meadow
For we have walked a mile.
One for you and one for me
And one left over;
Give it to the boy who shouts
To scare sheep from the clover.

XXIII

"Kookoorookoo! kookoorookoo!"
Crows the cock before the morn;
"Kikirikee! kikirikee!"
Roses in the east are born.

"Kookoorookoo! kookoorookoo!"
  Early birds begin their singing;
"Kikirikee! kikirikee!"
  The day, the day, the day is springing.

XXIV

Oh sailor, come ashore,
  What have you brought for me?
Red coral, white coral,
  Coral from the sea.
I did not dig it from the ground,
  Nor pluck it from a tree.
Feeble insects made it
  In the stormy sea.

XXV

A diamond or a coal?
  A diamond if you please.
Who cares about a clumsy coal
  Beneath the summer trees?
A diamond or a coal?
  A coal, sir, if you please.
One comes to care about the coal
  At times when waters freeze.

IX

Brown and furry
Caterpillar in a hurry,
Take your walk
To the shady leaf or stalk,
Or what not,
Which may be the chosen spot.
No toad spy you,
Hovering bird of prey pass by you;
Spin and die
To live again a butterfly.

X

What does the bee do?
  Bring home honey.
What does Father do?
  Bring home money.
And what does Mother do?
  Lay out the money.
And what does baby do?
  Eat up the honey.

XI

Rushes in a watery place,
  And reeds in a hollow;
A soaring skylark in the sky,
  A darting swallow;
And where pale blossoms used to hang
  Ripe fruit to follow.

XII

I dug and dug amongst the snow,
And thought the flowers would never grow.
I dug and dug amongst the sand,
And still no green thing came to hand.
Melt, O snow! the warm winds blow
To thaw the flowers and melt the snow.
But all the winds from every land
Will rear no blossoms from the sand.

XIII

What is pink? a rose is pink
By the fountains brink.
What is red? a poppy's red
In its barley bed.
What is blue? the sky is blue
Where the clouds float through.
What is white? a swan is white
Sailing in the light.

What is yellow? pears are yellow,
Rich and ripe and mellow.
What is green? The grass is green
With small flowers between.
What is violet? clouds are violet
In the summer twilight.
What is orange? why an orange
Just an orange.

XIV

Boats sail on the rivers,
  And ships sail on the seas,
But clouds that sail across the sky
  Are prettier far than these.
There are bridges on the rivers
  As pretty as you please.
But the bow that bridges heaven
  And overtops the trees
And builds a road from earth to sky
  Is prettier far than these.

XV

Who has seen the wind?
  Neither I nor you.
But when the leaves hang trembling
  The wind is passing through.
Who has seen the wind?
  Neither you nor I.
But when the trees bow down their heads
  The wind is passing by.

FRENCH GAMES

LORLEY ADA ASHLEMAN
The School of Education

A series of French games and songs, as played and studied in the School of Education, will be published during the year 1906. When two games bear the same name it is understood that the second game represents the work of students taking "Theory and Practice in the Teaching of French" in the College of Education; games, simple dramatic representations, and songs forming the basis of their pedagogical work.

NOTE 1.—The words in ordinary-sized type are intended for the child's vocabulary.

NOTE 2.—Complete vocabularies going with these games and "questionnaires," as well as games not published, may be obtained from the French Department, College of Education.

SIXIÈME LEÇON

LE CACHÉ MOUCHOIR

Ce jou se joue indifféremment en plein air ou dans un appartement.

LE DIRECTEUR: Guillaume, vous pouvez désigner par le sort un de vos camarades. Roulez et nattez votre mochoir.

GUILLAUME *(compte de la manière suivante):* Un, deux, trois, allons au bois; quatre, cinq, six, cueillir des cérises; sept, huit, neuf, dans mon panier neuf; dix, onze, douze, elles seront toutes rouges. Henri, c'est vous qui restez le dernier. Prenez ce mouchoir et cachez-le.

(Pendant qu'il accomplit cette opération, ses camarades restent à l'écart, sans regarder dans l'endroit qui sert de camp ou de but. Quand il a fini, il prévient en criant: "C'est fait!" *Et les autres commencent aussitôt leurs recherches. Celui qui a caché le mouchoir donne à ce moment une première indication vague; il dit:* "En terre," *si le mouchoir touche le sol ou le plancher,* "Au ciel" *dans le cas contraire. Les recherches continuent. Si un des joueurs, Paul, par exemple, approche de la cachette, le cacheur le guide ou l'encourage par les avertissements suivants:* "Paul a un peu chaud, Paul a très chaud, Paul brule!" *Si, au*

contraire, il s'éloigne par trop, les avertissements deviennent: "Dans l'eau, dans la glace," *etc. Dès que le mouchoir est découvert, celui qui l'a trouvé s'en empare et s'écrie:* "J'ai trouvé," *et en frappe ses camarades jusqu'à ce qu'ils soient rentrés au but ou au comp. C'est alors au tour de celui qui a trouvé le mouchoir de le cacher de nouveau.)*

SEPTIÈME LEÇON

CACHE-OBJET

LE DIRECTEUR: Mathilde, c'est-à-vous de désigner par le sort celle de vos compagnes qui devra sortir.

(Mathilde compte de la manière indiquée dans la sixième leçon.)

MATHILDE: Alice, c'est vous restez la dernière; sortez *(montrant les différents objets qu'il a sous les yeux).*

LE DIRECTEUR: Lequel de ces objets voulez-vous cacher?

GEORGES: Cachons le canif!

LE DIRECTEUR: Où allons-nous le cacher? dans l'armoire, dans le tiroir, etc.

ESTELLE: Dans la poche de Louise.

(Cela fait, on rappelle Alice.)

TOUT LE MONDE: Revenez et cherchez le canif que nous avons caché.

(Quand Alice se dirige du côte où l'objet n'est pas, on ne dit rien, à moins qu'elle ne s'en éloigne trop. Alors on s'écrie:)

TOUT LE MONDE: Vous brulez.

(Et lorsqu' elle est tout près:)

TOUT LE MONDE: Vous êtes dans le feu.

(Et si elle le touche:)

TOUT LE MONDE: Vous rôtissez.

(Lorsqu'elle l'a trouvé, elle désigne celle qui doit la remplacer.)

HUITIÈME LEÇON

LE CRI DES ANIMAUX

LE DIRECTEUR: Mes enfants, nous allons jouer au cri des animaux. Asseyez-vous en rond et choisissez un nom d'animal. André, venez ici que je vous bande les yeux. Prenez ce mouchoir, donnez moi la main que je vous reconduise dans le cercle. (*Et s'adressant aux joueurs*) Silence, la partie commence.

ANDRÉ: Attention, je lance le mouchoir.

(André lance le mouchoir qu'il tient par une extrémité, les joueurs cherchent à attraper l'autre. Un des joueurs—Charles, par exemple—saisit le mouchoir et imite le cri de l'animal, un mouton, qu'il représente en contrefaisant sa voix.)

ANDRÉ: C'est Charles qui fait le mouton.

(Car il doit reconnaitre l'animal et la voix du joueur. Si André se trompe, le groupe s'écrie:)

LE CERCLE: Vous vous trompez, recommencez.

(Alors il continue jusqu'à ce qu'il ait deviné, quand André a reconnu le joueur le cercle s'écrie:)

LE CERCLE: Oui, c'est cela; Charles, prenez la place d'André.

(*Les joueurs changent de nom, car il ne leur est pas permis d'en changer tant que c'est le même qui est au milieu du cercle.*)

VOCABULAIRE

Le mouton bêle
Le chien aboie
Le petit chien jappe
L'âne brait
Le taureau mugit
La vache beugle
Le cheval hennit
Le loup hurle
Le chat miaule
Le lion rugit
Le coq chante
La poule glousse
Le hibou crie
Le merle siffle
Le corbeau croasse
La pie jase
Le pigeon roucoule.

TREIZIÈME LEÇON

LE JEU DES HABILLEMENTS ET LE TOURISTE

LE MAITRE: Marcel, vous serez le directeur, choisissez tous vos marchands. Vous, Jacques, vous serez le tourist, voici votre bâton de voyageur.

(Marcel donne à chacun le nom de sa marchandise en touchant de sa baguette le vêtement du joueur.)

MARCEL: Françoise, vous êtes marchande de chapeaux. Hêlène, vous êtes marchande de jupons. Élizabeth, vous êtes marchande de manteaux. Georges, vous êtes marchand de gants, etc. Vous, mes marchands, formez un cercle. Touriste, mettez-vous au milieu du cercle. Un, deux, trois—marchands, dansez et chantez votre ronde: "Sur le pont d'Avignon."

(Le touriste s'approche des marchands, il étend son bâton et touche un marchand en disant:)

LE TOURISTE: Monsieur (ou madame), vous êtes marchand de———.

(Tout le monde s'arrête quand le touriste touche le marchand. Celui qui a été touché prend l'extrémité du bâton, tire le touriste hors du cercle, et répond:)

LE MARCHAND DE CHAPEAUX: A votre service, monsieur.

TOUS LES MARCHANDS: Dos à dos. (*Puis*) Un, deux, trois, partez!

(Le touriste et le marchand s'en vont dans des directions opposées. Quand ils se rencontrent, ils s'arrêtent et se saluent.)

LE TOURISTE: Bonjour, mademoiselle la marchande de chapeaux.

LA MARCHANDE: Bonjour, monsieur le touriste.

LE TOURISTE: Comment allez-vous ce matin?

LA MARCHANDE: Très bien, je vous remercie, monsieur. Désirez-vous voir des chapeaux aujourd'hui?

LE TOURISTE: Non, pas aujourd'hui, je vous remercie. Au revoir, mademoiselle.

LA MARCHANDE: Au revoir, monsieur.

(Ils se séparent et s'efforcent chacun de rentrer le premier dans le cercle, en marchant le plus vite possible à la place quitée par la marchande de chapeaux. Si la marchande ne peut regagner sa place la première, elle devient touriste.)

QUATORZIÈME LEÇON

LES GIROUETTES

NUMERO I

LE DIRECTEUR: Aujourd'hui, prenons le jeu des girouettes. Georges, voulez-vous tracer le carré dont les quatre coins représentent les quatre points cardinaux—nord, est, sud, ouest. Jacques, vous serez le dieu des vents—Éole. Madeleine, vous représentez le vent du nord. Guillaume, le vent d'ouest, Françoise, le vent du sud, et Charles, le vent d'est. A vous quatre, vous formez la girouette.

GEORGES: Monsieur, le carré est tracé.

LE DIRECTEUR: C'est bien; que les girouettes se placent chacune dans leur coin. Éole vous pouvez commencer.

JACQUES: Mes girouettes, chacune de vous devra tourner rapidement la tête et sans hésitation à l'opposé du point que je désignerai.

(Le jeu commence.)

ÉOLE: Nord *(toutes les têtes doivent se tourner vers le sud);* Sud *(toutes les têtes doivent regarder le nord. Si Éole crie* "Tempête," *chaque girouette doit tourner trois fois sur elle-même. Quand Éole dit* "Variable," *les girouettes se balancent de droite à gauche, en avant, en arrière jusqu'à ce que Éole ait fixé la direction du vent en disant par exemple:)*

ÈOLE: Variable, est. *(Alors les girouettes tournent doucement en inclinant vers l'ouest. Au commandement* "Ouest," *les têtes changent de direction et regardent l'est. Par exemple quant Éole crie* "Variable, est," *si Madeleine qui représente le nord s'incline vers l'est, Éole lui dit:)*

ÈOLE: Vous vous trompez, Madeleine, mettez un gage à mes pieds.

(Le jeu prend fin quand on a ramassé un certain nombre de gages. Ce jeu peut réunir plus de cinq joueurs; alors ils se placent en carré dans un ordre déterminé et non en troupeau. Les mouvements bien exécutés présentent un coup d'œil très agréable.

LES GIROUETTES

NUMERO 2

JESSIE FOSTER BARNES

LE DIRECTEUR: Formez un carré. Jeanne, vous serez la nature. Paul, vous serez le vent du nord. Pierre, vous serez le vent du sud. Jean, vous serez le vent de l'est. Gillaume, vous serez le vent de l'ouest.

(Que le différents vents choisissent les joueurs qui devront les représenter tous par des gestes.)

LE VENT DU NORD: Ooh, ooh, venez ici.

LA NATURE: Que voulez-vous, qu'avez vous à me montrer?

LE VENT DU NORD: J'ai l'hiver, et la neige, qui couvre la terre, j'ai des clochettes de noël et des dindons.

(Les enfants qui représentent ces choses se lèvent et tournent trois fois sur eux-mêmes. L'hiver frissonne de froid et laisse tomber des morceaux de papier; la neige la clochette tinte et le dindon glousse.)

LE VENT DE L'EST: Ooh, ooh, madame, venez à l'est.

LA NATURE: Que désirez-vous, qu'avez-vous à me dire?

LE VENT DE L'EST: J'ai le beau printemps qui revient si lentement, j'ai le vent qui siffle, j'ai le tonnerre et les éclairs; tout ce qui fait la tempête.

(Les enfants jouent leurs rôles en sifflant et en tournant rapidement.)

LE VENT DU SUD: Ooh, ooh, madame, venez au sud.

LA NATURE: Je viens, qu'avez-vous à me montrer?

LE VENT DU SUD: J'ai le bel été, la pluie qui fouette, la lune qui sourit et les fleurs qui croissent. *(La pluie fouette, la lune sourit, et les fleurs s'agenouillent et se relèvent.)*

LE VENT DE L'OUEST: Ooh, ooh, madame, venez à l'ouest.

LA NATURE: Pourquoi, donc, qu'avez-vous à me donner?

LE VENT DE L'OUEST: J'ai l'automne, le soleil qui brille, les feuilles qui tombent, le blé et les feux follets.

LA NATURE: C'est bien, mes enfants, je suis contente de vous. Mais, voici la nuit et les belles étoiles. Venez dormir, mes petits.

NATURE WORK IN THE SCHOOLROOM

ROBERT K. NABOURS
The School of Education

In studying live forms, both animal and plant, out in the field, the best possible equipment is the possession of the proper spirit—the abiding interest in the forms, and their varied relations to each other, to their environment, and to man. It is often found that if there be enough interest to induce a start, the larger abiding interest will develop.

To be in a hurry is a very bad thing, since nature does not sensibly pose for the benefit of the student. The forms do not arrange the times and places for displaying their breathing, feeding, breeding, hibernating, and æstivating habits and adaptations and wonderful stages of metamorphoses for the convenience of human beings, unless other than natural forces be brought to bear. Conditions of food and temperature largely determine these matters, and when one meets a favorable condition for observation, he must be prepared to stop and watch the processes, if he would see them. It is fortunate that the number and variety of interesting forms, and the places of their living, are very great, so that one may not pass through any strip of woods or marsh at any time of the year without seeing something worth observing, even if his time be limited.

However, there are many phases which cannot be thoroughly studied in the field, even if one should have much time at his disposal, but which may be brought in and observed under very natural conditions in the laboratory, where the whole school may have the benefit of the experiences, with little interruption of the regular activities. The whole school, however, should have a hand in gathering from their natural habitats the forms thus to be studied. Unless this be done, a valuable feature of the work will be lost. Besides, this material may be collected while

LADY BEETLES HIBERNATING

BUTTERFLIES AS SCAVENGERS

A WINTER FIELD TRIP

LIFE HISTORIES—FROG, SALAMANDER, AND WATER BUG

the students are on trips of observation of forms and areas and conditions which may better be studied in the field.

The life of ponds and streams is probably the most readily adapted for study in the schoolroom, as the conditions may be kept very nearly as they are in nature. In the aquaria stocked with plants and animals from the near-by swamps one may observe, from day to day and from month to month, the cycles of life as they develop and disappear or are displaced. The plants secure their subsistence from the decaying matter, water, and air; the lower animals—protozoa, crustaceans, etc.—feed upon the plants, and in turn are eaten by the higher forms; and these in turn live out their time and die, or the weaker succumb to the stronger, and their bodies again contribute to the plants and lower animal forms, and thus the cycle is completed. There are necessarily many animal forms which cannot be kept in the same aquarium, and the beginner will be dismayed with a good many accidents till he learns which forms have to be segregated. The principle of the "survival of the fittest" will manifest itself frequently.

A few Mason jars with tops which may be screwed on water-tight, a bag for carrying them, and a strong home-made net, will make up the necessary outfit for the field trip. A slowly running ditch, or a pond which has considerable algæ and pond-weed growing in it, will furnish the material. A few dips with the net into the water should be made, and the general contents of animal and plant life emptied into a water-filled jar. The jar may be crammed pretty full, the top screwed on tightly, and then placed in the bag, to be emptied into more water in an aquarium as soon as possible after the return to the laboratory.

In caring for an aquarium so stocked it may be necessary to change the water a few times and to take out some of the decayed matter; but if there be plenty of algæ and other plants, it usually clears up without help. Plenty of pond-weed and algæ should be kept in all aquaria, whether they be used for general observation or for the study of particular forms.

The possibilities for interesting and instructive study of aquaria so arranged are limitless. One may secure many helpful suggestions from several books and papers which have been published on the subject. The most helpful probably are Furneaux's *Life in Ponds and Streams* and Stoke's *Aquatic Microscopy.* Books on special forms and groups of forms should be consulted frequently, and there are many of these. The several volumes of the Cambridge *Natural History,* Miall's *Aquatic Insects,* Sedgwick and Wilson's *General Biology,* and Calkins' *Protozoa* are especially good. But hundreds of interesting observations which are not recorded in any book, and, in fact, some entirely new observations will most likely be made. A list of a few of the most probable observations may not be out of place: the manner of feeding, respiring, and breeding of hydra, cyclops, leeches, snails, the various larvæ of higher forms, beetles, and bugs, and the respiration and growth of algæ and other water plants. The study of the life-histories and habits of individual forms may be carried to any extent which the time and inclination of the teachers and pupils will admit. It is possible to give directions for the study of only a few in this paper.

The salamander.—During the last days of March or the first of April, in almost any small pond in a marshy area, one may find the eggs of our common *Amblystoma tigrinum,* one of the salamander group. They are very similar to those of a frog, except that the bunches are much smaller, being attached to weeds or bushes in the water in bunches a little larger than the thumb. Several bunches should be placed in a jar of water and taken to the laboratory, where in the ordinary temperature of the room they will hatch within a few days. They are carnivorous, and young tadpoles make choice food for them; so, some frog eggs should be hatched out in the same aquarium and at about the same time as those of the *Amblystoma.* When other food is scarce, they readily eat one another. The following account will to some extent describe their habits: About April 1, 25–40 *Amblystoma* eggs were hatched in an aquarium, and within a week 75–100 frog eggs were hatched in the same place. A few days later the *Amblystoma* larvæ (axolotls) were observed to be eating the tadpoles; but as there was much vegetable matter in the jar, the tadpoles soon became too large for their enemies.

By May 1, the *Amblystomæ* were seen to be eating one another, and this cannibalism continued till May 15 when but one fine large axolotl survived, and it was then able to eat the remaining tadpoles, 15 or 20 in number, by June 10.

For the purpose of saving stages in the life-history of the *Amblystoma,* it is well to have four or five of the larvæ in each of three or four jars. If tadpoles are not available for the later stages of the larvæ, insects, worms, or bits of meat may be fed to them. Much care, however, must be observed in using meat in any aquarium, as it is very easy to contaminate the water. When the axolotls have well-developed legs, they should be placed in a vessel with sand sloping up out of the water, so that, as the gills are lost and lungs are developed, the adult may crawl out of the water. The adult should be kept in a dark, moist place, and fed about the same as the larvæ.

The frog.—The life-history of the frog or toad is much easier to work out than that of the salamander, as they are omnivorous, eating anything from growing plants to decaying meat. It is probably better not to have anything in the aquarium with them for the first few weeks, except the usual plant forms; but pieces of bone and gristle should be provided for the later stages, and they will rasp off the softer parts. Persons engaged in cleaning and mounting skeletons sometimes use them in great numbers for cleaning the bones.

The water-bug.—The smaller water bug, *Zaitha,* is peculiar in its manner of breeding in that the female seizes the unwilling male, after a vigorous chase, and attaches her eggs on and all over his back. A specimen thus covered was secured early in August and placed in an aquarium, and within a few days a dozen or more young were hatched. The parent and two of the young were then killed and placed in formalin; the remaining young were allowed to grow, and about every ten days a specimen was taken out and preserved, till seven stages, from the egg to the adult male with the eggs on his back, were ready to mount permanently. The growing young frequently molted, and it was not easy to distinguish the molt, so perfect were they, from the dead specimens. The young *Zaithæ* are carnivorous, feeding on young of small crustaceans and snails by thrusting their beak like mouths into the body and sucking out the juices.

The bladderwort (Utricularia vulgaris).—This is one of the most common plants found in our ponds and sluggish streams, and it is one of the best to grow in the aquaria. It is very interesting in that it is carnivorous, feeding upon protozoa and small crustaceans which enter through trap doors into the pouch-like bladders at the bases of the leaves which are characteristic of this plant. During the spring and summer it reaches a length of several feet and floats around unattached in the water. In the late fall thick, dense buds are formed at the ends of the branches, ranging from the size of a pea to that of the thumb. These buds contain all the elements of the plant which is to come out the next spring. The greater portion of the bud appears to be composed of the long, slender leaves arranged longitudinally and very compactly together. In late November, when the buds are well covered with the slime from the decay of the surrounding vegetation, they are detached by their weight from the dead mother-plant, and sink to the bottom of the pond or stream, where they remain safely till the warmth of the spring causes them to expand and rise to the surface again, where they soon produce new plants. If these buds be brought in late in the fall, they soon open in the warm temperature of the room, and are excellent for keeping the aquaria in condition during the winter.

It was observed, upon tearing open some of the buds brought in late in December, that a great many small crustaceans, cypris, etc., were attached to them, or had crawled in among the longitudinally fitting leaves. This seems to indicate that these forms find the slime around the buds and, their interior substance, convenient places in which to spend the winter. Not only, therefore, does the plant perpetuate itself by the formation of these buds and through their habit of sinking, it also carries safely through the winter the very animal forms upon which it feeds during its growing season.

SCHOOL GARDENING AT THE NATIONAL CAPITAL

SUSAN B. SIPE

Each spring finds the garden work among children in Washington in vastly larger proportion than the previous year. The Department of Agriculture has provided the means for the work, in order that it might watch the development and establishment of a movement that has been so widespread, particularly in the cities of the East. The beginning, three years ago, was small. From a few successful home gardens of the Normal School students the work has found an established place in the school's curriculum. Every teacher in training for the schools of Washington now receives instruction in practical greenhouse work, in scientific principles of plant-raising, and in methods of teaching the subject to children.

In a short time the influence of this training has been felt throughout the graded schools. Every school in the city, but four, had gardens last spring. Some were pretentious, some were very small; but no matter what their size, the purpose for their existence was civic improvement through the children of the public schools. The plan followed for such gardens is about the same throughout the city. Where there is space at the front or the sides of a building suitable for decoration, the unbroken lawn in the center forms the main feature, with border planting on the side of shrubbery and annuals, and vines on the fences to complete the picture.

The interest aroused among 45,000 children has naturally spread to their homes. They have been encouraged to buy penny packages of seed for home planting. Simple instructions have been given them by means of experimental work in the schoolrooms. Many of the teachers have visited these home gardens, and the interest throughout the summer has been kept by urging the children to bring to school in the fall some result of their home efforts. In consequence of this, every building in the city last September held a flower show.

Until the present time the community garden—the garden in which each child has his own plot, and the garden established for the teaching of agriculture and horticulture—has not found its place in Washington. For three years one small garden of this nature has been in existence; but the Board of Education at the capital has its funds, and its power to use these funds, limited by Congress, so it has been powerless to connect such a garden with its schools. The secretary of agriculture, Hon. James Wilson, has recently made this possible by offering to the board the use of nearly two acres of lawn in the inclosure surrounding the main building of the Department of Agriculture for a children's garden. He proposes to fence the land, plow and manure it, and erect tool-houses. All the board has to do is to furnish the pupils and the teachers to demonstrate to the city and to the country at large the value of gardening as a form of manual training for the children of the public schools, and its value as a vacation movement for children. The board in its wisdom has accepted this offer, and has asked the teachers of five schools to undertake the work as a part of their regular school work. These teachers will be directed from the Normal School, and the plan of the garden also emanates from that school. For the vacation teaching the board must depend upon volunteer teachers, but there are earnest members of the profession in Washington who have volunteered their services for the summer for the privilege of studying the value of gardening in child-development.

These schools will work one afternoon a week, and the teachers, in so far as possible, will make the prescribed course of study bend to the garden. If, however, they cannot complete the course, the practical lessons brought into the lives of the children will much more than compensate for what the everyday world might consider a loss. Following the method pursued in the small garden mentioned, much attention will be given to the teaching of geography as connected with life. The winds, rainfalls, droughts, soil formation, and conditions affecting the

ONE DAY'S GATHERING FROM A PLOT NINE BY TWENTY

TRAINING IN THE PRINCIPLES OF PLANT-LIFE FOR STUDENT TEACHERS

AN ARITHMETIC LESSON IN THE FRANKLIN SCHOOLYARD

GROUND LAID OFF IN PLOTS BY PUPILS IN THE SIXTH GRADES

physical state of soils are taught at first hand. The garden will have a section devoted to the commonest products of the United States and the commonest local products. As these mature, they will furnish material for lessons in regard to their relation to man, the preparation of the raw material for man's use, and modes of transportation to markets. Only by such teaching is geography taken out of the realm of books and made a matter of life.

Much practical arithmetic is involved in measuring, in laying off the land, in calculating the cost of the manure to fertilize the land, the cost of fencing, and the amount of seed needed. Such arithmetic is of far more value and service than much laid down in the course of study which frequently has no application to the living of the present day.

Language, spelling, literature, drawing, painting, and designing will be correlated with the outdoor work, but care will be taken that the idea of correlation shall not make the garden dwarf in importance. The garden is not being cultivated for the sake of strengthening the other studies. Too frequently, particularly in composition work, to procure a variety of subjects, teachers are prone to take the spice out of every event by insisting upon a written account of it. During the great fire of Baltimore several years ago, one of our fifth-grade boys remarked to his teacher that he was so glad he didn't live in Baltimore, for he would have had to write a composition on the fire, he supposed. Such a feeling is death to love of work and interest in it.

As each child has his own plot, whatever he raises is his own—his own to bring to the highest state of perfection in his hands, to protect, to use. The rights of property-owners are most forcefully taught in a community garden.

The day is not far distant, it is hoped, when the Congress of these United States, in its capacity of educators, as it sits in judgment upon the schools of the District of Columbia, will grant to the boys who have no manual training until their seventh year at school, the benefits, now shared by a very few, of a practical development in the open air, by appropriating sufficient funds for school gardens.

NOTES FROM THE PARENTS' ASSOCIATION

MRS. ELLA ADAMS MOORE
Secretary

The February meeting of the Parents' Association was held on Thursday, February 15, at 8 P. M., in the School of Education.

Mr. G. H. Mead spoke on "Social Ideals of the School." He said: The child forms his own personality through social experience. His ego is the center of the organization of a social nature. It follows that his personality, his character, can be developed only through an environment which is socially organized. The child is not an individual first, and a social being afterward. He becomes an individual through his social experiences. The social organization of the school is bound, therefore, to reflect itself in the child's inner growth. If that organization is that of a crowd, the effect of his social environment upon the child will be that which a crowd has always proved itself to have, that of reducing the intellectual character of conduct, and lowering the standards of action. Even the virtues of the disciplined crowd are those of external order, obedience, routine, conformity, and the sort of devotion that is unthinking.

It is essential, then, that the school should be organized upon a higher plane than that of merely the crowd—that of a mass of children who are brought into merely external relations with each other. It is a precondition of any proper social ideals in the school that the groups should be small enough to allow the organization of the family type, not that of the factory or the army. In no case should the numbers of the groups go above sixteen. In the second place, it is essential that the work should be of a co-operative sort, that natural assistance may be rendered by the children one to another, that the children may be organized by what they do, not by what they must not do, and that the intellectual content of what they learn may pass over into their social conduct. It follows also that the work must be of a constructive character for the same reasons. Finally the social occasions, such as those of the dancing classes, the debating and other clubs, whose activities spring naturally from the life of the school, should be multiplied, especialy in the high school.

Mr. Mead was followed by Miss Emily J. Rice, of the Department of History, College of Education. Miss Rice spoke on "The Theory of Social Occupations." She said: I have asked many classes of student teachers, who come to us from all parts of the country, what they consider the greatest change in the schools within the last fifteen years. They invariably say that it is the introduction of active work into the curriculum, such work as cooking and gardening, sewing and weaving, wood-work and clay-modeling. It is being recognized by teachers everywhere, whether it is by the general public or not, that this active work is coming into the schools so rapidly as to form the most important educational movement of our times.

I believe that there are two leading causes for this change—one which may be called psychological, and the other sociological. The psychologists have taught us that the activities of children are largely motor in kind. Surely parents and teachers were not unacquainted with the fact that children are active before the psychologists told them so, but it took this scientific term to give them a true estimation of the value of activity. Activity has been considered in the past a thing to repress, at least in school. We have thought that teacher the best who could repress it the most thoroughly. The term "motor" influences the teachers in a wonderful way, because it frees them from the bondage of tradition. Perhaps it would be well to popularize it among the parents.

Some twenty-five or thirty years ago there was a wave of object-lesson teaching, as we called it, all over this country. The children were allowed to observe objects and describe them. This was a great reform for those times. The children might even touch the objects, but they must not do anything with them—use them in any constructive way. This object-teaching was the recognition of the fact that we have a sensory nervous system, and that our senses aid us in acquiring knowledge. It has taken all these years to teach us that we have a motor nervous system also, and that these are very closely connected. Thought and action belong together, and the child learns best when he has an opportunity of carrying his thought out in action.

At the same time that the psychologists were emphasizing the value of activity, the sociologists came to us with another lesson. Careful consideration of the conditions of modern life shows that there is very little opportunity for motor training in the average home of today. A few years ago the majority of people lived in the country and on the farms. The children came in contact with the raw materials of industry and had an opportunity to assist in their manufacture. The farm was a great manual-training school. Concentration in cities has taken this education away from the children. Specialization of industry and division of labor have also removed the industries from the homes. We no longer spin and weave, knit and sew. Such cooking and housekeeping as are left to the family are so complicated that the children cannot assist in them. If the value of such training is not to be entirely lost, the schools must take up the work abandoned by the homes, and it is interesting to see that one by one these industries have reappeared in the schools.

The social occupations change the whole character of the schools. The children come to have an active attitude toward learning instead of a passive one. This is true even of the older subjects of the curriculum, the history and geography, the science and mathematics. In their cooking and gardening, sewing and weaving, many problems arise in the children's minds in regard to the nature of the materials and the use which man has made of them, and these problems can be solved best in the lessons on nature-study and history. The children go to books to find answers to their own questions instead of learning lessons set by the teacher. The weakness of the old system lies in the fact that the teacher imposed the tasks upon the children, and the children worked without any impulse from within. With the social occupations, they gain knowledge which is of immediate interest to them, and which they can use in some direct way.

I have often thought that we have a marvelous faculty for introducing the best things into the schools in such a way as to get the least good from them. In many schools the occupations are put into the seventh and eighth grades only, the two highest grades in the elementary schools. The children's habits of study are largely formed before this time. They have not gained the physical strength nor the mental energy which come with the occupations, and these cannot be cultivated in two short years. Most of that time must be spent in the vain effort to counteract the tendencies already gained. The occupations are also introduced one hour, or an hour and a half, a week only. The children are engaged in active work one short period in the entire week, and all the rest of the time their work is of a passive character. We cannot expect by this means to secure those habits of self-control, patience, and endurance, and the feeling of the value of doing useful things, which should be the result of the industries. The occupations are taught by special teachers who know little of the work of the regular teachers, and the regular teachers are unacquainted with the work of the special teachers. Often they teach in separate buildings and cannot even consult with one another conveniently. Under such circumstances it is impossible that the spirit of the social occupations should enter into the methods of teaching of the other subjects.

Where the spirit of the social occupations permeates the whole school, even the discipline is transformed. The order becomes that of a group of people working together toward a common end. The test of success is no longer the quantity of knowledge acquired by each child in contrast or competition with the others, but what each contributes to the work of all. Many people believe that, if a textbook on morals were introduced into the schools, the children's conduct would be greatly influenced thereby. But the thoughtful teacher places very little reliance upon any such extraneous method. If we wish to have the children do right, we must give them conditions for right action. Habits are formed by doing, not by learning what others have done or what ought to be done. The school which makes the social occupations its center has an opportunity not only to give the children ideals of conduct, but also to help them to act in accordance with their ideals. I do not say that it does this. It may not live up to its possibilities, but it certainly has this unusual opportunity.

A discussion of these two papers followed.

NATURE-STUDIES WITH BIRDS FOR THE ELEMENTARY SCHOOL.

[*Continued from the April, 1905, number*]

ROBERT W. HEGNER
School of Education

V. BIRD PROTECTION

Before we can ask for protection of the birds, we must explain why and how they should be protected. This can be done most clearly by taking up separately the several phases of the subject. Accordingly the following arrangement has been adopted:

1. The benefits derived from birds.
2. The destruction of birds.
3. Bird enemies.

1. *The benefits derived from birds.*—Birds are of value æsthetically and economically. They possess and use freely voices that delight everyone. They furnish early morning concerts free of charge, and their songs still remain their own private property, as no one has ever been able to record them so that they can be reproduced on any musical instrument. Bird-songs contribute much to our happiness, and their value cannot be estimated.

Birds are beautiful to look at. Most of them play an important part in the enjoyment of a day in the country. Their plumage, always kept in perfect condition, is wonderfully diverse in its colors and varying effects. The flight of birds is beautiful and graceful, and no landscape is complete without the presence of bird inhabitants.

Economically birds are of undoubted value, and the benefits derived from them can be computed approximately in dollars and cents. A child may estimate the number of insects destroyed by a certain bird if he watches the parents of a family of young carry food to them. The wrens that built the nest shown on Plate XV of the *Elementary School Teacher* (opposite p. 412) for March, 1905, brought food to their young every few minutes. Both father and mother birds shared in this work, and the average number of times food was brought per hour was forty-three. This was continued, with short intermissions, for over sixteen hours each day.

A great amount of work has been done by the United States Department of Agriculture in determining the relations of birds to agriculture. The results may be obtained free of charge by addressing the Department of Agriculture, Washington, D. C. A few of the reports ready for distribution are given below.

Beal, F. E. L.:
1895. "The Crow, Blackbirds and their Food."
1896. "The Blue Jay and its Food."
1900. "How Birds Affect the Orchard."
1900. "Food of the Bobolink, Blackbirds, and Grackles."
Judd, Sylvester D.:
1898. "Birds as Weed Destroyers."
1900. "The Food of Nesting Birds."
1903. "The Economic Value of the Bobwhite."
Palmer, T. S.:
1898. The Danger of Introducing Noxious Animals and Birds."
Fisher, A. K.:
1901. "Two Vanishing Game Birds: The Woodcock and the Wood Duck."
McAtee, W. L.:
1905. "The Horned Larks and Their Relation to Agriculture."

We may take the kingbird as an example of the work done by the ornithologists named above. Mr. Beal examined 281 stomachs of the kingbird collected in various parts of the country, and came to the conclusion that about 90 per cent. of its food consists of insects, mostly injurious species, and that the vegetable food consists almost entirely of wild fruits which have no economic value. These facts, taken in connection with its well-known enmity for hawks and crows, entitle the kingbird to a place among the most desirable birds of the orchard or garden.

2. *The destruction of birds.*—Mr. William T. Hornaday has prepared the most important paper on this subject that has ever been published. It is entitled "The Destruction of Our Birds and Mammals," and was printed in the *Second Annual*

Report of the New York Zoological Society, New York, 1898. The office of the society is at 69 Wall Street.

Mr. Hornaday's paper was based on the replies received from persons all over the United States to the following questions:

a) Are birds decreasing in number in your locality?

b) About how many are there now in comparison with the number fifteen years ago? (one-half as many? one-third? one-fourth?)

c) What agency (or class of men) has been most destructive to the birds of your locality?

d) What important species of birds or quadrupeds are becoming extinct in your state?

The report compiled from answers to these questions includes thirty-seven states and territories.

The states of North Carolina, Oregon, and California reported that there were as many birds as fifteen years ago.

Four states—Kansas, Wyoming, Utah, and Washington—reported that bird-life was increasing.

The remaining thirty states and territories, comprising about three-fifths of the total area of the United States, reported a decrease in bird-life in the last fifteen years of from 10 per cent. in Nebraska to 77 per cent. in Florida. The exact figures are as follows:

State	Decrease	State	Decrease
Arkansas	50%	Missouri	36%
District of Columbia	33%	Montana	75%
Colorado	28%	New Hampshire	32%
Connecticut	75%	New Jersey	37%
Florida	77%	New York	48%
Georgia	65%	Nebraska	10%
Idaho	40%	North Dakota	58%
Illinois	38%	Ohio	38%
Indiana	60%	Pennsylvania	51%
Indian Territory	75%	Rhode Island	60%
Iowa	37%	South Carolina	32%
Louisiana	55%	Texas	67%
Maine	52%	Vermont	30%
Massachusetts	27%	Wisconsin	40%
Michigan	23%	Average of above, 46%	
Mississippi	37%		

The following conclusions were considered justified by the facts obtained by Mr. Hornaday:

a) Throughout about three-fifths of the whole area of our country, exclusive of Alaska, bird-life in general is being annihilated.

b) The edible birds (about 144 species) have been, and still are, most severely persecuted.

c) In many localities edible birds of nearly all species have become rare, and some important species are on the point of general extermination.

d) Owing to the disappearance of the true game birds, our song and insectivorous birds are now being killed for food purposes, and, unless prevented, this abuse of nature is likely to become general.

e) The extermination, throughout this country, of the so-called "plume birds" is now practically complete.

f) The persecution of our birds during their nesting season, by egg-collectors and by boys generally, has become so universal as to demand immediate and special attention.

g) Excepting in a few localities, existing measures for the protection of birds, *as they are carried into effect,* are notoriously inadequate for the maintenance of a proper balance of bird-life.

h) Destructive agencies are constantly on the increase.

i) Under present conditions, and excepting in a few localities, the practical annihilation of all our birds, except the smallest species, and within a comparatively short period, may be regarded as absolutely certain to occur.

j) If the present war of extermination is to be terminated, drastic measures must be adopted, and resolutely carried out; and the crusade for protection must be general. No half-way measures will suffice; and it is to be expected that some of the destroyers will be displeased.

Mr. Harnaday suggests that laws of the following character would be desirable to every state and territory, save two or three:

a) Prohibit all egg-collecting, except under license from state game commissioners, and the payment of a license fee.

b) Provide for the extermination of the English sparrow.

c) Prohibit the sale of dead game, at all seasons.

d) Prohibit the killing or capture of wild birds, and of quadrupeds, other than fur-bearing animals, for commercial purposes of any kind. (This will stop the slaughter of birds for millinery purposes.)

e) Prohibit all spring shooting.

f) Prohibit the carrying or using of a gun without a license.

g) *For three years* prohibit the killing or capture of any birds, except such birds of prey as may be declared by the United States Biological Survey to be sufficiently noxious to merit destruction. The only exception should be in favor of persons desiring to collect for scientific purposes, *in moderation,* and then only when properly vouched for by some scientific institution, and duly licensed by the state game commissioners.

h) At the end of three years restrict by legal enactment the number of game birds that may be killed or taken in one day, or in any given period, by a single individual.

3. *Bird Enemies.*—There is no better way to protect birds than to discover and dispose of their enemies. The most important bird enemies are the following:

a) Hunters.

b) Boys who shoot.

c) Market hunters.

d) Plume-hunters.

e) Egg-collectors, chiefly small boys.

f) English sparrow.

g) Collectors (ornithologists and taxidermists).

h) Cats.

i) Poisons used in gardens.

The above list includes two (*b* and *e*) that concern children directly. The teaching of children is of undoubted value in the future welfare of our birds. If boys and girls are taught to regard birds as beautiful and beneficial allies, there will be no more boys who shoot and collect eggs. And when these boys and girls grow up, there will be no hunters nor wearing of feathers on hats. And these same boys and girls will teach their children to love and protect their feathered neighbors.

Laws are very useful, but we must all help to enforce them, if they are to be of real benefit. Until the proper laws are passed and enforced, we must rely on the efforts of those who are sufficiently interested to contribute time and money to the cause of bird protection.

Birds may be protected as we find them, but we can attract them also. We can protect birds by discouraging egg-collecting and the wearing of plumes on hats, by *not* keeping a cat, and by waging war on the English sparrow. We can attract birds by furnishing bird-houses for them, by planting trees and shrubs where they can build nests or obtain food, by making bird-baths where they can drink and bathe, and by supplying them with food during the winter months.

EDITORIAL NOTES

One of the most interesting educational problems which in the near future will press for a solution relates to the teaching of religion. At present, this question is in the background, held in abeyance temporarily by an act of parliament, but it has been, by no means, finally settled. At this time the situation represents merely an armistice that the combatants, winded by a prolonged and relentless warfare, may regain their breath. As long, however, as education remains a topic of general interest, the subject of religion may be expected to claim the attention of the teacher because it seems to stand for something that we need in human character.

Religion in Education

The relation of religion to general education forms an interesting chapter of our history. The schools, at one time, were supposed to be essentially religious, being largely in the control of the clergy. One of their chief functions was to provide suitable training for the ministers of the gospel. But, with the rapid development of the country's material resources, religious instruction gradually became differentiated from secular, until at last they parted company entirely. This was because religion was anchored to a few dogmatic propositions that were held to admit of neither change nor question. It therefore dropped behind, and with many intelligent people it fell into disrepute.

Religious Instruction Isolated

The most virile thing in human life is a question; as a means of conquest and achievement, the interrogation point is mightier than the sword. The first symptom of moral decadence in a man, an enterprise, or an institution is found in the refusal to entertain an honest question. The vitality of anything is measured by its power to withstand the probes of Why and Wherefore. As religion became more and more restive under the questioning ordeal that was being applied to all secular matters, it gradually ceased to have a potent influence in the public schools.

Potency of a Question

The segregation of religious instruction has progressed until it is now found chiefly in the divinity schools, where it leads a hypersensitive existence, picking up crumbs from a full table where it once presided as host. Instead of breathing the atmosphere of religious life in everything they do in school, as they once did, the children now have to get their pious ozone from an occasional prayer-meeting, or once a week from an hour in the Sunday school. Even these sources of religious education are showing some drouthy symptoms. Not long ago, a conference of divinity-school teachers gave more or less anxious consideration to the fact that divinity students are diminishing in numbers. Prayer-meetings are not any longer strong rivals of the thousand and one other things that may be set for Wednesday evening, and from the nature of the case an hour a week in the Sunday school must wield but a limited influence. Nobody nowadays would seriously attempt to teach anything—even reading—under such unfavorable conditions.

The Divinity School

Prayer-Meetings and Sunday Schools

In American schools there are three R's, but in the German schools there are four: readin', 'ritin', 'rithmetic, and religion. In Germany, religion touches elbows on the daily program with geography on the one side and arithmetic on the other, and no one can doubt that it wields a strong organizing influence in their schools, as it once did in our own. For, when all other motives fail, as a last resort they can fall back upon religion and make the pupils learn their spelling, their grammar, and arithmetic, for the glory of God. Indeed, this motive was once held very closely before children in the schools everywhere, and, now that it has been taken away by legal enactment, it is pertinent to consider what we have put in its place.

Educational Four R's

The decadence of religion, so far as it is represented by an organized human institution, has been steady since the latter part of the eighteenth century, and within the past forty years its decline has been rapid. Religion, as we know it in history, has never been quite steady upon its feet since the thinking of Voltaire, Jefferson, Franklin, Paine, Henry, and a host of others finally overthrew the dogma which

Decadence of Religion

asserted the divine right of kings. Religious deterioration, already well advanced, was immeasurably hastened, when Darwin published *The Origin of Species.* Because the theory of evolution naturally led to a close investigation of three great tenets to which religion has always tenaciously clung—those pertaining to the soul, immortality, and God—and because it seemed likely that out of such study a reversal of opinion concerning the three dogmas might occur, the world at once jumped to the illogical conclusion that we, therefore, should have no further need of any religion. To this *non sequitur* from a superficial study of evolution, more than to anything else, we owe the present indifference in public and private morals.

In discussing the relation of religion to education, it is almost impossible to bring anyone down to the real point at issue. At the recent national meeting of school superintendents one of the topics before a general session was "Moral and Religious Education in the Public Schools." Both of the principal speakers were voluminous in their attempts to outline *moral* instruction, but neither one said a word about instruction in religion. This can mean but one of three things: first, that they were ignorant on the subject, for which they may be excused; second, that they were afraid of it, for which, if true, they should be ashamed of themselves; and, third, that religion is included in morality—an assumption by no means generally granted. Of course, the real trouble in such a discussion is that, when we are told a man "has religion" (a shocking phrase, utterly lacking in *finesse),* we first endeavor to orient him as a Presbyterian, a Methodist, a Baptist, a Catholic, a Quaker, or something else; once this is done, his religious quality is easily determined by the solution of a simple and definite formula as mechanical and bloodless as the binomial theorem. It is the habit that people have of thinking of religious instruction only in the terms of some ecclesiastical denomination that offers the greatest obstacle to teaching religion in the schools. When anyone has the hardihood to attempt to set up some sort of ideal for religious education, the various sects, with small exception, sit watching with blinking eyes and drooling chops ready to fall upon it and

Difficulty in Definition

Denominations as Obstacles

upon each other, the instant anyone discovers that his own particular theological formula has not been followed.

However, it is not the intention, primarily, at this time to rub salt into sore spots; nor is it the purpose to invite trouble by trying to define religion or by attempting to outline a course of religious instruction. It is proposed, though, to point out one thing so conspicuously absurd that it seems as if it might be easily remedied to the everlasting betterment of the schools and the race.

A Palpable Absurdity

The ideal of every religion has at some time found its incarnation in a living character. There is not a nation on the globe, outside of the jungles, that is not ensphered by the vitalizing influence of some such leader. These men, springing up centuries apart and in the remote places of the earth, were, each in his own time and place, the spiritual progenitors of a great people. Naturally these masterful prophets became a controlling force in the organization of whatever educational system such peoples may have developed. Now, here is the absurdity: while we are permitted, and expected, in shaping the ideals of the children, to make use of all the great influences of the past, in this American nation we are now barred by legal enactment from all reference to the one character which is incomparably the greatest in history. We may teach anything we please from Moses to Theodore Roosevelt—Buddha, Confucius, Mahomet, Washington, Benedict Arnold, anybody—if we except singly and alone the life of Jesus Christ. This, however, we must avoid as we would a contagion. Upon this point, the future will hold us convicted of inexplicable and indefensible folly. In this regard our present educational system represents neither philosophy, science, nor sense; we are the victims of mob control. We are playing an unholy farce. At Christmas we teach as neither myth nor fact, but as a strange confusion of the two, something about a heavenly heralded birth; and again at Easter we try to draw a doubtful analogy between the sprouting of seeds and the resurrection of the body—matters, by themselves, whether al-

Religion Incarnated

Blind Prejudice

What We Teach

legorical or real, having the least imaginable significance in human life. Of the great Teacher we must say nothing. As to his boyhood spent at the bench with his carpenter father; or his youth in which he developed a marvelous insight concerning the essentials of human character; or his manhood absolutely given over to teaching the plainest truths in the plainest manner—as to all these really stimulating influences of his matchless life, as set forth in his teachings, we must remain silent. The result is when the pupils leave school, instead of representing as it should, inflexible adherence to principle, unyielding devotion to duty, the cross of Christ now has no more significance for our children than has Hercules' club or the trident of Neptune. The "unspeakable Turk" is more deserving of respect; he is sincere enough, at least, in his fealty to Mahomet to base his educational system upon the teachings of his great prophet.

Essentials Omitted

Everyone acknowledges the tremendous educational effect produced by the study of a fine character. Our schools need now, and they always will need, the all-compelling personal influence of the life of Jesus. As the meridian sun seizes upon the seed lying in the darkened earth, and forces the expansion of leaf and flower and the ripening of the fruit, just so His teachings, as set forth in the Sermon on the Mount and in the parables, when learned and applied in the affairs of everyday life, must develop an irresistible spiritual control in the direction of righteousness.

Influence of Jesus

That there is some general sense of this need is evidenced by the almost clandestine attempt to readmit the Bible into the schools by the back door because of its claims as literature—apparently understanding literature to be largely a matter of euphonious sounds. It is as though we expected to make our children righteous by having them intone assemblages of pretty, but washed-out and meaningless, words. Whereas, unless we can persuade ourselves that present-day graft is an allegory, we need the Bible chiefly for neither its fables nor its myths, but for the straight-out-from-

Literature More Than Euphony

the-shoulder teachings that Jesus and the prophets leveled toward the evils of their day. Therefore, along with the piety of the heathen philosophers, I would see practically worked into every year of school life, and all the years thereafter, the plain and simple, the beautiful and understandable, teachings of Christ. If that means teaching religion, then teach it; if it means bringing the Bible into the public schools, bring it in—with all sincerity, candor, and earnestness, fetch it in.

Wanted: Direct Teaching

This appeal is not made, chiefly, to those who in the past have stood most urgently, perhaps, for so-called religious instruction. But few of such advocates are able to rid themselves of the notion that one's religion is inextricably mixed up with irrelevant beliefs that always must rest upon a speculative foundation. Nor is it made to that other large class of people who mistake indifference for tolerance. Least of all is the appeal made to the clergymen and the church; through nineteen hundred years of strife they have at last fought each other to a standstill. The address is, rather, to those of a younger generation having a clearer and broader vision who, from the fact that they are conscious of no religion whatever, are the best fitted to become the progenitors of the new. It must be made, strangely enough, to the men of science; for the axioms of conduct as laid down by Christ are more in harmony with the principles of evolution than they are with the dogmas of the old theology. It is the paradox of history that theology and not science is responsible for the present estrangement of religion from education.

The "Old Bottles"

Science vs. Theology

The teachings of Jesus are needed in the schools to reinforce everything else we do that makes for character. If the children could really be taught that grapes grow not on thorns, nor figs on thistles; if they could be made to feel the brotherhood of man through the story of the vine and the branches; if they could but once be shown the strait gate and made to realize the stupendous folly of any other way; if these, and a hundred other lessons of like import,

Influences Now Lacking

could be ground into their character so as to furnish the permanent background of all their thinking—a single generation of children so taught would be able to make human life on this planet the splendid thing that is hoped for in the millenium.

W. S. J.

BOOK REVIEWS

Elementary Physical Science. For Grammar Schools. By JOHN F. WOODHULL, Ph.D., Professor of Physical Science, Teachers College, Columbia University. New York: American Book Co. $0.40.

This course has been prepared owing to the widsepread demand that elementary physical science should be introduced into the grammar schools. From a study of this book many useful, common facts, relating to mechanics, fluids, and heat, are made clear to the pupil. He learns why earthenware, in order to hold water, must be glazed; why the brown-stone fronts of buildings disintegrate; and why edged tools must be tempered. City water and gas systems receive particular attention. The application of heat to thermometers and to propelling steamboats and railway trains, and the heating of buildings by the fireplace, stoves, hot-air furnaces, hot-water heating and steam heating, together with the ventilation of buildings, are taken up in an interesting and instructive manner.

Great Pedagogical Essays. By F. V. N. PAINTER, A.M., D.D., Professor in Roanoke College, Author of *A History of Education,* etc. New York: American Book Co. Pp. 426, 12mo, cloth. $1.25.

This volume introduces the student to the principal documents of educational history, from Plato to Spencer. Every important phase of education receives consideration. Selections from twenty-six of the world's greatest educators are given, prefaced in each instance by a brief biographical sketch. The book will meet the demand among students of educational history for an acquaintance with the original sources of information, and will form an acceptable and useful volume supplementary to any standard history of education.

A Primer. Pp. 92, 12mo, cloth. Illustrated. $0.30.
A First Reader. Pp. 127, 12mo, cloth. Illustrated. $0.35.
By JOSEPH H. WADE, Principal, Public School 186, New York City, and EMMA SYLVESTER, Assistant to Principal, Public School 186, New York City. Boston: Ginn & Co.

In this new series the best features of the various methods for teaching children to read have been utilized. The underlying principles of the lessons may be expressed as follows: (1) to help the pupils master as quickly and as readily as possible the printed forms of the words used; (2) to develop in the pupils power to acquire thought from the printed page by silent reading, and to reproduce this thought orally, with correct expression; (3) to lead the pupils to an early independence of the teacher in learning to read.

The books are the outcome of an actual experience in teaching reading to first-year pupils. They contain a large amount of concrete, practical work; the method of procedure is from idea to word, then to symbol. This feature makes the books especially valuable for classes of children who come to school with little or no knowledge of English speech.

The *Primer* is to be used in the first half-year of school, and the *First Reader* in the second half-year.

First Year in Algebra. By FREDERICK H. SOMERVILLE, the William Penn Charter School, Philadelphia. New York: American Book Co. Pp. 208, 12mo, cloth. $0.60.

This introductory course in elementary algebra furnishes a satisfactory one-year's work for grammar schools or for the first year in high schools. The book takes the pupil through fractions and simultaneous simple equations. Although remarkable for its simplicity and careful gradation, it is characterized by an unusually scientific presentation, which enables students to master the fundamental principles of the subject with less effort than is commonly the case.

Caesar: Episodes from the Gallic and Civil Wars. Edited by MAURICE W. MATHER, Ph.D., formerly Instructor in Latin in Harvard University. New York: American Book Co. Pp. 549, 12mo, cloth. $1.25.

This volume furnishes some of the most interesting and instructive portions of Cæsar's writings, which have hitherto been little read in schools. The sections on the *Gallic War* are equivalent in amount to the first four books. From the *Civil War* about two-thirds as much is taken, including Curio's disastrous African campaign and the struggle between Cæsar and Pompey. An innovation which will meet with general favor is the printing in full in the vocabulary of the principal parts of verbs and of the genitive of nouns, except in the first conjugation of verbs and in such nouns of the first, second, and fourth declensions as offer no possibility of mistake. The book is abundantly supplied with illustrations, maps, and plans.

Commercial Geography. By GANNETT, GARRISON, AND HOUSTON. New York: American Book Co. Pp. vi+415, and 30 pp. of index.

The enormous commercial and industrial expansion of the present time makes a book of this type of great value in school work. Geography is no longer a vague study of the earth's surface with general references to the occupations of men and with incidental descriptions of the various races. It deals closely with the great industrial output of the whole world, which makes it necessary that the pupils should know with exactness the means and methods of production and the routes of commerce. It is through this approach to the subject that we get the most intelligent introduction to the study of human life on the earth.

This book divides the subjects into three principal parts—"Commercial Conditions," "Commercial Products," and "Commercial Countries." The illustrations are numerous and excellent, showing the different phases of many interesting processes in manufacturing, etc. The maps are very valuable, some of which show the physical features, and others in single world-maps show at a glance the facts relating to distribution over the whole earth. There are many diagrams also that reduce the productions, etc., to a scale which renders comparison easy and instructive. The index of thirty pages is especially useful, as it enables one to follow easily any subject through all of its relations in the different countries. Teachers of geography will find the book most useful, and the pupils of the upper grades could use it with great advantage for at least one term's work.

W. S. J.

The Principles of Teaching Based on Psychology. By EDWARD L. THORNDIKE, Professor of Educational Psychology in Teachers College, Columbia University. New York: A. G. Seiler. Pp. vii+293.

This book seeks to connect closely the fundamental principles of teaching with certain equally important corresponding facts in psychology. In each chapter, after a statement of the psychological facts and a discussion of their relationship to the principles of teaching, there is a set of exercises which are intended to give the connection between the two a more definite shape. These exercises usually take the form of queries which compel the student to re-think the relationships for himself. The scope of the book covers the field of educational psychology, and its plan is consistent and clear. Abundant citations are made to results obtained in experimental psychology, which are used to point the way for teaching. These are useful in their general bearing, but the teacher needs to be on guard against a too specific application which the author himself would hardly justify. Reference here is made particularly to the chapter on the relation of special training to general ability. Mr. Thorndike is an example of his own doctrine that training in one direction does not give ability in another. It is manifest that his excellent work as a psychologist has not enabled him to think out fully the scope and nature of the teacher's function in school organization. In discussing "The Special Problem of the Teacher" he says: "It is the problem of the higher authorities of the schools to decide what the schools shall try to achieve and to arrange plans for school work which will attain the desired ends. Having decided what changes shall be made, they intrust to the teachers the work of making them." Space will not admit here a discussion of this point, but to allow the "higher authorities of the schools" the whole discussion as to what the schools shall be is to adopt a principle that is not less vicious, and it is fully as antiquated as the belief in "faculty psychology" which the author has long since discarded, or which, perhaps, he never held. It is not the intention here, however, unduly to magnify this point, for, while as an actual fact in school organization it is fundamental, in this book, it is of minor importance. The book does clearly what it, in the main, sets out to do—to couple up closely psychological theory with the theory of practice. It is a valuable addition to educational literature.

W. S. J.

VOLUME VI NUMBER 9

THE ELEMENTARY SCHOOL TEACHER

MAY, 1906

A SOCIAL SCIENCE OUTLINE—THE POINT OF VIEW

JOHN S. WELCH
Supervisor, University of Utah Normal Training School

History is a study of the stream of intellect and emotion flowing through the past and shaping itself in the institutional life of the people, social, industrial, political, religious. It traces the causes of these institutions—their formation, *trans*formation, and *re*formation. It deals essentially with the past, what man was as a fit background for an appreciation of what man is.

The student of history sees this stream, continuous, ever-varying, ever-broadening, ever-shaping itself anew, as it flows from the ancient civilizations of the Orient, through Greece and Rome, through Latin and Anglo-Saxon Europe, and finally culminating in democracy's latest hope, the Republic of North America. This is the philosophic aim and purpose of history.

Social science aims to utilize all that is vital in this organization of history, and to project it forward. It assumes that man can be understood as he is only when there is an intelligent appreciation of what man would be. *What is*, is transient. The abiding thing is *the ought to be:* the permanent thing, *the law of change.*

Social science is essentially the study of the present *in the process of becoming.* It links the future with the past, and makes intelligible the purpose divine that molds and shapes the institutional life of man. It is the study of the individual in his group-relations—the interdependence, the community of interests, the common hopes, aims, aspirations. Professor Horne says: "As the child merges from boyhood to manhood, the brook of promise must empty itself in the river of service."

Social science must therefore include a study of what we, the social group, are doing and whither we are tending. The organization of a social group in terms of effective, progressive service is a legitimate and vital topic for first-hand investigation. Its end and aim is purposeful citizenship through regnant character.

The school has an important function to perform, if ours is to continue a government of the people. A person is as his ideals are. So a nation. Children who leave school without worthy ideals of life, and without the real significance of a community of interests wrought into the very nerve and fiber of their beings, have been defrauded, and the school has failed to perform its most vital function.

Social science must foster the patriotism that germinates in the home, causing it to move out in ever-widening circles through the community, the city, the state, the nation, until there dawns a consciousness of world-citizenship in which the interests of one are the interests of all and the dream of Tennyson has indeed been realized:

> Then the war-drum throbb'd no longer, and the battle-flags were furl'd
> In the Parliament of man, the Federation of the world.

Let our aim and purpose be to plant a seed that may bud and blossom in a consciousness of the fact that we are the heirs of all that which the ages have accomplished through blood and toil, through heroic struggle and noble self-sacrifice. Therefore we are responsible, not alone for its preservation, but also for the contributing of our mite to the realization of the ideal toward which humanity has all the while been tending.

> Other futures stir the world's great heart,
> The West now enters on the heritage
> Won from the tomb of mighty ancestors,
> The seeds, the gold, the gems, the silent harps
> That lay deep buried with the memories of old renown.

GENERAL SUGGESTIONS

The justification of a public-school system lies not in the material success of the individual *per se,* his ability to make conditions better for himself; but it does lie in the gain to the state in terms of citizenship. The interests of the state and the individual are one just so far as his individual advancement means greater efficiency in terms of service, positive, dynamic.

The counting-chamber and the business office have dominated the schools too long. The first essential is a citizen fit to live; the second, his manner of making a living. It is no longer the problem of the survival of the fittest, but rather the problem of making fit to survive.

The N. E. A. regrets the revival in some quarters of the idea that the common school is a place for teaching nothing but reading, spelling, writing, and ciphering, and takes this occasion to declare that the ultimate object of popular education is to teach the children how to live righteously, healthily, and happily, and to accomplish this it is essential that every school inculcate the love of truth, justice, purity, and beauty.—Declaration of principles, N. E. A., 1905.

The children should early be imbued with the idea that it is their *privilege* to attend school, not an unquestionable, inalienable *right;* that the schools belong to the parents in the sense of the group, the state, but that no individual parent has any exclusive jurisdiction.

The aim and purpose should be: first, to secure a worthy citizenship of the room, the school, the neighborhood, with an intelligent, constructive appreciation of property rights and group-interests. Children who are not in the process of becoming good citizens here and now; who do not feel their mutual rights and responsibilities; in a word, who are not good citizens of the home, the school, the neighborhood, will scarcely reach the ideal citizenship which the state—the group—has a right to expect.

The school property of the United States is valued at $500,000,000; the income for school purposes, at $220,000,000 annually; the teachers of the United States number 500,000; the children, between the ages of five and eighteen, who attend school, more than 20,000,000. These schools are built, this money is expended, these children are accommodated by those who now constitute the state, in order that the accumulated wealth of the race, material and spiritual, may be preserved and the ideals of the race finally realized.

SPECIFIC STUDY

ALL GRADES IN TERMS OF AGE AND EXPERIENCE OF THE CHILDREN.

Estimate the value of school grounds, school buildings, equipment, cost of maintenance, etc. Who pays for all this? What do they receive for their money? Why a willingness to pay?

The aim and purpose of school organization. What we do *to help—to hinder*—the process. What should be expected of us.

Our obligations in terms of—

The lunch problem.

The waste-material problem.

The rainy-day problem.

The snow problem.

Our rights and the rights of others. Is there any conflict?

Consider the janitor service. The need for. What is he doing for us. How he is *helped—hindered*— in his work.

Consider the significance of forming in line, of marching, of forming in groups, of group-movements, etc.

In group or class-work, whose time can be squandered? If a group is hindered by an individual, by what right does he retain membership in the group?

Consider the function of teacher and pupil in the school process. The teacher can merely make conditions for growth. The child determines the growth.

Sum up in terms of individual privilege, opportunity, and *responsibility.*

PRIMARY GRADES

A study of individuals typifying a class in the social organization.

In making a study of the individual in terms of service, the teacher should keep in the foreground of the child's consciousness the fact that, while all human beings require food, clothing, and shelter, the differentiation of labor, in terms of these becomes justifiable only when by such means these problems can be solved more effectively and economically for all concerned.

KINDERGARTEN

GENESIS OF THE SOCIAL CONSCIOUSNESS

The socializing process in the kindergarten must begin with the dawning consciousness of the limits placed upon individual thought and movement through the rights and movements of others. This should be much more pronounced and definite than are any of the legitimate restrictions of the home.

In the games, plays, and group-work the idea of *service* through leadership, and of *being served* through the leader, is also brought to consciousness forcibly. The individual contributes to the social group through his promptness, initiative, and creative effort, and his interests are furthered through the promptness, initiative, and creative efforts of his little neighbors.

Another social factor of much significance is the direction of the energy of the kindergarten children, even through play, toward some definite, tangible end that is in itself worth while. In this manner the children become conscious of value, *pleasure,* in the doing and of value, *worth,* in the deed.

In a larger and more definite sense, the home may be made a topic for special study from the social, the group, standpoint. The factors of the home—father, mother, etc.,—and the activities of the home from the standpoint of service, may be so studied as to lead up to the general idea of a community of interests and of mutual rights and obligations.

This patriotism of the home, loyalty through service, is a fit foundation for the more pervasive patriotism, the more extended service of maturity.

FIRST GRADE

The Carpenter.—What does the carpenter do? What does he do it with? Whom does he do it for? What are his needs? Does his labor as a carpenter produce food, clothing, shelter? How can he produce all of these for himself? What effect will his so doing have upon his efficiency as a carpenter? In what other manner can he obtain food, clothing? What does he give us? What do we give him? What do we get? What do we give?

The dressmaker.—What does the dressmaker do? What does she do it with? Whom does she do it for? What does she need? What does she produce in terms of her needs? How are her other needs satisfied? What does she give? What do we give? What does she receive? What do we receive? How does she make our work easier? How do we make her work easier? What does she do for us besides making our work easier?

The blacksmith.—Who have seen a blacksmith? Where does he work? What does he do? How does he do it? What does he do it with? Whom does he do it for? What does he do it for? What does he produce for himself? What are his needs? How are they satisfied? What do we receive from him? What do we give him? How are we helped by his work? How could we get along without him? How would it affect us?

The postman.—Consider: what he does; how he does it; whom he does it for; how his needs are satisfied; what his work does for us; how we could do it for ourselves; the inconvenience in time, energy, and money; the significance of his uniform, etc.

The milkman.—Consider his work; what he does; how he does it; whom he does it for; how he serves us; where he gets the milk; how it is kept clean and wholesome; how we could get along without him; the inconvenience, expense, etc.; how his needs are satisfied; how he helps us; how we help him; etc.

SECOND GRADE

The farmer.—Where does the farmer work? What does he do? What does he do it with? Where does he get his tools? Who helps him? How does he help the carpenter? the blacksmith? the milkman? Can he get along without them? Can they get along without him? What would be the effect? How do we affect the farmer? How does he affect us? Can he get along without us? Can we get along without him? What would be the effect? What is our gain through the farmer?

The storekeeper.—Where does he work? What does he do? Name all the things we get from him. Where does he get them? Who helps him? How does he help them? How does he help the carpenter, the blacksmith, the milkman, the farmer? How does he help us? How do we help him? How could we get along without him? How would it affect us? What does he gain through us? What do we gain through him?

The bricklayer.—What does he do? Why does he do it? How does he do it? Whom does he do it for? What does he need?

What does he produce for himself? How are his other needs satisfied? Who satisfies them? Whom does he help? How? Who helps him? How? Why is he so necessary in Salt Lake City? Why is Salt Lake City essentially a city of bricks? What does the bricklayer gain through us? What do we gain through him?

The policeman.—What does he do? Where does he do his work? What is he for? How does he help strangers, the sick, the lost, the destitute? How does he help in crowded places? How does he help at fires? How does he help to protect health? In what other ways does he protect and serve us? How do we serve him? Why does he wear a uniform? A star? Who selects the policeman? What sort of a man do we want for a policeman? How can we help him? What do we gain by having him?

The doctor.—What is he for? What does he do for us? When do we use him? Why? How does he prevent disease from spreading? What does he do to warn others from disease? Why does he report? Why are the cards put up? What has the doctor to do with their removal? When a contagious disease has been in a house, how does he make it safe to live in? How does he prevent the spread of small-pox? How does he help a school? What does he need? What do we do for him? Who helps him to live and do his work? What do we gain through him?

THIRD GRADE

The baker.—Consider: where he does his work; what he does it with; where the materials come from; how they are produced, and by whom; what he does with them; whom he does it for; what his needs are; what needs are satisfied by his work; how other needs are satisfied; whom he is helping, and how; who are helping him, and how; how he helps us; how we help him; our gain through him.

The conductor.—Consider: who he is and what he is for; how he assists us in getting on or off the cars, finding seats, stopping the car at the right place, keeping people from getting off while car is in motion, etc.; what his needs are; how they are satisfied; his hours of labor; significance of uniform; the kind of man the conductor should be; how we help him in his work; how he helps us.

The motorman.—Consider: his work; how he does it; his hours of labor; how he protects life; his eyes; his habits; his uniform; the kind of man he should be; his service to us; our attitude toward him; how we serve him.

The engineer.—Consider: where his work is done; how it is done; the danger involved; the vigilance required; significance of switch-lights and signals; his eyes; his habits; his hours of service; what we do for him; what he does for us; the kind of man he should be; our gain through him.

The sailor.—Consider: what his work is; how he does it; where he does it; the dangers involved; the kind of man he should be; what he has an opportunity to see and to learn; how we are affected by his work; what his needs are; how they are satisfied; what boys are most apt to become sailors, and why; how the sailor's life benefits us; etc.

The lighthouse keeper.—Consider: location of lighthouses; why so located; purpose of the lighthouse; kinds of lights; how produced; how sailors are warned by the lights; the duties of the keeper; the dangers of; the importance of his work; his loneliness; privations; vigilance; the service he renders, and its importance in terms of human life; the kind of man he must be; etc. Make a specific study of some particular lighthouse and its significance.

FOURTH GRADE

The principal.—Consider: selection of teachers and books; arranging course of study; programming studies, noting progress of pupils and advancing them in their school-work; care of school property; of individual and school rights; health and safety of pupils; proper janitor service, etc; service to the social group.

The teacher.—Consider: what she is for; how she does her work; the preparation she has made; who benefits by what she does; how she is helped—hindered—in her work; whose loss when she is hindered; how hindrance can be avoided; what she has a right to expect; her service to the school group; to the social group.

The janitor.—What does he do? Why does he do it? Why is his work important? What results if his work is neglected? How it may affect us? How is he helped—hindered—in his work? What should be our attitude toward him? Why? What are his needs? How are they satisfied? He exchanges his labor for what? We satisfy his needs for what? What does he gain? What do we gain? Can we get along without him? How would our so doing affect our school work?

The pupil.—What is he here for? By what right? Who makes the privilege possible? What does he give in return? How are those who pay the expenses benefited? Who furnishes the pupil with conditions for his growth? What should be the attitude of pupil toward school property? Why? Toward school books? Toward his own books? Why? How is he helped to make wise use of books and materials? How is the teacher helped—hindered—in doing this? When the teacher's time is taken up with nonessentials, how is the pupil affected? What has a pupil a right to expect from the teacher? What has she a right to expect from him? What factors make a school? What conditions determine growth?

Pioneer life in Salt Lake City.—Consider: choice of location; allotment of land; problem of shelter-material, construction, co-operative effort, effect of co-operation; problem of food—allotment of food brought with pioneers, raising food, tilling soil, planting and care of, harvesting; flocks, how secured, how cared for, how made to contribute to the welfare of all; community effort in terms of food supply; clothing problem—sheep and wool industry, domestic manufacture, co-operative effort, difficulties involved in securing necessaries, effect on industry, on character; irrigation problem—necessity for, irrigation ditches, care of; water master, his service, his compensation, necessity for; method of exchange—its cumbersomeness, dissatisfaction with; discovery of gold and silver; coining money and issuing script as a measurer of values; water problem for homes—how solved; problem of protection—Indians and wild animals—the protecting wall; fire problem—bucket brigade, etc.; amusements and recreations; differentiation of labor—cause and effect; city organization—special systems, means and purpose, growth toward modern city.

GRAMMAR GRADES

In the upper grades the differentiation of labor in terms of group-needs will differ from individual study of lower grades merely in terms of complexity. The spirit that moves, shapes, controls, must be the vital force; not the cold, dead machinery of the social process. The motive is to make a study of social groups functioning themselves in terms of effective public service as a basis for intelligent tax-paying, tax-spending, and a proper understanding of the dignity and responsibility of casting a ballot.

The pupils should be led to see, in the quality of the service, the duties of citizenship in terms of taxpayer, voter, and office-holder.

The psychological value of the study will lie in the formation of habits of perceiving clearly, imaging rationally, remembering acurately, judging wisely, reasoning logically; through which changes will be wrought in the fiber and structure of the brain itself. The matter and method will render children strong or weak; self-reliant or dependent; dynamic factors or passive recipients. We must bear in mind the fact that a broad generalization is reached through a series of painstaking investigations, not by a flippant deduction. It is the end of a series determined by reason, not the beginning, the result of a guess.

This course provides definite lines of investigation, local and individual to the child, but of world-wide sweep to the teacher.

FIFTH GRADE

Police department.—Organization of; officers, how chosen; compensation; qualifications; why so officered; qualification of policemen; how chosen; compensation; daily hours of service; days per week.

Function of department in terms of the social group: (*a*) suppress lawlessness; arrest disturbers of the peace; protect property; protect life; note suspicious characters; assist other cities in suppressing evil-doers; (*b*) guard street crossings; railway crossings; stations; direct strangers; visit sick and destitute; report and relieve; care for sick and injured on public thoroughfares; note condition of teams and attitude of teamsters; seek lost children or others; report unsanitary conditions and contagious diseases; note condition of streets in terms of safety; assist in guarding life and property at fires; etc.

Significance of uniform and star; of club and gun; secret service men; how helped; how hindered; attitude of mind toward this department as it is; as it ought to be.

The gain to the social group through this department.

Suggestions: Visit police stations, witness drill, and gather all available data at first hand. If possible, have a discussion with the chief of police.

The attitude of mind through this study should be that the policeman is merely an expression of public will, not an enforcer of arbitrary rules. Therefore he is entitled to unqualified approval and support.

Fire department.—Organization of; officers and fire-men; qualifications; how chosen; compensation; significance of organization. Compare and contrast with the police department in terms of qualifications, salaries, daily hours of service, manner of choosing, duties, dangers, service, etc.

Visit fire stations; note organization; drill; make a detailed study of apparatus used; study alarm systems and means of locating fires; number of fire stations and location of.

Consider power to destroy property in case of fire, and on whom conferred; why fire limits and fire districts are established; why buildings must conform to fire ordinances; etc.

Emphasize efficiency of service through differentiated fire-group; contrast with bucket brigades.

Consider fire insurance; the relation of rate and amount to effective service; significance of.

Plat of city locating fire districts and engine-houses.

Consider the gain to the social group through this department.

SIXTH GRADE

Health department.—Officers of; how chosen; salaries; duties; qualifications; health, or sanitary, districts; justification of; inspectors, purpose and duties; quarantine, purpose of; contagious-disease cards, purpose of; birth reports, burial permits, purpose of; means to prevent spread of contagious diseases; regulation of sewage, plumbing, garbage; relation to city prisoners; city poor; public vaccination; why jurisdiction beyond city limits; why reports of contagious diseases; why order buildings disinfected; why condemn buildings, etc.; relation to water supply.

Importance of this department.

Gain, through efficiency, to social group. How helped, hindered, by public attitude toward this department.

Garbage system.—Officers of; how chosen; compensation; duties; garbage districts, location and purpose of; receptacles for garbage; how collected and disposed of; frequency of collection; laws regarding collecting and disposing of garbage; justification of.

Consider: garbage and irrigation ditches; penalties for corrupting waters of irrigation ditches; justification of; laws governing private burning of refuse; justification of; condition of back-yards, alleys; etc.

Gain to social group through this department.

Contrast with health and garbage systems in other cities.

Children should know their own garbage districts, and ought to know the quality of service (*a*) contracted for, (*b*) rendered.

Water system.—The water problem of a large city is literally "a fight for life."

Members of water department; how chosen; compensation; function and duties; why a water system instead of private wells; why public instead of private ownership and control; location of head-waters; how determined; how secured; how controlled; meaning of "water rights;" relation of Liberty Park wells to head-waters.

Means employed to keep water pure; how enforced; how water is brought to the city; the homes; cost of; who pays; location of reservoirs; problem of getting water to upper stories of business blocks. Make a detailed study of the siphon, and apply principle to water system and artesian wells.

Consider special water tax, how adjusted; sprinkling lawns and streets; regulation of irrigation flow; relation of snowfall to water supply.

Suggestions: excursions to head-waters, reservoirs, water office, etc., for data. Consult city engineer; consult city chemist for tests and means taken to preserve the purity of the water supply.

Consider the interrelations of health, garbage, and water systems.

Consider how the social group functions itself through this department, and the social gain through effective service.

SEVENTH GRADE

In this grade the study should become more intensive and extensive in an historical and social sense.

I. Study individual family severing connections with social group, temporarily, and moving into the wilderness. Make a detailed study of problems that arise and of the attempts to solve them.

Consider physical features of new home; climate; plant and animal life; soil; water; rainfall.

Consider equipment in terms of goods; personality; individual and race experience.

Problem of shelter.—Consider site; materials; labor; furniture; barns; roads; protection; defense.

Problem of food.—Consider cultivation of the soil; care of the flocks; division of labor; marketing surplus and contact with the outside world.

Problem of clothing.—Consider raw materials for domestic manufacture; processes of; labor involved; community of interests.

Consider also education of children; religious training; growth of settlement; highway for travel; village problem. (Adapted from Small and Vincent.)

II. Consider primitive mode of city life; lack of organization; no real differentiation of labor; lack of economy and progress in terms of effective service; lack of civic virtue in a large sense; prevalence of plagues; famines; pestilences.

Illustrations: the Black Death; the London Plague; New Orleans and yellow fever, past and present; Havana before the Spanish-American War; Colonel Waring and his white-robed angels. Port Arthur and the cholera in the late Russo-Japanese War; and others of historical significance that emphasize the point.

III. Modern society contrasted with primitive conditions; social and industrial reasons for the change. Advantage of people serving themselves through differentiated branches of *public service* instead of through a collective service. Disadvantage: the people lose sight of the *functioning process,* hence a corrupt service.

Consider the meaning of one-man power in a democracy: Folk in Missouri; La Follette in Wisconsin; Weaver in Philadelphia; Jerome in New York.

IV. Study of Salt Lake City. The city should be thought of as a social group with specialized functions—we, the people, protecting ourselves through taxes which return to us in terms of public service.

Consider the machinery of the social group, or the mode of organizing different departments with special functions.

Study the city as the social unit within which the special groups find place and meaning. Study it as organizing itself through legislative, executive, and judicial branches.

The *why* of the organizing process should be kept vividly in the foreground at all stages of the development of the subject.

Consider the organization of the city into municipal wards, and the manner in which each ward functions itself in terms of city government; how the ward is represented in the city council; how councilmen are chosen; term of office; duties; salary; function; why represented by wards instead of by city as a whole? why not two branches, by city and by ward? Function of council as a whole; why not initiative and referendum? What gain to the social group through functioning itself through the city council?

Consider the chief executive; how chosen; when; term of office; salary; why greater than councilman's; duties in general; executive, legislative, appointive power; relation of mayor to the city council; significance of office.

Consider judicial branch in similar manner.

Consider interrelations of various departments and the gain of the social group through them.

Taxes.—Consider: how funds for supporting the different departments are secured; justification of; why tax all? Apportionment of taxes; collection of taxes; who should see that the taxes are properly expended and why? In the study of taxation the children should see again through form to content; should see that the taxpayer, through taxes, merely hires someone to look after his share of interest in the general welfare; should see that his responsibility as a member of the social group does not end with the payment of taxes, but that it is also his duty to see that the same are wisely, effectively, and economically expended. In short, through the study the children should lay a foundation for intelligent tax-paying and tax-spending.

EIGHTH GRADE

Paving.—Consider: kinds of material—asphalt, macadam, brick, blocks, etc.; what governs choice; residence districts; business districts; compare with other cities; relative cost; durability; access to material; water vs. oil for street-dressing; cost, durability, sanitary effect, etc.

Consider the significance of the "good roads" movement. Consider the "road" movement from the standpoint of history. Contrast Greece and Rome in terms of roads, and their effect on national life. Significance of, "All roads lead to Rome."

Consider the municipal-ownership movement, its purpose and significance. Study effects of, in London, Glasgow, Birmingham.

Consider government control of public utilities. (The children of the eighth grade won't settle this question, but, as many do not go beyond this grade, they should have an intelligent appreciation of its significance.)

County organization.—Consider: genesis of; legislative, executive, judicial departments; officers of; how chosen; compensation; duties; public service rendered; social gain through county organization.

State organization.—Consider: officers in various departments; how chosen; term of office; compensation; duties; service rendered; social gain; relation of city and county to; relation of state to nation.

Industrial development.—Consider the industrial development from the adoption of the Constitution of the United States to the present day. Trace development through home and factory from local area to world-markets. Consider: our present supremacy; coal and iron as factors; probable effect of Panama Canal; competitive forces; world-service vs. individual gain.

Army and navy.—Consider: organization of; cost; function; non-productiveness of; necessity for. Contrast with England, France, Germany. Cost of war in men and money.

TEACHERS' READING COURSE ALONG SOCIOLOGICAL LINES

Nash, *Genesis of the Social Conscience;* Henderson, *Social Spirit in America,* and *Social Elements;* Small and Vincent, *Introduction to the Study of Society;* Small, *General Sociology;* Giddings, *Principles of Sociology;* Horne, *Philosophy of Education;* Thurston, *Economics and Industrial History;* Gibbins, *Industry in England;* McVey, *Modern Industrialism;* Arnold, *Culture and Anarchy,* and *Essays on Democracy;* Ruskin, *Crown of Wild Olive,* and *Open Sesame;* Emerson, *The American Scholar.*

FICTION DEALING WITH SOCIAL PROBLEMS

Dickens, *Hard Times;* Reade, *Put Yourself in His Place;* Kingsley, *Alton Locke* and *Yeast;* Eliot, *Felix Holt;* Hugo, *Les Misérables* and *Toilers of the Sea;* Mrs. Humphrey Ward, *Marcella;* Besant, *All Sorts and Conditions of Men;* Allen, *The Reign of Law;* Elizabeth Stuart Phelps Ward, *The Singular Life.*

Typical poems, articulating the cry of the social spirit, may be found worthy of study, such as:

Elizabeth Barrett Browning, "The Cry of the Children;" Tennyson, "Rizpah," "Despair," and " Locksley Hall Sixty Years After;" Whittier, "Massachusetts to Virginia;" Lowell, "The Present Crisis;" Lanier, "The Symphony;" Whitman, "Song of the Open Road;" Markham, "The Man with the Hoe," "The Toilers," and "Brotherhood."

BIOGRAPHIES FOR CHILDREN IN GRADES

John Howard, Elizabeth Frye, Florence Nightingale, Peter Cooper, Frances E. Willard, George Waring, Governor Folk, Governor La Follette, William Travers Jerome, Mayor Weaver.

The author ackowledges his indebtedness to Mr. Henry W. Thurston for insight into, and interest and inspiration in, this phase of school work

BIRD BOXES FOR THE CITY PARKS, MADE BY THE UNIVERSITY ELEMENTARY SCHOOL

CULTIVATE CHILDREN LIKE FLOWERS

LUTHER BURBANK

Which has the more influence in building the life of a child, heredity or environment? And are acquired characters inherited?

My own observations prove that all characters that are inherited have once been acquired, and that heredity is only the sum of all these past environments, which, if impressed on the heredity long and strong enough in any specific direction, will become part of heredity itself, and this new heredity, already slightly changed by these late environments, will have to meet new environments as before, which will, by repetition, become fixed in the ever new and constantly fluctuating heredity.

Did you ever think what is the most pliable and the most precious product of all the ages? It is not pigs, mules, books, or locomotives, cotton or corn—but children.

Children cannot all be treated alike; each has his or her special individuality, which is the most valuable of all endowments. If all were alike, no progress could be made and right here comes the weakest point in the present educational systems.

I have long been studying the intricate complexity of the action of heredity and environmental forces on life, both in plants and in man, and these comparisons and deductions came clearly, sharply, and naturally. It has been said that to improve a child we should begin with the grandparents. This is only a half-truth, which perhaps had better never have been said. Do not waste any of your time on grandparents unless you commence on them in earliest pliable childhood. If we hope for any improvement on the human race, we must begin with the child, as the child responds more readily to environment than any creature in existence. The change may come in the first generation, and it may not. It may not show at all for many generations, but patience and constant attention will finally be rewarded in the survival of the most beautiful, the most precious, or the fittest, whichever you may wish to call it.

In child-rearing, environment is equally essential with heredity. Mind you, I do not say that heredity is of no consequence. It is the great factor and often makes environment almost powerless. When certain hereditary tendencies are almost indelibly ingrained, environment will have a hard battle to effect a change in the child; but that a change can be wrought by the surroundings we all know.

A child absorbs environment. It is the most susceptible thing in the world to influence, and if that force be applied rightly and constantly when the child is in its greatest receptive condition, the effect will be pronounced, immediate, and permanent. There is no doubt that if a child with a vicious temper be placed in an environment of peace and quiet the temper will change. Put a boy born of gentle white parents among Indians and he will grow up like an Indian. Let the child born of criminal parents have a setting of morality and decency, and the chances are that he will not grow up to be a criminal, but an upright man.

I do not say that heredity will not sometimes assert itself, of course. When the criminal instinct crops out in an individual, it might appear as if environment were leveled to the ground, but in succeeding generations the effect of higher environment will not fail to become fixed.

We in America form a nation with the blood of half the peoples of the world in our veins. We are more crossed than any other nation in the history of the world, and here we meet exactly the same results that are always seen in a much-crossed race of plants; all the worst as well as all the best qualities of each are brought out in their fullest intensity, and right here is where selective environment counts.

All the necessary crossing has been done, and now comes the work of elimination, the work of refining, until we shall get an ultimate product that will be the finest human race which has ever been known. It is perhaps this country which will produce that race. Many years will pass before the finished work is attained, but it is sure to come. The characteristics of the many peoples that make up this nation will show in the composite, with many of the evil characteristics removed, and the finished product will be the race of the future.

In my work with plants and flowers, I introduce color here, shape there, size, or perfume, according to the product desired. In such processes the teachings of nature are always followed. Its great forces only are employed. All that has been done for plants and flowers by crossing, nature has already accomplished for the American people. By the crossing of bloods strength has, in one instance, been secured; in another, intellectuality; in still another, moral force. Nature alone could do this.

Man has by no means reached the ultimate. The fittest has not yet survived. In the process of elimination the weaker must fall, but the battle has changed its base from brute force to mental integrity.

Statistics show many things to make us pause, but after all the proper point of view is that of the optimist. The time will come when insanity will be reduced, suicides and murders will be fewer, and man will become a being of fewer mental troubles and bodily ills.

Wherever you have a nation in which there is no variation there is comparatively little insanity or crime, or exalted morality or genius. Here in America, where the variation is greatest, statistics show a greater percentage of all these variations.

As time goes on in its endless and ceaseless course environment will crystallize the American nation. Its varying elements will become unified, and the weeding-out process will probably leave the finest human product ever known. The color, the perfume, the size and form that are placed in plants will have their analogies in the composite, the American of the future.

And now, what will hasten this development most of all? The proper rearing of children. Don't feed children on maudlin sentimentalism—give them nature. Let their souls drink in all that is pure and sweet. Rear them, if possible, amid pleasant surroundings. If they come into the world with souls groping in the darkness, let them see and feel the light.

Don't terrify them in early life with the fear of an after-world. Let nature teach them the lessons of good and proper living, combined with an abundance of well-balanced nourishment. Those children will grow to be the best men and women. Put the best in them by contact with the best outside. They will absorb it as a plant does the sunshine and the dew.—*Chicago Tribune.*

SOCIAL ACTIVITIES IN THE FIRST GRADE OF THE FRANCIS W. PARKER SCHOOL

ROSE B. PHILLIPS

At the beginning of the fall term three social needs presented themselves to the first grade:

1. The making of a Christmas gift for home.
2. The planning of a pleasing curtain for our dressing-room.
3. Making candles for the kindergarten Christmas tree.

I. A CHRISTMAS GIFT

Plants to blossom indoors, and to blossom preferably at Christmas time, were chosen for gifts. After looking at flower catalogues, we decided that freesias and jonquils were best suited to our purpose. The children filled low four-inch bulb-pots with sandy loam from a field near the school, first putting in a small stone or two for drainage. Each child planted in his pot five of the kind of bulb he preferred. To make the gift a more complete one, we decided that bowls of clay should be made to hold the pots and plants.

The following reading-lessons, which were first written on the board by the teacher as the children told each step of the process, give an account of the work. These reading-lessons, with a kodak picture of the bowls and plants, and two working-plans of the bowls, made by each child for his use in the clay-room, were tied between stiff paper covers, as a book to accompany the gift.

FIRST-GRADE READING LESSONS

MOTHER'S CHRISTMAS GIFT

In October we planted some freesia bulbs.
We planted jonquil bulbs, too.
These may blossom by Christmas.
They are for our mothers' Christmas gifts.

THE PLANTING

We planted our bulbs in flower-pots.
The pots are four inches wide.
They are two inches high.
We put stones in the bottom of the pots.
What was that for?
We filled the pots with sandy soil.
We planted the bulbs one inch deep.

PUTTING BULBS IN THE DARK

We put our bulbs in a dark place.
This was to let the roots grow.
Strong roots help to make strong plants.
The light makes the leaves grow well.
At first we watered the bulbs well.
The soil stayed damp.
We did not water them again.
We left them in the dark place for twelve days.

GROWTH IN THE DARK

We brought the plants from the dark.
We held them upside down.
We took the pots off.
We could see many roots.
They were all through the soil.
We put the plants into the pots again.
The freesia leaves were two inches high.
The jonquil leaves were one inch high.
The leaves were white.

PUTTING PLANTS IN THE LIGHT

We first put the plants in a dim light.
We watered them.
We left them there for two days.
Then they could bear sunlight.
We put them in a sunny window.
The leaves turned green.
We water them often now.
Look at this picture.
It shows how our plants look now.
The taller ones are the freesias.

ANOTHER PART OF MOTHER'S CHRISTMAS GIFT

We are making dishes of clay.
The bulb-pots will be put into the dishes.
The dishes will be five inches wide.

They will be two and one-half inches high.
They will be dried.
They will be baked in the kiln.
They will be glazed.
They will be baked again.
The color will be light green.

II. THE DRESSING-ROOM CURTAIN

The entrance to our schoolroom has a dressing-room on one side, and a cupboard with glass doors on the other. The dressing-room has no door, the cupboard no curtains. To make this entrance more attractive was what we wished to do. Curtains for each place was the suggestion of most of the children, and was the only feasible one. Tan-colored linen was being used elsewhere in the school, and this was shown to the children. They liked it. We went to the eighth-grade room to see curtains of linen which the eighth grade had stenciled with pine trees. The first grade thought it would be nice to decorate their curtains in such a way.

We went to Lincoln Park to see what suggestions for decorations might offer themselves there. The park was beautiful that morning, and rich in suggestion. Beautiful leaves were picked up, and one of the park gardeners gave generously of flowers and curious seed-pods, as a result of his pruning in "Grandmother's Garden." We made several trips to the park, the school garden, and to fields near by. The children painted and drew trees, flowers, seeds, and vegetables. They then decided that leaves would make the nicest decoration for the curtains.

FIRST-GRADE READING LESSONS

THE DRESSING-ROOM CURTAIN

Our dressing room has no door.
All who come into our room pass the dressing-room.
We thought it needed curtains.
Tan linen was bought for the curtains.
We decided to decorate them with leaves.

CUTTING PATTERNS

We cut patterns of oak, maple, poplar, and willow leaves.
We pinned the patterns on a curtain.
We liked the oak patterns best.

CHOOSING THE COLOR

We had to choose the color for the leaves.
Leaves out-of-doors were red, green, and yellow.
We cut leaves of green and yellow paper.
We had no red paper of the right shade.
We pinned the yellow and green leaves on the curtain.
We chose the green for our leaves.

THE ARRANGEMENT OF LEAVES

We did not know how to arrange the leaves.
Each played a sheet of paper was a curtain.
With green crayon each arranged leaves on the paper.
We chose Adrian's arrangement.
You may see it on our curtain.

MAKING THE STENCIL

A stencil was cut from one of the oak-leaf patterns.
The stencil was cut in heavy, brown paper.
The paper was shellacked on both sides.
This was done to keep the color from passing through.
We painted the leaves on the curtain with green dye.
The dye was boiling while we painted.

III. CANDLE-MAKING

The first thing to do was to choose the material of which the candles were to be made. Wax, paraffin, spermaceti, stearin, and tallow were shown to the children. Spermaceti and stearin were excluded on account of expense. To help in making a choice of paraffin, wax, or tallow, candles of each of these materials were burned. The paraffin flame was the largest, and that material was the one chosen.

How to make the candles was the next question. One of the boys said his father had read to him of boys making candles in bamboo canes. This idea was quickly taken up by the children and modified in various ways.

The children were asked to work out their plans at home. The result was candles made in five different ways.

One was made in a paper mold. A piece of heavy paper had been wrapped around the handle of a duster and the edges of the paper glued. Darning-cotton was used as a wick and the tube stood upright in a low tin can, being held in place by

Plants and Clay Bowls for "Mother's Christmas Gift"

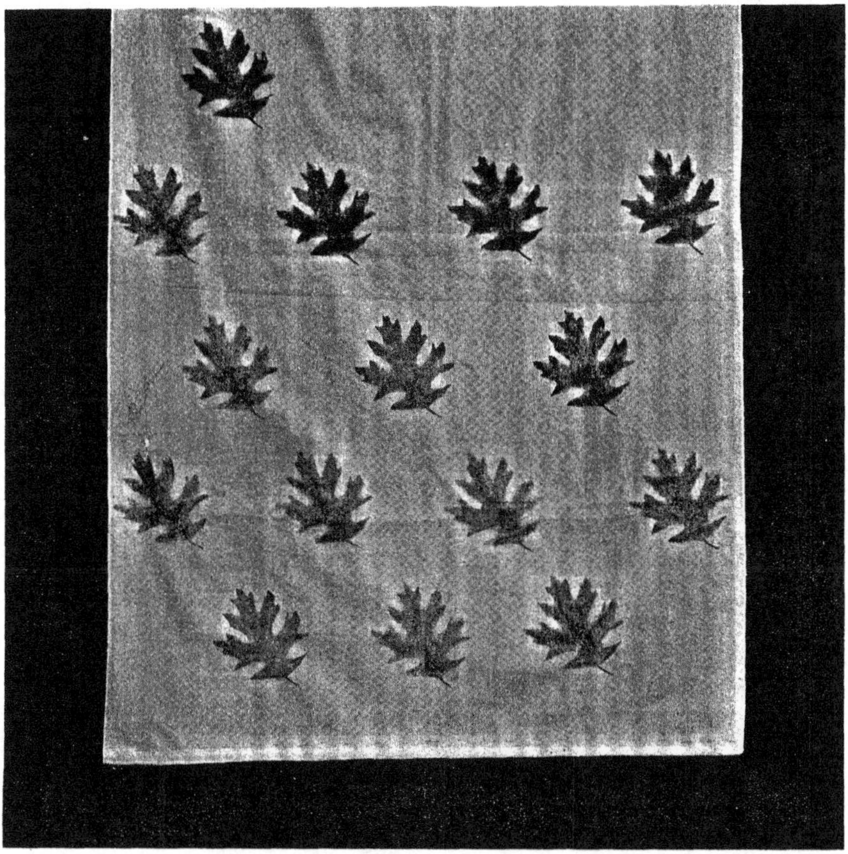

Curtain Showing Stencil Design—First Grade

DIPPING CANDLES FOR THE CHRISTMAS TREE

CANDLESTICKS AND MOLD CANDLES FOR VALENTINE GIFTS—FIRST GRADE

paraffin that had solidified around the tube. Paraffin was poured into the mold—the mold, of course, having to be broken to release the candle. Another was made in a bottle, and another in a wooden mold.

A wooden mold was made from a block 7×2×2. A half-inch hole was made lengthwise, almost through the block. The block was split, and the two pieces fastened together with hinges and a clasp. (Help had been given in putting on the hinges and clasp.) A piece of string was used for the wick.

Another candle was made by dipping a piece of string in and out of wax repeatedly; another, by rolling paraffin, partly warm, around a string.

We liked the size and appearance of the dipped candle, and thought, too, that it was the easiest of the five ways shown for making candles; so it was decided to make the Christmas-tree candles by dipping.

Five pounds of paraffin were melted. Three wicks were tied to each of two sticks, nails being tied to the wicks to make them sink easily into the paraffin. These nails were cut off as soon as the paraffin stiffened the wick. Two dozen candles were made in this way.

The children thought they would like to make candles for home, so we planned to make larger candles, and candle-sticks of clay to fit them, as Valentines or Easter gifts.

The children were shown some tin candle molds. These they thought would make nice candles of just the right size. To the paraffin for these candles was added some stearin to make them harder. A candle made of paraffin alone will bend in a warm room.

The children drew plans for their candlesticks. They were then shown some simple candlesticks of good design, and their second plans were better.

Many wished that the candles might be colored. Green is the only color we have managed successfully. This is made by dissolving green and yellow aniline dye in stearin.

The candlesticks for the green candles were glazed green; for the white candles blue.

CAN THE COLLECTING INSTINCT BE UTILIZED IN TEACHING?

ELIZABETH HOWE

The collecting instinct seems to arise in the majority of children; comparatively few have never collected. Is it not possible, since this habit seems to be almost universal, to develop this instinct along certain lines in schools?

Dr. G. Stanley Hall, Professor Earl Barnes, and Mrs. C. F. Burk [1] have made investigations on the collecting instinct of children, and have found it to be very common. So far as known, the public schools as yet have not recognized the value of this instinct. My investigation was along the same line as that of the above writers, and the results in the main agree.

Dr. Hall says: "The habit could be put to great advantage; that is, to collect scraps on literature, geology, etc. Children gather blindly, with no knowledge of the geography of the country from which the stamps come, nor the species of birds which lay the different eggs collected." With the knowledge confronting us that this instinct does commonly exist, two questions arise: first, What are the principal varieties of this collecting instinct? and, second, What varieties can be utilized to advantage? Investigators have tried to solve the first by having a group of children write answers to a number of questions; but, of course, there is one great fault to be found with the questionaire method, because when a teacher asks questions of her pupils, there is a tendency for them to give what they think the teacher wants. This was so to some extent in the papers from which I got my data.

The ideal method for finding out the individual instincts would be to take each child separately, and find out from him

[1] G. S. Hall, *Pedagogical Seminary,* Vol. I, p. 234; Earl Barnes, *Studies in Education,* Vol. II, p. 144; C. F. Burk, *Pedagogical Seminary,* Vol. VII, p. 179.

in an unguarded moment the things he collected and the reason for doing so. This method would take time and trouble, which probably could not be given by the average school-teacher.

Nevertheless, it is quite clear that the teacher who had such information would have an insight into the children's inner life which she would hardly be able to get in any other way. It would bring out some of the desires of a child which the teacher could encourage or check.

The following list of questions was asked of 135 pupils, from eleven to seventeen years old, belonging to the sixth, seventh, and eighth grades of a school situated in a very much congested district of Chicago:[2]

1. Tell all the things you have collected.
2. How old were you when you began?
3. Have you stopped? If so, how old were you at that time?
4. Why did you begin?
5. If discontinued, why have you done so?
6. Tell the number in each collection.
7. Did you arrange the things collected? If so, how?

Of the 135 there were 17 who did not understand the meaning of the word "collection" and fourteen who had made none. This leaves 104 papers from which I have drawn my conclusions. Of this 104, 52 were boys and 52 were girls. Forty-six different things were collected by boys and 45 by girls. The interests of the girls as a whole seemed more trivial than that of the boys, although this might not be true if a larger number were considered.

The following is a list of the things collected:

BOYS	
Books	20
Stamps	8
Money	7
Pictures	5
Pencils	4
Old and foreign money	4
Stones	3
Marbles	3
Railroad folders and time-tables	5
Photographs	2
Buttons	2
Papers	2
Electrical things	2
Pins	2
Pens	2
Cord	
Coal with iron in it	
Blank checks	
Tools	
Brushes	
Magazines	

[2] Through the kind interest of Mr. Joseph A. Bache.

Bibles
Music-books
Outcast animals
Bats
Balls
Footballs
Drawing-paper
Paints
Neckties
Scarf-pins
Tickets
Tops
Twigs and branches
Shoe-laces
Coupons
Spelling-papers
Boxes
Rulers
Notes
Seeds
Flag buttons
Departments of government
Articles made in manual training

GIRLS

Books	19
Pictures	11
Stamps	7
Postal cards	5
Dolls	5
Ribbons	4
Notes	4
Money	4
Photographs	4
Souvenirs	3
School papers	3
Shells	3
Spoons	2
Flowers	2
Handkerchiefs	2
Old and foreign money	2
Cups and saucers	2
Songs	2
Drawings	2

Rags
Marbles
Arithmetics
Magazines
Receipts
Railroad maps
Plates
Calling-cards
Sunday-school papers
Sheet music from Sunday *American*
Turfs from Ireland
Paper
Chalk
Pens
Pencils
Time-tables
Birds' wings
Berries
Corn
Stones
Tubs
Desks
Leaves
Pocket-books
Fancy-work
Music

Collections of books were made more often than any other thing. This is true both of the boys and of the girls. In Dr. Stanley Hall's investigation he found that stamps were collected more often than anything else; in that of Earl Barnes, buttons and picture cards; in that of Mrs. Burk, nature interest ranks the highest. These observations seem to show that the things which interest children most are different in different localities. As Mrs. Burk's children all live in California, where flowers and plants are more common than here, it is barely possible that this would explain their preference for nature.

The reasons for collecting are interesting. Things were collected, in the majority of cases, without any thought of value, but apparently, first, simply to own something, and, second, to increase the quantity of that something. Nine wanted to see how many they could get; eight collected for remembrance; eight, because it was right or they were told to do so; seven collected books because they wanted to read; six collected, but did not know why; three, to see how much money they could save (not for its value at first). The other reasons stated were "amusement," "curiosity," "interested," "ornamental," "useful," and some "because they liked to do so." One boy collected bats and balls because as he said: "I got crazy over playing ball;" another collected electrical apparatus because he thought it would be good as a trade. Another boy began to collect things so as to have something to leave to his brothers and sisters.

Earl Barnes states that he found emulation to be the reaosn given for collecting in 22 out of 128 cases; and a curious thing is that not one of the children in the group I had gave evidence of having had emulation or imitation as a motive. None said anything about color or beauty, but quantity was their special aim.

In Dr. Hall's paper he gives "marbles" as one of the first on the list, while comparatively few of my children collected them. One girl has 579 and is still collecting them. She is now sixteen years old and started her collection at the age of ten.

Out of the 104 who made collections, 77 are still collecting; 27 have stopped. Twenty-seven commenced to collect at the age of ten years, 36 after they were ten and 41 before they were ten. There were a few who started as early as the fifth year. Forty-eight of the children are now fourteen or over, and 56 are under fourteen years. Some of these who are now collecting are fifteen and sixteen.

Of the 52 girls who made collections, 30 had schemes of arrangement, and 22 did not. One arranged her postal cards according to the months, to see how many she received in each month; one held each kind of examination papers together with a rubber band; another put books on a shelf according to the men and women who wrote them; and another put her leaves and flowers in a book made for that purpose.

Twenty-four boys made no arrangement, and 28 did. The one who collected buttons arranged them in the form of a crescent and hung them on the wall. The stamps of one boy were arranged in a book according to their value; another arranged them in an album according to the country to which they belonged; another one put his United States stamps in packages of 100 each, and the foreign ones he pasted in a book. One boy arranged petrified animals according to the family in which they belonged; another arranged his books by numbering them with a paper and putting them in a bookstand. A considerable number stated that they had arranged their collections so that they could find them.

This investigation has shown that there were almost as many different kinds of things collected as there were children to collect them. It might seem at first that, on account of this great diversity of interest, it would be almost a hopeless task for a teacher to try to direct these young ideas into proper channels. On further study, however, it will be noted that many of the things collected can easily be divided into a few groups. For example, we could put under the head of "educational" the collections of books, minerals, electrical apparatus, paints, leaves, branches, flowers, etc.; under the head of "remunerative," money, possibly coupons and stamps, etc.; under "æsthetic," pictures, neckties, scarf-pins, souvenirs, shells, fancy-work, etc.

This paper has been written with a view to raising the question as to how the collecting instinct can be utilized in teaching. But first of all it is very desirable to learn of instances in which it has already been utilized. The writer would be grateful for answers to the following questions:

1. Have you ever made any use of the collecting instinct of children in your teaching?

2. What methods of enlisting and developing the instinct were used.

3. What results were obtained?

Answers to these questions may be sent to

ELIZABETH HOWE,
Care of *Elementary School Teacher,*
School of Education.

ANIMAL COVERINGS: FROM THE STANDPOINT OF THE TEXTILE WORKER

ROBERT W. HEGNER
Zoölogical Department, University of Chicago

The material in the following paper was originally prepared for the college class in textiles at the School of Education. It was considered of sufficient value to place before other teachers, not only as an aid in textile work, but also as a means of increasing the points of contact between the child and the lower animals, thus fostering a natural love and sympathy for the creatures that live out of doors.

Before we can consider in logical order the various facts of animal coverings, we must have some knowledge of how the animal kingdom has been divided into groups, classes, etc. Zoölogists recognize a number of groups, or phyla, of animals, which they have arranged, according to their complexity and supposed relationships, into a series beginning with the one-celled forms and ending with the genus *homo*. At one point in their classification, a new character, the backbone, appears, which is so important that the whole kingdom is often divided primarily into two large assemblages, namely, those with backbones, and those without backbones. A simplified form of the classification employed by prominent scientists is given below:

GROUP A. *INVERTEBRATA* (*ALL ANIMALS WITHOUT BACKBONES*)

Phylum 1. *Protozoa* (one-celled animals, mostly microscopic).
Phylum 2. *Porifera* (sponges).
Phylum 3. *Coelenterata* (jellyfish, coral, etc.).
Phylum 4. *Platyhelminthes* (tapeworms, etc.).
Phylum 5. *Echinodermata* (starfish, sea urchin, etc.).
Phylum 6. *Annelida* (earthworm, leech, etc.).
Phylum 7. *Mollusca* (clam, snail, cuttlefish, etc.).
Phylum 8. *Arthropoda* (crayfish, insects, spider, etc.).

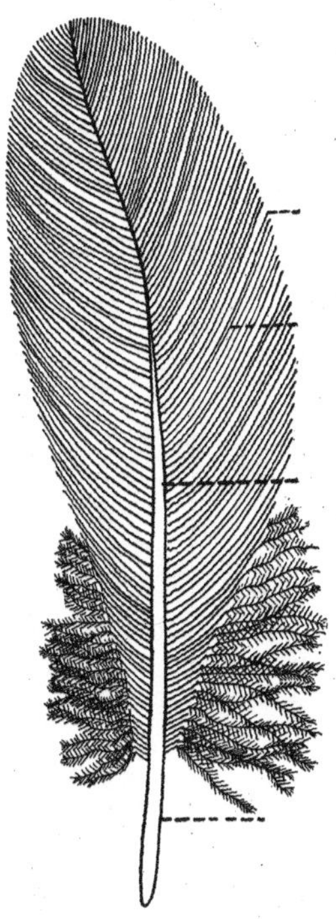

FIG. 1

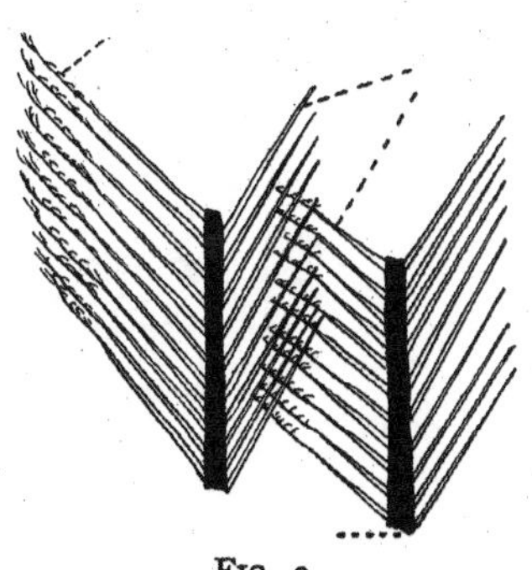

FIG. 2

FIG. 3

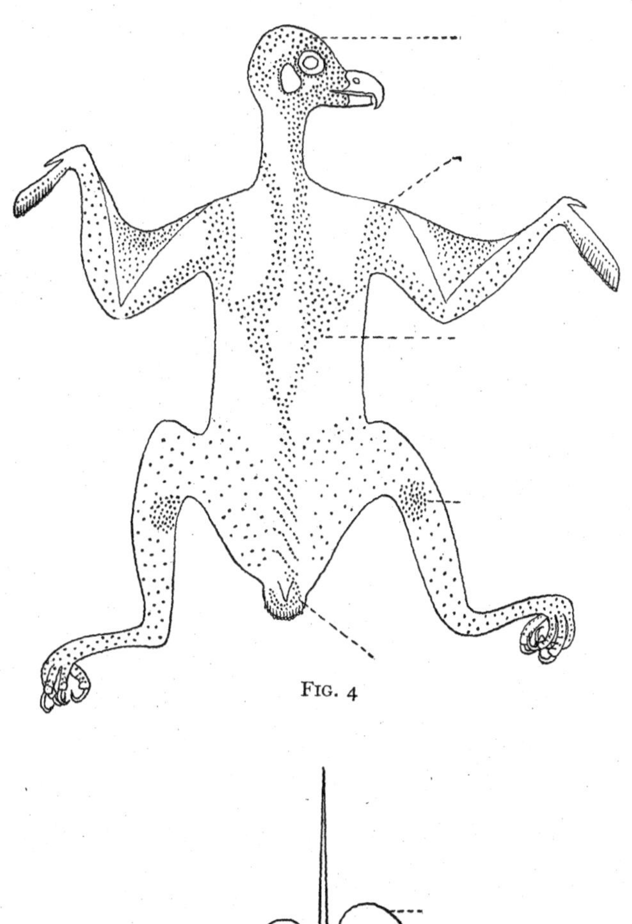

FIG. 4

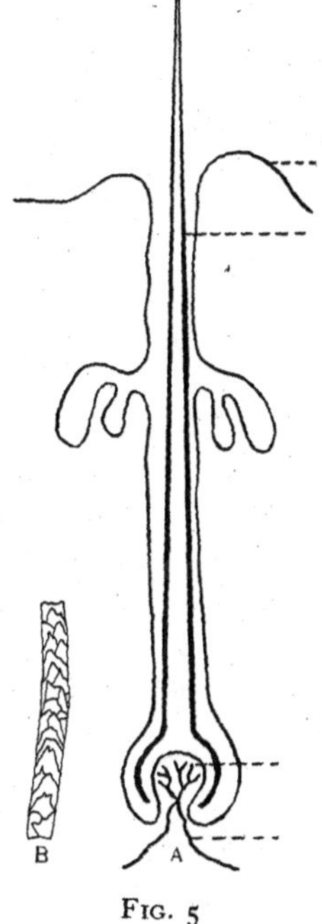

FIG. 5

GROUP B. *VERTEBRATA (ANIMALS WITH BACKBONES)*

Phylum 9. *Vertebrata.*

It is necessary for our purpose to divide the last phylum into its five classes, giving the characteristics that separate each class from the others.

PHYLUM *VERTEBRATA*

Class 1. *Pisces.* (Animals with backbones that spend the whole of their lives in the water. They are usually covered with scales, possess fins instead of jointed limbs and fingers, and breathe by means of gills.)

Class. 2. *Amphibia.* (Vertebrates that spend part of their lives in the water and part on land. They are usually without scales, and breathe by means of lungs.)

Class 3. *Reptilia.* (Vertebrates, usually covered with scales, that breathe by means of lungs.)

Class 4. *Aves.* (Vertebrates with a covering of feathers.)

Class 5. *Mammals.* (Vertebrates possessing mammary glands from which they feed their newly born young. They always have hair on their bodies.)

A fact of interest to us is that these five classes just outlined are distinguished from one another by the *nature of their coverings.*. Thus no animal except a mammal has hairs on its body; only birds have feathers; only reptiles have scales and also lungs; only amphibians have naked skins; and only fishes have scales and also gills. This, of course, is only a superficial examination, and there are rare exceptions in each of the above groups. The natural classification depends on the skeleton and other structures that are of more importance, and do not vary as greatly as does the external covering.

The coverings of animals serve various purposes. (1) They prevent serious injury from ordinary accidents, (2) they keep the natural warmth of the body from escaping, and (3) by their colors they protect the animal from its enemies.

The first benefit derived from the coverings need take up little of our space, for it is perfectly obvious how valuable hair, feathers, scales, and shells are to their owners as a protection from injury. We may, however, draw a comparison between these coverings and our own clothing, which gives us a similar immunity from accidents. Shoes, hats, gloves, the headgear of football players and many other articles of apparel are donned expressly to escape injury. In southern warm climates the shoes are reduced to sandals, and hats to sunshades, and in the daytime all clothing becomes a refuge from the burning rays of the tropical sun, while at night it serves to shield the body from the dew and chilly winds.

In considering the second benefit, that of warmth, we must exclude all cold-blooded animals. All invertebrates, fishes, amphibians, and reptiles, are cold-blooded; that is, the temperature of their bodies is generally only several degrees higher than their surroundings. Only birds and mammals then come under discussion here. Birds have a temperature up to 112°F. This is higher than that of man, which is normally 98.3-5°F. It is evident that these animals must have some means of keeping this warmth in their bodies, and this is accomplished by their coverings.

The feathers of birds are remarkable structures, and no organs like them are possessed by other animals. The structure of feathers is very interesting. An ordinary one (Fig. 1) has for its central support a main *stem,* on each side of which is a *vane.* The part of the main stem free from the vane is called the *quill;* the remainder is called the *shaft.* The vane is composed of a number of *barbs* (Fig. 2). Each barb bears smaller structures called *barbules* (Fig. 3) on either side causing it, when viewed under a microscope, to resemble an entire feather. These barbules in turn, in many cases, notably the large wing and tail feathers, carry on their anterior surface—that is the surface toward the tip of the feather—small *hooklets* (Fig. 3). This complete structure is remarkably well adapted for an aërial life. The barbules of one barb overlie those of the preceding barb, forming a diagonal mesh-work (Fig. 2). Each hooklet of one barbule catches in the barbule from the next barb in front, thus further increasing the interlocking. The result is an extremely strong and resistant, though pliant, mechanism—just such as is necessary for the use of the bird in flying.

In the majority of birds there are two kind of feathers. The large ones with vanes are called *contour feathers,* and the small fluffy ones are the *down feathers.* Both kinds lie in sacs in the outer layer of the skin, the *epidermis.*

Just at the base of the rudimentary tail, or "pope's nose," is a gland that secretes an oil. When the bird presses a drop of oil with its beak and dresses its feathers, it is said to be pruning. It is very difficult to wet a bird's feathers, and, as everyone knows, the aquatic birds—ducks, gulls, etc.—can remain in the water indefinitely without any disasters. The oil aids the feather in shedding water, just as a raincoat does for us, and when a bird "prunes" it is simply putting on its waterproofs.

Feathers do not occur over the entire body of a bird, but are restricted to certain tracts caled *pterylae.* The illustration (Fig. 4) shows the feather tracts on the back of a great horned owl.

All birds change their feathers frequently. The young, when newly hatched, are either naked or covered with down. They soon outgrow this, just as young children outgrow their clothes, and in the course of a week or two true feathers begin to appear, and all that remains of the down are a few spots where the baby clothes still show through the contour feathers. The first plumage is worn only a short time; then it gives way to a second plumage. The loss of one set of clothing and the acquirement of another is called "molting." In adult birds molting is annual or semi-annual. All birds shed their feathers in the autumn, after they have finished their household duties for the season, and put on their heavy woolen winter clothing in the shape of a beautiful new set of plumage. In the spring there are many birds that do not consider their ordinary clothes good enough in which to do their wooing; so they change again, and at this time acquire the gorgeous ornaments that are everywhere noticeable just before the breeding season, such as the elegant plumes of the snowy heron, known as "aigrettes."

A much-disputed theory which attempts to account for the beauty of the feathers of male birds at the breeding season is that called "sexual selection." The females are supposed to be attracted by the most brightly colored males, and select them for their mates, the result being that more beautiful males have been bred generation after generation, until by sexual selection the present strikingly ornamental effects have been produced; for example, the birds of paradise, lyre birds, humming birds, etc.

The characteristic covering of mammals is hair. This is undoubtedly extremely well fitted to keep the possessor dry and warm; for humans are ever ready to take the beautiful fur away from them to make coats, boas, muffs, etc., for themselves. Hairs are much simpler in their structure than feathers. They arise from sacs in the epidermis (Fig. 5). Each hair has at its base a papilla, which contains nerves and blood-vessels, and from which a new hair grows if the old one is destroyed. At the sides of the sac are sebaceous glands, which serve to oil the hair and keep it pliable.

Fur is generally composed of one kind of hair; but some animals possess two kinds: (1) long, coarse structures scattered over the body, but not so numerous as (2) the finer underfur. The fur seals are thus covered. Many modifications are found in hairs on different parts of mammal bodies. The long hairs on the tails of horses, the eyelashes of man, the sensitive hairs on the snout of the cat, the spines of hedgehogs and porcupines, are all modifications.

The most useful and most important of all hairs is that found on the sheep, called wool. The fiber of wool is more or less waved. It is a "peculiar modification of hair characterized by fine transverse or oblique lines from 2,000 to 4,000 in the extent of an inch, indicative of a minutely imbricated surface" (Prof. fessor Owen; Fig. 55). These serratures interlock firmly when the hairs are twisted together, and give to wool its felting quality.

In most mammals there is a periodic shedding and renewal of the hair, the new hair arising from the old papilla. This usually occurs in the spring. Low temperatures seem to stimulate the growth of hair, as we find the coats of horses becoming thick and woolly in autumn, and the wool of arctic animals is heavier than that of like creatures found in warm climates.

There is a seasonal change in the colors of certain mammals. The polar hare and the arctic fox show this to a remarkable degree. In them the hair becomes pure white in the winter. This, of course, makes them inconspicuous against a background of snow, and helps them escape the sharp eyes of enemies. "In the case of Ross's lemming, we know that this change is due to the influence of the cold, and depends in great part on the appearance of gas bubbles inside the hairs" (Thomson).

The value of color in nature, our third topic, cannot be overestimated. Large volumes have been written regarding the various benefits derived from advantageous colors, and indeed the very lives of most animals depend on their power to conceal themselves amid their surroundings so effectually as to escape their enemies. Obviously only the principal and most easily explained phenomena can be considered in this paper.

Color is caused by white light being broken up into its various wave-lengths. When an object appears black, it is because it has absorbed the entire complex of white light. When an object appears red, it has absorbed all the elements of white light except the red wave-lengths, which are reflected and make an impression on our eyes. Colors have been divided into (1) structural and (2) pigmental. The former occur to perfection in the gorgeous raiment of birds and butterflies. The changeable colors seen on humming-birds, on the neck of the pigeon, and on numerous other birds are optical effects due to modifications of the feather structure. The exact physical causation of the colors is unknown. Pigmental colors are due to the presence in the organism of substances of definite chemical composition that react to light always in the same way. The green color in plants is a good example. It is due to a pigment called chlorophyll that acts when extracted from the plant body exactly as when within the tissues.

Poulton, in his book on *The Colors of Animals,* gives in concise form the uses of color, and later gives a full explanation with examples under each.

I. Non-significant colors.—These are colors that are due to chemical or physical structure, valuable to the animal not because of their color itself, but because the organs that contain it are of value. For example, blood is red and fat is white.

II. Significant colors.

1. *Colors of direct physiological value.*—Included under this head are those colors that are of importance in retaining and giving off heat. Dark colors readily absorb radiant heat, and light colors do not. For this reason black clothes are the warmest in hot weather and white most comfortable. This may account for the change of colors at different seasons of the year. However, a dark surface readily parts with heat, while a white surface tends to retain heat, and this may be a factor in the coloration of animals. For example, the white appearance of arctic birds and mammals must be advantageous for concealment in a region so largely covered with snow, but it is very probable that advantage is also secured by checking the loss of heat through radiation.

2. *Protective and aggressive resemblance.*—An animal is *protectively colored* when it resembles its natural surroundings in such a way as to elude its enemies. Almost all animals are thus protected, familiar examples being the insect known as the walking stick, which so closely resembles a twig as to be practically invisible among the branches of trees; and the owlet-moths belonging to the genus *Catocala,* which are safe from discovery while resting on the bark of trees. *Aggressive coloration* is possessed by animals that resemble their surroundings so closely that they can steal upon their prey unseen. This style of coloration is found in many snakes, lizards, etc., whose skins harmonize with their habitat and enable them to get close to their victims.

3. *Protective and aggressive mimicry.*—In this case the animal gains advantage by superficial resemblance to some other form. *Protective mimicry* occurs when one animal resembles another which is immune from attack from other animals because of its sting, offensive taste, or smell. An animal shows *aggressive mimicry* when it resembles another so that it can injure the latter or some other form which accompanies it or is not afraid of it. A well-known case of protective mimicry occurs in two species of butterflies belonging to the group of which the common monarch or milkweed butterfly is an example. *Danais erippus* is immune because of its offensive taste, and is mimicked by *Limenitis aichippus.* These both live in Central America.

4. *Warning colors.*—Bright colors are of advantage to animals that possess unpleasant qualities, such as taste and odor, as other forms can easily recognize one so colored and "pass by on the other side." This is a rather common condition among the butterflies. The above example, *Danais erippus,* serves here also, as its bright colors advertise it from afar and lessen the danger of a bird mistaking it for another species.

5. *Colors displayed in courtship.*—These are colors that appear only during the breeding season and are of common occurrence among the birds. The presence of brilliant plumage is accounted for by sexual selection, as has been explained in the discussion of feathers.

The insects are the most diverse and highly colored of animals, and examples of all the above styles may be found easily among the members of that class. They are more frequently used by authors than other forms to illustrate the various color classifications and theories. Among the vertebrates, birds undoubtedly hold first place, and one has but to examine a book on ornithology that contains colored plates to realize that the feathered animals carry all the colors of the rainbow on their backs. Bright colors in mammals are comparatively rare, their coats being usually uniform, with stripes and spots by way of variety.

A few animals are especially interesting with respect to their coverings, and I wish to discuss these separately.

1. *Whales* were for hundreds of years thought to be fishes. Their structure, when they were examined by morphologists, proved them to be mammals. They are covered with a heavy skin, and the hairs are reduced to a few isolated specimens in the neighborhood of the muzzle. The presence of blubber just under the skin no doubt accounts for the absence of hair, as it prevents the dispersal of the body heat.

2. *Elephants* are restricted in their habitat to Africa and Asia, although they once inhabited America. There are only two species now living: (1) *Elephas indicus,* with small ears, and (2) *Elephas africanus,* with large ears. Other forms have become extinct. The elephant of today has very few hairs on its body, but it has a very thick skin, which protects it from injury

and keeps in all the warmth that is necessary considering the temperature of its present home. The elephants of former times were very differently clothed. They lived in colder climates and needed more protection than that afforded by their skins. Specimens found frozen in ice in Siberia have close woolly hair, in some places three feet long.

3. *Armadillos* are small animals confined entirely to South America except one that comes as far north as Texas. They are unique among living mammals in having an armature of bony plates united into shields and rings, and covered by horny epidermis. This is just such a coat of mail as the knights of olden times used to wear when they sallied forth to do battle. The armadillo, despite these bony plates, still comes under our definition of a mammal, because here and there hairs are found protruding from the joints of the shields.

4. *Rhinoceros.*—Species of this animal occur in Africa and parts of India. The skin is very thick, with scanty hair. Similar arguments may be used here to account for the decrease of fur as were suggested with the elephants.

5. *Snowy owls, snow-buntings, ptarmigans,* and numerous other northern birds become white in winter, for no other reason apparently than that they may be better protected from enemies. Natural-selectionists account for the change by claiming that those birds with this advantageous tendency of bleaching survive and transmit this characteristic to their progeny until the tendency results in a fully developed seasonal change.

6. *White mice, white rats,* and other animals with white fur or feathers are called "albinos." There is no coloring matter in their hair or feathers. These animals cannot exist under natural conditions, because they are conspicuous both day and night. The opposite condition is called 'melanism." This is the result of an excess of pigment in the hair or feathers. Black wolves and rabbits are melanic forms.

7. *Chimney swifts and woodpeckers* make special use of their tail feathers to brace themselves when clinging to sides of trees or chimneys. The vanes have disappeared from the end of the tail feathers of the swift, leaving a strong sharp spine.

Grouse that stay with us all winter have slender toes in the summer, but in the autumn, when snow comes, they acquire a comblike fringe on either side, which they wear instead of snow-shoes until the following spring.

The tails of birds that are continually on the wing have become adapted to their mode of locomotion, and act as rudders in flight and balancers when perching.

LITERATURE

Every textbook of zoölogy will give more or less in detail information on the subjects treated in this paper; but no one book gives all. Thomson's *Outlines of Zoölogy* is the simplest and most comprehensive of the host of zoölogical textbooks. Besides a review in order of the groups of animals with a detailed study of a type under each, there are chapters on comparative physiology, geographical distribution, and the theories of evolution. Parker and Haswell's textbook is larger, and is valuable for reference. The volumes of the *Riverside Natural History* and the *Cambridge Natural History* pay more attention to the habits of the various animals and less to their anatomy. These are of great value to textile workers. All the books mentioned are well known, and are to be found in every good scientific library.

1. Thomson, J. Arthur. *Outlines of Zoölogy*. New York: D. Appleton & Co., 1899. Third edition, 819 pages, 322 illustrations. $3.50.
2. Parker, J. F., and Haswell, W. A. *Text-Book of Zoölogy*. New York: The Macmillan Co., 1897. Two volumes. Vol. I, Invertebrates; Vol. II, Chordates. $9.
3. *Cambridge Natural History*. New York: The Macmillan Co. Ten volumes by special authors.
4. *Riverside Natural History*. New York: Houghton, Mifflin & Co. Six volumes by special authors.

There is an infinite amount of literature relating exclusively to birds. Perhaps the best of these for our purposes is that by Beddard on the *Structure and Classification of Birds*. Frank M. Chapman's *Bird Life* contains a very clear account of avian peculiarities in the first eight chapters, pp. 1–83. Newton's *Dictionary of Birds*, Cone's *Key to North American Birds*, Part II on "General Ornithology," pp. 59–244, and Headley's *Structure and Life of Birds* treat very fully such questions as the structure of feathers, molting, seasonal changes in color, migration, etc.

1. Beddard, Frank E. *The Structure and Classifications of Birds.* New York: Longmans, Green & Co., 1898. 548 pages.
2. Newton, Alfred. *A Dictionary of Birds.* London: Adam & Charles Black, 1896. 1088 pages.
3. Chapman, Frank M. *Bird Life.* New York: D. Appleton & Co., 1901. 270 pages, 75 colored plates, appendix for teachers. $2.
4. Cones, Elliott. *Key to North American Birds.* Boston: Dana, Estes & Co., 1903. Two volumes. 11552 pages.
5. Headley, F. W. *The Structure and Life of Birds.* New York: The Macmillan Co., 1895. 412 pages.

There are three books that give the general facts and theories of color in nature. Many other references might be given, but these are the ones most easily obtained, and give as full an account of the subject as is necessary for textile workers:

1. Poulton, Edward B. *The Colours of Animals.* New York: D. Appleton & Co., 1890. 360 pages, 66 figures. $1.25.
2. Beddard, F. E. *Animal Coloration.* New York: The Macmillan Co., 1895. 288 pages, 36 illustrations, 4 colored plates. Second edition.
3. Newbigin, Marion. I. *Colour in Nature.* London: John Murray, 1898. 344 pages.

EDITORIAL NOTES

The aim of education in terms of community life is civic virtue. This is the cap sheaf. If, in a democracy, one fails as a citizen, nothing else can guarantee public service. In the earlier days of our history, when the blood was made hot by the irritating relations with the mother-country, and later when questions of territorial expansion and human slavery arose, the duties of the citizen were very closely related to those of the soldier. The trappings of war, made familiar to most people by the parade ground and by heroic description, appeal strongly to the imagination. By a proper presentation of such pictures it is easy enough to make every boy resolve to die for his country—when the time comes. It has been chiefly by such means that the spirit of our civic life has been engendered. It was developed by circumstances of which war was the central fact. Before these dramatic culminations, and for a long time after them, our wars have furnished the motive for a study of the duties of citizenship. But today the orations of Henry and the Adamses, of Clay, Calhoun, Webster, Phillips, and Sumner, have practically passed from our school literature. The masterful oratory of these men that once determined the channels of our national life is now taught to the pupils as the incident of history, utterly lacking in the vitalizing effect it once possessed. For the issues which they represented are dead; the questions that inspired the genius of those men were settled at Yorktown and Appomattox. The leaven of the Hague tribunal is beginning to work, and the real high-priest of our civilization in these days is not the devotee at the shrine of the warrior.

Training in Citizenship

Citizenship and the Soldier

The tendency is unmistakably toward universal peace, and in the education of the children it is much more important to keep in mind the civil qualifications of the voter than the martial characteristics of the soldier and marine. It is the vote and not the bullet that, hereafter, will transmute the theories of the citizen into the realities of practice,

Vote vs. Bullet

despite the fact that as a means of firing the young imagination the ballot-box is not to be compared with the gun.

Voting Remote from Children

Education into citizenship, like that toward any other goal, is a growth. Citizenship, as everything else, must gradually take shape from the experiences of life, and it follows, therefore, that its political aspects which are most closely related to the voter, and which are finally determined by him, are very remote from children. And yet the science which deals with the civil administration of the affairs of society, like every other science must have its roots in the simple experiences and relations of childhood. To the pedagogic analyst it is a matter of interesting research to discover what individual experiences of his pupils are related directly to those duties of citizenship which belong to their maturer years. To synthesize in a natural way from these experiences a civil code under which the individual may both give and receive the best from society, and under which society itself may best develop—that would seem to be the chiefest aim of the teacher.

Mimic Government

We used to begin our formal training for citizenship by having the pupils commit to memory the Constitution of the United States. This in itself was enough to incite a rebellion. The plan was often supplemented by establishing a kind of a scheme for self-government, so called, which was laid down upon the same general lines as those prescribed by the Constitution for the country at large. I can well recall having helped elect a president, and other officers belonging to the republic, and of having been chosen to Congress; of having assisted in establishing a supreme court and magistracies of lesser degree—all in a small-sized school. As a bit of by-play this was an interesting diversion, but it had really nothing to do with the citizenship that belonged to our years. The fact is, our plan finally fell through because nobody ever did anything that was wicked enough to get himself into trouble by starting our legal machinery in motion. We regarded our scheme of government as a kind of elaborate net that was spread to catch somebody—and our fish were all too small!

The study of civics is often approached from a point of view that is diametrically wrong. The negative side of life is over-emphasized. The children get the idea that government is wholly a matter of restraint; that it is a trap set to catch offenders. Whereas, it is no less its real purpose to aid directly the well-doer.

Government Not a Trap

It is this aspect of civics that should be kept uppermost in the minds of children. Everything that adds to economy and efficiency in the individual and in society pertains to good government and lies at the foundation of civics. It follows that the more opportunities the school offers for the children to put themselves into some piece of work of real value, the more clearly the essentials of good government will appear to them, and the more tractable they will become. It is not without deep significance in its bearing upon the theory of government that pupils are most difficult to control in those schools that provide least for the individual physical activities of the children, and the negations of government are fewest in those schools where a great variety of handwork abounds. And, still further, it is important to observe that schools for delinquent children are laying more and more stress upon manual training of various types as an indirect means of civic control. The foundations for this study are not, therefore, to be found in those external forms of a repressive character that impose themselves upon a school, but they are in those constructive acts of adjustment, positive in character, which are intended to promote the welfare of the individual and of the whole.

Relation to Industry

Control of Delinquents

Anything that is done in a community which bears upon the organization and administration of its affairs has to do with civics. Good citizenship implies in the child, as well as in the adult, that in some way he is able to affect favorably the general good. There is no other class in the community, equaling the schools in size, teachers and pupils, that exerts so little influence, directly, upon the civil organization. This fact is usually accounted for on the theory that civic influence can be exerted only *through* the

Test for a School

ballot, and there is no other equally large part of the community that is practically disfranchised. It is still true, however, that this body should have some kind of a civic influence that should be in evidence to the boundaries of the school district. A stranger approaching the school should know when he reaches these boundaries by the marks which this influence makes upon the general welfare. This is rarely true, because the maxim, "Learn to do by doing," has seldom been applied in the study of civics. That subject is still a matter of books, lectures, and theory.

Home Interests

The paramount interest of the child is in his home. This is the corner-stone of good citizenship, for the home is the unit of the national life. Upon the integrity of the home everything depends. It is for this reason that manual training and the crafts in all of their artistic and utilitarian forms may be a direct means of upbuilding a robust civic spirit, since the output can be immediately utilized in the home. This spirit would be immensely reinforced if the care of the grounds and home surroundings were also placed largely in the hands of the children. The public-spirited parents who support local improvement associations are robbing the community of one of its chief means of training the children in citizenship. In caring for their private grounds and the affairs of the household wholly, or almost so, with hired help, parents frequently deprive their children of the best means of putting themselves into direct touch with civic life. There is no estimating the benefits that children derive from such experiences, if the parents are also participants in this work. Children cannot and will not peform these duties alone, but they will gladly join with their parents. The command "Go" is rarely heeded; the invitation "Come" always is; that is the whole secret. The movement on the part of schools and of certain associations to enlist the interests of the children in home gardening is the best work in civics that has ever been undertaken for young people. If he is thoroughly trained in the care of his home, and if he have a well-developed civic taste, the voter is apt to deposit a ballot on the side of virtue in public life. If the parents who are the patrons of

Civics and Improvement Associations

THE UNIVERSITY ELEMENTARY SCHOOL would join with their children in the planting of flowers and vines on a plot of ground about the home, however small, and, where this is not possible, if window-boxes were used, it would not only transform a large section of our city into something beautiful, they would also place a mortgage on the future through the civic ideals which such work would create in their children.

Civic Training by Newspapers

In the general movement toward better things in citizenship, there is one instrumentality, that we have been accustomed to depend upon as a leading influence in civic training, that is not living up to its opportunities. It is the public press as represented by the daily papers. There is nothing more ambitious to be classed among the educational forces of a people than the daily newspaper, and yet it is the last thing that anybody would prescribe as a part of the curriculum in any school. It is difficult to say which is the more baneful in its influence, the matter that is published or the grossly vulgar form through which the ordinary sheet offers its wares to the eye. As a debaser of public taste and opinion there is nothing now, except the crime of the "bill-boards, that is equal to it. Although the papers claim that they are catering to the public, I have yet to meet the first man who is willing to give the yellow-journal methods his approval; I have yet to meet the first person who is willing to have the average daily turned over to his children. Besides, even though it were a matter of money, the newspaper men, as well as the school-teachers, are under obligations to put some conscience into their work. They have no more right to debauch public morals and to debase the taste of children than anyone else. It need not be argued that what the pupils get from the dailies by clandestine and unwholesome methods goes a long way toward undoing the work of the school-teacher.

The average newspaper seems to think that, in order to be reputable, a paper must be dull, and that to be bright and readable it must be shocking. It therefore crams its first page with the startling, the horrible, and the vulgar, set in type of such preposterous dimensions that a self-respecting man is ashamed to be found with a copy in his possession. The papers make a mistake. The public does not demand this—simply takes it because it must, and it does so under protest. The part of the public they seem to have most in mind is made up of the sports, the gamblers, and the sensation mongers. The papers do not commit the crimes they describe—not all of them—and therefore cannot be held responsible for them, but they are responsible for presenting them in such a way as to give the impression that practically everything on earth is rotten.

We need a new régime in editing. The first page should be devoted to a summary of the news, with a reference possibly to a fuller statement elsewhere. A large percentage of readers would never go beyond this page, unless personal interest led to a further investigation. The space now given to murders, prize fights, and other crimes could be cut to one-sixth the amount really used, and still tell all that anybody need to know. By having to read less the public might be induced to believe more.

Better Editing Needed

At present the editor and the school-teacher are working at cross-purposes. They should be together. The school-teacher is compelled to prepare his material so that decent people can feed upon it and grow better; there is no reason why the editor should not do the same. Both the press and the school live in the same world and deal with the same facts—it is all a matter of editing, a question of relative values, of perspective. It may be necessary for us to know the plain facts about crime that we may be ready to deal with it; but it is far more important to realize that the steady persistence of one honest man has a deeper significance in terms of citizenship and civilization than all the schemes and peculations of a thousand rogues. This is the chief article in the school-teachers' creed, which both the press and the school should magnify, for upon it rests our hope in the future civic life.

The Teacher vs. the Editor

W. S. J.

FRESCO MADE BY PUPILS OF THE TENTH SCHOOL YEAR, FROM LANDSCAPE STUDIES ON WOODED ISLAND, JACKSON PARK
(Placed above the blackboard of their room)

VOLUME VI NUMBER 10

THE ELEMENTARY SCHOOL TEACHER

JUNE, 1906

THE UNIVERSITY ELEMENTARY SCHOOL
THE YEAR IN REVIEW AND THE OUTLOOK

WILBUR S. JACKMAN
Principal

THE PROPER MEASURE OF A SCHOOL

The test of a school, like that of any other enterprise, is found in its output. Gathered together in the schoolrooms, in the persons of teachers and pupils, is a tremendous amount of vital energy which, as a rule, is still almost wholly unproductive. From this source the community expects but little help directly, and it gets even less. The real educational problem, therefore, would seem to be that of transforming the non-productive into the productive in some form that has an actual value to the community. It is the larger aspect of the old problem of making two blades of grass grow where but one grew before; and it is to this end that THE UNIVERSITY ELEMENTARY SCHOOL has largely directed its efforts during the past year. This conception of the function of a school need not obscure the fact that in the last analysis the educational output is a spiritual product; but we have learned by bitter experience to question severely the character of a spiritual product which does not manifest itself at once in some objective and tangible form having a definite and beneficent function. It is this idea that is at the bottom of the art, the industrial, and the civic work in the school.

COMMUNITY-INTERESTS AS SUBJECTS OF STUDY

In organizing the activities of the school community, it should be the aim to have represented, as far as possible, the interests that bind together the various elements of society at large. The chief difficulty encountered in doing this lies in the fact that the instant an industry or an art is introduced into the school-room the tendency is to erect it at once into a "subject of study." This means to the average person that it must have its special teacher, its abitrary place on the program, and in other ways take a definite setting in the curriculum. Now, there is a vast and an essential difference between this kind of so-called organization attempted by the school, and the actual organization which takes place in true community life. If, for example, under normal conditions, in the latter, a wagon is to be made, the various activities that contribute to that particular end are so correlated as to combine efficiency and economy. Everybody's efforts are directed to that result. There is just so much wood needed and no more. A premium is placed upon the endeavor to use as little as may be consistent with the character of the wagon desired. The same is true of the iron work—no more bolts or bands are made than are actually needed. So, also, it is with the paint; what the wood needs for its preservation and adornment is used, and nothing beyond. But bring these industries into school as "hand-work," and we find only so many more "subjects of study" that in some way must be juggled into an already overcrowded program; only so many more teachers that are to increase the wear and tear in already overwrought children. It is no longer a question of doing *just as little as is needed, but as much as possible!* It is as though the wagon-maker were to go ahead blindly and make a dozen wheels where only four can possibly be used; as though the blacksmith should forge a hundred pieces of iron where but twenty are needed; and as if the painter should demand forty hours for his work when five would be altogether adequate. We are in an incipient stage of development, where there is insufficient attention given to the relation between demand and supply. The work generally in any particular subject represents the strength and the personal push of the teachers, or the reverse. If by superior wit, or by greater cunning, or by sharpness of tooth or strength of claw the ambitious teacher is able to get a lion's share of the program, his particular subject may be correspondingly magnified, even to the detriment of all others.

The faculty of THE UNIVERSITY ELEMENTARY SCHOOL, recognizing to some extent the great need for a truer form of organization, has given a good deal of attention to the question, and the subject will probably be in the foreground of discussion for some time to come. Meanwhile, the public has no right to become testy or impatient because, so far, it has not yet made an astonishing success in organizing itself on the community plan; and the problems which face us in the schoolroom are not less difficult—they are, in fact, of precisely the same type.

THE BASIS OF ORGANIZATION

The cardinal principle to be observed in the newer organization of the school is that everything which the pupils do should be a genuine response to a real need. It must not only be a need that the child himself can appreciate; it must be one which, on its own merits, appeals to the teacher also. Whenever this is true, the work assumes its highest possible educational value. To illustrate: A member of the Civics Club of the ELEMENTARY SCHOOL came to the office a few days ago and said: "We have been looking over the building, and we think there should be a waste-basket put upon each landing on the stairways. We believe that, if this were done, the pupils coming down from the lunchroom would not scatter wrappers and other scraps of paper on the stairs, as they now do." This was a suggestion well worthy of the oldest and the wisest head in the school. Such work makes the pupils participants in the vital interests of the whole; through these opportunities they actually partake in a perfectly natural and genuine way in the real life of the place, and the chief virtues desired in human character receive a direct and lasting stimulus. As we multiply such opportunities for co-operation between the teacher and the pupils, the school becomes less a matter of aimless play, on the one hand, and less a matter of dull drudgery, on the other; it becomes a scene of normal activity and a field for reasonable accomplishment. The relationship of *mutual* helpfulness between pupil and teacher is vitally important. The feeling on the part of the pupil that he can actually do something which the teacher cannot do for himself at once transforms him from a time-serving lesson-learner into a real social factor. The year just passed has still further demonstrated what tremendous possibilities there are in children for accomplishing things that have intrinsic and lasting merit in the fields of civics, industry, and art. It has also emphasized how trifling still are the demands which the school makes upon the pupils for creative work that has a permanent value.

TYPE OF TEACHER THAT IS NEEDED

The plan of reorganization here proposed requires teachers of fine training and insight, who can discern and properly estimate values. There is no greater obstacle to progress than the "special teacher," so called, of narrow attainments. The high-school graduate who begins at once to "specialize" in some training-school for teachers is the particular pest that is just now most to be dreaded, discountenanced, and avoided. It is this type of specialist that insists on the pupils' making five wheels for a wagon. The specialist we must have, it is true; not the one, however, who pretends to know a single subject, though never so well, but rather one who has sufficient breadth of vision to see the whole educational situation from his particular and special point of view. The kind of teacher needed, now as never before, is found in the ideal citizen; one who is in vital touch with the demands of life, and who knows how to work with people—including the children—in finding the supply. We educate only as we train the children to consider the fields of nature, of history, of literature, and of art as original sources of materials that are demanded by the public welfare. The so-called specialist of today *deliberately and purposely limits his pupil to one field,* and too often to but a small part of that. Under such instruction people cannot grow up otherwise than circumscribed in view and prejudiced in judgment. On the contrary, every teacher must know how to tap the primal sources of strength that lie on all sides, and how to train his pupils to turn toward them and appropriate them for his personal needs of growth and for the general weal.

A careful review of the year justifies the observation that we have advanced only as we have learned to discriminate more closely between artificial and genuine needs, and as we have displayed insight in appraising the relative values of subject-matter as a means of supplying them. Every study on our program can be scaled as to its importance in the school and as to its hold upon the pupils according to these two criteria.

The tremendous development of all the industrial work in the direction of both utility and art is due to the fact that both teachers and pupils have found a place in human life—in their lives—hitherto unoccupied, that needs filling, and they have proceeded to fill it.

SCHOOL WORK HAS A VALUE PROPORTIONED TO THE PERMANENCY OF ITS OUTPUT

It is most instructive to note how much the fact of permanency has enhanced the value of certain lines of study. While the work with clay, for example, was confined to models that were allowed to dry up and crumble away, the subject had almost no significance in the school. The use of the kiln, however, and the adoption of processes for reproducing the modeled forms in plaster, have aroused an interest in the subject, and given it an energy and directive intelligence, that in earlier days were unknown. Similarly, the work in wood has advanced enormously, not only in the quantity, but also in the quality, of the product, as the pupils have vitalized their efforts with the idea of making things that are *permanent* as well as *useful* and beautiful. The same may be said of textiles. Cooking to a pre-eminent degree enlists the best efforts of the pupils, as the results have an immediate and recognized value in both the school and the home, and by teachers as well as by parents and pupils. It is interesting, also, to observe how easily the pupils solve the much-vexed problem as to the relation of utility to art. They instinctively avoid the ugly in the work, as though it were a kind of maladaptation to the end desired. Every movement is toward the artistic, and under intelligent instruction in design they, seemingly without much conscious effort, blend the useful and the artistic into a harmonious unity.

THE ORGANIZATION OF SCHOOL CLUBS

At the opening of the spring quarter the teachers adopted a plan that was designed to break down somewhat the barriers formed by the grading system, and to offer additional opportunity for the display of initiative on the part of the pupils. This is in line with the discussion of the subject in last year's handbook. The school, as a whole, regardless of age, was given the privilege of organizing itself into some eighteen groups or clubs. The central idea of each club was developed in part by the teachers, and the matter was laid before the pupils with the statement that each one could choose the line of work which he wished to pursue. The following is the list of clubs, with the number of members in each: Civics, 18; Wood-Working, 17; Gymnastics, 44; Metal-Working, 16; Cooking, 33; Bookbinding, 9; Camera, 12; Field Club, 16; Dancing, 18; Sketching, 13; Dramatics, 13; School Paper, 8; Electricity, 18; Garden, 9; Tool-House Construction, 12; Textiles, 10; Clay-Modeling, 30; Microscope, 2.

Inasmuch as it was anticipated that some of the clubs would be too large if all were assigned according to their first choice, it was deemed wise to ask the pupils to name their second and their third choices also. In the main, however, the clubs represent the first choice of the children. As the plan was so new to all of them, there were, of course, a number who made mistakes in selecting their work; when it seemed advisable, such children were permitted to change before the clubs were really organized; but when once under way, transfers on all grounds were prohibited.

It has happened in this case, as it always does, that where the real responsibility was placed upon the children themselves, their steadiness and all-around efficiency have been worthy of note and a matter of astonishment to the teachers. The spirit, generally, was that manifested by a little boy in the early stages of organization of one of the clubs, who, becoming somewhat impatient with the proceedings, rose and said: "Well, I move that we *do* something."

As it was to be expected, the significance of the movement was not apprehended equally well by all the teachers nor by all the pupils. On the side of the faculty it revealed, as nothing else could have done, how firmly fixed upon us is the traditional attitude of the teacher toward the class. This was shown by the disposition to "step in" and assume responsibility, when really the teacher should have "stepped out." The essence of the whole plan is that the club shall assume the entire responsibility, and the teacher shall have no more authority or influence, necessarily, than any other member. The teachers have given the plan their heartiest support, but the greatest obstacle to success on their side is the inherited and acquired disposition to "boss." On the side of the children, with many, the individualistic and selfish motive was strong. They wanted to make use of the club to further personal ends; whereas the cardinal idea is that of being able to make some contribution to the welfare of the whole.

The work in many of the clubs, however, has been exceptionally good. The school has been distinctly helped by the Civics Club that has devoted much attention to the care of the building and grounds, and they are creating a healthy public spirit in the school at large. The Tool-House Club is building a much-needed storeroom for the garden implements. It is a frame structure, about twelve by sixteen feet. The Garden Club has been industrious in trimming up the trees and bushes, and in doctoring those that were badly trimmed in previous years. The Dramatic Club is preparing to make a contribution in kind to the approaching spring festival in the garden. The Dancing Club is preparing the May Pole and other dances for the occasion. The Press Club is publishing regularly *The Elementary School Reporter*—a small paper edited by themselves and published under their direction. They make it pay expenses through advertising and subscriptions.

One interesting result of the club organization has been to bring together in something of a common interest children of widely different ages. In the Textile Club the membership includes pupils from the fifth, seventh, and tenth years. The Sketching Club contains those from the fourth, seventh, eighth, ninth, and tenth years; the Clay-Modeling Club, from the second to eighth, and so on. Once in a while, as might be expected, there is an atavistic outcrop toward grade conditions, but generally the association of the older and younger has shown some distinct advantages. There is no doubt that we suffer an enormous social loss in our schools from the fact that the grading system effectually prevents the development of any bonds of sympathy between the older and younger pupils. The clubs have been useful in revealing the school as a state of society. This was brought out in the work of the clubs themselves, and through discussion in the town-meetings held by the pupils and in the conferences of the faculty. They have shown a social condition of which the ordinary classroom work gives almost no indication. The clubs have disclosed the selfishness on the one hand, and the clannishness on the other, as well as a certain amount of public-spiritedness, which one finds in the community at large. These inner aspects of the pupils' character are almost untouched by the prescribed classroom work. It is only when the children begin to act for themselves, and when they endeavor to enhance those actions through organization of their own, that character growth really takes place. It is only as the school furnishes the opportunity for such work and such organization that it becomes a help and not a hindrance to mental and moral development.

The proper unfolding of the club idea requires an insight and training that is of a distinctly higher type than that now possessed by the average parents and teachers. The former, more or less unwittingly no doubt, instil into the minds of their children the same feelings of indifference toward the needs of the school as a social organization that they themselves exhibit toward the interests of the general public. The teachers, on their side, know too little about actual citizenship. They are too easily disconcerted by the inevitable turmoil which is created when the children really enter upon the work of self-organization. They are too apt to long for the peace of the "well-ordered" classroom which is made possible when each pupil works for himself and all are under the complete domination of the teacher.

The sole purpose of the club is to develop a public spirit that shall correspond to, and even outrun, the public need. The children must have, therefore, the inspiration and help that can come only from a teacher who is alert and sensitive to the demands of the school community and the community at large. He must understand democracy and be a thorough believer in it.

Crude and imperfect as the work with the clubs has been this year, it is a consensus of opinion on the part of both pupils and teachers that it must be continued in some form. The plan will be modified so as to give the pupils more completely their freedom. As a need appears, in either the school or the community, the pupils that so desire will be given opportunity to organize themselves for the purpose of supplying it. When the end is accomplished, the club may then dissolve, and a new issue may be taken up by another organization. The usefulness of the clubs has been demonstrated; it only remains to develop during the coming year a more effective plan of administration.

THE OLDER SUBJECTS IN THE CURRICULUM

In the radical reorganization of the curriculum which, through the slow processes of evolution, is now taking place, a question perennially green is: "What is to be the future of such studies as history, geography, arithmetic, English, spelling, grammar, and others that have formed, traditionally, the core of the course of study? It must be remembered that evolution involves not only the modification, but also the extinction, of many existing forms. Both of these operations are actually taking place in the schools. Some parts of arithmetic, fomerly considered important, have become extinct; as for instance, alligation, true discount, and partial payments. It is safe to say that corresponding eliminations are taking place in all the other subjects named. In spite of vigorous protest, the inclination is decidedly toward less, rather than more, formal grammar, and the sequel will show that the tendency is correct. And after a while our English will be all the better for it. That will be when we learn how to make it less of a misfit in the pupil's life. There is not another subject in the whole school course, from the kindergarten to the junior year in college, that is taught with the same uniform lack of regard for the actual experiences of the learners. In the whole of this long, long period there is scarcely an exercise in English that is not written, chiefly, that the teacher may have a chance to criticise the form—let him deny it who will! It is the lowest possible motive under which the human mind can act, and the results in the pupil's character correspond.

During the past year I happened to be present at a meeting of the junior class of a high school. The president announced that one of the members wished to make a statement to the class concerning the need for funds for some school enterprise, and this is the way the young man delivered himself: "Now see here, I just want to say that you fellows have got to hustle up and get some money. You can't expect two or three fellows to rustle round and do all the work, for they can't do it. The sophomore class last week got a move on and got a lot of advertising, and we've got to do the same. So I want you fellows to wake up and get busy."

This young gentleman represented about three years of high-school English, in addition to the training he had received in some elementary school, all of which, of course, stands for the best that all the numerous college-entrance requirements committees have been able to bring forth in two decades. The real irony of the matter is in the fact that he will probably go up to some college next year and answer all the stock questions which they choose to ask him on *The Faerie Queen*, *The Nun's Tale*, the *Roger de Coverley Papers*, and the sanity of Hamlet; and he may pull through even if he is called upon to sketch in "his own words" some character in *Silas Marner* or George Eliot. To be sure, there will be a wail later when some accident like the class-meeting episode unmasks the young man; but the college should not complain—he gave them what they asked for! The pity is, however, that out of it all the boy gets so little for himself.

It is not the intention here to underestimate the value of good literature in education; it is only intended to show that the present common use of it as a means of teaching English in the earlier stages of development is but little better than a farce. To a perpetuation of this serio-comic procedure in education we must refuse to be a party.

When the thinking of the pupil makes the same direct demand

for expression in English that it now makes for forms in metal, wood, clay, and textile fabrics, then, and not till then, will language become equally clear, graphic, and artistic. The malady affecting the young man here described is not to be reached by an additional dose of technical rules, nor by further attention to the classics; but rather by cultivating a thoroughgoing respect for his own thinking. Like every other form of art, English is a matter of taste, and taste is not a concern of rules, but of thinking. As before noted in connection with clay-modeling, the quality of permanency has a tremendous effect upon a pupil's effort. Children are frequently asked to write something about nothing; this is done upon any kind of a scrap of paper with any kind of pen or pencil; this is later inspected, "blue-penciled," and sent eventually to the waste-basket. There is not a step in the procedure that is not intellectually and morally downward. Instead of compelling the pupils to write for the sake of their English, it would be far better for their English if they were not permitted to write except when they had something to say which must be written, and which when written must be preserved. To this end it is proposed during the coming year to devise some means for binding all written work in a permanent and artistic form, and greatly to extend the use of the printing-press as a further means of giving to this form of expression a higher and more genuine value.

THOROUGHNESS IN SCHOOL WORK

The application of the principles herein discussed is in no wise inimical to all the thoroughness that a given subject may demand at any particular age. It may not preclude the possibility, or even the necessity, of drill. If in his cooking lesson the pupil finds out that there are two pints of milk in a quart, there is no reason why the fact should not be fixed in the mind. The sane teacher will not become panic-stricken, however, if such facts are not at once readily remembered. If he finds, after the frequent recurrence of similar operations, that the facts still escape, he will as a last resort give it the special attention secured by drill.

The most discouraging struggle in the schoolroom is with the spelling. While it is believed that our children are learning to spell more words than their elders did in the days when the spelling book reigned, the hopelessness of the task lies in the unphonetic character of the language. We are dutifully teaching the pupils to spell correctly, but it is no part of our intentions or duty to teach them to respect the traditions that place upon their shoulders such a heavy and useless burden. It is our ambition, rather, to send every pupil out of the school charged with the mission to do what he can to strengthen and hasten the great work undertaken by the Committee on Spelling Reform.

The year now closing has been full of encouragement. The school is particularly fortunate in securing a deep interest on the part of the patrons, who through the Parents' Association have most effectively supported the labors of the teachers. Without the generous spirit of tolerance and co-operation which marks the attitude of all the patrons, the solution of the difficult problems which rise in the school would be practically impossible.

Our school, owing to its newness, has been handicapped in some measure by the absence of all traditions among the pupils. During the years past, however, customs and habits have become established upon the lines that lead toward steadiness of effort, and much has been done to create in the children those feelings of pride and self-respect that are the most precious possessions of any school.

The paramount interest in our institution at this time lies in readjustment. The school is slowly changing its organization from a competitive to a co-operative form, and it is endeavoring to do this without impairing the vitality of individual initiative. The movement necessitates constant resurveys of scholastic values, and the new estimates given frequently do violence to academic traditions, and cause apprehension. The needed and sufficient safeguards are found in the directive function of the trained teacher who can intelligently comprehend the organizing forces at work in society at large, and who will conscientiously heed the children's responses to these forces as they make themselves felt in the schoolroom.

THE DRAMATIC CLUB IN THE SPRING FESTIVAL
The Musicians of Bremen, Scene 1
(An original adaptation as played in the Garden Theater)

THE DRAMATIC CLUB IN THE SPRING FESTIVAL
The Musicians of Bremen, Scene 2

OUTLINE OF WORK FOR THE YEAR 1906–7

DIVISION A

KINDERGARTEN, FIRST AND SECOND SCHOOL YEARS

Many of the children in a kindergarten enter at the age of three years and remain for three years; hence, to avoid repetition, it seems to be necessary to change at least the phase of the subjects considered from year to year. The center about which the work and play of the kindergarten gather is found in the home life in some of its aspects, and in a few of the activities most closely associated with the home, such as the work of the grocer, the milkman, and the postman. To this are added some other social phases of neighborhood life. An outline can do little else than suggest the possible subjects to be considered, and can show even less of the adaptation of these subjects to the needs of each group of children. The arbitrary divisions into history, nature-study, etc., found below are made only to connect more closely the work of the kindergarten with that of the other groups of the school.

History.—Autumn Quarter: Subject—homes. Some of the things that contribute to the making of a comfortable, convenient home. (1) The house; rooms; closets. (2) The work contributed by each member of the household. (3) Thanksgiving and Christmas as celebrated at home. (4) Surroundings of the home: back yard; homes of animals in back yard. (5) What the farm contributes to the home (drawing on the country experiences of the children during the past summer).

Winter Quarter: Subject—grocer, milkman, postman. Equipment of a home in light, heat, water supply, telephones, bells; winter sports and industries.

Spring Quarter: Spring cleaning; the cleaning and beautifying of our homes, yards, and parks; making a school garden; relation of the market gardener to the home.

Science or nature-study.—Autumn and Winter Quarters: The areas around which the year's work centers are: (1) garden, (2) lake-shore, (3) the Midway, (4) Washington and Jackson Parks. Observations: daily changes of weather—sun, clouds, rain, frost, wind, snow; seasonal changes—effect of frost on plant life, animals, and people; movement of sun (by noting through which windows we have the sunlight); habits of late birds; gathering seeds, and watching how they are distributed, as we go to the parks or lake; study of nuts, fruits, and vegetables, according to the way they may be preserved and stored for the winter; collections of cocoons, leaves, and seed; noting the effect of frost on all vegetable life.

Spring Quarter: Effect of warm winds and sun on the earth; effect of moisture, heat, and light, on growth of seeds, incidentally noted; return of birds and insects; work of bees in the garden begun; earthworms and their work in the earth; ants; spring flowers noticed as they appear.

Literature.—Rhymes and Poetry: From Lear, *Nonsense Rhymes* and *Mother Goose:* "Hickory Dickory Dock," "Sing a Song of Six-pence," "Little Bo-peep," "Mary, Mary, Quite Contrary," "Jack, Be Nimble," "Old King Cole," and others; Christini Rossetti: "Mix a Pancake," "What Does the Donkey Bray About?" "What Does the Bee Do?" (from *Sing Song*); Robert Louis Stevenson: "The Rain is Raining," "Birdie With the Yellow Bill," "When I Was down Beside the Sea," "The Swing," "My Shadow."

Stories: From *Six Nursery Classics,* edited by O'Shea; "The Old Woman and the Six-pence," "Chicken Little," "The Three Bears;" from Dasent, *Stories from the Field:* "The Pancake," "The Pig and the Sheep," "The Lad Who Went to the North Wind;" from Dasent, *Popular Tales from the North:* "Billy Goats Gruff;" "The Gingerbread Man;" Thaxter: "Peggy's Garden and What Grew Therein;" Helen Hunt Jackson: "St. Christopher;" adapted from Cary: "Peter at the Dike;" Æsop: "The Lion and the Mouse."

Gift-work.—Building with large and small blocks—houses, rooms, closets, furniture; basements and furnishings; designing with tablets, sticks, and lentels; floor and wall papers; making steam- and gas-pipes, furnaces, and radiators with second gift beads and sticks; building fences and outhouses for yards; swings, see-saws, horizontal bars, toboggan slides; chicken yards and houses; doghouses built for back yards and parks.

Hand-work.—Christmas presents; work incidental to the celebration of Hallowe'en, Thanksgiving, and Christmas. The construction and furnishing of a basement, a kitchen, and possibly a bathroom in a pasteboard box with the simplest possible form of water- and heat-piping—for the basement, a furnace, coal-bins, and laundry; for the kitchen, the stove, boiler, and radiator or register; for the bathroom, the usual equipment. Making of telephones; valentines, May baskets, and garden stakes, and possibly the simplest little flat boats, made in the manual-training room.

Modeling.—Autumn Quarter: Dishes, kitchen utensils, flower-pots, tea-rests, marbles, seeds, and fruits.

Winter Quarter: Furnaces, pipes, gas and electric chandeliers, telephones.

Spring Quarter: Birds, nests, twigs, vegetables; illustrating story or poem.

Cooking.—Used only as a social industry, and employed by the teacher with the children as the mother in the home would use it. Its special function in the Autumn Quarter is in the preparation for a Thanksgiving celebration of grape-juice, jelly, and cookies, or for Christmas candies, and popcorn balls, or for Valentine heart cookies in the winter.

Rhythm and games.—Simplest skipping, marching, and running; simplest ensemble dances; romping games: of skip and hop tag, changing chairs; "Chickemy, Chickemy, Craney Crow," "The Little Mice Are Hiding," "Cat and Mouse;" Rythmic games: making and throwing snowballs, skating, seesawing, swinging, wind-mills, pendulums, rocking-chair and boat movements; "The Farmer in the Dell," "London Bridge;" races; nature games; dramatizing stories.

Painting.—Fruits, vegetables, wall-paper designs, or in all-over washes, with paper-cutting units pasted in different designs —flowers, plants, etc.

Number.—Used as a limitation in single groups and combinations, and used constantly in building, making, and designing at the table and in the games.

Music.—Exercises in tone-placing in plays of whistles and bells, simple scales, songs, and exercises; appropriate songs from kindergarten and primary song-books by Eleanor Smith, Jessie Gaynor, Patty and Mildred Hill, and Mrs. Crosby Adams; Elliot's *Mother Goose.*

DIVISION B

SECTION 3 (THIRD SCHOOL YEAR)

During the year following the kindergarten, the attempt will be made to help the children to understand the activities around them under the general headings of food, clothing, and shelter.

History.—The work is closely related to the social occupations of the children, cooking, gardening, and playhouse-making. These lead into a study of various forms of shelter, and modes of living among peoples of primitive conditions.

The children will work in two groups, their subject-matter differing somewhat, one group constructing a miniature farm and the other a playhouse. It is hoped that in this way each group may gain something of the experience of the other.

The basis for the study of the farm will be the children's experiences in the country and a visit to a farm in the neighborhood in the early fall. Some products will be traced in their production and transportation to the city. General activities of farm life will be relived in dramatic plays and games.

The other group of children will show with building-blocks, stick-laying, and chalk lines on the floor something of the appearance and arrangement of their own homes, and will then make plans for a large playhouse. Each child will make a model in paper or cardboard of the house he would like. After the best plan is selected, the house will be made for them.

During this time of preparation for their playhouse, they will visit houses and buildings in process of erection, and observe the various kinds of work required. In addition, the children will study the different building materials, look into the lumbering industry, and, if possible, visit a quarry and brickyard.

When the playhouse frame is finished, they will paint the outside, paper and decorate the walls, make rugs of coarse materials, and fit up the rooms with furniture of wood. By working with not more than two children to each room of the house, it is hoped there will be a chance for individual taste and initiative.

In order to give a little more color and significance to their thought of their own homes, the building materials and kinds of shelter used in extreme climates will be touched upon, as, for instance, the snow houses of the Eskimos, and rush huts of the tropics. The shelter and general life of the American Indians will be gone into in more detail. In this connection the children will visit the Field Museum.

Wood.—During the autumn the new children will need to learn the handling of tools, and also the necessity for careful measuring and accurate work. They will make name-tags for drinking-cups, and dressing-room hooks, boxes for school materials, and some simple Christmas presents. Later the furnishings of the playhouse will fill the time of one group. (See history outline.)

The other group will make farm buildings, house, barn, sheep-fold, chicken-coops, etc. They will also make sheds and help the other children with the playhouse furniture.

Home economics.—Home economics in this year has an important place in furnishing a social activity that appeals strongly to the children. It aims to give experience with different foods and processes, and to develop muscular control. It demands reading, writing, and especially number, in order that its activities may be carried on.

Cooking: Baked apples; apples cooked in syrup; dried fruits stewed; lemonade; fruit lemonade; sherbet. Different ways of thickening liquid: by gelatine, as illustrated in lemon jelly; by sugar, in cranberry jelly; by eggs, in baked custard. Making of cocoa, sandwiches, and doing other cooking demanded by the social life of the children. The beginning of the care of the house in the setting of tables and serving of simple luncheons.

Science: Study of different kinds of apples and the effect of heat upon them; meaning of the fruit to the plant; fruit juices;

replacing of water in dried fruits. Boiling- and freezing-points of water; observation of the solution in water of different substances. Hot and cold water as a solvent.

Clay-modeling.—Fruits, animals, etc., to illustrate work in nature-study, history, and literature; bowls, cups, trays, etc., for Christmas gifts. The aim is to give much opportunity for expressing freely in so plastic a medium as clay, and incidentally to develop a more definite feeling for shape.

English.—(1) Literature: Rhymes and poetry: Lear's *Nonsense Rhymes* and *Mother Goose;* repetition of those given in kindergarten; Christina Rossetti: "What is Pink?" "Brown and Furry," "If a Pig Wore a Wig;" Robert Louis Stevenson: "Bed in Summer," "The Wind," "Foreign Children," "The Whole Duty of Children," "The Cow," "Singing;" "Little Gustava," Celia Thaxter, "I'll Tell You How The Leaves Come Down," Susan Coolidge.

Stories: From Dasent's *Popular Tales from the Norse:* "Boots and His Brothers," "Princess on the Glass Hill," "Gudbrand on the Hillside," "Why the Bear is Stumpy Tailed;" adapted from Grimm: "The Wolf and the Seven Young Kids," "Cinderella;" from Grimm's *Fairy Tales:* "The Shoemaker and the Elves," "One Eye, Two Eyes, and Three Eyes," "The Town Musicians;" from Howell's *Christmas Every Day in the Year and Other Stories:* "The Pony Engine," Christmas Every Day in the Year;" "The Sleeping Beauty," "Perrault," "The Gingerbread Man;" Whittier's *Child Life in Verse;* "The Bell of Atri," Baldwin, *Fifty Famous Stories Retold;* "German Legend of the First Christmas," *St. Nicholas;* "The Birth of Christ," read from Luke; *Fables of Aesop:* "The Wind and the Sun," "The Lion and the Mouse."

(1) *Reading.—Mother Goose,* published by D. C. Heath; *Heart of Oak,* No. I.

(2) Reading and language: The children will see constantly words and sentences in connection with their work on the blackboard. Through much repetition they will learn to recognize some words and be able to follow simple written directions. Work in phonics is begun and is carried on throughout the

year. They will learn the sounds of all the consonants, and many of the simpler combinations of vowel and consonant, such as *ig, in, et, it, ill,* etc. Recipes and directions will be written and printed in large chart form.

The children will begin to read from printed slips and simple readers. They will make and have printed a kind of calendar of the various "signs of spring."

During the year they will dramatize Mother Goose rhymes, fables, "The Three Bears," and "The Sleeping Beauty."

(3) Writing and spelling: The writing will at first be entirely board work, and will consist of words and short sentences and numbers in connection with other work. There will also be much free-hand exercise. Free-hand exercises extended to paper with large crayons or charcoal. Short records will be kept of cooking and weather observations.

Whatever of spelling there is during this year will be in this reproduction of words written on the board, and in the making of words in phonic drill. It is probable that by the end of the year the children will have mastered the spelling of many of the common words through constant repetition in writing and reading.

Music.—One of the first and principal objects with these children is to train them to *hear* musical tones. They will learn to sing the scale with syllables. They will write the scale and simple scale songs. The seasons, festivals, and general work in the grade will determine the songs to be learned by rote.

Nature-study.—Basis: actual work with pets, gardening, and excursions. The children will have a hen, raise chickens, provide these with shelter and food.

Gardening: The yard at the east end of the building is assigned to this grade. The soil is prepared by the older grades. The children will plant flowers and ivy, and set bulbs for spring flowering; water, weed, etc. Window-boxes outside in summer, and in the house in winter, will give opportunities for closer acquaintance with some plants. The children will lay out a miniature farm, planting appropriate grains and vegetables.

Visits will be made to the school garden, Jackson Park, and

the lake-shore. On these trips the children will gather whatever material that pleases them—stones, seeds, flowers, etc. From the excursions they will gain acquaintance with some birds, as the robin, bluebird, and woodpecker, with cocoons, butterflies, ants, etc. Some seeds gathered may be placed in envelopes and kept for use in the spring; some may be used for decoration.

In connection with the history work, some of the domestic animals of our homes and of the farm will be studied, as the horse, cow, dog, cat, and sheep. By weekly paintings of outdoor scenes the children will notice the gradual change in color.

The "burning glass" may be shown. Simple experiments with paper will show the intensity of light at different windows (this with reference to placing window-boxes). Direction of the wind noticed in play; weather-vane on the building.

Geography.—Meteorological observations are made daily and records kept of temperature, sunshine, clouds, rain, frost, and direction of the wind. The children will observe the changes in the length of day and night. Through noting the direction of the wind, the children learn to orient themselves in the immediate vicinity, and are led to observe the directions followed upon the excursions taken. These are used in the sand models which the children make of the places visited.

In connection with the study of building materials, the children learn to recognize some stones, such as limestone, sandstone, and granite.

The consideration of the shelters of peoples of extreme climates leads to graphic picturing of some details of these regions, as barren or snowy fields of polar regions, luxuriant tropical vegetation, grassy plains, and forested hills.

Excursions are taken to the south shore, Beverly Hills, a farm, Washington Park conservatory, and a stone quarry.

Mathematics.—The making of the playhouses requires much excellent number work. Most of the number work is incidental to this making, and it is only when the opportunity seems fitting that certain facts or processes are fixed by special drill. It is hoped that by the end of the quarter the children will have learned to use: (1) all combinations of numbers under 12; (2) units of measure, inch and foot; (3) half-inch and half-foot; (4) the reading of the thermometer which necessitates counting to 100 by 1's, 2's, and 10's.

The cooking brings in another use of number. The children will use, generally, the cup as a unit of measure, and will become familiar with one-half, one-third, one-fourth, two-thirds, and three-fourths. They will also learn to tell the time in connection with sun-rising and setting.

Attention will be given to the writing of numbers and the signs of addition and subtraction; measuring in feet and yards in garden.

Drawing and painting.—At six the seeing is indefinite and general even at its best. It seems to be important to introduce the children to a wide range of visual material, rather than to force the accuracy of observation in any one direction. The subject-matter includes the seasonal coloring of plants and landscape, the illustration of the dramatic incidents of the history and literature and the decoration of such articles as the children have occasion to make during the school year, as portfolios, Christmas presents, valentines, invitations, etc. The materials used are water-colors with large brushes, chalks, and charcoal. The technic of the year includes the use of large washes, mixing of green, orange, violets, recognition of at least two values of light and dark, and the co-ordination necessary to render the action in silhouette of animals and the human figure. While the dominant motive of this age is the utilitarian, there is an unconscious exercise of the æsthetic instinct, and it is the intention to develop this in all of the work which has been indicated.

Gymnastics.—Marching, running, body movements and breathing, jumping and games; short daily periods; work arranged to require little form or application; largely initiative; proportion of formal work to jumping and games one-third. Music accompanies all parts of the lesson. Games of sense, inexact imitation, of no purpose, of variety of motion, and games involving all the players. One lesson each week in rhythm. Relation of directions and the different parts of the body discovered; their relation to various musical rhythms.

DIVISION B

SECTION 4 (FOURTH SCHOOL YEAR)

Industrial history.—City children of today have food and clothing at their disposal, with very little appreciation of their sources, the processes by which they come to hand, or the labor involved. To give an understanding of the interrelation of workers and the consecutive steps in the process which puts these necessities at our doors is the immediate aim of the industrial history of the second grade.

Excursions will be taken to a farm, to South Water Street, Booth's fish-market, a wholesale grocery, the Rush Street docks, an express depot, and a wholesale bakery. These put before the children effectively Chicago's food supply, its sources, and its means of transportation. To bring these conditions into forms within the comprehension of children, stories of simple and primitive life are told. Waterloo's *Story of Ab* is told in considerable detail, allowing the children to work out primitive means of milling, harvesting, fire-making, cooking, pottery-making, stone and shell tool-making, etc.

During the year the children are given experience in spinning, dyeing, and weaving (see "Textiles" below). In this connection they study the history of clothing and of shepherd life, considering how a hunter people might become a shepherd people. This type of life is illustrated by stories of the shepherds of Palestine, Arabia, Greece, and Switzerland. Trips are taken to the Field Museum, a carpet-weaver's, the Hull House Industrial Museum, Marshall Field's rug department, and a wholesale tailoring establishment.

The next step in history, and that which gives background to their garden-making, is the transition of a nomad, hunter, or shepherd people into an agricultural permanent community. The lake-dwellers of Switzerland are taken as a type, and their story is told as adapted from Kellers' *Lake Dwellers of Switzerland.* Trips are taken to a farm, to the Field Museum, to the McCormick Reaper Works, and to the office of a patent lawyer, where models of agricultural implements can be seen. (For reading in this connection see that heading below.)

Nature-study and geography.—A pair of ring doves has been given to the children. They will build a house in the garden for them, and take full charge of them. In the house they have a canary, the plan being to add a female in the spring and to raise a family if possible.

Gardening: Flower-beds on the east side of the building; planting of ivy and of window-boxes; a tree nursery; planting from seeds; a part of the wild-flower garden will be the gardening for this year. The work will aim to give daily experience with the simplest phenomena of plant life, to preserve the personal attitude of the child toward nature, and to develop more and more his responsibility to all living things.

The following trips will be taken: To the beach south of the German building, the Wooded Island in Jackson Park, South Shore, Stewart Ridge, Flossmoor, Beverly Hills, Dune Park, and Glencoe; the harbor and lighthouse at the mouth of the Chicago river, the life-saving station in Jackson Park, and the shipyards in South Chicago.

The children will make fire and cook outdoors, build huts from available outdoor materials, and play in a swift flowing brook.

Through the field trips, and the study of material collected upon these trips, the children get personal experience with various means of seed distribution, the life-history of frogs and moths, hibernating habits, habitat and food of animals placed in an aquarium, names and some characteristics of common minerals, names and places to look for the following common wild flowers: hepaticas, spring beauties, violets, mandrakes, and trilliums; names and some habits of the following birds: bluebird, blue jay, woodpecker, red-winged blackbird, summer warbler, catbird, nuthatch, brown creeper, and thrush.

Children observe the directions followed upon the trips, and adhere to these in the sand models which they make of the trip upon their return. These form the beginning of map-making.

The making of a sun dial and the keeping of time by means of the shadow of the house on the stone wall about the school give definite observations of the movement of the sun.

Out-of-door paintings of the landscape once a week will

give a graphic picture of the change of seasons during the year.

The domestication of animals forms an important study in connection with the history of shepherd life (see "History"). We shall aim to tame our doves and canaries, thus showing the underlying principle of domestication—patient kindness.

Mathematics.—The aim in this work is to put mathematical power in the hands of the children just so far as they need to use it. Drill will be given at the time that the need for a fact or a process arises. The following processes are demanded, and should be so mastered as to be used with skill and accuracy: (1) counting, reading, and writing of figures to 100; (2) addition of two columns of figures and subtraction of quantities under 100; (3) recognition of pieces of money; (4) counting by two's to 100; (5) adding of simple mixed numbers; (6) use of halves, fourths, thirds, eighths, twelfths, and sixteenths of one thing and of a few things; (7) making of plans to a scale; (8) use of gram and square inch as units of measure; (9) construction of square, oblong, right triangle, equilateral triangle, circle, and hexagon.

These principles and relations are involved in the actual work to be done as follows: (1), (2), and (3) are used in keeping accounts; (4), in reading and recording of thermometer and plotting of curve; (5), (6), (7), in construction of portfolio, dictionary, Christmas presents, plan of garden, mineral box and bags; (8), in science work, weighing and measuring, and in construction of mineral box; (9) in laying of garden in circular and rectangular beds, making of paper weights in geometric forms, devising of valentines and May baskets, and use of these forms in designs.

Textiles.—The children will experiment in shearing, spinning, dyeing, and weaving of wool. They will examine oriental rugs and experiment to reproduce a similar weaving effect. These rugs will be made for the playhouses of the younger children in the school. They will design and make hangings for the French window, a frieze of stenciled burlap for the wall space above the blackboard, and a bag with design in cross-stitch to be used on field excursions.

Clay-modeling.—The first half-year the modeling will be in close relation to the nature-study work. The children will design, model, color, and glaze paper-weights to be used as Christmas gifts. These will be in geometric forms, the unit of design being some natural form found on the field trips and of interest in itself.

They will make typical scenes from the hunter and shepherd life, and will experiment in making dishes to hold water for their painting materials.

Drawing and painting.—The children of this year are strongly imaginative. Free from the self-criticism which later retards creative effort, they are fearless in the pictorial expression. Conditions are favorable to the emphasis of imaginative drawing at this age. The interest in the idea should be the means of developing a closer observation of natural phenomena as the symbols of expression.

The technic of the year includes use of large washes, three tones of dark and light, expression of plane relations by variations of size and value, in landscape work, and action of figure. The æsthetic qualities emphasized are rhythm and balance. The more formal design will be developed in the weaving, and will include the use of symbols, two values of dark and light colors of two intensities.

English.—(1) Literature: Rhymes and poetry: Repetition of Robert Louis Stevenson's verses given before; the following ones added: "The Lamplighter," "Young Night Thoughts," "The Sun Travels," and "Nest Eggs." "Clouds," Frank Dempster Sherman; "Snow-Storm," Sherman; "Hunting Song," Coleridge; "The Lamb" (first stanza) and "The Shepherd," William Blake; "Fairy Folk," and "Wishing," Allingham; "Seven Times One," Jean Ingelow; "March," Wordsworth; "The Wonderful World," (three stanzas), William Rand; "The Birds in Spring," Thomas Nashe; "Seal Lullaby," Kipling; "Ariel's Song," and "I know a bank whereon the wild thyme grows," Shakespeare; "The Swallow's Nest," Edwin Arnold; "The Sun with His Great Eye," John Keats (a fragment). Most of the poems mentioned above may be found in *The Posy Ring,* edited by Kate Douglas Wiggin.

Stories: Adapted from Grimm: "Snow White and the

Seven Little Dwarfs," "The Enchanted Stag;" from Hawthorne's *Wonder Book:* "The Golden Touch," "The Miraculous Pitcher," and "The Chimera;" "Little Thumbling," Perrault; "Old Pipes and the Dryad," Stockton; "Muleykeh," adapted from Robert Browning; "Mowgli's Brothers" and "Toomai and the Elephants," Kipling.

(2) Oral reading and dramatic art: The poems given above under "Literature," and the selections to be printed for the children's reading, listed above, offer the opportunities for gaining skill in reading aloud. Certain of these will be memorized for morning exercises and festivals, and will be used as a means of entertainment at our social periods.

"Snow-White and the Seven Little Dwarfs," "Old Pipes and the Dryad," and other old tales will be dramatized as simply as possible, using pantomime for the most part. If any costumes are necessary, they will be planned and made by the children, and therefore will be crude and simple.

The children will construct the plot, write the dialogues, and stage two plays during the year for morning exercises. These will be made one from the stories of Ab and the other from the stories of the Arabian shepherds.

For the annual spring festival the children of this group, together with those of the group below and above them, will give "Sleeping Beauty" in the garden.

Bible stories: Abraham, Isaac, Jacob, Joseph, Ruth, David—read in part from the Bible.

(3) Reading: The children's own reading will be from books, printed slips, and script. Each child will have at the beginning of the year covers for printed slips. These will cover the following subjects: Sketches and stories of shepherd life and descriptions of the desert, by Jennie Hall; stories of hunter life and adaptations from Waterloo's *Story of Ab;* descriptions of Arabia, Palestine, and Switzerland; "Threshing in Greece," by Jennie Hall; selections from children's poetry, some rhymes of Christina Rossetti, and the words of the children's songs. We shall use "Little Black Sambo" and "Peter Rabbit," and selected

articles from the following readers: *Lights to Literature; Heart of Oak,* Vols. I and II; *The Blodgett Reader; The Culture Readers; The Tree-Man; The Cave-Man;* and *Stories for Children.*

(4) Writing: The aim in the writing is to gain freedom and legibility. The drill comes through daily demands for written expression. An alphabetically classified list of words which have been used frequently is kept by each child as a means of independent reference and as a record of progress. The above-mentioned daily written expression together with the general conversation gives constant opportunity for the teaching of English.

In the written work the definite points to be made are the feeling for a sentence; use of capitals at the beginning of a sentence in proper nouns and in direct address; use and meaning of question mark, apostrophe, quotation mark, and hyphen; agreement of subject and predicate, and of pronoun and antecedent; logical sequence of tenses.

Music.—Rote song-singing; writing of simple melodies; analysis of two-, three-, and four-pulse measure; names of lines and spaces; placing of bars; time symbols (whole, half, quarter, and eighth notes); songs for school festivals, seasons, and such as correlate with the history and literature of the grade.

Gymnastics.—Beginnings of formal work in marching and running; odd fancy steps; postural work and breathing still imitative; beginning of exercises on apparatus (hanging); games. Short daily periods. Proportion of formal work to apparatus and games, one-half. Music accompanies all but apparatus and games. Begin games of exactness of motion.

One lesson each week in rhythm. The simple rhythms—walking, running, skipping, hopping, sliding, etc.—woven into combinations and combined with rhythmical movements of the arms and body.

Dancing.—Positions for feet; exercises; bows; beginning of the waltz and two-step; galop square; grand right and left; clap dance.

DIVISION C

SECTION 5 (FIFTH SCHOOL YEAR)

Activities and occupations which will be carried on during the year are: (1) walks in the park and excursions into the surrounding country; (2) gardening; (3) cooking, baking, preserving; (4) pottery; (5) textiles; (6) woodwork; (7) housekeeping and care of rooms, halls, and grounds; (8) a store, as a distributing point of supplies; (9) celebrations; (10) parties and daily morning exercises.

Subject-matter.—The children are encouraged to acquire knowledge from every available source in order to carry on these activities in the most effective manner, and also in order to appreciate some of the social activities which they see around them. For this purpose it is necessary to visit shops, factories, markets, docks, and wharves in the vicinity, where similar occupations are engaged in, and to visit museums and collections of all kinds. It is necessary to perform experiments, to use books and pictures for information, as well as objects and specimens from the school museum. Each activity has a scientific and social aspect, both of which receive due attention. Records of the work are kept in the form of finished articles, plans, collections of objects studied, written notes, essays, drawings, and paintings.

History.—Basis: (1) observations of trade conditions; South Water Street; boats and freight-cars loading and unloading; stores; children's own desire to barter and exchange; (2) children's occupations in making boats and carts, and keeping a store for supplies.

Topics: Beginnings of trade, of exploration, and of travel; development of means of transportation and of a diversity of arts; expansion of industrial, social, and political life. As concrete illustrations of the era of early trade and discovery, some phases of Greek and Norse history have been selected for study.

Geographical conditions which encourage early navigation and commerce—islands, harbors, overproduction of some commodity, desire for other products. Industries and occupations of the early Norse and Greek. Development of trade. How trade

THE FIELD CLUB—COOKING BACON

FIELD TRIP—ON THE SAND DUNES

was carried on; means of transportation by land and water. Discoveries and expansion of geographical knowledge. The Vikings, their mode of life. Discovery of Iceland, Greenland, and America (Vinland). The Homeric Greek—based on a study of the *Odyssey.*

Standards of measurement, currency, use of metals. The children make furnaces, melt metals (lead and tin), make molds, and carry on the whole process of molding in lead and tin. Arrow-points, spear-points, battle-axes, money, weights, etc., are made. Social condition of the people, classes of people, the king, the assembly, games and sports, warfare and warlike conditions; ideals of the time, and religious beliefs.

The story of Columbus will be told as embodying the spirit and aims of exploration. For comparison stories will be told of modern explorers, as Nansen, Livingstone, Stanley; their equipment and aims as compared with those of the ancient explorers.

Geography.—(1) The neighborhood. On all excursions the natural features will be observed. The lakeshore—shore line, bluffs, different kinds of beaches. Beverly Hills—the ravines, brook-basins. Swamps—ridges with trees. (2) Typical environments. Mountain landscapes; Norway and Greece as types; narrow valleys, rapid rivers, falls, lakes; forest-covered, barren, and snow-covered mountains. Coasts: bays, headlands, fjords, islands, harbors. Animal life in the northern forests; animals of the northern seas. Study of such typical environments with relation to their social occupations, fishing—lumbering, hunting, trade (See "History").

Given typical physiographical features, the children will plan routes of travel by sea and land; construct maps in sand and on blackboard. These maps will first be made to record imaginary trips, and later the journey of the Norsemen to America, the caravan travel through the deserts, Columbus' discovery of America.

Picture Arctic scenery with Nansen's journey, and tropical scenes with Livingstone and Stanley. The earth as a ball will be introduced with the study of Columbus, and the different oceans and land masses noticed with relation to one another. The children will construct simple compasses, and learn to use them on their excursions.

Nature-study.—The children have charge of the beehives in the garden. This responsibility necessitates a close study of these insects as to cleaning hives, winter conditions, removing honey, making new hives, etc. This work interests the children in the life-history of bees and other insects; the bumble-bee, ant, and butterfly are especially studied.

Garden: This grade is responsible for three flower beds in front of the school building in which tulips bloom in the spring and asters in the fall (transplanting); also for planting ivy and climbing-roses. Window-boxes in the house allow care of plants during the winter; the children are encouraged to have gardens and window-boxes at home, seeds being supplied by themselves. Note is made of trees that blossom early (food for bees). Sweet alyssum planted for the bees.

Excursions: To Jackson Park, Wooded Island, South Shore, Beverly Hills, Lakeside. The special interests of the children are noted and followed up as far as demanded by them. Birds, bird-notes, building of nests, some ways of food-getting; the woodpeckers, kingfisher, swallows, robins, etc. Materials gathered on these excursions will be cared for, and different kinds of seeds mounted to show seed distribution, classified as to means of dissemination; insects, cocoons, etc., will be placed in an insect case; frogs' eggs, tadpoles, salamander eggs, snails, larvæ of mosquito, dragon-flies, etc., in an aquarium in the room; turtles, snakes, and toads are cared for in the school museum. The habits of the animals with which the children have become acquainted during the summer are discussed, such as the squirrel, chipmunk, bat, muskrat, and others. Stories of the same are told and read.

Temperature studied in relation to bees, bulbs, and other plants out-of-doors. Barometers made and compasses constructed (see "History"). Phenomena of the Arctic day and night (history) compared with our own conditions lead to more interested observations of the sun's position. Experiments on evaporation (see "Cooking"). Paintings made of out-of-door scenes often enough to be a record of the changes of the seasons.

English.—(1) Literature: Poems: Robert Louis Stevenson, "The Land of Story Books," "The Little Land," "North-West Passage," "Travel," "Where Go the Boats," "Escape at Bedtime," "Windy Nights," "Foreign Lands," "Fairy Bread," "Farewell to the Farm," "Looking Forward;" "The Fairy Folk," Robert Bird (Posy Ring); "Is the Moon Tired?" C. Rossetti; "The Wind and the Moon," George MacDonald; "Robert of Lincoln," Bryant.

Stories: the saga of King Harold the Fair-Haired, the Volsunga saga, and the sagas of Eric the Red and Leif Ericson told and read to the children; the *Odyssey,* parts read by children from Palmer's translation, parts read or told by the teacher; Norse myths: "Thor's Journey to Jotunheim," "The Death of Balder," "The Gifts of the Dwarfs," and others (Mabie's *Norse Stories* are recommended); Greek myths and hero-stories: "Apollo and the Python," "Hermes and the Cave of Winds," Perseus, Theseus, and Hercules (Hawthorne's *Wonder Book* and Kinsley's *Greek Heroes* are used). Fairy-tales to be told: "The Land East o' the Sun and West o' the Moon," "The Twelve Wild Ducks," Dasent's *Popular Tales from the Norse.* Fables: "The Country Mouse and the City Mouse," "The Man, the Boy, and the Donkey," "The Fox and the Grapes," "The Shepherd and the Wolves," and others from Æsop.

Poems and stories with which the children are familiar from previous grades will be used constantly in the story-telling time.

(2) Oral reading: Poems and stories, of the greatest literary value, which at the same time are easy enough for the children to read, are selected for oral reading; they are studied especially with a view to rendering them in a beautiful way to others. All of the selections from *A Child's Garden of Verse,* some of the fables, the selections from the *Odyssey,* and the sagas are included in the oral reading.

(3) Reading: For some of the children considerable phonic drills and reading of very simple stories will be necessary. Others will use silent reading mainly for study in science, history, and geography, oral reading being used only for social purposes. At

the end of the fifth year in school (third grade) the children should have acquired ease in reading whatever thought-matter is adapted to them, and in giving an intelligent oral rendering of the same.

(4) Writing: The children have many opportunities to feel the need of writing, which cause them to use it for reasons which they themselves think valid. Written expression is used in the following instances: (1) note-taking (*a*) while experimenting, (*b*) while on excursions, (*c*) while studying books; (2) notes written up to present to the class; (3) dictation: (*a*) recipes for cooking, (*b*) directions for experiments; (4) original stories and verses; (5) invitations, letters; (6) to give direction for work to other children. In writing, the pupil needs many words which he cannot spell. The teacher writes them on the blackboard, or the child looks them up in his "dictionary"—a notebook in which each child writes the words he has misspelled or asked for in previous lessons. This dictionary, consisting of words which the child actually needs and uses constantly, becomes a spelling-book, if so it may be called, the children often taking it home to learn the words. When a paper is read aloud and the class does not gain the thought which the writer desires to convey the language is reconstructed by the help and criticism of the other chidren. The use of punctuation marks is discovered, and rules for the use of capitals, etc., are established. The oral as well as the written language of the pupils is constantly corrected.

Music.—Rote song-singing; sight-reading exercises in two-, three-, and four-pulse; notes and rests; simple melodies written; six-pulse rhythm analyses; original songs.

Home economics.—Cooking: Drying of grapes; grape jelly. Sugar cookery; candied fruit. Preserving of meat and fish by salting, smoking, and drying, to illustrate work in history. Starch cookery; making of white sauce; cooking of starchy, sweet-juiced, and strong-juiced vegetables; vegetable soups; baking of bread. Milk and its products; making of butter; junket; sour milk; cheese. Christmas candies.

Science.—Quantitative work in evaporation; effect of the skin of the fruit on evaporation; study of individual plants; parts of the plant used for food; classification of vegetables according to their composition and the parts of the plant used; starch grains seen under microscope; iodine test for starch; determination (roughly) of the amount of water and starch in some foods; change of starch to sugar by sweet taste developed in the chewing of starchy foods; density of different liquids from the study of milk and cream; determination of the amount of fat in milk through butter-making; and through the preparation of sour-milk cheese.

Mathematics.—If the children are actually doing work which has social value, they must gain accurate knowledge of the activities in which they are engaged. They will keep a record of all expenses for materials used in the school, and will do simple bookkeeping in connection with the store which has charge of this material. In cooking, weights and measures will be learned. The children will also keep accounts of the cost of ingredients. Proportions will be worked out in the cooking recipes. When the children dramatize the life of the trader, in connection with history, they have opportunities to use all standards of measurements. Number is demanded in almost all experimental science work; for instance, the amount of water contained in the different kinds of fruits, or the amount of water evaporated from fruits under different conditions (in drying fruits). All plans for woodwork will be worked to a scale and demand use of fractions. When the children have encountered many problems which they must solve in order to proceed with their work, they are ready to be drilled on the processes involved until they gain facility in the use of these. The children should be able to think through the problems which arise in their daily work, and have automatic use of easy numbers, addition, subtraction, multiplication, short division, and easy fractions.

Woodwork.—At the beginning of the second half of the year the time scheduled for wood-working will be devoted to the construction of portfolios—an exercise valuable not only for the concrete result, but because of the careful measurements involved. As a natural sequence, library fittings may follow, and penholders, trays, paper-knives, desk-boxes, blotting-pads, and paper-files be constructed from wood. These are the personal property of the children who make them, and may be taken home or donated to the school for use. The tools involved in the construction of these articles are the plane, ruler, trysquare, saw, hammer, gauge and mallet, bit and brace, spokeshave, and file. The children are expected to have acquired a fair degree of skill in the use of tools previous to this year, and the articles are designed with reference to a natural sequence in the use of the tools and the increasing power of technic on the part of the child.

Textiles.—Use of grasses, twigs, leaves, corn-husks, and other primitive fibers in the making of baskets and mats; sewing of bags for school purposes.

Experimenting with the weaving, braiding, and sewing processes, and application of design so discovered in the making of bags of jute; dyeing of the jute fibers with vegetable colors; preparation of flax fiber; spinning.

Clay-modeling.—Vases, jars, and bowls for flowers. Having become familiar with some characteristic Greek and Norse design, the children often choose these for their own purposes. Statuettes illustrative of the work in nature-study, history, and literature are made.

Drawing and painting.—This is a year when the children make a rapid transition. Up to this period they put meaning into crude symbols, showing but little discontent with the crudeness of the effort. After this age they rapidly take an objective interest in their drawings. Their imperfections discourage and disgust them. It is important that the subject-matter should lead to a closer visual analysis, and that it should be of such a nature as to enable the children to "check up" their results by comparison with real things. The nature-study, with its wide range of interests, offers a class of subjects by which visual as well as æsthetic powers may be developed.

Gymnastics.—Marching, running, fancy steps, postural work and breathing, and jumping and games. Work still imitative, but increasing importance attached to proper respect for command and response to it. In increasing the emphasis upon the advantages of method and system, begin methods of formally placing the class on the floor for postural work. All formal work still accompanied by music. Begin games of low organization, and simple games of competition and co-operation.

Dancing.—Positions for feet; exercises; bows; beginning of the waltz and two-step; galop square; grand right and left; clap dance.

DIVISION C

SECTION 6 (SIXTH SCHOOL YEAR)

During the previous years the children have studied some of the conditions that bring people together in a city. In the sixth year they will trace the growth and development of their own city, Chicago. It is necessary to make a study of the present physiographic conditions; for Chicago represents man's struggle with his environment.

History.—This approach to the study of Chicago is through the consideration of the early French explorers and early settlers of the Northwest.

First half-year: (1) Early French settlers—their motives: (*a*) religion, (*b*) adventure, (*c*) acquisition of territory. (2) Industries naturally developed on the St. Lawrence: fishing, fur-trading, and trapping. (3) Story of Marquette and Joliet. (4) Story of LaSalle and his attempts to establish a chain of forts in the country south of the Great Lakes, and to control the fur trade; development of trading-posts at Kaskaskia, Detroit, Vincennes, and Fort Dearborn. (3) Fort Dearborn: (*a*) development of trading-post; (*b*) building of fort; (*c*) coming of pioneers.

Construction work: (1) Marquette's fort at Michillimachinac; (2) Fort St. Louis at Starved Rock; (3) Fort Dearborn.

Second half-year: Civics. Chicago as a village—development of the city: (1) streets and bridges; (2) water supply; (3) illumination; (4) fire department.

Geography.—First half-year, first six weeks (only). Special point: agencies which change topography. Excursions to (1)

South Shore: (*a*) formation of sand bars, lagoons, swamps, and ridges; (*b*) reasons for piers; (2) Glencoe: (*a*) formation of cliffs and ravines; (*b*) river action; (*c*) character of beach; (*d*) piers; (3) swamps: conditions for formation and change; (4) Dune Park; (*a*) formation of dunes and swamps; (*b*) cause of succession of dunes; (5) Beverly Hills: special features—forests, wide ravines, swamps, and prairies.

In connection with history: (1) the St. Lawrence and Mississippi basins; (2) geography and topography of Illinois: (*a*) the old river routes; (*b*) appearance of the country; (*c*) routes to the East.

Lumbering (see "Woodwork").

Second half-year: (1) study of mining (see "Metal-Working"). (2) Study of clay (see "Modeling"). (3) Special study of Mississippi basin industrially considered: (*a*) cotton belt, (*b*) grain belts, (*c*) sugar-cane belt, (*d*) rice belt, (*e*) grazing belt, etc. (4) Excursions.

The last six weeks will again be devoted to excursions. Special point, ravines: (*a*) Thornton, (*b*) Beverly Hills, (*c*) Fraction Run.

NOTE.—For reference each child owns Carpenter's *North America.*

Nature-study.—(1) Animal life: The children will build squirrel boxes in the garden and have special charge of a pair of gray squirrels. The question of taming them will lead to a close study of the habits of these and kindred animals. (*a*) Prehension of food, comparison of prehensile organs, nature of food, ways of obtaining it, are some of the points for comparative study. (*b*) Birds: habits of winter birds, children placing suet, meat, and grain for them; relation of claws and beak to food-getting. (*c*) Insects: grasshoppers, lady-bugs. (*d*) Spiders. (*e*) Earthworms: place in boxes; observe relation to soil.

(2) Garden: This grade has charge of four flower-beds, the ivy and climbing-roses in front of the school building, one flower-bed and an herb-bed in the school garden, bulbs for spring and winter blooming, six large window-boxes outside the windows, and three boxes inside. In explanation of problems which arise, the following experiments will be peformed:

Those explaining (*a*) the relation of light and heat to growth under perfectly natural conditions; (*b*) germination and rate of growth in various soils with similar conditions; (*c*) effect of roots on rock; (*d*) ways of getting moisture; (*e*) relation of moisture to growth of root. Buds: examine; note modes of protection. Grafting fruit trees and house plants. Twigs of common trees: (*a*) find comparative growth for several seasons; (*b*) note modes of protection.

(3) Excursions: Excursions will be made to (*a*) the Wooded Island, (*b*) South Shore, (*c*) Glencoe, (*d*) neighboring swamps, (*e*) Beverly Hills. Special points for observation: (*a*) plants—recognition of known species, identification of some new ones, where found, the nature of the soil, mode of growth, relation of seed to plant, meaning of color in fruit, meaning of shells on nuts; (*b*) observations of animals' life as noted under the first heading.

Meteorology.—(1) Slant of sun's rays; measurement taken weekly. (2) Average temperature; daily record taken at 9, 11, and 1 o'clock. (3) Direction of wind at the time noted above. (4) Relation of direction of wind and slant of sun's rays to temperature.

Mathematics.—In the correlation necessary to the general work, the following should be the outcome in arithmetical knowledge: (1) familiarity with the use of the multiplication tables through the 12's; (2) dry and liquid measure in connection with cooking; (3) linear, square, and cubic measures in the study of ventilation; (4) simple fractions and decimals with nature-study, manual training, and cooking; (5) ability to add, subtract, multiply, and divide whole numbers, as rapidly as is consistent with the general development of the individual; (6) keeping simple accounts.

English.—(1) Literature: Story of Siegfried. This will be read and told by the teacher, from William Morris, *Sigurd the Volsung*. They will also read "Aladdin, or the Wonderful Lamp," "Ali Baba, or the Forty Thieves," from the *Heart of Oak Books,* No. 3; "Sinbad the Sailor," from *Heart of Oak*

Books, No. 4; Hawthorne's *Wonder Book* and *Tanglewood Tales;* and Kipling's *Jungle Book.*

(2) Reading in connection with history and geography,—Catherwood, *Heroes of the Middle West;* Baldwin, *Discovery of the Old Northwest;* Eleanor Atkinson, *History of Chicago;* Jennie Hall, *History of Chicago;* Carpenter, *Geographical Reader: North America.*

(3) Special oral reading, and dramatic art: (1) dramatization of a part in the celebration of the yearly festivals. (2) Study of a group of celebrated horse-back rides in literature: (*a*) "John Gilpin's Ride;" (*b*) "How the Good News Was Carried from Ghent to Aix;" (*c*) "Sheridan's Ride;" (*d*) "Paul Revere's Ride." (3) Other poems and dramatic stories which develop the power to express intelligently the reader's interpretation of the author's meaning.

(4) Writing: The demands for writing are numerous. Papers are written for (1) records of (*a*) science work, (*b*) excursions, (*c*) cooking; (2) stories; (3) letters; (4) invitations; (5) expense accounts; (6) songs. The skill to be acquired through this demand is: correct use of capitals, periods, interrogation point, and quotation marks; the use of the apostrophe; some uses of the comma; simple paragraphing. Spelling: The plan suggested in the third grade is followed.

Drawing and painting.—(1) Landscape: (*a*) immediate landscape, showing weekly change; (*b*) typical areas visited. (2) Trees and plants—from these areas. (3) Illustrative work in history, etc. The technic is constantly improved, or there is dissatisfaction with the work. (4) Design. The crafts in which the children engage form the basis of the design. The emphasis will be placed on the following technical points: form, proportion, and spacing; the decoration of the rectangle and the circle; straight lines and simple units used in borders.

Modeling.—(1) Pottery—i. e., vases, jars, tiles, etc. (2) Tiles illustrating a scene in high or low relief from literature. Excursions: Marshall Field's and Burley's, to see pottery exhibits; Art Institute; Teco potteries at Terra Cotta. (3) In connection with prehension of food each child will model some animal in the round. (4) Tiles for window-boxes in frames of metal or wood.

Wood-working.—First half-year: (1) Desk-boxes, fern-stands, doll furniture, etc., for Christmas presents, made in hardwood, in which the child meets the same problems of previous years; (2) a hardwood screen and other articles needed by the school.

Applied science.—A collection of woods representing the trees of the environment will be cut and polished to show the graining. Geography: Lumbering; (1) life of the people engaged in it; (2) their work; (3) the preparation of the wood for use; (4) trees used for other purposes—rubber, maple, etc.; (5) location of the great forest areas of the world.

Metal-working.—Second half-year: The fifth section has studied the use of metal in the beginning of trade and barter. In Section 6 it is taken up as a material in which the children can express themselves socially and artistically. They will (1) hammer from sheet copper such articles as bowls and trays; (2) or make articles which call for sawing and etching, as book-ends, letter-files, calendar-frames, picture-frames, etc. Science: Simple experiments in smelting. Geography: Mining; the life of the miner; the source of the ore; the preparation of metal for use; the location of mines.

Music.—Rote song-singing; preparation for two-part singing; rounds; sight-reading exercises in various measure-rhythms, with special emphasis on time problems; melodies written; original songs notated in blank books; rules for finding keynotes.

French.—Songs and games illustrating manner of living, customs and festivals in France; dramatizing of French Christmas play. Reading material will be taken from *Chansons et rondes populaires de France.* Writing of grammar; records to be printed by the eighth grade. Masculine and feminine of nouns and adjectives, singular and plural forms, agreement of subject and predicate.

German.—Beginning German. Instruction mostly oral; no textbook used. Conversation is based on everyday experiences of the children at home (meals, etc.) or at school (excursions, etc.). Many games, rhymes, riddles, songs, and dialogues will be learned. Free expression is encouraged as much as possible. Some writing.

Gymnastics.—Lesson plan same as for third grade. Proportion of lesson given to formal exercise increases. Shorten reactions by the addition of commands while running. Dumbbells and wands introduced in postural work, also combination of movements demanding finer discrimination and co-ordination. Begin games of a higher type of co-ordination.

Dancing.—Waltz, two-step, galop, polka; London dance; two folk-dances; (1) sailor's hornpipe, (2) clap dance.

DIVISION D

SECTION 7 (SEVENTH SCHOOL YEAR)

History.—The Pilgrims in America, their relations with the Indians, and their life amid primitive conditions appeal to the child's spirit of adventure. Not only is the life amid these conditions of vital interest, but the beginnings of the improvement of them are equally interesting, and the substitution of the candle for the pine-knot, and of the rug for the sand floor, leads to a study of colonial industries and investigation as to the best methods of production. The greatest value of interest in work is secured by presenting to the pupil subjects for study in some relation to his own life and experience. He expends effort, and realizes to a degree the effort which must have been made by all pioneers to produce more comfortable living; and this is a great factor in enlarging his social interest.

By repeating the experience of other peoples, he is not only interested in their life, but in weaving and cooking, and in candle- and soap-making, he satisfies his own desire for activity. The mere doing generally satisfies him, and care in manipulation comes only after he has failed by careless work to produce good results.

Study of the Pilgrims: Plymouth Harbor will be modeled in sand, and the town constructed on the sand-table, including Governor Bradford's house, the fort, the town brook, Leyden Street, Priscilla's home, and Burial Hill. The story will continue with

Governor Bradford's "Journal" as a basis, and the chidren will read Nina Moore Tiffany's *Pilgrims and Puritans.* The study of the New England home will include the houses and furniture, fireplaces and furnishings, preparing and serving meals, spinning, dyeing, weaving, and making candles and soap. During the study of Pilgrim life, and because of the historical setting obtained, Longfellow's *Courtship of Miles Standish* will be read.

The Virginia colony: The study of the Virginia colony begins with the plantation as contrasted with a New England farm. After describing the large plantation, with its great fields of tobacco, many laborers, mansion house, river, wharf, and the ship from England with its freight of manufactured articles, the causes for the difference between the life in Virginia and in New England will be seen. This will lead to the reasons for the introduction of slave labor, and the effects upon later history will be very simply traced. The causes of the colony and events connected with the history of its founding will be studied. The children will construct a miniature plantation.

The New York colony: Hans Brinker furnishes a vivid picture of life in Holland, and the siege of Leyden illustrates the character of the people. The characteristics of the colony will be studied and compared with those of New England and Virginia—occupations, classes of society, labor, education, government. A miniature New Amsterdam on the sand-table, and drawings of scenes in old New York, will illustrate the work. The *Legends of Sleepy Hollow* and *Rip Van Winkle* will be read, and the latter dramatized by the class.

Some functions of our own civic government are contrasted with similar functions of colonial government. The work of the fireman with that of the "bucket brigade;" the work of the policeman with that of the tithing-man and other officers. This continues the civic study of the sixth year.

English.—(1) Literature. The literature of this grade is Pyle's *Robin Hood,* Irving's *Rip Van Winkle,* and *Legends of Sleepy Hollow. Rip Van Winkle* will be dramatized by the pupils and put upon the stage at one of the morning exercise periods.

(2) Writing: By means of the writing in cooking, history, and science, it is expected that the class will gain a free and correct use of English. The pupils will formulate simple rules for punctuation, capitalization, and spelling, and write them in their notebooks. By analysis of the thought of their work in history, geography, and literature they will gain a knowledge of sentence structure. In this year the children begin to use the dictionary —Webster's *Academic*. They will also write simple verse and original stories.

Speech, oral reading, and dramatic art.—The interpretation of *Miles Standish* by the teacher; study and dramatization of *Rip Van Winkle;* dramatic training in the staging of the French and German plays. Oral reading: "The Revenge," Tennyson; some of the ballads of *Robin Hood.* Poems of the seasons will be interpreted to the children and some of them committed and recited at morning exercises. This class will take an active part in the Thanksgiving festival.

French.—Dramatizing of scenes from the life of Samuel de Champlain; playing of rounds and games taken from *Chansons et rondes populaires de France,* and popular French games; review of the sixth-year grammar Record Book; first conjugation in indicative and imperative modes; pronouns of first, second, and third persons; reading of historical and literary anecdote-book printed by the seventh grade.

German.—The greater part of the work is still oral. Topics for conversation are found in the experiences of the children. A story-book, Foster's *Geschichten und Märchen,* is introduced. There is no translation, only sight-reading, and, in connection with the work, retelling and dramatization of the stories. The writing which is done at this time is mainly for ear-training. No formal grammar, but some drill in singular and plural of common nouns, is given.

Geography.—The general work in geography will be a study of North America. During the first half-year the geography will be closely allied to history, which is a study of the colonies. (See "History"). A general study of glaciation will be made with special application to New England. From a knowledge of the soil, and also through the use of pictures and descriptions, ıss will study the rivers, forests, hills, bowlders, water and climate of the region, in relation to the principal in- s—manufacturing, agriculture, and fishing. Excursions made to Stony Island, where the influence of the glacier -rock and glacial drift can be seen, and to Purington for deposits. The location of many towns and cities, as ined by topographic causes, will be noted. Other sections :ountry will be studied by different groups of children, who ɔrk out characteristic occupations of the areas and present class the results of their work.

ring the second half-year the study of the entire continent, ng the polar and tropical regions, will be continued. Visits made to industrial plants in or near the city, which will nent the work of the classroom. In the work on New ıistory, constant reference is made to Holland, and, in o make this work more vivid, the general geography of d, including the subjects of erosion, formation of islands, nsportation of soil will be studied.

ring the entire year current geography will have an im- place in the curriculum, and a period each week will be l to current events.

ure-study.—This class will make a special study of a in its different aspects and relations. There are several ampy areas near the Midway, and more extensive ones easy reach along Stony Island Avenue. The children will e swamp often, taking note of the changes in plant and life from time to time, and explaining the changes by g the interdependence of the various forms of life. This ill have charge of the water garden—a tank 8 feet long, wide, and 4 feet deep, made by the children last year. ill use the water garden for the cultivation of the various f swamp plants brought in by the children. Frogs, toads, nakes, and fishes may be introduced into the tank and in ıria the children may establish in the schoolroom. The f the swamp will involve such topics as: the food of the animals and their dependence upon plants; the "balance of life" between animals and plants; the changes in the flora and fauna due to changing character of the swamps; the ways in which swamp animals and plants survive the winter; the temperatures of the ground at different depths; the temperatures of the air; etc. The children will, so far as possible, solve their problems by experimentation, as well as by reference to the books in the school library and at home.

The expression of the changing phases of the swamp will take the form, among others, of paintings, made at regular intervals. The complete set of these will be a history of the swamp in color for a year.

Many problems in meteorology grow out of the work; the application of the principles learned will be made to the country as a whole, in the study of the geography of North America. (See "Meteorology").

In addition to the planting of ivy on Arbor Day, and to the care of the window-boxes, this class will have charge of the strawberry bed in the garden.

The class will take several longer trips to Stony Island and Purington (see "Geography"), to Stewart Ridge near West Pullman, and to East Chicago. (See "Cooking" or "Applied Science").

Home economics.—(1) Cooking: Making of jelly, and drying of corn and beans, as a preparation of food for winter use; review of sugar cookery and making of maple sugar; cooking of cereals. Preparation of dishes to illustrate colonial history: hominy, corn pone, baked beans, brown bread. Albumin: Cooking of eggs, meats, and meat soups. Combination of starch and albumin. Visit to flour-mill and bakery.

Science: The science is the basis for much of the work in cooking and industrial history. Cereals: value as food, distribution, conditions for growth, milling. Review of starch test and finding of starch in foods. Sugar test and finding of sugar in vegetable foods and milk. Cooking temperature of albumin; comparison of albumin of egg and milk curd. Composition of meat; ways of extracting and retaining juices of meat.

(3) Soap-making: Leach lye from wood ashes; test properties; let it combine with oil to form soap. The class will make

hard soap by using caustic soda, and soft soap by using caustic potash. Visit soap factory.

(4) Candles: Work out conditions under which oils and fats burn, and study different kinds of wicks as to volatilization of oil. Make candles of tallow and paraffin. Discover use of chimney. Study convection currents. Discover need of oxygen and production of carbonic-acid gas.

(5) Pewter: Perform experiments in melting and mixing lead and tin in different proportions to make an alloy suitable for dishes. The children will originate methods, as far as possible, and perform the experiments independently. The apparatus is simple, and mostly made by the children.

Meteorology.—Climate of North America, direction of winds, rainfall, weather maps, barometer, thermometer. Weather charts as records.

Mathematics.—The number work of the year will be correlated with other studies. The four fundamental processes will be studied especially, and simple problems performed in fractions, common and decimal; averaging temperatures, long division; garden: linear and square measure; material for looms and Christmas gifts—linear and square measure; recipes—addition, subtraction, multiplication, and division of fractions, dye for textiles—fractions and metric weights; supplies for school use—United States money.

Art.—The work is the beginning of a somewhat more conscious study of the æsthetic elements of art expression. These are developed in both the formal decoration of wood and textiles, and in the drawing and painting which arise from various subject-matter. The use of color opposites will be studied.

Textiles.—The work in textiles will be a general outlook upon the different materials used in making of clothing, including the manner of production and preparation for use.

First half-year: The children will make Christmas gifts upon linen and hand-frames, of small bags, mats, or doilies, using cross-stitch in design where practicable. They will experiment in making an indigo vat, and the use of fustic and logwood chips in dyeing various shades of yellow, green, gray, and purple.

Second half-year: The class will make a study of different

fibers used in weaving, spin wool and flax on spindle and wheel, and study the processes used in weaving and dyeing employed by the early American colonists. A simple stencil pattern will be applied to portfolio of linen.

During the year excursions will be taken to Hull House, Mungo Reid rug and curtain manufactory, Field Museum, Fine Arts Building, and Art Institute.

Manual training.—The second half-year. The use of woodworking is especially to reinforce class work. With the colonial history as a basis, the miniature Mount Vernon begun this year will be completed and furnished with the hangings, rugs, and furniture characteristic of that period. The Sheraton, Chippendale, and Heppelwhite styles of furniture will be discussed, and furniture planned with reference to them.

Music.—In the early part of the year emphasis is laid upon sight-reading and singing of unison songs. Later, two-part work is taken up; first by means of rounds—"Frère Jacques," "We Merry Minstrels"—and later by simple two-part exercises. By the end of the winter work two-part songs are sung correctly: "There are many flags," "Waken, Lords and Ladies." Rules for finding the keynotes of the various scales are worked out. Phrases in all keys are notated by the children.

Physical exercises.—Further development of volitional control through problems in new co-ordination in postural and apparatus work and jumping will be sought. This age of children demands the addition of antagonistic and competitive work which requires special adaptation of running, vaulting, and jumping exercises. Games involve increased endurance and skill.

Dancing.—Waltz, two-step, galop, polka, London dance; two folk-dances: sailor's hornpipe, clap dance.

DIVISION D

SECTION 8 (EIGHTH SCHOOL YEAR)

The children are interested in the many industrial and commercial problems arising in the city around them. Their father's business appeals to them; they visit his office or shop; they do shopping, and have a general interest in commercial values. The

WORK IN BASKETRY

WORK IN METAL—COPPER

alien peoples about them suggest questions that carry the children into geography and history and civics with real zest. Questions of government are becoming interesting to them. They have a tendency to generalize in this as in much of their thinking. They are organizing their artistic and æsthetic tastes.

Civics and history.—This group of children help very materially in making beautiful the school grounds, having charge of the flower-bed and urns in the court. Out of this grows an interest in the general work of beautifying the place in which we live. At this time children are alive to the problems of government in the concrete, and are beginning to enjoy something of the science of government. The outcome of these interests is a study of the work of our "civic improvement" societies, and Athens is taken as a type of the "city beautiful."

The children's interest in our own problems of government and their desire to know more of the foreign people around them (which is given at length under "Geography"), make desirable and profitable a study of a people other than the English in the exploration and settlement of America. The French life in the early days in Canada and the Mississippi Valley is full of many simple, beautiful stories of the hunter, the trapper, the priest guiding his own people or teaching the Indian, which give the children a feeling for the French people, and an appreciation of the difference between the French life, social and political, and that of the English and our own.

History.—A study of civic beauty; how to make our city beautiful; what the civic improvement societies of our city are doing. Greek history: Athens as a beautiful city; Greek education, music, art, games; Greeks' struggle for liberty. The *Iliad* is used as the foundation for this work.

The French in America: conditions, geographical, social, and political, that led to their coming; their fishing industries in the New World, Cartier on the St. Lawrence, at Stadaconé and Hochelaga. Fur-trade monopoly, DeMonts and Champlain in Nova Scotia. Champlain on the St. Lawrence: Quebec, Montreal, summer fairs; trapper, soldier, explorer, missionary; church, school, seigniorage. Spread into Great Lake region and

Mississippi Valley; contact with the English in the Ohio Valley. In much of this work the children are in touch with the original papers, journals, diaries, and letters of the Frenchmen as found in Champlain's Journals and the various State Historical Society Papers.

Comparison of French and English colonial life; account for difference in government. French and Indian War—the importance of its results.

Growth of English colonies: industrial development; hand and home manufacture; growth in factory system; lumbering; ship-building; manufacture of barrels, linen, paper, etc.; trade with West Indies and Europe; Navigation Acts. These acts and internal taxation lead to the Revolution; result, the birth of the nation.

Sand-modeling, map-drawing, clay-modeling, painting, and story-writing help the work. In the Greek work the clay-modeling is very significant. (See "Clay" under "Art"). Woodwork will help toward an appreciation of colonial homes, through study of furniture and building of the times.

Home-reading: Andrews' *Ten Boys on the Road from Long Ago to Now;* Guerber's *Story of the Greeks;* Kipling's *Captains Courageous;* Martineau's *Peasant and Prince;* Weir Mitchell's *Hugh Wynne.*

English.—(1) Literature: The *Iliad* will be the principal selection of literature for the year. We shall use Bryant's translation. The children will read and tell stories from the *Iliad,* from books they may have or find in the library. Some books of the poem will be left untouched, and others read only in part.

Prose and poetry of the seasons will be read. Burroughs' "Signs and Seasons," "Wake Robin," "The Apple;" parts of Thoreau's *Excursions;* extracts from Bradford Torrey; Riley's "Dream of Autumn;" Whittier's "Fisherman," and "Paul Revere's Ride."

(2) Writing: Writing is part of the work in every subject; the aim toward legibility, ease, and rapidity.

(3) Spelling: Oral and written spelling of words heard and used; some attention to simple rules of spelling.

Speech, oral reading, and dramatic art.—Parts of the *Iliad* interpreted by the teacher to the class. Construction of a drama founded upon some of the incidents of the *Iliad;* the selection will be determined by the feeling of the class. Dramatic training in French and German plays. Oral reading of parts of *Hugh Wynne,* of *Paul Revere's Ride* (review), *King Olaf's Christmas* and other Norse sagas, and Browning's "Herve Riel." Interpretation by the teacher of season poems. Some of these will be committed and recited by the children. Interpretation by the teacher of Browning's "Phidipides" and other poems; also of the "The Ship That Found Herself."

This class will take an active part in the Christmas festival.

Modern languages: (1) *English.*—Composition in its various forms—narration, description, character sketch—grows out of the wealth of material in history, geography, nature-study, and literature, and in excursions, travels, and other experiences. The heroic in history and literature, and the beauty of nature often appeal to the poetic in the children, and the result is simple verse. The aim is to foster a desire to express, and to gain the power to express interestingly and beautifully, what one has to tell. Clearness and conciseness are emphasized in appropriate places. Choice of words, flow of sentences, style, in a simple way, are noted. Letters and invitations are written. Records of experiments, and recipes are written.

(2) *French.*—Dramatizing scenes from the life of Francis I; original play of Jacques Cartier's visit to Hochelaga at Mount Royal. Scenes from the life of Samuel de Champlain, Pontrincourt, and Lescarbot at Port Royal. Reading of Lescarbot's *Adieu à la France.* Reading of historical and literary anecdote-book printed by ninth-year pupils. Christmas work taken from illustrations of play. Reading and grammar work taken from *Popular Games of France, Chansons et rondes populaires de France,* and *The Dramatic French Reader.* Second conjugation, demonstrative and possessive adjectives and pronouns.

(3) *German.*—Conversation based on the same topics as in the lower grades. The children learn how to go shopping in Germany. They become acquainted with German life and cus-

toms through pictures, dialogues, and stories that are told them. Dictation work increases. Some original composition work comes in. Begin Guerber's *Märchen und Erzählungen,* Vol. I. Method the same as the previous year. Presentation of Christmas play. No formal grammar; drill on singular and plural of nouns; and endings of regular verb in present tense.

Geography.—The children are coming in contact with foreign people at school, at home, and in the great city outside; they are seeing products of foreign countries in the stores as they go shopping alone or with their parents; they or their parents have traveled abroad, or are anticipating such travel. The scope of their interests is great enough now to include the many people and countries contributing to the life around them. They are ready to see the interdependence of peoples; to appreciate the contributions of nations to progress, material and otherwise; are really very open-minded and sympathetic in this direction. At this time much can be accomplished by a somewhat thorough study of foreign people here in our city, and in their own countries abroad. If this study is deferred a year or two, the children's questions are answered haphazard outside; the children make abstractions and come to wrong conclusions, which the truth, learned later, does not always eradicate. So, to satisfy the demands of the children at this time, Eurasia is studied.

Eurasia. Physical features: great mountain systems, plateaus, and plains, and rivers. Climatic features: tundras, forest belt, steppes, desert belt; characteristic products of each; effect of each upon human life. Regions of wheat, flax, etc.; grazing, mining, etc. A general picture of the great continent.

We shall see the three great civilizations: the European, pressing ever on and on over the great western peninsula, and even across the sea to the New World; the Chinese (Japanese, Corean), ever clinging to its own soil, looking backward always, with its wonderful background of written history; the Hindu in the southern peninsula, looking to the spiritual, living in the future life, as it were, leaving only buildings to tell its past.

A study of France, England, and Greece, somewhat in detail, will be made in connection with history. The European will be studied as a traveler, a discoverer, an explorer.

Our commercial relations with the leading countries of the continent will be emphasized.

Sand models, chalk models, maps, drawings and paintings, and excursions to the Field Museum, Art Institute, Stony Island, and Dune Park, will be an integral part of the work.

Nature-study.—This class will make a study of birds. The children will make frequent excursions to the Wooded Island of Jackson Park. Other wooded areas, such as Beverly Hills, will be visited occasionally. Attention will be paid to the changes in the nature picture, and frequent records in color made. The children will make a bird calendar, showing the date of the first appearance of each kind of bird, and will explain as far as possible the migrations of birds by discovering the nature of the food of the birds.

Last year this class had charge of the tulip-bed around the fountain in the court; after the tulips had bloomed, the children planted asters for fall blooming. This year the class has charge of the planting of bulbs for winter blooming in the different classrooms, as well as of the tulip-bed in the court. They will set out clumps of lilies-of-the-valley and other lilies in the garden. They will also make a wildflower garden, using the plants brought in from excursions.

Arbor and Bird Day is a special feature of the spring work. Excursions to Stony Island, and Dune Park. (See "Geography.")

Applied Science.—(1) Cooking, first half-year: Making of vinegar; canning, preserving, and pickling of fruit, as a beginning of study of fermentation. Study of doughs and batters, and methods of lightening them; sponge cake (air), pop-overs (steam), baking-powder-mixtures (as cake, etc.), sour milk and soda mixtures (ginger bread), bread raised with yeast.

(2) Science: Expansion of gases, change of water into steam. Study of acids; products of fermentation; determination of amount of gluten in flour. Yeast, molds, and other germ-life; conditions of growth of yeast, food, temperature, and moisture; yeast seen under microscope.

(3) Mechanics: Simple machines in use at school, at home, on the streets; universal principles in machines; find lever in many phases, construction of simple machines.

(4) Garden: Study of fertilization. Care of beds of vegetables.

Æsthetics.—Beauty of seasons; special attention to beauty of sky, sunsets, sunrises, color and form in nature. Songs of birds; original songs about birds. Literature—snatches from the nature prose-writers and poets.

Drawing and painting, and design.—Landscape, weekly, to show change in nature. History, geography, and literature call for expression in pencil and color. Notes taken on excursions are material for composition in color; particular trees and flowers are studied in detail. Designs for pottery, textiles, and wood are worked out. Emphasis on invention; composition of plant and animal forms.

Mathematics.—Study of rectangle, parallelogram, octagon, trapezoid, circle, parallel lines and circles, radius, diameter, circumference of circle, area and perimeter of first four figures—all growing out of planting and covering tulip-bed in early fall; drawing to a scale, estimating sizes in same connection. Ellipse, foci, horizontal, vertical, perpendicular; angle, measuring angle, degree, use of compass and protractor. This work is done in connection with change of seasons, revolution of earth around sun. Finding the center of a circle and bisecting a line are two interesting problems that will assert themselves here.

Business problems—how business is done, values, gain and loss; geographical problems, scientific and commercial; simple discount expressed in per cent. This last arises in home economics. Common and decimal fractions; emphasis laid upon the free use of the latter.

Mathematical language, the equation; generalized number with formal statement of principles.

Music.—Practice in sight-reading is continued. A few difficult songs are given by rote. In two-part songs the entire class occasionally sings the alto part, in preparation for school ensemble-singing. The scale is analyzed, its structure noted, and rules for key progression formulated. Original songs are composed by each class.

Wood-working.—Second half-year: The study of colonial

history by the children of this group suggests the opportunity of making a brief study of colonial furniture. Its chief features will be taken up: (*a*) the principal articles of furniture in a colonial house; (*b*) the kinds of wood used; (*c*) the characteristics of the "colonial style." An excursion will be made to a leading furniture store for the purposes of further illustration and identification of colonial furniture. It is hoped that in some of the articles which the children make for the school-room, or the school, or for their own use, it will be possible to carry out simple outlines and designs suggested by the study of colonial furniture.

Free-hand sketches for outline and proportion precede the making of all articles in wood. These will be followed by a working or mechanical drawing. A few blue-prints will be made by the children of those designs which the class, as a whole, consider the best.

Textiles.—Second half-year: Design costumes for dramatic work, Greek, and colonial French and Indian. Designs stenciled for decoration of costumes on leather, cotton, linen. Comparison of vegetable with other dyes. Study of woven and printed patterns.

Cooking.—Given under "Applied Science."

Modeling.—First half-year: Building of pottery, modeled after shapes of Greek vases, the decoration chosen from Greek motives of design.

Gymnastics.—Lesson plan the same. Additional control of distance and direction in running and marching; increased mental and physical values through tactics executed without music at command. Training for increased dexterity and alertness through introducing insistence upon form, as well as uniformity in the details of changing the direction of facing or position of the class upon the floor. Games still involve all players, but emphasize the element of additional choice.

Dancing.—Waltz, two-step, square dance, prairie queen, Highland fling, sailor's hornpipe. Gymnastic dancing for eighth-year girls: (1) Highland fling, (2) cachucha, (3) Greek dance, (4) Irish lilt.

DIVISION E

SECTION 9 (NINTH SCHOOL YEAR)

At the age of eleven or twelve the child is not so much interested in activities for their own sake as he is in their relation to the world-activities about him. In studying the different phases of the development of the United States, such as the development of the steamboat or the railroad, he constantly refers to the present and tries to interpret the significance of the present in the light of the past. This is the keynote of the work in history: the study of some of the social and economic questions of the past, to be able to interpret present-day problems. To be able to understand this, and to appreciate what is going on around us more fully there must be a study of geography and the physical sciences. In all this study there is a constant demand for mathematics, which must become, if it is not already, an efficient tool. The children are not yet able to generalize broadly, but are able to organize their knowledge in the solution of a problem. At this age interest in adventure is strong, and the reading for home and school follows this interest and seeks to develop a greater love for the good in literature.

History.—The history of the United States from the Revolutionary War to the present time is the year's work. Special features of the work: the geographical, industrial, and social phases of the expansion of the American people; the great westward movement which began with the early emigration to Kentucky and continued across the continent to the Pacific Ocean.

Pioneer life. The child's conception of life on the frontier is built up from a study of such topics as the following: the migration of a family across the mountains to Kentucky; the cause of the migration; the possible routes across the mountains; the geographical factors involved in choosing a tract of land for a farm; the clearing and tilling of the land for a farm; the necessity for some form of community life; Daniel Boone as a type of the early explorer and pioneer; the governmental problems presented to the pioneers and their solutions; the settlement of Kentucky and Tennessee; the work of George Rogers Clark in saving the

Northwest territory to the United States; the settlement of the Northwest Territory; the Ordinance of 1787; the Ohio Company and other land companies in the settlement of Ohio.

Reading: Extracts from original sources; two of the following: Thwaites, *Daniel Boone;* Churchill, *The Crossing* (first part); Thwaites, *How George Rogers Clark Won the Northwest.*

Economic and industrial conditions in the West. Topics to be considered: the demand for a market, and for the right to navigate the Mississippi River; the purchase of Louisiana Territory; improvements in transportation by invention of the steamboat, and the building of national and local roads and canals; the War of 1812, a struggle for commercial independence; the expedition of Lewis and Clark; the growth of the slavery questions, including the Missouri Compromise and the annexation of Texas; the development of railroads; the effect of railroads and steamboats in the development of the trans-Mississippi country; the discovery of gold in California; the Oregon country; the economic conditions leading up to the Civil War; the geographic factors in these conditions; the Civil War; the great industrial revolution following the Civil War; the factory system; the industries of the North and South.

Reading: Extracts from original sources; three of the following as home reading: Lighton, *Lewis and Clark;* Kinzie, *Wau Bun;* Brady, *The Conquest of the Southwest;* Parkman, *Oregon Trail;* Irving, *Astoria;* Hale, *The Man without a Country;* Taylor, *Eldorado;* a biography of Lincoln.

Excursions to a farm, railroad shops, and other industrial plants, will be made.

English.—(1) Literature: King Arthur Legends; the children read Lanier's *The Boy's King Arthur,* and selections from Mallory's *Morte D'Arthur.*

(2) Reading: The books named under "History" for home reading; also Stevenson's *Treasure Island and Kidnapped.*

(3) Writing: When the children reach this year, they are expected to have the power to write legibly and easily. There is constant demand in history, geography, science, and literature

for written reports, stories, and descriptions. The correction of these papers by the children requires a knowledge of the simpler rules of grammar. The papers are filed and furnish a record of the individual work.

Care is exercised to present the oral and written expression that should accompany the growth and complexity of idea. Drill is given in the forms and their use whenever the pupil feels a need for it, or whenever it is apparent that the form will not be learned without it.

Some facts in grammar are taught incidentally. The outcome of this work during the year should be a knowledge of sentences and sentence structure; subject and predicate; words, phrases, and clauses and their functions; parts of speech, with emphasis on nouns, pronouns, adjectives, and verbs, and functions of each.

German.—Half of the work for this year in German is oral. The children are encouraged to use the vocabulary they have acquired as much as possible in class, and frequently a child takes the place of the teacher for a portion of the recitation hour. The class reads: Guerber, *Märchen und Erzählungen.* A few of the more difficult songs are learned. A story is dramatized and given either at one of the morning exercises or at a school festival. Grammar: the principal tenses of the verb, use of genitive and dative.

French.—Printing of historical and literary anecdote-book for the seventh and eighth years from material prepared by pupils of the seventh and eighth years. Making and illustrating of programs for French carnival party given to French students of University High School; dramatizing and writing of scenes characteristic of Breton sailors and fishermen in connection with the reading of "Herve Reil;" photographs and postal cards from Brittany to be used as illustrations. Reading of French historic sketches selected and printed by tenth year; review of sixth, seventh, and eighth years' grammar record book. Fourth conjugation, indicative, conditional, and imperative modes; gender and number of nouns and adjectives; exceptions to the general rule. Reading-lessons and grammar work taken from the *Dramatic French Reader*. La Fontaine's *Fables*.

Speech, oral reading, and dramatic art.—Old English and Scotch ballads. Browning, "Herve Riel;" Kipling, "The Ballad of East and West." Interpreted to the children: Kipling, "The Explorer;" Longfellow, "The Building of the Ship;" Lowell, selections from *Biglow Papers*.

The reading and recitation of poems, orations, and other selections for the school festivals. The dramatic training required for the presentation of the children's English, French, and German plays.

Geography.—(1) North America: The study of North America begun in Section 7 is reviewed in this section from the standpoint of the relation of the geography of the country to the history of the development of the people. Points considered: topography of the continent as a whole; the topographic divisions; the climate of each in connection with the daily weather maps of the United States Weather Bureau (see "Science"); the agricultural, mineral, and commercial advantages of each; state of development; the effect of these geographic factors upon the life of the people; the relation of the geography to the history. Blackboard chalk-modeling of topography; field trips and the geographic laboratory are used as aids in the study of physiographic processes. Maps, pictures, lantern slides are also used. A collection representing the resources of the United States is made.

(2) South America: A continent similar to North America in structure, but differing in its climatic conditions, hence differing in its agricultural, commercial, and social relations. The same general plan is followed as in the study of North America. The museum collection is used to illustrate the trade relations between Chicago and South America.

(3) Africa: "The continent of contrasts" (Keane); a continent differing in structure from those already studied; a continent greatly retarded in its development because of its desert conditions, plateau formation, and slightly eroded river valleys.

Points to be considered and purpose to be attained are the same as in the previous study.

(4) Australia: A continent similar to South America in location, but differing from it in climatic, industrial, and commercial features.

A study of current events continued during the year serves to unite all continents with our own. References for pupils Carpenter, *North America, South America, Africa, Australia;* Shaler, *The Story of Our Continent;* books of travel; magazine articles. For textbooks, see list of textbooks on another page.

Nature-study.—This class will make a special study of trees, their characteristics, their habitats, and the character of the wood. Frequent visits will be made to Washington Park and to Jackson Park to study trees. The children will label for the younger children the trees in our own garden. Each child will keep a history of the year in color, showing by frequent paintings the changing aspects of nature.

This class will plant the new shrubs in the garden, including raspberries, blackberries, currants, and grapes, and will be responsible for their care.

There is much material for nature-study in the lower grades which can be made available by the older children. The ninth-year class will this year make for the lower grades: observation ants' houses, stocked with ants; aquaria stocked with various water plants and animals; earthworm boxes; and will be responsible for the gathering of cocoons, etc. These older children will suggest ways by which the younger children can get most good out of the nature-study material.

This year hot-beds and cold-frames will be made in the garden, for the use of the entire school. The class will study the principles involved in making hot-beds. These children will also have charge of the urns in the court.

The nature-study and forestry bulletins of the United States Department of Agriculture and of the state experimental stations will be of great use, as well as other books in the library. A special study will be made of the meteorological instruments of the school; weather charts made for a while, and the weather maps of the United States Weather Bureau, will be used in making out the weather and climate of the United States. (See "Geography"). The principles thus learned will be applied to the determination of the climate of the other parts of the world studied.

The longer excursions are to Dune Park, Glencoe, Palos Park, and Willow Springs.

Applied science.—First half-year: A child living in a vortex of mechanical forces in a great industrial center like Chicago is constantly coming in contact with natural forces applied by man in a multiplicity of ways to aid him in his work. Hitherto this changing panorama has held him transfixed with its play on his senses, but at about this period in his development the spell is broken somewhat. He is no longer satisfied with mere seeing and wondering. As he sees each mechanical wonder, whether a dynamo, a locomotive, a steamship, or any of the myriad machines, he must know what runs it, why it runs, and how it works. He wants to control it himself.

Many of the boys have shops at home. They have begun to make simple machines, to theorize about and plan various mechanical devices. Chief among their interests is electricity. Because of its great interest for them, and because of its almost universal application along industrial lines, it is given special attention at this time.

They are interested in making electrical machines and apparatus, in experimenting, in telling their various experiences in and out of school, and in studying about the men who have accomplished things in the electrical world.

Static electricity is not given much attention except from a historical standpoint. Each pupil is expected to plan and construct electrical machines or apparatus, and to do experimental work. Any of the following may be constructed: wet and dry cells, storage cells, batteries of each, electro-magnets, a simple telegraph instrument, electric switches, buttons, motors, electric furnaces, electrical signals, a small trolley-car system and an arc light.

Each one is encouraged to work along individual lines as

soon as he understands the principles well enough to do so without wasting his time. As the classes are doing work in wood in the shop at the same time that they are studying electricity, they are encouraged to execute their plans at school under supervision as well as at home independently.

The telegraph, the telephone, the submarine cables, the X-ray, wireless, the phonograph, the great electrical achievements, and the part each plays in our present complicated social and industrial life, will receive as much emphasis as the children can appreciate; the aim being to make this a study of a phase of the life about them, rather than a study of a thing interesting in itself apart from the life of which it is a part. To this end excursions will be made to the university electric plant, a municipal lighting-plant, the Western Electric Company at 269 S. Clinton Street, and the annual electric show.

Second half-year (see "Cooking"): Hygienic physiology; digestion in relation to health; experiments; respiration; proper breathing; composition of air; experiments; carbon dioxide; proper ventilation; circulation—the transference of nutrition and respiratory gases.

Meteorology: Constituents of atmosphere; effects of changes in temperature and air-pressure; the barometer; the United States Weather Bureau; the weather-recording apparatus in the Elementary School; weather records kept by children as a basis for study.

Drawing and painting.—Drawing and painting are forms of expression used in many phases of school work in this year, but especially in nature-study, geography, history, and literature. The class will make a series of frequent paintings as records of the changes in the nature picture. Design is based upon the experience which has been gained previously in the crafts, and hence will not depend upon the initiative of those subjects. It will represent the individual interest in creating beauty. The designs, when made, will be carried out in some craft. The creative exercises will be in line, dark and light, and color, illustrating the principles of rhythm, balance, and harmony.

Mathematics.—The subject-matter for mathematics is

selected as far as possible from the pupil's experience: from problems growing out of his activity in and out of school, and problems growing out of his study of the commercial and industrial life about him. This involves work in (1) arithmetical processes, (2) geometrical constructions and applications, and (3) algebraic representations of arithmetical processes and equations.

Arithmetical processes: (1) Through a study of the organization and operation of modern business institutions the pupils will become familiar with the commercial transactions involved in banking, handling stocks and bonds, loans, promissory notes, interest, taxes, discount, insurance, and commission. This will require the solution of numerous problems demanding a knowledge of operations in percentage. (2) Ratio and proportion as related to field and shop work. (3) Square root worked out through geometry and number; application to the square and right triangle. (4) Constructions in cardboard and paper, and drawings and diagrams, to work out methods for field-work. (5) Volumetric mensuration: calculate cost of digging foundations, tunnels, and canals, filling for railroad constructions and elevations; finding area and volume of bins, boxes, railroad cars, and tanks; finding area and volume of cones.

Geometrical constructions and applications: (1) Working-drawings for manual training. (2) Representative drawings to scale of tracts of ground; of farms, maps, field measurements. (3) Designing for simple electrical and mechanical appliances. (4) The bisecting of a line, the construction of a perpendicular, of angles and of triangles; the bisecting of an angle. (5) Similar triangles; indirect measurements by the use of similar triangles; ratio and proportion through the laws of similar triangles (similar right triangles being used); English and metric systems of weights and measurements used.

Algebraic work: (1) Syncopated algebraic laws of number and of mensuration formulated into equations by abbreviating words into letters, the resulting equations being read as sentences. (2) The use of the equation in percentage and interest. (3) Equations in ratio and proportion. (4) Solution of problems by both arithmetic and algebra.

Sufficient emphasis is given terminology for a clear and intelligent use of it. In all cases enough practice is given to fix the mathematical principles and processes involved.

Textiles.—First half-year: A study of the development of the textiles industry; weaving on Swedish looms; fabric analysis; collection and classification of fabrics; evolution of looms; biographies of inventors of textiles machinery; excursions to shops and factories with a view toward understanding American textile products.

Suggested excursions: Textile Rug Co., Fine Arts Building, Field Museum, public-school textile classes, and Art Institute. The work will be related to the history work, which at this time is dealing with the pioneer conditions of the westward movement.

Woodwork.—First half-year: Method; working-drawings for each construction; a careful study of plans and principles involved. Articles made; those for use in home and school; the pupil given a choice when practicable. The class design electrical machines and apparatus (see "Applied Science"), demanding part of the construction in wood. A study of the history and distribution of some important cabinet woods; characteristics of bark, branching, and leaves by which trees may be recognized; grain and finish of woods; lumbering.

Home economics.—Second half-year: Study of different foods; classification of food: (1) carbohydrates, (2) fats, (3) proteids. Application of heat to each of these food principles, and temperature at which each is cooked. Different processes of cookery. Review of previous work with more definite organization of previous experience. Study of cooking apparatus and utensils.

Science.—Heat and methods of transmitting it. Comparison of conducting power of different substances. Boiling point of different materials; effect of pressure on boiling-point; effect of substance in solution on boiling- and freezing-point of water. Tests for different food principles. Beginning of food analysis.

Metal-working.—Second half-year: The children hammer from sheet copper and brass articles of social use, such as trays, bowls, candle-sticks; or cut and bend into shape such articles as book-ends, calendar-frames, picture-frames, candle- and lamp-shades. Designs will be applied by means of etching, piercing, or perforating. This work necessitates riveting and possibly soldering.

Music.—Two-part songs are read. Two parts of three-part songs to be sung in the general assembly are learned. The minor scale is analyzed, and rules for its formation are formulated. The chromatic scale is learned by syllable. Chromatic exercises are used.

Gymnastics.—Lesson plan the same as in previous grades. Girls and boys in separate classes. Marching and running as well as postural exercises and apparatus demanding increased volition and concentration of attention; rhythmic exercises for the girls developing into folk-dances; tactics introducing an increasing number of evolutions, calling for greater concentration and alertness. This is a period of rapid growth—new functions develop, as well as large amounts of new tissue. Hence all exercises tend to special development of heart and lung actions, care being taken to avoid strain. Games of higher organization are added which prepare for team play and require endurance and develop judgment.

Dancing.—Waltz, two-step, square dance. Folk-dances: Irish washerwoman, Rejane, Swedish weaving dance.

DIVISION E

SECTION 10 (TENTH SCHOOL YEAR)

History.—The European history immediately preceding the discovery of America: Following the American history of the ninth year, the tenth year takes up that period of European history which immediately precedes the discovery of America. The work which centers about the Renaissance, is selected because it is the background of American history; because it may be used in solving some of the social and governmental problems which appeal to these pupils; because the spirit of chivalry, service, and heroism finds a ready response in the adolescent years; because knowledge of the conditions which surround modern labor will show the value of the freedom in work which resulted in the art and architecture of the thirteenth, fourteenth, and fifteenth centuries. The subject will be presented according to the following outlines:

1. The period of discovery and the growth of geography: (*a*) Geographical knowledge previous to the fifteenth-century voyages; ideas of the Greeks and Romans. (*b*) The Crusades, their effect upon the routes of travel. (*c*) The journeys of the Polos; increase of geographical knowledge and the breaking-up of routes of trade. (*d*) The invention of printing; books of the Middle Ages; mural paintings; effect of printing upon knowledge.

2. Feudalism and chivalry; the growth of feudalism; the life of the people; the growth of the church.

3. The guild system of labor contrasted with our modern factory system. Art: (*a*) The towns of the Middle Ages; their position on lines of trade; trade guilds. (*b*) Florence and Nuremberg—typical expressions of the thirteenth century; the cathedrals of Europe, illustrations of Gothic architecture. (*c*) Results of the guild system of labor—compared with modern factory system.

English.—(1) Literature: Shakespeare, *Julius Cæsar;* Aldrich, *Friar Jerome and His Beautiful Book;* Arnold, *Little Flowers of Saint Francis*; Henry Van Dyke, *The First Christmas Tree;* Tennyson, *Gareth and Lynette* (selected parts); Lowell, *The Vision of Sir Launfal;* Scott, *Marmion and Douglas*, and selections from *Ivanhoe.*

(2) Home reading: As throwing light upon the history, the following poems and books are recommended for home reading. Some of the poems may be read with the class. Longfellow, "Venice," "The Belfry of Bruges," "Nuremberg," "Giotto's Tower," "The Sermon of Saint Francis," "Walter von der Vogelweide;" Scott, *Ivanhoe, The Talisman;* C. M. Yonge, *The Little Duke;* Pyle, *The Story of King Arthur, Robin Hood, Men of Iron;* Lanier, *The Boy's King Arthur;* Gunsaulus, *Monk and Knight;* Pitman, *Stories of Old France;* Harding, *The Story of the Seven Hills;* Brooks, *Historic Girls, Historic Boys.*

(3) Languages: Pupils who have previously studied French or German will continue that study. Any who are not studying a modern language may begin Latin. The syntax of these languages, by conscious comparison and contrast, will be used to aid in the understanding of English syntax. Latin in this grade will not take the place of the high-school Latin, but will form a basis for it, consisting of simple exercises planned in accordance with Professor Hale's *First Year Latin* lessons. Pupils are expected, before completing the work of this grade, to have acquired the habit of spelling correctly, skill to write legibly, and power to express their thoughts clearly in both oral and written language. Systematic instruction in grammar to this end will be a part of the work in English. There will be a study of the sentence (subject and predicate, modifiers, phrases, clauses, kinds of sentence, declarative, imperative, etc., forms—simple, complex, and compound). The parts of speech will be learned, and some work done in inflection. Scott and Buck's *Brief English Grammar* will be used as a textbook.

German.—The eighth grade will be led on to do original work in German either in writing or in oral work. The oral work will be connected, if possible, with the history or field-work. This class will read Seligmann's *Altes und Neues.* The method will be the same as in previous years, translation being avoided if possible. Grammar: the declension of the nouns and adjectives, and the conjugation of the verbs.

French.—Planning and carrying out of a French carnival party to be given by the Elementary School French classes to the French students of the University High School; selecting and printing of brief sketches of French history, dramatizing of scenes from *La Chanson de Roland* and *La Vie de Charlemagne.* Christmas work: Writing of scenes from *La Vie de Sainte Geneviève,* illustrations of Puvis de Chavannes used; Panthéon. Reading lessons and grammar work taken from *The Dramatic French Reader.* Review and printing of grammar record-book for the fourth, seventh, eighth, and ninth years. Reflexive and impersonal verbs; a few irregular verbs in common use; rules of past participle. *Le petit Robinson de Paris-Foa,* L. de Bonneville; the history to be selected in Paris, 1906.

Speech, oral reading, and dramatic art.—Subjects for oral reading are chosen from the general work in nature-study, history, and geography, from the subjects listed under "Literature," from Julius Cæsar, and selections from Scott, and from other orations and dramatic selections to be used in the morning exercise. The oral reading of subject-matter bearing on these general topics is used to give the class information not otherwise to be obtained. The study of oratory has for its object the training of the pupils to speak with purpose and power to an audience.

Geography.—In this year the class will sum up the geography of the preceding years, including the physiography and political geography, but from a new point of view. The geographical conditions under which man is living on the earth, and the effect of these conditions upon his life, form the background of the work.

Starting with the world as a whole, attention will be directed to the distribution of land and water on the earth, the mountain masses, the great plains, river basins, deltas, flood-plains, and coastal plains, the glaciated areas, tundras, and forests. This will involve the study of the distribution of sunshine and heat on the earth, and the terrestrial winds. The children will review their work of former years on weather and climate, and learn by experiment more definitely the principles of governing atmospheric pressure, and winds and rainfall.

The class will visit several of the large commercial stores and maunfacturing plants, to learn what the different countries are sending us, and what we are sending them in return. This will involve a thorough review of the commercial and political geography of the preceding years.

In the study of climate the class will use the meteorological instruments and records in the school museum, and will make a visit to the United States Weather Bureau Station in the Federal Building.

In studying the relation between the nature of a country

and the lives of a people, constant reference will be made to the books in the school library, to magazine articles, and especially to Herbertson's geographies, which are a series of extracts from the best books of travel.

The excursions will be to the following regions: (1) Glencoe; (2) Fraction Run, near Lockport, and the Drainage Canal; (3) Dune Park; (4) Thornton (see "Nature-Study"). On these excursions the class will use the contour maps of the United States Geological Survey (see "Mathematics" and "Geography").

Nature-study.—This class will have general oversight of the garden, with the specific work of mulching the beds in the fall, pruning the shrubs and trees, and guarding against injurious insects; it will also make a study of the relations of insects to plants. The beneficial relations will be studied through the work of the bees in pollination, and the injurious effects through a study of the scale insects, the rose beetles, and the different moths. The depredations of the harmful insects will be combated with the various spraying mixtures, and in other ways.

During the year the class will make frequent excursions to Jackson Park to observe the changes which are taking place, and to make sketches of the landscape. Last year these sketches gave the *motif* for a large mural drawing in the classroom. (See frontispiece.)

In the spring longer excursions will be made in connection with the geography: (1) to the north shore, to study the action of running water in making ravines, and the action of the waves and of the wind; (2) to Thornton, to study river valleys of a later stage, with broad flood plains; (3) to Fraction Run, a rock ravine; (4) to Dune Park, to study the action of the waves and the wind in making sand-dunes. The pupils will study the development of the topography of the regions, the distribution of plants and animals found there, and the factors which control it. They will also draw contour maps (see "Mathematics"), on which they will locate these life-areas. They will study the borderland which lies between these vegetation areas, to emphasize the constantly changing conditions—physical evolution and the influence on life.

Home economics.—First half-year: Beginning with the homes of the Middle Ages, and instituting a comparison between them and the homes of the present day, the class will make a study of the modern house. The plan of the house and its furnishing; the methods of heating, ventilating, and lighting; the water supply and the plumbing, will be considered and studied experimentally. Visits will be made to buildings in process of construction. The study of the care of the individual home will lead to that of municipal housekeeping, and emphasis will be laid upon the responsibility of each household in helping to secure healthful conditions throughout the city, and in making the city beautiful.

Mathematics.—(1) Algebra viewed through arithmetic. By means of the equation, solve simple arithmetic problems, force problems, laws of simple machines, and mensuration laws, lead up to work with purely formal equations, and justify all reasoning by the five laws of the equation.

(2) Mechanical drawing: Scale plans and elevations of accessible objects; scale drawings in manual training; representative drawings of accessible and remote tracts of ground; topographic work from data taken in the field; construction of ornamental designs; study of government land surveys.

(3) Geometry: constructive, experimental, and quasi-demonstrative; relation of angles of polygons, shown experimentally and by measurement; construction of square corners on paper and in the field; running parallels and laying out curves; staking out lines at any angles to given lines; proofs of principles by actual superposition of representative figures; laws of similar triangles and their uses in field-work.

Wood-working.—First half-year: The making of articles for use in the school. The making of articles for individual use, with emphasis upon staining, polishing, and care of wood. In drawing there will be: (*a*) free-hand drawing for proportion and design; (*b*) reduction of these drawings to working-drawings; (*c*) blue-prints.

OUTDOOR GYMNASTICS

THE COOKING CLUB

Metal-working.—First half-year: This group has had two quarters of metal-work, and is able to design more intelligently for this material. Designs will be applied to all pieces, either in etching, piercing, chasing, or in combinations of the three ways. The process of soldering and riveting may be freely used. Very simple buckles, hatpins, or brooches are possible.

Modeling.—Second half-year: Illustrations of various phases of the life of the Middle Ages, emphasizing the spirit of chivalry and the work of monastic orders. Illustrations to be in the round or in relief, and colored when that is deemed advisable.

Textiles.—Second half-year: Study of fabrics for clothing and for household use; classification of fabrics; some practice in fabric analysis; chemical tests for the different textile fibers; use of aniline dyes in the preparation of embroidery materials; preparation of maps, charts, and illustrative samples for the school museum to show the textile centers of the world, and regions of production and manufacture; history of the evolution of textile machinery.

Music.—The work of the first half of the year will include a review of the major, minor, and chromatic scales, with their intervals; also the singing of unison and two-part and three-part songs. Where interest in music technic seems to be lacking, special emphasis will be laid upon chorus work.

Physical culture.—Results more than ever depend upon the attitude and interest of the pupil. The training should begin to show dexterity and co-ordinate action and power of endurance. Proportion of formal exercises to games now becomes two-thirds. Rhythmic work largely folk-dances. Exercises chosen for direct bearing upon the growth and development of the period. Exercises of skill and precision with hand apparatus. Fundamental exercises on hanging and resting apparatus. The best games of the previous years are used for the free play at the close of the lesson, and, in addition, preparatory work for the highly organized competitive games.

Dancing.—Waltz, two-step, square dance, Cecilian circle, bow dance, Irish washerwoman.

TEXTBOOKS

FIFTH SCHOOL YEAR

Literature: Robert Louis Stevenson, *Child's Garden of Verse* (Rand, McNally).

Arithmetic: Myers and Brooks, *Rational Elementary Arithmetic.*

SIXTH SCHOOL YEAR

History: Jennie Hall, *History of Chicago.*

Arithmetic: Myers and Brooks, *Rational Elementary Arithmetic* (bought in previous year).

Geography: Carpenter, *North America.*

French: *Popular French Games.*

SEVENTH SCHOOL YEAR

History: Governor Bradford's *Plymouth Plantation* (paper cover); *Description of New Netherlands* (paper cover).

Geography: Longmans' *New School Atlas;* Carpenter, *North America* (bought in previous year).

Literature: Irving, *Rip Van Winkle* (paper cover).

French: *Jeux, chansons et rondes populaires de France* "Popular French Games" (bought in fourth year).

German: Foster, *Geschichten und Märchen.*

Dictionary: Webster's *Academic.*

EIGHTH SCHOOL YEAR

History: McMaster, *School History of the United States.*

Arithmetic: Myers and Brooks, *Rational Grammar School Arithmetic.*

Geography: Tarr and McMurry, Book III., Longmans' *Atlas* (bought in previous year).

Science: Walter, *Wild Birds in City Parks.*

French: *French Dramatic Reader.*

German: Guerber, *Märchen und Erzählungen,* Vol I.

Dictionary: Webster's *Academic* (bought in previous year).

NINTH SCHOOL YEAR

History: Sparks, *Expansion of the American People;* Roosevelt, episodes from *Winning of the West;* McMaster, *School History of the United States* (bought in previous year).

Arithmetic: Myers and Brooks, *Rational Grammar School Arithmetic* (bought in previous year).

Geography: Tarr and McMurry, *Complete Geography;* Tarr and McMurry, *North America* (bought in previous year); Longmans' *Atlas* (bought in seventh year).

French: *French Dictionary; Dramatic French Reader* (bought in previous year).

German: Guerber, *Märchen und Erzählungen.* Vol. I (bought in previous year).

Dictionary: Webster's *Academic* (bought in seventh year).

TENTH SCHOOL YEAR

History: Harding, *The Story of the Middle Ages.*

Geography: Herbertson's *Descriptive Geographies: Asia, Europe, North America, South America;* Longmans' *Atlas* (bought in seventh year).

Literature: Shakespeare, *Julius Cæsar.*

French: L. Bonneville, *Le petit Robinson de Paris-Foa.*

German: Seligmann, *Altes und Neues.*

Grammar: Scott & Buck.

Dictionary: Webster's *Academic* (bought in seventh year).

EDITORIAL NOTES

The last great debate of national import in which the foes of manual training made their final stand was in the meeting of superintendents held in Washington, D. C., in March, 1889. The subject formed one of the chief topics on the program, and the result seemed to be so indecisive that one of the principal opponents, who at that time was an influential man in education, said: "Well, didn't we do them up?" But its right to a place in the course of study has never been really seriously questioned in an equally important body since! "How beggarly appear arguments in the face of a defiant deed." It is the "defiant deed" alone that shapes the things that are to come to pass, even after they have been disproved by the logician and howled down by the mob. It was much later than the Washington debate—almost a decade—when Colonel Parker went down to a public meeting in Chicago which packed the council chamber, and met a smart lawyer, then a member of the Board of Education, to discuss the fads, of which clay-modeling was the chiefest sinner. It was the old struggle over again of the seer with the "practical man": Each was as inexplicable to the other as though they spoke strange tongues. For, the one was estimating values in terms of human character, and the other was appraising clay at two cents a pound.

Struggle for Manual Training

Since those days manual work, in a great variety of forms which then were scarcely heard of, has come into the schools, and it has done much to make the term "fad" respectable. The annual meeting of the Western Drawing and Manual Training Teachers' Association enables one through its exhibits to keep step with the progress of this work from year to year. To one familiar with the character of the meetings of this body a decade ago, the recent sessions held at the University of Chicago show a marvelous development in both quantity and quality. Whereas

Western Drawing and Manual Training Teachers' Association

the exhibits were once small and made up, chiefly, of comparatively few drawings in black and white and in colored crayons, with here and there a few water-colors, the whole being liberally interspersed with copies, now one is confronted with a bewildering amount of material illustrating a half-dozen or more interesting kinds of artistic hand-work, in addition to the much-improved products of brush and pencil. The present exhibits of the society show in graphic terms the rapid and radical changes taking place in the schools.

Ability of Children to Work

A few years ago the present industrial and artistic output of school children would have been deemed impossible. The children have demonstrated as never before their ability to conceive and carry out a large amount of work having intrinsic merit. It remains only to organize further these efforts toward more useful and more definite ends. The teachers, the pupils, and the parents must bestir themselves to find what needs there are in the school, in the home, or in the community at large which the schools can fill. A genuine purpose, that can be easily appreciated and clearly understood by the children, must lie behind every piece of work that is done. It is doing things with a distinct realization of the needs that leads to the highest quality in the educational result. If this point is not clearly wrought out as the fundamental principle in organization, the art and handwork will be confined forever to the low level of the "pretty" and the "cunning."

Study of Design

The introduction of the study of design is an important step in the direction of proper organization. This subject fastens the attention of the pupils upon the relation of form to function; and as the adaptation becomes more and more refined, the merit of the result continues to rise. The work in design will be more useful as it becomes freer from the tendency to copy its forms from other days—an inclination not at all unnatural. The art of a people is their most enduring monument, and it is the embodiment of their ideals. These two facts will always cause it to command a respectful attitude of mind in those who study its significance, from which it is but a short step to actual imitation.

Of course, there are certain axioms in design, relating to arrangement and proportion, which always hold, and which always have controlled really artistic work; but the need now is that these principles be applied to the development of themes that belong to the present; to the embodiment of higher ideals than ever before—not of art alone, but of life as a whole. It must be remembered that ideals have not only changed; they have grown and are still growing. The proper development of design, therefore, requires that the children shall draw directly upon nature—not from other art—for their forms and materials. Otherwise they cannot remain original; they cannot become productive; they must degenerate into copyists.

The Artist vs. The Scientist

The thing most needed at this time for the furtherance of art is that there shall be a better understanding between the artist and the scientist. No artist ever plays an important rôle in his age until he goes to his work thoroughly saturated with the highest ideals of the time. Most of the art teachers today who are in contact with the children are not only almost wholly deficient in technical science training, but they have not studied nature enough to enable them to see even in dim outline the tremendous import of the theory of evolution. They have not yet caught the distinction between the older idea of a static creation and the newer idea of a dynamic creation. They face nature and really interpret it as the artists did in the days when the race was under different intellectual and moral control; and hence they see no special incongruity in allowing the children to repeat the art forms which are not significant now because they represent radically different conceptions of nature. Post-Darwinian art, whether better or worse, at least will never repeat the art of the Orient. In some way and in some form, neither of which at present may be clearly understood, it must involve the notion of movement; it must embody the idea of a continually rising goal, of a growing ideal in human life.

The oriental is controlled by his idea of a static creation. He sought and attained a dead level. He found a pattern and repeated it for centuries, until even its origin was lost and its significance had disappeared. Beautiful as the art forms are, as much as they tell of simplicity, skill, and patience, they are valuable to us as warnings rather than as models. The excellences of oriental art correspond to the perfections of a dead level; they represent a fixed horizon of thought, above which almost nothing new arose in centuries. This was necessarily true because the notions of nature and of its relation to man remained throughout this long lapse of time practically unchanged.

Oriental vs. Western Art

In the higher sense, therefore, the older art is not true to nature as we now know it, though it is true to nature as the latter was then understood. By being "true to nature" I do not mean that there shall be that microscopic faithfulness that limits every line of art to the actual nerve filaments of the individual thing. Nor does truthfulness to nature call for that rigid adjustment of "facts" which made Thomas Gradgrind object to flowers in the carpets because in nature we do not walk upon flowers. It does mean, however, that the unity which the new science seems to find in nature shall be made to appear in those forms of art which choose to use its materials. The scientific mind now sees in every bit of landscape, and in every clump of bushes, an immense variety in form and color, but withal an interrelationship among all the parts that makes a complete unity. The single, isolated leaf is meaningless, but in its place on the bush it is essential in explaining the meaning of the whole. If, now, in some piece of art which essays to use such materials, this unity is not preserved either in fact or by clear suggestion, then there is a fatal infidelity to nature as the man of science sees it. There is no just cause for quarrel between the artist and the scientist at any other point. This is a fact which the greatest nature artists have always recognized.

Art "True to Nature"

Unity of Nature in Art

On the other hand, we are educated beyond the point of being satisfied with the fragmentary and unrelated representations of nature, no matter in what field of art they may be found. This growth, which is not less scientific than it is artistic, is gradually relegating to oblivion the older wall-papers of maniacal pattern. Indeed, unless some invention soon comes to the rescue, wall-paper as a means of mural decoration is doomed. We are coming to see how preposterous it is to plaster over the four walls of a room a repetition of the same pattern. In a room with windows in one wall, a fireplace in another, a doorway in a third, and a blank space on the fourth, there is no possibility of treating the room well as a whole if the walls are all to be covered with the same set figures. It is out of the question to suppose that these, having the same light and space values, can be adapted equally well to all sides. The two determining factors in such a case are light and space. The intensity of the light will decide where the decoration focus, so to speak, will be, and the distribution of the light will regulate the depth and variety of color and shade that can be used. The shape and size of the various spaces will determine the forms that may be employed, and the artist who is also versed in nature will not plan to use unrelated figures and groups whose unity will be marred or destroyed by the nature of the spaces in which they are placed.

Decadence of Wall-Paper Art

The study of design, therefore, which will be sufficiently broad to organize the art work in schools in its present condition must comprehend a good deal more than the problem of merely filling spaces with well-balanced forms; it is of equal importance that the artist and teacher should be so thoroughly saturated with the modern scientific views of nature that, in perfecting his design, he will show, on the one hand, as much conscience in the selection and treatment of natural forms as, on the other hand, he displays judgment in filling spaces. Design requires not only training of the sense of proportion; it also involves scientific insight into the facts of nature.

Double Problem of Design

It is at this point that the recent exhibit showed its greatest weakness. The work in design will always present an anæmic condition, until it is associated with an exuberant study of nature; it will starve to death though in the midst of a great plenty. The exhibit, as a whole, indicates that the work of the schools is weakest upon this side. The advance made in the study of nature is not abreast of the improvement in the technics of expression. It is still irregular and scrappy, giving small evidence that the pupils have any grasp of the underlying thought of development. It is inevitable, therefore, that this weakness should appear in the art work.

Better Study of Nature Needed

The remedy lies in a broader, a more persistent, and a more intelligent study of nature. The teachers of both art and nature-study must get not only the modern point of view that science offers; they must make a closer personal study of the methods of development that are found in nature. They must through personal observation and study derive the dynamic conception and apply it in their teaching, instead of the static conception which is now, practically, in control. The pupils must have still freer access to the larger aspects of nature, and they must be allowed to represent directly what they see. The beautiful landscape work which children can do, and which may tell so much of the movement in nature, had practically no place in the exhibit. The tendency is still too strong to have the pupils learn to draw first and then learn to see afterward. This is especially true of the landscape sketching, which is so essential in nature-study.

There is no reason, however, for impatience or discouragement. The future seems assured of great things from biological considerations alone. In a recent magazine article Mr. Burbank points out the probable significance of the fact that we have in this country the mingling of all the races on the globe. In the year 1904 there were over 750,000 emigrants, representing over fifty nationalities. What the virility of this great composite may mean in future achieve-

Promise of American Art

ment one can but dimly forecast. Under the stimulus of a matchless environment, that includes almost every influence to which a human being can respond, it would seem that the embellishments of art and the inventions and discoveries in industry must indefinitely move forward and upward. To take a practical part in this growing individual and material life is the teacher's inspiring work.

W. S. J.

BOOKS RECEIVED

American Poems. By AUGUSTUS WHITE LONG. New York: American Book Co. Cloth, 12mo. Pp. 368. $0.90.

Advanced Arithmetic. By ELMER A. LYMAN. New York: American Book Co. Cloth, 12mo. Pp. 235. $0.75.

Carpenter's Geographical Reader: Africa. By FRANK G. CARPENTER. Illustrated. Chicago: American Book Co, Cloth, 12mo. Pp. 336. $0.60.

Commercial Geography. By HENRY GANNETT, CARL L. GARRISON, AND EDWIN J. HOUSTON. Maps and Illustrations. New York: American Book Co. Half leather, 8vo. Pp. 451. $1.25.

Composition—Rhetoric. By STRATTON D. BROOKS AND MARIETTA HUBBARD. New York: American Book Co. Cloth, 12mo. Pp. 442. $1.

Elementary Latin Writing. By CLARA B. JORDAN. New York: American Book Co. Cloth, 12mo. Pp. 270. $1.

Elements of German Grammar. By THOMAS H. JAPPE. New York: American Book Co. Cloth, 12mo. Pp. 133.

Essentials in American History. By ALBERT BUSHNELL HART. Illustrated. New York: American Book Co. Cloth, 12mo. Pp. 554+31.

Essentials of Latin. For Beginners. By HENRY CARR PEARSON. New York: American Book Co. Cloth, 12mo. Pp. 330. $0.90.

Excursions sur les bords du Rhin. Par ALEXANDRE DUMAS. Introduction and Vocabulary by THEODORE HENCKELS. New York: American Book Co. Cloth, 12mo. Pp. 176. $0.40.

Fishing and Hunting. By SARAH M. MOTT. New York: American Book Co. Cloth, 12mo. Pp. 127.

In Field and Pasture. By MAUDE BARROWS DUTTON. New York: American Book Co. Cloth, 12mo. Pp. 190.

Manual of American Literature. By JAMES B. SMILEY. Illustrated. New York: American Book Co. Cloth, 16mo. Pp. 336. $0.60.

Nine Choice Poems. By JAMES BALDWIN. New York: American Book Co. Cloth, 12mo. Pp. 112. $0.25.

Thirty More Famous Stories Retold. By JAMES BALDWIN. Illustrated. New York: American Book Co. Cloth, 12mo. Pp. 235.

Robinson Crusoe. Written for Children. By JAMES BALDWIN. Illustrated. New York: American Book Co. Cloth, 12mo. Pp. 191.

Stories of Great Musicians. By KATHERINE LOIS SCOBEY AND OLIVE BROWN HORNE. Illustrated. New York: Amercian Book Co. Cloth, 12mo. Pp. 189. $0.40.

The Fairy Reader. Adapted from Grimm and Anderson. By JAMES BALDWIN. Illustrated. New York: American Book Co. Cloth, 12mo. Pp. 188. $0.35.

The Rose Primer. By EDNA HENRY LEE TURPIN. Illustrated. New York: American Book Co. Cloth, 8vo. Pp. 128. $0.30.

Waste Not, Want Not Stories. Retold by CLIFTON JOHNSON. Illustrated. New York: American Book Co. Cloth, 12mo. Pp. 260. $0.50.

The Brooks Primer. By CLARENCE F. CARROLL AND SARAH C. BROOKS. Illustrated. New York: D. Appleton & Co. Cloth, 12mo. Pp. 128.

Culture Readers. Book III. Edited by EDITH A. SCOTT. Illustrated. New York: D. Appleton & Co. Cloth, 12mo. Pp. 144.

The Mind and its Education. By GEORGE HERBERT BETTS. New York: D. Appleton & Co. Cloth, 12mo. Pp. 265.

Twentieth Century Speller. In two Books. By WILLIAM L. FELTER AND LIBBIE J. EGINTON. New York: D. Appleton & Co. Paper, 12mo. Book I, pp. 88; Book II, pp. 138.

The False Entry and Other Stories about Schools. By C. W. BARDEEN. Syracuse, N. Y.: C. W. Bardeen. Cloth, 12mo. Pp. 244.

Berry's Writing Books. Chicago: B. D. Berry & Co. Five Books. Books I and II. Illustrated. Book I, *The Jingle Book;* Book II, *The Mother Goose Book;* Book III, *The Bird and Beast Book;* Book IV, *The Mother Goose Book;* Book V, *The Proverb Book.* Paper.

Business Speller. By G. S. KIMBALL. Indianapolis, Ind.: Bobbs-Merrill Co. Cloth, 12mo. Pp. 140. $0.30.

Colonial Stories. Retold from *St. Nicholas.* Illustrated. New York: Century Co. Cloth, 12mo. Pp. 194.

Lion and Tiger Stories. Retold from *St. Nicholas.* Illustrated. New York: Century Co. Cloth, 12mo. Pp. 186.

Our Holidays. Retold from *St. Nicholas.* Illustrated. New York: Century Co. Cloth, 12mo. Pp. 204.

A Watcher in the Woods. By DALLAS LORE SHARP. Illustrated by BRUCE HORSEFALL. New York: Century Co. Cloth, 12mo. Pp. 205.

Book of Indoor and Outdoor Games. By MRS. BURTON KINGSLAND. New York: Doubleday, Page & Co. Cloth, 12mo. Pp. 610. $1.50.

The Geography of Commerce and Industry. By W. F. ROCHELEAU. Boston: Educational Publishing Co. Cloth, 12mo. Pp. 408

First Reader. By JOSEPH H. WADE AND EMMA SYLVESTER. Illustrated. Boston: Ginn & Co. Cloth, 12mo. Pp. 127.

Paper Sloyd. By EDNAH ANNE RICH. Illustrated. New York: Ginn & Co. Cloth, quarto. Pp. 55. $0.85.

Primer. By JOSEPH H. WADE AND EMMA SYLVESTER. Illustrated. Boston: Ginn & Co. Cloth, 12mo. Pp. 92.

The Principles of Rhetoric. By ELIZABETH H. SPALDING. Boston: D. C. Heath & Co. Cloth, 12mo. Pp. 275.

Fifty English Classics Briefly Outlined. By MELVIN HIX. New York: Hinds, Noble & Eldredge. Cloth, 12mo.

Poems for the Study of Language. Edited by CHESTINE GOWDY. New York: Houghton, Mifflin & Co. Paper, 16mo. Pp. 207. $0.30.

Historiettes et poésies. Par MARIE M. ROBIQUE. New York: William R. Jenkins Co. Cloth, 12mo. Pp. 107. $0.60.

Word Studies. By EDWIN S. SCHEPPE. Advanced Book. Richmond, Va.: B. F. Johnson Publishing Co. Cloth, 12mo. Pp. 127.

Webster's Modern Dictionary. Elementary School Edition. Chicago: Laird & Lee. Cloth, 8vo. Pp. 416.

Webster's Modern Dictionary. Adapted for Intermediate Grades. Illustrated. Chicago: Laird & Lee. Cloth, 12mo. Pp. 458.

Webster's New Standard Dictionary. Compiled by E. T. Roe. Chicago: Laird & Lee. Cloth, 12mo. Pp. 745.

Webster's New Standard Dictionary. Student's Common School Edition. Illustrated. Chicago: Laird & Lee. Cloth, 12mo. Pp. 750.

Webster's New Standard Speller. By Alfred B. Chambers. Edited by E. T. Roe. Chicago: Laird & Lee. Cloth, 12mo. Pp. 216.

Bryant's Poems: Thanatopsis, Sella, and Other Poems. Edited by J. H. Castleman. New York: Macmillan C. Cloth, 16mo. Pp. 238.

Dynamic Factors in Education. By M. V. O'Shea. New York: Macmillan Co. Cloth, 12mo. Pp. 320.

How to Write. A Handbook based on the English Bible. By Charles Sears Baldwin. New York: Macmillan Co. Cloth, 12mo. Pp. 200.

How We Are Sheltered. By James Franklin Chamberlain. Geographical Reader. Illustrated. New York: Macmillan Co. Cloth, 12mo. Pp. 184. $0.40.

Joan of Arc. By Thomas De Quincey. Edited by Carol M. Newman. New York: The Macmillan Co. Cloth, 16mo. Pp. 296.

Language Readers. For First Five Grades. By Franklin T. Baker, George R. Carpenter, and Katherine B. Owen. Colored Illustrations. New York: Macmillan Co. First Year Book, Pp. 138, $0.25; Second Year Book, Pp. 152, $0.30; Third Year Book, Pp. 284, $0.40; Fourth Year Book, Pp. 345, $0.45; Sixth Year Book, Pp. 479, $0.60.

Language Speller. By Elizabeth H. Spalding and Frank R. Moore. New York: Macmillan Co. Cloth, 12mo. Pp. 144. $0.30.

Macmillan's Pocket American and English Classics. New York: Macmillan Co. Carlyle's *Heroes and Hero Worship,* Emerson's *Essays,* Shakespeare's *King Henry V,* Bacon's *Essays,* Hawthorne's *Wonder Book,* Carroll's *Alice's Adventures,* Church's *Story of the Iliad,* Church's *Story of the Odyssey,* Longfellow's *Miles Standish,* Horner's *Iliad, Memorable Passages from the Bible,* Dicken's *Christmas Carol.* Cloth, 16mo. Each $0.25.

Special Method in Language in the Eight Grades. By Charles A. McMurray. New York: Macmillan Co. Cloth, 12mo. Pp. 192.

Washington's Farewell Address and Webster's Bunker Hill Orations. Edited by William T. Peck. New York: The Macmillan Co. Cloth, 16mo. Pp. 128.

Lads and Lassies of Other Days. By Lillian L. Price. Chicago: Silver, Burdett & Co. Cloth, 12mo. Pp. 175.

Elements of English Grammar. By Arthur Le Roy Bartlett and Howard Lee McBain. New York: Silver, Burdett & Co. Cloth, 12mo. Pp. 345.

The Making of the American Nation. By Jacques Wardlaw Redway. For Elementary Schools. Illustrated. New York: Silver, Burdett & Co. Cloth, 12mo. Pp. 476. $1.

The Bird Woman at the Lewis and Clark Exposition. By Katherine Chandler. Illustrated. Silver, Burdett & Co. Cloth, 12mo. Pp. 109.

War for Independence. By Everett T. Tomlinson. Chicago: Silver, Burdett & Co. Cloth, 12mo. Pp. 178.

Algebra for Grammar Schools. By CHARLES HOBBS. New York: Parker P. Simmons. Cloth, 12mo. Pp. 138.

Basketry, Clay and Paper Weaving for the Elementary Grades. By ARTHUR HENRY CHAMBERLAIN, ELLA V. DOBBS, JANE LANGLEY, AND HARRY D. GAYLORD. San Francisco: Whitaker & Ray Co. Cloth, 12mo. Pp. 78. $0.50.

Library Method in American History. By GEORGE R. CRISSMAN. Dansville, N. Y.: World's Events Publishing Co. Paper, 12mo. Pp. 231. $0.30.

Graded Lessons in English. By REED AND KELLOGG. New York: Maynard, Merrill & Co. Cloth, 12mo. Pp. 281.

Graded Poetry Readers. Edited by KATHERINE D. BLAKE AND GEORGIA ALEXANDER. Book I, first and second grades; Book II, third grade; Book III, fourth grade; Book IV, fifth grade. New York: Maynard, Merrill & Co. Paper, 16mo. Pp. 95. $0.20 each.

Graded Literature Series. Edited by HARRY PRATT JUDSON AND IDA C. BENDER. Eight Books. Illustrated. New York: Maynard, Merrill & Co. Cloth, 12mo.

Introductory Language Work. By ALONZO REED. New York: Maynard, Merrill & Co. Cloth, 12mo. Pp. 386.

Nature-Study in the Poets. Arranged for School Use. By MARY ROENAH THOMAS. Boston, Mass.: Palmer Co. Paper, 12mo.

The Choral Song Book. Edited and Arranged by WILLIAM M. LAWRENCE AND FREDERICK H. PEASE. New York: Rand, McNally & Co. Cloth, 8vo. Pp. 224. $0.50.

Occupation for Little Fingers. By ELIZABETH SAGE AND ANNA M. COOLEY. Introductory Note by MARY SCHENK WOOLMAN. New York: Charles Scribner's Sons. Cloth, 12mo. Pp. 154.

The Elementary School Teacher

June, 1906

Vol. VI, No. 10

THE UNIVERSITY OF CHICAGO PRESS
CHICAGO AND NEW YORK
OTTO HARRASSOWITZ, LEIPZIG

The Elementary School Teacher

PUBLISHED MONTHLY EXCEPT IN JULY AND AUGUST

Editor . . WILBUR S. JACKMAN
Assistant Editor, BERTHA PAYNE
WITH THE CO-OPERATION OF
THE FACULTY OF THE UNIVERSITY OF CHICAGO SCHOOL OF EDUCATION
AND
THE FACULTY OF THE FRANCIS W. PARKER SCHOOL

CONTENTS FOR JUNE, 1906

Editorial communications and manuscripts should be addressed to Mr. Wilbur S. Jackman, Editor, The University of Chicago, Chicago, Ill.

Business correspondence should be addressed to The University of Chicago Press, Chicago, Ill.

Subscription, $1.50 per year. Single copies 20 cents. Postage prepaid by publishers for all subscriptions in the United States, Canada, Mexico, Cuba, Porto Rico, Panama Canal Zone, Republic of Panama, Hawaiian Islands, Philippine Islands, Guam, Tutuila (Samoa), Shanghai. For all other countries in the Postal Union 50 cents for postage should be added to the subscription price. Remittances should be made payable to the University of Chicago Press, and should be in Chicago or New York exchange, postal or express money order. If local check is used, 10 cents must be added for collection.

Claims for missing numbers should be made within the month following the regular month of publication. The publishers expect to supply missing numbers free only when they have been lost in transit.

European subscriptions, 9 marks (postage included), should be remitted to Otto Harrassowitz, 14 Querstrasse, Leipzig, Germany, European Agent.

Entered October 12, 1903, at the Post-Office at Chicago, Ill., as second-class matter, under Act of Congress March 3, 1879.

The Best TONIC

For the restoration of energy and vitality; the relief of mental and nervous exhaustion, impaired digestion or appetite, there is no remedy so beneficial as

HORSFORD'S Acid Phosphate

(Non-Alcoholic.)

It is a scientific and carefully prepared preparation of the phosphates that provides the tonic and nerve food needed to improve the general health.

If your druggist can't supply you, send 25 cents to RUMFORD CHEMICAL WORKS, Providence, R. I., for sample bottle, postage paid.

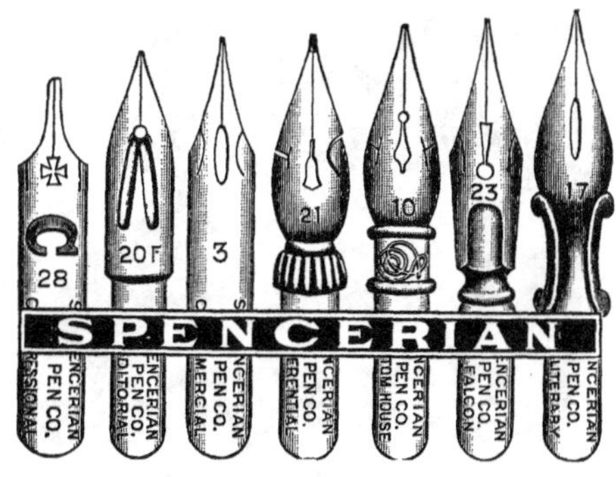

The STANDARD BRAND in the UNITED STATES

They are the best Steel Pen that can be made. Each pen is carefully examined before packing. Their reputation has been national since 1860. Twelve samples (different patterns) sent postpaid on receipt of six cents in stamps.

SPENCERIAN PEN CO.

349 BROADWAY, NEW YORK.

MENNEN'S

BORATED TALCUM

TOILET POWDER

The Freshness of Roses

and balmy June days are not more delightful and refreshing than the soothing touch of Mennen's. Gives immediate and positive relief from **Prickly Heat, Chafing, Sunburn** and all skin troubles. Everywhere used and recommended by physicians and nurses for its perfect purity and absolute uniformity. Mennen's face on every box. See that you get the genuine. For sale everywhere, or by mail, 25c. Sample free.

Gerhard Mennen Co., Newark, N.J.

Try Mennen's Violet (Borated) *Talcum.*

A Colorado-
Yellowstone Tour

Have you two vacation weeks at your disposal?

Do you want to do something different, something better than you have ever done before?

Then here is a brief outline of a tour that will bring you the best two weeks you ever lived.

Leave Chicago (for example) any day after June 1 on either of the Burlington's famous fast trains to Denver. You may travel via Omaha, Pacific Junction, St. Joseph or Kansas City, just as you like. Stop-overs permitted (no extra charge) at the Missouri River and points west.

From Denver take a side trip to Colorado Springs (no extra charge) and see the Cheyenne Canyons, Garden of the Gods, Pike's Peak and other attractions.

Returning to Denver, spend from one to three days in making some of the numerous and inexpensive little journeys into the mountains.

Leave Denver on the Burlington's Yellowstone Park train, the route of which is thro' the interesting formations of Northwest Nebraska; along the picturesque Black Hills (into which inexpensive side trips may be made); over the Big Horn Mountains; past Custer Battlefield, the most tragic upon which our sun shines; and, finally, thro' famed Yellowstone Valley to Gardiner, the official entrance to the Park.

This tour provides for a stay of five and a half days Wonderland — a complete tour of the Park — coachi each day, viewing what is by far the most interesti scenery on the globe and being entertained at the b hotels. Stay longer, if possible, for this is the finest o ing place known. Only extra charge after five and a h days is for hotel accommodations — $4.00 and up per d after seven days $3.50 and up per day.

After leaving Yellowstone Park, you travel to Min apolis and St. Paul, following the Yellowstone River th Montana, making a bee line thro' North Dakota's fer fields and crossing Minnesota's Lake Park region.

It would be well to provide for a day or two in a about the Twin Cities, for there is much to do and to s

Then come home on one of the Burlington's handso observation trains running over the Mississippi Ri Scenic Line. This will give you a splendid view of finest river scenery east of the Rocky Mountains, and, addition, a cool and comfortable journey.

Don't you think you would like to make this tour?

Too expensive? No! Indeed not!

The cost of a railway ticket for the entire tour (exclusive of side trips other than that to Colorado Springs), and including the coaching trip and five and a half days hotel accommodations in the Park, is only $85 from Chicago, Peoria or St. Louis; only $79 from Missouri River points, Kansas City to Omaha, inclusive.

Let me tell you more about this grand trip. Just write "Colorado-Yellowstone Tour" above your address on a postal card, sending it to

P130 **P. S. EUSTIS, 350 "Q" Building, Chicago.**

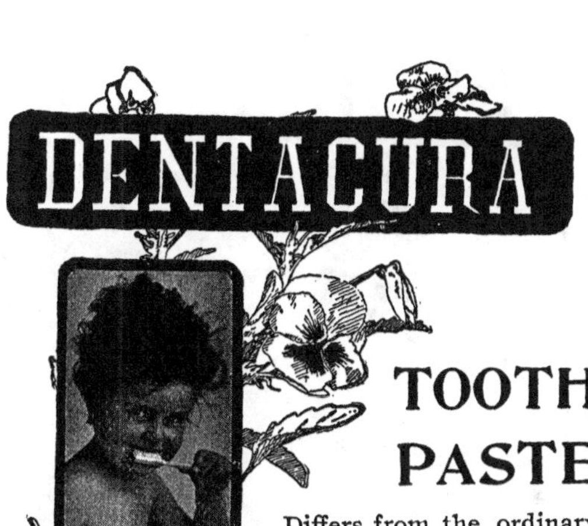

Differs from the ordinary dentifrice in minimizing the causes of decay. Endorsed by thousands of Dentists. It is deliciously flavored, and a delightful adjunct to the dental toilet. In convenient tubes. For sale at drug stores, **25c.** per tube.

AVOID SUBSTITUTES

DENTACURA COMPANY,

Newark, N. J., U. S. A.

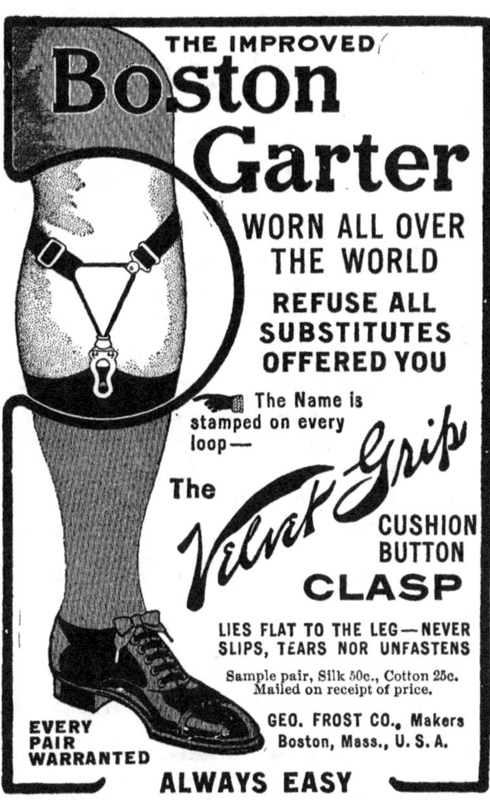

Chickering

PIANOS

THE Chickering Piano is at once the earliest Piano manufactured in America, and the model of all later makers. It has a peculiarly rich tone that has been equalled in no other instruments that have ever been produced. This exquisite tone is the standing mystery of the industry. Nearly every other maker has tried to copy it, but none have succeeded.

¶ A Chickering may mean an outlay slightly greater than would be necessary for an ordinary, good Piano, but the enjoyment that will accrue from its use—and the knowledge that you are securing a Piano that is "just right," make the small additional expense a trivial matter.

REPRESENTED IN CHICAGO BY

CLAYTON F. SUMMY CO.

220 WABASH AVENUE

PUBLISHERS AND IMPORTERS OF MUSIC — DEALERS IN MUSIC OF THE BETTER CLASS

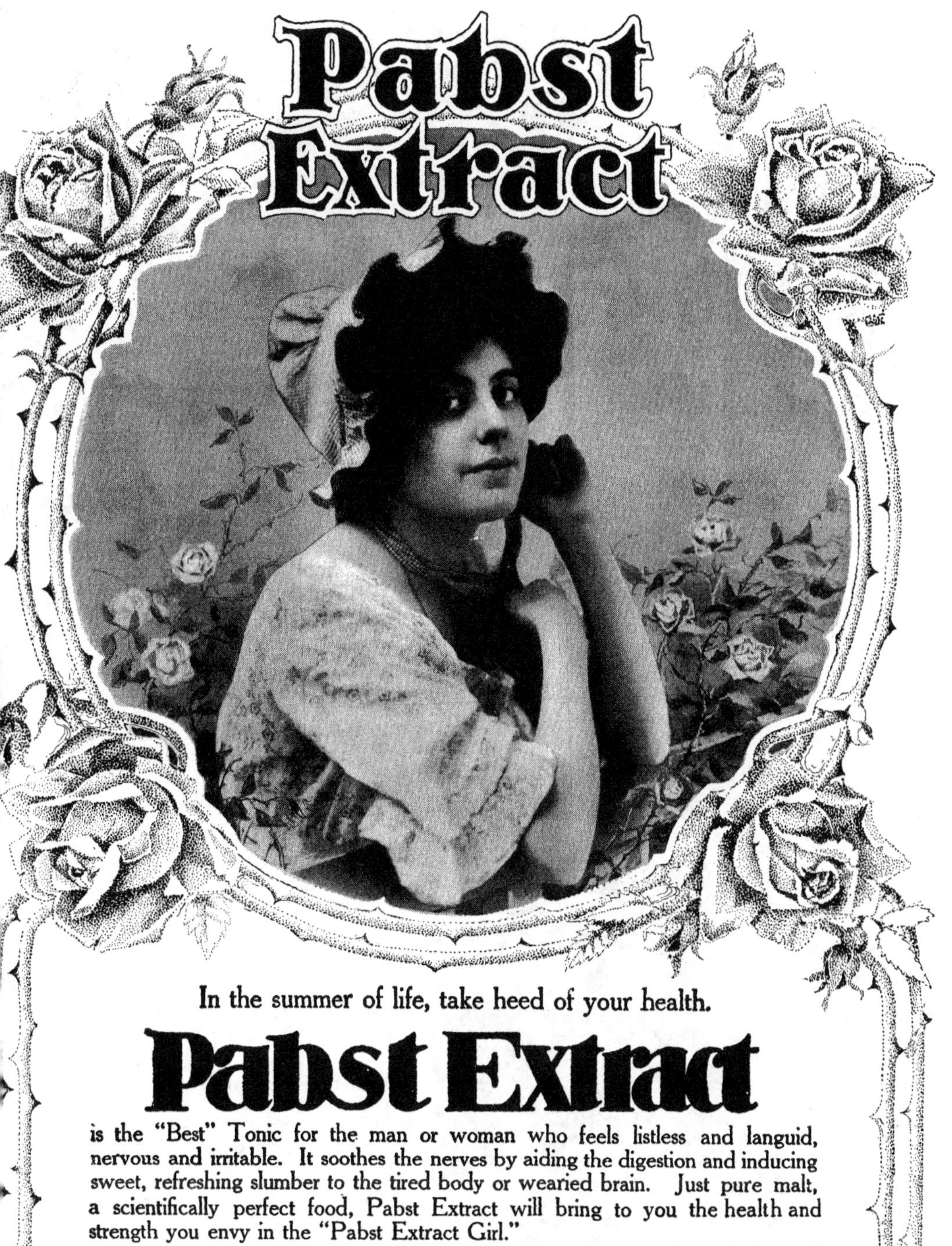
Pabst Extract
In the summer of life, take heed of your health.
Pabst Extract
is the "Best" Tonic for the man or woman who feels listless and languid, nervous and irritable. It soothes the nerves by aiding the digestion and inducing sweet, refreshing slumber to the tired body or wearied brain. Just pure malt, a scientifically perfect food, Pabst Extract will bring to you the health and strength you envy in the "Pabst Extract Girl."
25 cts. at all druggists. Insist upon the original.
Pabst Extract Department, Milwaukee, Wisconsin.

THE
HAMBURG-AMERICAN
LINE
has issued a special pamphlet setting forth the attractions that their delightful summer cruises offer the seeker of health and pleasure.
FROM NEW YORK LEAVING
JUNE 23, 1906
TO ICELAND
SPITZBERGEN
AND NORWAY
by the twin-screw express S. S. "Oceana"—8,000 tons—specially equipped for pleasure cruising. Superb accommodations. Rates including all side-trip expenses, if desired.
12 OTHER SIMILAR CRUISES
by the well-known steamers "Blücher," "Prinzessin Victoria Luise," "Meteor," during JUNE, JULY, and AUGUST.
For programmes, rates, etc., apply
HAMBURG-AMERICAN LINE
OFFICES
NEW YORK: 35-37 Broadway.
PHILADELPHIA: 1229 Walnut St.
BOSTON: 90 State St.
CHICAGO: 159 Randolph St.
ST. LOUIS: 901 Olive St.
FROM STEREOGRAPH, COPYRIGHT 1906 BY
UNDERWOOD & UNDERWOOD, N.Y.

COOL BREEZES GUARANTEED

NORTHERN STEAMSHIP CO.'S

STEAMSHIPS

NORTH WEST

in commission between Buffalo and Duluth, leaving Buffalo Saturdays and Duluth Tuesdays. First sailing from Buffalo June 23d.

NORTH LAND

in commission between Buffalo and Chicago, leaving Buffalo Wednesdays and Chicago Saturdays. First sailing from Buffalo June 20th.

EUROPEAN OR AMERICAN PLAN

TICKETS OPTIONAL, RAIL OR STEAMSHIP

Write for Particulars and Printed Matter to
W. M. LOWRIE, G. P. A., 379 BROADWAY, NEW YORK

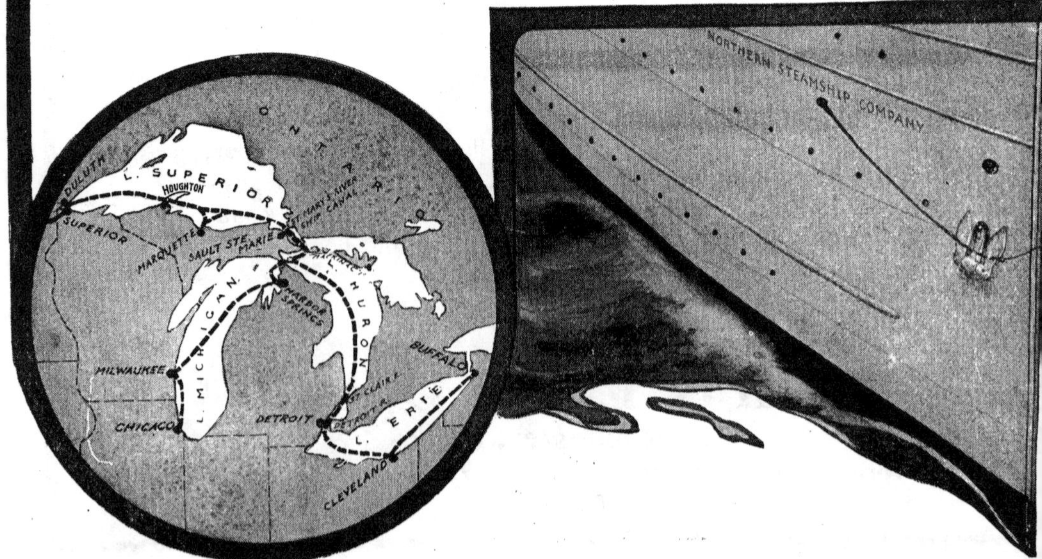

www.ingramcontent.com/pod-product-compliance
Lightning Source LLC
LaVergne TN
LVHW010515100826
845148LV00001B/14

* 9 7 8 1 4 2 5 5 7 3 9 9 7 *